Pete Wood
10-21-2006

THE PAPER BOY

A COLLECTION OF MEMORIES

FROM THE MIDDLE OF THE TWENTIETH CENTURY

IN SMYRNA, GEORGIA

CHARLES "PETE" WOOD

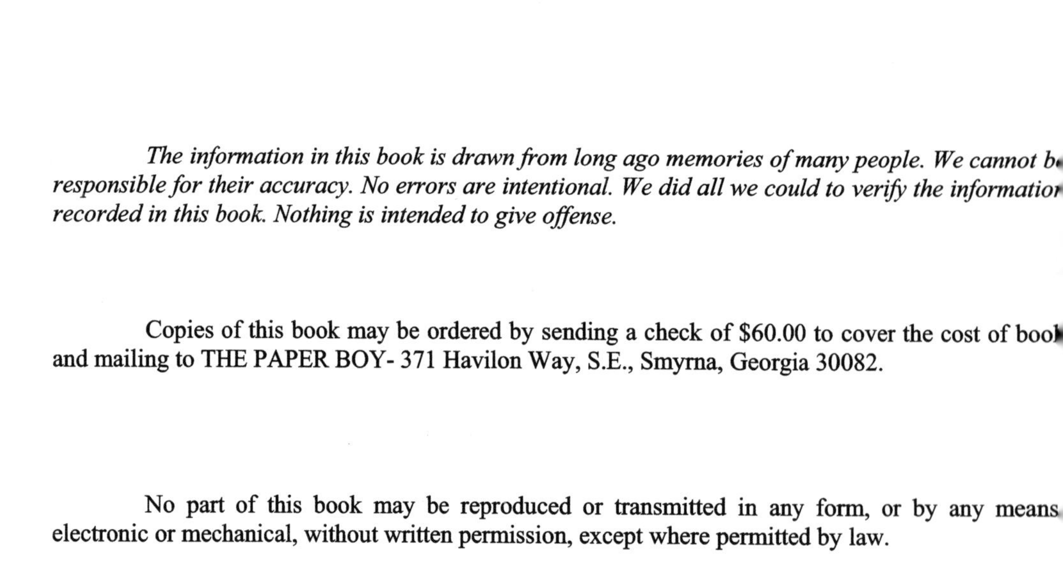

The information in this book is drawn from long ago memories of many people. We cannot b responsible for their accuracy. No errors are intentional. We did all we could to verify the informatio recorded in this book. Nothing is intended to give offense.

Copies of this book may be ordered by sending a check of $60.00 to cover the cost of boo and mailing to THE PAPER BOY- 371 Havilon Way, S.E., Smyrna, Georgia 30082.

ISBN 1-4243-1293-0

Printed in the United States of America
2006

Dedication

This book is dedicated to our grandchildren, Chase, Carson, and Lily Rose Wood, who are the joy and light of mine and Lillie's life. They are our future. May this book help them to grasp the importance of family and community history, and give them a legacy that will become theirs to remember.

ACKNOWLEDGEMENTS

Appreciation is extended to the many people who contributed to this book and also to the people who lived in Smyrna, in the middle of the Twentieth Century, for their dedication to a way of life that is worth remembering.

Consulting and Advice

Al Cochran, Attorney at Law
Rebecca Landers
Jim and Ann Wooten

Cover Art and Title Page

Charcoal Drawing of The Paper Boy
Claire Colquitt Curtis

First Edit

Linda Beasley
Betty Burruss Brown
Jeane Springer Travis

Final Edit

Joyce Reagin

Research

Lillie Wood
Janet Brown

Typing

Lillie Wood

Indexing

Millie Clayton Broyles
Benjamin Duncan
Stephanie Duncan
Carolyn Duncan

Format

Marilyn Wood Strickland

Special Thanks

In memoriam to one of my longest and dearest friends, Sonny Davenport, who was the first person I turned to for information for this book!

A special thanks is extended to my good friends and neighbors, Miller Davis and Joyce Lovern Davis, who hardly went through a day for eighteen months without answering at least one question. To my friend, Councilman Bill Scoggins, who answered so many questions he ran out of answers, and to our friends, Betty Burruss Brown and Janet Brooks Brown, who knew more people than were counted in the census.

A special thanks goes to Sara Anderson Gentry who was born in Smyrna in 1912 and remembered everyone she ever knew. It has been a refreshing experience to work with her throughout the writing of this book.

A special thanks also to Betty and Harold Smith, who came to Smyrna in 1954, as a young couple from Atlanta. She was working with Southern Bell Telephone Company and he was fresh out of the United States Navy, working for Equifax in Atlanta.

Betty and Harold quickly adopted Smyrna as their home. They became involved in First Baptist Church and the politics of Smyrna and were supportive of their neighborhood and the young people of their church.

In their senior years they organized the Smyrna Historical and Genealogical Society and founded the Smyrna Museum. They were instrumental in encouraging the people of Smyrna to record their memories and to preserve their history. Many historical documents and artifacts are preserved because of their untiring dedication to the establishment of these two institutions. It was their influence and his continued dedication that led to the building of the new museum located on Atlanta Street. They were also instrumental in staffing the museum with volunteer help. After Betty's death in 1993, Harold continued to serve as director of the museum, which is still currently staffed with volunteers by Harold's "good friend," Norma McHann.

INTRODUCTION

I grew up in Smyrna Georgia, in the middle of the Twentieth Century, in an era when time stood still. It was a time of innocence, when we youngsters enjoyed kicking rocks in the street and, for the most part, didn't know when things were bad.

This book is mainly about the people of Smyrna in my earliest memories, from about 1938 until 1951, when I graduated from high school. It is also a collection of memories of many people my age and some older and younger all of whom chose to share their memories. The people, streets, and places are the way they have remembered. I deeply regret if someone's name is omitted or misspelled. Those who assisted me in the organization of the family data have tried to make sure that didn't happen. I have intentionally avoided gossip and "scuttlebutt." I purposely left out events and incidents that could cause further pain to the family or friends of those involved. Some events mentioned are a matter of public record.

Since I have grown up and realized what the real world was like then, I am amazed how the people of that era made the best of the conditions and the times in which we lived. The Great Depression began when the stock market crashed in October 1929, and caused many people to lose their jobs. The attack on Pearl Harbor, December 7, 1941, propelled America into World War II, which was already raging in Europe. Both of these events caused great pain for many people for years to come. Some of those people who contributed memories to this book were adults when these events occurred, and willingly shared their personal memories of the hardships and sorrows they and others experienced during those difficult times.

It was a privilege for me to know so many of the people who withstood the Depression and those young men and women in my town who went off to fight World War II, one unlike any other—and to win! Many of those same people lived to enjoy an economic revival unequaled in modern history. Having enjoyed technological advances far beyond their imaginations, they have passed on to their children a heritage of education and technology that is "mind-boggling."

These memories are about the people of Smyrna at a time and place in history when its uniqueness and character shaped the lives of the people it touched. They vividly recalled the lack of material things, they emphasized the importance of people who made a difference, of stability and steadfastness in the homes, the churches, and the schools. They understood that cooperation among these institutions produced good citizens who were taught to value themselves and others. Therefore, the human spirit of these people proves what people are willing to endure to maintain their freedom.

Smyrna was a small town. Actually, when I started to school in 1940 (two months short of my seventh birthday), there were only 1,440 people counted in the census. It was a town with several grocery stores, a dentist, more than one doctor, two drug stores, a telephone office, cafes, some sidewalks, a library, the Jonquil Garden Club, the Smyrna Social Club, the Smyrna Men's Club, a Masonic Order, and American Legion Post #160. On a streetcar line between Marietta and Atlanta, Smyrna was my home and the foundation of my life, that has influenced me, schooled me, and created within me a "thought process" which has directed me long after the principal people in my life of that time are no longer living.

My parents were both active in First Baptist Church and the community. I saw the difference their Christianity and community involvement made in our family; therefore, I always had a desire to follow their example. My dad was my mentor and my friend. Drawing strength from my association with him, I have felt his influence in my decision-making experiences. I continue to draw strength from my up-bringing, and I am very appreciative to my mother and dad for their faithfulness in going to church regularly with my sister, Hilda, brother, Sammy, and me throughout the days of our youth.

My early life revolved around the home, the church, and the school. My parents taught me that faith in God was important, and thus I was taken to church regularly. Furthermore, they taught me that if I could read well, I could learn anything; conversely, if I could not read well, I would probably limit my opportunities. I still believe their teachings.

It was in my early family life that I learned to enjoy sporting events, especially baseball. Mother and Dad loved sports and passed that love on to us children. As a family, we enjoyed many baseball and basketball games together. Sporting events served two purposes for me: firstly, they were something I enjoyed with my family; secondly, they kept me busy and out of trouble. That is what my dad told me, and I believed him. (I remember that my mother, the night before she died, enjoyed a Braves game via television.)

The churches in Smyrna were First Baptist, First Methodist, Smyrna Presbyterian, Spring Street Baptist, and Second Baptist on Atlanta Street. Late in the 1940s Sharon Baptist was built. Bethel Baptist was out Spring Street in the country. The "Colored people" (as was said then) had two churches in Davenport Town. (These and other churches in the out-lying areas were very influential in the lives of many Smyrnans of that day.)

The schools were Smyrna Elementary and Smyrna High, both located on Church Street, across from First Baptist Church. According to information from long-time residents of Davenport Town (the Black community of that time), there was a school in their community for elementary school students, and the high school students from Davenport Town attended Perkinson High School in Marietta.

To each of the people who contributed to this book, I am deeply grateful for taking time to share personal and family information. Acknowledgements of their recorded memories are given at the beginning of each contributor's respective street(s). Should there be any statements that are not completely accurate, I apologize. This book, I must add, is not intended to be history but an account of memories.

The ability to remember is one of our most precious gifts from God. I hope you will enjoy this book and find it helpful in reminiscing your "Good Ole Days."

Biography
Charles "Pete" Wood

Charles "Pete" Wood was born in Smyrna (Cobb County) Georgia in 1933, and has lived there all his life. He attended Cobb County schools, then graduated from the University of Georgia in 1955 with a BBA degree. Pete also graduated from the School of Banking of the South at Louisiana State University in 1975.

In 1960 Pete married Lillian (Lillie) Fulgham, and they have two children, Marilyn and Stephen, as well as three grandchildren, Chase, Carson, and Lily Rose Wood. He and Lillie are members of First Baptist Church of Smyrna.

Pete was Vice-President of Bank South (formerly Fulton National Bank) and retired after thirty seven years in the banking industry.

MILITARY:

- Commissioned Second Lieutenant from ROTC, 1955 stationed at Fort Eustis, Virginia
- United States Army Command and General Staff College graduate
- Numerous command and staff positions in Army Reserve; retired with the rank of Colonel in 1985
- Member of Reserved Officers Associaton of the United States
- Member Veterans Memorial Association of Smyrna

CHURCH ;

- First Baptist Church of Smyrna, entire life.
  Chairman, Budget and Finance Committee, 1974-1987 and 1999-2000
  Treasurer 2000-2004
  Chairman, Building Committee during a major building and renovation program 1987-1991

CIVIC/ COMMUNITY SERVICE:

•Founding Trustee of Hospital Authority of Cobb County in 1962 that built Cobb General Hospital (now WellStar Cobb Hospital). He has served on the Authority Board since 1962 and was Chairman for 16 years.

•Founding Trustee of Northwest Georgia Health Systems (now WellStar Health Systems). He has been on the Board since 1993 and served as Finance Chairman and Member of Executive Committee. Elected Chairman of Board of Trustees July 1, 2006.

•Blind and Low Vision Services - based in Smyrna.
Chairman 1990-1995
Vice-President, Board of Directors
Board Member since 1988

Board of Directors:
WellStar Health Systems, 1993-Present
Cobb Hospital Regional Board, 1997-Present
Cobb Senior Services, 1997-Present
MUST Ministries Capital Funds Campaign Chairman, 1998
The Center for Family Resources, 2003-Present
Cobb County Public Schools Education Foundation, 2004-Present

Member:

American Legion, Smyrna Post #160
Friends of Smyrna Library
Taylor-Brawner House Foundation
The Smyrna Historical and Genealogical Society

PROFESSIONAL and POLITICAL SERVICE:

•Cobb County Chamber of Commerce:
Board Member 1994-1996
Chairman, Smyrna Area Council, 1995-1996
Honorary Commanders Association 1993

•Downtown Smyrna Development Authority, Founding Board Member 1989-1991

•Smyrna Business Association Member

•Consumer Credit Counseling Service of Greater Atlanta, Chairman 1989-1993

•Cobb Convention and Visitors Bureau:
Chairman, 1998-2001
Secretary, 1996
Member since 1991

•Smyrna City Councilman 1991-Present:
Finance and Administration Committee, Chairman 1992-1996 & 2001-Present
Police Committee, Chairman 1991
Human Resources Committee, Chairman 1997-2000
Economic Development Committee, Chairman 2000-Present
Parks and Recreation, Library and Community Relations, Chairman 2000-2001
Cobb County Economic Development Incentive Advisory Board 1993-1996
Public Works Committee
Veterans Memorial Committee

AWARDS:

Smyrna's Young Man of the Year, 1963
Outstanding Local President, Georgia Jaycees, 1962
Outstanding National Director, Georgia Jaycees, 1964
Smyrna Civitan's Citizen of the Year, 1969
Life Membership Junior Chamber International, 1969
Cobb Chamber of Commerce, Public Service Award, 1971
Outstanding Board Member, Blind and Low Vision Services, 1989
Mr. Smyrna, 1993
Smyrna Citizen of the Year, 1998
WellStar Cobb Foundation named "Pete" Wood Therapeutic Gardens, 2000
Community Leader of the Year: Cobb Senior Citizens Council, 2000
Cobb Chamber of Commerce Mack Henderson Public Service Award, 2001
Smyrna Rotary Club, Outstanding Citizen Award, 2001
South Cobb Citizen of the Year, 2005

TABLE OF CONTENTS

PAPER BOY

I began carrying *The Atlanta Constitution* to homes on the east side of the railroad when was eleven years old. I carried the morning paper throughout the time I was in the sixth and sevent grades.

The paper route required me to be at Sam Reed's Sinclair Service Station on Atlanta Stre by six o'clock in the mornings in order to be at school by eight o'clock. (Being late was not acceptab to my parents.) The route would take about an hour and a half. Then I would go home and get ready go to school. I would usually just make it! Of course, during the two summers of those years delivered the newspaper, I had no time problem.

My co-worker and mentor in the paper business was W.H. Scoggins, known as "Bill." Thre years older than I, he was already experienced in the paper delivery business when I started. He said me, "Arley," that is what he called me, "you stick with me, and I will make you a professional delivering newspapers."

To be professional, according to "Bill," there were several things I had to do. "You 'gotta' b on time with the people's papers and deliver them as near their houses as possible, and you 'gott keep the papers dry." He also said that it is very important to be professional in collecting. "Yo 'gotta' keep good records. You 'gotta' be prepared to let them know that unless you get paid, the won't get a paper." "Bill" made it clear to me, that, if I would build good customer relations, I woul make money. I heard what he said. "Bill" was a good mentor and friend. He is still my friend!

Being on time to deliver papers was not any problem. But delivering them dry when it w raining was another matter. We did not have the little plastic bags in which to protect the papers fro the rain. As far as we knew, there was not anything called plastic. What I used was a tarp bag that w called a paper bag. I also carried an umbrella and wore a rubber raincoat. One of my jobs was to figu out ahead of time where to put the paper when I delivered it so that it would not get wet. Also, I d not want to leave it where the dog might chew it up. This was part of my being professional, and wanted to be a respected paper boy.

If the customer had a screened door, sometimes I would leave the paper behind the scree especially if it were raining. That would take care of the rain and the dog. But there still could be problem. Sometimes that dog did not want me to get to the screen door!

As far as collecting was concerned, I always made sure I kept accurate records. I did not wa the customer to catch me in an error, for that would make me vulnerable and give the customer cau to question my record keeping. Most of my customers paid regularly, but I had a few who just seem not to be at home when the "paper boy" would come to collect. Now and then, I would just "stop t paper" if they did not pay; otherwise, I would have been losing money.

I walked my paper route for the first year. It was rough to carry those papers on my back a walk that distance because the route encompassed about two miles. Life was easier for me when I g my bicycle. However, carrying those papers served a purpose for me. Professional or not, I learn that I did not want to carry papers for the rest of my life. But, I hasten to add—I did make some mon at a time when I really needed it.

I left the paper business when I started the eighth grade and began playing basketball. M dad said that if I were going to be a ball player, I would have to put time and practice into it. I believ what my dad said.

CHAPTER ONE

BANK STREET

North Side

Appreciation is extended to Mildred Clayton Broyles, known as "Millie." For sharing information about her parents, Mr. and Mrs. Paul Clayton, who moved to Bank Street in the early 1940s when that section of the street was unpaved. I also want to thank Ruth and Steve Skelton and J.B. Westbrook, who provided information about the Westbrook Family, and Beverly Wallace Head for sharing information bout her grandparents, the Criders.

First House

Mr. and **Mrs. Talmadge Pharr Westbrook** lived here with their six children: **Elizabeth**, **Henry**, **Ruth**, **Harold**, known as "Hamburger," **Marion**, and **John**, known as "J.B." Mrs. Westbrook was the former Ellen Mae Bramlett of East Ellijay. Mrs. Westbrook's mother, **Martha Bramlett**, also lived here. The Westbrook house was located immediately behind the Smyrna City Hall (formerly a bank that closed during the Great Depression), on the northwest corner of Bank and Atlanta streets. (Over time, the Westbrooks lived in several houses on Bank Street.)

Talmadge Pharr Westbrook, known as "Hoke," was fourteen years old when he came to Smyrna from Roswell early in the Twentieth Century. Mrs. Westbrook came to Smyrna with her mother in or about 1920. Ellen Mae worked at Montag's (a stationery company that made Blue Horse writing paper and envelopes). She and Talmadge met and married in Smyrna.

Talmadge's father, Henry Bascomb Westbrook, was a builder, and, according to family information, constructed First Methodist Church, which was completed in 1912 on the corner of Atlanta and Church streets.

Also a builder, Talmadge Pharr Westbrook was instrumental in building many homes in the Smyrna area, including Dr. D.C. Landers' home on Church Street. According to information in *But Thou Art Rich,* A History of Methodists in Smyrna (Cobb County) Georgia 1990, Talmadge was the building contractor for the educational building, a wing of First Methodist Church, completed in 1940.

T.Y. Westbrook, known as "Doc," was a brother of Talmadge and was a pharmacist in Dr. Pace's Drug Store on Atlanta Street in the earlier part of the Twentieth Century. This drug store was located near the Smyrna Depot, on the southeast corner of Atlanta and Spring streets.

Elizabeth Westbrook married Russell Larson. They had no children. After they divorced, she took back her maiden name.

Henry Westbrook married Dee Jones. They had three children: Ellen, William Henry, known as "Hank," and Paul Talmadge. Henry was in the United States Army Air Corps during World War II. He was active in American Legion Post #160, in Smyrna, where he served as Commander and his picture hangs. After the War Henry worked for Lockheed Aircraft Corporation, from which he retired. He moved back to Bank Street, where he raised his family and lived the rest of his life.

Ruth Westbrook married Blake Skelton of Kennesaw, a nephew of Mr. Ed Skelton, who lived on Sunset Avenue. Ruth and Blake raised their family on Oakdale Drive, where Ruth still lives. They had three children: Stephen Blake, known as "Steve," Cheryl Elizabeth, and Richard Mason, known as "Dick." Blake Skelton is deceased.

Ronnie Howard
Casualty of War
Vietnam

Cheryl Skelton's first husband, Ronnie Howard, was killed in action on March 16, 1969 while serving in the United States Marine Corps during the Vietnam War. After Ronnie's death Cheryl married Zahid Hussain. They had one son, Imran, who married Lisa Fouts, a granddaughter o C.J. and Betty Fouts. See *Fouts, Atlanta Street, from Mrs. Mazie's to Pearce Matthews.*

"Steve" Skelton also served in the United States Marine Corps during the Vietnam War While he was stationed in Okinawa, he met and married his wife, Sumiko Shinzato, known as "Aiki, a native of Japan. They had two children: Stephen Scott and Joy Leiko. I have known both "Steve" an Scott, electricians, for many years.

Richard Mason Skelton, known as "Dick," married Patti Hall of Smyrna. They had on daughter, Lindsey Blake. "Dick" served in the United States Army in Korea during the Vietnam War.

Harold Edgar Westbrook, Sr., known as "Hamburger," married Irene Lewendowsky fror Chicago, Illinois. They had one son, Harold Edgar, Jr., known as "Hal." A graduate of Georgi Institute of Technology, he served in the United States Air Force during peace time. Harold, Sr served stateside in the United States Army during the Korean Conflict. Afterwards he worked fo Lockheed Aircraft Corporation, from which he retired.

Edith Marion Westbrook married Donald Sanders. They had two sons: Donald, known a "Donnie," and Dr. Philip Sanders, a chiropractor who had his practice on Spring Road. Donald i deceased.

Marion Westbrook Sanders later married Jimmy Phillips, also a chiropractor. They had tw children: a daughter, Jamie, and a son, Jay. Jimmy is deceased.

John B. Westbrook, Sr., known as "J.B.," married Julia Carter of Sandy Springs. They ha one son, John Bascomb Westbrook, Jr.

"J.B., Sr.," graduated from Campbell High School, where he was known as "Pige" (short fo Pigeon) on the Campbell High School Football Team. Afterwards he earned a Bachelor of Scienc degree in biology from Georgia State College of Business Administration. After finishing colleg "J.B." taught at Campbell High School for three years. He later earned a Ph.D. in zoology (anim physiology) and was the Chairman of the Division of Natural Sciences including biology, physics, an chemistry at the University of South Carolina, in Aiken, from which he retired. "J.B." and Julia live i Aiken, where she is a licensed marriage and family therapist in private practice.

The Westbrook house was torn down in 1950 to make way for the Colonial Store, Smyrna' first self-service food store, which opened in the first quarter of 1951.

Second House

Mr. and **Mrs. Job Carroll Dunton**, known as "Job," lived next door to the Westbrook hous on Bank Street. Mrs. Dunton was the former Elizabeth Lester. They had eleven children, six sons an five daughters: **Louella**, **Hollis Jewel**, known as "H.J,"and by some as "Joby," **Francis Barlow** known as "Frank," **Margaret Linda**, **Ralph Carrol**, known as "Rabbit," **Mary Louise**, **Jame Raymond**, **Marvin Dean**, known as "Big Head," **Earl Lingo**, known as "Doc," **Martha Ann**, an **Doris**. Louella Dunton, a good seamstress, spent much time in New York City, where she sewed fo residents. "Joby" Dunton had a brother who lived on Concord Road. See *Dunton, south side o Concord Road, south side of Concord Road, The Country Road, north and south sides of Churc Street, and south side of Church Road, The Country Road.*

Job Carroll Dunton
Born: July 6, 1871 Died: February 21, 1943

Frances Elizabeth Lester Dunton
Born: September 29, 1881
Died: March 23, 1958

Willie Wood, father of Roy Wood, wearing overalls is standing in the center front. Employed by Georgia Power Company, he was electrocuted in 1914 while working on a streetcar in Atlanta.
Circa 1910 Courtesy of Pete Wood

NOTE: We have established that "Joby" Dunton probably was a son of Mr. Hollis Jewell Dunton, who bought much property in the Smyrna area, in 1892.

Third House

Mr. and **Mrs. J.J. Hill** lived in this house. Mrs. Hill was the former Belle Valentine. They had no children. Mr. Hill, named Judge, was never connected to the legal system. He worked in Atlanta; though I never knew where, I knew he must have been a professional man because he always dressed in a suit and tie. I remember that Mrs. Hill was an aunt of Gennie Valentine Haralson and Millie Valentine Brinkley Mitchell, who always referred to her as "Aunt Belle."

Gennie and Millie grew up in the Log Cabin community, south of Oakdale, where the streetcar line ran between Smyrna and Atlanta. Amenities of that area were the Log Cabin Sunday School and Boy Scout Troop # 1's hut being located there. Gennie married Cecil Haralson, whose parents lived on Brown Circle. Millie married Dr. Claude Mitchell, who practiced medicine in Smyrna from 1933 until 1980. See *Brinkley, north side of Love Street* and *Haralson on Brown Circle*, and *Mitchell on Atlanta Street, from Marlowe's to Creatwood.*

I cut Mrs. Hill's grass for a long time, always using her push mower. She always paid me fifty cents because her yard wasn't as large as Mrs. Reed's, on the other side of the street. Mrs. Reed always paid me a dollar.

Sarah and Betty Burruss, daughters of Mr. and Mrs. Chesley Burruss, boarded with Mrs. Hill in the late 1940s. By this time Mr. Hill had died. Sarah was working in Atlanta at the Fulton National Bank, and Betty was employed by Stewart Insurance and Real Estate on Atlanta Street. Later on, Betty worked for Lockheed Aircraft Corporation, which opened in 1951. See *Burruss, Atlanta Street, from Miles Streetcar Stop to the Motters.*

Lillie and Mrs. Hill became very well acquainted with each other. Lillie remembered her with cards on her birthday, April 30th, and Christmas for many years.

There were two vacant lots between the Hill property and our house; these provided a very crude ball field. I remember that Billy and Lamar Akins, "J.B." and Harold Westbrook, "Bill" and "Buddy" Scoggins and I, along with other boys, gathered there to choose sides and play baseball with our ball gloves, a taped-up bat or two, and a very used baseball. The terrain was rocky and uneven, but it was a place to play. After World War II and my dad had purchased these two lots from Pitner Dorris; we also played football and various other games on this field. (Brinkley Park was the only park in Smyrna at that time.)

Judge and Mrs. Hill were our next door neighbors until Dad sold one of the lots to John and Leila Fowler, who built a beauty shop there in the early 1950s. After Lillie and I married, Lillie patronized that shop for several years; Blanche Guice was her stylist. Leila Fowler operated Leila's Beauty Shop for many years. Another business was operated in this building after the beauty shop closed and before the City of Smyrna acquired the property; I believe it was a gun store,

NOTE: Bank Street was a residential street in the days of my youth. The first business to open there was Colonial Store; then came Leila's Beauty Shop

Fourth House

Roy H. Wood
Smyrna City Councilman
1956-1959
1962-1969

My parents, **Roy Hampton Wood** and **Dora Inez Crowe**, married December 24, 1929, on olk Street in Marietta. The house (home of friends) where they married, still standing, is the second ouse on the right from the northeast corner of Marietta Parkway and Polk Street. They had four hildren: **Hilda Joanne, Charles Ronald**, known as "Pete," **Willie Ellison**, and **Roy Samuel**, known s "Sammy." Willie Ellison died immediately after his birth on August 17, 1936.

This house, where my siblings and I were raised, was located on the north side of Bank treet, directly across from the end of King Street. Dad traded two lots that he owned on Hughes Street Ralph Argo for our house, which stood about midway between Atlanta and Hamby streets, where he street ended. My early years were spent within a one-square-mile radius of downtown Smyrna. chool, church, sports, extended family, and friends were all within walking distance. The Twentieth entury Veterans Memorial is located where our house stood. A street was cut to the Village Green, ast of the Veterans Memorial, between the site of our house and Leila's Beauty Shop.

When the memorial was built, a large oak tree, which stood in the Ingle yard next door, had be removed because of root damage. We hated to see it go! Robert Lewis has related that his aughter, Marsha Lewis Turner, asked him to get one of the huge limbs for her and that she now has a eautiful clock that was made from that limb.

When we moved to Bank Street in 1940, the population of Smyrna was 1,449. There were bout 400 hundred families that made up that number. Several of those families, whom I knew well, ad ten or more children.

Dad lived in the Bank Street house until he died in 1970. Mother continued to live there until 975, when she sold the property and moved to the Southern Manor Apartments on Reed Street, across om Smyrna School. She resided on Reed Street for ten years, after which she moved to Smyrna owers, a high rise apartment for senior citizens, located on South Cobb Drive.

Dad, Roy Hampton Wood, was born in the northwest section of Atlanta, on October 15, 909. The son of Willie and Mamie Langley Wood, who married March 24, 1907, he had one sister, ardelle, born March 30, 1911.

Willie Wood, the son of Mary Colvin Wood, a widow, was born March 12, 1888. (The place f his birth is unknown.) His family migrated from Connecticut in the late Nineteenth Century. Willie, as employed by Georgia Power Company in Atlanta; there he worked as a serviceman on the reetcar lines. He was killed at work in 1912 and is buried in Hollywood Cemetery in northwest tlanta.

Mamie Langley, whose family moved from Suwanee to Atlanta in the late Nineteenth entury, was born in Atlanta, October 16, 1883, to James Thomas Langley and Julia Ellen Pittman.

Several years after Willie's death, Mamie Langley Wood married Robert Guy Tucker. They ad two sons: Harold, known as "Boob," born in 1915, and Thomas, known as "Tom," born in 1920. I as very close to both of them as long as they lived and also to my grandparents, whom I called "Ma-a" and "Pa-Pa" Tucker. "Ma-Ma" and Pa-Pa" moved to Smyrna in 1918. "Pa-Pa" died in Smyrna, ctober 18, 1939, and "Ma-Ma" died in Atlanta, February 5, 1955. "Ma-Ma" and "Pa-Pa" Tucker are ried in Providence Cemetery in Sandy Springs (Fulton County).

Ralph Pair and **Dora Crowe (Wood)**
Maloney Springs Cemetery Fair Oaks Community
Circa Mid 1920s Courtesy of the Roy Wood Family

Roy and **Dora Wood** on their Wedding Day, December 24, 1929 On Polk Street in Marietta. Courtesy of Roy Wood Fami

Dora and **Roy Wood**, in front of 164 Bank in 1966. Dora wore this hat in the Easter Pa in Atlanta. Courtesy of Roy Wood Family.

When my grandparents, the Tuckers, first came to Smyrna, they lived on Powder Springs Street. They also lived on Hill Street before moving to the west side of Roswell Street, where they were living when "Pa-Pa" died.

My mother, Dora Inez Crowe, was born March 24, 1912, in Cobb County's Fair Oaks community, south of Marietta. Her parents were George Ellison Crowe, known as "Ed," and Callie Eva Brewer. "Papa Crowe," as his grandchildren called him, was born November 12, 1873, in Marietta; my grandmother, Callie Eva (whom I do not remember), was born in Marietta, July 29, 1879. They had three daughters: Myrtle, Lula, and Dora Inez. Callie Brewer Crowe died February 1, 1934, in Smyrna; "Ed" Crowe died April 20, 1951, in Marietta. Both are buried in the Maloney Springs Cemetery, located in the Fair Oaks community on the southeast corner of South Cobb Drive and Austell Road.

My dad had only eight grades of formal schooling but placed a high value on education. Though I do not know where Dad started to school, I do know that he, nine years old when the family moved to Smyrna, attended Smyrna School when the classes were held in the Masonic Lodge Building on West Spring Street. To my knowledge, he never attended class after the new Smyrna School was built on Church Street in 1925.

My dad's days were spent working at Brooks Foundry and Machine Works in Atlanta. As a moulder, he was involved with hot iron and dangerous work. (I recall his moulding manhole covers.) I believe the heat from so many years of handling hot iron and steel shortened his life. Suffering from what the doctors called "little strokes," Dad (at the age of sixty-one) died November 23, 1970, at Kennestone Hospital, in Marietta.

My dad was a good and just man. Very civic and community minded, he loved his family and worked very hard to provide for each family member. There is no doubt that he was the most influential person in my life. Even today, as I grow older, I sometimes ask myself "What would Dad do or think about this?" I feel that I am still guided on many occasions by his teachings. Dad was fortunate to do several things that he loved doing during his lifetime. Firstly, as a young man, he managed the Smyrna Amateur Baseball Team for many years. Secondly, he was on the Smyrna City Council and served for twelve years. Thirdly, he was Chairman of the Building Committee when the sanctuary of First Baptist Church was built in the late 1950s. Always conscientious about the things he did, he always believed in doing what was right, regardless of the political fallout. Dad left a legacy of which I am very proud!

SMYRNA AMATEUR BASEBALL TEAM

While we were living on Grady Street before I started to school, my dad was the manager of the Smyrna Amateur Baseball Team. I can't remember when he started managing, though I remember going with him to the games. I was about five years old when I became the water boy for the team; I remember feeling very important to have that job. Because the players needed much water, Dad said it was my job to make sure it was there for them between innings. I took my job very seriously.

I became very close to the men who played ball as part of that team, as well as to their families. Those people became role models for me in the earliest stages of my life. I remember their traits, their personalities, and their thinking. It was as if I would know when they wanted water, even before they asked for it. As the closest people around me at that time, they helped to shape my life.

These are some of the people that I remember best from that ball team: Ralph Cobb, J.C. Austin, "Sonny" Davenport, Woodrow Lutz, Spurgeon Ware, Homer Brooks, O.L. Pinson, Harry Mitchell, Alvin Austin, Aubrey and Clyde Herren, and my uncle, Tom Tucker.

I also remember some of the team sponsors who would furnish money to buy the uniforms: Black and Webb Grocery Store, Smyrna Drug Company, Collins Pharmacy, Saul's Department Store, and W.F. "Bill" Stewart Insurance Company.

Roses Were Presented To Mrs. Dora Wood

Roses were presented to **Mrs. Dora Woo** of Smyrna, shown seated at her switchboard at the Peoples Bank in Atlanta, for her "most pleasant voice." Mrs. Leona Bartholmew of Southern Bell is making the presentation. Courtesy of Roy Wood Family

THE SMYRNA AMATEUR BASEBALL TEAM

Standing Fourth Row L-R: Fleming Jolley, Alvin Austin, Spurgeon Ware, Homer "Joby" Brooks, J.C. Austin, Ralph Cobb and "Sonny" Davenport. **Third Row L-R:** Aubrey Herren and Tom Tucker. **Second Row L-R:** O.L. Pinson, Richard Pierce, Robert "Hoofy" Fortner, Roy Wood and Frank Mitchell. **First Row L-R:** Richard Smevog, "Pete" Wood and Bobby Fortner. Circa 1946
Courtesy of Corrine Austin Ware (Cates) and "Sonny" Davenport

The following letter was written by Scott Edwards, Jr., to Roy Wood during World War II. The hand-written note was written by Marvin Daniel, both Scott and Marvin played on the Smyrna Amateur Baseball Team.

Some Where in the Philippines.
July 14, 1945. (Saturday)

Dear Roy:-

Sure appreciated your nice newsy letter of July 1st which arrived this morning. It really helps a fellows moral to hear from an old pal who is giving you the news about your other pals.

Roy, I too, was sorry to learn of Ralph Argo's death for more reasons than one. Ralph was a mighty fine fellow to all the boys and even though he use to tease you about the ball team and the fellows he told me a number of times about what a good team he thought we had and what a good job of managing you had done with such little financial help. Roy, you will never realize it, but you are directly responsible fo for a lot of people in Smyrna enjoying themselves by watching a ball game played by home town boys on Saturday and Sunday afternoons. A lot of the kids around town have sent me letters asking me when would Roy Woods start having another base ball team. You know, Roy, kids like little Pat, Sunny and Quition Hamby, and Tommie Coker. You made a lot kids mighty happy when thier mothers would let them go to the ball game and you are going to make a lot more of them happy after this war is over with by useing those same kids that use to watch the games as players. Only yesterday I wrote little Quintion Hamby a letter and told him to keep on playing ball every day because someday he would be playing for the big team. Frankly, I believe that you will be able to put a first class team on the field in forty seven, but all the old faces will be on the side lines watching. I don't guess I will ever play again, but you can count on me in a big way for financial aid and all the help that I will be able to give you.

Sure wish I could have been at home to see J.C. Austin, Paul Morris, and Woodrow. I feel pretty sure that I might be home by April of forty six or maybe just a little sooner. At the present I have only seventy seven points and almost two years overseas so you see my chances of getting home this year are mighty slim. We haft to stay over here much longer than the boys did in Europe for I know of a lot of cases where the boys over on the other side were home at the end of twenty to twenty four months. It dosen't seem fair to me for we have had a much harder time over here than the boys in Europe. There is absolutly no place to go or see when you are stationed away from a town over here and the climate is awful. A lot of our boys haven't seen a train or anything that resembled civilization in almost two years. At the present we are eating very good, having a lot of shows, and get plenty of P.X. supplies and even though the Jap's are not bothering us we still get mighty lonesome. Infact, Roy, I would come home right now if Uncle Sam would say the word and not feel bad about leaving at all for two years is a long time to be stuck in hell holes.

Marvin is getting a long fine, looks good, and seems to like being with us. The other day we got a ball and glove to play a little catch and it wasn't long until we were talking about all the ball teams we had ever played with and both agreed that you had the finest bunch of boys to play with. We didn't have any great ball players, but we did have plenty of team work and that is what counts.

Well, Roy, that is all for this time except bear in mind that I think of you and the rest of my friends in Smyrna often and am looking forward to the day when we can have a good bull session together. Tell your wife, your family, and the rest of my friends hello for me.

Your pal,

Scott Jr.

(P.S) Hi Roy: Just a note but hope this finds you and your family in the best of health. Scott and I often talk of you and the swell ball teams you put out. Keep sending those planes over here and we will soon be home and winning another championship for you. Best of luck. Marvin

THE ROY WOOD FAMILY is pictured with Larry Bell, President of Bell Aircraft Corp., as they toured the plant in 1944. On the left is Pete Wood, standing next to his sister, Hilda, now Mrs. Grady Chaffin. Mr. Wood is holding Sammy, 4. The group is shown in front of a B-29.

Sammy, Hilda and **Pete Wood** 1947

Sammy Wood, Bank St., Spring 1942
Courtesy of Roy Wood Family.

There was also a large group of people that always went to the games, mostly the players' families, who were loyal supporters. My mother and sister hardly ever missed!

Because I was only thirty-seven years old when I lost my dad, I have often wondered what it would be like to associate with him in my latter years. He loved sports and gave me an appreciation for the games. One thing he said I have never forgotten: "The hardest thing in any sport is to hit a baseball with a bat. It takes tremendous coordination of the eyes, the mind, and the body." Dad knew the game of baseball and was a great manager. Therefore, today one of my most enjoyable pastimes is a good Braves baseball game. Rarely do I miss the opportunity to revel in the sport of baseball.

My mother, Dora Crowe Wood, graduated from Marietta High School in the Class of 1929. In my early childhood, she was a "stay-at-home mom." After my brother, Sammy, was born in 1940, she began working at Davison-Paxon Department Store. (It later became Macy's.) After that, she worked for the Fulton National Bank in the Candler Building on Atlanta's Peachtree Street. Afterwards, having trained to become a switchboard operator, she was employed by People's Bank at Atlanta's Henry Grady Square, where she retired after twenty-seven years. Upon retiring from People's Bank, she worked for Bank of Smyrna, from which she retired in 1975. Mother was a smart lady, having received a good education at Marietta High School. She always stayed in touch with her classmates, even attending her sixtieth class reunion in 1989. Mother died on February 9, 1992, six weeks prior to her eightieth birthday.

Mother was fifty-eight years old when my dad died. She continued to work and stay busy for the rest of her life. One of the things she enjoyed most and was the proudest of was holding the position of Worthy Matron in the Smyrna Chapter of the Order of the Eastern Star. Mother, baptized at Olive Springs Baptist Church, taught us the importance of church attendance by her example. She and dad had both been members at First Baptist Church but, for the last twenty years of her life, she was a member of King Spring Baptist Church. My family and I still miss her and gain strength from our memories of her.

Roy Samuel Wood, known as "Sammy," was born in the Bank Street house on October 4, 1940. "Sammy" married Beverly Jane Walker on August 14, 1964. They had two daughters: Julia, known as "Julie," and Cynthia, known as "Cindy." Jane, the daughter of Buna Walker and Julia Worley Walker, and "Sammy" attended Smyrna Elementary School and graduated from Campbell High School: "Sammy" Class of 1958 and Jane, Class of 1964. See *Walker, Atlanta Street, from Mapps to R&M Café* and *south side of Spring Street.*

"Julie" Wood married Chris Haddox of Smyrna. They had two sons: Stephen and Drew. Julie, Chris, and their sons attend Mt. Paran Church of God (Central), in Atlanta. Julie graduated from Campbell High School in 1988 and from Georgia State University, in Atlanta, where she earned a Bachelor of Science degree in medical technology. She is a lab technician at WellStar Cobb Hospital, in Cobb County. Chris, who graduated from Campbell High School in 1989, is an electrician with Taylor Electric Company.

"Cindy" Wood graduated from Campbell High School in 1993. She began high school in the year that Campbell and Wills merged and the school was named Smyrna High School. "Cindy" actually attended classes only one year at Smyrna High School, for the name change was rescinded: the next year the name reverted to Campbell High School. Cindy, attending Atlanta Christian College on a basketball scholarship, earned a Bachelor of Science degree in early childhood education there. She received her Masters degree in early childhood education from Kennesaw State University. Cindy is a second grade school teacher at Powder Springs Elementary School, in Powder Springs. A member of First Baptist Church, she is active in the singles ministry.

Hilda Joanne Wood was born on Fleming Street, September 1, 1931. She attended Smyrna Elementary and is a member of the Smyrna High Class of 1948. She married Grady Chaffin from the Fair Oaks community, December 16, 1950, in First Baptist Church, the rock building, known now as the First Baptist Church Chapel.

Smyrna High School girls at B & H Skating Rink on Access Road (Now South Cobb Drive)
L-R: Jean Scoggins, Doris Bailey, Peggy Lutz, Jean Black, Joan Bennett and Mildred Clayton.
Circa 1951 Courtesy of Mildred Clayton

Mildred Clayton on Bank Street Circa 1952
Courtesy of "Millie" Clayton (Broyles)

Hilda Wood (Chaffin)
On Roswell Street Circa 1948
Courtesy of Ruby Langley Hunter

Grady graduated from Osborne High School, located then on Joyner Avenue in the Fair Oaks community. He was the son of Mr. and Mrs. Hubert Chaffin, of Marietta, long-standing members of Olive Springs Baptist Church. Hilda and Grady had three sons: Alan, Kevin, and Jeffrey, known as "Jeff." Grady is retired from Atlanta Gas Company, where he worked forty-five years.

Alan Chaffin married Robin Young of Marietta. They had no children. He graduated from Wills High School in the Class of 1973. From Georgia State University, in Atlanta, in 1978, he earned a Bachelor of Business Administration degree in accounting. Alan is employed with National Employees Solutions as an insurance underwriter.

Kevin Chaffin, a graduate of the Wills High School Class of 1976, married Brenda Fincham from Marietta. They had three children: Justin, Jeremy, and Rebecca. Kevin is employed by Yellow Freight Transport Company.

"Jeff" Chaffin, a graduate of the Wills High School Class of 1981, married Nancy Scott of Atlanta. They had no children. Jeff earned a Bachelor of Business Administration degree in computer science from Georgia State University, in Atlanta; he is employed by SunTrust Bank, in Atlanta.

Charles "Pete" Wood
Smyrna City Councilman
1991-2003: 2004-
Member, Downtown Development Authority
1989-1991

I married Lillian Annette Fulghum, known as "Lillie," from Douglas County, while I lived on Bank Street. We had two children: Marilyn Elaine and Stephen Charles known as "Steve."

Lillie and I met in 1956 at Fulton National Bank in Atlanta, where we were both employed. We married in the Frances Winship Walters Chapel of Saint Mark Methodist Church, on Atlanta's Peachtree Street, October 1, 1960. Our first home was in the Southern Manor Apartments, owned by Raymond Reed. We lived in the second apartment of the first building on the east side of Davis Street. (Quinton and Annette Bell Hamby lived in the first unit.) On April 1, 1961, (six months after we married) we moved to 458 Pinehurst Drive. From the intersection of Concord and King Springs roads, Pinehurst Drive is the first street to the right. Our house, which is still there, was the sixth one on the right. We lived there until 1969, when we built our house at 371 Havilon Way in Smyrna's Bennett Woods subdivision. We moved into the house on Havilon Way on Labor Day, 1969.

Lillie's parents were Mr. and Mrs. Frank Freeman Fulghum. Her dad, a native Georgian, was born and raised in Meriwether County. Her mother, the former Susie Harrel, was a native of Gadsden, Alabama, but was raised on Sand Mountain, Alabama. In 1957 Lillie's parents moved to Cooper Lake Road in Mableton, where they lived for the rest of their lives. Her mother passed away August 2, 1985, at the age of seventy-five; her dad passed away November 18, 2002, at the age of ninety-seven. Both are buried in Powder Springs Community Fellowship Cemetery, which is adjacent to the Powder Springs City Cemetery. Lillie had two sisters, Maxine and Peggy, and five brothers, Charles, John W., known as "Jake," Melvin, known as "Bo," Wayne, and Byron.

Our daughter, Marilyn, married Adam Strickland of Smyrna, November 17, 2001. Having graduated from Campbell High School in the Class of 1984 and attended Young Harris College and Kennesaw State University, she is employed at Home Depot Corporate Offices. Adam is the son of Mr. and Mrs. Jack Strickland of Smyrna. He graduated from Wills High School in the Class of 1984 and Chattahoochee Technical College, in Marietta. Adam, an automobile mechanic, owns his business, Auto Pro, in Peachtree City. Marilyn and Adam live in Senoia.

Our son, Stephen married Kimberly Joanne Cox, known as "Kim," from Pike County. They had two sons and one daughter: Stephen Chastain, known as "Chase," Carson Cox, and Lily Mae Rose.

Stephen graduated from Campbell High School in the Class of 1986. Having earned a Bachelor of Business Administration degree in marketing in 1991 from West Georgia State University, in Carrollton, he is employed with Staples Business Advantage.

"Kim" graduated from Pike County High School in Zebulon in the Class of 1985 and earned a Bachelor of Science degree in early childhood education at West Georgia State University, in Carrollton, in 1990. "Kim" was employed by the Cobb County Board of Education as a teacher at Ford Elementary School in West Cobb County for several years. She is currently the director of the Children's and Preschool departments of Johnson Ferry Baptist Church at Cedarcrest. Maxie Cox of Zebulon and Judy Hatcher Roberts of Forsyth are the parents of "Kim," who has a sister and two brothers.

Two months short of my seventh birthday, in 1940, the year we moved to Bank Street, I started to Smyrna School. The school building was a wing off the two-story building that faced Church Street; built in 1925 with school district tax money; it was my school home for seven years. I attended first grade in one of the two first grade classes in that section of the school. (Because many of the families in Smyrna had small children, two first grade classes were required. My first grade teacher was Miss Fannie B. McClure.) See *north side of Church Street.*

Miss McClure was from Acworth. Her sister, Miss Charlotte McClure, who also taught at Smyrna School, was my second grade teacher. Both of the McClure ladies were very nice. Miss Fannie B. taught three years in Smyrna before leaving to teach at Acworth Elementary School, from which she retired.

I had the privilege of knowing Miss Fannie in her senior years. After she retired from teaching, she went to work for Rich's Department Store at Cobb Center Mall, in Smyrna, upon its opening in 1964. I had the privilege of seeing her there from time to time. A big booster of mine in the years that I was working through the ranks of business, she was always interested in my progress, or, as she called it, "my success." Miss Fannie was a teacher from "the old school," as my generation terms the roles of instruction and discipline. The progress her students made were her pride and joy. I feel very fortunate to have had a first grade teacher who was as dedicated to teaching as she was.

I also remember Miss Charlotte McClure fondly although, after leaving Smyrna School, I didn't have any contact with her.

Miss Elizabeth Wills was my third grade teacher. Miss Wills, who also taught Hilda and Sammy, was the only teacher that all three of us had for our homeroom classes. It was for Miss Will's father, Mr. F.T. Wills, Cobb County School Superintendent, that Wills High School was named. Her brother, Zelan Wills, became the United States Postmaster in Smyrna and held that position for many years.

Doris Arrington Quarles was my fourth grade teacher. I liked her very much and thought she was so pretty. When she started teaching at Smyrna School, she was not married. Having grown up on Sunset Avenue, she married Jimmy Quarles, who was Mayor of Smyrna, 1955-1957. They had one son, Harry. I was always fond of Doris, as I later called her, and was fortunate to have known her; she had a lot of influence on my life. See *Quarles, Atlanta Street from Marlowe's to Creatwood.*

In the fifth and sixth grades my teacher was Miss Barron. My seventh grade teacher was Mrs. Hannah Bible Curtis. (My friend Joyce Reagin shared with me that she taught with Mrs. Curtis at Floyd Junior High School, in Mableton. Mrs. Curtis retired before the school became Floyd Middle School.)

When the County crew started wrecking the Smyrna School building, my friend, Buddy Mason called and said, "Pete" they are wrecking the old school building. Do you want the corner stone?" Because I certainly wanted that physical part of historical Smyrna, I took some of my friends to get that marker. We placed all thousand pounds of it onto the back of a truck and took it to my house. From that truck it was placed in the corner of my front yard, where it has been ever since. The marker will become property of the Smyrna Museum when space becomes available for it to be housed properly. The names of the Smyrna School District Board of Trustees on that marker are listed below:

Smyrna School District
1938-1939
Board of Trustees
W.T. Hanson, Chairman
B.B. Jones, Secretary and Treasurer
L.H. Baldwin
J. R. Bramblett
T. B. Martin
J. T. Lowe, Principal
Frank W. Manning, Architect
G.G. Wells, Builder

I started high school in the new facility that was built by the Works Progress Administration (WPA) and completed for the 1938-1939 school year, (WPA was one of the programs that President Franklin Delano Roosevelt initiated to help create jobs during the Depression.) This building was only ten years old when I began my eighth grade year. I remember that we were very proud of this building and felt very fortunate to have such a nice facility in which to attend school.

NOTE: To my knowledge, Smyrna High School was the only physical structure that was built by the Works Progress Administration in Smyrna. The other programs offered were housed in existing buildings.

The gym, which was in the elementary school building (built in 1925), became a gathering place for the citizens of Smyrna. I was fortunate to play on the basketball team during my high school years; thus I spent many happy times in that gym.

NOTE: First Baptist Church purchased the land and both buildings from the Cobb County Board of Education in 1974. This information is from *A Beacon for Christ*, A Centennial History of The First Baptist Church of Smyrna Georgia.

DURING THE WAR YEARS

We raised chickens all through World War II years. A man in Marietta, with whom Dad worked at Bell Bomber Plant, hatched baby "chicks." On days Dad planned to meet him at the streetcar to purchase the "chicks," I would ride with Dad to carry the "chicks" home. Placing them in the garage, where Dad had made preparations for them, I would settle the "chicks" down, feed and water them, and then go to school.

Dad had a platform area, with mesh wire around it, for the "chicks." He used light bulbs hanging from the ceiling for warmth. The "chicks" were kept in that environment for two weeks, or until they were large enough not to get trampled by the larger chickens.

My family ate a lot of chicken during the War because meat was rationed. Even if we did have enough ration stamps issued by the United States Government to buy meat, we did not have it often, due to our family's limited income.

Therefore, our purpose of raising chickens was to have chicken and fresh eggs to eat. We used most of our eggs, but I did get a few to sell to some regular customers who would buy what we had available. Some customers that I remember included Mrs. Howard Hames, on Spring Street, and Mrs. B.F. Reed, Jr., and Mrs. J.J. Hill, on Bank Street. Their purchases would give me spending money to go to the "picture show" or to the "five and dime" store. I always liked to get new marbles or a *Big Little Book,* or maybe a comic book now and then. (I was big into Dick Tracy in those days.) It was also good to go to Landers Drug Store and get a milk shake or a soda. I was also fond of BB Bat suckers. All these things cost money; thus I made sure that I always had a means of supporting myself in such buying ventures.

DISCIPLINE IN THE FAMILY

In my family I don't remember any of us children getting a spanking or a whipping very often. When we did, it was with "peach tree" switches and because of minor offenses. My mother did not think her children did anything really wrong. If someone wanted to hear from her, all that person had to do was to say something critical about one of her children. As a child, I remember thinking how awful it would be if I did something to change her mind about me. From my earliest memories I always wanted her to be proud of me. Therefore, I tried to do things in a way that would be pleasing to her—and to my dad.

As for Dad, he would always say, "Son, I didn't get much education, but I would like for you to get all you can." He said that it would make my life more fulfilling and successful. He impressed on me that education was very important. From my earliest memories I can remember his saying. "I will do all that I can to help you, but I can only teach you what I have learned. You must learn what you want to know for yourself."

Going to school and to church were not optional in my family. I don't know what my parents would have done had we children not gone, but I do know they would have been very displeased. I did not want to displease them.

However, one time I went against their principles and left school without their permission. I must have been a junior in high school. (I hope these guys don't mind me telling this.) Mickey Walker was one of the few guys in those days that had a car. One day a group of us guys drove over to Sunnyside Inn, a restaurant, bar, and tourist court, owned and operated by A.T. Parks. Sunnyside Inn was located on South Atlanta Road, across from where Campbell Middle School is currently located. None other than Jasper Griffin, the principal, caught us. I don't remember if he told my parents or insisted on my telling them; but one thing I do remember is the session I had with my dad afterwards!

Dad and I took seats in the living room. He was on the sofa, and I was sitting in a chair. He asked, "What was your reason for doing that? He just wanted a reasonable explanation that made sense. Also, he wanted to know what I thought the experience would accomplish for me. I didn't have any real reason, nor did I especially remember having had such a good time. When I told him I did enjoy being with the guys, he said he thought that was a good reason except for the timing and the place of our going. I was never able to tell him more than that. He thought a good time was not worth giving up some things.

There were many times in my life when Dad and I would talk about how I should act. Most of them were when we would be cleaning the chicken house, walking to a ball game, cutting grass, or riding the streetcar to Marietta or Atlanta. But none of those times stand out in my memory as much as our talk about that trip I took to Sunnyside Inn. It taught me how fragile one's reputation is; also, I leaned how important it is for me to feel good about my actions. I owe so much to my dad for his teachings: not so much by what he said but by the way he lived. As the years have passed, it is amazing to me how much those "talks" still influence my life.

NOTE: At times during the days of my youth, Smyrna and Cobb County were "dry," as we said then—meaning it was illegal to serve alcoholic beverages. When I left school with a group of guys that day, Cobb County allowed beer and packaged alcohol to be sold but prohibited alcohol being served by the drink.

My mother, on the other hand, had a different kind of influence on me. Hers was a type of unyielding trust that made me feel she believed I would always do the right thing. I think the only thing she did not trust me with was washing my face and hands and brushing my hair when I was going to Mrs. Mazie Nelson's, to church, or to school. Until the day that she passed away, I knew she still had that trust in me. I often think about that and the importance of children's having the responsibility to live up to that kind of expectation. I always felt that Mother loved me unconditionally. The discipline I received because of that trust, I believe, is why I did not want to disappoint her.

This feeling carried over to my classrooms, for I never wanted to disappoint my teachers. I don't ever recall being sent to the principal's office. (I would like to mention that most of my teachers have passed away and can't dispute this; maybe that is the reason I haven't written this sooner.) It was a good feeling to know many of my teachers in my adult life and to have them recall that I was a good student. I was fortunate to be good friends with several of them as the years passed. I had the opportunity to see Jasper Griffin many times during my adulthood, and he always showed me the utmost respect. The Sunnyside Inn incident never surfaced!

Work was one of the things that disciplined my life. I knew that if I were to have spending money, I would have to work. My first big earnings came from my paper route.

One of the things that I remember most about my paper route was that I learned to save money for things, one of which I both wanted and needed—a bicycle. Bicycles could not be bought during World War II years because metal and rubber were required for the defense effort. The district manager for the newspaper had a friend who took old bicycle parts and put them together as reconditioned bicycles and this is how I obtained a bicycle. The district manager said that, since I carried a paper route, if I would save the money, he would get his friend to make me a bicycle. (The friend's surname was Fulghum, my future wife's maiden name, but no relation.) Mr. Fulghum charged $36.00 for a bicycle, which I saved by giving my dad $1.00 per week for 36 weeks. I shall never forget the day that I got that bicycle, the prettiest red bicycle I had ever seen or ever will see! That bicycle, which I kept for many years, made a big difference in my delivering papers. I really enjoyed those two years that I delivered papers with "Bill" Scoggins and afterwards with "Buddy" Scoggins.

"Bill" Scoggins, unlike me, already had a bicycle. A few years older than I, he delivered papers to the customers that were farther away, and I delivered papers to the closer-in customers, My route covered Spring, Roswell, and Matthews streets and their surrounding areas. "Bill" would deliver to Davenport Town and farther out Roswell Street. We made a good team. In fact, Bill and I are still good friends and have served on the Smyrna City Council together for the last 15 years, with his already being on Council prior to my retiring from BankSouth. I really treasure my friendship with "Bill."

I had a lot of freedom as a child. When I reminisce now, I realize what a privilege it was to be in a town where it was safe for a boy of eleven or twelve to arise at five o'clock in the morning and deliver papers before going to school.

There has never been a time in my life since those paper-delivering days that I didn't make enough money to meet my needs. I can truly say that I am grateful for the discipline that my mother and dad gave me.

FAMILY ENTERTAINMENT

Of course, baseball was the main attraction in our family because we all loved it; therefore, baseball was the subject of frequent discussions. I can't remember when we didn't go to baseball games. Apparently my parents took me even when I was a infant. For the first twenty something years of my life, my dad was always the manager of the Smyrna Amateur Baseball Team. We had a lot of good times, and I established my lifelong love of baseball and sports in general.

Games were always scheduled somewhere, and all of my family attended the games. Some of the team players or family members had cars; my family would always ride with one of them. My parents didn't own a car until after I graduated from high school in 1951; I remember that when we bought that car, we thought we had "arrived."

As a family, we went to the movies frequently, for Mother and Dad both loved movies. We would board the streetcar on Atlanta Street and go to Marietta or Atlanta to a movie. I remember going to the Rialto Theater on Forsyth Street in Atlanta. I loved to go to that theater! We would get off the streetcar at Marietta and Forsyth Streets and walk three blocks to the "picture show," which is what we called a theater in those days.

One of the movies that I remember seeing with my parents was *Dagwood and Blondie*, one of our favorite comedy series. Other movies I remember most vividly are *Laurel and Hardy, Abbott and Costello,* and *Red Skelton.* I remember that my mother and dad would laugh and talk about those movies on the streetcar all the way home. We would refer to some scenes for days after seeing one of those movies, some of which are still shown as reruns. I remember going to see Elizabeth Taylor in her first movie, "*National Velvet*," playing at the Loew's Grand Theater, in Atlanta. We would also go to see Bing Crosby movies, one of my favorites being *Going My Way.*

As a family, we also liked to listen to the radio. It was so much fun to sit and hear a voice coming through "that box," as we called it. I remember that my sister and I would sit and listen to it. One of the programs we loved to listen to was *The Amos and Andy Show.* Always funny, it contained "clean" dialogue; I always looked forward to the next show.

My dad was a quiet, serious-minded person, not stuffy—but very good at conversation. Not a loose talker, he spoke only when he had something to say. He also had the ability to have a good time and enjoy himself. He smiled often, too, particularly at punch lines on the radio.

I really hated to see *The Amos and Andy Show* come to an end. Still remembering statements with truth and humor, I can't imagine a show on today's radio that would hold kids spellbound for thirty minutes to an hour, as that one did. I still remember that most of the punch lines had good moral lessons within them; I think that kids who listened also learned to be attentive when someone was talking with them, both at home or in public.

The characters on *The Amos and Andy Show* were excellent communicators, two white men pretending to be a "colored" duo (terminology for that day). They were always funny, with just clean dialogue.

Another of my favorite radio programs was the *Lone Ranger,* which to me was the most exciting show. I would envision myself on Silver, the Lone Ranger's horse, riding off into the "wild blue yonder" with Tonto; it did not matter that the phrase "wild blue yonder" normally refers to the sky. "Riding off into the sunset" gave me the thrill of the sky's touching the barren land as my eyes were almost blinded by the sun. Tonto was so smooth. I still can almost hear his conversing with the Lone Ranger as they "rode along." It seemed to me that they, like true friends, really understood what each other was thinking. Therefore, they became my friends. I loved to listen to the horses' hooves as they would hit the rocks and sand. I could almost see the sand flying in the background as they trotted along. I especially loved to hear the Lone Ranger and Tonto when they crossed a stream or a river. It seemed to me that they were always looking for water, which they always found. They would also get the bad guys and bring them to justice. This was something I knew would always happen, for they were trustworthy.

One of the highlights of *The Lone Ranger* show was discussing it the following day with my friends because most of them also listened to that show. Lamar Akins, my age, who also enjoyed the show, and I sometimes would listen to the show together, either at his house or mine. Because the show was ongoing, sometimes we had to wait until a later show to find out what happened after a crucial episode. Often I could hardly stand the wait because I wanted to know so badly what would happen. I remember that Lamar and I often would speculate as to what would happen; it would be exciting to have guessed right. But I knew, no matter the outcome, that Tonto and the Lone Ranger would do the right thing.

Other radio shows that were fun to listen to were *Dagwood and Blondie, Superman, and Henry Aldrich.* Henry was so funny, for he was always getting into mischief.

The Major Bowls Amateur Hour was the setting for our family listening. My mother and dad always said it was a program we really needed to listen to, for it engaged aspiring singers, musicians, and comedians. Wishing that I didn't have to sit through it and pretending to listen, but turning my thoughts elsewhere, I don't remember much about that show. It might have been good for us children, but I barely endured it.

One of the radio programs that I do remember listening to most as a small child, in companionship with my dad, was the heavyweight boxing matches. I am not sure, but I think that I may have listened to the heavyweight boxing championship of the world, in 1937, when Joe Louis won. I was just a little guy, about four, but I later remember my dad and the other men talking about the match when I was in their company.

Of course, the baseball games were exciting for us I remember the New York Yankees, my dad's favorite team. He would tell me that he would listen to the game on the radio and imagine that he was a devoted fan, cheering them on from the stadium seat. It was always a big desire of his to attend a Yankee baseball game in Yankee Stadium, or better yet, the World Series. One of my biggest regrets is that he didn't get to do either. Dad died at age sixty-one, but I wouldn't be surprised to learn that he is managing a baseball team in Heaven and, furthermore, to know he has Ralph Cobb, Babe Ruth, and Mickey Mantle on his team. (Sometimes, when a game would be on the radio and the moon would be shining brightly, he would say, "I wonder if the moon is shining like that in New York at Yankee Stadium tonight.")

The year I graduated from high school, Mother and Dad purchased a television. I remember how much, thereafter, my dad enjoyed watching the major league games! Television was as close as he ever got to a major-league game. He would have loved the Atlanta Braves!

I remember a radio station would carry games when the Atlanta Crackers would play teams from cities like Birmingham, Alabama; Nashville and Memphis, Tennessee; Little Rock, Arkansas; and New Orleans, Louisiana. Dad said the game was teletyped. The station personnel would receive the teletype and transcribe it over the local radio stations; they would hear the game before the listening audience did. In addition, the announcers and other station personnel would create an environment as if they were at the game; therefore, I always thought the game was happening right then as I was listening to it.

In the days of my youth, the Atlanta Crackers played their home games at Ponce de Leon Park. The park was located on the north side of Ponce de Leon Avenue, across the street from the huge Sears, Roebuck and Company Catalog and Retail Center. It was easy to get there and a "fun" place to go. My family would board the streetcar in Smyrna and ride to the Georgia Power Building at Walton and Poplar streets, in Atlanta, walk down to Broad Street, and catch a streetcar that read "Ponce de Leon Park." (The park was also used for other events, including the Billy Graham Crusade in 1949.) The streetcars ran every half hour. It took about thirty minutes on the streetcar to get to Walton and Poplar streets and another fifteen minutes from Broad Street to the ball park. Some of the people, other than family, with whom I remember attending the games were "Buddy" Scoggins, Bobby Fortner, Hoyt Dorris, and "Bill" Scoggins.

NOTE: The streetcar lines were closed down in 1947, and Georgia Power Company began using trackless trolleys in Atlanta. Trolleys were buses with overhead power lines that provided smoother riding than did the streetcars, which ran on rails. Both systems were very effective modes of transportation. The trolley system did not extend into Cobb County, whereas the streetcar did. When the streetcar operation into Cobb County ceased, Georgia Power Company sold the route to a company that provided bus service into Cobb County, Smyrna, and Marietta for a few years. I believe the name of the company was Atlanta Northern Lines.

Fifth House

Reed and **Mary McCollum** lived in this house, next door to us, when we first moved to Bank Street. Later on, they built a house on the south side of Bank Street and moved there. See *McCollum, south side of Bank Street.*

Mr. and **Mrs. Dave Ingle**

Edith and **Dave Ingle** and their daughter, **Sue**, moved into the fifth house after the McCollums vacated. Sue and my sister, Hilda, were good friends, both graduating in the Smyrna High School Class of 1948. Sue was also in Hilda's wedding, in 1950.

Sue married Robert Lewis, who was a member of the large Sam Lewis Family on Highland Avenue. They had two daughters: Marsha and Mary Jane, who as small children, along with their mother, Sue, lived with the Ingles. I can remember Marsha and Mary Jane crawling through our door often when they were just toddlers. See *Lewis Family, Highland Avenue.*

Dave Ingle worked at the Grinnell Company in Atlanta. A pipe fitter with this company, he installed fire sprinkler systems, among other things. Dave died sometime in the 1960s. Edith, who outlived my mother, lived past the age of eighty; she and my mother remained friends until Mother died on February 9, 1992. The Ingles were faithful members of First Baptist Church.

Sixth House

Mr. and **Mrs**. **George Groce** live on the west side of the Ingles. They had one son, **Keith**. Mrs. Groce was the former Eunice Miller. I remember well the day that George died suddenly. I was at home that day and went over to see if I could help. After George's death, Eunice maintained her home on Bank Street for more than a quarter of a century, until her health failed. She lived the rest of her life with Keith and his family.

Keith Groce and his wife had one child, George. Keith divorced and later married Tammy Johnson, whose daughter, Jessica, Keith adopted. He and Tammy had a daughter, Christi. Keith worked for Atlantic Steel, in Atlanta.

George Groce, a very large man, was very likeable. George, whose mother and dad lived on Spring Street, was a member of First Methodist Church. See *Groce, south side of Spring Street.*

Eunice Miller Groce's family originated in Sweden. Her parents were immigrants to this country in the early part of the Twentieth Century.

Eunice, a faithful member of First Baptist Church, taught in the First Baptist Church Kindergarten, from which she retired. Lillie had the privilege of being associated with Eunice for many years through the preschool and kindergarten programs at the church, especially in the 1960s and 1970s.

Seventh House

Mrs. Mary Voss resided in the next house. She was a widow with three children: **Martha**, **Jimmy**, and **Mary**.

Eighth House

Mr. and **Mrs. Emory J. Paris** were residents of the house next door to Mrs. Voss. They had one son, **Emory Duane**. Mrs. Emory Paris died in an automobile accident sometime in the early 1940s. See *Paris, King Springs Road.*

Duane Paris married Marilynn Edmonds, the daughter of Mr. and Mrs. Sam Edmonds. Duane and Marilynn had three children: Mike, Nancy, and Sam. Marilynn, along with her mother, Mrs. Sam (Hester) Edmonds, taught at Smyrna School. Duane, Marilynn, and Mrs. Edmonds were members of First Methodist Church.

NOTE: After I finished high school and entered college, there were two other houses built between our house and Hamby Street.

Ninth House

Carolyn and **Denny Jerome** built next door to the Paris house in the early 1950s and were residents there for some time. The Jerome Family were members of First Baptist Church.

Tenth House

Martha and **Sam Cochran** lived in the house on the northeast corner of Bank and Hamby streets. Sam was a member of the large Cochran Family who lived on the east side of Roswell Street. Martha and Sam were members of First Baptist Church. See *Cochran, east side of Roswell Street.*

NOTE: Bank Street westward from Hamby Street early in the 1940s was a gravel street. This part of Bank Street was paved in the late 1940s and early 1950s.

Eleventh House

Clyde and **Sara Herren** lived in this house, west of the vacant lot at the northwest corner of Bank and Hamby streets. They had three children: **Bonnie, Clyde Herren**, **Jr**., known as "Buster," and **Johnny**. Sara was a member of the Gentry Family who lived near Carmichael's Streetcar Stop, between Log Cabin Drive and Atlanta Road. Clyde and Sara moved to Oakview Drive in 1955. Both are deceased. See *Smyrna Amateur Baseball Team, north side of Bank Street.*

Bonnie Herren married Jimmy Potts; they had two children: Cary and Ann Whitten.

Ann Whitten Potts married Tom Bourne of Stone Mountain.

Clyde Herren, Jr., known as "Buster," married Nena Caviness of Canton. They had two daughters: Jessica and Jill.

Jessica Herren married Jeff Llewallyn of Smyrna.

Johnny Herren married Denita Cheek of Smyrna: they had two sons: John, Jr. and Justin. Denita and Johnny divorced; he then married Joy Llewallyn of Smyrna. They had one son, Jake. After Johnny and Joy Llewallyn divorced, he married the former Joan Jackson of Smyrna. They had twin daughters: Jean and Jamie.

Twelfth House

Mr. and Mrs. Dudley Cooper were residents here. Mrs. Cooper was the former Nell Tatum from Atlanta's Bolton community. They had three daughters: Sylvia, Nancy, and Sue. See *Cooper, Pickens Street.*

Nell Tatum Cooper was the daughter of John and Addie Tatum of Habersham County. She worked at Whittier Mills in Atlanta's Bolton community.

Dudley Cooper served two years in the United States Army during World War II. After the War, he drove a truck until he became employed at Lockheed Aircraft Corporation when it opened in 1951, he retired from Lockheed. The family attended Riverside Baptist Church in Atlanta's Bolton community. Dudley had two sisters, Ruth Dunton and Cora Fowler, and two brothers, Gideon and Carl Cooper. See *Fowler, King Springs Road* and *east side of Concord Road*

Sylvia Cooper married Edward Daniel Cherry of Bowling Green, Kentucky. They had two daughters: Dana Jill and Kimberly Jane. Dan and Sylvia moved to Bowling Green, Kentucky, after he retired from the United States Air Force, where he had been a leader of the "Thunderbirds," a special unit like the "Blue Angels." According to family information, Dan's grandfather was very instrumental in the building of a college in Bowling Green, Kentucky.

Dana Jill Cherry married Brian Tweed from North Carolina. They had two children: Madeline and Claire.

Kimberly Jane Cherry married Steve McGowen from Las Vegas, Nevada. They had two children: Maggie and Amelia.

Nancy Cooper married Joseph Daniel Logan, known as "Joe." The Logans had two sons: Joseph Mark and Scott Daniel. "Joe," the son of Mr. and Mrs. Pete Logan, had a twin brother, Brown, and another brother, Eddie. Brown and Eddie are both deceased. See *Logan east side of Old Concord Road.*

Joseph Mark Logan married Donna Roland from Greensboro. They had two children: Katie Leigh and Joseph. Donna is deceased. Mark and his children live in Marietta.

Scott Daniel Logan married Colleen Marie McGetterick from Chattanooga, Tennessee. They had two children: Brandon Scott and Hanna Marie. Scott and Colleen live in West Cobb County.

Sue Cooper married Richard Brooks from Marietta. They had two children: Richard Lane and Susan Kelly. Sue and Richard live in Acworth.

Thirteenth House

William Marcus Reed, known as "Bill," married **Virginia Lee Pepper** of Bloomfield, Missouri. They had three children: **William Marcus Reed II**, **Cynthia Pepper Reed**, and **Bruce Thomas Reed**. After World War II, "Bill" and Virginia built a house about midway between Hamby Street and the Clayton house. See *Reed, Atlanta Street, from Mrs. Mazie's to Pearce Matthews.*

"Bill" Reed founded Reed Realty in Smyrna in 1949. Mark Reed continues to own and operate Reed Realty, which is now located in Roswell.

William Marcus Reed II, known as "Mark," married Michelle Davis. They had two sons: "Bill" III and Lew.

Cynthia Pepper Reed married Larry Savage.

Bruce Thomas Reed married Beth Ingram. Bruce is now married to Katherine Leonard; they had two daughters: Laura and Paula

Fourteenth House

Mr. and **Mrs. Hubert Colquitt** moved to Smyrna in the late 1940s. She was the former Frances Corley of Thomaston. They had three children: **Gayle**, **Wayne**, and **Claire**.

Gayle Colquitt married Stephen Ruddell, known as "Steve," who grew up in the Oakdale community. He was the son of Mr. and Mrs. Herbert Ruddell, who also had a daughter, Sandra. Mrs. Ruddell was the former Ruby Patterson. Gayle and Stephen had three children: Russell, known as "Russ," Jeffrey, known as "Jeff," and Leslie. See *Patterson, Medlin Street* and *Concord Road, the Country Road.*

"Russ" Ruddell lives in Smyrna and is a member of First Baptist Church.

"Jeff" Ruddell married Mandy Phillips, who grew up in the Vinings area. They had two sons, Chandler and Chapman. Jeff and our son, Steve, have been close friends since they were very young children. They both live with their families in West Cobb County.

Leslie Ruddell married Brandon Moore, who grew up in Smyrna.

Wayne Colquitt married Donna Tilly from Jonesboro. They had two sons: Gavin and Bryce.

Claire Colquitt married Mark Curtis of Smyrna. They had two daughters: Megan and Sarah. Mark passed away in autumn of 2004.

Megan Curtis married Jeff Leathers, and Sarah Curtis married Paul Bennett.

The Colquitts came to Smyrna from Thomaston and opened Wayne's 5, 10, & 25 Cents, a store in downtown Smyrna. Later on they moved the store to Dickson Shopping Center, where it was Wayne's. When Belmont Hills Shopping Center opened in 1954, Hubert and Frances opened Colquitt's Gift Shop there. In 1972 they opened Colquitt's Dress Shop in Dickson Shopping Center and operated it up into the 1980s. Hubert was also a director of Security National Bank in Smyrna. The Colquitts, in business in Smyrna for thirty-five years, were members of First Baptist Church. See *Waynes Five and Ten, Atlanta Street, from Marlowe's to Creatwood.*

Frances and Hubert built a house on Northview Place, off Collier Drive, in the 1950s. Hubert died in September 2003, and Frances died in February 2004. Frances was still living on Northview Place when she died.

Fifteenth House

Mr. and **Mrs. Martin Ruff, Sr.**, were residents here. They had four children: **Martin, Jr.**, **Virginia**, **Kitty**, and **Rex**. See *Concord Road, the Country Road.*

Sixteenth House

Mr. and **Mrs. Clifford Crider** lived in this house. They had a son, Leonard, who bought this house for his parents sometime in the late 1940s or early 1950s. Mrs. Crider was formerly Esther Spruill from Sandy Springs. Mr. Crider died in the 1950s, and Mrs. Crider continued to live here until she died, in 1978. Mrs. Crider was also the mother of Jewell Wood Wallace. See *Walker Street.*

Leonard Crider served in the United States Army during World War II. Being a cook while he was in military service may have been Leonard's beginning as a cook. After returning from the military, he cooked at G.B.'s Place. Leonard married Ethelle Davis from Fairmount; they had two daughters: Joan and Risa. Afterwards, Leonard bought a house on Hurt Road next door to G.B. and Vonceil Williams.

Seventeenth House

Mr. and **Mrs**. **Roy Hunton,** who resided here, had two children: **Sammy** and **Betty**. Mrs. Hunton was the former Edith Williams. According to family information, G.B. Williams built this house in the mid 1940s for his sister, Edith, and her husband, Roy Hunton. This property abutted property owned by G.B. Williams on Powder Springs Street, where he built four other houses. See *south side of Powder Springs Street.*

Eighteenth House

The Wehunt Family were residents of this house, according to Beverly, the Crider's granddaughter.

The Bailey Family

"Millie" Clayton Broyles remembered that a **Bailey Family** also lived in this house. She recalls that they moved to the North Georgia Mountains, where she spent a weekend with them once.

Nineteenth House

Mr. and **Mrs**. **Paul Clayton** lived in the last house on Bank Street. They had two daughters: **Mildred**, known as "Millie," and **Pauline**. Mrs. Clayton was the former Ida Mae Black.

Mildred Clayton, known as "Millie," married Vic Broyles of Kirksville, Missouri. The couple had one son, Robin. Vic was a charter member of the Smyrna Jaycees and was employed by the City of Smyrna as Public Works Director. "Millie" Clayton was a member of the Smyrna High School Class of 1951.

Robin Broyles married Pamela Stevens of New Hampshire. They had two children: Kevin and Kellie. Robin is currently Chief Building Official for the City of Smyrna.

"Millie" Clayton Broyles shared some memories she has of a murder that occurred in Smyrna in the late 1930s. This is the way she remembers it: "A father, his daughter and her son were attacked at their homes. After the father was murdered outside his home, the assailant went next door, raped and murdered the daughter, and attempted to murder the son. The little boy, who was about ten years old, was left for dead but survived and was able to assist the authorities in identifying the attacker."

Ida Mae Clayton, "Millie's" mother, knew the assailant. He had delivered firewood to her home many times.

The Claytons were living on Foster Street at the time, and "Millie" was playing in her yard while the lady's funeral was being held at Spring Street Baptist Church. "Millie" says, "I remember seeing, in the front of the church at that time, members of the Ku Klux Klan in full 'white-sheeted' attire."

Pauline Clayton married Harold Wood from Manchester, New Hampshire. The couple had no children. Pauline worked for Fulton Savings and Loan Association in Atlanta for many years. In fact, I believed she retired from there. Harold came to Marietta in 1953 to work at Lockheed Aircraft Corporation, from which he retired after forty-one years of service. Harold, a member of the Smyrna Jaycees (1960 and 1970s), and Pauline live in Marietta.

Ida Mae Black and Paul Clayton married March 25, 1933. Ida Mae grew up on Terrell Mill Road in east Cobb County, near Powers Ferry Road. She was not a member of the Roy Black Family that also lived on Terrell Mill Road.

Standing L-R: Pauline Clayton (Woods), "Millie" Clayton (Broyles), and Paul Clayton. **Seated**: Ida (Black) Clayton in front of their Bank Street House. Circa 1970s Courtesy of "Millie" Broyles

Charley and **Paul Clayton**, with their mother, **Ella Elizabeth Clayton**.
Circa 1930s Courtesy of "Millie" Broyle

Ella Elizabeth Clayton. At a relatives home in Jonesboro, in 1941, with grandson**;** Johnny Clayton sitting on car. **Granddaughters L-R:** Betty, Martha, Pauline, Mildred and Edna Clayton. Circa 1940s Courtesy of "Millie" Clayton Broyles

Ella Elizabeth Clayton holding **Pauline Clayton. Betty Clayton** sitting next to Grandmother, in front of the Paul Clayton Home on Bank Street. Circa 1940s Courtesy of "Millie" Broyles

Paul Clayton, who grew up in Ellijay (Gilmer County), came to Smyrna as a young mar seeking work. He and his mother, Ella Elizabeth Quinn Clayton, lived on "Sally's Alley" (thought tc be what later became Fuller Street). After Paul and Ida Mae married, they lived on "Sally's Alley,' along with Paul's mother, who continued to live with Paul and Ida Mae for twenty-five years, until he death, April 6, 1958. In 1932 there were two houses located in the area called "Sally's Alley": th Claytons living in one, and John and Bessie Martin living in the other. See *Walker Street.*

The Claytons moved from "Sally's Alley" to Matthews Street, Next door to Mrs. Lula Byrd Their first child, Mildred, known as "Millie," was born there May 18, 1934. The delivering physicia was Dr. Ralph Fowler, who had a medical office in Smyrna. At an early age "Millie" became ill an had to learn to walk again. The Claytons moved from Matthews Street to Spring Street, next door tc the McDowell/Robinson families, where daughter Pauline was born August 21, 1938.

Paul and Ida Mae moved from Spring Street to Foster Street and from there to a small house on the west side of Roswell Street, just south of the ice plant. From there they moved to Pickens Street In 1942 Paul and Ida Mae moved to Bank Street, where Paul lived until his death, in 1993. Ida Mae maintained the yard and paid the utility bills at the Bank Street house for the next ten years, but she never spent another nigh there after Paul's death. She is currently living with Pauline. See *Clayton Pickens Street.*

Paul and Ida Mae personally built the house on Bank Street. Never having done any building before, they constructed the house almost entirely of cement blocks and used discarded lumber fron Bell Bomber Plant for door and window facings and other areas requiring wood. The house was buil at the back of the lot because Paul's idea was to build another house at the front and use the origina house as a garage. But that never happened. For forty years the Clayton Family lived in the house a the back of the lot.

Ida Mae was a homemaker except for the time when she was the cook at Paul's Café "Millie" has shared, "Mother and Dad prepared breakfast at Paul's Café for all of my classmates wher we were going on our Senior trip to Jacksonville, Florida, in 1951."

After her daughters were grown and married, Ida Mae became employed at Sonoco Pape Company, where she worked for twenty years, or until her retirement. That was the only job she eve had in the business world, and she really enjoyed it.

Early in his life Paul Clayton worked for the Standard Feed and Seed Company. Later h owned and operated Paul Clayton Gulf Oil Station on Atlanta Street for many years. He sold tha business to Gil Lynch.

Paul also had a small print shop in his home, where he would print invitations, notices, an other types of items for citizens in the community. Janet Brooks Brown remembers that when she wa young, he did some printing for her on special occasions. When the house on Bank Street was sold Mrs. Clayton left the printing equipment in the house; everything was claimed by the wrecking crew ir the early 2000s.

Paul, very civic minded, was involved in many activities. A charter member of the Smyrn Lions Club in 1946, he, at the time of his death, had forty years perfect attendance. Just before he died he received the Melvin Jones Award, the highest award given by Lions Club International.

Ella Elizabeth Clayton was the widow of Thomas Jefferson Clayton, whom she married i 1908. Prior to their marriage, Mr. Clayton had one son, James, known as "Jim." Ella and Thomas ha two sons together: Charles, known as "Charlie," and Paul. See *nineteenth house, north side of Ban Street.*

"Charlie" Clayton married Maude Fraser. See *Clayton, south side of Powder Springs Street.*

James Clayton married Vera Belle Hughes of Douglas County, where they settled and raised ive children: Betty, James Dilmus, known as "Dink," Doris, Tommy, and Terry.

In 1948 Paul Clayton's nephew, **James Dilmus Clayton**, known as "Dink," came to Smyrna rom Douglasville and lived with Paul and Ida Mae until he married. See *nineteenth house, north side f Bank Street.*

James Dilmus Clayton, known as "Dink," married Betty Garnto in 1950. At the time of her arriage to "Dink," Betty was living with an aunt and uncle, Frank and Grace Gardner, north of myrna, off Dixie Avenue. Betty grew up in Dublin (Laurens County). After their marriage, Betty and Dink" bought a house on Wayland Court, where they raised their family. They had two children: erry and Beverly.

Betty Garanto Clayton began working at Lockheed Aircraft Corporation when it opened in 951 and retired from there in 1995. "Dink" retired from Black and Decker in 1985, after thirty-two ears of service. He then joined his son, Terry, in the sporting goods business. The original store was cated in Belmont Hills Shopping Center for many years before being relocated to Concord Road; the usiness was sold in 2002. Betty and "Dink" still live in Smyrna, in the Cheney Woods community. etty and "Dink" are members of First Baptist Church, where Betty is active in the Friendship Sunday chool Class.

Terry Clayton married Deborah Chupp from Sparta. They had two daughters: Caroline and athleen. Terry and Deborah live in Smyrna, where Deborah teaches school.

Beverly Clayton married Michael Stephens. They had one son, Adrian Thomas. Divorced om Michael, Beverly and Adrian live in Smyrna.

BANK STREET
South Side

Appreciation is extended to the following Bank Street residents for sharing information about eir families on Bank Street in the days of my youth: William Austin Atkins, known as "Bill," orothy Moseley Bacon, known as "Dot," Eleanor Reed Bruce, Gayle Martin Gober, Ruth Adams ancock, Helen Blackwell Hanson, Barbara Adams Porter, William H. Scoggins, known as "Bill," and ohn Thomas Thatch.

Eleanor Reed Bruce, Gayle Martin Gober, Barbara Adams Porter, and "Bill" Scoggins grew p on Bank Street; "Dot" Bacon and Helen Hanson moved to Bank Street as new brides in the 1940s. With all of these I share many memories.) "Dot" moved to the street immediately after World War II, nd Helen and her husband, B.H. Hanson, Jr. moved to their new house on Bank Street in 1948. "Dot" nd Helen still reside on Bank Street in the houses where they lived with their husbands. They have bserved many changes that transformed Smyrna from a small town of a little more than 2,000 citizens the 1950 census to a thriving city of 42,000 in the 2000 census.

I remember most of the people who lived on Bank Street during my growing up years. It as my street, and I loved living there. I fondly recall the peace and contentment I felt while growing p in my home and living among the people who were my neighbors.

My dad and Arthur Bacon were both in politics. Arthur and Dad respected and supported ach other in their efforts to improve Smyrna and keep it a good place in which to live and raise amilies. One time in the 1950s they became "crossed up" and ran against each other. Dad won the ection for City Councilman.

The Bacons were always active in First Methodist Church. "Dot" Bacon shared the llowing story. "On the following Sunday morning after the election, Arthur went to church and flashed a pistol in his Sunday School class. Mr. John Matthews, the teacher of the class, asked Arthu 'Why do you have a gun in the Church?'

"Arthur replied, 'Anyone as unpopular as I am needs protection.'"

Dad's last term on the Smyrna City Council expired in December 1969, eleven months before he died.

Arthur returned to politics. He served six years as City Councilman from Ward 3 and wa elected Mayor in 1976. Arthur died in office October 26,1985. Like my dad, he was a hometown gu that loved Smyrna and always had the City's best interest at heart. Arthur and Dad served in an e when real politics were the norm.

"Dot" related to me that in that era she would buy buttermilk from Mrs. McLean o Stephens Street and the Paul Austin Family on North Cooper Lake Road. A common practice in thos days for people to make extra money was selling their churned buttermilk, butter, eggs, chicken vegetables, and other consumables.

First House

Mr. and **Mrs**. **Kary Jackson** lived in this house with their three daughters: **Caroly Frances**, and **Muriel**. Mrs. Jackson was the former Jeanette Parnell, the daughter of Mr. and Mr Fletcher Parnell. This was the first house on the south side of Bank Street from Atlanta Street. In th days of my youth it was located directly behind Walker Akins Grocery Store, which faced Atlan Street. According to information from the Jackson Family, this house, built by John Fletcher Parne was the oldest house on Bank Street at the time the Jacksons lived there. See *Parnell, west side of Kin Street,* and *Parnell* and *Lewis, Highland Avenue.*

Carolyn Jackson married William Curtis Thatch from Apison, Tennessee. They had tw children: John Thomas and Brenda Carol. The Thatch Family moved to Chattanooga, Tennessee, i 1954.

Brenda Carol Thatch married Jim Barber and lives in Marietta.

John Thomas Thatch and his family live in Marietta.

Frances Jackson married Hugh Echols. They had one daughter, Pamela, who married Lonni McCurry. Pamela and Lonnie currently live in Chickamauga.

Muriel Jackson married Jim Evans. They had one son, Cliff, who lives on Love Street.

Second House

Mr. and **Mrs**. **Ralph Martin** resided next door to the Jacksons. Mrs. Martin's given nam was **Jewett**. In 1945 the Martins moved to 109 Bank Street, where they lived until 1954, when the moved to Pinetree Drive, in the Forest Hills community. They had four children: **Shirley**, born i 1934; **Judy**, in 1940; **Gayle**, in 1944; and **Doug**, in 1946.

Shirley Martin married Sammy Sanford, the son of Mr. and Mrs. Grady Sanford. The coupl had three children: Buck, Sheri, and Stacie.

Judy Martin married Stan Nix. The couple had two children: Stan and Alicia. Judy current lives in Marietta.

Gayle Martin married Phil Gober; they had two children: Gary and Sandy. Gayle and Phi who are members of First Baptist Church, Live in Marietta.

Sandy Gober married David McIntosh, the son of Aubrey and Hazel McIntosh.

Gary Gober married and had one daughter, Emma. Gary, who grew up with our son, Stephen, now deceased. See *fourth house* and *McIntosh, west side of King Springs Road.*

Doug Martin married Linda Prince. The Martins had three children: Andrew, Russ, and Lori. ug and Linda live in Pensacola, Florida.

In the 1930s and 1940s, tuberculosis was a raging, contagious disease that affected many ople. Drastic measures were required for the patient to get well and for the public to be protected m exposure. Around the state were located hospitals for the treatment of the disease

Ralph Martin, because of tuberculosis, in 1948 had to go to Batty State Hospital in Rome for atment. He was there for five years, not an unusual time frame, for it took a long time for a person recover from tuberculosis. Ralph was lucky because many people did not survive.

According to family information, while Ralph was hospitalized, his wife, Jewett, supported family by renting out part of their house and sewing for the public. During that time she made the oir robes for First Baptist Church.

Ralph Martin was a builder. Gayle shared that, when her dad returned home in 1953, he built ouse for the family and three other houses on Pinetree Drive, in the Forest Hills community, about t time. She also shared that Pinetree Drive was not paved then and that a professional archery range s located at the end of the street.

Gayle remembers that, when her family lived on Bank Street, she and her siblings were not owed to go to the Pressley Farm, which was in the next block, because it was too far for them as ung children to go alone. She said they loved going there, for Mr. and Mrs. Pressley had chickens, ws, an apple orchard, and a clay pit. To them it was like going to the country. See *Pressley, sixth use.*

Third House

Mr. and **Mrs. B.F. Reed, Jr.**, lived in this house. Mrs. Reed was the former Jessie Belle ok. The Reeds had five children: **Mary Eleanor**, **Rita Frances**, **Benjamin Franklin Reed III**, own as "Ben," **Clifton Webber,** and **Jessie Mae**. Mr. Reed, a builder in Smyrna, developed anklin Heights subdivision, off Church Street, which he named after his first son, Benjamin Franklin ed III. Three streets in the subdivision were named for three of his children: Eleanor Way, Rita ay, and Clifton Road.

Mary Eleanor Reed married Robert Tye Bruce, from the Oakdale community. They had four ildren: Robert Marshall, Margaret Angela, known as "Angel," William Ronald, known as "Ronnie," d Clifton Reed, known as "Cliff."

Robert Bruce married Kem Mansfield. They had two children: William Christopher and uren Kemberly.

Angel Bruce, a CPA, owns her own company. Angel, who has no children of her own, loves nieces and nephews.

Ronnie Bruce married Anna Pickelsimer. They had two children: Bridgett Renee and Hunter le. Ronnie is a policeman in Smyrna.

Cliff Bruce married Lisa Chastain; they had one daughter, Kelsey Angela.

Eleanor, a stay-at-home mom and homemaker, began working after her children were grow Over the past thirty years, she has been serving in a secretarial position to pastors in Cobb Count churches. Eleanor lives in Acworth in the home that her "beloved husband," Bobby, literally built fc her. He worked night and day for two years to complete this country home. Bobby Bruce died Januar 11, 2003.

Rita Frances Reed married Charles Larry Harper from Cordele. They had two childre Wendy Leigh and Mickey. Rita, once a full-time homemaker, has, over the past fifteen year performed secretarial duties in churches in Douglasville. Charles is a teacher and a coach.

Wendy Leigh Harper and her husband, Mick, had one child, Bay. Wendy is in administratic at Six Flags over Georgia; Mick is a coach.

Benjamin Franklin Reed III, known as "Ben," married Donna Marie Reiman. The two c them attended school together. "Ben" earned a Bachelor of Architecture degree from the Georgi Institute of Technology and a Masters degree from Harvard University. He recently retired as cc owner of Laubmann-Reed Associates, Inc., located in Atlanta. Ben served as Chairman of the Board Deacons at First Baptist Church of Atlanta. Donna worked for over thirty years with Reverend Joh Glover, who directs *The Passion Play* for First Baptist Church of Atlanta. The Ben Reeds had n children.

Clifton Webber Reed married but divorced Donna Leigh Lancaster. They had no children. H trained in Dahlonega as a paratrooper and was a ranger. Cliff retired from active service in the Unite States Army as a Lieutenant Colonel after serving for over twenty years. He served in Vietnam an was awarded three purple hearts and other medals of commendation; he was also stationed in Kore and in Germany during his tenure. He is an active member of First Baptist Church of Atlanta.

Jessie Mae Reed married Gregory Bruce McGahee of Smyrna. They had two sons: Grego Reed McGahee and Christopher Shane McGahee. Jessie has been a manager in the insurance busine for many years. She lives in Douglasville.

Christopher Shane McGahee married Jacqueline Leigh Galbraith. They had one so Michael.

Mrs. Jessie Cook Reed was the daughter of Reverend John E. Cook and Emma Bruce Coo who came from Polk County, Tennessee, to Hemp, Georgia, late in the Nineteenth Century. Emn Bruce Cook's grandparents migrated from Pickens County, South Carolina, to Hemp, Georgia, late i the Nineteenth Century.

Emma Bruce and John Cook had five children: Arkie, Charles, Lura, Jessie, and Ella. All the girls were educators; Charles was a chemist in Copperhill, Tennessee.

Jessie Cook Reed graduated, in 1935, from Piedmont College, in Demorest, with a Bachel of Science degree. She taught high school mathematics in the Smyrna High School School, 1935-194 and married B.F. Reed, Jr. ., in May 1940.

Charles Cook, a brother of Jessie Belle Reed, shared the following information on the parents: "Early in their marriage our parents, Reverend and Mrs. John Cook, began planning for the children's education. Mother became an agent for Aladdin Lamps with the aim of providing adequa light so that we children would not injure our eyesight while studying. Reverend Cook, a Methodi minister, was farmer and apple orchard owner.

"Both our parents made many sacrifices. There were two winters when Mother took us Epworth Grammar School. Dad stayed home, keeping house and tending the livestock and chicken All household chores were his. We would come back from school in the early spring to help pla crops.

"All of us children except Ella went to Epworth Seminary and then to Tennessee Wesleyan Junior College, where we graduated. Ella went to Fannin County High School. She attended two years at Piedmont College and earned a Bachelor of Science degree in 1953 from Oglethorpe University, in DeKalb County. She taught school one year in Fannin County, then taught forty-three years in Cobb County as a first grade teacher."

Ella Cook, who taught at Smyrna Elementary School, married Murphy McBrayer; they had one son, Mac. Murphy owned and operated a Gulf station on Atlanta Street. At one time, they lived on the north side of Bank Street. Mrs. "Mac" McBrayer still lives in Smyrna, in the Forest Hills community, on Pinetree Drive. See *McBrayer, north side of Sunset Avenue.*

When I was growing up, I cut Mrs. Jessie Reed's grass with a push mower. The property extended through to West Spring Street. The back yard was a steep hill before it was graded down for the building of the Smyrna City Hall in the late 1950s. Mrs. Reed, a teacher at Smyrna Elementary School, paid me a dollar. It was rough for me as a kid on a hot day to cut that grass with a push mower, but I just kept that dollar in my mind. I liked Mrs. Reed a lot; she was a very nice lady.

B.F. Reed. built the Southern Manor Apartments next door to the school property, which is across the street from First Baptist Church. This was the first apartment complex built in Smyrna; Raymond Reed, an attorney in Marietta and B.F. Reed's brother, retained ownership of the apartments into the early 2000s. Raymond still maintains a home on Atlanta Street. See *Atlanta Street, from Marlowe's to Creatwood.*

In addition to being a builder, B.F. Reed, Jr., owned and operated the Don Ree, which was a restaurant and bar located on Atlanta Road in Marietta. The Don Ree was north of the intersection of South Cobb Drive and Atlanta Road at the overpass in Marietta. Atlanta Road in the days of my youth was to the south of the railroad tracks and did not cross the railroad until about a block before reaching the Marietta Cemetery.

Fourth House

Reverend and **Mrs. H.B. McIntosh** lived in the next house. They had three children: **Aubrey, Agnes**, and **Grover**, who were all grown when I was only a child. Reverend McIntosh was a barber and a part-time preacher. I remember him well; however, I do not remember his cutting my hair or my hearing him preach. The McIntoshes, both very kind people, were members of First Baptist Church. Aubrey McIntosh and his sister, Agnes, joined First Baptist Church during a revival that was held during the months of April and May of 1934. Grover McIntosh was baptized at First Baptist Church on June 28, 1936.

Grover McIntosh
Casualty
World War II

Grover was killed in World War II in the Normandy Invasion. Though only about ten years old, I remember that day so well. Mrs. McIntosh was a two-star mother, hanging stars in her window to indicate that she had two sons serving in the War. She hung a gold star in her window after Grover was killed.

On the day of the news that Grover, who loved his country, had been killed, I remember, my dad went up to see the family. It was a sad time on Bank Street. People were saying that we should be very grateful that Grover had been willing to go and serve and die that we might have freedom.

My dad had several friends serving in "that foreign War," as people called it. He corresponded with them while they were serving overseas. Two of them were Scott Edwards, Jr., who became an attorney in Marietta, and J.C. Austin, a friend and neighbor. Both of them were members o the Smyrna Amateur Baseball Team. .

Years after Aubrey was discharged from the service, he married a lady named Hazel, whos maiden name I never knew; she was not from Smyrna. In the late 1940s or early 1950s they built nice brick house on King Springs Road, just south of Concord Road on the west side of the street Hazel McIntosh died a few years ago; Aubrey continued living in this house until he required assiste living. He and Hazel were members of First Baptist Church

NOTE: The house, on King Springs Road, mentioned in the previous paragraph, wa demolished late in 2004 for redevelopment.

Agnes McIntosh married a minister whom I never knew; Reverend McIntosh preached a several small churches in the area.

Fifth House

Mr. and **Mrs. Howard Akins** were residents of this house. She was the former Ruby Wallace. They had two sons: **Billy** and **Lamar**. See *Wallace* on *Gilbert Street,* and *Akins* on *North Avenue.*

Lamar Akins and I were born the same day, November 29, 1933, twelve hours apart. I remember being told that I was born at four o'clock in the afternoon. Both of us were born in ou homes.

Lamar and I started to school together the same day and graduated together in the Smyrna High School Class of 1951. Growing up, we were good friends. My family moved across the stree from his family on Bank Street in 1940 before we started to school. However, we had known each other at First Baptist Church, where both of our families were members.

After we graduated from high school, Lamar went into the United State Air Force. Upon his discharge from the military, he settled with his family in Ohio. Lamar married Isabelle Rebfrew from Luton, England. They had three children: Blake, Kara-Dee, and Alia. I have seen him only a few times in our adult lifetime. However, I still feel very close to him, for he was my true friend and I have many memories of our playing in the vacant lots near our houses and in the deep back yard behind his house.

We had so much fun! Bank Street was a great area in which to grow up. I remember that the Akins Family had a horseshoe "pit" in their backyard. We always had plenty of room to play. I am sure there were ever-watchful eyes of some adult who knew what we were doing, but I did not mind that. In fact, looking back, I guess I thought that was the way it was supposed to be.

Billy Akins was older than Lamar and I but often played with us. Billy married Martha Barnett, who grew up in the Oakdale community, south of Smyrna. Martha, very active in sports, played on the Fitzhugh Lee High School Girls' Basketball Team.

Martha was the daughter of Mr. and Mrs. Milton Barnett. Mrs. Barnett was the former Lucille Brooks, a member of the large Brooks Family on Roswell Street. See *east side of Roswell Street.*

Martha and Billy Akins moved to the Bennett Woods subdivision in the 1960s before Lillie and I did. When our children were growing up, Martha and Billy were members of King Spring Baptist Church. Still our neighbors, they are members of Saint James Episcopal Church in Marietta.

Mother and Mrs. Ruby Akins were good friends from the time I can first remember, even before we moved to Bank Street. Later on Mrs. Akins, an attractive lady and well groomed, worked at Rich's, a department store in downtown Atlanta. Mrs. Akins was always nice to me; therefore, I knew she was my friend. She was a member of the Wallace Family who lived on the east side of the railroad. Mr. and Mrs. Akins were active members of First Baptist Church. Mr. Akins worked at NC&St.L, formerly the Nashville, Chattanooga & St. Louis Railroad.

Sixth House

William Pressley
Smyrna City Councilman
1945-46

Mr. and **Mrs. William Pressley** had five children, all in their adulthood when we moved to Bank Street in 1940. Mr. Pressley was a widower with two children, **Thurston** and **Faye**, when he married his second wife, Ella Gaines. He and Ella had three children: **Gaines**, **James**, and **Elizabeth**.

The Pressley house stood where the present day Smyrna City Hall is located, on the corner of King and Bank streets. Even though the porch faced King Street on the east side of their house, I always considered the Pressleys as living on Bank Street.

I remember that, during World War II, Mrs. Pressley had a star in her window to represent her son who was serving our country. Their son-in-law, Woodrow Lutz, also served in the United States Army Air Corps. Many of the people in Smyrna who had someone serving in that War would hang a star in their window.

In the early 1930s, Mr. and Mrs. Pressley moved to Bank Street from Concord Road, the country road toward the covered bridge. The house they moved from is still standing on the southeast corner of Concord Road and Highview Drive, at the entrance to Bennett Woods subdivision.

Mr. Pressley was a streetcar conductor, but I do not think he was still working when we moved to Bank Street. He also served a term on the Smyrna City Council in the 1940s. A farmer, he always had a cow and some chickens. In fact, most of the people on Bank Street had chickens. I remember going to Mr. Pressley's barn and watching him milk his cow. I liked to watch him milk! Mr. Pressley, who owned the entire block between Stephens and Bank streets, had a garage, a barn, a pasture, and a garden. Also, he had fruit trees, beehives, and a well in that block. Mr. Pressley's barn was across the street from where West Spring Street ended at King Street. The Smyrna City Hall currently stands on what was Mr. Pressley's property.

The Pressleys were the nicest, kindest couple. I thought they were always old, maybe even born that way; it never occurred to me that they were once young. The Pressleys were also both short in stature. Being short myself, I always thought it was okay to be short, since they were both so nice.

Mr. and Mrs. W.M. Pressley were members of First Baptist Church, where he was a deacon and she was a member of the Women's Missionary Union.

Thurston Pressley, at the time of this writing in 2005, is ninety-eight years old. He lives in Detroit, Michigan, where he has been successful in operating several beauty salons and a beauty college. He now works for the person to whom he sold his beauty college that had two hundred students.

Faye Pressley married Chess Lovern, a first cousin of Jim Lovern, who lived on Powder Springs Street. I remember Faye and Chess coming to visit Mr. and Mrs. Pressley. Mr. Chess Lovern, a minister who rose to the position of Bishop in the Methodist Church, and Faye lived in Texas.

Gaines Pressley married Frances Massey. They had two children: James Patrick, known as "Jimmy," and Barbara.

Mrs. **Jeanette Parnell Jackson's** home on Bank Street. Circa 1957 Courtesy of Gerald Eaton

Evelyn and **James Pressley** pose beside the pecan tree (which is still standing on the north side of Smyrna City Hall) in Mr. And Mrs. William Pressley's yard on Bank Street NOTE: The Roy Wood house in the background. Early 1940s Courtesy of James and Evelyn Pressley

Mr. and **Mrs. William Pressley**
Circa 1940s Courtesy of James and Evelyn Pressley

"Jimmy" married Ann Cobb, the daughter of Edna and Ralph Cobb. Jimmy and Ann had a daughter, Kellie.

Barbara married Huey Hammond. They had three daughters: Beth, Susan, and Grace.

Gaines Pressley was a hairdresser who owned and operated a salon in Marietta and, later, one in Smyrna, in the Belmont Hills Shopping Center. He was President of the State Beauty School Association. One evening after having dinner and while speaking to a group from the Beauty School Association, he collapsed and died on stage. See *north side of Church Street.*

James Pressley married Evelyn Edwards, a member of the Pat Edwards Family, who lived on Love Street. They had three children: James, Jr., Mary Faye, and Melda. (Melda died in January 2004.) The Edwards house was located where First Methodist Church is today. See *Edwards, Love Street* and *Roswell Street*

James graduated from Oglethorpe University, in DeKalb County. After serving in the United States Army during World War II, he became the head football coach at Marietta High School. He recruited many guys from Smyrna to play football, one of whom was Pat Edwards, Jr., his brother-in-law. James later operated Pressley Insurance Agency, at the corner of Atlanta and Powder Springs streets. He and Evelyn built a house on Collier Drive in the Forest Hills community when it was developed sometime in the early 1950s. They are faithful members of First Methodist Church. See *north side of Love Street* and *Forest Hills community.*

Evelyn Pressley remarked that she and James, after his military service was finished, could have purchased the property where Bennett Woods subdivision is located for $10,000.00. But she told James, "I do not want to live in the country." To him, buying the property would have been like moving back home because he had grown up in the house that still stands at the southeast corner of Concord Road and Highview Drive. James' family left this area to move near the streetcar line for him to have transportation to Marietta High School in the 1930s.

Elizabeth Pressley married Woodrow Lutz. After World War II they moved to Florida. I recall that we would always receive a Christmas card from them. My dad kept in touch with Woodrow, who for many years was the pitcher on the Smyrna Amateur Baseball Team that my dad managed. Woodrow Lutz grew up in Marietta.

Seventh House

J.C. Austin and his wife, the former **Stella Mae Chandler**, were living here when J.C. joined the United States Navy after the beginning of World War II. Throughout the War, he served as a boatswain's mate on a destroyer in the Pacific Ocean. He and my dad corresponded during the War; I still have at least one of those letters. J.C. was the son of Mr. and Mrs. Paul Austin, who raised their large family on North Cooper Lake Road. J.C. Austin joined First Baptist Church at a revival meeting which was conducted in April and May of 1932. He was also a player on the Smyrna Amateur Baseball Team.

Stella Mae Chandler grew up on Austell Road, not far from the Milford community, near Hicks Road in Marietta. Sometime after the War, later in the 1940s, J.C. and Stella moved to Dunn Street, where their children grew up. See *Austin, Dunn Street* and *North Cooper Lake Road.*

The Horace Adams Family

Mr. and **Mrs. Horace Adams** moved to the seventh house after the Austins vacated. Mrs. Adams, the former Sallie Mae Morris, and Horace had two children: **Barbara** and **Curtis**. Sallie's parents, **Mr.** and **Mrs. Sam Morris**, lived with them. Sallie had two brothers: **Harley** and **William Pinkney Morris**, known as "Pinky," who also lived here at one time. The Morris Family later lived in two locations on Roswell Street. See *Morris, Roswell Street.*

Horace Adams worked for Atlanta Paper Company in Atlanta, which was later known as Mead Packaging Company. Sallie Mae Adams worked for Nunnally Candy Company, in Atlanta, and later with the Cobb County Board of Education, in the Smyrna and Campbell High School lunchrooms.

Barbara Adams married Charles Porter of Paulding County. They had no children. Barbara graduated from Campbell High School and worked for AT &T, from which she retired.

Curtis Adams married Carol Daniel. They had two children: a son, Charles Lamar, known as "Chuck," and a daughter, Stacey. Curtis and Carol graduated from Campbell High School.

Carol Daniel Adams was the daughter of L.N. and Ruby Daniel, who lived on Pierce Avenue. Carol had a brother, Michael Daniel, who married Elizabeth Fridell. Michael and Elizabeth both graduated from Campbell High School.

Curtis worked for Long Banknote Company in Atlanta, and Carol was employed by Massachusetts Mutual Insurance Company in Atlanta and later by the Cobb County Board of Education in the Human Resources Department.

Charles Lamar Adams married and divorced, but had no children. "Chuck," as he was known, died from a heart attack at the age of thirty-seven.

Stacey Adams had two sons: Jordan and Joshua, known as "Josh."

Eighth House

Mr. Reed McCollum
Smyrna City Councilman
1934-1937

Mary and **Reed McCollum** lived here. Mrs. McCollum was the former Mary Austin from Acworth. Her mother, Mrs. Austin, lived with them. Mrs. Austin and Mary were not related to J.C. and Stella Austin, who lived next door to them, nor were they related to Bob and Lucile Austin, who lived in the eighteenth house.

The McCollums had this house built in the mid 1940s. Before they built this house, the McCollums lived next door to our house, which was on the opposite side of the street. I thought their new house was the biggest and prettiest house I had ever seen. It was "kinda" like a Cape Cod style, except it did not have dormer windows. Before that time, due to the Depression and World War II, not many new houses had been built in Smyrna. Therefore, I was fascinated as I watched the construction of the McCollums' house.

Mary and Reed had the prettiest yard, and they always grew a garden. Their garden was between their home and a lot where Arthur and Dot Bacon built their house after the War. It was in their yard that I worked for Mrs. McCollum, whom I called "Mary." It was very unusual for me as a child to call my elders by their given names, especially since I had always been taught to call elders "Mr." or "Miss" or "Mrs." because it was the respectful thing to do. I did odd jobs for Mary, such as pulling weeds, hoeing, and gathering vegetables. She would not let me operate her lawn mower or use the hedge trimmers and shears. I do not know who used those—Reed, I suppose. I cannot recall ever seeing anyone cut shrubbery. She paid me twenty-five cents an hour. Mary and Mrs. Austin really liked me; though they did not say they did, I could just tell. Mary and her mother never worked outside the home; thus they were always at home. For some reason, I felt they had an eye out for the kids in the neighborhood: I think they expected children to be small adults.

NOTE: The McCollum, Adams, and Pressley houses were torn down in the 1990s for the building of the current Smyrna City Hall and parking lots.

Reed worked at Simmons Mattress Company in Atlanta. Occasionally I think about Reed, and I say to myself: "I wouldn't be surprised to learn he's up in heaven making mattresses." He walked by our house every morning on the way to the streetcar and was so punctual that one could set a clock by the time he walked up the street. In fact, I thought everybody in the world was punctual because all the residents of Bank Street were. They did things the same time and way every day.

Reed was elected to the Board of Trustees of First Baptist Church in November 1947 and was ordained a deacon on September 1, 1952. He was as good a man as I ever knew. Mary and Reed, who did not have any children, both lived into their upper senior years: Mary died first, and Reed lived into his mid-nineties. Mary, Reed, and Mrs. Austin were very good to me. I liked them! See *Austin, Walker Street and McCollum, Marston Street.*

Ninth House

Arthur T. Bacon
Smyrna City Councilman
1970-1975
Mayor
City of Smyrna
1976-1977,1981-1985

Mr. and **Mrs. Arthur Bacon** lived in the next house. They had four children: **Linda, Max**, **David**, and **Virginia Ruth**, known as "Jenny Ruth." Max was named for Max Parnell, and "Jenny Ruth" was named for Virginia Duckett Parnell.

The lot next door to Reed and Mary McCollum was vacant until Arthur and "Dot" married after World War II, and built their house on this lot. I believe the year was 1947.

Max Bacon married Marsha Hamby, of Smyrna. They had two children: Ashley and Ty. Max and Marsha later divorced. See *Hamby, south side of Concord Road.*

Ashley Bacon married Nathan Mize; they had one daughter, Abigail Jean, known as "Abby."

Ty Bacon married Heather Masters of Marietta. They have one son Harrison Arthur Bacon..

Max later married the former Patty Wilson Pate, of Marietta. She had two daughters, Alicia and Elizabeth Pate, whose father is a pharmacist in Statesboro. Max and Patty, who live in the Bennett Woods subdivision, are members of First Methodist Church.

David Bacon married Denise Clanton from Atlanta. They had two children: David Andrew and Jordan Lee. David and his family live in Kennesaw.

Linda Bacon married Joe Keeney from Atlanta. They had two children: Amanda, known as "Mandy," and Melissa.

Mandy Keeney and her husband had one child.

Melissa Keeney is married and lives in Florida, where she works in broadcasting.

Virginia Ruth Bacon, known as "Jenny" Ruth, married Steve Douglas of Smyrna, they had one daughter, Neely Deane Douglas. "Jenny" Ruth later married Charles Black, they had one son, Branden Black ; still later "Jenny" Ruth married Dale Williams of Smyrna, they had one son, Arthur Cole Williams. Dale and "Jenny" Ruth are graduates of Wills High School.

"Dot" Bacon was the former Dorothy Moseley from Sumter, South Carolina. She and Arthur both served in the military during World War II. Dot was a registered nurse in the Women's Army Nurse Corps, and Arthur was in the 78th Infantry Division of the United States Army. He received a battlefield commission and was promoted to First Lieutenant. The military had a rule that prohibited officers and enlisted personnel from fraternizing with each other. Because Arthur was an enlisted man and nurses were classified as officers, Dot and Arthur had to wait until they were discharged from the military to be married.

The Bacons were both very active in the American Legion. In fact, they were instrumental in the building of the present day Post # 160 facility, on Legion Drive. I also remember that Arthur was employed by the American Legion, for which he also did volunteer work and to which he was faithful for the rest of his life. Dot and Arthur were also members of First Methodist Church, where Dot is still a faithful attendee.

As is mentioned elsewhere, after the War, Arthur and his brother, Robert, opened a dry cleaning service on Atlanta Street. Later on, Arthur worked for the United States Post Office as a rural mail carrier until his United States Air Force Reserve unit, in which he held the rank of Captain, was called to active duty during the Korean Conflict; he served stateside. After the Korean Conflict he entered the real estate business with Bill Moore. Arthur served as Smyrna Councilman for Ward Three for three two-year terms, 1970-1975. Then he ran for and was elected to the position of Mayor for the 1976-1977 term; he was re-elected in 1981 and sworn into office in January 1982. Arthur served as Mayor until October 26, 1985, when he died.

"Dot" Bacon has two sisters who live in Smyrna: Irene Mosley Ferguson Dow and Ruby Moseley Spradley Atkins. Mrs. Dow had a daughter, Patsy Ferguson, who attended Smyrna Elementary School and was in my class before her family moved away from Vinings. I remember her riding the school bus from Vinings and my thinking how exciting it would be to ride the school bus. Her dad was Mr. Bruce Ferguson, who in later years, with his second wife, Alice, lived in the same neighborhood where Lillie and I live. We knew him well, for Alice was in the Bennett Woods Garden Club with Lillie. Alice and Bruce are both deceased.

Max Bacon
Smyrna City Councilman
January 1980-November 1985
Mayor of Smyrna
November 1985-

When Arthur was Mayor of Smyrna, his son Max was elected as the Smyrna Councilman for Ward Two. After Arthur's death, Max ran for and was elected to the mayoral office that had been left vacant when his father died. To my knowledge, Arthur and Max are the only father and son to hold the office of Mayor of Smyrna. At the time of this writing, Max is still Mayor of Smyrna and holds the record as the longest serving Mayor in Smyrna's history. He has led the City of Smyrna through the great revitalization period, beginning in the 1980s and extending into the early years of the Twenty-first Century.

The Griffins

Jasper and **Bess Griffin** lived in the terrace apartment of the Bacons' home. They were living there when their daughter **Susan** was born. (I remember seeing her when she was just a baby.) Later they had another daughter, **Betty**. The Griffins became good friends with Reed and Mary McCollum, who lived next door and remained very close to them for the rest of their lives. I remember that when Reed was aging, frail and alone, how faithful Betty was to him. She saw that his needs were met, helped him make the transition from his home to the nursing home, and handled all of his final affairs.

Linda Bacon and Mary McCollum's Bob Tail cat. Bank Street, 1949
Courtesy of "Dot" Bacon

Arthur and **"Dot" Bacon with Linda**
("Max" is on the way.) McCollum house is in the background Bank Street, 1949
Courtesy of "Dot" Bacon

Linda Bacon pushing **Max Bacon** in the carriage.
Bank Street, Winter of 1949
Courtesy of "Dot" Bacon

Linda, Max and **"Dot" Bacon** Easter, 1950
In front of the Bacon House
Courtesy of "Dot" Bacon

L-R: David, **Max**, **"Jenny Ruth"** and **Linda Bacon** Circa early 1950s Courtesy of "Dot" Bacon

Betty Griffin and **Linda Bacon**
Bank Street, 1949 Courtesy of "Dot" Bacon

Linda Bacon in front of the Bacon House
Bank Street, 1949 Courtesy of "Dot" Bacon

L-R: Max Parnell, Arthur Bacon and **Sam Lewis**. "Catch of the Day". Bacon house on Bank Street. Circa 1940s Courtesy of "Dot" Bacon

Linda, "Dot" and **Max Bacon**
Max's 1st birthday
Circa 1950 Courtesy of "Dot Bacon
NOTE: (View looking east on Bank Street)

Jasper Griffin, whose wife, Bess, taught music, came to Smyrna to assume the position of principal of the Smyrna School. I was in the eighth grade at the time. He was my principal from then until I graduated from high school in 1951. Jasper became the first principal at Campbell High School when it was opened in 1952.

Smyrna citizens were fortunate that Jasper and Bess Griffin moved here. The Cobb County Board of Education rewarded Jasper's outstanding leadership by naming Griffin Middle School for him in the early 1970s, during his lifetime. He was very deserving of this honor; thirty years later the school still stands, honoring his legacy.

Bess Griffin had a long and distinguished teaching career also. I believe she finished her career at Argyle Elementary School, on Spring Road.

The Griffins, members of First Methodist Church, moved to Dunn Street, in the Forest Hills community, after it was extended beyond Collier Drive. At the time of this writing, Bess still lives here.

<u>Tenth House</u>

Mr. and **Mrs**. **Howard Scoggins** lived next door to the Bacons. Mrs. Scoggins was the former Victoria Dean Crowe, known as "Vicki." The Scoggins, who moved to this Bank Street house in 1943, had four children: **Sue**, **William H**., known as "Bill," **Hugh O'Neal**, known as "Buddy," and **Jean**.

The Scoggins Family attended First Baptist Church, where Mr. Scoggins taught Sunday School, was ordained a deacon June 1, 1976, and served as a lay preacher. In the late 1950s, First Baptist Church began sponsorship of the King Spring Mission. When it was organized as King Spring Baptist Church, Howard Scoggins became the first minister.

Howard Scoggins worked for Southern Railroad, and Vicki Scoggins was a registered nurse. Virginia Gann McDaniel shares that, when her mother, Irene Gann, was very ill, Vicki Scoggins would go to the Gann home and give her mother injections and excellent care. This was the small town quality of Smyrna that is so rare today.

<u>Sue Scoggins</u> was also a nurse. She married Warren Cargal, who grew up on Concord Road. Warren was employed by The Container Corporation of America. For many years Warren and Sue lived in Amsterdam before moving to Albany, where they raised their family. Sue and Warren had four children: Warren, Jr., Connie, Bill, and Matthew. See *Cargal, east side of Concord Road.*

Warren Cargal, Jr. is a doctor of holistic medicine in Buckhead, with a practice in acupuncture.

Connie Cargal married Irvin Woolsey. Both Connie and Irvin are managers for George Strait Company.

Bill Cargal is employed by George Strait Company.

Matthew Cargal, an attorney, lives in California.

William H. "Bill" Scoggins
Smyrna City Councilman
1988–

<u>William Howard Scoggins, Sr.</u>, known as "Bill," and his wife, Gerrye, live on Roswell Street. They have resided for more than twenty-five years in this house, which was occupied by the large Elmer Anderson Family during the first half of the Twentieth Century.

"Bill" Scoggins, Sr., and his first wife, Frances Houston, had one son, William Howard Scoggins, Jr., known as "Bill." The Scoggins lived on King Springs Road when "Bill," Jr., was growing up.

"Bill" Scoggins, Jr., married Lori Ann Tiller. They had three children: Suzanne Marie, Jason William, and Travis James.

Gerrye Scoggins, by a previous marriage, had seven children who are now grown: Richard H. Wright; Beverly Jo Wright Dolan; Lisa Ann Wright Bacon; Teresa Jeanne "Cookie" Wright Stringfield; Stephanie Gayle Wright Polo; Gerrye Michele Wright Gaissert; and Christopher S. Wright.

"Bill," Sr., has served on the Smyrna City Council, representing Ward Three, since 1988. His ward covers most of the area of Smyrna east of the railroad, including Davenport Town. The ward also encompasses the area on the west side of the railroad around the Smyrna City Hall, Fire and Police stations, Community Center, Market Village, and Smyrna Public Library (the only city-owned library in the State of Georgia). "Bill' was employed with Fouts Brothers GMC Truck Sales on Atlanta Road, north of Smyrna, until his retirement. He and Gerrye are members of First Methodist Church.

Hugh O'Neal Scoggins, known as "Buddy," married Edna Earl Moon, who grew up on Matthews Street and was the only child of Mary and Earl Moon. "Buddy" and Edna had one daughter, Dani Beth. See *Moon, west side of Matthews Street.*

Dani Beth married Brad Whitecotton. They had three children: Jeff, Mary Elizabeth, known as "Beth," and Reed.

"Buddy" was ordained a deacon at First Baptist Church on May 16, 1972. He also served as Sunday School Superintendent, 1973-1974. For many years, "Buddy" was the announcer at the Campbell High School football games. He worked for Lockheed Aircraft Corporation and later, for many years, owned and operated Scoggins Real Estate Company, from which he retired. The Scoggins, along with Dani, Brad, and children, are living in Clarksville.

Jean Scoggins, my age, graduated with me in the Smyrna High School Class of 1951. She was one of the nine players on the Smyrna High Girls' Basketball Team, winning the Cobb County Championship our Senior year.

Jean, who had a beautiful voice, pursued singing as a profession. She went to Nashville, Tennessee, where she established her own recording studio. She married Jerry Zimmerman; they had four children: Susie, Keith, Tammy, and Rusty. Jean died from cancer in her late fifties.

NOTE: After World War II ended, the City of Smyrna extended Bank Street from Hamby Street to Fraser Street. The following houses were built and occupied after that time.

Eleventh House

John Porterfield
Mayor
City of Smyrna
1972-1976

Mr. and **Mrs. Joe Porterfield** lived in the eleventh house. Joe and his wife, Alma, had two sons: John and Bobby. Joe Porterfield was Smyrna Fire Chief for many years.

Bobby Porterfield, known as "Bob," and his wife had three children: Bobby, Ann, and another son who died from cancer in his young teenage years.

GEORGE DANIEL'S HILLBILLY BAND, August 1926 **Front Row:** "Spooks" the dog and James Cook, known as "Black Face." **Middle Row:** Seated, George Daniel, Robert McBrayer (head showing, playing white guitar), Edward Richardson (playing the banjo), Myrtle Richardson, Ewing ("Shorty") Underwood, George Dunn (standing) playing the bass fiddle. **Back Row:** Bogue Richardson, Howard Scoggins, Kim Wiley, Luke James (striped tie), Bill See (in black suit) and Jake Groover (in plaid suit, playing rhe scrub board). Herbert Wallace, not pictured was also in the band. Courtesy of "Bill" Scoggins, see *south side of Bank Street.*

J.C. and **Stella Austin**
Circa Mid Twentieth Century
Courtesy of Johnny Austin

Smyrna City Council Members - National League of Cities, Boston, MA. December, 1988
L-R: John Patterson, City Mgr., Bob and Joyce Betenbaugh, Judy and Jimmy Hawkins, "Bill" and Gerrye Scoggins, Louise and Bob Davis. **Front Row**: Kathy Brooks Jordan
Courtesy Gerrye Scoggins.

Councilman, **"Bill" Scoggins**, and wife **Gerrye**. Circa 1988
Courtesy of Gerrye Scoggins

John Porterfield married Betty Shumate; they had one son, Mike. John served as Mayor of Smyrna, 1972-1976. Betty passed away in the 1990s. John and Mike still live in Cobb County.

Twelfth House

Mr. and **Mrs. B.H. Hanson, Jr.**, lived in the twelfth house. They had three sons: Mike, Danny, and Scott. Mrs. Hanson, the former Helen Blackwell, grew up on Spring Road, next door westward to Bethel Baptist Church. B.H., Jr., who grew up on Love Street, died a few years ago; Helen still lives on Bank Street, where they reared their three sons, all of whom still live in Cobb County.

Danny Hanson and his wife, Maggie, served as missionaries in Thailand for several years.

B.H. Hanson, Jr., worked for Southern Bell Telephone Company, and Helen Hanson was a teacher in First Baptist Church Kindergarten, from which she retired. See *Hanson,* on *Love Street* and *Spring Road.*

Thirteenth House

Mr. and **Mrs. H.F. Hancock** lived next door to the Hansons. Mrs. Hancock was the former Ruth Adams. They had three children: **Gary**, **David**, and **Nancy**. Mrs. Hancock still lives on Bank Street, where she and her husband raised their children. Ruth was a sister of Horace Adams, who lived on Bank Street. See *Adams,* on *Bank Street* and *Roswell Street.*

Gary Hancock married Vicky Noland. They had two children: Adam and Jessica. Adam, in the United States Air Force, is stationed in Pensacola, Florida.

David Hancock married Sue Switzer from West Virginia. They had one child, Jennifer. They live in Woodstock.

Nancy Hancock, who lives in Marietta, works for a dentist in Smyrna.

Fourteenth House

Mr. and **Mrs. J.D. Daniel** built this house on Bank Street in the late 1940s. Mrs. Daniel's given name was Eddie Lee. They had three children: **Stephen**, known as "Steve," **Judith**, known as "Judy," and **Kathy**. Eddie Lee Daniel died March 21, 2004.

J.D. grew up in East Cobb County, in the Lower Roswell Road area. In fact, the Eastside Baptist Church is located on land that was part of his family's farm. J.D. first operated a grocery store at the corner of Spring and Atlanta streets. He was later instrumental, along with Henry Konigsmark and others, in the development and building of Jonquil Plaza Shopping Center. Becoming the major tenant, he owned and operated the Red Dot Food Market in Jonquil Plaza for many years. He still owns the shopping center. One of J.D.'s sisters, Frances, is married to Don Barnes, who also grew up in Smyrna. See *Barnes, east side of Roswell Street.*

When the new area off Collier Drive was developed, J.D. and Eddie Lee had a house built on Northview Place, where they lived for several years; afterwards they had a house built on Pinetree Drive, in the Forest Hills community. The Daniel Family are members of First Methodist Church. J.D. Daniel is a charter member of the Smyrna Rotary Club, chartered in 1964.

"Steve" Daniel and his wife, Penny, live in the Forest Hills community, off Collier Drive and next door to his parents' home. They had two children: Melanie and Joseph, known as "Jay."

"Judy" Daniel married and had a daughter, Christine. "Judy," who divorced, lives in Smyrna.

Kathy Daniel married and had two children: Daniel and Jennifer Bishop. Kathy lives in Albany.

Fifteenth House

Mr. and **Mrs. Dallis Guthrie** built this house in the 1940s. Mr. Guthrie and his wife, the former Colene Reed, moved from this house to Atlanta Street in the early to mid 1950s. See *Guthrie, Atlanta Street, from Marlowes to Creatwood and west side of Dunn Street.*

The Austin Atkins Family

Mr. and **Mrs. Austin Atkins** moved to Bank Street from Dixie Avenue after their oldest son, "Bill," graduated from Smyrna High School in 1950. Their house on Dixie Avenue was near the Belmont House. Mr.and Mrs. Austin Atkins had five children: **William Austin,** known as "Bill," **Gene**, **Charlene**, known as "Sharkey," **Ralene**, known as "Babe", and **Gary**.

Mr. Atkins served as United States Postmaster in Smyrna for ten years.

Members of the Atkins Family are very active in the community life of Smyrna, Marietta, and Cobb County.

William Austin "Bill" Atkins
State of Georgia Representative
1982-1994

William Austin Atkins, known as "Bill," married Mary Jo Ellerbee from Thomaston. They had two children: William Austin Atkins, Jr., known as "Chip," and Paige. Jo Ellerbee Atkins is deceased.

"Chip" Atkins and his wife, the former Ruth Ann Mitchell, had two children: Will and Tate. "Chip" followed in his dad's footsteps as a pharmacist.

Paige Atkins married Dan Post, a certified public accountant. They had two children: Ari and Ryder. Paige and Dan live in West Cobb County.

"Bill" was born in Tate, August 16, 1933. Having earned a Bachelor of Science degree from The Southern School of Pharmacy of Mercer University in 1954, he owned and operated Atkins Pharmacy in Smyrna for more than twenty-five years: first on Atlanta Street in downtown Smyrna, then on Spring Road, and later on Concord Road.

"Bill" served in the Georgia House of Representatives, 1982-1994. During that time as State Representative, he was a member of these committees: Appropriations; Regulated Beverages; and Industry and Trade.
Since 1994, "Bill" has been the Director of the Georgia Drugs and Narcotics Agency. He is also a director of the Mercer University School of Pharmacy Governing Board.

Present titles for "Bill" are the following: leader and vocalist for *The Bill Atkins Band*; member of the Administrative Board of First Methodist Church; member of the Georgia Association of Chiefs of Police; and member of the Cobb County Chamber of Commerce.

Past titles for "Bill" include: President of the Seventh District Pharmaceutical Association; Chairman of the Board of Pharmacy for the State of Georgia, 1978; member of the Governing Board of Brawner Hospital, 1993-1996; member of the Smyrna Hospital Long-Range Planning Board, 1993-1996; and, as a pharmacist, Specialist Third Class, in the United Sates Army, 1955-1957.

"Bill" has received numerous awards: Appreciation plaque from the Georgia Division of th American Cancer Society; Legislator of the Year Friendship Award from the Personal Care Homes c Georgia, 1991; Liberty Bell Award, Phi Delta Chi, 1978; One of a Kind Award from Cobb Clea Commission; the Meritorious Service Award from Southern School of Pharmacy of Merce University, 1982; and Community Service Bowl of Hygiea Award, 1997.

The Smyrna/Oakdale Loyal Order of the Moose and the National Sheriff's Associatio named "Bill" Mr. Cobb County in 1993. He has also been included in *Who's Who in America.*

"Bill" Atkins is married to his second wife, the former Jennifer McGahan, daughter o Richard and Shirley McGahan. When Jennifer was in high school, her family moved to the Smyrn area from Kentucky. She enrolled in R.L. Osborne High School, from which she graduated. He parents still live in Cobb County, on Gray Road near Smyrna.

Jennifer was first married to John Yarbrough. They had two children: a daughter, Stacy, an a son, Justin. John is deceased.

John Yarbrough was the son of Glenn and Nan Edwards Yarbrough of Smyrna. Nan was member of the Pat Edwards Family on Love Street, and Glenn was a long-time Smyrna City Clerk See *Yarborough, Love* and *Lee streets.*

<u>Gene Atkins</u> married Harriet Wright, his sweetheart from Campbell High School. Gene own and operates Atkins Apothecary in Marietta. Gene and Harriet had three daughters: Kim, Jill, an Hope. See *Hanson, south side of Love Street.*

<u>Ralene Atkins,</u> " known as "Babe", married Bill Byrne, who served as Chairman of the Cob County Board of Commissioners, 1992-2002. Babe is the administrative assistant to Cobb Superio Court Judge George Kreeger.

Bill Byrne
Chairman, Cobb County Board of Commissioners
1992-2002

<u>Charlene Atkins</u>, known as "Sharkey," is married to Bob Gill. They had two children: Cand and Bart. Charlene and Bob live in Marietta.

<u>Gary Atkins</u> married Anne Pyle. They had two children: Austin and Hannah. Gary and hi family live in Ballground, where he works for the United States Postal Service.

<u>Sixteenth House</u>

Mr. and **Mrs. Charles Kelley** and their family lived in this house. They had three daughters Charlotte Linda, Lane, and Jane, the latter two of whom were twins. Mrs. Kelley was the forme Frances Baucom from Clay County, Alabama, and Mr. Kelley was from Oxford, Alabama. They cam to Smyrna from Chattanooga, Tennessee, for Mr. Kelley to work for King Plow Company in Atlanta He later worked at Baldwin Foundry. Both Charles and Frances Kelley are deceased.

<u>Charlotte Linda Kelley</u> married Jim Alexander from Atlanta. They had two children Anastasia and Charles Nathan, and four grandchildren.

<u>Seventeenth House</u>

Mr. and **Mrs. J. Calvin Johnson, Jr.**, built this house on Bank Street in the 1940s. Mrs Johnson was the former Betty Brooke, the daughter of Virgil and Myrtle Brooke. Betty and Calvin ha two children: John Calvin III and Susan. Betty Johnson, my first cousin, is deceased.

Susan Johnson died from leukemia when she was in her upper teenage years.

John Johnson III married Cindy Affalter. They had three children: Kathy, John Calvin IV, nd Elizabeth Susan. John and Cindy live in the Mableton area, where they raised their family.

Kathy Ann Johnson, born June 28, 1974, married Tracy Ezzell. They had two children: ayna Brooke and Grayson Kennedy. Kathy, a graduate of Pebblebrook High School and the Jniversity of Georgia, teaches part-time in Paulding County.

John Calvin IV was born January 10, 1977. A graduate of Pebblebrook High School and ennesaw State University, he is employed as an electrician with Askea Electric Company. John IV is ow living in his grandparents' former home, on Bank Street.

Elizabeth Susan, born December 5, 1981, is a graduate of Pebblebrook High School and 'aldosta State University. Known as "Beth," she is the assistant band director at North Cobb High chool in Cobb County.

J. Calvin Johnson, Jr., was the son of Mr. and Mrs. J. Calvin Johnson, Sr., Calvin Johnson, r., and his dad, both Masons, were members of Nelms Lodge, in Smyrna. Calvin's son, John III, and is grandson, John Calvin IV, are also Masons and members of Nelms Lodge.

J. Calvin Johnson, Jr., worked for Georgia Power Company, from which he retired. Betty Brooke Johnson was the financial secretary at First Baptist Church for a long time. Later on, she vorked for Allstate Insurance Company in Atlanta. Long-time members of First Baptist Church, the ohnsons later joined King Spring Baptist Church, where John and Cindy Johnson and their family vere members. See *Johnson, south side of Fleming Street* and *Brooke, east side of Roswell Street.*

Eighteenth House

Robert "Bob" Austin
Deputy Cobb County Commissioner
1964-1984
Smyrna City Councilman at Large
Mid 1950s

Mr. and **Mrs. Robert J. Austin** lived next door to the Johnsons. Mrs. Austin was the former ucille Hanson. Mr. Austin, known as "Bob," and Lucille had their house built in 1947 and lived ere for the rest of their lives. They had two children: Karen and Wayne. "Bob" and Lucille and their amily were members of First Methodist Church.

NOTE: On August 18, 1947, a building permit was approved for Mr. M.J. Hensley to build a ouse for Robert J. Austin on Bank Street.

"Bob," serving in the United States Navy during World War II, was a parachute packer in iamond Head, Hawaii. Because of a health problem, he was discharged from the Navy. He then erved stateside in the Georgia Air National Guard at Dobbins Air Force Base, in Marietta, until he etired.

Ernest Barrett
Chairman, Cobb County Board of Commissioners
1964-1984

Bob" Austin was active in politics in Cobb County. He served for twenty years as Deputy ommissioner to Ernest Barrett, who was elected Chairman of the Cobb County Board of ommissioners in 1964 and served until 1984. Lucille and "Bob" were both members of "old Smyrna" amilies. See *Austin, North Cooper Lake Road* and *Hanson, south side of Love Street.*

Betty Lou Brooke (Johnson) Circa 1938
Courtesy of Pete Wood

Betty Brooke and **Faye Camp**
Downtown Atlanta Late 1940-Early 1941
Courtesy of Pete Wood

Betty Brooke and **J. Calvin Johnson, Jr.**
Engagement Picture, December 1944
(They married January 16, 1945)
Courtesy of Johnny Johnson IV

Bob and **Lucille Austin**, Wedding Day
September 20, 1946
Courtesy of Vera Austin Blackburn.

Nineteenth House

Mr. and **Mrs. Roy Howard** were residents of this house. Mrs. Howard was the former Villie Shaw, a sister of Annie Mae Davenport, who lived on Hill Street. In the 1940s, the Howards uilt this house, which was located across the street from the corner of Guthrie and Bank streets. (Roy vas a brother of George Howard.) See *Howard, west side of Lee Street.*

Roy Howard ran a service station and auto shop in downtown Smyrna, south of the ntersection of Spring and Atlanta streets. See *Atlanta Street, Marlowe's to Creatwood.*

HAMBY STREET

Hamby Street is a short street only two blocks long. It runs north and south from Powder prings Street to Bank Street. In the days of my youth there were two houses on Hamby Street.

First House

Mr. and **Mrs. Sasser** lived in the first house off Bank Street on the west side of Hamby treet.

Second House

Mr. and **Mrs. Edward Darwin Cox** built this house while I was still in high school. It was the middle of the block on the west side of the street. Her name was Ola. They had a daughter and a on, Billie Jo and Stan. The Cox children were younger than I.

The Cox family was very active at the First Baptist Church. Ed and my dad were close in ose years. By the time they came into my family's life I was out of school, in the Army and working.

Across the street on the corner of Hamby Street and Sunset Avenue was a neighborhood rocery store. The people who ran that store were named Harbin. They lived on Sunset Avenue in a ouse to the side of the store. The store faced Sunset Avenue.

CHAPTER TWO

ATLANTA STREET

West Side

From Miles Streetcar Stop to the Motters'

Atlanta Road/Street, heavily traveled, was U.S. Highway 41 through Smyrna from Atlanta to larietta and northward. The streetcar route ran parallel with Atlanta Road. The section of the road side the Smyrna City Limits began near the Pinecrest Streetcar Stop at Fleming Street, on the north de of Smyrna and ended near Collier Drive, on the south side. (According to common knowledge, e city limits of Smyrna ran ½ mile in each direction from the intersection of Spring and Atlanta reets.) This section of the highway was known locally as Atlanta Street. The section of the highway orth of the Smyrna City Limits was called North Atlanta Road, and the section of the highway south f the Smyrna City Limits was called South Atlanta Road.

The people who lived north and south of the city limits were very much Smyrna people ecause they attended school and church in Smyrna and many of them worked here. Today, many of e people who grew up in the area are now living within the extended boundaries of the city limits of myrna. The have contributed greatly through the years to the success of both Smyrna and Cobb ounty.

Appreciation is extended to Al Brasill, Betty Burruss Brown, Sarah Burruss Dunn, Mary Motter owler, and Robert J. Motter, known as "Bobby," for providing information concerning their families n Atlanta Street. Al, Betty, Sarah, Mary, and Bobby grew up in Smyrna, married, and raised their milies here.

First House

Mr. and **Mrs. John Chesley Burruss**, with eleven children, had one of the many large milies in Smyrna when I was growing up. They were: **A.L. Burruss**, known as "Al," **Sarah**, **Betty**, **immy Lee, Sr.**, **Shirley**, **Peggy**, **Hymon Herschel**, known as "Buddy," **Gerald**, **Linda**, **Jane**, and **anny**, known as "Dan." All of their children lived into adulthood except one, and all but two of them ave remained in Smyrna and/or Cobb County.

Nine of the surviving Burruss children attended Smyrna Elementary, Smyrna High, and/or ampbell High schools. Dan, the youngest, was among the students in the Smyrna area who were ansferred to Pebblebrook High School to relieve overcrowding at Campbell High School.

The Burruss Family is an influential family in Smyrna, Marietta, and other Cobb County eas. Members of this family have been significant contributors to the progress of the County through e years.

Mr. John Chesley Burruss, known as "Chess," owned and operated "Chess" Burruss Eggs, a isiness that delivered eggs to stores and to some homes. I remember that my mother would buy eggs om him on occasion.

Mrs. Burruss was the former Eula Corn. She was related to Homer, Jack, Denver, Bentley, id Sara Corn, all of whom lived in the Smyrna area.

Mr. and Mrs. Burruss moved to Pat Mell Road, from Cumming in 1935. Pat Mell Road hich at that time extended from Atlanta Street east of the railroad, was later changed to Broad Street, om there they moved to Davis Road. The Burruss' later moved to the west side of Atlanta Street, ar the site of the drive-in theater, which was built in the late 1940s, and is now the location of the myrna Public Works Department.

NOTE: The drive-in theater era was short lived. Most of those theaters did not stay business any longer than twenty years. We citizens who grew up in that era fondly remember going the drive-in with our dates. Because it was in the middle 1950s before I got a car, I did not take a dates to the drive-in theater.

In 1958 "Chess" and Eula Burruss bought a house located at 3922 South Atlanta Road, the southwest corner of South Atlanta and Westwood roads. This had been a country cottage built ju prior to the Twentieth Century by L.R. Aiken, a state senator from Brunswick, for his family to u while the Georgia State Legislature was in session. Senator Aiken sold this cottage to Mr. and M Frank Dabney in 1922. (Mr. Frank Dabney was the father of Ham Dabney, who was a homebuilder Smyrna in the middle of the Twentieth Century.) After the Dabneys died, "Chess" Burruss bought t house, where several of his ten children were reared. After Mr. Burruss died, his widow, Eula, liv here until her death in 1997. Their son, Gerald, remained in the home place until 2002. This area Atlanta Road is changing rapidly due to much redevelopment in the area. See *Dabney, Brown Circle.*

"Al" Burruss
Member, Cobb County Board of Commissioners
1965-1968
Georgia State Representative
1968-1986

A.L. Burruss, known as "Al," was the oldest of the eleven children. He married Bobbi Elr from Cornelia. They had three children: Robin, Renee, and Michael, who died when he was fourte months old.

Robin Burruss married Penny Owens, They had two daughters: Meghan and Ashley. Megh is married to Brad Respress; they had a son, Jack. Ashley is married to Dr. Valery Akapov.

Renee Burruss married Ken Davis. They had three children: Jared, Whitt, and Hunter.

"Al" owned and operated Tip Top Poultry in Marietta, in partnership with "Chet" Austin, h long-time friend. "Al" and "Chet" were closely associated with a group of young men in Marie known as "The Young Turks." Some of them were these: Ernest Barrett, Bill Bullard, Romeo Hudgir Harold Dellinger, Wyman Pilcher, and Garvis Sams. They all became leaders in Cobb County duri the surging growth years: 1950s-1970s.

In 1964 Ernest Barrett was elected chairman of the first multiple commission in Co County. "Al" Burruss was elected as one of the commissioners to serve with him. Having complet his term on the Cobb County Board of Commissioners, "Al" was elected to the House Representatives in 1968 and served for eighteen years. He died in 1986 while he was still in office.

The "Al" Burruss Family were members of Tillman Methodist Church on Concord Road Smyrna for a number of years when the children were young. After moving to Marietta, where th raised their family, they became faithful members of First United Methodist Church of Marietta.

Sarah Burruss was the second child of Eula and Chess. She married Charles Dunn, who gre up north of Smyrna. He was from the large George Dunn singing family. Sarah, a member of Fi Baptist Church, was employed by the Bank of Smyrna and its successors until she retired. (T banking industry went through a period of mergers and acquisitions, and this bank changed nam several times.) Sarah and Charles, who live across the street from Lillie and me, have been o neighbors for more than thirty years. Charles and my mother, Dora Wood, were first cousins. Sar and Charles had two children: Judy and Charles, Jr., known as "Chuck."

Judy married Troy Cannon. They had two children: Shane and Shawn. Both boys, wi beautiful voices, have followed in their grandfather Charles' footsteps by singing publicly. Sha Cannon married Lisa Baker; they had three sons: Max, Sam, and Ben. Max Cannon is named for M arnell, Lisa's Smyrna relative who was a prisoner of war during World War II. Sam Cannon is named or his great-grandfather, Sam Lewis, the patriarch of the large Lewis Family on Highland Avenue. hawn married Nikki Sims; they had two daughters: Allysa and Taylor. See *Lewis Family, Highland venue.*

"Chuck" Dunn and his wife had two daughters: Ansley and Crystal, the latter of whom is arried to Sam Bryant. Crystal and Sam had two sons: Adam and Ben.

Betty Burruss was the third child of Chess and Eula. At Second Baptist Church in Smyrna, etty married Richard Brown from Marietta, the son of Ola Garrard Brown and V.T. Brown, who ere from Boaz, Alabama. Betty and Richard live in Smyrna and are active members of First Baptist hurch, where Richard is on the Board of Deacons. Richard has a sister, Bonnie Brown, who also lives Smyrna. Betty and Richard Brown had three children: Dawn, Rick, and Brent.

Dawn Brown married Randy Harris; they had four children: Tiffany, Brandon, Christy, and athan. Dawn and Randy, who live in Marietta, are members of Olive Springs Baptist Church. Randy the son of Reverend and Mrs. Mack Harris. At one time, Reverend Harris was the pastor of Locust rove Baptist Church in the Oakdale community.

Rick Brown married Caroline McHugh from Atlanta. They had three children: Brian, icholas, and Cassidy. The Rick Browns live in West Cobb County.

Brent Chesley Brown is married to Carla Mathis, who grew up in Florida. They live in ableton. Brent is the Chairman, President, and Chief Executive Officer of Chesley Brown ternational, Chesley Brown Companies, Inc., and Chesley Brown Associates, Inc., respectively, cated on Atlanta Road at I-285. All three companies are security management services providing ecurity to large malls, Class "A" Office Towers, and Corporations in 28 states and three countries. arla Mathis Brown is an employee of the Cobb County Convention and Visitors Bureau. Brent and arla had twin daughters: Elizabeth Ann, known as "LizAnn" and Madison Chesley, known as Maddie".

Jimmy Lee Burruss, Sr., the fourth child of Chess and Eula Burruss, married Betty Ann asey from the Fair Oaks community. They had five children: Sherrie, Jimmy Lee, Jr., Rodney, Al ichard, known as "Al," and Johnny. Jimmy, Sr., retired from Tip Top Foods, of which he was the ounder and owner; his sons are now running the business. Jimmy Lee, Sr., and Betty Ann lived in arietta. Jimmy Lee, Sr., died November 25, 2004.

Sherrie Burruss married Charlie Schwartz. They had two children: Tracy and Casey.

Jimmy Lee Burruss, Jr., married Sharon Marcinko. They had four children: Jimmy Lee III, rant, Day, and Michael. Jimmy Lee III, having earned a scholarship to the United States Naval cademy in Annapolis, Maryland, is now serving in the United States Navy.

Rodney Burruss married Lynn Melton. They had one son, Ryan.

Al Richard Burruss and his wife, Robin, had two children: Kerry and Kimberly.

Johnny Burruss married Kay Brown. They had three children: Wesley, Brian, and Laura.

Shirley Thomas Burruss, the fifth child of Chess and Eula, died when he was fourteen onths old.

Peggy Burruss was the sixth child born to Chess and Eula Burruss. She married Horace ulsey; they had one daughter, Jennifer. Peggy and Jennifer, members of First Baptist Church, live in nyrna and are neighbors of Lillie. and me. Horace is deceased. See *Hulsey, Whitfield Street.*

Hymon Herschel Burruss, known as "Buddy," is the seventh child of Eula and Che Burruss. Named for his Uncle Hymon Herschel Corn, "Buddy" works with Tip Top Poultry Marietta. He married Linda Cochran of the Fair Oaks community. Having reared their two sor Michael and Todd, in Smyrna, they now live in Marietta.

Michael Burruss married Tonya Bennett. They had one son, Michael Lane, and a daught Kayla.

Todd Burruss married Kate Tumlin in September 2003.

Gerald Burruss, the eighth child of Eula and Chess Burruss, married Kathy Wilson; they h no children. Kathy passed away in their third year of marriage. Gerald, a member of First Bapti Church of Atlanta, lives in Smyrna.

Linda Burruss is the ninth child of Eula and Chess Burruss. She married Charlie Moore fro Atlanta, where they now live; they had no children. Linda is a member of the Smyrna Social Club.

Hugh Ragan
Smyrna City Councilman
1984-1987
Georgia State Senator
1987-1995

Jane Burruss, the tenth child of Eula and Chess, is married to Hugh Ragan from Perry. Th had two daughters: Shanda and Whitney. The Ragans, members of First Baptist Church, live in t West Cooper Lake Hills community. Hugh served two terms as a Smyrna Councilman for Wa Seven, as well as two terms as Georgia State Senator.

Danny Burruss, known as "Dan," is the eleventh child of Eula and Chess. He married Ja Lloyd from Griffin, whom he met at Auburn University while attending college. They had thr children: Matthew, Chesley, and Kathryn, the first two being twins. Dan and his family for eight yea lived in Japan, where he was employed by Delta Airlines, from which he retired. Dan and his fami now live in Hawaii, where he works for Hawaiian Airlines. Jane and Dan are of the Lutheran faith.

NOTE: In the days of my childhood, the Belmont Streetcar Stop was on Atlanta Street Cherokee Road, north of Smyrna. Cherokee was a narrow dirt road which ran east to west, fro Atlanta Street to the Access Road (now South Cobb Drive). West of the Access Road it was call Jones Shaw Road. When, in more recent years, Windy Hill Road was extended to Atlanta Road, Co County and the City of Smyrna renamed all of this road (from Powers Ferry Road in East Cobb Austell Road in South Cobb) Windy Hill Road.

NOTE: There were other houses between the Burruss' and the Smith House, but I do n recall who lived there.

Second House

Mr. and **Mrs. Gordon Smith** lived in the first house south of the little dirt road known Cherokee Road, which currently is the part of Windy Hill Road between Atlanta Road and South Co Drive. Gordon Smith was a plumber who operated a business from his home. The Smiths had tw sons: **Alec** and **Sonny**. I remember that Alec and I started to school together, and were in the san class.

Alec Smith had a long career in the United States Marines Corps, from which he retired. I married Peggy Spradley, the daughter of James and Ruby Spradley, who lived on Matthews Stre Ruby and Dot Bacon (the widow of Arthur Bacon, who served as Mayor of Smyrna, and the mother

Max Bacon, the current Mayor of Smyrna) were sisters. See *south side of Bank Street,* and *east side of Matthews Street.*

One of the things that I remember about Gordon Smith is that a black man, Forrest Bedford, of Davenport Town, worked for him. My dad really liked Forrest and trusted him; when we needed plumbing done, he always asked Gordon to send Forrest. Dad said he was an expert plumber. I remember that after Lillie and I married, we would also call Forrest to do work for us.

Mr. and **Mrs. Ernest Peek**

Mr. and **Mrs. Ernest Peek** were residents in this house after the Smith Family moved. Mr. Peek was the Smyrna Chief of Police at one time. I remember one of the Peeks' daughters, **Gayle,** married Judson Hamby. Mrs. Peek was the mother of Mae Davenport. See *east side of Matthews Street* and *south side of Love Street.*

Third House

This house was known around Smyrna as the Dr. Yancey House.

Virgil and **Myrtle Brooke** later resided here. Aunt Myrtle Brooke was my mother's sister. In the 1940s, I remember visiting the Brookes many times in this large white house on Atlanta Street, next door to the Gordon Smith Family.

The Stuart Murray Family

The **Stuart Murray Family** purchased this house after Aunt Myrtle and her family moved. I never knew this family, but I heard it said that the Murrays moved in and completely renovated the house.

Fourth House

Mr. and **Mrs.** **Albert C. Brasill, Sr.**, lived in this brick house, which was located on the north side of the Motters. They had six children: Dole, Geneva, Evelyn, Albert C., Jr., known as "Al," and twin daughters, Vivian and Vera.

Mrs. Brasill was the former Arlintie McClure, the daughter of Mr. and Mrs. Sam McClure, who were farmers in the Sandy Plains area of Cobb County and had ten children.

Mr. Albert Brasill, Sr. 's family lived on a farm east of Marietta, near Black Jack Mountain, on what was then Brasill Road, but now Piedmont Road.

Dole Brasill passed away with pneumonia in 1914, when he was only a few months old.

Geneva Brasill died from complications due to pneumonia at the age of six months, in 1924.

Evelyn Brasill was born in 1916. She married Ernest Underwood; they had five sons. In 1952 the family was in a terrible automobile accident in Graysville, Tennessee, near their home. Evelyn, a passenger in the front seat, was killed while holding her youngest son, Ernest. Her husband and the young son, plus their four sons in the back seat, were all injured; however, all recovered.

Vera Brasill married Fred Matthews of Marietta; they had one son, Richard, known as "Ricky." Fred passed away in 2003; Vera still resides in their home on Dunn Street. "Ricky" Matthews, who died December 24, 2004, is survived by his wife, Deborah.

Vivian Brasill married Raymond Motter of Smyrna; they had four children. Vivian passed away in her sleep on April 9, 1999, from complications due to congestive heart failure.

L-R: Vera Brasill Matthews, Vivian Brasill Motter, Albert Brasill, Sr., Arlintie Brasill, "Al" Bra Jr., and Evelyn Brasill Underwood standing in front of the Brasill home on Atlanta Street.

Circa 1941 Courtesy of "Al" Brasill, Jr.

Al and **Mary Edwa** **Brasill**, sitting on th 1941 Ford in the side of the Brasill house Atlanta Street, (Mary pregnant with thei daughter).

Circa 1946

Courtesy of

"Al" Brasill, Jr.

Back Row (L-R): Albert Brasill, Sr., Arlintie Brasill, Vivian Brasill Motter, Mary Edwards Bra and Vera Brasill **Front Row** (L-R): Evelyn Brasill Underwood and her sons, David and Haro Underwood, in front of the Brasill's Atlanta Road Home.

Circa 1942 Courtesy "Al" Brasill, Jr.

NOTE: Raymond Motter's brother, Kelly, died on April 8, 1999, after a long illness and troke, only a few hours before Vivian's death. See *Motter, north side of Spring Road.*

Albert C. Brasill, Jr. , known as "Al," was born in 1922. He met Mary Edwards in 1938, and hey married March 13, 1942. Mary was living at that time on Roswell Street in Smyrna with her arents, Joe and Mona Edwards, and her brother and sister. Mary's dad was an engineer with L&N ailroad.

"Al" and Mary, who now live on the north side of Hurt Road, near the intersection of oncord and Hurt roads, had one daughter, Gayle, who lives with her husband, C.F. Duke, in Apollo each, Florida. Gayle and C.F. had one daughter, who lives with her husband in Brandon, Florida.

Knowing "Hoot" Gibson well, long before "Hoot" became Mayor of Smyrna, "Al" has hared: "I sold 'Hoot' the first automobile that I ever owned, a 1933 Plymouth Coupe for $150.00 in 939, and 'Hoot' drove that Plymouth throughout World War II. I bought a 1936 Ford with the money received from that sale."

I have known "Al" through the years; we worked together on several "tough" zoning issues n the area. "Al," Chief of Transit Police at MARTA when he retired in 1982, set up the MARTA ransit Police Department from "scratch" in 1972 and held statewide authority wherever MARTA perated.

According to "Al," Mr. and Mrs. Albert Brasill, Sr., who came from a long line of Baptists, ere wonderful parents. "They were both devoted Christians who lived their religion every day," he marked.

"Al" also shared that, after they married, his parents moved to Atlanta, where his dad, orked for Georgia Power Company. "Because he loved carpentry work, Dad left Georgia Power and egan building houses. In 1924 my dad and his business partner learned that the building business in iami was booming and big money could be made. When the Depression hit, he and his partner were uilding seventeen houses in Miami; they lost everything they had. Dad brought my family back to obb County, to a farm on Sandy Plains Road, where we were able to raise our own food. Although e didn't have any money, we had plenty of food and fared better than a lot of people during that time.

"In 1936 we moved back to Marietta, and Dad went back into the building business. We oved to Smyrna in 1938, and I met Mary shortly thereafter at the Strand Theater, in Marietta, where I as working at the time. (I was employed at the Strand when *Gone with the Wind* premiered at the oew's Grand Theater in Atlanta, in 1937.) Mary and I had our first date the following Sunday after e met. We went to Preacher Marlowe's church on Spring Street. We married Friday, March 13, 1942, out three years after we met.

"Mary worked for Southern Bell Company in the business office in Marietta, and I was udget Manager at Cowan Auto Supply, on the Marietta Square. I continued to work on weekends at e Strand Theater, where I learned to operate the projector. Knowing I was going to be drafted into ilitary service when I turned twenty years old on August 25, 1942, Mr. Clarence Smith, the long-ne manager of the Strand Theater, gave me a really nice letter, stating I was an experienced movie ojector operator; this, along with the fact I was also a licensed electrician, helped me get into the gnal Corps on November 17, 1942.

"I was sent to Camp Crowder in Joplin, Missouri, for my basic training and then to wire hool to train in telephone installation and repair. In January, Mary came to the Camp, and we rented converted chicken house with a pot bellied stove with an oven on the stove pipe to cook in—plus an thouse, in the little town of Neosho, Missouri. It was a little 'hick' town that was the boon docks of boon docks. Because all nicer places were rented, the converted chicken house was the only thing could get. I could live off the post while I was in wire school training and could go home every ght as long as I got back to camp by 6:00 A.M. roll call.

"Mary and I lived off the post until March 6, 1943, when I went back to camp that morning th no knowledge that I was going to ship overseas and wouldn't see Mary again until November 24, 45. They wouldn't let me call Mary or anything; they said they would send her a telegram telling her to go home because I was shipping out. I joined the 3196 Signal Service Company that already had a their equipment. We boarded the troop train and went to Fort Dix, New Jersey, and from there Staten Island, New York, to board the *SS Andes* with 5,000 troops. As we boarded the ship, Preside Roosevelt, sitting in his wheel chair at the entrance ramp, shook hands with each of us and said, 'G Bless America.' That surely gave us a lift! We didn't know where we were going until we landed Casablanca, North Africa, five days later, A very fast ship! We encountered German Submarine ' Boats' all the way and would drop depth charges, zigzag, and outrun them."

NOTE: "Al" shared that he was told by some of the crew that the *SS Andes* was a Briti luxury liner converted for use as a troop ship, with a top speed of 30 knots. Making almost three rou trips a month to America, it was bringing 5,000 troops each time. The skipper and all the crew we British. The British were desperate, afraid that Hitler was going to invade England. (History tells what happened.)

"Al" continued, "We set up camp at the edge of the desert, about twelve miles north Casablanca, North Africa. We supported the troops all the way to Bizerta, North Africa. The heat w terrible, and the malaria-carrying mosquitoes were so rampant that we had to sleep under a mosqui net and cover all our skin with clothes or mosquito nets. We had to take Abadern, a quinine tabl every day to prevent our contracting malaria; the Adabern tablets made us deathly sick. We were North Africa in tents six months, and not a drop of rain fell. The temperature would reach 110 degre at sun up, and at night it would drop to 45 degrees.

"Clean water was very scarce. Our water was kept in several large canvas lister bags different parts of a 50-tent area. With no ice or refrigeration, by noon the water was just about boilir All of our food was dehydrated or canned, and we were rationed a quart of water per day.

"In late August of 1943, at the Port of Bizerta, with all our gear, we boarded open landi craft to go across a 150-mile stretch of the sea from Bizerta, North Africa, for the invasion of Salerr Italy. Our company was split into several landing crafts. We joined a convoy of ships that w stretched out as far as the eye could see. Half of our company made the landing in Salerno; the otl half of us went on up about fourteen miles to the Italian coast and made a second landing, on the sou side of Naples, right behind the 82nd Airborne Division. We didn't have to get our feet wet, for th just dropped the gate on the sea wall, and we walked off onto dry land. It looked like the City Naples was on fire all over.

"It was about September 3, 1943, when we landed in Naples, after having been in three ma battles: Naples-Foggia, Rome-Arno, Appenines, and all the way up the Italian boot until the War Europe ended May 12, 1945. Our unit received a bronze battle star, one for each battle. We were al presented the Meritorious Unit Service Award. We were the first unit overseas to receive this award had a lot of close calls and still thank the good Lord almost every night for getting me through alm three years without serious injury. Many others were not so lucky, and some didn't come hon Thanks to our President Harry Truman for having the courage to order the Atomic Bomb to dropped on Japan to end the War, thus saving thousands of our lives!

"My rank was Sergeant T/4. I served with the 319th Signal Service Company under Gene Mark Clark's 5th U.S. Army, 1943-1945, in North Africa, in three major battles. I would hate to thi what would have happened if we had not had God with us.

"It was planned that we would get a two-week furlough back to the states and then ship to Pacific. On November 24, 1945, after two years, eight months, and four days, I got to see Mary aga There was no telephone or no e-mail back then; there was v-mail, but sometimes, particularly when were on the move, we would go a month with no mail."

"Al" concluded his story: "We had a company of three hundred of the finest dedicated n with whom it was a pleasure to serve, under all kinds of conditions. I love every one of them lik brother. There are only sixty of us left, and only a small group is still able to attend our reunion e ear. When one of us is sick, others of us pray for that one. God has always been a part of our lives. 'e made a sizable contribution toward the construction of the World War II Memorial, in 'ashington, D.C., and we have all been delighted with the beauty of the monument."

Fifth House

Mr. and **Mrs. Robert Motter** lived here with their two children, **Robert Jones**, known as 3obby," and **Mary**. Mr. Motter was known as "Rob."

Robert Jones Motter, married Thelma Cantrell of Rome. They had three children: Sam, Paul, id Nancy. Thelma and "Bobby" are active members of First Baptist Church, where he is a deacon. hey live on Dunn Street, where they raised their children. "Bobby" worked for Southern Bell elephone Company, from which he retired.

Before she married "Bobby," Thelma spent time in Washington, D.C. There she worked for iil Landrum, Congressman of Georgia's Seventh Congressional District, which at that time included obb County.

Sam Motter married and had two sons: Michael Paul and Samuel Jones Motter. Sam married. He and his second wife, Lorraine, had a son, Clinton. Lorraine had two sons, Michael mes and Justin Nunnery, from a previous marriage. Sam's son, Michael Paul, is married and has two iildren.

Paul Motter married Vicki Davis, who grew up in East Cobb County. They had a daughter, ssica. Vicki passed away in the spring of 2004.

Nancy Motter married Ricky Williams, who grew up in the Smyrna area. They had two ughters: Nicole and Danielle. Ricky works for Georgia Power Company, and Nancy works for ome Depot Corporate Office, on Paces Ferry Road in Vinings.

Mary Motter married Pete Fowler from the Oakdale community, south of Smyrna. They had e son, Michael Pete, known as "Mike." Mary, my age, and I started first grade together and aduated in the Smyrna High School Class of 1951. Pete attended Fitzhugh Lee Elementary and High hool, in the Oakdale community. He and his brothers founded Complete Garbage Company, to my owledge, the first company to put out service containers at businesses in the City of Smyrna. Pete d his brothers operated throughout Cobb County and developed a large, successful business.

Michael Pete Fowler, known as "Mike," married Lisa Giles of Marietta. They had one son, ichael Kyle. "Mike" and Lisa live near Smyrna on Fowler Road, west of the Covered Bridge. Iike" is the owner of Commercial Disposal on Smyrna Hill Drive.

Mr. Robert Motter, known as "Rob," was born in Greene County. His father was Mr. David enry Motter, who, according to information from family members, was the grandson of German migrants who settled in Pennsylvania. His mother was the former Rebecca Mable Mapp, a sister of r. Willie Mapp, who also lived on Atlanta Street. The Motters came to the Smyrna area early in the ventieth Century. They purchased a farm that was located on Spring Road, about one mile west of iat is now Cobb Parkway. Their house faced a country road (Hargrove Road), which is now known Cumberland Parkway. Their house was just north of Bethel Baptist Church. In addition to Robert, re were three daughters: Essie Mae, Mable, and Virginia, known as "Jennie." See *Motter, north side Spring Road, the Country Road.*

Mrs. Robert Motter, the former Zelma Jones from Dawsonville, was the daughter of Mr. and s. James Aaron Jones. Zelma moved to Atlanta as a young woman to attend a business school. hen she came to Smyrna, she boarded in the home of Mr. and Mrs. David Henry Motter to be near thel School, where she would be teaching. The school was on the south side of Spring Road in the inity of the present intersection of Cumberland Parkway and Spring Road.

When Zelma Jones started boarding with the elder Motters, their son Robert, known "Rob," was boarding on Atlanta Street with the Mapp Family, whose home was located near t Pinecrest Streetcar Stop. This arrangement was convenient for "Rob" to take the streetcar to work. T Motter home in those days was out in the country. Mrs. Mapp was Mr. David Henry Motter's sist See *Mapp, Atlanta Street, Mapps to R & M Café.*

All the while that Zelma Jones was boarding with the Motters, all she heard was "Rob" t and "Rob" that. The way his parents talked, he was the most wonderful person in the whole wor One day he happened to stop by to see his parents while Zelma was present. She thought to herse "So this is 'Rob!'" It took him a while to live up to the reputation that his parents had built up for he

After that first meeting, "Rob" started coming by to see his parents more often although was still boarding with the Mapps. He and Zelma would sit on the porch and talk for long periods time.

Later on, Zelma moved back to Atlanta, where she became employed at the Atlanta Belti Company and lived at the Y.W.C.A. (It was customary in those days for young women to live th and work in the area.) "Rob" started going to the Y.W.C.A to see her.

At some point "Rob" asked Zelma to marry him, and she said, "Yes." They did not sh their marriage plans with anyone. One day, boarding a train for Chattanooga, Tennessee, they elop They came back that night as if they had never married. Both continued to work at their jobs and out with each other as they had done before that trip to Chattanooga. It was some time before they t their families that they were married.

Mrs. Zelma Motter was known for her daylilies and often arranged flowers for the Sund services at First Baptist Church. The Church services were held in the rock building. (Mary Mot Fowler still has the flower vases her mother used for those arrangements.) Zelma, a Charter member the Jonquil Garden Club, was later instrumental in organizing the Dogwood Garden Club.

NOTE: All of the houses from the Gordon Smith House to the Motters, was affected by building of Belmont Hills Shopping Center, which opened in 1954.

NOTE: The Jonquil Garden Club was chartered on September 21, 1937. It is still a v vibrant garden club, often decorating for functions that are held by the City of Smyrna a organizations in the area. See *Atlanta Street, west side, from Mapps to the R & M Café.*

ATLANTA STREET
West Side
From Mapps to the R & M Café

First House

Appreciation is extended to Mary Motter Fowler_ and her brother, Bobby Motter, for shar their memories of the Mapp Family, and to Carol Fuller for sharing memories of her grandpare who lived on "Fuller's Hill." Appreciation also goes to Clifford Poston for information about family and Poston Realty and Insurance Company, and to Charles Gustafson, Jr. for information ab the Gustafson and Sprayberry families.

Mr. and **Mrs. W.H. Mapp** lived in this house on the northwest corner of Atlanta Fleming streets. This large white frame house was imposing for that day and time. The Mapps w affectionately known as "Willy" and "Aunt Betty." They had two daughters, **Louise** and **Elizabe** who was known as "Libby." I personally do not remember Mr. Mapp, but my sister, Hilda, rememb him well as an active deacon in First Baptist Church for many years. I do remember Mrs. Mapp Elizabeth, who were both very active in First Baptist Church Sunday School and Women's Mission Union (WMU). They were both good Christian women.

"Willy" Mapp, a policeman in Smyrna, was a great uncle of Bobby Motter, who well remembers him. "Willy" Mapp's sister, Rebecca Mable Mapp, was the grandmother of "Bobby" and Mary Motter.

Louise Mapp married Johnny Cameron of Lithonia; they had one son, Larry Mapp Cameron.

Elizabeth Mapp never married and lived with her parents to the end of their lives. I recall that she worked in Atlanta and rode the streetcar or bus to work because she never owned a car. Elizabeth, in her late fifties or early sixties, was murdered in her home in the early 1960s, a few years after her mother died. I remember my dad, Roy Wood, was serving on the Smyrna City Council when she was killed, and the Mapp home was in his ward. He knew the Mapp Family well and had attended school with Elizabeth. It was very perplexing to him that her murder was never solved. The investigation was finally closed, although it is a matter of public record.

Second House

Mr. and **Mrs. Fred Matthews** resided in this house, on the southwest corner of Fleming and Atlanta streets. She was the former Vera Brasill, one of the twin daughters of Mr. and Mrs. A.L. Brasill, Sr., who lived in the fourth house on Atlanta Street. They had one son, Fred Matthews, Jr. See *Brasill, Atlanta Street, from Miles Stop to the Motters* and *east side of Lee Street.*

Third House

Mr. and **Mrs. Robert Paul Alexander** and their daughters, Kay and Paula, moved to this house on Atlanta Street, between Fleming and Hill streets, in 1948. They bought this house after their apartment on 14th Street in Atlanta burned.

A pharmacist, Mr. Alexander, from Rome, was working at a drug store in Toccoa when he met Laura Ramsey, who was in high school; later she became his wife. He continued his career at Reed's Drugs in Atlanta; after moving from Toccoa to Smyrna, he rode the bus to and from Atlanta, as did many others in that era. Mrs. Alexander, who worked at Western Electric, also rode the bus to and from work. They bought their first car in 1952. The Alexander Family were members of Smyrna Presbyterian Church.

Kay Alexander, a member of the Campbell High School Class of 1958, married Jimmy Moss, a member of the Campbell High School Class of 1954. They had two children, a daughter, Ansley, and a son, Jarrett, and three grandchildren. Jarrett Moss is a medical doctor, specializing in anesthesiology and pain management, at Northside Hospital in Atlanta.

Jimmy attended Fitzhugh Lee Elementary School, where his mother was a teacher. He and his family lived on the south side of Atlanta Road, next door to Mrs. Cagle, also a teacher at Fitzhugh Lee School; their neighbors on the other side, in the Spanish style house, were the McConnells. The Moss Family was also active in Smyrna Presbyterian Church.

NOTE: The Devonshire Court subdivision is now located where the Moss house stood.

Paula Alexander, a graduate in the Campbell High School Class of 1957, married Jerry Cofield. They had three sons, Greg, Gary, and Jimmy, and three grandchildren. Paula and Jerry now live in Kennesaw.

Fourth House

Mrs. Harvey Jackson Sprayberry, the former Julia Antoinette Gunnell, and her youngest daughter, **Mae Sprayberry Gustafson**, and her husband, **Charles Gustafson, Sr.**, in 1940 moved to 2950 Atlanta Street from their farm near Acworth. Mae and Charles had two children born in this

Mrs. Sprayberry
Sprayberry/Gustafson House on Atlanta Street
Circa 1940s
Courtesy of Charles Gustafson

The Tatum House on Atlanta Street
Circa 1940s
Courtesy of Smyrna Museum

house: **Charles, Jr.**, in 1940, and **Carol Ann**, in 1945. This house was located on the northwest corner of Atlanta and Hill streets. While living in Smyrna, Mrs. Julia Spraybery, along with Mae, was a faithful member of First Methodist Church, where they were active in the Woman's Society of Christian Service. At the age of 80, Mrs. Sprayberry died in this house in1948. See *Gustafson, north side of Hill Street*

While reminiscing about Smyrna, Charles Gustafson, Jr., remembered sitting on the front porch of this house on Atlanta Street and seeing Mr. Powell, a deaf neighbor, being struck and killed by a train.

Mr. and Mrs. Harvey Jackson Sprayberry raised their family on their farm, near Acworth, in Cobb County, where Mr. Sprayberry died in 1924. They had five sons and another daughter besides Mae: Ralph, W. Paul, Herbert, Inman, Butler, and Lena, none of whom ever lived in this house on Atlanta Street.

Ralph Sprayberry was wounded in France while serving in the United States Army during World War I.

W. Paul Sprayberry, known as Paul, was principal of Acworth School (elementary and high school) and later served as Cobb County School Superintendent. Sprayberry High School is named for him. Paul attended Red Rock School in West Cobb County, Young Harris College, and earned a degree from the University of Georgia.

Herbert Sprayberry, who served in the United States Navy during World War II, owned and operated a well-known restaurant in Atlanta—Sprayberry's Cafeteria on Peachtree Street.

Inman Sprayberry.

Butler Sprayberry.

Lena Sprayberry married Sam Laird of Atlanta.

NOTE: The Sprayberry house is still standing on McLain Road in West Cobb County, near Acworth. The house was built very early in the Twentieth Century. While living on the farm, the Sprayberry Family were active members of County Line Methodist Church, on County Line Road, in West Cobb County. Mrs. Julia Sprayberry was a member there for over sixty years.

Mr. and Mrs. W.W. Kidd

This house was later the home of **Mr.** and **Mrs. W.W. Kidd**. I do not remember their living here until the early 1950s. Mr. Kidd, called "Captain" by many, and my dad were very close friends. When I first knew him, he was the building inspector for the City of Smyrna. He also supervised the construction of the King Street Library in the late 1950s. The library building was dedicated in 1960. T.P. Allen, who lived on Collier Drive, was the masonry contractor for this building and was assisted by his sons Danny and Tommy. T. P. and Danny are deceased.

Fifth House

Mr. and **Mrs. George Skelton** resided in a brick house on the southwest corner of Hill and Atlanta streets.

Sixth House

Mr. and **Mrs. Robert DeBoard** lived here with their five daughters: **Frankie**, **Mildred**, **Jean**, **Betty**, and **Joyce**. Both Mr. and Mrs. DeBoard were from Pickens County.

I remember that Mr. DeBoard worked at one time for the City of Smyrna Parks Department. My dad, who was on the City Council and chaired the Smyrna Parks and Recreation Committee, worked with him very closely in those days. Mr. DeBoard later worked for Cobb County Water Department, where he continued to work into his late 80's. At the time of his death, *The Atlanta Journal* printed an article about his having worked such a long time.

The DeBoards bought this house from Sidney Ruan of Macon, who obtained the house in some kind of land swap. Mr. Ruan continued to live in the house with the DeBoards because he had no family and no place to go. Through the graciousness of the DeBoards, he lived with them for about thirty years, even moving with them when they returned to Pickens County to reside. Mr. Ruan is buried in the DeBoards' family plot, in Philadelphia Cemetery in Pickens County.

Frankie DeBoard. See *DeBoard, seventh house.*

Mildred DeBoard married Richard Brooks, Jr., known as "Junior." He was a member of the large Brooks Family on Roswell Street. See *Brooks, east side of Roswell Street.*

Jean DeBoard married Henry Holland of Cobb County. They had one son, Michael, and two granddaughters.

Betty DeBoard married Winfred Aenchbacker. They had a son, Wendell, a daughter, Linda, two granddaughters, and four grandsons.

Joyce DeBoard married Doyle Cantrell. They had a son, Randall, a grandson, and a granddaughter.

NOTE: Later on, in the 1950s, Cecil Grogan, a chiropractor, had his office in one of these houses. Various other professional people occupied these buildings from time to time. Still later, in the 1960s, the Fouts Brothers, C. J. and Jerry, bought this property and built Fouts Brothers Auto Parts Store and Service Station. According to family information, they established the first Datsun dealership at this location in 1969. See *Fouts, Atlanta Street, from Mrs. Mazie's to Pearce Matthews.*

Seventh House

Frankie DeBoard married **Jack Maddox** from Griffin. They lived here with their son, **Carl.** This wood frame house, built about 1949, is one of two still standing in this area in the early part of the Twenty-first Century. It is the only owner-occupied house; the brick one next door is now owned by the City of Smyrna.

Eighth House

The Blackwell Family lived in this house in the days of my youth. They had a daughter, **Mary Beth**, and a son, **Buddy**.

Ninth House

John Tatum
Mayor of Smyrna
May 1941-November 1942
Smyrna City Councilman
Dates Unknown

NOTE: The dates recorded above are posted on Mayor Tatum's picture which hangs in the Smyrna City Hall.

This was the home of **Mr.** and **Mrs. John Tatum** and their daughter, **Elizabeth**. Those who knew Elizabeth said they would never forget her because she was so "tiny." Mr. Tatum, the Railway

Express Agent in Smyrna during the days of my youth, was on the Smyrna City Council for a period of time and served as Mayor from May 1941 until November 1942. Mr. Tatum's short term was due to his job at the railroad necessitating his being on duty because of World War II.

The Tatum house, along with the DeBoard house, the two rental houses and all the property to Powder Springs Street, is located on what the locals referred to as "Fuller's Hill." This area is now the location of Smyrna Fire Station # 1 and Police Headquarters; both of these buildings were part of Smyrna's downtown revitalization, 1990-2002. All of the property from Hill Street to Powder Springs Street is owned by the City of Smyrna, with the exception of Second Baptist Church and one house that stands between the fire and police stations.

Jones Walker Fuller
Mayor of Smyrna
1913-1917

Mr. and **Mrs. Jones Walker Fuller** lived on Atlanta Street in this area, early in the Twentieth Century. Mrs. Fuller was the former Ollie Morris. They had four children: **Ollie Francis**, **J.B.**, **Morris**, and **Harold**. This house was located on "Fuller's Hill," which, along with Fuller Street, was named for Jones A. Fuller, a soldier in the Confederate Army and the father of Jones Walker Fuller. (Fuller Street was a short street that was located off Powder Springs Street, behind the Fuller property; it was first named Sally's Alley, then Lemon Street.) See *Fuller, Atlanta Street, from Marlowe's to Creatwood.*

NOTE: The following house was located near or on the property that was formerly the Fuller property.

<u>Tenth House</u>

Mr. and **Mrs. Buna Walker** built this house on Atlanta Street sometime in the mid-to-late 1940s. It was located near the bottom of "Fuller's Hill." I remember when the Walker Family moved into this house, which I recall as being pretty and nice. I am sure the Walkers moved here before Mickey or Phillip graduated from high school. I can remember going to their house when they lived on Spring Street and we boys were still in elementary school. See *Walker, south side of Spring Street* and *Worley, south side of Church Street.*

Poston Insurance and Real Estate Company

A.M. "Red" Poston
Smyrna City Coucilman
1954-1956

Mr. and **Mrs. A.M. "Red" Poston** moved to Smyrna in 1952, after buying, from Bill Stewart's estate, the **Bill Stewart Insurance and Real Estate Company**, which was located on the east side of Atlanta Street. "Red" and his wife Clifford, moved the agency in 1955 into the Poss Building on West Spring Street and from there to this house on the west side of Atlanta Street. "Red" served as President of the Cobb County Real Estate Board in 1959 and again in 1962.

"Red" Poston and his wife, Clifford, had two sons, Milburn and Bill, and a daughter, Marian. 'Red' died April 15, 1963, at age 53. After "Red's" death Clifford continued to operate the business, with the help of "Bob" Fowler and Dallis Guthrie while the children finished their education.

In 1971 Clifford and her sons, Milburn and Bill, established Traton Homes: "Tra" for Milburn's daughter, <u>Tra</u>cie and "ton" for Bill's son, Clif<u>ton</u>. The Poston children and some of the grandchildren continue to operate Traton Homes, one of the largest homebuilders in Metro Atlanta, which is quite a success story. Clifford said; "It was established around the kitchen table." Clifford, at age 86, continues to work full time. See *Poston, Whitfield Street.*

Clifford Poston
Circa 1990s
Courtesy of Poston Family

A.M. Poston
Circa 1950s
Courtesy of Poston Family

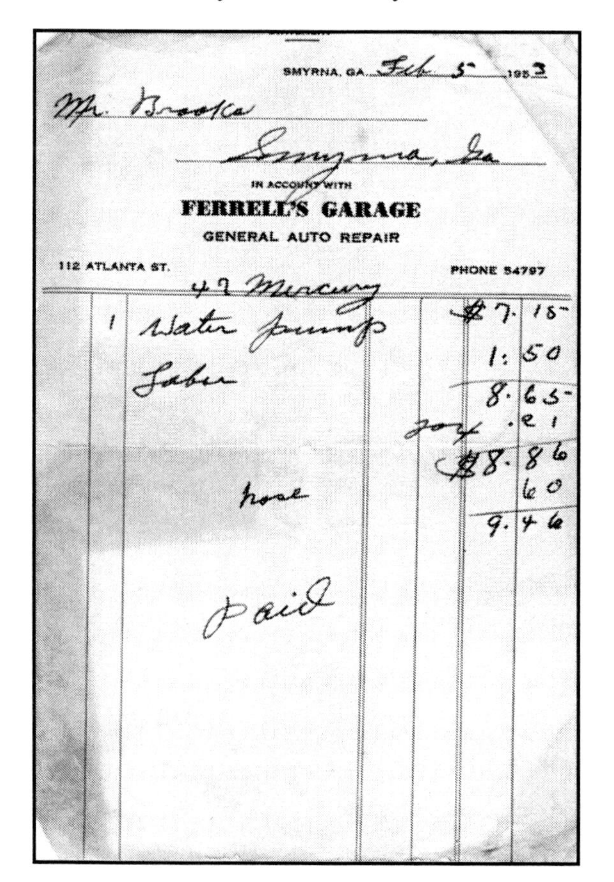

SMYRNA, GA. Feb 5 1953

Mr. Brooks

Smyrna, Ga

IN ACCOUNT WITH

FERRELL'S GARAGE

GENERAL AUTO REPAIR

112 ATLANTA ST. PHONE 54797

47 Mercury

1	Water pump	$7.15
	Labor	1:50
		8.65
	tax	.21
		$8.86
	hose	60
		9.46

Paid

Courtesy of Janet Brooks Brown
Circa 1953

Lillie and I bought our first home from "Bob" Fowler and "Red" Poston in 1961. One unday evening after the church service, "Bob" approached us and said, '"Red"' Poston told me to sell ou a house that is located on Pinehurst Drive." Though we thought we were a year away from buying home, it was certainly to our advantage financially to purchase a home that soon. We had been narried only six months when we moved into this house. We both give "Red" credit for helping us to nake that move in our lives earlier than we might otherwise have done.

NOTE: Long-time local residents remember a vacant lot between the above house and econd Baptist Church. Those who remember say that this area was "A sea of yellow jonquils in the pringtime."

SECOND BAPTIST CHURCH

Second Baptist Church stood next door to the Walker house. I do not remember when the hurch was built. It seems it has been there from my earliest memories. So far, it has survived amid all he renovation going on in that area of the City.

Next door to the church was an electrical business run by Mr. John Bradfield. I do not know ow long he was in business there, but I remember his being there in the late 1940s. **Mr.** and **Mrs.** **ohn Bradfield** had two children: **Wendell** and **Norma**.

The next structure was a service station that was owned and operated by **Earl Cobb,** who onstructed it in the late 1940s or early 1950s. This station replaced Earl's business located next door o The Telephone Exchange Building.

Ray and **Fred Ferrell** were brothers who owned and operated **Ferrell's Garage** in the asement of Earl Cobb's Service Station. Ray Ferrell was employed as a mechanic by the City of myrna for many years.

Eleventh House

The **Lemon Sisters**, along with their mother and brother lived in this house. One of the isters was married. Throughout my childhood, this old frame house with a porch across the front tood in this location. I can see, weather permitting, the Lemon Sisters sitting there, with their mother r brother, in the middle of Smyrna, at the foot of "Fullers Hill." I never saw them anywhere except on hat porch. I thought they probably shopped at Mr. Southern's store because I never saw them at Black nd Webb. I always heard the Lemon Family was good Christian people.

NOTE: According to family information, the **Gillham Family** lived in the above house in 935. See *Gilham, north side of Fleming Street*

The Smyrna Woman's Club

The Smyrna Woman's Club owned a building on the southwest corner of Powder Springs nd Atlanta streets. It was a small brown building with two entrances. One side of the building was sed for the Smyrna Library. I remember that, as a child, I frequented the library, where I read many hildren's books and did some research for my school projects. Mrs. Mazie Nelson, the unpaid ibrarian, was usually there. I remember she was always kind to kids.

I seem to remember that some organizations, e.g. The Jonquil Garden Club and The Smyrna Voman's Club, held their meetings in this building. The community room in The Smyrna Woman's Club building was also rented out for showers and small parties. Janet Brooks Brown remembers a ridal shower was given for her there.

Appreciation is extended to Harold Lee Smith, Director of the Smyrna Museum and the founding President of the Smyrna Historical Society, for the information about The Smyrna Woman's Club members as listed below. This information was published in the April 2004 issue of *Lives and Times,* a publication of the Smyrna Historical and Genealogical Society.

THE SMYRNA WOMAN'S CLUB

1944 Officers

Mrs. David Cano, President
Mrs. Paul Gresham, First Vice President
Mrs. M.C. Clarkston, Second Vice President
Mrs. Robert Baugh, Recording Secretary
Mrs. Thomas Kent, Corresponding Secretary
Mrs. C.L. Groce, Treasurer
Mrs. R.R. Manning, Sr., Elle F. White
Mrs. G.C. Green, Parliamentarian and Historian

Foundations

Mrs. A.H. Carson, Tallulah Falls
Mrs. E.C. Bird, Student Aid
Mrs. R.R. Manning, Sr., Elle F. White
Mrs. W.E. Patterson, War Service

Committee Chairmen

Mrs. Paul Gresham, Membership
Mrs. M.C. Clarkston, Program and Music
Mrs. C. L. Deal, Welfare
Mrs. L. T Eskew
Mrs. G.B. Williams, Citizenship
Mrs. W. A. Quarles, Education
Mrs. C. E. Wagoner, Fine Arts
Mrs. Mazie Nelson, Legislation
Mrs. E.B. Awtry, Spiritual Education
Mrs. Robert Motter, Constitution and Gardens

Mrs. S. W. Turner, Safety
Mrs. Jimmy Pierce, Health
Mrs. Paul Hensley, Civic
Mrs. Joe Pruitt
Mrs. G.C. Green, Library Service
Mrs. Robert Baugh, Publicity
Mrs. L.T. Eskew, American Home
Mrs. Z. A. Hardage, Rural/Urban
Ways & Means, The Executive Board

JONQUIL GARDEN CLUB

The Jonquil Garden Club was chartered on September 21, 1937, and became a member of The Federated Garden Clubs in April 1939. The following Smyrna Citizens were charter members of The Jonquil Garden Club.

Mrs. W.H. Medlin, President

Members

Mrs. Lewis Anderson
Mrs. C. B. Austin
Mrs. Robert F. Baldwin
Mrs. Homer Bell
Mrs. John Bush
Mrs. Fannie Crawford
Mrs. P. F. Brinkley
Mrs. D. J. Ray

Mrs. Fred Dowda
Mrs. C. L. Groce
Mrs. Henry Konigsmark
Mrs. W.H. Medlin
Mrs. Robert Motter
Mrs. W.E. Patterson
Mrs. W.A. Quarles

(The above information is typed exactly as it was in 1937, when the club was chartered.)

The Jonquil Garden Club from Smyrna planted the first jonquils at the Georgia Baptist Children's Home in Hapeville, Georgia. The members planted two rows of jonquils across the front lawn.

NOTE: The above Jonquil Garden Club information was furnished by Mrs. Robert W. (Jacque Hyde) Landers. The ladies, as can be seen, were identified by their husband's names.

THE UNITED DAUGHTERS OF THE CONFEDERACY

The United Daughters of the Confederacy in Smyrna was chartered ten years after I graduated from Smyrna High School. Many of the ladies who helped organize were leading citizens in the community when I was a child. Some of the members in this organization are not listed elsewhere in this book, probably because they lived outside the area about which I have been writing.

UNITED DAUGHTERS OF THE CONFEDERACY
PHILLIP'S LEGION CHAPTER
NUMBER 2300
CITY OF SMYRNA
COUNTY OF COBB
STATE OF GEORGIA

This charter authorizes the above mentioned chapter to perform all acts pertaining to the purposes of this association and to enact for its own government such by-laws as may be deemed necessary, provided they do not conflict with the charter or constitution of this association.

In testimony of which we have hereunto affixed our signatures at Jonesboro, Georgia, this 27th day of June 1961.

United Daughters of the Confederacy
Signed by Elizabeth Cody Elaine Bachman, President-General
Doris Walker Lyle, Recording Secretary-General

Charter Members

Baldwin, Jennie Legg
Beshears, Ina Ruff
Brinkley, Evelyn Osburn
Brown, Mildred Barnett
Carmichael, Ruby Hamby
Colston, Martha Joe McCleskey
Cummerford, Emily Dunn
Dorris, Catherine Baldwin
Echots, Ida Mae Poss
Eubanks Caroline Lee
Farrar, Sara Green
Fowler, Jennie Lou Hamby
Gann, Estelle
Green, Lena May
Gresham, Erma McLain
Groover, Mittie Luna Hamby
Hamrick, Laura Alice Green
Harper, Louise Lindley
Harris, Dorothy Petty
Howard, Alice Guthrie
Jolley, LeoDelle Lassiter
Jones, Lucile McLain
Landers, Julia McCleskey
Manning, Leila Sewell
Mountcastle, Ruth Potts
Nash, Gladys Wright
Paris, Maude Baldwin
Pettett, Woodrow Petty
Petty, Lula Legg
Poss, Will Mae Millwood
Pruitt, Lorena Pace
Ray, Willie Alta
Siddall, Anna Vene Garrison
Terry, Mary Baldwin
Whittington, Willie Sewell
Windsor, Ruth Morris
Witham, Vera Poss
Wood, Clara Morris

The above information was copied from the original charter of the Phillip's Chapter of the United Daughters of the Confederacy. The original charter is in the possession of the Julia McCleskey Landers Family. Jacque Hyde Landers, the daughter-in-law of Mrs. Julia McCleskey Landers, loaned this charter and gave permission for it to be retyped.

Smyrna Women's Club, Corner of Atlanta and Powder Springs streets
(Library on the left: Women's Club on the right) Circa 1940s
Courtesy of Smyrna Museum

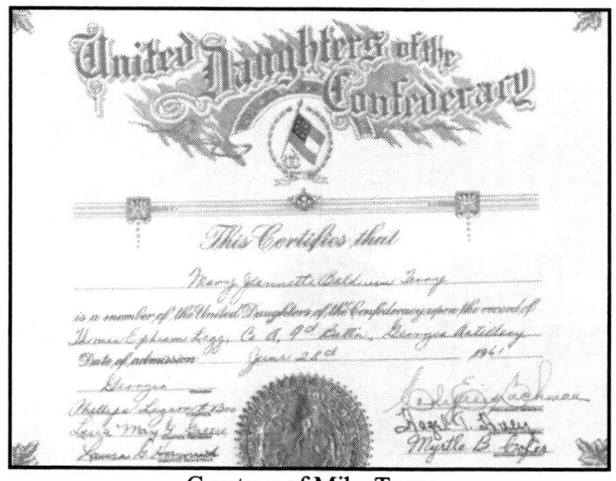

United Daughters of the Confederacy

This Certifies that

Mary Jeannette Baldwin Terry

is a member of the United Daughters of the Confederacy upon the record of

Thomas Ephraim Legg, Co. A, 9th Battn. Georgia Artillery

Date of admission June 22d 1961

Georgia

Courtesy of Mike Terry

United Daughters of the Confederacy District Meeting in Carrollton. Seated: Mrs. John F. Petty (Lula), a real daughter of the Confederacy seated between her daughter far right Mrs. Carlton Harris (Dorothy), and Mrs. Petty's nieces, (L-R): Mrs. Pitner (Catherine) Dorris, Mrs. Emory (Maude) Paris, and Mrs. J.J. (Mary) Terry.
All Members of Phillips Legion Chapter # 1300
Courtesy of Mike Terry

Paul and **Ida Mae Clayton** in Paul's Café
Circa 1951
Courtesy of "Millie" Clayton Broyles

Paul Clayton and **Robert Day**, owner of Day's Taxi, in Paul's Café
Circa 1951
Courtesy of "Millie" Clayton Broyles

Harvey Yardage and **"Millie" Clayton** in Paul's Café
Circa 1951
Courtesy of "Millie" Clayton Broyles

R & M CAFÉ

The R & M Café, located on the southwest corner of Sunset Avenue and Atlanta Street, was owned and operated by Mr. Morgan. Probably the "M" was for Morgan. I do not know where the "R" came from. I personally do not recall ever going into the R & M Café, which was there for a number of years. I do not believe my family did either, for we mostly ate at home or at G.B.'s Place, where we might buy hot dogs before going to a movie. I do not even know what kind of food was served and do not remember talking with anyone else that may have eaten at R & M; but somebody must have, for it stayed in business.

PAUL'S CAFÉ

Later on, Paul and Ida Mae Clayton operated Paul's Café at the same location as the R & M Café. They were operating this café when I graduated from high school. Their daughter "Millie" and I were in the Smyrna High School Class of 1951. The Senior Class chartered two buses for our Senior trip to Florida: one for the boys and one for the girls; the morning we left, Paul and Ida Mae served all of us breakfast at Paul's Café. See *Clayton, north side of Bank Street.*

ATLANTA STREET

West Side

From Marlowe's to Creatwood

Appreciation is extended to Rebecca Nash Paden for information she shared regarding the residents of Atlanta Street. Rebecca grew up on Atlanta Street in the middle of the Twentieth Century. Appreciation is also extended to Councilman "Bill" Scoggins for his memories of working in the downtown area from the 1940s through the 1960s; to "Mike" Terry, who contributed the history of the Cano/Gautchey House; to Carol Fuller, who grew up on Atlanta Road; to Gayle Colquitt Ruddell for information about Wayne's 5, 10, & 25 Cents, a store on Atlanta Street; and to Claudia Mitchell Harper and Lucy Mitchell Evans for information about the Dr. Mitchell Family.

MARLOWE'S FIVE AND DIME STORE

Marlowe's Five and Dime Store was on the west side of Atlanta Street, next door to the café. We always called it the "ten cents store." It was owned and operated by Mr. and Mrs. Marlowe, who worked in the store full-time. When I would get a nickel or a dime, I would go to Marlowe's and buy marbles and BB shots for my rifle. One time I remember buying a ball and a kite. A ball in those days would last a long time. I always enjoyed going into that store!

My mother, Dora, had a little corner shelf in our living room. We called it a "what not." I remember that little shelf was bought at Marlowe's. I don't remember if she bought it or if someone gave it to her, but I know that is where it came from. On that "what not" she had little items that we called "do dads," some of which were stamped "Made in Japan." They were small items like many of you would have bought in a "ten cents store." When my mother sold her home in 1975 and moved to an apartment, that "what not" and some of the little "do dads" went with her.

Arthur and **Robert Bacon** opened a dry cleaning business in a new building located here after World War II. The name of the business was **Smyrna Cleaners**. See *Bacon, south side of Bank Street* and *east side of King Street.*

Bob Lewis owned and operated **Bob's Pool Room** in the next building. He opened this business after World War II. See *Robert Lewis, east side of Hughes Street.*

The next location was **Earl Cobb's Service Station. Wes Pass** operated a **garage** that was located behind Earl's service station. The **Southern Bell Telephone Exchange Building** was next door.

TELEPHONE EXCHANGE

The Telephone Exchange was in the front of a small, attractive red brick building about four or five buildings from Bank Street. All of the phone equipment was located here. The operators who handled all the calls would sit on stools that were bar high. I liked to go in and watch them switch calls.

NOTE: Southern Bell Telephone Company owned the Exchange; in fact, I didn't know there were other telephone companies.

The back of the building was living accommodations for the Exchange supervisor, who in the days of my youth (until the system changed) was Mrs. Mamie Daniel, whose husband, Mr. Fuller Daniel, was employed by the Simmons Mattress Company in Atlanta, where many men in Smyrna worked in those days. The Daniels lived at the Exchange much of the time, although they had a home on South Atlanta Street in front of what is now Campbell Middle School.

If we wanted to make a long-distance call, we would need to know whom and where we were calling. Atlanta was long distance in those days; in fact, the only places we could call locally were Smyrna and Marietta. Calling long distance was not an easy procedure, especially if the town or city being called were a long way off. This is the system that we still had when I graduated from high school. In fact, when Lillie and I started dating in 1956, Atlanta was still long distance.

When phone numbers were lengthened, people just went "bonkers." They would say, "This is a lot to remember." Our new number was HE 5-4228 (HE, short for Hemlock); and this did seem like a lot to remember. People complained for a long time about having to dial such a long number, but they finally adjusted. There were some good things about the change: we were not on a party line, and we did not have to go through a third party. It was still a big change! This happened while I was a student at the Atlanta Division of the University of Georgia, now Georgia State University.

Argo and McLarty Barber Shop was next door.

NOTE: There was a vacant lot between Argo and McLarty Barber Shop and Jimmy Pierce's Pool Room, where the Bank of Smyrna was constructed in 1946.

JIMMY PIERCE'S POOL ROOM

Jimmy Pierce's Pool Room was located in this building and afterwards, **Atherton's Drug Store**, which later became **Atkins Pharmacy**.

UNITED POSTAL SERVICE

The United States Post Office in Smyrna was located in the next building until it was moved to West Spring Street, within the Masonic Lodge building in the late 1950s. The post office stayed there until 1969, when it was relocated to a new building on Cherokee Road, now known as Windy Hill Road.

The Market Village is now located on the West Spring property where the **Masonic Lodge** stood. The Masons sold their property to the City and bought land on Concord Road, near Hurt Road, where they built a beautiful new lodge. See *Nelm's Lodge, West Spring Street* and *Concord Road, the Country Road.*

The next building at one time housed a bank, which failed during the Depression years. Smyrna did not have another bank until 1946, when the **Bank of Smyrna** opened. In the days of my youth this building, located on the northwest corner of Atlanta and Bank streets, was our city hall, police station, and jail. In the late 1930s, Dessie Brooks Cochran operated a restaurant here.

L-R: Paul Gresham, B.F. Reed, Dr. G.C. Green, Jake Nash, Tommy Richardson and Dr. D.C. Landers
Bank of Smyrna Directors and Head Teller, Tommy Richardson Circa 1940s

Arthur Bacon
Site Unknown
Circa 1949
Courtesy of "Dot" Bacon

FIREWORKS AT CITY HALL

As told by "Bill" Scoggins

The City Hall was on the northwest corner of Atlanta and Bank streets. When a person entered the City Hall, he would walk across the room and take two steps up to a wooden four-foot door. This entrance would take him down to four jail cells.

In the jail area, the first door to the right was the men's room. The wall of the men's room was also the inside wall of the City Hall reception area. The police chief had a young enterprising police officer on duty. Those who seem to know said the young officer had bought himself a new 357 Magnum pistol, so powerful that it would shoot through a V8 engine block of a car.

On a certain day, he was in City Hall, showing off his new gun to City personnel. All of a sudden, without any warning, the gun went off. The slug went through the wall between the reception area and the men's room and blew the commode all to pieces!

It is reported, by those who seem to know, "The chief was seen running real fast down Bank Street, having a hard time holding his britches up."

WALKER AKINS' GROCERY STORE

Walker Akins' Grocery Store was on the southwest corner of Bank and Atlanta streets. This store was later **Saul's Department Store**.

Ed and Jeff Crowe

Two of the people I remember vividly from my childhood are my grandfather, Ed Crowe, and his brother, Uncle Jeff Crowe, who was the older of the two. My grandfather was a carpenter. I remember he was always building a chicken house, screening a porch, fixing a leak on a roof, or doing some other kind of carpentry work. He was already an old man from my earliest memories, and so was Uncle Jeff, who had a wooden leg, or a "peg leg," as we called it. I do not think I ever knew how he got that "peg leg." See *south side of Church Street*, *east side of Old Roswell Road,* and *north side of Bank Street.*

What I remember most about Uncle Jeff is that he would come to my Aunt Myrtle Brooke's home to visit his brother, Ed. Aunt Myrtle lived on Roswell Street, across the railroad from G.B.'s Place. She was my mother's sister.

At times Uncle Jeff and my grandfather would come across the railroad to Atlanta Street and Walker Akins' Grocery Store. There was a ledge on the front of the store, and the older men in the neighborhood would use that ledge as a bench. They would sit there on that ledge and discuss politics or anything else of interest in the news in those days. Whether it was local, state, or national news, they knew something about it. I would see them frequently and would stand for long periods of time and listen. It was interesting, for it seemed to me, as a child, that they knew everything. Ed and Jeff, who were both old men at that time, were gone from us a few years later.

I remember well the 1946 State of Georgia Governor's race, mostly because of the old men's conversation. I was only thirteen years old. One of the things that became a very heated discussion on that ledge was the "Jimmy" Carmichael and "Gene" Talmadge race. They called "Jimmy" Carmichael "Jimmy Car-mick-el." (That was their pronunciation.) The County Unit System was the rule in Georgia in those days. Whoever won the most county unit votes won the election. That happened in this race. My grandfather always said that "Jimmy Carmickel" won because he got the most popular votes, but he lost the election by a large margin under the County Unit System.

The County Unit System worked like this: The 8 largest counties in the state had 6 unit votes each; the next 30 largest counties had four unit votes each; the next one 121 counties had two unit votes each. This gave control to the rural counties where the populations were small and, typically, gave rural county candidates an advantage. In 1946, the 8 largest counties were Bibb (Macon), Chatham (Savannah), DeKalb (Decatur), Floyd (Rome), Fulton (Atlanta), Muscogee (Columbus), Richmond (Augusta), and Troup (LaGrange). Statewide Jimmy Carmichael got 313,389 popular votes over Eugene Talmadge who received 297,245. This information was lifted from Bill Kinney's column in *The Marietta Daily Journal.*

This electoral process was later declared unconstitutional. I learned a lot from those men sitting on that ledge. It was through them that I came to understand the workings of the County Unit System. Even as old as they were Papa Crowe and Uncle Jeff realized this was not a fair process.

NOTE: This electoral process was repealed in 1962.

James V. Carmichael
Georgia State House of Representatives
1937-1941
1946 Gubernatorial Candidate

I learned that "Jimmy" Carmichael was a local boy from the Log Cabin community, south of Oakdale. The local citizens called the community "Carmichael's" because the Carmichael Family for years ran a store in the area and were prominent in the Log Cabin community and the Log Cabin Sunday School. "Jimmy" Carmichael and my mother, Dora Crowe Wood, were members of the Marietta High School Class of 1929.

Attorney "Jimmy" Carmichael, a graduate of Emory University, was instrumental in bringing to Cobb County Bell Aircraft (commonly called the Bell Bomber Plant). He served as Vice-President and General Manager of the plant during World War II. He later became President of Scripto, an old Atlanta company that manufactured writing instruments, such as ball point pens, and cigarette lighters. Prior to World War II, Jimmy served two terms in the Georgia State Legislature. In 1946 he ran for governor but was defeated by Eugene Talmadge, who ran on the County Unit System.

When I was a small boy, there was a restaurant in the building next door to Saul's Department Store. It was owned and operated by **G.B. Williams** and **Lee Black**. This was before G.B. opened his place on Spring Street at the railroad.

WAYNE'S 5, 10, & 25 Cents

Hubert and **Frances Colquitt** opened Wayne's 5, 10 & 25 Cents, a store in downtown Smyrna, next door to **Saul's Department Store,** in the late 1940s. Hubert and Frances moved the business from this location to the Rice Building on Atlanta Street; then, in 1954, they moved it again—to the new Masonic Building, on West Spring Street; from there in 1958, it was relocated to Dickson Shopping Center, where it became **Wayne's**.

Belmont Hills Shopping Center, advertised to be the largest shopping center in the Southeast of that time, was opened in 1954. Frances and Hubert opened **Colquitt's Gift Shop** there in 1955, shortly followed by **Colquitt's Record Shop**.

In 1963, they closed Colquitt's Gift Shop and Record Shop in Belmont Hills to consolidate it with Wayne's at Dickson Shopping Center. In 1972 Hubert and Frances opened **Colquitt's Dress Shop** in Dickson Shopping Center, on South Cobb Drive. The Colquitts retired in the mid 1980s.They were in business in Smyrna for almost forty years.

NOTE: Gayle Colquitt Ruddell shared that, when her family first moved to Smyrna, they first lived on Pierce Avenue, outside the city, for a very short time. The upstairs over the store became available, and they lived there while the house on Bank Street was being prepared for them to move

Wayne's 5, 10 & 25¢
Circa 1940's
Courtesy of Gayle Colquitt Ruddell

THE COLQUITT FAMILY, L-R, CLAIRE CURTIS, FRANCIS COLQUITT
Wayne, The Son After Whom The STore Was Named, Hubert And Gayle Ruddell

Photo of the Culquitt Family and article appeared in the *Marietta Daily Journal* in the late 1970's when Wayne's in the Dickson Shopping Center ceased operation.

into. Gayle also shared that she has fond memories of living upstairs over the store and riding her tricycle on the sidewalk out front.

There was a dentist's office upstairs over Wayne's 5, 10 & 25 Cents store. At one time, **Dr. White** had his practice there, and at another time **Dr. Charles Blain's** office was there. Later on in the 1950s, **Dr. Joe Collins** practiced dentistry in this office before moving to the Mitchell Building.

COLLINS PHARMACY

Collins Pharmacy, operated by Dr. and Mrs. M.L. Collins, was located in the next building. **Dr. W.C. Mitchell's Medical Office** was upstairs over Wayne's 5, 10, & 25 Cents Store. Dr. Mitchell had the Mitchell Building constructed, in the 1940s, on the northwest corner of Atlanta Street and Sunset Avenue. There he practiced until his retirement.

CHAT 'N' NIBBLE

Chat 'N' Nibble, a restaurant owned and operated by "Butch" Alexander, opened in 1946 in the "Old Post Office" building. ("Butch" was formerly the butcher at Rogers Store.) I remember, as a small boy, going to the United States Post Office when it was in this building. The post office was later moved to a building, which was specifically designed for it, next door to the Smyrna City Hall. As a kid living on Bank Street at the time, I thought this was the biggest and nicest building I had ever seen.

GENE RICE'S FURNITURE STORE

Gene Rice's Furniture Store was next door to the "Old Post Office" building. Gene Rice married Virginia Mitchell, who grew up on Church Street. See *west side of Lee Street* and *south side of Church Street.*

Leila Cochran shared with me that she and Al came to Smyrna in the mid 1950s, after Al completed his tour of military duty in the United States Army during the Korean Conflict. **Al Cochran** opened his first law office in the rear of Gene Rice's Furniture Store. He has maintained a law office on Atlanta Street ever since. His firm, **Cochran**, **Camp**, and **Snipes**, is currently located on Atlanta Street, just south of Church Street. Though it has not always carried the same name, the law office has been in its current location for more than 40 years. According to Al, he was the second attorney to maintain a law practice in Smyrna. The first one was **Raymond Mulkey.**

Al Cochran came to Smyrna from Jasper. He and Leila lived in Smyrna for many years before moving to East Cobb County. They had two children, Karen and Scott, and four grandchildren. Al is an ordained deacon and Sunday School teacher at King Spring Baptist Church, where he and Leila have been faithful members since the church was constituted.

NOTE: King Spring Baptist Church, formerly a mission of First Baptist Church, was constituted in October 1958.

Scott Cochran is Smyrna's current City Attorney, a position he has held since he was sworn in, the first Monday of January 2000. Scott and Erika are active members of North Metro Church in West Cobb County.

Charles E. Camp, known as "Chuck," and his wife, Jane Woods Camp, came to Smyrna in the early 1960s. They had two children: Matt and Camilla. Matt is an eye surgeon with a practice in Atlanta. Camilla is an attorney in Marietta. Her attorney husband, Mike Williams, is currently an attorney in the Cochran, Camp, and Snipes Law Firm. They had two daughters: Savannah Jane and Chloe. Mike is the son of Pete and Mary Williams. See *Manning, east side of Gilbert Street.*

"Chuck," who received his law degree from the University of Georgia, served as Smyrna's City Attorney from the late 1970s until his death in December 1999. He was a devoted "Bulldog" fan;

1948

Chat 'N' Nibble "Open House" Wed.

Open House will be observed at Chat 'N' Nibble. Wednesday from 6 to 9 p. m. in celebration of the second anniversary of the business. Favors will be given children and refreshments will be served.

Established in April two years ago, the popularity of Chat 'N' Nibble has grown to such an extent that it has been necessary to remodel the building in order to accommodate the crowd. It is a popular meeting place for teenagers, adults and children.

Meals, short orders, sandwiches, drinks and ice cream are served. The business opens at 7:30 a. m. and closes at 11 p. m.

Butch Alexander is the popular manager and Mrs. H. O. Swain is assistant.

he and I shared that passion! "Chuck" was a fun guy. The following statement is one I always enjoyed hearing him say, "There is nowhere I would rather be than between the hedges." Jane, "Chuck," Matt, and Camilla were members of First Baptist Church.

H.G. Snipes married Nancy Jones, a daughter of Mr. and Mrs. Charlie Jones. See *Jones south side of Spring Road.*

Mr. H. B. McIntosh operated a barber shop near the northwest corner of Atlanta and West Spring streets. It was a little brown wooden building set back from the street and offset from the other stores. There was an unpaved parking space behind the barber shop.

Corner Grill was built on the same site where Mr. McIntosh operated his barber shop. This property is now part of the Market Village redevelopment.

Smyrna Taxi was in a small rock and cement block building located at the rear of Corner Grill. The taxi business faced West Spring Street and was surrounded by an unpaved parking lot that was utilized by downtown shoppers.

SMYRNA DRUG STORE

Smyrna Drug Store was on the southwest corner of West Spring and Atlanta streets. This store was owned and operated by **Dr. D.C. Landers**, a pharmacist. His son, **Bobby Landers**, worked with him and later operated the store after Dr. Landers retired. Jack Taylor worked at Landers' Drug Store when he was a teenager. He told about selling streetcar fare ticket books there: "Many people who rode the streetcar in those days would buy weekly or monthly supplies of fare coupons at the drug store on pay day."

TACK-TA-CAL MEDICINE

One time when I was very small, I was helping my mother decorate for my sister Hilda's birthday party. We were hanging crepe paper streamers. My Grandfather Crowe was a carpenter, and I had seen him put tacks in his mouth to hold while he used his hands to hold a nail and hammer. I decided this was a good idea, since I was having a hard time holding the paper and the "tack."

Well, as luck would have it, I swallowed the tack. My mother went berserk and, of course the first thing she did was call Dr. Landers at Smyrna Drug Store. Dr. Landers said that, since I wasn't choking to death, it would be better to leave the tack alone and let it pass. That is what was done except they didn't trust me to pass it alone. They decided to pour Milk of Magnesia down me.

I don't think I was ever in any danger of dying from that tack, but the Milk of Magnesia almost killed me. From that time on until he died, Dr. Landers forever after called me "Tack."

Dr. Herbert Fowler had a medical office in the rear portion of Smyrna Drug Store. Because he had a practice in Marietta, he opened the office in Smyrna only two to three days a week. Dr Fowler was the attending physician when I was born, November 29, 1933. My friend, Miller Davis who grew up on Church Street, told me that Dr. Fowler delivered him also. He was born December 5 1933, six days after my birth. We have wondered if Dr. Fowler delivered anyone else during the six days between our births. If any other Smyrna residents, were delivered by Dr. Fowler between these dates, I wish for them to let me know.

Miller and I grew up together, even attending school from first grade through high school and have lived on the same street, Havilon Way, since 1969, when Lillie and I moved here. We raised our families together, and we are still good friends.

ROGERS GROCERY STORE

Rogers Grocery Store was next door to Smyrna Drug Store. I worked for Rogers Store part time while I was still in high school. Henry Duncan was the manager, "Bill" Scoggins was the assistant manager, and Clarence Newton was the butcher when I started working there in 1949. Harry Lovingood succeeded Henry Duncan as manager shortly after I started working there. Some of the other people who worked at Rogers Store were Wendell Anderson and a Mr. Green, who was the produce manager.

THE DAY SMYRNA BURNED

As told by "Bill" Scoggins

"There was only one traffic light in Smyrna in 1945. It was at West Spring Street in front of Smyrna Drug Store and Rogers Grocery Store. In fact, it was the only traffic light between the Chattahoochee River and Marietta.

"It was Sunday afternoon about two o'clock. Most of the stores in Smyrna didn't open on Sunday, but Rogers opened at two o'clock p.m. A group of teenage boys was standing on the sidewalk, waiting for Rogers to open. The guys were Mac Camp, Charles Ray Eaton, Martin Cantrell, Martin Ruff, and I." (Charles Ray Eaton ran the soda fountain at Smyrna Drug Store, and I worked at Rogers Store.)

"Mrs. Ruby Carmichael was a widow, but we always just called her, 'Miss Ruby.' She and her daughter, Virginia, came across the railroad from their home on Spring Street on their way to First Methodist Church for a meeting. They spoke to us boys and kept walking.

"When they passed Rogers Store, 'Miss Ruby' stopped and called out, 'Scoggins, (that is what she called me) come here!' I walked over to where she was, and she asked, 'Is that store on fire?' I looked up and saw smoke just pouring out the rear of Rogers Store. I took off running to the Police Department, which was also the Jail and the City Hall.

"Chief Sexton was sitting in a chair, leaning up against the building, resting. I shook him real hard and said, 'Chief, Rogers Store is burning down, and I am afraid for Smyrna.'

"He asked, 'Boy, can you drive?'

"I said, 'Yes, sir, I sure can.'

"He hollered, 'Get that truck down to that store right now.'

"I did. When I got there, he had 'high tailed it' down the street and was giving orders. He told us boys standing around to get the hose off that truck and hook it up to the fire hydrant. We finally did.

"He said, 'Get that hose to that fire.' The trouble was we didn't know where in the store the fire was located.

"About that time Paul Clayton, a volunteer fireman, came up. He said, 'Boys, beat those front doors in.' We chopped them all to pieces.

"The Chief told Paul and me to take the hose through those doors and find the fire. When we got inside the building, the smoke was so thick we couldn't see anything. Paul said, 'Bill, get down on your belly and crawl.' I did. You could see all the way to the back of that store.

"Paul yelled, 'Bill!' shoot that water.' I did. All of a sudden, I could hear jars bursting, and I could smell mustard, catsup, pickles, and who knows what.

Rogers Store
Atlanta Street
Walker Akins, Far Left; **Lilla Akins**, Far Right
Circa 1940s
Courtesy of Cecile Akins Martin

Smyrna Fire Truck
Near Bank and Atlanta Streets
Circa early 1950s
Courtesy of Smyrna Museum

"All of a sudden Paul shouted, 'Let's get out of here!' We left the building and went around o the back.

"Somebody had said the fire was in the meat market. ("Rip" Matlock ran an independent neat market in Rogers Store.) We climbed on top of the building and started chopping through the oof. We chopped right through to the top of a freezer. It didn't budge. That freezer didn't even know e had an axe.

"About that time we heard a siren. Knowing that Smyrna didn't have a siren, we knew it had be the Marietta Fire Department. When he arrived, the Marietta Fire Chief assessed the situation.

"What had happened was a small motor to the meat case had overheated and was smoking. here wasn't any fire at all, but we tore up that store.

"By this time Henry Duncan, the store manager was there. He said, 'Bill, ya'll get to work. Ve gotta open this store tomorrow morning.'

"I looked around to see bags of grits, flour, corn meal, and other 'stuff' all over those floors. Vhat a mess!

"About that time Mr. W.W. Cary appeared at the door. He took one look inside that store and aid, 'We ain't going to open this store no more.' (All of a sudden I was out of a job.) Then he said to ne, 'Bill, you be here tomorrow morning. We are gonna salvage what we can from this store.'

"We saved everything we could. Employees from the warehouse picked that 'stuff' up and arried it away. We didn't know what they did with it.

"After we finished that job, the supervisor sent me to the Big Star Store on Forrest Avenue in tlanta. I rode the streetcar both ways to work. About two weeks after I started working there, they ent a shipment of 'stuff' for us to sell. It was the same merchandise that we had salvaged from the myrna Store. I couldn't believe I was handling that 'stuff' again!

"I learned that Miss Ruby and Virginia went on to First Methodist Church to their 'Tea arty' and had a nice afternoon."

NOTE: There were several different stores around Atlanta, Marietta, Smyrna, and other eighboring cities: Big Star, Little Star, Rogers, and Pender. They later consolidated and became olonial Stores, one of which was operated successfully in Smyrna for many years.

Colonial Store opened on Bank Street early in 1951, replacing Rogers Store on Atlanta Street, here I had been working before I graduated from high school. I transferred to Colonial Store, the first elf-service grocery store in Smyrna, and worked there most of the year after I graduated. Two long-me cashiers who started working at the new store on Bank Street were Louise Motter and Jennie hitener.

The next building housed **Johnson Shoe Shop**. This shop was owned and operated by ubert Johnson, who was married and had two daughters. The Johnson Family lived in Marietta. I member Mrs. Johnson as being an attractive woman I would see around town from time to time, e.g. G.B.'s Place or the drug store. Mr. Johnson was a nice person but a man of few words. Johnson hoe Shop was a unique place! The shoes were piled so high that a person had to go through the shop deways. Many people did their shoe shopping with Mr. Johnson, who had a wide variety of styles nd colors. One had to have plenty of time to look through the huge collection of unclaimed shoes he ad for sale.

JOHNSON SHOE SHOP

by: Johnny Fulton

NOTE: The following memory of Johnson Shoe Shop was written by Johnny Fulton, wh grew up on King Street. It is a good description of the place that I feel many people who grew up i Smyrna could have shared.

"Johnson Shoe Shop was a legend. The place was always filled with shoes that were either i need of repair or had been repaired. Each pair had a hand-written tag (attached to the shoelaces) wit the owner's name. There was a smell of fresh leather and shoe polish that made the confused look c the place acceptable. Mr. Johnson was always gluing a new sole on a shoe or cutting off excess leathe with a hand-cranked machine that followed the outline of the shoe and added a little 'knurlec finishing touch to the new sole. There was a large noisy sewing machine that added a 'ka-chunk, ka chunk' sound while stitching the sole to insure that it would stay in place. A nail machine clampe down on the shoe and popped down a brad that attached to the heel. The fancy metal taps were adde by hand. With a little sole black, some shoe polish, and the buffing by the different whirling pads on long spindle that looked like a lathe, the old worn-out shoes would become new before your eyes an ready to wear."

Hubert Johnson had an African-American man who worked for him. I think his name wa Lamar, but Hubert always referred to him as Lee-mar. Therefore, he became known by this name. Le mar, who worked there for many years, was synonymous with Johnson Shoe Shop. I do not believe was ever there without seeing him. I never knew anything about Lee-mar except that he worked Johnson Shoe Shop.

Roy Fowler's Beauty Shop stood to the south of Rogers Store. Roy was in business the for many years. I can still see in my mind's eye the sign on that shop, *ROY FOWLER'S BEAUTY AN BARBER SHOP*. His sister, **Leila**, a hairdresser, also worked in the shop.

Later, their nephew, **John Fowler**, bought a lot from my dad on Bank Street and built beauty shop. He owned the shop, and Leila Black operated it. That shop was built and opened after graduated from Smyrna High School in 1951. The sign on the shop read, LEILA'S BEAUTY SHO Roy and Leila had a brother named Lee, who, I seem to recall, was Leila's twin. Later on, Lei married Harry Black, who was one of the owners of Black and Webb Grocery Store. See *Leila Beauty Shop, north side of Bank Street.*

OLD SMYRNA CEMETERY

Next door to Fowler's was a vacant lot used for parking. This lot was adjacent to the **Ol Smyrna Cemetery**, known today as the **Smyrna Memorial Cemetery.**

SMYRNA PRESBYTERIAN CHURCH

Across the street from the south end of the Old Smyrna Cemetery was Smyrna Presbyteria Church. What I remember is that the street was short and unpaved, with the Old Smyrna Cemetery o the west side and C.T. Osborn's Garage and Smyrna Presbyterian Church on the east side. (Th Church at that time was a small wooden building painted brown.) The street is known today Memorial Place.

South on Atlanta Road past the business district was **D.C. Osborn's Service Station an Garage**, located in the triangle at Memorial Place and Atlanta Street.

Just beyond the garage was a florist and gift shop. According to long-time Smyrna residen this shop was owned and operated by **Elizabeth Davis Konigsmark**, a very talented and artist

D.C. Osborn at his Garage on Atlanta Street
Circa 1940's
Courtesy of Smyrna Museum
NOTE: Smyrna Hotel and First Methodist Church in the background

Downtown Smyrna
Circa 1950s
Courtesy of Alice Gibson Vaughn

person. After she closed her shop in Smyrna, Elizabeth worked for Owens Flower Shop on Atlant Road in Marietta, where she was noted for designing beautiful flower arrangements.

THE SMYRNA HOTEL

Next door to the garage was The Smyrna Hotel, a wooden structure which, I seem t remember, was painted green. The hotel was a two-story box-type building. I think it may have been boarding house during my childhood. People used to say that workmen from the railroad and othe transient workers would stay there. This building was about where the north parking lot of Wachovi Bank is currently located.

The hotel was not on one of my regular footpaths. As a kid walking, I had no reason to g that far down Atlanta Street. When I went to church or school, I walked King Street; I also walke King Street to Brinkley Park. I would go Spring Street and across the railroad to run my paper route and my egg customers were on Bank Street,and across the railroad. The only time I would see Th Smyrna Hotel was from the streetcar going to or from Atlanta, and that was not very frequent.

NOTE: According to page 81 of *But Thou Art Rich*, A History of Smyrna First Unite Methodist Church, this hotel building was originally First Methodist Church.

I recall several houses, maybe three, between the Smyrna Hotel and First Methodist Church one of them being the parsonage of First Methodist Church.

FIRST METHODIST CHURCH PARSONAGE

The house just north of First Methodist Church was the parsonage before the Church bough other property and built a new one on Dunn Street, probably in the 1950s. First Methodist Church ha three pastors during the years I was growing up: Rev. James W. Stephens, 1937-1944; Rev. Roy C Owens, 1945-1948; and Rev. Lewis F. Van Landingham, 1948-1952.

FIRST METHODIST CHURCH

First Methodist Church stood on the northwest corner of Atlanta and Church streets. It wa a red brick building with beautiful stained glass windows. A bell hung inside the steeple and was run on Sunday mornings. I used to go there for special occasions, e.g. Boy Scout meetings and othe community-related events. The atmosphere was very serene and worshipful.

Miller Davis is a lifelong member of First Methodist Church. He shared with me: "The da World War II was over, in 1945, a group of us boys got together and rang the First Methodist Churc bell. Those in the group were Sammy Mitchell, Parker Lowry, Clark Davis, and I. We were so prou the War was over."

I thought the church building on Atlanta Street was so pretty. I remember riding home fro Atlanta on the streetcar when I was a little boy. I would look for the church, and then I would know w were almost home. I recall being sad when the decision was made to raze the First Methodist Churc building. But the church members did Smyrna proud with the building of their stately sanctuary o Concord Road. They preserved the beautiful stained glass windows and displayed them for all to enjo in the new structure.

<u>First House</u>

Mr. and **Mrs. D.J. Ray** lived on the southwest corner of Church and Atlanta streets, whe Ken's Corner Grill is currently located. Mrs. Coral Ray and Mrs. Alma Konigsmark, both Reeds, we sisters. .

First Methodist Church

CORNER S. ATLANTA AND CHURCH STREETS

SMYRNA, GEORGIA

Picture printed from order of Sunday service bulletin of First Methodist Church
Courtesy of Nancy Pearson Black

REGISTER OF ATTENDANCE & OFFERING
ATTENDANCE TODAY 117
ATTENDANCE LAST SUNDAY 143
OFFERING TODAY 932
OFFERING LAST SUNDAY 1050
ATTENDANCE A YEAR AGO TODAY 114

TOM THUMB WEDDING
SMYRNA METHODIST CHURCH June 13, 1940

TOM THUMB WEDDING-First Row (L-R): Betty Gibbs, Quinton Hamby, Lois Hiate, Dianne Candler, Laura Helen Jones, and Gail Hiate. Second Row (L-R): Bobby Gibbs, Jeanette Hanson, Charlotte Theodocian, Pat Edwards, Jane Copeland (bride), Don Woodliff (groom), Joanne McBrayer, Bobby Latta, Bud Theodocian, Sonny Hamby (preacher). Third Row L-R: Gabriel Ray, Ella Ray Griggers, James Woodliff, Dan Theodocian, Sam Hensley, Rebekah Austin, Leonard Gibbs, Margaret Mann, Joy Hamby, Bobby Fowler, and Joyce Hamby.

Program

Fifth Nocturne——————Eloise Williams
Wedding of Jack and Jill—Ellan Ray Griggers
Wedding of the painted Doll—Jeanette Hanson
At Dawning
I love you Truly——Charlotte Theodocian

CAST

Preacher——————Sonny Hamby
Bride——————Jane Copeland
Groom——————Don Woodliff
Maid of Honor——————Nancy Candler
Best Man——————Dicky Latta

Brides Maids-Groomsmen

Ruth Marlow——————James (Bud)Theodocian
Betty Davis——————Bobby Gibbs
Beverly Ann Anderson——————Quentin Hamby
Lois Hiate——————Joe Davis

Flower Girls

Laura Helen Jones——————Gail Hiate

Ring Bearer

Robert Bowman

Ushers

Bobby Fowler, Danny Theodocian, Gable Ray, James Woodliff

Mothers

Joann McBrayer——————Margaret Mann

Fathers

Leonard Gibbs——————Danny Theodocian

Grandmothers

Rebekah Austin——————Sue Davis

Grandfathers

Bobby Latta——————Pat Edwards

Old Maid Twin Aunts

Joy Hamby——————Joyce Hamby

First Methodist Bible School, June 19, 1947 Made by Fisco Studio, Rt.1, Smyrna Ga. Phone# 325

Note: Original belonged to Jeanette Hanson Taylor

Standing: (1) Bud Theodocian, (2) Hal Shields, (3) Frank Stewart, (4) ___ Mitchell, (5) Presbyteria Minister, (6) Bill Pavalosky (7) Mrs. Blair, (8) ___ Chastain, (9) Jeanette Hanson, (10) ___.
Seated: (1) ____ (2) ____ (3) Jean Pierce, (4) June Gravely.

Pearce Matthews Sunday School Class, Smyrna First United Methodist Church
Circa 1974
Courtesy of Lois Matthews

Front Row (L-R): J.P Crenshaw, James Pressley, Reverend Larry Caywood, Gill Hand, James Hale, H.H. Cumbee, John Matthews, Howard Hames, and Early Cobb. **Second Row (L-R)**: Hen Koningsmark, Sr., James Spradley, Eanest Vick, Bo Vaughan, Robert Johnson, Jim Lovern, J Gabriel, Lewis Anderson, and Jack Brooks. **Third Row (L-R)**: Bill Lovejoy, J.W. Pittman, Char Oakley, L.P. Reynolds, Leland Williams, John Simms, Al Barrett, Luther Williams, Don Suessmi Hansel Parks, James Gaston, and Joe Latanzi.

I seem to remember that **Miss Eunice Padgett** and her dad rented an apartment in Mrs. ay's house where she lived for a long time. Miss Padgett taught at Smyrna High School and later at ampbell High School. She was a lovely lady and a devoted member of First Baptist Church.

Second House

This house was a two-story framed one, owned by Mrs. D.J Ray. She rented it to her nephew, **eed Konigsmark**, and his family.

Third House

A rental house was located here. Through the years many families lived in it.

Fourth House

Mr. and **Mrs. Jake Nash** lived here. They had a daughter, **Becky**, and two sons, **Jim** and **hn**. This house stood where Cochran, Camp and Snipes Law Firm stands today. Their daughter, cky Paden, is a member of the Smyrna Social Club and the Smyrna Historical and Genealogical ciety. She is also a member of the Cobb County Historic Preservation Commission. Mr. Nash vned and operated a wholesale produce business at the Farmer's Market on Murphy Avenue in lanta. See *Atlanta Terrace, from Mrs. Mazie's to Creatwood.*

NOTE: Rebecca Nash, a graduate of Campbell High school, is a writer. At one time she was the staff of the *Marietta Daily Journal.* She, along with Joe McTyre has written two books, the est one, *Images of America, Cobb County*, was published in 2005.

Fifth House

Mr. and **Mrs. David Cano** were residents here. They had two children: **Al** and **Dora Lee.** rs. Cano, known as Eva, was a hairdresser. She styled hair for many of the ladies in Smyrna, one of m being my mother, until she closed her shop. My sister, Hilda Wood Chaffin, also remembers tting her hair styled by Mrs. Cano. The Cano House, a unique, two-story, masonry block structure, s known as the Gautchey House.

Mr. Cano was also a hair stylist. He worked in the salon at Rich's Department Store located Broad, Forsyth, and Alabama streets in Atlanta. He worked at one time in a shop in the Henry Grady tel at Cain and Peachtree streets, also in Atlanta.

Mr. and Mrs. Cano kept a nice yard. In the spring and summer they had a variety of pretty wers blooming, and the grass was always cut. Their house, a very attractive one, was located in the art of Smyrna.

THE "GAUTCHEY HOUSE"
A Brief History
by Mike Terry

"Known locally as the 'Gautchey House' (pronounced 'Gow-chee'), this all-concrete house located on Atlanta Road across from Jonquil Plaza Shopping Center. It was built between 1895 and 00 by the Gautchey Family, who immigrated to America from Germany in the mid-to-late neteenth Century. When the Gautchey Family first came to Smyrna, they took up residence in a use that was located on the corner of Concord and King Springs roads; it was on this site that Mr. utchey operated a legal liquor distillery. Because business was good, he eventually decided to build family a more elaborate home on Atlanta Street. He sold his home on Concord Road to the John ldwin Family, who farmed the surrounding land the next fifty years. (This farm was closer to the ner of Concord Road and what was then known as Cooper Lake Road, changed in the late 1930s to ng Springs Road.)

The Gautchey House
Known in the 1940s as The Cano House: children unknown
Circa 1940s
Courtesy of Smyrna Museum

Young Matron's "Pajama Girls"
Circa early 1930s
Courtesy of Evelyn Edwards Pressley
L-R: Ada McCreary, Pauline Dunn, Mrs. Holcomb, Margie Manning, Alta Ray, Eva Edwards, Ann Lou Fowler, Mary Willis Morris, Nina BeShears, Nancy Lee Pollock, Irma Gresham, Maggie Edwards, J. Gid Morris, Blanche Brawner, Emmy Dunn, and Mary Sue Pollock.

Picture was made at the home of Mary Willis and J. Gid Morris on Cherokee Road, now Windy Hi Road, between Atlanta Road and South Cobb Drive.

"Mr. Gautschy built his new Atlanta Street home by using concrete molds purchased from Sears, Roebuck and Company; his workers mixed the concrete right on the job site. The blocks he produced were made to resemble cut stone, and there was little doubt that the German background of his family was an influence on their choice of a home design. They also wired for electricity, something not found in many Smyrna homes.

"The Gautchey Family and their distillery business eventually was moved to Atlanta, for in 1920 federal prohibition laws forced them to close the family liquor business here.

"The all-concrete Gautchey House has had numerous owners. It was sold sometime prior to 1916 to Mr. Frank Rawls, a bachelor, who lived in the house until 1923, when he sold it to his sister. I believe his sister was Leila Harrison, who sold the house in 1929 to the Cano Family. Mrs. Eva Cano operated a beauty parlor in the home, where many local ladies had their hair styled. The Canos sold the house in 1966 or 1967 to Judson Strickland, who operated an upscale antique shop. The Gautchey House was sold once again in the early 1970s to Bob and Mary Kilpatrick and then again in 1983 to Milton and Janice Hill. The Hills did a great deal of restoration of and renovation to the house before operating their business ('Automobilia') here for several years.

"In more recent years, the house has been a business office and an antique shop. Currently it is the home of **Ruby Jeans**, a clothing store. Pete Wood tells me that of all the people that have owned this unusual property, the Cano Family is the one that he remembers best." See *John Baldwin, east side of Concord Road.*

Sixth House

Mr. and **Mrs. Roy Manning** lived in this house, where their daughter, Marie, grew up. As a plumber, Mr. Manning, on the back of his property, had a large metal building he used to store his plumbing supplies. Marie, who graduated from Campbell High School in the mid 1950s, is currently living in the western part of the United States.

Seventh House

Mrs. Callie Jay resided here. She was the mother of Mrs. Roy Manning, who lived next door. They were both widows for a long time. Mrs. Jay at one time was the librarian at the Smyrna Public Library: she also taught at Campbell High School. Her picture, along with all the previous librarians' pictures, is hanging in the Smyrna Public Library, on the Village Green. The Mannings and Jays were active members of First Methodist Church.

Eighth House

Grayson and **Maude Brown**, along with their only child, **Ferd Brown**, his wife, the former **Mary Ruth Sorrells**, and their sons, **Ronnie** and **Jerry**, lived in this house on the northwest corner of Atlanta and Love streets (current location of CVS Pharmacy). According to family information Grayson and Maude owned land on the opposite side of Atlanta Street. See *Sorrells, Atlanta Street, from Marlowe's to Creatwood* and *Brown, east side of Dunn Street.*

Ninth House

Mrs. Marion Coppenger's home stood on the southwest corner of Atlanta and Love streets, back off the road and facing Atlanta Street. An active member of First Baptist Church, Mrs. Coppenger was involved in Sunday School and the Women's Missionary Union. Mrs. Coppenger worked, but I never knew where.

I remember Mrs. Coppenger would bake cakes, which people of the community would buy from her. Mother bought cakes from her for special occasions, and I remember going to her house to get them. Her home was furnished with very old, nice furniture made of dark wood. I always believed she inherited it.

According to family members connected to the Pollock Family, Mr. Pollock, earlier in the Twentieth Century, owned the property where Mrs. Coppenger lived and all the tract of land to Lee Street. His wife was a sister of Mrs. Quarles, who lived two doors south of Mrs. Coppenger. The Pollocks also owned a coal yard by the railroad, across from Atlanta Street. See *King Street.*

Tenth House

Mr. and **Mrs. Beal** at one time resided in the house located between the Coppenger and Quarles houses.

Eleventh House

W. A. Quarles
Smyrna City Councilman
1944-1947

Mr. and **Mrs. W.A. Quarles** and their daughter, **Martha**, lived in this house. Their son, Jimmy Quarles, also grew up in this house. Martha Quarles taught at W.F. Slaton Elementary School in southeast Atlanta, along with Colene Reed Guthrie and Judith Rice Lowry, in the years when Miss Ira Jarrell was principal. After Judith Lowry became the principal of Bolton Elementary School in Atlanta, Martha Quarles and Colene Guthrie transferred to Bolton Elementary School, from which they all retired. The Quarles Family were faithful members of First Baptist Church, where Martha and her mother were active in Sunday School and the Women's Missionary Union. Mr. W.A. Quarles served on the Smyrna City Council, 1944-1947.

NOTE: Later on, Miss Ira Jarrell became Dr. Jarrell and Superintendent of Atlanta Public Schools, 1944-1960. She was holding this position when the editor of this book, Joyce Abbey Reagin, was a student at Hoke Smith High School in Atlanta and a teacher at Fulton High School in Atlanta.

"Jimmy" Quarles
Mayor of Smyrna
1955-1957

James E. Quarles, known as "Jimmy," married Doris Arrington; they had one son, Harry. Doris, the daughter of Mr. and Mrs. Harry Arrington, grew up on Sunset Avenue. She was my fourth grade teacher. After Dunn and Lee streets were extended in the 1950s, Doris and Harry built a new home on Lee Street, where they lived the rest of their lives. Jimmy Quarles served as Mayor of Smyrna, 1955-1957. He and my dad were friends

The James E. Quarles
Water Treatment Plant
4402 Lower Roswell Road
Marietta, Georgia 30068
770-971-1911.

For many years, "Jimmy" Quarles was a member and Vice-Chairman of the Cobb Marietta Water Authority. In fact, James E. Quarles Water Treatment Plant was named in honor of him in recognition of his service to the Authority and Cobb County. See *Sunset Avenue.*

QUARLES AVENUE and **WILLS STREET**

Quarles Avenue was the street cut from Atlanta Road to Lee Street when the growth started in the late 1940s. Wills Street was also cut about the same time; it was a north/south dead-end street off Quarles Avenue. I knew some people who lived there, two of whom were Charles and Patsy Cook; they had four sons: Andy, Chip, Lee, and Doug, all of whom are in my children's generation. Charles was one of the sons of Jesse and Ruby Cook, who lived on King Street and later, Lee Street. Charles was very instrumental in the growth and upkeep of Brinkley Field during the years my children were growing up. Cook Field at Brinkley Park is named for him.

Twelfth House

Mr. and **Mrs. D. C. Osborn** lived in a brick house next door to the Quarles Family. They had three daughters: **Louise**, known as "Bill," **Sara**, and **Mardelle**. Mr. Osborn owned and operated D.C. Osborn Garage on Atlanta Street.

Louise Osborn, known as "Bill," married Reed Konigsmark. They had two daughters: Ann and Nancy.

Later "Bill" Osborn Konigsmark married Alan B. Morton. The Mortons built a house on Atlanta Terrace, across the street from Mr. and Mrs. Osborn, on part of the large parcel of land that was owned by Emory Chastain.

Ann Konigsmark married Dr. James Johnson, a veterinarian in Vinings. They had two children: Jim and Beth. James and Ann Johnson are members of First Methodist Church. Ann is a member of the Smyrna Social Club, founded in 1908.

Nancy Reed Konigsmark was active in the 1976 campaign to elect Jimmy Carter as United States President. She has been on the staff at the Carter Center for many years, working closely with President and Mrs. Jimmy Carter. Nancy is a member of First Methodist Church and the Smyrna Social Club, founded in 1908.

Sara Osborn married Dr. Albert Brawner

Mardelle Osborn, a school teacher, married and moved to Cartersville.

Thirteenth House

Dr. and **Mrs. W. C. Mitchell** lived in the second brick house on the west side of South Atlanta Street. She was the former Louise Jones. They had two children: Lucy and Bill.

Lucy Mitchell and Harry Evans married in 1949. Harry, who grew up on Fleming Street and Highland Avenue, graduated from Smyrna High School. Lucy, who graduated from Marietta High School, worked in Dr. Mitchell's office for seventeen years. See *Evans, Fleming* and *Bank streets.*

Bill Mitchell currently lives in this house on Atlanta Street.

Dr. and Mrs. Mitchell and their family were members of First Baptist Church. Mrs. Mitchell was active in the Alathean Sunday School Class, which was chartered in 1933 and in which she served as president in 1935. According to information received from the King Davis Family, Mrs. Mitchell gave a baby shower for Nell Davis when she was pregnant with Miller Davis in 1933. Louise Jones Mitchell died in 1948.

From my very earliest memories, Dr. W.C. Mitchell maintained a medical practice in downtown Smyrna. For a long number of those years, his office was on Atlanta Street, on the second floor of a building located between Walker Akins Grocery Store and Dr. M.L. Collins' Drug Store.

Dr. Mitchell was a leader of the Smyrna Men's Club, which included most of the business men in the community. The Men's Club sponsored community events and activities; in many ways it was like a forerunner of civic clubs that came later, such as Lions, Rotary, Civitan, and Kiwanis clubs.

Later, in the mid 1940s, Dr. Mitchell was one of the founders of the Bank of Smyrna, where he served on the Board of Directors; he also served as a Director of the Cobb Exchange Bank in Marietta.

It seems that Dr. Mitchell was always in the forefront of community activities. He was appointed to the Cobb County Board of Education by the Cobb County Grand Jury. (This was the system in the middle of the Twentieth Century.) According to *The People of Smyrna*, written by Bill Miles, Editor of *The Smyrna Herald*, 1952-1961, "Dr. Mitchell served on the Cobb County School Board for eleven years (1954-1965), during the crucial years of school integration with great success and diplomacy. Smyrna was one of the few systems never taken to court and with never a serious racial incident." See copies of *The People of Smyrna* in The Smyrna Public Library and The Smyrna Museum.

NOTE: The following information regarding Dr. Mitchell's career was furnished by Dr. Mitchell's daughter, Lucy Mitchell Evans, and the Smyrna Museum.

"Having earned his medical degree form Emory University School of Medicine in 1931 and completing his internship at Grady Memorial Hospital in Atlanta from 1931-1933, at the age of twenty-six, Dr. Mitchell practiced medicine on Atlanta Street in Smyrna from 1933 until 1980. He was a member of the Cobb County Medical Society and the Smyrna Men's Club. Dr. Mitchell was a charter member of the Smyrna Lions Club, chartered in 1946. He was also a participant in many civic projects through the years.

"During the 1930s and 1940s, Dr. Mitchell treated diseases that today are almost history–typhoid, smallpox, polio, and tuberculosis; pneumonia, associated with colds and flu, was often fatal in the 1930s. He saw the advent of sulfa drugs and then penicillin. During World War II, Dr. Mitchell became all too familiar with the dirt roads in the Smyrna area. The only doctor between Marietta and the Chattahoochee River for a two-year period, he was 'on call' seven days a week, 24 hours a day, with no one to relieve him. 'I made mostly house calls at the time,' said Dr. Mitchell. 'Most people had trouble getting enough gas for their cars because of rationing during the War. As a doctor, I could get what I needed.' He explained that, in the early days of his career, many of the house calls were for newborn deliveries. When Dr. Mitchell came to Smyrna, there were only thirteen doctors in Cobb County." See *Lions Club, Sunset Avenue.*

Dr. Mitchell married **Millie Valentine Brinkley** in 1950. She had two children: **Patricia,** known as "Patsy," and **Milton Scott Brinkley**, known as "Mickey," from a previous marriage. See *Brinkley, north side of Love Street.*

Dr. Mitchell and Millie Valentine Brinkley had two children: **Claudia** and "**Skipper**," who grew up in this house on Atlanta Street.

Millie Valentine Brinkley Mitchell, raised in the Log Cabin community, south of Smyrna, was a graduate of Marietta High School. She was a lifelong member of First Methodist Church and a member of the Susannah Wesley Sunday School Class. Millie was also a member of the Smyrna Social Club. While serving as President of the Cobb County Medical Society Auxiliary, she was one of the organizers of the Kennestone Gift Shop, in Kennestone Hospital in Marietta

Claudia Mitchell married and had three sons: Thomas Matthew Owens, known as "Matt," Samuel Gentry Owens, known as "Sam," and William Mark Owens, known as Mark.

Claudia married Bill Harper of Marietta in 2002. Claudia is a member of the Smyrna Social Club. She and Bill live in Marietta. Claudia shared that her dad built this house on Atlanta Street in 1939 for $5,000.00

Benjamin White Mitchell, known as "Skipper," was the youngest child of Dr. W.C. Mitchell and "Millie" Valentine. A graduate of Campbell High School, "Skipper" married Pam Bryan of Thomaston. They had two children: a son, B.J., and a daughter, Maggie. "Skipper" and Pam live in Douglasville.

"Skipper" owned and operated an insurance business for twenty years. Having been accepted at Candler School of Theology at Emory University, he is serving as a part-time minister in Waco.

NOTE: Janet Brown noted that "Skipper" looked like a young Dr. Mitchell when she saw him at his mother's funeral.

Fourteenth House

John D. Corn
Mayor of Smyrna
1938-1940

The next dwelling I remember was that of **Mr.** and **Mrs. John D. Corn, Sr.**, They had one son, John D. Corn, Jr., who played football for Georgia Institute of Technology in the 1950s and lived in this house with his mother until her death. Mr. John Corn, Sr., served as Mayor of Smyrna, 1938-1940.

Fifteenth House

NOTE: According to information from Mr. Raymond Reed, this house was built by his father, Mr. B.F. Reed, Sr., and Mr. B.L. Walker in 1910. **Mr.** and **Mrs. B.F. Reed, Sr.**, lived here in those early years with their young family. They later moved to the east side of Atlanta Street. See *Reed, Atlanta Street, from Mrs. Mazies to Pearce Matthews.*

J. Gid Morris
Mayor of Smyrna
1925-1926

Mr. and **Mrs. J. Gid Morris** lived in this house sometime in the first half of the Twentieth Century. He served as Mayor of Smyrna, 1925-1926, and was a railroad man. Long-time Smyrna residents remember Mr. Morris wearing "blue serge suits." Younger residents remember Mr. Morris living on Cherokee Street, where he owned farm land. According to information from long-time Smyrna residents, Mr. Morris was a close relative of the Dabney Family who lived in Smyrna; Mr. Frank Dabney, a builder, constructed many homes in Smyrna in the middle of the Twentieth Century.

The Sorrells Family

The Sorrells Family resided in this house in the 1940s while I was growing up. The Sorrells' daughter, Mary Ruth, married Ferd Brown. See *Ferd Brown, Atlanta Street, from Marlowe's to Creatwood* and *east side of Dunn Street.*

Dallis and **Colene Reed Guthrie**

Mr. and **Mrs. Dallis Guthrie** bought and renovated this house in the 1950s. They had two children: **Rufus** and **Palma Ann**, known as "Pam." Mrs. Guthrie was the former Colene Reed, a member of the B.F. Reed, Sr., Family. Dallis was in the real estate business, and Colene taught at W.F. Slaton Elementary School in Atlanta when Miss Ira Jarrell was the principal. When Julia Rice Lowry transferred to Bolton Elementary School to be the principal, Colene transferred there also. According to family information, she retired from that school, which was also in the Atlanta School System. See *B.F. Reed, Sr., Atlanta Road, from Mrs. Mazie's to Pearce Matthews* and *Quarles, eleventh house.*

Rufus Guthrie married Sandra Brown; they had three children: Denise, Benjamin Reed, and Robert Dallis. Rufus, a graduate of Baylor Prep School in Chattanooga, Tennessee, was an All-American football player at Georgia Institute of Technology in the early 1960s. Rufus and Sandra are both deceased. See *Guthrie, south side of Powder Springs Street; Howard, west side of Lee Street; Reeds, east side of Atlanta Street.*

Denise Guthrie married Tim Sperier. They had two sons: Parker and Peyton.

Benjamin Reed Guthrie married Allison Payne. They had two children: Reagan and Benjamin Reed III.

Robert Dallis Guthrie married Lori Chalebois. They have no children at this time.

Palma Ann Guthrie, known as "Pam," married John David Tempel from Decatur. They had three children, Steve, Kelly, and Scott, and six grandchildren. Pam and David both sell real estate in Florida.

Steve Tempel and his wife, Sheree, and their children, David and Ashley, live in Athens.

Kelly Temple married James D. Killingsworth, Jr., known as "Jamey." Kelly and James Killingsworth, Jr., are the owners of Moe's Southwest Grill in the Market Village in Smyrna. They live in Marietta.

Scott Tempel lives in Alabama with his wife, Nancy, and two children, Dallis and Madelyn.

The Guthries moved from this house in the mid 1960s to a community which was being developed off Cobb Parkway in the Vinings area.

From the middle of the Twentieth Century and until the present time, the above house has been known as the Guthrie/Reed House.

The Raymond Reed Family

Mr. and **Mrs. Raymond Reed, Sr.**, in 1964 moved to this house with their three children: **Patricia Marie**, known as "Tricia," **Deborah Joan**, known as "Debbie," and **Raymond Morgan Reed, Jr.**, Mrs. Reed was the former Mary Frances Taylor, who grew up on Atlanta Street. Raymond Reed, Sr., an attorney in Marietta, was the son of Mr. and Mrs. B.F. Reed, Sr. Raymond grew up on Atlanta Street. See *Reeds* and *Taylors, Atlanta Street, from Mrs. Mazie's to Creatwood.*

Patricia Marie married Benjamin Munnerlyn Carter, an attorney in Atlanta. "Ben," as he is known, was one of the developers of the Mall of Georgia. Patricia Marie and "Ben" live in Atlanta.

Deborah Joan married Paul Hudson. They live in Atlanta.

Raymond Morgan, Reed, Jr., married Antonia Bonnie Kirkland. They live near Cornelia.

Mary Frances Taylor Reed was killed in a car accident in 1971.

Raymond Reed later married Mary Love. They reside in this house on Atlanta Road. Mary Love Reed was an administrator at The Walker School in Marietta for many years. See *Reed, Atlanta Street, from Mrs. Mazie's to Creatwood.*

Sixteenth House

Appreciation is extended to Margaret Londeau Woods for sharing the following information about her grandparents, Mr. and Mrs. Frank M. Collier, Sr.

Mr. and **Mrs. Frank M. Collier, Sr.**, lived in this large white clapboard house, located on he northwest corner of Atlanta Street and Collier Drive. Mrs. Collier was the former Coopie 'homason from Atlanta. They had three children: **Frank M. Collier, Jr.**, **Margaret**, and **Alice**. Their laughter, Margaret, was born in this house in 1911. She and her family lived here with Mr. and Mrs. Collier until their deaths. Margaret Collier Londeau continued to live here until she was 92 years old. After her death, her daughter, also named Margaret sold the property, and Collier Place community vas developed there in the late1990s.

<u>Frank M. Collier, Jr.,</u> married and moved to Columbus.

<u>Margaret Collier</u> married Steve Londeau. They had one daughter, also named Margaret, who s a graduate of The Westminister Schools in Atlanta. Margaret Londeau Woods lives in Roswell.

<u>Alice Collier</u> married Howard Marler. They had two sons: Charles and Frank. Alice Collier Marler lives in Cartersville, Georgia.

According to family information, Mr. Frank M. Collier, Sr., came to Smyrna from the Buckhead community in Atlanta. Collier Road in Atlanta bears his name because, at one time, he owned much acreage in that area.

Mr. Frank M. Collier moved to Smyrna by wagon, pulled by a white horse named "Jim." According to family records, "His dog, named 'Trail,' walked every step of the way from Atlanta to Smyrna behind the wagon."

In 1911 Frank Collier. purchased 126 acres of land about a half mile south of Smyrna. The and was on the west side of Atlanta Street, just north of Brawner Sanitarium, built in 1910. (The Collier house stood where Collier Place subdivision is currently located.) Mr. Collier's farm encompassed the land extending from Atlanta Street and covered most of what is known today as the Collier Heights and Forest Hills communities; it extended westward toward the property on Cooper Lake Road, now King Springs Road, which was later purchased by P.F. Daniell and Mr. Quinton Petty. See *Petty* and *Daniell, east side of King Springs Road.*

From the beginning, the Collier Farm was a working farm. It contained tenant houses, barns, and smokehouses. Mr. and Mrs. Collier, both excellent gardeners were known for their zinnias and dahlias. On many weekends Mr. Collier would gather bouquets of flowers and take them up the street for the Baptist, Methodist and Presbyterian churches to use in their sanctuaries for the Sunday services. Though Mr. and Mrs. Collier died many years ago, some of the older people in Smyrna still remember their beautiful flowers and delicious vegetables.

Mrs. Collier was a good, close friend of Mrs. Lena Mae Green, who lived on Love Street. According to family information, the two of them together merged their thinking and supported an effort to create a library in the Smyrna Woman's Club Building on Atlanta Street in the mid 1930s. Mrs. F. M. Collier, Sr., also sang in the choir of First Methodist Church.

<u>Seventeenth House</u>

Mr. and **Mrs. Ollie Francis Fuller** lived on the southwest corner of Atlanta Road and Collier Drive. They had one daughter, **Carol Francine**. Mrs. Fuller was formerly Nellie Leona Daniell, daughter of Mr. and Mrs. George Newton Daniell, who owned property at one time in the valley of Spring Road, where the Highlands subdivision is currently located. Ollie Francis was the son of Jones Walker Fuller and his wife, the former Ollie Morris, who also had three other sons. See *Fuller, Atlanta Street, from Mapps to R & M Café.*

Nellie, who worked for an insurance company, rode the streetcar to work until Carol Francine was born in 1941. Carol married and had two children: Lisa and Shawn; she also had one granddaughter, Erika.

Carol remembers that "Sunday dinner was a chicken that I had chased down. My mother would put it on a chopping block to cut its head, pluck the feathers, then clean and cut it up for frying." In addition to chickens, the Fullers also had rabbits, a cow, and hunting dogs.

According to family information, Ollie Francis was a locomotive engineer for Seaboard Coastline Railroad—and its subsequent name changes. Garry Daniell, a first cousin of Carol Fuller, remembers riding with Ollie on his last trip before the steam engines were retired. During the Depression, Ollie Francis also worked at the ice plant.

According to information from the Fuller Family, a cousin of Ollie's, Captain William A. Fuller, was the conductor of one of the famous engines in the Civil War, "The General" in the Great Locomotive Chase. See *Kennesaw History* and page 545 of *The First Hundred Years,* a short history of Cobb County.

Eighteenth House

Miss Nettie Fuller resided in this house, located between Nettie's great nephew, Ollie Fuller, and Brawner Sanitarium. A very large house, with a wrap-a-round porch and numerous antiques, it burned early in 1956. Nettie, who never married, was a sister of Jones A. Fuller, who was a soldier in the Confederate Army.

According to information from the family, Nettie was active in some organization(s) pertaining to the Confederacy, which met in the Kennesaw House in Marietta. She was also a member of the Smyrna Social Club, and a long-time greatly committed member of First Methodist Church.

In 1962 the Fuller Family sold the home sites and property of Mr. and Mrs. Ollie Fuller and Miss Nettie Fuller to Smyrna Presbyterian Church. In the mid 1960s, the Church constructed a new building on this property and sold their property on Memorial Place to the Smyrna Assembly of God. Smyrna Presbyterian Church today is a vibrant congregation, also operating on their Atlanta Road campus the Covenant Christian School, a popular private school that offers a broad curriculum and enjoys a reputation of respect.

BRAWNER SANITARIUM

Dr. James Brawner, Sr established Brawner Sanitarium in 1908 to treat people of all ages for drug, alcohol, and psychological problems. Built in 1910, this large hospital building with Greek Revival architecture, including massive columns, is located on part of the 85-acre farm purchased in 1909 from Mr. and Mrs. S.A. Taylor, who, in 1908, moved to Spokane, Washington.

Dr. Brawner modeled his facility after the European hospitals where he had studied psychiatry. Two of Dr. Brawner's brothers, Dr. Albert Brawner and Dr. Charles Brawner, both of whom were psychiatrists, practiced here. His son, Dr. James Brawner, Jr, joined the staff at Brawner in 1940. He was a graduate of Johns Hopkins University School of Medicine, where he was chief resident in gynecology. Prior to coming to Brawner, Dr. James Brawner, Jr. had returned to Atlanta in 1935 to teach at Emory University School of Medicine and to establish a private practice. Later on, his son, Dr. James Brawner III, a medical doctor, practiced medicine in Atlanta.

NOTE: At one time, Dr. Charles Brawner lived in the small white house just south of the hospital.

Over the years portions of the Brawner property were sold, and the hospital was not under the control of the Brawner Family. The last member of the Brawner Family to work here was Dave

Miller, the son of Nell Brawner Miller and a grandson of the founder; Dave lived in Buckhead. Patients were still treated at Brawner Hospital until the mid 1990s.

NOTE: In 2001 the City of Smyrna purchased the remaining 11 acres and all the buildings, including the hospital building and Taylor-Brawner House. Plans are under way to restore the hospital building and develop the acreage into a park.

HOSPITAL ADMISSION

The Atlanta Constitution Circulation Department would send us paper boys four extra papers every Sunday. After servicing my regular paper route customers across the railroad, I would take any extras down to Brawner Sanitarium. The staff there would pay me for the papers and, in turn, sell them to the patients. The cost of the Sunday papers was 15 cents each, thus giving me a little extra cash. This sales trip was the only one I would make to Brawner because it was not on my regular route.

Mr. Lawrence Butler, a huge man who worked at Brawner Sanitarium, lived with his family in one of the houses furnished by the hospital. He was the father of Mary Butler, who graduated with me in the Smyrna High School Class of 1951.

One Sunday after I had finished my regular paper route, I was dropping off my extra papers at Brawner when someone brought a man to the Brawner Sanitarium for treatment. As the man walked into the reception room, it became obvious that he had been imbibing something very potent. About the time he reached the reception desk, he pulled two bottles of liquor from under his coat, plopped them down on the desk really hard, and said in a loud tone: "Hold this 'expletive' liquor for me till I get out of this 'expletive' place."

About the time he pulled that whiskey out from under his clothing, Mr. Lawrence Butler, with two other men, appeared on the scene. They really took charge of that man. He was gone before I hardly knew they were there. I never knew what happened to him. Those that seem to know said, "The staff strapped him down until he sobered up." What did I know? I was just the paper boy!

Nineteenth House

THE TAYLOR-BRAWNER HOUSE

Mr. and **Mrs. S.A. Taylor** built this house in 1883 as a summer residence. The historical significance of the Taylor-Brawner House is twofold: firstly, it is one of the oldest houses in Smyrna; secondly, it was at this house where the first jonquil bulbs in Smyrna were planted. The Taylors' son sent a burlap bag of jonquils by train from Spokane, Washington. Year after year, Mr. and Mrs. Taylor shared bulbs with their neighbors; eventually the town was covered with yellow blossoms every spring. This led to Smyrna's being named the "Jonquil City."

After receiving permission from the Smyrna Mayor and Council to preserve and restore this house, a group of local citizens formed The Taylor-Brawner House Foundation, Inc. Plans are for the house to be available as a meeting place for civic and community groups, as well as a facility for small weddings and other activities. The house will remain a part of the park area being developed by the City of Smyrna.

NOTE: The historical facts concerning the Taylor-Brawner House were obtained from the Smyrna Museum, and members of the Brawner Family.

Taylor-Brawner House
Picture taken in 1926
Courtesy of Smyrna Museum
Via Mary Brawner Rambo

Dr. and Mrs. Albert Brawner

Dr. and **Mrs. Albert Brawner** lived in the Taylor House located on Atlanta Road, south of the hospital, from the early 1920s until the 1940s. They had three children: **Albert**, **Jr.**, **Mary,** and **Harriette**. Mrs. Brawner was the former Blanche Rice, the daughter of Mr. and Mrs. P.M. Rice, who lived on the corner of King and Church streets. She was a descendant of the Ruff Family, who operated Ruff's Mill at the Covered Bridge in the Nineteenth Century. Blanche Rice Brawner was a member of the Smyrna Social Club and First Methodist Church. See *Brawner, east side of King Street.*

Dr. Albert Ferguson Brawner graduated from the Medical College of Georgia at Emory University. He practiced psychiatric medicine at Brawner Sanitarium for forty years and also maintained a practice in Atlanta. He died in 1960.

Albert Brawner, Jr., was born in 1923. He died in 1939 from a ruptured spleen, which occurred during a football game at Marietta High School.

Mary Brawner married Albert Loton Rambo. They had three children: Albert Loton, Jr., Martha, and James D. Rambo. Mary and Albert live in Marietta. Mary Brawner Rambo is currently a member of the Smyrna Social Club, founded in 1908.

Albert Loton Rambo, Jr.., and his wife, Elizabeth, live in Denver, Colorado.

Martha Rambo married Charles Wyatt of Decatur. They live in Franklin, North Carolina.

James D. Rambo lives in Marietta.

Harriette Brawner graduated from the University of Georgia and shortly afterwards married George Matthews. They first moved to Cuthbert, then to Birmingham, Alabama, and then to Florida. Harriette was born in 1929 and died in 1978.

NOTE: The Information about the family of Dr. Albert Brawner was furnished by Mary Brawner Rambo. She and her husband, Albert, aided the Taylor-Brawner Foundation in the restoration of the Taylor-Brawner House, in the early years of the Twentieth-first Century.

CREATWOOD FARM

Creatwood Farm once was the site of a thriving herd of Guernsey cows and a pastoral scene on South Atlanta Road. Owned by the Crowe Family since 1892, Atlanta surgeon Dr. Walter A. Crowe bought the property to build a summer home. The brick house, built in 1916, faced Atlanta Road, just north of Brawner Sanitarium. The farm name was derived by using the first letter of each of the surnames of the new owners (all former residents of the West End section of Atlanta), who bought summer homes in the area: thus the name "Creat" for the Crowes, Rays, Eubanks, Awtrys, and Taylors. The dairy farm ceased operation in 1951.

NOTE: The information regarding the name of Creatwood Farm is from Mrs. Mazie Whitfield Nelson's book: *Past...Present...Future.* A copy can be located in the Smyrna Public Library.

Twentieth House

Mr. and **Mrs. Arthur Crowe, Sr.**, lived in the large brick house on the west side of Atlanta Road, south of Brawner Sanitarium. The parents of **Arthur L. Crowe, Jr.**, and **Edith Crowe Ingram**, they took great care in the way the property was developed into a residential community in the last decade of the Twentieth Century.

Mr. Pat Crowe built the large house that stood across the street from Brawner Sanitarium and raised his family there. He was one of the first members of the Crowe Family to grow up in this area, known today as The Heritage at Vinings. The Crowe farm extended all the way to the railroad and covered the area known today as Vinings Forest.

There were several houses located on the east side of Atlanta Road in a pine thicket. The people who lived in those houses were employees of Creatwood Dairy, the Guernsey Jug, or other farm enterprises operated by the Crowe Family. Some of these included the Davis Family, who lived and worked at Creatwood Dairies. They had two sons that I remember: J.O. and Richard, with whom I played ball. J.O. died in 2004.

THE GUERNSEY JUG

Another building located south of the Crowe home on the Creatwood Farm property was the **Guernsey Jug**, a restaurant specializing in ice cream, milk shakes, sandwiches, hamburgers, and snacks. It was a quaint place, a nice white brick structure located on Atlanta Road, which was U.S. Highway 41 and referred to as the Old Dixie Highway between Chattanooga and Atlanta. (Once the Four Lane was completed, it was designated U.S. Highway 41; the Old Dixie Highway became Georgia State Route 3.)

Edith Hudgins Crowe, the widow of Dr. Crowe, opened the Guernsey Jug Restaurant in 1931. It flourished through the early 1940s. The Guernsey Jug was a favorite stopping place for travelers taking that route in those days. It was a special place—a place where one looked forward to going. Although it has been closed fifty years, the Guernsey Jug still stirs strong feelings in the hearts of many Smyrna residents, including mine. It was a most enjoyable place of which I have fond memories! The Guernsey Jug building was moved from its location on Atlanta Street to the entrance of The Heritage at Vinings, located on the former Crowe property.

The Creatwood Dairies delivered milk to area residents. My family bought our milk from the Black and Webb Grocery Store, which may have purchased milk from Creatwood Dairies. I know other stores did.

Arthur Crowe, Jr. ., a veteran of World War II, served in some of the major battles in Europe. A major contributor toward the building of the Twentieth Century Veterans Memorial Park in downtown Smyrna, he served on the Park's Board of Directors and was a major fundraiser. He is also a member and supporter of both the Smyrna Public Library, the Smyrna Historical and Genealogical Society, and the Taylor-Brawner House Foundation.

After the War, Arthur, Jr. returned to Cobb County and practiced law for many years in Marietta. Although he resides in Marietta, he continues to have a keen interest in Smyrna and its redevelopment efforts.

The Creatwood Dairy Farm and its adjoining property remained in the Crowe Family until the mid 1990s, when Arthur, Jr. and his sister, Edith Ingram, decided to sell some of their property. Very selective in choosing a developer, Arthur, Jr., and Edith sold the property to John Weiland Homes and Neighborhoods for the building of Heritage at Vinings. This decision on their part played a major role in the quality of future redevelopment on South Atlanta Road.

NOTE: Most of the information about the Crowe Family, Creatwood, and the Ingram property was obtained from the Smyrna Museum.

RUST CHEESE COMPANY

Rust Cheese Company, owned and operated by **Mrs. Mae Rust**, was located on a large tract of land between the Creatwood Dairies and the Gray Family. Mrs. Rust's home was located on the property. One of their products, a big favorite, was their liquid ice cream mix. See *Mingo, Dixie Avenue.*

The Guernsey Jug at Creatwood Farm
Circa 1940s
Courtesy of Smyrna Museum

Rust Cheese Company
Atlanta Street, South of Creatwood Dairies
Circa 1940s
Courtesy of Ed Mingo

Twenty-first House

Mr. and **Mrs**. **Charles Henry Gray** built this house in 1941. Mrs. Gray, the former Betty Hamby, was a member of the large Hamby Family. They had two sons: D.C. and Jack, both graduates of Campbell High School. D.C., who served in the United States Navy, married Carolyn Captin; Jack, who served in the United States Air Force, married Dawn Morrison, also a Campbell High School graduate.

Twenty-second House

Mr. and **Mrs**. **Fuller Daniel** resided in the white frame house south of Creatwood Dairies. They owned this property and also some vacant land behind it. Mr. Daniel, a good friend of my dad, allowed dad to use that land for a baseball field, where I remember going many times for ball games. After Campbell High School opened in 1952, there was an upholstery business in this house. A small building was later constructed next door for this business. See *Telephone Exchange, Atlanta Street.*

SUNNYSIDE INN

Sunnyside Inn and Tourist Court was located just south of the Daniel House. This business was located directly across Atlanta Road from where Campbell Road ends at Atlanta Road and just south of what is known today as Campbell Middle School. The Inn was "kinda" like a sports bar of today, where both food and beer are served. Of course, there was no television at first, but they had a bar, radio, and jukeboxes. There one could get a good hamburger, among other food items. This restaurant and tourist court, owned and operated by the A.T. Parks Family, was like many located along this highway, from Florida northward, in that time.

STONEWALL RESTAURANT AND TOURIST COURT

Another business establishment along south Atlanta Road in the days of my youth was the Stonewall Restaurant and Tourist Court, owned and operated by Edgar Anderson. Located directly across from where Paces Ferry Road ends at Atlanta Road, the restaurant was a stone building where good food was served; behind the restaurant there were several cottages, which, I seem to remember, were also stone.

In the days of my youth, Sunnyside Inn and Stonewall Restaurant and Tourist Court were successful enterprises. (Long before interstate highways and large hotel chains came to the area, Atlanta Road in those days was part of U.S. Highway 41.)

I remember one well-publicized event, a matter of public record, that took place at the Stonewall Tourist Court. According to those who seem to know, several local "ladies" and "gentlemen" from Smyrna were there one evening without their spouses. Sometime in the early morning hours the Cobb County Police decided to check out the "goings on" at the Stonewall Tourist Court. Well, as I said, it is a matter of public record.

Ray Brown remembers when Stonewall Court Restaurant burned in the late 1940s. He also recalls that an extensive collection of Civil War memorabilia within the restaurant was destroyed. Ray remembers seeing the explosions ("popping like firecrackers") and a lot of black smoke. Then, he, along with his brother, Ted, rode their bicycles from Oakdale to the site of the fire. The restaurant was rebuilt.

Circa 1940s
Courtesy of Janet Brooks Brown

Stonewall Restaurant and Tourist Court
Circa 1940s
Courtesy of Janet Brooks Brown

ATLANTA STREET

East Side

From Mrs. Mazie's to Mr. Pearce Matthews

I want to thank Miller Davis, Harold Flynn, Melvin Holleman, Nancy McGee, "Bill" Scoggins, and Jack Taylor for sharing their memories of the places and people on the east side of Atlanta Street. Appreciation is also extended to Henry Konigsmark III, known as "Hank," for sharing information about his family on Atlanta Street, and to Lois Broome Matthews, who shared information on the Pearce Matthews Family.

THE GEORGIA POWER STREETCAR SUB-STATION

The Georgia Power Streetcar Sub-station was located on the west side of the railroad, almost directly across the street from The Smyrna Woman's Club Building. It was an imposing brick building that really stood out in Smyrna. The station furnished power for the streetcar line that ran from Marietta to Atlanta via Smyrna. (The streetcar line operation began in 1904 and continued until 1947.) At one time a group of business people operated some antique and gift shops in the sub-station building. They were unsuccessful because there was no parking area on that side of the street. Finally, in the late 1980s, when Atlanta Road was widened, the building was torn down. I hated to see it go, for it was a Smyrna landmark, which had been there all of my life.

Just north of the sub-station was a street that crossed the railroad and ran between the Nelson and Reed houses through to Gilbert Street. Long-time residents of the area across the railroad referred to this street as "Reed's Alley." At some point in time, before the road was closed, the City of Smyrna named it Nelson Street. When I was a kid growing up in Smyrna, I never remember the street's having a name other than "Reed's Alley." When Atlanta Street was widened in the late 1980s, Nelson Street (Reed's Alley) was closed at the railroad.

NOTE: In the middle of the Twentieth Century, when I was growing up, the first four houses listed below were separated from Atlanta Street by the railroad but were considered to be located on Atlanta Street.

First House

Mrs. Guy Ray and her son, **Reuben**, lived in the first of these four houses, which faced Atlanta Street.

Later on, **Mrs. Vicky Griggers**, one of the daughters of Mr. and Mrs. B.F. Reed, Sr., lived in this first house. "**Jim**" and **Sara** (Anderson) **Gentry** moved to this house in 1950 and lived here for a short time. Later on, another owner, whose name I do not recall, changed the entrance from Atlanta Street to Gilbert Street. The house is still standing, but it now has a Gilbert Street address.

Second House

Mrs. Mazie Whitfield Nelson was the resident of the second house, the rear of which backs up to Gilbert Street. Mrs. Nelson was born in 1890 to Mr. and Mrs. Thomas P. Whitfield. Her mother was known as "Miss Emma." Her father, Thomas P. Whitfield, was in the grocery business; he was also on the Smyrna City Council.

NOTE: Harold L. Smith, Smyrna historian, stated that he had an interview with Mr. Hugh Marston, who served on the Smyrna City Council in the late 1920s. Harold received the following information from Mr. Marston: "The area east of the railroad was a rural route, and the Smyrna City Council voted at that time to name the streets in that area for some of the people who were living there. Whitfield Street was named after Thomas M. Whitfield, Mrs. Mazie Nelson's grandfather."

Thomas P. Whitfield
Smyrna City Council
1901-1907

Any kid growing up in Smyrna had to know Mrs. Mazie Whitfield Nelson. She was one of
e ladies who volunteered in the library when it was located in The Smyrna Woman's Club Building.
remember going there as a student to do research and to study; she was always kind and very helpful.
Irs. Mazie was also an insurance agent for the Macabees, underwriting insurance for every member
f the family. As an insured, I was a Macabee when I was a small child. After a family would buy an
isurance policy, one of the "perks" for the insured was that Mrs. Mazie, along with others she
ngaged to help, would conduct group sessions for the children of the policyholders. We would go to
er house, where games, refreshments, and other amenities, such as arts and crafts, reading and/or
torytelling, were available. It was fun to get together with other children in the community. I
emember my mother was always very particular about how I looked when I went to Mrs. Mazie's
ouse. My teeth had to be brushed, and my clothes had to be clean; I also had to wear shoes, even in
e summertime.

Mrs. Mazie Whitfield Nelson wrote a book, *Past...Present...and Future*, a delightful book
bout her life in Smyrna. (A copy of this book is in the reference section of the Smyrna Public
ibrary.) Mrs. Mazie joined First Methodist Church between 1900 and 1910 and was an active
ember there for the rest of her life. She is buried in the Smyrna Memorial Cemetery. See *Woman's
lub, Atlanta Street, from Mapps to R&M Café.*

Third House

Mr. and **Mrs. Benjamin Franklin Reed, Sr.**, lived in the third house facing Atlanta Street.
hey had ten children: **Gertrude Webber**, **Victoria Melvina**, known as "Vicky," **Colene Webber**,
enjamin Franklin, Jr., known as "B.F. Jr.," **Earl Stephens**, **Rebecca Hilda**, **Raymond Morgan**,
lice Palma, **William Marcus**, **and Ruth**. Mr. and Mrs. Reed's children were all adults who were in
ny parents' generation. Mr. B.F. Reed, Sr., was an elderly gentleman when I was a child, but I knew
im well. The Reeds were members of First Baptist Church. See *Church Street, both sides of Bank
treet,* and *the west side of Atlanta Street.*

NOTE: Mr. B.F. Reed, Sr., is reported to have founded the first Real Estate Brokerage and
end Company in Cobb County, in the early part of the Twentieth Century.

Gertrude Webber Reed married Mark Humphrey.

Victoria Melvina Reed married Rayford Ezra Griggers. They had three children: Elaray,
ictor Curtis, and Myrtle Joan.

Robert E. Flournoy, Jr.
Georgia State Representative
1963-1964
Mayor of Marietta
1982-1985
Superior Court Judge, Cobb Judicial Circuit
July 14, 1987–January 1, 2001
Superior Court Chief Judge, Cobb Judicial Circuit
January 1, 2001–August 10, 2003

NOTE: The above dates were obtained from the State of Georgia Archives, respectively.

Robert E. Flournoy III
Superior Court Judge, Cobb Judicial Circuit
Elected July 14, 2000–

Ella and **"Murph" McBrayer**
Beside the B.F. Reed Home on Atlanta Street
Circa World 1942
Courtesy of Ella McBrayer

Walker Akins, (L) in Akins Grocery Store
Corner of Bank and Atlanta Streets
Circa 1940
Courtesy of Cecile Akins Martin

Elaray Griggers Reed, known as "Pam," married Robert Edward Flournoy, Jr., known as "Bob," who served as Georgia State Representative from Cobb County, Mayor of Marietta, and Cobb Superior Court Judge. They had two sons: Robert III and Matthew, both of whom have practiced law in Marietta, Robert Flournoy III is Superior Court Judge, Cobb Judicial Circuit, and a daughter, Gwen Flournoy Ross, a real estate leasing agent in the Galleria area.

Victor Curtis Griggers married Ellen Dixson.

Myrtle Joan Griggers died in a jeep wreck when she was eleven years old.

Colene Webber Reed married Dallis Rufus Guthrie of Smyrna. See *south side of Atlanta Street.*

Benjamin Franklin Reed, Jr., . known as "B.F., Jr.," married Jessie Belle Cook. See *south ide of Bank Street*

Earl Stephens Reed married Madeline Duncan. They had two children: Jacqueline Faye Reed and Earl Stephens Reed, Jr. Jacqueline married John Pruitt Ogletree; Earl Stephens, Jr., married acqueline Simonton.

Rebecca Hilda Reed married John Franklin Leonard. See *north side of Church Street.*

Raymond Morgan Reed married Mary Frances Taylor. They had three children. After Mary Frances died in 1971, Raymond married Mary Love, who was the administrator at The Walker School, in Marietta. See *south side of Atlanta Street.*

Alice Palma Reed, who never married, was a very successful real estate agent in the Smyrna area for many years.

William Marcus Reed married Virginia Lee Pepper. See *north side of Bank Street.*

Ruth Reed was born July 6, 1924, and died three days later, July 9, 1924.

Fourth House

Mrs. Fanny Crawford lived here with her daughter, **Pauline**, the pianist and later the organist at First Methodist Church. Pauline was a very talented and beautiful woman. This house, the fourth of the houses across the railroad from Atlanta Street, backs up to Nelson Street and the lot where the ice plant was located. The ice plant was razed in the late 1990s. See *Ice Plant, west side of Roswell Street.*

NOTE: Now we are back on Atlanta Street, on the west side of the railroad, in downtown Smyrna. The first building past the sub-station was a little wooden structure that housed the dispatch office for **Day's Taxi Service**. "Papa" Day and his son, **Robert**, owned and operated this business. **Day's Used Cars** was later operated at this site. See *north side of Sunset Avenue.*

W.F. Stewart Insurance and Real Estate was located next door to the taxi service. See *Hughes Street.*

J.Y. Wooten
Mayor of Smyrna
1945

J.Y. Wooten Real Estate was in the same building with W.F Stewart's Insurance and Real Estate. Mr. Wooten later moved his office to Concord Road in the vicinity of the present Tillman

Methodist Church. This was after Rem Bennett, Sr. began building the small frame houses along Concord Road in the late 1940s.

South of the insurance agency were two liquor stores, next door to each other. B. F. Reed, Jr., owned and operated the **Don Ree**, and the **Stonewall** was owned and operated by Edgar Anderson.

NOTE: In addition to the liquor store, Edgar Anderson also owned the Stonewall Restaurant and Tourist Court, located on South Atlanta Road at the intersection of Paces Ferry Road. See *Atlanta Road, Marlowe's to Creatwood.*

CITY JAIL

A small building that stood by itself at the rear of the liquor stores and adjacent to the railroad served as the Smyrna City Jail, and the inmates were called convicts. When I was a boy, I thought: "How convenient! The convicts can break out of jail, 'hop on' a train, and be gone."

The building next to the Stonewall Liquor store was a two-story brick structure that backed up to the railroad. A grocery store on the first floor had several different owners through the years. The two that I remember were **Ralph Stephens** and **Clarence "Shorty" Black,** the son of Roy Black. "Shorty" had worked for his uncle, Harry Black, at Black and Webb Grocery Store until it closed. Later on, Harry Black married Leila Fowler, who ran Leila's Beauty shop on Bank Street. See *Fowler, north side of Bank Street,* and *Atlanta Street from Marlowe's to Creatwood.*

The second floor above the grocery store was used for different kinds of meetings in the community. Also, from time to time different businesses were operated there. I remember the **Smyrna Men's Club** held some meetings in this place. Most of the citizens who belonged to this club were local business owners and community leaders. Some that I recall were these: **Dr. W.C. Mitchell, Dr. M. L. Collins, Dr. D.C. Landers, Harry Black, Paul Clayton**, and **D.C. Osborn**.

The basement of this building was used for various types of businesses and activities. I remember the Work Progress Administration (WPA) had a mattress factory there when I was a kid. I am sure that business was still operating when World War II began. From what I have read, President Franklin D. Roosevelt's New Deal programs (such as the WPA) were enacted with the intent of putting people back to work during the "Great Depression," which brought on widespread unemployment throughout the nation. I remember that, as a young boy, I peered through the basement window to see ladies using sewing machines and other workers assembling the mattresses.

There was a path alongside the basement of this building that led to steps going down to the railroad. I would use those steps when going to visit my relatives across the railroad. Many people did likewise. The steps saved having to go down to the Spring Street railroad crossing to get to Roswell Street.

The next building was **Paul Clayton's Gulf Station**. At this station there was an outside canopy, under which was a bench where men would play checkers. My dad was one of the men who played checkers there in the evenings and on the weekends. I remember his playing frequently with **Speer Stone**. I do not remember others by name. (**Gil Lynch** later owned this service station.)

During the World War II years, **Paul Clayton** had a tire retread operation at his station. Because rubber was rationed and tires were in very limited supply, the people who had automobiles would go to Paul Clayton to get their old tires retreaded. Because the technology was not all that good in those days, sometimes the retreads would just peel off the tires. One would frequently see those retreads lying around the streets.

I also remember that Paul Clayton was one of the Charter Members of the Smyrna Lions Club, organized in the mid 1940s.

Smyrna Jail on West Spring Street, at the foot of the Water Tank
Circa 1940
Courtesy of The Smyrna Museum

Parade in "Downtown Smyrna" in 1958 with **"Fibber" McGee**, (on the far left) in front of "Gil Lynchs' Gulf Station
NOTE: Smyrna's only traffic light, Davis Department Store, and Campbell High School Band in the background and on the left, the middle car, belonging to Ray Brown.
Courtesy of Janet Brooks Brown

Next door to Paul Clayton's Gulf Station was the **Smyrna Barber Shop**, owned and operated by **Carl Carson**, **T. G. Rogers**, and **V. J. DuPree**. This shop was opened after World War II. T. G. Rogers, a barber in Smyrna for over fifty years, retired in the early part of the Twenty-first Century. He cut my hair when I was still in high school, and he was cutting my hair just before he retired. Having had a long-time relationship with T.G. Rogers, I found him to be a man of honor and a faithful Christian member of First Baptist Church, where he was ordained as a deacon on January 18, 1984.

T.G. and **Ruth Rogers** came to Smyrna in 1950 or 1951. Ruth, a hairdresser, and T.G. lived with his parents on West Dixie Avenue, between Smyrna and Marietta. Later on they moved to a house on the south side of Smyrna, across from the Burruss home, on South Atlanta Road. They built their own home on Old Concord Road, two doors south of Church Road, and lived there the rest of their lives. T. G. and Ruth had one daughter, Cheeka Rogers Nelson, and one granddaughter, Sherida Nelson. T.G. was a Master Mason in Nelms Masonic Lodge and a member of American Legion Post #160.

The **Smyrna Hardware** was next door to the barber shop. **Mr. Baugh** owned and operated this store for a long time. After World War II, Pitner Dorris was the owner, and later George Howard owned and operated the store for a while.

Mr. George R. Miller ran a shoe repair shop in a small building between the Smyrna Hardware Store and Sam Reed's Sinclair Service Station. My friend Miller Davis remembers going as a child to the shoe shop and looking out the back door to see the Edwards/Shipp house, where he once lived.

Next to the shoe repair shop and on the northeast corner of Spring and Atlanta streets was a **Sinclair Service Station** that was operated by **Sam Reed**. From under the station's canopy I would pick up my newspapers each morning to begin my paper route. This station was later owned and operated by **John Baldwin** and **James Petty**, a brother of Watson Petty. James and Watson grew up on their family farm on King Springs Road, previously named Cooper Lake Road. Both James and Watson were prisoners of war: Watson, during World War II, and James, during the Korean Conflict. See *Petty, east side of King Springs Road.*

The Fouts Brothers

C.J. and **Jerry Fouts** came to Smyrna in 1948 from Dawson County. They owned and operated the aforementioned Sinclair Service Station until 1963. Afterwards, they built an auto parts store and service station on the west side of Atlanta Street, near Hill Street, in the same location as the present Smyrna Fire Station # 1. C.J. and Jerry established at this location, in 1969, the first Datsun dealership in Cobb County.

The Fouts Brothers Datsun dealership moved in 1970 to a new location, on the west side of Atlanta Road near Pat Mell Road. The Datsun dealership was later moved to a location on Cobb Parkway; it then became known as Fouts Brothers Nissan, Inc.

Before moving Fouts Brothers Nissan dealership to Cobb Parkway in 1985, Fouts Brothers built a facility for Nissan UD trucks at the Pat Mell and Atlanta roads' location. At that time, "Bill" Scoggins became their first and only full-time truck salesman for a long time; his total sales time there was twenty-one years. When he retired in November 2002, there were six full-time truck salesmen. The Fouts Brothers have been big contributors to the Smyrna business community for more than a half century.

The C.J. Fouts Family owns and operates Smyrna Truck Equipment Company, as well as Fouts Brothers Fire Equipment Company, at the Atlanta Road location. The Jerry Fouts Family now owns and operates UD-GMC Trucks at the Pat Mell/Atlanta Road location.

The Fouts Family

Carl and **Lottie Fouts** had five sons: Jerry, C. J. , Charles, Richard, known as "Bud," and lvin. They also had three daughters: Barbara, Shelba, and LaVerne. After Mr. Fouts' death, Lottie outs married Johnny Lindsay, who is now deceased. Mrs. Lottie Fouts Lindsay is a devoted member f First Baptist Church.

Jerry Fouts married Margie Frisbee Poss. Margie was previously married to Claude Poss, vho is deceased. Jerry and Margie adopted two daughters: Carolyn and Sarah. Jerry, Margie, and arolyn are deceased.

C. J. Fouts. married Betty Austin from Acworth in 1949. They had three children: Jan, arry, and Tim. In 1952, Betty and C.J. lived on Turner Drive, off Belmont Circle. Later they moved Lee Street, in the Hickory Hills community. Betty and C.J. lived on Nowlin Drive, off North Cooper ake Road until recently, when they moved to West Cobb County to be close to their children. C.J. ied in June 2006.

Jan Fouts married Billy Edens. They had two sons, Scott and Jacob, known as "Jake," and a aughter, Stacey.

Barry Jay Fouts married Melanie Ross. They had four children: Amy, Lisa, Bradley, and onathan.

Tim Alan Fouts married Melissa Chaffin; they had one child, Benjamin Alan, known as Ben."

Charles Fouts married Gayle Hiatt; they had three daughters: Angela, Jane, and Patricia.

Charles Fouts later married the former Carole Shadix. They are the parents of one son, John. harles Fouts operated a Texaco Service Station on Atlanta Road in Smyrna for many years; he still wns the property and building, adjacent to Jonquil Plaza. Charles, Carole, and John Fouts are embers of First Baptist Church, where Carole is very active in Women on Missions.

Richard Fouts and his wife had one daughter, Tammie.

Alvin Fouts married Kathy Shirley, the daughter of Newton and Kathryn Shirley of Smyrna. hey had two children: Karla and Keith. Alvin has owned and operated an automobile business on outh Cobb Drive in Smyrna for many years.

Barbara Fouts married Wayne Little; they had three children: Dennis, Michael and Cheryl.

Shelba Fouts married Johnny Holland from West Cobb County. They had two daughters: inda and Diane.

LaVerne Fouts married William Moore, known as "Bill." They had one daughter, Connie. aVerne is now deceased

BLACK and WEBB GROCERY STORE

Black and Webb Grocery Store was on the southeast corner of Atlanta and Spring streets. his store was owned and operated by **Harry Black** and **Sam Webb**. Later on, **J.D. Daniel** ran **Red ot Grocery Store** in this building; afterwards, he moved the Red Dot Store a block down Atlanta reet to a new store building. It was from this building that he relocated the business to Jonquil Plaza the 1950s.

Harry Black lived on Hill Street, off Atlanta Road in the Oakdale community, south of Smyrna. Mr. and Mrs. Sam Webb also lived on Hill Street. I remember that Mrs. Webb and Mrs. Black worked in the store sometimes. Mr. and Mrs. Black had a daughter, Evelyn, who attended Fitzhugh Lee High School. See *J.D. Daniel, north side of Bank Street,* and *Red Dot Grocery Store, east side of Atlanta Street.*

Sometime in the 1950s, **Mr.** and **Mrs. Harold Davis** operated Davis Department Store in this building.

Glover Auto Repair Shop was next door to Black and Webb Grocery Store. Later on in the 1950s **Mangum's Studio** (photography) was also in this building.

<u>Fifth House</u>

There was a house that stood just past the Glover Auto Repair Shop. I do not recall who lived there. According to information from long-time residents, this was a rental house during the days of my youth. During the late 1950s and early 1960s it was the medical office of **Dr. Huenegardt**. Afterwards, he moved his office to Cherokee Road, now Windy Hill Road, in the Belmont Hills area; then Buddy Scoggins operated Scoggins Real Estate in this house.

At some time in the 1940s **J. D. Daniel** constructed a building near the fifth house, to which he moved the **Red Dot Grocery Store**. He operated the store here until the Jonquil Plaza Shopping Center was built in the late 1950s.

NOTE: J. D. Daniel, who operated a grocery store in Smyrna for about 50 years, grew up in East Cobb County on a farm that encompassed the area of the present Eastside Baptist Church, on Lower Roswell Road. Coming to Smyrna, he became the butcher at Rogers Store. According to his Smyrna contemporaries, before then he worked at the ship yards, during World War II.

Roy Howard operated a service station next door to the Red Dot Grocery Store. This is the same Roy Howard who later moved to Bank Street after it was extended in the late 1940s.

<u>Sixth House</u>

Lorena Pace Pruitt
Mayor of Smyrna
1946-1948
Smyrna City Councilwoman
1945

Joe and **Lorena Pace Pruitt** and their son, **Rex**, lived in this house, where Lorena grew up. "The Pace House," as it was called, was almost directly across from First Methodist Church, on the northwest corner of Atlanta and Church streets. Lorena Pace Pruitt served as Mayor of Smyrna, 1946-1948. Lorena was the only lady to ever hold the office of mayor in Smyrna. The daughter of Dr. and Mrs. W.T. Pace, Lorena was a member of First Baptist Church, where her family had also worshiped

Dr. W.T. Pace
Georgia State Representative
1929-1932

Dr. and **Mrs. W.T. Pace**, according to long-time Smyrna residents, lived in this house earlier in the Twentieth Century. They had three children: **Lorena**, **Helen**, and **Sidney**. Dr. Pace practiced medicine in Smyrna. He also operated a drug store in the building at the southeast corner of Atlanta and Spring streets, prior to Black and Webb Grocery Store being located there. Dr. and Mrs. Pace were faithful members of First Baptist Church, where the WMU named a circle for Mrs. Linda Pace. Dr. Pace served two terms in the Georgia State House of Representatives, 1929-1932.

Dr. W. T. Pace
Medical Doctor and Pharmacist
Georgia State Representative
Two Terms 1929-1932
Picture Courtesy of Janet Brooks Brown

Dr. Pace, who was the only physician in the Smyrna area for a number of years, is shown on the far right, also pictured left to right are **"Doc" Westbrook**, pharmacist, **Wallace Arrington** and **Charlie Walker**.

Pace's Drug Store in 1926 (one of the first in Smyrna when this picture was taken, was located on the southeast corner of Atlanta and Spring Streets.)
Courtesy of Janet Brooks Brown

Dr. and **Mrs. W. T. Pace** are pictured after their marriage in 1900. Mrs. Pace was the former Linda Bentley.

his above picture and the following information from Dr. Pace's obituary, courtesy of Janet Brooks Brown. The obituary clipping is assumed to be from *The Marietta Daily Journal.*

and Mrs. Pace had three children: Lorena Pace Pruitt of Smyrna, Mrs. Helen Pace Thompson of anta, and Sidney Pace of Marietta. Dr. Pace practices medicine in Smyrna for thirty-five years and l the distinction of having the number "1" for his telephone number. Dr. Pace two terms in the orgia Legislature as Cobb's Representative and pioneered in the introduction of bills which were olutionary in his day: sterilization of the mentally unfit, sale of automobile tags by counties, and lishment of capital punishment.

IOTE: Mrs. Pace's long devotion and service to the First Baptist Church WMU was kept alive for many years by the circle that bore her name.

Helen Pace married Schley Thompson, known as "Sly." Together, in Buckhead, they owne Peachtree Road Bank. During their ownership, they initiated a banking facility at Lawson General, a military hospital. (Peachtree DeKalb Airport is currently located on the former hospital property.) Th military hospital service was still offered when I began working for Fulton National Bank in 1952. Th Thompsons sold Peachtree Road Bank to Fulton National Bank, which they continued to manage fo many years. Over time, I became acquainted with Mr. and Mrs. Thompson. Helen kept close ties wit Smyrna, and I remember when my dad, Roy Wood, was on the Smyrna City Council, she owne several Smyrna properties, one of which was part of the land where Nash Junior High School was buil in 1963. (Nash Junior High became Nash Middle School in the 1970s, and is now a part of Campbel High School.)

Miller Davis told me that he was born in the Pace House in 1933. Miller's family move from this house to the Edwards/Shipp house on Roswell Street and from Roswell Street to Churc Street, where he grew up.

NOTE: On the south side of the Pace House was a driveway used as an entrance to th **Konigsmark Coal Yard**, which was located alongside the railroad.

Seventh House

Mr. and **Mrs**. **Henry Konigsmark**, **Sr**., resided here. Henry Konigsmark and the forme Alma Reed were married after he came to Smyrna in the early 1900s. They had twin sons: **Henry**, **Jr** and **Reed**. Mr. Konigsmark, Sr., was affectionately known to his grandchildren as "Daddy K."

"Henry Konigsmark, Sr., came to Smyrna in the early 1900s from Konigsmark, Iowa, whic is near Cedar Rapids. He was the secretary for the Belmont Farm, which covered all the area wher Belmont Hills Shopping Center is currently located, north of Smyrna on Atlanta Street. The Belmo House stood east of the railroad and the Belmont Streetcar stop."

NOTE: The above information is from Mrs. Mazie Whitfield Nelson's boo *Past...Present... and Future.* A copy is located in the Smyrna Public Library, in the referenc department.

Mr. Henry Konigsmark, Sr., was a postal inspector at the United States Post Office in Atlan for many years. Alma Reed Konigsmark, who served as postmistress in Smyrna for many years, als owned and operated the Konigsmark Coal Company. Alma was a sister of Miss Coral Reed, who fir married Mr. S.A. Love and, after Mr. Love's death, married D.J. Ray. See *Love Street* and *Atlan Street, from Marlowe's to Creatwood.*

Henry Konigsmark, Jr.
Smyrna City Councilman
Elected 1948

Henry Konigsmark, Jr. ., married Elizabeth Davis, the daughter of Mr. and Mrs. Grov Warren Davis on Church Street. They had two sons: Henry III, known as "Hank," and Reed. Se *Konigsmark, east side of Dunn Street* and *north side of Church Street.*

Reed Konigsmark, a twin brother of Henry, Jr., married Louise Osborn, known as "Bill." S was the daughter of Mr. and Mrs. D.C. Osborn. They had two daughters: Ann and Nancy. See *Atlan Street, from Marlowe's to Creatwood.*

Eighth House

Marion Taylor
Casualty of War
United States Army
World War II

Mr. and **Mrs. Howard Taylor** lived in this house. They had seven children: **Charles**, **uise**, **Gordon**, **Marion**, **Robert**, known as "Bob," **Jack**, and **Mary Frances**. Mrs. Taylor, the mer Marie Gonzales from Louisiana, was of French descent. Mr. Howard Taylor grew up in rida. The Taylor Family were members of Smyrna Presbyterian Church.

Marion Taylor married Bobbie Bramblett of Smyrna. According to family information, rion Taylor was a manager at Rogers Store, the grocery store in Smyrna where Arthur Bacon and nes Pressley worked with him on weekends while they were in high school. Marion left Smyrna l went to Miami, Florida. Having been there for a few weeks, he enlisted in the United States Army l volunteered to be a paratrooper in an airborne unit. Marion had lived in Smyrna all of his life ept for that short period of time in Florida before his military enlistment. Marion was killed in rld War II during combat in Europe. Because of his enlistment in Miami rather than in Cobb unty, he was not eligible to be listed among the Cobb County citizens who lost their lives in the vice of their country. However, his body was brought back to Smyrna and buried in the New yrna Cemetery, on Hawthorne Avenue.

Louise Taylor married Max Pavlovsky. They had a son and a daughter. Louise was the first y to serve as Smyrna City Clerk. Her service was during the mayoral term of Guye Duncan and at time Smyrna had only one policeman, Ralph Argo. See *east side of Dunn Street.*

Robert Taylor, known as "Bob," earned a Bachelor of Architecture degree from Georgia titute of Technology. He joined the United States Navy and was assigned during World War II to USS Hornet. He was on board when it was torpedoed; though he was not injured, he received ors for meritorious service. Bob served as building inspector for the City of Smyrna during the yoral term of Guye Duncan; Belmont Hills opened while he was building inspector. During this e Bob wrote a book detailing his plans for the redevelopment of Smyrna. According to family rmation, a copy of his book is in the Smyrna Museum.

NOTE: The above information was shared by Jack Taylor.

Jack Taylor married Barbara McCrary, known as "Bobbie," who was the daughter of Mr. and . Charles McCrary. Jack was in the United States Navy and served in the Pacific during World r II. Early in their marriage Jack and Bobbie lived on the corner of King and Stephens streets; later moved to Spring Street. After the War, they built a house on Dunn Street. In the late 1940s or y 1950s, they built another house in the Forest Hills community, where they currently live.

Jack, who was an account executive with the stock brokerage firm Dean Witter, in Atlanta, lso a member of American Legion Post # 160.

Bobbie's family came to Smyrna from Cassville. She grew up on South Atlanta Road in the nd house north of Ridge Road. (That area has been redeveloped and is now covered with beautiful homes.) Fletcher McCrary, "Bobbie's" uncle, and his family lived in the first house north of ge Road. Both of the McCrary houses were demolished for the building of Oak Ridge Estates, on corner of Ridge and Atlanta roads.

The McCrary men married sisters, thus making their children double first cousins. One of the sins, Ruth McCrary, the daughter of Fletcher McCrary, married Michael Mackay. Ruth continued to live in the area at Ridge and Atlanta roads until she sold her property for the redevelopment in th late 1990s. She still lives in Smyrna, on Memory Lane, in the Forest Hills community. Ruth recentl married "an old school chum," Barney Barnett, who grew up in the Log Cabin community, south c Smyrna.

Mary Frances Taylor married Raymond Reed. They had three children. See *Reed, south sid of Atlanta Street.*

Ninth House

W.H. Beshears
Smyrna City Councilman
1924

This was the home of the **Beshers** (pronounced "Be-shears") **Family**, who had a son name **Edward**. Mrs. Beshers was the former Nina Ruff, a member of the Ruff Family, associated with Ruff Mill. I am sure that this is the house where **Lewis Day** established his **State Farm Insurance Agenc** in the middle 1950s. I remember that, when I had an automobile wreck in the triangle at Memori Drive and Atlanta Street in the 1950s, Lewis had his office in this house. See *Woman's Club, Atlant Street, from Mapps to R & M Café.*

Tenth House

Jesse and **Ruby Cook** and their family lived in this house, which was located where th northwest corner of Spring Road and Atlanta Street come together today. At that time, this proper was elevated to an almost steep bank. (Atlanta Street then intersected with Love Street; today; becau Spring Road was cut through, Atlanta Street intersects with Spring Road.) Helen Blackwell Hansc remembers that her dad took her and her brothers to the Cooks' home to stay while her mother gav birth to Neil, Helen's youngest brother. See *Cook, west side of King Street, east side of Lee Street,* ar *Blackwell, north side of Spring Road, the Country Road.*

Eleventh House

Mr. and **Mrs. Howard Wheeler** were residents here after the War. Because Mr. Wheel lost both of his legs in World War II, the United States Government gave him a new Linco automobile. Harold Flynn shared with me that, when he rode to work with Howard Wheeler, h thought the way Mr. Wheeler was able to maneuver that car was so remarkable.

Emory Chastain owned the tract of land between the streetcar line on Atlanta Street and th railroad. According to Chastain Family information, Emory sold this property, which later becan Atlanta Terrace, to Rem Bennett, Sr., who developed the property in the early 1950s. Thus th following three homes did not exist in the days of my youth. They were built sometime after graduated from high school.

Mr. and **Mrs. Henry Konigsmark, Jr.**, **Mr.** and **Mrs. Alan Mortin**, and **Mr.** and **Mr** **Jake Nash** built new homes on Atlanta Terrace at that time.

Twelfth House

Mr. and **Mrs. Horace Mulkey** lived on the east side of Atlanta Road, across from whe Smyrna Presbyterian Church is today. Mrs. Mulkey was the former Evelyn Wildberger. Evelyn mother, **Mrs. Ida Wildberger**, lived with them until her death. Evelyn's dad, Mr. Jacob Wildberg was from Switzerland. Both parents, along with Evelyn and Horace, are buried in the New Smyr Cemetery. The Mulkeys had no children.

Evelyn and **Horace Mulkey** at their home on Atlanta Road
Circa early 1950s
Courtesy of Janet Brooks Brown

Horace Mulkey was a Private in the United States Army in World War I. Horace and Evely both very gifted musicians, sang and played at many weddings. Their wedding was held in Fi Baptist Church in 1926. A picture from their wedding is in *A Beacon for Christ, A Centennial Histo of The First Baptist Church of Smyrna, Georgia.*

Evelyn was active as a Brownie leader in the 1950s. Both Horace and Evelyn were active the ministries of Locust Grove Baptist Church, in the Oakdale community. They also served in t music ministry at Green Acres Baptist Church, where she was the organist and he was the song lead In their senior years they moved their memberships back to First Baptist Church, where th worshiped until their deaths.

Horace once told Janet Brown proudly, "Nothing but a Ford has ever been parked in o garage." Their property on Atlanta Street was left as a trust to the Georgia Baptist Foundation. T Montclair subdivision is now located where the Mulkey house stood.

<u>Thirteenth House</u>

Marion McGee, known as "Fibber," and his wife, **Helen Terrell McGee**, lived here. Th had two daughters and a son: Suzanne, Nancy, and David. "Fibber" McGee served in the 8 Airborne in the United States Army during World War II. He was a paratrooper in France and Ital After he came home from the War, he and Helen built this house on Atlanta Road. He was a faith member of American Legion Post # 160, where he served as Commander. See *Terrell, west side Roswell Street.*

<u>Fourteenth House</u>

Mr. and **Mrs. Leslie Morgan Camp** lived here with their three children: daughter, **Sar Paige**, and twin sons, **Tim** and **Tom**. Mrs. Camp, the former Mona Whitley, was born in Cordo Alabama, but grew up in Atlanta. She had one sister, Rebecca Newman, of Atlanta. Leslie Camp w from Marietta; he had two sisters, Edith and Lucille, and a brother, Paul. Mona Camp was a teacher Smyrna High School and later at Campbell High School, from which all of the Camp childr graduated.

<u>Sarah Paige Camp</u> married Lamar Tedder, who grew up on Fleming Street. They had t children: Kellie and Charlie. Lamar Tedder was the president of the Smyrna High School Class 1951. Kellie and Charlie both graduated from Campbell High School. Lamar and Sarah Paige deceased. See *north side of Fleming Street.*

<u>Tim Camp</u> married Sandra Stephens of Alabama. They had a son, Timothy Stephens Can and a daughter, Katherine Faith Camp. Tim died in 1994.

<u>Tom Camp</u> married Marsha Green from Fort Payne, Alabama. They had twin daughters: L Michelle and Charissa Nichole. They also had one granddaughter.

Several years after Leslie Camp's death, Mona Camp married Mr. Francis E. Bedient. Th lived into their senior years and were very active members of First Baptist Church until their deaths.

<u>Fifteenth House</u>

In a pine grove between South Atlanta Road and the railroad was a large red brick house t was somewhat secluded. This was the home of one of the **Crowe** families associated with Creatwo Dairies.

Sixteenth House

There was a two-story white frame house farther down the street, next door, on the north side, to the present Campbell Middle School. In the days of my youth, it was referred to as the McMillan House because several generations of McMillans had lived there.

Mr. and **Mrs**. **Franklin Lamar McMillan** lived in this house earlier in the Twentieth Century. Mrs. McMillan was the former Silina Gartrell. They had several children. The following are those that we know about: Mary Bertha, Frank, and Alice. Franklin Lamar McMillan was an engineer for L & N Railroad and a Baptist preacher.

Alice McMillan never married.

Frank McMillan, known as "Red," led the congregational singing at First Baptist Church. Frank was a member of the McMillan Quartet, often singing in the area.

Mary Bertha McMillan married Luther Abernathy. According to family information, the Abernathy Family lived in this house at one time. They had several children, including Lina, Nell, Orthella, and L.H. Mary Bertha operated a millinery shop in Blairsville. She died in the flu epidemic of 1918, when her daughter, Lina, was a little girl.

Lina Abernathy married Quinten Steppe from Blairsville. Mr. Steppe was a funeral director in Blairsville before he and Lina moved to Smyrna in 1950. See *Steppe, east side of Lee Street.*

Nell Abernathy married Gene Charles McMullan; they had three children: Jean, Gene, and Carl.

Gene and Carl McMullan were both pharmacists. Gene worked in the drug store across from Fitzhugh Lee elementary and high schools in Oakdale, south of Smyrna, and later bought a drug store in Dallas.

Orthella Abernathy never married.

L. H. Abernathy. lived in a garage apartment at the McMillan Atlanta Road property, where he farmed and operated a greenhouse. Jane Steppe Chastain remembers her "helping, as a child, in the greenhouse." L.H. grew tomato plants, which he sold to nurseries and to the public. Says Jane, "I remember my job was to put mud on the roots of the plants as they were being wrapped in newspapers and tied with a string. (This was before the use of plastic containers.)"

Seventeenth House

Mr. and **Mrs**. **Pearce Matthews** lived in this large brown frame house that was on a slightly elevated hill on the northeast corner of Atlanta and Jane Lyle roads, directly in front of the Atlanta and Ridge roads' intersection. (Post Properties apartment homes are now located in this area.)

Mr. Matthews married Laura Candler from Blairsville. She was affectionately called "Mom Pick" by all of her grandchildren. Laura and Pearce both attended Young Harris College; Pearce earned his law degree from the University of Georgia. They had three children: **John**, **June**, and **Mary**.

Mr. Matthews was a prominent Atlanta attorney and Executive Vice-President of Lawyers Title Insurance Corporation, where he worked throughout his career. I knew who he was, but I never knew him personally when I was growing up. After I graduated from college and began working at Fulton National Bank in Atlanta, I knew him in the business arena.

Mr. and Mrs. Matthews were very active in First Methodist Church. During World War II with many of the men in the Church being drafted into the armed services, Mr. Matthews began teaching a Sunday School Class for those who were left. The class became known as the Pearce Matthews Sunday School Class. Mr. Matthews has been deceased for a number of years, but the class continues to be a vibrant part of First Methodist Church. After his death, his son, John Matthews taught the class for 38 years.

First Methodist Church installed the stained glass windows from the old sanctuary on Atlanta Street into the chapel of the present church building. The Church voted to name the chapel "The Matthews Chapel" to pay tribute to Mr. Pearce Matthews and Mr. John Matthews.

John Matthews married Lois Broome from Greene County. They had two children: Betty and Nancy. John earned his law degree from the University of Georgia. He, like his father, worked throughout his career with Lawyers Title Insurance Corporation in Atlanta. Lois Matthews, a teacher at Smyrna Elementary School, taught my sister, Hilda, in the fourth grade. The John Matthews Family were faithful members of First Methodist Church. In the 1940s they moved to Collier Drive, in the Forest Hills community, where John lived until his death in 2000.

Betty Matthews, who graduated from Campbell High School, received a degree from the University of Georgia. She married William Bennett, known as "Bill;" they live in Seattle, Washington.

Nancy Matthews graduated from The Westminster Schools in Atlanta and St. Mary's College in Raleigh, North Carolina. She also received a degree from the University of Georgia. Nancy was married to Jerry Musarra; they had two children: John Matthew, known as "Matt," and Amy.

"Matt" Musarra graduated from The Westminster Schools in Atlanta and the University of Georgia. He is employed with King and Spalding Law Firm in Atlanta.

Amy Musarra, who graduated from The Westminster Schools in Atlanta and the University of Georgia with a degree in art history, now works with Ainsworth Noah at Altanta Decorative Arts Center.

June Matthews married Earl Blackwell. She graduated from Agnes Scott College, in Decatur with honors.

Mary Matthews married Harold Scott, the son of a Methodist minister. She graduated from Agnes Scott College, in Decatur, with honors.

Eighteenth House

Mr. and **Mrs. Eugene Duncan**, known as "Gene," and their daughter, **Peggy**, resided here. Peggy was a member of the Smyrna High School Class of 1951. The Duncan Family were members of First Baptist Church.

Peggy Duncan married Lamar Dickson, the son of Mr. and Mrs. T. L. Dickson, who owned and operated Dickson Shopping Center, on South Cobb Drive. Peggy and Lamar had two children: Cindy and Cliff.

NOTE: Dickson Shopping Center, now owned and operated by Lamar's brother, John, faces Concord Road as well as South Cobb Drive

CHAPTER THREE

WEST SPRING STREET

West Spring Street was about one block long. It ran from King Street, across from Mr. Pressley's barn, to Atlanta Street. This is the area where the Market Village is today.

Nelms Lodge was immediately behind Smyrna Drug Store. When I was a child, I thought all the men in Smyrna belonged to the Lodge: in fact, I thought that was where men went on Saturday nights, for my dad was a Mason. Later on, my mother was a member of the Smyrna Chapter of the Order of the Eastern Star, which met in the Lodge.

Appreciation is extended to Sam Whitfield, a Past Worshipful Master of Nelms Lodge # 323 and Past Worthy Patron of the Smyrna Chapter of the Order of the Eastern Star. Sam has also held the offices of Senior Warden, Junior Warden, and Treasurer and has been active on the state level through the years. He loaned me *A Brief History of Nelms Lodge # 323*, from which the following information was obtained.

The Lodge was named in honor of Mr. John W. Nelms, a long-time Mason. He moved to Cobb County, near Smyrna, about 1886 and was affiliated with Kennesaw Lodge # *33*, in Marietta. Brother Nelms, together with other local Masons, then became desirous of establishing a lodge in Smyrna. On November 3, 1886, the Grand Lodge of the State of Georgia, located in Macon, granted Mr. John W. Nelms a charter and established a Masonic Lodge in Smyrna. Because Mr. John W. Nelms had so endeared himself to the Lodge, the local Masons named the Lodge for him.

In September 1887 the Lodge formed the first "Eastern Star Degree for the ladies entitled to receive (those) instructions." The sick and needy were, then as now, of primary concern to Nelms Lodge.

THE FIRST MASONIC HALL

In September 1888, the Masons approached the elders of Smyrna Presbyterian Church about building a schoolhouse with a room on the second floor for the Masonic Hall.

In 1889 the Masons paid Mr. Pace the sum of $12.50 for a lot that faced Atlanta Street, in front of what would become the new Lodge site. This location was between the Smyrna Cemetery and what is now First Baptist Church property. (West Spring Street did not exist at that time.) Construction was completed on the two-story structure in the fall of 1889, and the Masons held their first meeting in the new Lodge to install the officers in 1890.

According to the history of Nelms Lodge, records are sketchy from 1890 until 1923. However, Mr. Robert L. Baldwin, a lifetime resident of Smyrna and a member of Nelms Lodge since 1923, said that he attended school in this building, which remained in this location until it was destroyed by fire in March 1924. Lodge records were fortunately saved because they had been kept by the secretary at his home.

NOTE: My dad, Roy H. Wood, attended school in the Nelms Lodge building from about 1918 until 1923.

NOTE: The Smyrna District Public School constructed a new building on the north side of Church Street. Smyrna School opened for classes in 1925. Mr. J. T. Lowe was the principal. See *picture of the marker from the 1925 school building on the north side of Church Street.*

After the school was moved to its new location, the Lodge building was completely renovated, and a new street, which became West Spring Street, was graded in front of the building. Mr. Baldwin stated that an elephant is buried in front of what was the original Smyrna Fire Station #1 property. The elephant, which died during a carnival held at this location, could not be moved away from the area because there was no equipment available.

NOTE: Fire Station #1 was on the south side of West Spring Street next to the Masonic Lodge, about where the first townhouse in the Market Village is currently located.

THE SECOND MASONIC HALL

In April 1925, Nelms Lodge members began holding meetings in the newly renovated school building, located just north of the Smyrna Cemetery. The building occupied by Nelms Lodge in April 1925 had a history of its own. Before the Civil War, it was the Boys Military Academy; during the Civil War (from 1861) it was used as the first Confederate Officers' Training Headquarters, known as Camp Joseph E. Brown. The two-story Lodge building was also used by Smyrna Presbyterian Church in the 1870s and 1880s, and First Baptist Church was organized in this building in August 1884. In 1905 Smyrna Presbyterian Church, in receipt of $1,600.00, deeded the property to the Cobb County Board of Education.

Because records are sketchy, it is not known how much the Masons actually paid for the old school building. However, it is known that they spent between $4,000 and $5,000 for the acquisition and renovation. The Masons demolished the front section, which faced the cemetery, and refurbished that portion which was the first brick structure in Smyrna (1840).

Through those early years, the Lodge building was used for meetings of the following groups: the Smyrna City Council; the "Matrons' Club"; the Ku Klux Klan, at least one time, in October 1926; and, beginning in 1925, the Woodmen of the World, a social organization, having to do with insurance. The old Lodge building held many memories of my watching my dad as he would leave to attend meetings on Saturday nights.

THE THIRD MASONIC HALL

In 1954 the Nelms Lodge members voted to construct a new building on the site of the second Masonic Hall, on West Spring Street. The ground floor was rented to Hubert Colquitt, who moved Wayne's 5, 10, & 25 Cents store there, where it remained until 1958, when he moved Wayne's to Dickson Shopping Center. In April 1959 the United States Post Office rented the ground floor for use as the Smyrna Post Office, which remained until the new Post Office building was erected in 1969 at its current site on Windy Hill Road. See *Wayne's, South Cobb Drive* and *Concord Road.*

Mother was a member of the Smyrna Chapter of the Order of the Eastern Star, which was chartered by the Grand Chapter of the Georgia Order of the Eastern Star in 1950. (They met in the second Lodge building until the third one was constructed in 1954.) For many years she was very active, "going through the chairs" and holding the position of Worthy Matron. Her participation in the Eastern Star was very important to her. When Mother was installed as Worthy Matron, in the early 1970s, she asked my children, along with the sons of my sister, Hilda, to be a part of the ceremony. The dress that Mother wore for the occasion was lavender. Lillie made for our daughter, Marilyn, a white satin dress trimmed in lavender to match Mother's dress. Mother was very pretty that day!

Janet Brooks Brown shared that, in the late 1950s, the Masons sponsored and organized Rainbows, a Masonic Chapter for teenage girls, and DeMolay, a Masonic Chapter for teenage boys. These became some of the best chapters in Georgia. Masons and Eastern Star members were leaders of these groups, where adults and teenagers shared many happy times. These two groups in Smyrna disbanded in the 1980s due to lack of interest.

The third Nelms Lodge building was in use until the early part of the Twenty-first Century; it was located on part of the land that was purchased by the City of Smyrna in 1999 for the development of the Market Village.

SMYRNA WATER TANK
(60,000 gallon)
Constructed in 1927
Dismantled in 1984
Watercolor by and Courtesy of Clare Colquitt Curtis

THE FOURTH MASONIC HALL

The Masons built a new Masonic Hall near the triangle at Concord and Hurt roads. The Masons held their "Groundbreaking Ceremony" here September 23, 2001. Masons of Nelms Lodge conducted their first meeting in the building on December 8, 2001. Portable chairs were brought in for the Masons'116th Annual Communication and their election of officers. The officers were installed by Sam R.Whitfield, Grand Treasurer of the Grand Lodge of Georgia.

Following completion of the building and delivery of certificates of occupancy, the building was officially opened on April 27, 2002, at a dinner meeting, with home-cooked food provided by the ladies of Nelms Lodge. Many guests attended this very nice occasion for presenting Twenty-Five and Fifty-Year Aprons, Certificates, and Pins by C.E. Horne, the Grand Master of Georgia. The recipients of the Fifty-Year awards were Jack Diemer and Sam Whitfield.

Lillie and I felt privileged to be invited to both the groundbreaking and the official opening of the new Lodge. One of our friends, T. G. Rogers, who was a barber in Smyrna for fifty years, was also honored at this meeting, where Lillie and I were T.G.'s guests. Because T. G. had raised the money to purchase the new flagpole for the Lodge, the Masons dedicated the flagpole to him. The Masons are very proud of the new building, and those of us in the community are pleased to have it in this location. T. G. Rogers died in 2004.

THE WATER TANK

Smyrna's water came from several wells in various geographical locations within the City. Water was pumped from the wells into a large metal storage tank towering over the City. Since the City was dependent on wells for its water supply, the storage tank was essential. Bearing the name "City of Smyrna" in black letters on two sides, the tank was located between West Spring Street and First Baptist Church, near Nelms Lodge and the Smyrna Memorial Cemetery. The tank was in a good place for boys within the community to play. Some of them attempted to climb to the top; few succeeded. Because this was a dangerous practice, official measures were taken to discourage unauthorized access.

n the early 1950s the City of Smyrna became a member of the new Cobb/Marietta Water Authority that provided water to unincorporated Cobb County and the cities located within Cobb County. After more than fifty years this is still the water source for these governments. The Water Authority, drawing its water from the Chattahoochee River and Lake Allatoona, eliminated the need for wells and a water storage tank in the City of Smyrna. (The Smyrna Water Tank was constructed in1927 and dismantled in early 1984.) See *Quarles, Atlanta Street, from Marlowe's to Creatwood* and *Wyckoff, east side of Hughes Street.*

THE CANNERY

Next door to the Nelms Lodge was a building known as the **Cannery**. My mother always told me to be careful and not get too close to the equipment. I remember, as a small lad, walking to The Cannery and, standing around, watching the employees work. The food smelled so good! However, I don't ever remember eating anything there. The man who ran the Cannery was very nice to me.

In that era, people who grew fruits and vegetables would take their produce to The Cannery to be processed and canned. I am not sure, but I believe The United States Government provided an overseer and supplies (i.e. hot water, cans) which were needed to safely preserve the food. The people who utilized the Cannery contributed a portion of their food to the operator of The Cannery for distribution to people in need, for there were no food stamps in those days. (I have never studied this program, but I think the people furnishing the fruits and vegetables received the larger share.)

This program was phased out after the Great Depression. I am not sure when it ended, but I believe the Cannery was still operating when Pearl Harbor was bombed, December 7, 1941.

THE BLACKSMITH SHOP

Next door to the Cannery was a **blacksmith shop**, which was in a wooden building on property that had two or three big oak trees between it and the gristmill next door. I do not remember anyone in particular working at the blacksmith shop, but according to family information, Mr. Richard Brooks from Roswell Street was a blacksmith on West Spring Street in the 1930s—and maybe into the early 1940s. I do know that I could stand for hours, watching work being done. This was another place I had been told to keep my distance. Mother laid out rules for me to follow; and if I did not obey them, I would lose the privilege of moving around the neighborhood so freely.

The blacksmith would heat the coals until they were red hot. (It was fun to watch those coals turn red!) He would put the iron horseshoes into those hot coals. The horseshoes, turning red from the heat, were shaped to fit the horse's or mule's hoofs and then dipped into a barrel of cold water prior to being nailed onto the animal's hoofs.

One of the things that concerned me was that, when the blacksmith put the shoe on the horse, the horse would always shiver. I just knew the horse felt the nails going into his hoof! I remember thinking how awful it would be if someone were to nail my shoes onto my feet. After I expressed this thought to the blacksmith on one occasion, he told me that it would hurt the horse more to walk without the shoes on his hoofs and, therefore, the horse or mule had to have protection for his feet.

It seemed to me that there were always several mules to be shod. But still there were times when the blacksmith and his helper would not be busy. It was at these times that they would explain to me how the shoeing procedure worked. The heat would soften the iron, of which the horseshoes were made. While the iron was hot, it was pliable and would adjust to fit the horse's hoof. I also learned that it is an art to put the shoe on the horse's foot without its breaking off the horse's hoof. I gained respect for the blacksmith, who really had to know how to do this "hot" job. I remember not feeling as sorry for the horses after I learned the procedure.

THE GRISTMILL

Another place that was intriguing to me was **Stamper's Gristmill**, which was next door to the blacksmith shop. The miller had a huge grindstone fueled in part by water, in addition to electric power. The corn was fed to the grindstone via a big belt that would carry it into the grinding area. After the corn was ground into meal, it would fall into large bins, from which it was bagged for selling.

I knew Mr. Stamper and spent much time watching the meal being ground. He would talk to me about the operation of the mill. I remember his letting me watch as long as I wanted to, but he would always be cautioning me as to where to stand so that I would not get too close to the working area. I especially liked to watch that big stone wheel turn and crush that corn. I am not sure when the mill was closed, but it seems to me that it may have been gone by the time I started to high school.

Appreciation is extended to Dr. and Mrs. Robert Mainor for the following information regarding his medical practice, and their family.

DR. ROBERT MAINOR

Dr. Robert Mainor had his medical office on the corner where the gristmill had been.

Dr. Robert Mainor, who grew up in Macon, was stationed at Fort Benning in Columbus. Having been discharged from the United States Army, he and his wife, the former Alma Allen of Waverly Hall, came to Smyrna in 1953. They had two children: Janet and Robert, Jr. Dr. Mainor was a long-time member of the Smyrna Lions Club, and was still a member when the club disbanded June 1, 2000. The Mainors are members of First Methodist Church. See *Lions Club membership list, south side of Sunset Avenue.*

In World War II Robert, Sr., a First Lieutenant with the Seventh Armored Infantry, served during the Ardennes Campaign—known as the Battle of the Bulge. His citations included European Theater of Operation (ETO) Ribbon, three Battle stars, Bronze Star with Oak Leaf Cluster, and the Purple Heart with Oak Leaf Cluster.

After the War he attended The Medical College of Georgia and received his Medical Doctorate degree in 1951. He interned at Madigan Army Hospital in Tacoma, Washington, and Fort Benning (one year) before coming to Smyrna.

Dr. Mainor was an active staff member of Kennestone Hospital for over forty years. He was President of the Cobb County Medical Society in 1965, President of the Georgia Academy of Family Practice in 1967, and a member of the American Board of Family Practice.

Robert Mainor, Jr., . married Donna Chastain; they had two daughters: Jennifer, known as "Jennie," and Katie. Robert, with a Masters degree in Physical Education, currently teaches at Belmont Hills School. He and Donna are divorced.

Janet Mainor, a psychologist, is the Administrative Director of The Link Counseling Center, a non-profit organization.

When Dr. Mainor closed his practice, toward the end of the Twentieth Century, he donated his x-ray machine to the Smyrna Museum and other medical equipment to The Cobb County Health Department.

"Dr. Charles Garland came to Smyrna in the early 1950s and began his practice with Dr. Mitchell on Atlanta Street," so says Dr. Mainor.

NOTE: In the days of my youth, there were no houses on the north side of West Spring Street, only the back yards of the residents of Bank Street. Later on, Smyrna Taxi had a small building located near a parking lot, used by downtown shoppers, located to the rear of the Corner Grill, which faced Atlanta Street.

SPRING STREET
North Side

Appreciation is extended to Joann McDowell for the information she furnished about her relatives, the Robinson and Pinson families, many of whom lived on Spring Street for more than a century; to Jane Rutledge Yausi for her help with the Rutledge Family information; W.F. Osburn, who grew up on Spring Street in the early years of the Twentieth Century; Barbara Lesley Burson, who moved to Spring Street in the mid 1940s; Ruby Bowles, regarding her family on Spring Street, where she grew up and still lives; Nellie Poss Lacy McTyre, for information about the Poss Family; Evelyn King Jenkins, for information on the King Family; to Linda Whelchel Bennett, for information regarding the Lacy family; and to Howard Gunn, a descendent of the Simpson Family, "Land Barons," on Spring Road from the middle of the Nineteenth Century until the Great Depression years.

G.B.'S PLACE

G.B.'s Place, an eating establishment, was on the north side of Spring Street in a small painted brick building between Atlanta Street and the railroad and across Spring Street from the Depot. G.B. Williams owned and operated this café, where he sold hamburgers, hot dogs, and other short order foods, i.e. soup and chili. He had a big supply of Moon Pies and other packaged items. His drink supply included R.C. Colas, Coca-Colas, Orange Crush, and other popular drinks of the day. G.B.'s

G. B's Place Circa 1940s Picture Courtesy of Chad Williams

G.B. Williams inside G.B.'s Place
Circa mid-1940s
Picture Courtesy of Chad Williams

"Shorty" Black standing in front of G.B.'s Place
Photo Courtesy of Smyrna Museum
Circa 1940s

place offered an environment for good conversation and association. It appeared to me that almost everyone in town was a frequent customer.

I worked at G.B.'s Place from about age thirteen to sixteen and, by doing so, created some of my best memories. I enjoyed getting to know people who came into the café. (For many years I dreamed of having my own restaurant, but the closest I ever got was short order cooking for Lillie and my children, who always made me feel so important. Only in my upper years did I learn that they did not want to cook; therefore, they complimented me.)

Leonard Crider, known as "Critter," managed G.B.'s Place. Though G.B. was there often, he was also involved with his other enterprises: supervising the building of houses, buying and selling livestock, and renting properties. He built several houses on Powder Springs Street, including the one in which he lived, and he also built his house on Hurt Road. See *south side of Powder Springs Street* and *north side of Bank Street.*

Many young guys in Smyrna worked for G.B. over the years. Two of the first people that I recall are Joe Barnes and Raymond Motter, both long-time employees. Raymond worked for G.B. until the beginning of World War II, when he joined the United States Marine Corps.

I also worked for G.B., after he bought a farm on Hurt Road, by helping him string a barbed wire fence around the farm and the lake he had developed and stocked for fishing, which later became known as G.B.'s Lake. He also built a barn and stables, where he boarded horses. G.B. always had plenty of work.

G.B. was good to me. I remember that, after I had finished college and my "stint" in the United States Army and had come home to live, I was working in Atlanta and needed transportation. G.B. took me to Anderson Chevrolet, in Marietta, to meet the sales manager, Gilbert Johnson; thus G.B. helped me purchase an automobile. Because of G.B.'s involvement, I am positive that I got a better deal on that car. (By the way, it was a 1956 Bel Air Chevrolet and such a "beauty"!) G.B was like that, for it was his nature to become involved with people and help them when he could. In a lifetime most people do not see a person like him, the unique G.B.!

The following story, told by G.B.'s grandson, Chad Williams, entails a well-known event that many people in Smyrna could tell about.

"Mayor Hoot Gibson and G.B. always butted heads. Granddad said, 'Me and Hoot never did gee haw much.'

"Granddad said that 'Ole' Hoot would come in the café and ask, 'You going to be for me this time, G.B.?'

"G.B. replied, 'No more than I was the last time you ran.'

"Granddad told this: 'at night, after the café closed, Hoot would have the curb in front of the café painted yellow so my café customers could not park there. He claimed the traffic was getting quite heavy at the main intersection.'

"The next morning G.B. would go around to Fouts Brothers Service Station and get the Fouts' tar buckets, the ones from which they painted tires; then he would paint that curb just as black as it could be. Hoot would stand up there and just watch.

"G.B. said, 'They would paint it back yellow before morning, and that is what made me so mad. I would go there in the morning, and that yellow curb would put my eyes out.'

"C. J. Fouts will laugh about that today and tell you, 'G.B. would come running around the corner just a *diggin' it and huntin'* for that tar bucket.' "

"Pete" Wood and **Leonard Crider** known as "Critter"
In G.B.'s Place
Circa 1946

The **W.O. Robinson, Sr.** Homeplace-Site of Ivy Springs Townhomes from the late 1990s
Circa late 1880s: Picture Courtesy of Joann McDowell

G. B. WILLIAMS
1917-2002

Chad Williams, G.B. Williams' grandson, provided the following family and historical Information.

"G.B. Williams, whose birthday was September 8, 1917, was the youngest of ten children born to Green Berry Williams and Genie Young Williams in the small northwest Cherokee County community called Salacoa. His family was 'dirt poor,' surviving as subsistence farmers. In the mountains the family became so monetarily desperate that G.B.'s father made moonshine for a few years.

"In 1922 G.B. and his family moved to Cobb County and bought their first home, in Marietta. Unfortunately, because of an unpaid debt by the previous owner, they 'lost' the house.

"G.B. had often dreamed of owning his own business; but when the Great Depression hit, he knew that would be out of the question, at least at that time.

"Because of having to work and help the family make a living, G.B. was only able to go to school through the third grade, with just basic reading, writing, and arithmetic. Even though the obstacles seemed endless, G. B. bought his first restaurant in 1936 for $400.00. The little building between Atlanta Street and the railroad tracks seemed to be a poor location; besides, in the middle of the Depression people could not afford to feed their children, much less go out to eat.

"In the following years, things improved. Even though World War II was brewing, money began to circulate. The War brought jobs; but, with many of the men serving in the military, that left women for the first time to go out of the home to work. Many of those women worked at Bell Aircraft Corporation (known locally as The Bell Bomber Plant), where those who were riveters were called 'Rosies'; and, after a long day at work, the women would stop by the restaurant and buy food to take home. This revolutionized the restaurant industry.

"During the War, people needed places to live, and many could not afford to own a place of their own. G.B. began buying and building homes, which he would rent out. Eventually he had ten to fifteen homes that he kept rented. This way he had income from sources other than the restaurant.

"Smyrna was a small town, but the opening of Bell Aircraft Corporation and other new businesses in the area evoked a need for a local bank. To meet this need, G.B. and a group of other businessmen invested money to organize the Bank of Smyrna, which opened its doors in 1946.

"In 1949, for $5,000, G.B. bought a hundred acres of land on Hurt Road. This was the same land that he had worked as a young man, plowing and making a dollar per day. With this purchase he had acquired the one thing he most wanted: a large tract of land. In 1953 G.B. developed a fifty-acre lake, where one of his cattle pastures had previously been located, and a smaller five-acre pond. In 1956, he had the lake fully stocked with several types of fish and opened it for public fishing at a dollar per day, per person." See *Williams, south side of Powder Springs Street.*

G.B. WILLIAMS PARK

On April 24, 2004, the City of Smyrna dedicated G.B. Williams Park, on Roswell Street in Smyrna, near the location where G. B. operated his restaurant for more than thirty-five years. This park will be a lasting memorial to a man that made a positive difference to both the City of Smyrna and the surrounding areas. G.B. Williams died in the summer of 2002.

First House

Mr. and **Mrs. Ollie Harris** lived in the first house, a large white one with a screened porch, on the north side of Spring Street, across the railroad. They had two daughters: **Maggie** and **Alice**. Mrs. Harris, whose given name was Bess, hailed from South Carolina. According to family information, Mr. Harris at one time ran the Smyrna Depot.

NOTE: When I was growing up, apparently Mr. Harris must have been deceased, for I only remember Mrs. Harris' living there. At that time **Scott Edwards, Sr.**, lived there also. I seem to remember that he and Mrs. Harris were related: it appears that he may have been married to one of her daughters, Maggie. I also remember that the Coker Family that lived on the south side of Spring Street was related to them. See *Coker, south side of Spring Street.*

Second House

Mr. and **Mrs. William Jasper Osburn,** known as "W.J.," moved to this house sometime prior to November 1, 1925, because their oldest child, **"W.F". Osburn**, was born here that day. Their daughter, **Janie Bell,** was born here also. Mrs. W.J. Osburn was the former Flora Lee Dobbs of Cherokee County. William Jasper Osburn, known as "W.J.," whose family has been in Cobb County from the 1800s, was born in Cobb County in 1874. The Osburns sold this house to Mr. Green, who lived on Love Street, and the Osburns moved to Roswell Road (now Windy Hill Road). When the United States Government purchased much property north of Smyrna, the Osburns moved to Walker Street, where they lived for about four years before selling that house to the Newman Wallace Family. The Osburns then moved to Bank Street, to the former Dunton house. See *Osburn, south side of Spring Street* and *Duntons, on the north side of Bank Street.*

NOTE: The Mr. Green mentioned above was probably Dr. G.C. Green. The property bought by the United States Government, which began at the end of North Matthews and Roswell streets, encompassed the area where Fox Creek and Legacy golf courses and Dobbins Air Force Base are now located; it extended northward to Lockheed Aircraft Corporation's present location.

W.F. Osburn—see *W.F. Osburn Family below.*

Janie Bell Osburn married Thomas William Oglesby. They had one son, Thomas William Oglesby, Jr. Janie Bell Oglesby is deceased.

Mr. W.J. Osburn, who made venetian blinds, also had a weather stripping business. After W.J. died, one of his brothers, Claude Osburn, continued to run the businesses.

Mrs. Bluford Osburn, W.J. Osburn's mother, after she was widowed, lived here with W.J. and his family. In addition to W.J., she had three other sons, Claude, Ed, and "Doc," and at least three daughters, "Teen", Laura, and another one, who was the mother of Maude Turner. Mrs. Osburn's husband, Bluford, fought in the Civil War. See *Osburn* and *Cochran, south side of Spring Street,* and *Cochrans, Spring Road, The Country Road.*

"Teen" Osburn Cochran was the mother of Benjamin Bluford Cochran, known as "B.B.," and "Jack," who was named after his grandfather. See *Cochran, east side of Elizabeth Street.*

Laura Osburn married Mr. Conn.

Claude T. Osburn, see *Osburn, south side of Spring Street.*

The W.F. Osburn Family

W.F. Osburn married Carrie Lee from Dallas. They had three children: **W.F. Jr.**, **Janice Lee**, and **Vickie Lynn**. W.F. and Carrie Osburn are currently living in Dallas.

W.F., having entered the United States Navy on October 4, 1942, served during World War II. After the war, he served in the United States Naval Reserves until he was called for active duty in 1951, during the Korean Conflict. After being discharged in 1953, he remained in the Naval Reserves until 1966, when he retired. W.F. worked at Georgia Power's Plant Atkinson.

W.F. Osburn, Jr., known as "Frank," lives in Woodbridge, Virginia. He had two sons: Nathan and Chris. Nathan is deceased.

Janice Lee Osburn, known as "Jan," is married to Ray Mashburn; they live in Roopville. They had two sons, Russell and Zack, and a granddaughter.

Vickie Lynn Osburn married Mickey Paris. They had two daughters, Kim and Carla, and four grandchildren (including twin boys). Vickie and Mickey live in Dallas.

NOTE: According to Osburn Family information, the Osburns were some of the original settlers in Smyrna.

Mrs. Ada Camp

Mrs. Ada Camp lived in this house for a while after the Osburns moved. Madge Dobbs Jackson remembers they had lots of children.

Mr. and Mrs. Ben Waters

Mr. and **Mrs. Ben Waters** and their family moved to this house in 1951. They had three children: **James**, **B.J.**, and **Marie**. Mrs. Waters' daughter by a previous marriage, **Margaret Wheeler**, also lived here.

Ben Waters, now 89 years old, lives on Lee Street.

Margaret Wheeler married Calvin Cowart, who grew up on Roswell Street. They had two sons: Dwayne and Darrell, who live in Cobb County. Margaret and Calvin are deceased. See *Cowart, west side of Roswell Street.*

James Waters married Barbara from Marietta. They had no children.

Marie Waters married Larry Cox; they had two daughters, Paula and Lori, and one grandson.

B.J. Waters was married and had one daughter, Debra. He remarried and had twin sons: Christopher and Kenneth. B. J. Lives in Haralson County.

NOTE: The Waters Family sold the property where their house was located to Southern Bell Telephone Company, still there but is now known as BellSouth.

NOTE: The west entrance into Mimosa Circle was just past the Waters House.

In the mid 1940s, four new homes were built on the north side of Spring Street. The first one was just past the Waters House. Mimosa Circle was later developed, the house now stands on the northeast corner between Mimosa Circle and the Hamby House. The other three were built between the Hamby and Bowles houses.

Third House

Nolan Medley, known as "Polo," was the first resident of this house. His mother, Mrs. Burton, lived across the street. See *Burton, south side of Spring Street.*

Ruby and **Virginia Carmichael**

Later **Mrs. Ruby Carmichael** and her daughter, **Virginia**, moved from Dunn Street, to this house. From here they moved to Mimosa Circle. See *Mimosa Circle.*

Fourth House

Mr. Thomas Lee Hamby, known as "Tommy Lee," built this large, dark red brick structure with a circular porch in 1902. It was among the nicest houses in Smyrna during the days of my youth. Thomas Lee married Mae Love; they had two daughters: **Ruby Lee** and **Emmaline**, who grew up in this house, they were in my parents' generation. Mr. Thomas Lee Hamby was a railroad engineer. He and his family were active members of First Methodist Church. Thomas Lee Hamby was born October 5, 1864, and died in June of 1943. His wife, Mae Love Hamby was born May 20, 1873, and died August 20, 1939.

Thomas Lee Hamby was the first child of Tandy Kay Hamby, and his wife, the former Mary Ann Moore, known as "Mollie." They had ten children: Thomas Lee Hamby, Benager Hamby, Eugenia Caroline, Adrian Dearburg, Eula Amanda, Isaac Be-Bee Hamby, Tandy Kay Hamby, Jr., Joseph Elijah Hamby, Benjamin Hill Hamby and Olive. See *Hamby, south side of Love Street, south side of Concord Road, north side of Concord Road, and east side of Roswell Street.*

NOTE: The Genealogical information on the Thomas Lee Hamby Family was furnished by Marcellus and Betty Hamby, from their history of the Hamby families in and around Smyrna.

Ruby Hamby married Loyd Carmichael. They had one daughter, Virginia. In the days of my youth, Mrs. Carmichael (whose husband was deceased) and Virginia lived in this house. Mrs. Carmichael worked at the Bill Stewart Insurance and Real Estate Agency. According to local "lore," Winston Burger, Vice President of the Bank of Smyrna, found "Bill" in his office, where he died, one morning before Mrs. Ruby arrived for work. Afterwards she worked for the Bank of Smyrna, on Atlanta Street, where she was an "icon." "Mrs. Ruby" and Virginia were also well known in First Methodist Church, where they were faithful members, and long-time members of the Smyrna Social Club, founded in 1908. It is believed that Mrs. Carmichael and Virginia, moved from this house, to Dunn Street, where they lived for several years. See *Osborn, Atlanta Street, from Marlowe's to Creatwood.*

According to family information, Loyd Carmichael's parents were J.H. and Emma (Stanback) Carmichael. Loyd was a brother of Mrs. D.C. Osborn, on Atlanta Street, and of John Vincent Carmichael. John Vincent and his wife, the former Emma Mae Nolan, were the parents of Jimmy Carmichael, President of the Bell Bomber Plant, in Marietta, during World War II. John Vincent owned and operated Carmichael's Store on Log Cabin Drive, south of the Oakdale community.

NOTE: Former residents of the Oakdale community remember that Mrs. J.H. (Emma Stanback) Carmichael lost her eye sight completely before she died at age 100.

John Collier
Smyrna City Councilman
1951-1955

Emmaline Hamby married John Stratton Collier, a cousin of Mr. F.M. Collier, who lived on Atlanta Street. John Collier served on the Smyrna City Council, 1951-1955.

According to family information, Emmaline, as a realtor, helped develop Mimosa Circle, where she and John were residents at the time of her death.

NOTE: Several long-time residents of Spring Street remember Mrs. Ruby Carmichael, in early 1946, renting out rooms while she still lived in her family home, the Hamby House.

The Charles Rumsey Family
Kay
"English War Bride"

Charles and **Kay Rumsey** and their small daughter, **Sandra**, (who was born in England) rented a room from Mrs. Carmichael. Everyone shared the kitchen and bath. The Rumseys lived there for several months before moving upstairs to the apartment. Two years later, in June 1948, their daughter, **Rosalind**, was born. After the Gresh Family bought this house, the Rumseys continued to reside in the upstairs apartment. They had lived here twelve years when, in 1958, they bought a house on Linwood Court, off Powder Springs Street.

Charles Rumsey, from Athens, was stationed with the United States Army in England during World War II. While there, he met and married Kay Kettle of Stoke-on-Trent, England. Kay was working in the medical arena when they met and married.

When the family came to the United States, they lived with Charles' family in Athens for a short time before moving to Smyrna. Mr. Rumsey worked at Western Electric, which he rode the bus to and from—for they did not have a car until much later.

Sandra Rumsey, married Charles Beckett of the Oakdale community. They had five children, Todd, Leighann, Sharon, Steven, and Amy, and twelve grandchildren.

Rosalind Rumsey married Wilson Brock. They had one son, Scott, who grew up in Green Acres subdivision. After Rosalind and Wilson started dating, they learned that their dads had attended school together in Athens. Both dads had been riding the Greyhound bus to and from work for years, never knowing their children were dating.

Sandra shared her memories of her young years: "I would go to the Jonquil Theatre and stay all day—using a Capitola token from a cloth bag of flour as a ticket. I remember a Black man who would drive his green wagon with wooden wheels, pulled by a mule up Spring Street, in the late 1940s or early 1950s, to town. I also remember walking to a creek beyond Smyrna Elementary School, catching crawfish, and putting them into a glass jar.

"Dr. Hugh Colquitt delivered my sister, Rosalind, in 1948. Later after Dr. Robert Mainor began his practice in Smyrna, he made house calls. Once when my sister, Rosalind was sick, Mother called him to see Rosalind. When the doctor arrived, he did not immediately come up to see Rosalind. Mother called down to Dr. Mainor, 'What do you mean standing there, picking muscadines when my child is up here sick!'

"I remember the upstairs as having a screened back porch. In the summer my mother would put the kitchen table out there so that our family could have our meals in a cool place among the trees—before air conditioning."

The Rumseys were members of First Methodist Church until the founding of the Christian Church, on Concord Road, which they joined. Mr. Rumsey had been raised in a Christian Church in Athens.

NOTE: After Charles, their dad, had died, Sandra and Rosalind, while going through his belongings, found a telegram he had sent to his dad, which read, "I got married. Send money." Charles had been sending his money home to his parents for safekeeping. (This was a common practice with people in the United States Military at that time.)

The Walter Gresh Family

Mr. and **Mrs. Walter Gresh, Sr.** bought this house in 1948 from Emmaline Hamby Collier. Mrs. Gresh was the former Margaret Reinoehl. Mr. and Mrs. Gresh, from Pennsylvania, had one son, Walter Gresh, Jr., known as "Wally." Mr. Walter Gresh, Sr., worked for the United States Government.

<u>"Wally" Gresh</u> married a daughter of Mr. and Mrs. S.A. White of Marietta.

Several people in the neighborhood told Janet Brown that the Greshes had an arbor of muscadine vines behind their house, to which Mrs. Gresh encouraged neighbors and others to "help themselves." The fruit made delicious jelly.

Larry and **Jill Jones**

Larry and **Jill Jones**, who renovated this house in the early part of the Twenty-first Century, live here with their young son, **Augustus Levi**, known as "Gus."

<u>Fifth House</u>

Becky
"English War Bride"

Marvin and **Becky Long** lived in this house, which was built after World War II. They had no children. Marvin, an "American Indian," and Becky, an "English war bride," married while Marvin was serving in the United States Military during World War II. They moved from here to Tennessee, where Marvin had grown up.

Mr. and **Mrs. "Red" McMillan**

Mr. and **Mrs.** "**Red**" **McMillan** moved here in 1947. She was the former Nell Worley. They had three children: **Dorothy Jean**, **Charles**, and **Larry**.

<u>Dorothy Jean McMillan</u> graduated from Smyrna High School in 1944. She married Harry Peacock; they had three children: Stephen, known as Steve, Barbara, and Linda. The Peacock Family are living in Woodstock. See *McMillan, south side of Church Street.*

<u>Charles McMillan</u> graduated from Smyrna High School in 1947 and entered North Georgia College, in Dahlonega. Afterwards, Charles received a degree from Mercer University. Then he entered Southeastern Seminary in Wake Forest, North Carolina. He married Greta Hensley and they had three children. See *Hensley, west side of Roswell Street* and *McMillan, south side of Church Street.*

<u>Larry McMillan</u>. See *Goodwin, ninth house, west side of Roswell Street.*

<u>Sixth House</u>

In the 1950s, after her husband, Paul had died, **Mrs. Ober Hensley** moved from her home on the west side of Roswell Street, where they had raised their family, to this house. At that time, Mrs. Hensley's youngest son, **Sam**, was a student at Georgia Institute of Technology.

Seventh House

Mr. and **Mrs**. **Charles T. Lesley** moved from Atlanta to this house in 1946. Mrs. Lesl the former Mary Parks, along with her husband, was originally from South Carolina. They had tv children: **Barbara Ann** and **Charles H**., known as "Butch."

The Lesleys had previously lived on 14th Street in Atlanta, in a house they rented from a la whose husband was in the United States Military. After the soldier's return, the Lesleys had to fi another place to live. Though there was a shortage of housing, they bought this house in Smyr Barbara shared, "This house had two bedrooms, one of which the children shared. Can you imagin Later they added on to the back of the house. Here Mr. and Mrs. Lesley lived until their deaths.

Mr. Lesley worked for Walthour and Hood Sporting Goods in Atlanta. He later owned appliance store before becoming a manufacturing representative for kitchen cabinets; he traveled ofte

After her children were grown, Mary Lesley became employed at Allstate Insuran Company, where she worked until her death.

Barbara Lesley married James Burson; they had three daughters, Leslie Ann, Leigh Ann, a Laurie Ann, and two grandchildren. Barbara Ann and James are graduates of Campbell High School.

James was the son of Thomas Ezekiel Burson and the former Ruth Morris. He had one sist Ann, who married Charles Pittard of Marietta. See *Burson, Forest Hills.*

Charles Lesley., known as "Butch,"a graduate of Campbell High School, married Pau Norton, who also graduated from Campbell. They had three sons. See *Norton, North Cooper La Road.*

Eighth House

Bea and **Mitt Parsons** lived in this house.

NOTE: Walker Court is between the eighth house and the Bowles.

Ninth House

William Brown Bowles, known as "Will," and **Fannie Kate Black Bowles**, known "Frances," and "Kate," purchased this house, which is the first house on Spring Street past Walk Court, directly across from Elizabeth Street. There they lived with their children: **Frances Lee**, know as "Teen," **Billy Martin** and **Ruby Lois**. They also had two children that died.

"Teen" and Ruby Bowles never married.

Billy Bowles married Barbara Simpson; they had four children. Billy also adopted Barbara two children from a previous marriage.

"Will" and "Frances" Bowles married during a 1920 ceremony performed by Reverer George Crowe while they were sitting in a buggy in his yard (in Cobb County). They came to Smyr in 1932 and lived in several rental houses until 1946. They bought, from Rachel Simpson, a house c Foster Street which they sold to Howard Barfield, who still lives there with his daughter, Linda.

According to information from the Bowles Family; in 1946 Mr. Bowles bought a thi house, this one on Spring Street, from Earl Medford Real Estate Agency, in Marietta. (A lady who last name was Stephens and who married a man with the last name of Lyles built this house in the m 1800s, when she was eighteen years old. The windows have wooden pegs in them. Mrs. Lyles died 1933 at the age of ninety-eight.)

Robert Day, who ran the car lot in Smyrna, also lived in this house at one time and put the as pipes into the house so that it would be ready when the gas lines were run. Mr. and Mrs. Bowles nally received gas service in 1950.

Still in the house are non-functioning electric meters, the readings from which, in years long ast, the family mailed to the power company. Functioning meters are now outside the house.

Ruby Bowles remembers that there was no sewerage system, at least on Spring Street, until e 1950s: "My family had two outside toilets. I remember my sister's asking one winter, 'Don't you ink we're lucky to have two toilets?'

"My reply was, 'I'll talk to you about it in August, when I thaw out.'

"When the Bowles Family first moved to this house, water was pumped from the branch that ame from below the Gibsons, across Walker Street, and onto Spring Street, at the bottom of the hill rom the Bowles' home. A water line was built in the early 1950s.

"Mr. Claude Osburn had the only telephone in the neighborhood for a long time, and veryone used it. Mr. Osburn owned a lot of property in the area: on Foster, Elizabeth, and Spring treets," Ruby further commented.

Ruby also remembers her dad as a smart man. "At one time he worked at Mr. Tribble's Feed nd Seed Store and would have the customer's total bill added in his head by the time the customer ad finished shopping."

When my dad was a Smyrna City Councilman, "Will" worked for the City of Smyrna as ead of the Sanitation Department and, before that, for the State of Georgia when Herman Talmadge vas governor. "Will" Bowles is a good man," my dad always said.

As a kid, I, along with many other students remember Mr. Will Bowles would pick up food craps at the Smyrna School Lunchroom, to feed his pigs. *Recycling!*

Mr. and Mrs. "Will" Bowles were members of Spring Street Baptist Church. Their children vere grown when I was in high school.

William Brown Bowles' parents, Bartlett N. Bowles and Eliza Charlotte Stephens Bowles vere pioneers in the Sardis community. Bartlett was originally from North Carolina; Eliza Charlotte tephens Bowles, a teacher, hailed from Connecticut. They had four children: "Will," Eugene Chester, /ernon Lee, and Edna.

Eugene Chester Bowles, known as "Gene," lived with "Will" and Fannie Kate until his leath. "Gene" had worked as a ship builder in St. Simons during World War II.

Vernon Lee Bowles
Casualty of War
World War I

Vernon Lee Bowles, another brother of "Will," died during World War I.

Edna Bowles married James Alexander Hyde, known as "Jim." (He was a cousin of J.C. Iyde, who was the last large landowner near the Chattahoochee River in southeast Cobb County.)

After William Brown Bowles' mother "Frances Kate" died, his dad, Bartlett remarried and ad five additional children: Jim, John, Fonnie, Emma, and Nan.

Jim and John Bowles lived in Atlanta's Riverside community.

Fonnie Bowles was the father of Lula Bird, see *east side of Matthews Street.*

Emma Bowles married Newt Haney, they lived on Atlanta Road in the Oakdale community

Nan Bowles married a Mitchell.

NOTE: Janet Brooks Brown asked Ruby Bowles how her grandmother got here fro Connecticut. She was told that Eliza Charlotte Stephens' daddy's brother, Robert Roy Stephens, professional gambler, won property in a gambling game. The property he won is the area of Sar Cemetery, Sardis Church, and Sardis School (now closed), as well as other land located across fro their home, near Sardis Church.

Fannie Kate Black Bowles' Parents

The parents of Mrs. Fannie Kate Bowles were Andrew Jackson Black and Frances Dickers Black. They had two children: Fannie Kate and Martin Black. Martin always lived with "Will" a Fannie Kate Bowles.

Andrew Jackson Black had a brother, Casson Black. His children, cousins of Fannie Ka Bowles, are as follows: Elsie Mae Black (Spinks); Ada Black (Frisbee Stephens); Reuben Black; To Black; Claude Black; Daniel Black, who lived in Marietta; and Carrie Lou Black (Neary). See *we side of Roswell Street* and *north side of Walker streets.*

Tenth House

Mr. and **Mrs**. **Ralph Lewis** resided in this house. They had two children who were old than I. Their house, with a bird bath and many large trees in the front yard, was located betwe Walker Court and Wright Street. Everything was always neat and in order, including their paper bi Ralph was the son of Mr. and Mrs. Glenn Lewis.

Mrs. Lewis was always nice to me when I delivered her papers. I did not see her husba very much, as he worked irregular hours for the railroad.

Eleventh House

Mr. and **Mrs**. **W.A. Blan** lived on the northwest corner of Spring and Wright streets. Th had two children: **Louise** and **Jack**. Mr. Blan was an insurance agent who ran a debit route by car. knew him because he would often go to G.B.'s Place. Mrs. Blan was the former Mattie Denson.

Louise Blan married James Huddleston. They still live in Smyrna, on North Cooper La Road. Mr. Huddleston, a minister, preached for many years at a church that was located at the end North Cooper Lake Road near the former railroad (now the Silver Comet Trail). He had a broth named Thomas Huddleston. I think James is now retired from preaching. See *Huddleston, Wrig Street.*

Jack Blan served in the United States Navy during World War II. Later on, he owned ar operated a sawmill in the Smyrna area.

Twelfth House

Mr. and **Mrs**. **Larkin Simpson** were residents on the northeast corner of Spring and Wrig streets. They had four children: **Florence**, **Henry**, **Mary**, and **Margie**. The Simpsons were members Spring Street Baptist Church prior to moving their membership to Second Baptist Church, on Atlan Street.

Mr. Larkin Simpson was a member of the Simpson Family who owned much acreage on pring Road from the early 1800s into the early part of the Twentieth Century. See *north* and *south ides of Spring Road* and *east side of Matthews Street.*

<u>Thirteenth House</u>

Mr. and **Mrs**. **Leonard Rutledge** lived here. They had three daughters: **Barbara Ann**, **Mary Jane**, and **Shirley Elizabeth**, known as "Betty."

<u>Barbara Ann Rutledge</u> married Howard Witt from Austell. They had two children: Terri ynn and Denise.

Terri Lynn married Louis Courette; they had a daughter, Chloe.

Denise married Clifton Webb; they had two children: Jeremy and Lindsey.

<u>Shirley Elizabeth Rutledge</u>, known as "Betty," married Lanier Ledford; they had two hildren: Malinda and Kim. Betty later married Ray Anderson.

Malinda Ledford married Rodney Brown of Paulding County. They had three children: ason, Robbie, and Eric.

Kim Ledford married Jeff Arthur; they had two children: Justin and Christian.

<u>Mary Jane Rutledge</u> married Steve Law; they had one son, Christian. Jane is now married to Nick Yausi.

Christian Law married Lauranda Greenway, who had a son, Taylor Proctor, from a previous narriage. Christian and Lauranda had a daughter, Calea.

Leonard Rutledge worked in downtown Atlanta at Muse's, advertised as George Muse Clothing and located at the intersection of Peachtree, Walton, and Broad streets. It was a very upscale tore that catered to the more distinguished gentlemen of that era. Mr. Rutledge, who was always well lressed, was a deacon at First Baptist Church.

Leonard's family came to Cobb County in 1920, or maybe earlier. According to family nformation, Leonard's father, John Toliver Rutledge, who came from DeKalb County, bought a farm hat encompassed the area where Dickson Shopping Center is currently located, near the southwest ntersection of South Cobb Drive and Concord Road.

NOTE: South Cobb Drive was not a road at the time Mr. Rutledge owned the above property. t was built during World War II as an access road to the Bell Bomber Plant.

On Spring Street, near the feed store, John Toliver Rutledge also owned a dwelling, which he used as a boarding house. Additionally, he owned land around what is now G.B.'s Lake, on Hurt Road; and, according to family information, he owned on Hawthorne Avenue some land which he donated for the New Smyrna Cemetery. See *Tribble's Feed Store, south side of Spring Street.*

Leonard Rutledge had three sisters: Lillian, known as "Tee," who married Mr. O'Kelly; Allene Rutledge, who never married; and Nellie Mae Rutledge, who worked for the FBI in Washington for a long time, retired from AT&T, and never married.

Mrs. Leonard Rutledge, the former Stella Knapp, was born in Nebraska but spent her hildhood in Michigan. Her daughter, Jane, shares how Stella and Leonard met while living in separate oarding houses across the street from each other in Fulton County. Stella would not date Leonard at first but did allow him to walk to church with her for months before she agreed to date him. Prior her marriage, Stella was a nurse's aide at Crawford Long Hospital in Atlanta.

After their marriage, Stella and Leonard lived in a garage apartment on Mr. Rutledg mother's property near the corner of what is now known as Concord Road and South Cobb Drive. 1935 they moved to the Spring Street house.

Stella, a short lady with red hair, was a Sunday School teacher at First Baptist Church. La she became the first paid Director of First Baptist Church Kindergarten, a position she held from time the kindergarten began, in 1953, until she retired, in 1974.

The Williams Family

Dorothy Williams and her family lived in a house in the vicinity near the Rutledge Famil could not establish the house in which the Williams may have lived. Dorothy married Phagan Durha who lived on the south side of Spring Street. See *Durham, south side of Spring Street* and *Willia north side of Love Street.*

Fourteenth House

Mr. and **Mrs. O.L. Pinson, Sr.**, lived in this house. They had two children: **O.L., Jr.**, a **Ruby**, who were in my parents' generation. Mrs. Pinson, the former Annie Mae Robinson, the fi child of Georgia Alice Cannon Robinson and William Oliver Robinson, Sr., was born in her paren house (next door), about 1888. Mr. O.L. Pinson, Sr., was very active in Nelms Masonic Lodge. S *tenth house.*

Ruby Pinson married E.W. Camp. They had no children.

O.L. Pinson, Jr. ., served in the United States Army Air Corps during World War II. married Thelma Frady, the mother of Reverend Marvin Frady, at one time Pastor of Calvary Bap Church in Smyrna and now Pastor of First Baptist Church of Clarkdale, as well as Chaplain for Cobb County Jail. O.L. and Thelma, both older adults when they married, had no children.

O.L., Jr., who played baseball on the Smyrna Amateur Baseball Team, and Dad were go friends. There is an interesting story about O.L., Jr., as a player. Though his position was catcher, would not play ball on Sunday because his Christian commitment would not allow him to do "Sunday is the Lord's Day," he said. I remember how my dad always respected that. O.L. served Chairman of the Board of Deacons in First Baptist Church; he was also my Sunday School teac when I was in the Junior Department.

The elder Pinsons were very hospitable. I knew them well from my delivering their pap and seeing them at ball games.

Fifteenth House

Mr. and **Mrs. William Oliver Robinson, Sr.**, resided in the house next door to their old daughter, Annie Mae Robinson Pinson, and her family. The Pinson and Robinson houses were wh the Ivy Springs town homes are currently located. The Robinsons had seven children: **Alonzo**, kno as "Lonnie," **Mamie Lou**, **Tommy**, **Nolan**, **Sarah**, known as "Sadie," **Annie Mae**, and **Willia Oliver, Jr.**

William Oliver Robinson, Sr., was a roofer and a builder. He constructed this house Spring Street more than a century ago.

Several of the Robinson/Pinson relatives, the Cannons, are buried in the old Smyr Cemetery, now known as the Smyrna Memorial Cemetery.

"Lonnie" Robinson never married. He maintained the family home for the rest of his life.

Mamie Lou Robinson married William Neary.

Tommy Robinson never married.

Nolan Robinson married Wynelle Free.

"Sadie" Robinson married Joe McDowell. See *Dixie Avenue* and *Whitfield Street.*

W.O. Robinson, Jr., married Barbara McBride.

Sixteenth House

Mr. and **Mrs. Jack Lacy** lived in the house on the northwest corner of Spring and Matthews streets. Mrs. Lacy was the former Edna Brown. They had four sons: **Ralph**, **Bobby**, **James**, known as "Jimmy," and **Fred**, known as "Freddie." The elder Mr. Lacy was a carpenter and a roofer.

NOTE: Mrs. Edna Brown Lacy was a sister of Dovie Brown Whelchel, Clara Brown Lawler, Fred Brown, and J.T. Brown, who ran a plumbing business in Smyrna for many years.

Ralph Lacy married Jeanette Lawler. They had a son, Raymond, and two daughters, Lynn and Lisa.

Bobby Lacy married Betty Emmett. They had three children: Mike, Melonie, and Marlene.

Jimmy Lacy married Nell Poss. They had two sons: Jeff and Ken. Jimmy and Nell divorced and married again. Nell married Everett McTyre and Jimmy married Janice Doby.

Freddie Lacy and his wife, Sara, had two sons, Darren and Matthew. In later years, Sara and her sons attended First Baptist Church, where the children attended the church preschool and where Sara was employed. Freddie is deceased.

Seventeenth House

Mr. and **Mrs. Joe Poss** resided in this well-maintained, five-room, white house with a screened porch, located on the northeast corner of Spring and Matthews streets. Mrs. Poss' given name was Nora Lee. They had no children. Mr. and Mrs. Poss were members of Second Baptist Church, where he was a deacon. Mr. Poss had five brothers, Lee, Claude, Bill, Jess, and Ike, and one sister, Sara. See *Fouts, Atlanta Street from Mrs. Mazie's to Pearce Matthews and Poss, Davis Road.*

I remember that, while I was working at G.B.'s Place, Mr. and Mrs. Poss would come by every Sunday night after church to get something to eat. (They were faithful Sunday night church attendees.) Mr. Poss, a "stocky" man with big arms and large chest, was always happy and friendly. I never saw him when he appeared to be downhearted or upset, and he always demonstrated a Christian demeanor. To my knowledge Mrs. Poss, always pleasant, was a homemaker, not working outside the home. They, to whom I delivered newspapers, were always nice to me.

Brothers and Sister of Joe Poss

Bill Poss married Edna Crowe. They had four children: Hazel, Edna, William, known as "Buck," and Ed.

Jess Poss married Mae Hiatt; they had two daughters: Faye and Joyce.

Lee Poss married Imagean McPherson. They had two daughters: Nell and Sandra.

Sara Poss married Morris Tanner. They had three children: Margaret, Morris, Jr., known "Buck," and Johnny. See *Gilbert Street.*

Claude Poss married Margie Frisbee. They had a son, Eugene, who died at birth. See *Walk Street.*

Ike Poss married Coy Richards. They had five children: Frances, Doyle, Barbara Ar Charles, and Jerry.

They also had a half-brother, Charlie, who lived in Fayetteville.

Eighteenth House

Mr. and **Mrs**. **Lester King** were residents of this house. Mrs. King, the former Nel Richards, was from Douglasville. They had two daughters: **Marguerite** and **Evelyn**. (Marguerite a "Bill" Scoggins were the same age.) Mrs. King ran a neighborhood grocery store across the street fro their home, in what today is a triangle formed by Spring Street, Spring Road, and Jonquil Drive. M King worked for the NC& St.L Railroad, which later was the L&N Railroad, from which he retire The King Family were members of Bethel Baptist Church.

Marguerite King's husband, Ralph Groover, was from the Elizabeth community in Mariet They had four children: Ralph, Jr., Raymond, James, and Ann Marie, known as "Jackson." Aft Ralph's death, Marguerite married Velton Fowler; they still live in the area.

Matthew Beadles
Casualty of War
Iraq 2003

Evelyn King married Gordon Jenkins of Acworth. They had two children: Gordon, Jr., a Joyce. A grandson, Matthew Beadles, was killed in Iraq in 2003. Evelyn and Gordon still live in Co County.

Nineteenth House

Mr. and **Mrs**. **Wright** resided here with their daughter, Janice.

Twentieth House

Mrs. **Roach** was an elderly lady who lived in this nice brick house, almost directly across t street from the Freeman Family. According to Howard Gunn, neighborhood children of that day sa Mrs. Roach "as a very articulate lady, whose home was attractive and well maintained."

Twenty-first House

Mrs. **Mary Prater**, Mrs. Roach's daughter, lived a very short distance away from h mother.

Howard Gunn, the Harpers' grandson, remembers the Prater house like this: "The Pra home was a moderately sized house that was located about three to four hundred feet off the roa There was a long, nicely paved driveway, rare in those days. I would say the Praters were somewh 'upper class' folks! They always seemed to have a new car. According to those who may have know they probably socialized in Atlanta. Their house was located almost directly across the street from o house."

SPRING STREET
South Side

Appreciation is extended to Pat McAdams Barnett; Paul Chastain; Priscilla Durham amwell; Virginia Ransom Collins; and Madge Dobbs Jackson, all of whom grew up on Spring Street the middle of the Twentieth Century; and to Howard Gunn, who grew up on the south side of Spring oad during that time—each of whom has contributed invaluable information. Appreciation also goes W.F Osburn; Helen Emmett Massey Stymest; Carl Marlowe; Rebekah Austin Walker; Patricia urham Baldwin; and June Emmett Chesser for sharing information regarding their families, who ved on the south side of Spring Street; to Steve Harris regarding his maternal grandparents, the ttys; Betty Burruss Brown; also to, Mary Lou and Bobby Cochran.

Appreciation is further extended to Linda Barfield, and Janet Brooks Brown, for sharing their emories of attending Sunday School when they were growing up, in the Petty House after Spring reet Baptist Church bought it from the Pettys.

THE SMYRNA DEPOT

The Smyrna Depot was located on the south side of Spring Street, just west of the railroad. ssengers could enter the Depot from Spring Street. When I was growing up, Mr. John Tatum was e Railway Express agent who managed the Depot. He was responsible for shipments in an out of the epot, such as documents, money, and appliances. Sometimes there would be shipments of fertilizer d farm implements. I also remember shipments of bread for Rogers Store. See *Tatum, Atlanta Street, om Mapps t R & M Café.*

NOTE: The Smyrna Museum was built as a replica of the Smyrna Depot and is located very ar to where the original depot stood.

Incoming and outgoing mail was also handled from the Depot. I can remember that, when the ail was "light," it was put on a pole at the edge of the railroad track. The Little Hook Train would run om Atlanta to Chattanooga each morning and return around five o'clock in the afternoon. If there ere no passengers, packages, or boxes to be unloaded, the train would not come to a complete stop. meone on the train, in such cases, would take the mail from the pole.

NOTE: In the days of my youth, most of the mail was shipped to Smyrna by train.

At one time the railroad that ran through Smyrna was called the Louisville and Nashville &N). Later, due to mergers, it was called the NC&St.L, which stood for Nashville, Chattanooga, and . Louis. Still later it became the CSX Railroad.

I remember that, during World War II, military troops would come through on the train, hich would stop on the sidetrack next to G.B.'s Place. I was intrigued in those days by the uniforms orn by the men and women on the trains; to me they always looked sharp!

MR. TRIBBLE'S FEED STORE

Mr. L.H. Tribble ran a feed and seed store on the south side of Spring Street, immediately st the railroad. Besides different types of food for domestic and farm animals, he always had a good sortment of flower, vegetable, and grass seeds, as well as fertilizers and tools. He carried a wide riety of groceries, such as dried beans, flour, cornmeal, cheese, crackers, cookies, canned meats, anut butter, BB Suckers, Moon Pies, and candy. He also sold meat products, fresh eggs, and fruits d vegetables in season. I remember that one could buy chewing tobacco and snuff at Mr. Tribble's. ere, women could buy their cleaning supplies, such as mops, brooms, and household cleaners. I member going to the store to buy Dutch Cleanser and/or Bon Ami for my mother. We also used ory Soap, bought there. Remember *99-44/100th % Pure*?

Smyrna Depot
Circa 1940
Courtesy of Smyrna Museum

Spring Street Baptist Church Cornerstone on old Building Reads
Organized and Dedicated to the Service of Our Lord
October 15, 1933
Bldg. Lot Donated
Circa 1940s
Courtesy of Shirley Barnett

I could always depend on Mr. Tribble's being nice, friendly, and upbeat. Smiling often, he as a very gracious person; he never failed to thank the customers for their business. I thought it so eat, with my being just a kid, that he would tell me, "I appreciate your business."

Joann McDowell shared the following story about going with her dad to Mr. Tribble's store hen she was eight or nine years old. Her father gathered his purchases and told Mr. Tribble to put em on his account. Another day, when Joann was in the store and saw a Hershey candy bar, her vorite, she took the candy to the register and told Mr. Tribble to put it on her dad's account. He did. r some time after that, she would go by and get a candy bar and charge it to her dad—as if she could t resist. At some point she began worrying about charging without her dad's permission and, coming so uncomfortable, she stopped. She was afraid of what would happen when her dad found t. One day, about a year later, Joann overheard her dad telling her mother about her charging the ershey bars; then she heard him chuckle.

The practice of having an account with local stores was common at that time. Store operators ould grant credit to their customers from pay day to pay day. To my knowledge the proprietor did not arge interest on the accounts.

The first two houses on Spring Street, the rental house and the Walker house, were razed, and lumberyard, which was owned by Travis Sanders and "Ed" Herren, was established there. Later on, P. Stephens Lumber Company in Marietta acquired this business.

First House

The first house was a rental one, in which different families lived through the years.

Second House

Mr. and **Mrs. Buna Lewis Walker** resided here before they had a house built on Atlanta reet. Mr. Walker came from Dallas to Smyrna in 1926. Mrs. Walker, the former Julia Worley, was e daughter of Gordon and Emma Worley, who lived on Church Street. Buna and Julia had four ildren: **Mickey**, **Phillip**, **Don**, and **Beverly Jane**. See *south side of Church Street* and *Atlanta Street, om the Mapps to the R & M Café.*

Mickey Walker married Rebekah Austin, who grew up on Sunset Avenue. They had four ildren: Lewis Austin, known as "Bo," Donald Joseph, known as "Joey," Gregory Adair, known as Greg", and Rebekah Ann, known as "Becky." Mickey and Rebekah are members of First Methodist hurch.

Lewis Austin Walker, known as "Bo," a graduate of Campbell High School, married Susan rner from Mableton. They had two children: Cardi and Heather. Cardi Walker married Philip Early, .; they had two children. Cardi and Philip are graduates of Campbell High School. Heather, also a aduate of Campbell High School, married but has no children.

"Joey" Walker, a graduate of Campbell High School, married Teresa King; they had one ild, Allen. Joey's second marriage was to Adele Contrata; they had a daughter, Kristen. Adele is ceased.

"Greg" Walker married Marilyn McDermott; they had two children: a daughter, Jackie and a n, Luke. "Greg" is a graduate of Campbell High School.

Rebekah Ann Walker married Christopher Beck, known as "Chris." They had three children: daughter, Addie, and two sons, Lee and Mitchell. Both Rebekah Ann and Chris are graduates of mpbell High School.

Phillip Walker married Peggy Jo Addison, who grew up in the Oakdale community, sout Smyrna. They had two children: Beverly Katherine, known as "Kathy," and Phillip Eugene, Jr., knc as "Chuck." Peggy's parents, Mr. and Mrs. Sloan Addison, who had another daughter, A Katherine, were very active in Locust Grove Baptist Church, in the Oakdale community, where Phi served as a deacon and Peggy was the pianist for many years. Phillip, who has a beautiful bass vo and Peggy have provided the music (vocal and instrumental) for many funerals and weddings thro the years. Peggy and Phillip are now members of First Baptist Church, where he has been a dea since June 13, 1983.

"Kathy" Walker married Mike Fennell. They had one daughter, Judith Joanna, known "J.J." "Kathy" later married Tom Hembree.

"Chuck" Walker. married Linda Bates from Atlanta. They had two children: Tony Christopher.

Donald Lewis Walker, known as "Don," married Linda Nalley from Smyrna. They had th children: Julia Carol, known as "Carrie," Donald Andrew, known as "Andy," and Daniel, known "Dan." "Don" and Linda had one grandchild.

Beverly Jane Walker married Roy Samuel Wood, my brother, known as "Sammy." They two daughters: Cynthia, known as "Cindy," and Julia, known as "Julie." Jane and "Sammy" members of First Baptist Church, where he is a deacon. Jane, "Sammy," and both of their daugh are graduates of Campbell High School. See *Wood, north side of Bank Street.*

"Julie" Wood married Chris Haddox; they had two sons: Stephen and Drew. "Cindy" W is not married.

FEEDING THE TROOPS

by Mickey Walker

"World War II was in full force. Troop trains loaded with soldiers being transferred from place to another came through Smyrna. I know that at least one troop train passed through Smy daily.

"We lived on the south side of Spring Street, across the railroad from G.B.'s Pl Sometimes the trains would stop for various reasons. More than likely they would be held on sidetrack so that other trains could pass. Some of the guys on the train near G.B.'s Place wo purchase cold drinks and snacks. You might say G.B. ran a 'track side' restaurant.

"One day Sonny and Quinton Hamby, my brother, (Phillip), and I (the 'gang') were ea apples from a bucket while standing at the railroad. Some on the train offered to buy the apples f us. I remember giving them what I had left. Though the passengers wanted to pay us, we would take their money.

"After this incident, 'the gang' decided to prepare snacks (crackers with peanut butter cookies) and meet the trains when they came through. Sometimes we would have some kind sandwich or whatever else we could come up with. The troops were always glad to see us and re appreciated the snacks. Of course, we never saw the same guys twice.

This is one of the great memories that I have from my living close to the railroad dur World War II, in the days of my youth."

FLY BOYS

by Mickey Walker, "Master Sergeant"

"In 1943 World War II was going strong, and I had developed a very strong interest in iation. I became very good at building model airplanes, an interest that I have maintained throughout y life.

"My father, Buna Walker, owned and operated Walker Motor Company. It was an auto repair rage and a used car lot. The business was located on Atlanta Street, near where the Smyrna Museum today. We could walk from our back yard and across the railroad to my dad's business.

"We lived on Spring Street. Our house was on the south side of the street, across the railroad. d had many used cars and car parts in our back yard. I saw potential in those old parts that would be ry useful in making an airplane that would fly. I worked sometimes in the automobile repair shop d was positive that I could make an engine that would fly a plane.

"There was a 'gang' of us guys that had 'military ranks.' I was the leader of the 'gang'; in ct, I was the 'Top Sergeant,' Sonny Hamby was 'Sergeant,' and Quinton Hamby and Phillip Walker re 'Privates.'

"The following incident happened in our back yard on Spring Street. I took some bamboo hing poles and covered them with silk from a parachute that was given to me by a friend. Of course, nade the engine from old car parts. The 'gang' decided to make rubber bands from old inner tubes in scrap pile. I got this idea from the model airplanes that I had built. I had a piece of wood, about ree feet long, from which I carved the propellers. When the airplane was finished, I wound up the opellers, which worked pretty well. All of the controls were in the airplane, just like in a real one.

"In our back yard, my family had a garage with a steep roof that was covered with tin, from ich we planned to launch the plane. Dad had a chain hoist that he used to remove engines from cars. e worked about two days, rigging that chain to hoist the airplane to the top of the garage. My plan s to fly the plane myself. Because of the age and size of the other 'gang' members, we discovered t I was the only one that had enough strength to wind up the motor propelled by the rubber band. ter much discussion, it was decided that Phillip would have the honor of flying the plane. member the Wright Brothers?

"I gave Phillip instructions that, as soon as Sonny and Quinton released the ropes, he was to l back on the stick to elevate the plane. I wound that propeller up full force and, on my signal, nny, and Quinton released the rope. That plane fell from the roof of the garage and went straight wn and became a large pile of rubble. It almost killed Phillip, but I remember that he did not cry. I d him that I was sure that he did not pull back on the stick quickly enough. He was promoted to orporal!'"

<u>Third House</u>

C. L. Groce

Smyrna City Councilman

1920, 1929-1930, 1946

Mr. and **Mrs. Curtis L. Groce** resided next door to the Walkers. She was the former Hepsie onard. They had seven children: **Nadine**, **Kathleen**, **Blanche**, **Claude**, **Anita**, **George**, and **Norma**.

Mr. and Mrs. Groce grew up in Cave Springs. They moved to Atlanta in 1901 and came to yrna in 1917, the year their third child, Blanche, started first grade. Mr. and Mrs. Groce and their nily were active members of First Methodist Church. Mr. Curtis Groce served three different terms Smyrna City Council and was an appointed member of the Cobb County Board of Education.

Mr. Groce worked for the King Plow Company as a pattern maker. It was the only job t the family can ever remember his having. Mr. Groce was still employed when he died suddenly at age of sixty-five.

Nadine Groce married Howard Hames of Marietta. They had one son, William, who had t children. Howard worked for Georgia Power Company as a master electrician. See *fifth house, so side of Spring Street.*

Kathleen Groce married Harry Haggerty of Philadelphia, Pennsylvania. They had t daughters: Camille and Kathleen, known as "Kathy."

Blanche Grocemarried Charles Dobbs. See *ninth house, south side of Spring Street.*

Claude Groce married Martha Land. They had no children. Claude worked for Colo Bread Company as a deliveryman. He rose through the ranks and retired as an executive of Colo Bread Company.

Anita Groce married Kenneth Tapp of Chamblee. They had three children: Kenneth, El and Jane, all of whom raised their families in Chamblee. Kenneth worked for Georgia Power Comp as a mechanic in the boiler room.

George Groce married Eunice Miller. They had one son, William Keith. Eunice's pare were Swedish immigrants in the early part of the Twentieth Century; Eunice was born after they ca to America. George, a member of First Methodist Church, was a volunteer fireman for the City Smyrna and a school bus driver for the Cobb County School System. Eunice Groce was a teache First Baptist Church Kindergarten. See *north side of Bank Street.*

Norma Groce married Fred Morris of Lyons. They had one son, Phillip, and one grands Matthew Sloan. Fred was a brick mason and a builder. Norma, who worked for the Cobb Cou Water System from the time it was created, helped to establish a business office in Smyrna. Prio her marriage, Norma was still living at home with her parents when I delivered her parents' pa Phillip Morris died February 11, 2005, at age fifty-eight.

Fourth House

Mrs. Burton owned this house. From a previous marriage, Mrs. Burton had a son, **No Medley**, known as "Polo." She also had, from another marriage, a son, **Howard**. Mrs. Burton's sis Gladys, known as "Snooks," a practical nurse, also lived here.

"Polo" Medley had been married but was divorced when he was discharged from the Uni States Army, at which time he came to live here with his mother. "Polo" remarried and had t daughters.

Madge Dobbs Jackson remembers "Polo" as being a "good looking man." She also rec "Polo" as being the original owner and operator of Smyrna Taxi.

NOTE: Prior to the time "Polo" started Smyrna Taxi, another cab company under ano name had provided service in Smyrna. Between Smyrna Taxi and the earlier one, there was a perio time when cab service was not available in Smyrna.

Fifth House

Howard Hames
Smyrna City Councilman
1951

Mr. and **Mrs. Howard Hames** lived in one side of this duplex. She was the former Nadine roce. They had a son, Billy, who was several years younger than I. Mr. and Mrs. Hames were on my per route and also bought eggs from me. Mrs. Hames, always prompt in paying the "paper bill" eekly, never failed to offer me a glass of lemonade when I would go by to collect.

Mr. Hames worked for Georgia Power Company. I remember he had a nice, new car. Mr. and rs. Hames, members of First Methodist Church, were neat and attractive people, who impressed me ry much!

I never knew those who lived in the other side of the duplex, for they did not subscribe to the per. See *third house, south side of Spring Street.*

Sixth House

Mr. J. O. Hargis
Smyrna City Councilman
1944

Mr. and **Mrs. J. O. Hargis** resided next door to Mr. and Mrs. Hames. They had a nice home, cated on the southwest corner of Spring and Alexander streets. Mr. Hargis was a big man, very stinguished looking though gray and balding. Wearing suits often, he was very dignified and carried nself accordingly. In fact, every time I saw him I would think he might be going to church though I ver knew where or if he was a member. He served on the Smyrna City Council in 1944. I delivered s paper every morning for about two years and never had to worry about the "paper bill." He was a ry nice man.

NOTE: Alexander Street was located between the sixth and seventh houses on Spring Street. was a short street with only three houses. See *Alexander Street.*

Seventh House

Mr. and **Mrs. Norwood Coker** lived on the southeast corner of Spring and Alexander eets. They had a son, **Joe**. From a previous marriage, Mrs. Alice Coker, the former Alice Harris, had on, **Tommy Oglesby**, whose dad was deceased.

Alice Harris Coker was a sister of Maggie Harris, who married Scott Edwards, Sr. Maggie d Scott had a son, Scott Edwards, Jr., who practiced law in Marietta. See *Harris, north side of ring Street.*

Mr. Norwood Coker, a suit-and-tie man, was an accountant for the Civil Air Administration. am not sure about the proper name of his employer.) The Cokers, fine people and good paper stomers, were always very nice to me. I remember when I was working at G.B.'s Place, the Cokers re regular customers. They moved to Alaska in 1951. Norwood and Alice Coker are both deceased.

Tommy Oglesby was one of the Smyrna guys who played football for Coach James Pressley Marietta High School. He was the charter president of the Smyrna Jaycees, in 1959. Tommy and his fe, Beverly, later moved from Smyrna.

Joe Coker married Sue Boss Watkins, a widow from Atlanta. Joe and Sue had three children d seven grandchildren. Joe is now retired from Lockheed Aircraft Corporation.

There was a relationship between the Cokers and the Harris/Edwards, Sr., families who li on the north side of Spring Street, near Roswell Street. See *east side of Roswell Street.*

The Warren Asa Candler Family

After the Cokers moved in 1951, the **Warren Asa Candler Family** moved to the seve house from Gilbert Street. They had two daughters: **Diannah** and **Nancy**.

Nancy Candler graduated from Marietta High School. Diannah graduated from Camp High School in 1958. The Candler Family later moved to Pretty Branch Drive in the Forest H community.

Eighth House

Mr. and **Mrs. John Franklin Petty** resided in this house. Mrs. Petty, the former Lula M Legg, was born October 1, 1882, and Mr. Petty was born in 1884, and died in 1934. They had ei children: **Lula Belle**, **Dorothy Elizabeth**, **John Thomas**, **Woodrow Wilson**, known as "Wood **Charles Legg**, **James Franklin**, known as "Jim," **Mary Myrtle Harriett**, known as "Mell," and A **Evelyn**. Mrs. Petty was a member of The United Daughters of the Confederacy. Her parents, T.E. Amanda Legg, were founding members of First Baptist Church, where the Pettys were also act members. See *Baldwin, east side of Concord Road.*

Lula Belle Petty was born July 15, 1908, and died July 15, 1970. She married Marion Hammock.

Dorothy Petty married Carlton Harris. See *south side of Whitfield Street.*

John Thomas Petty, a bachelor, who lived with his mother, was born March 1, 1911.

"Woody" Petty married Harold Pettet. They had one daughter, Dorothy Ellen, known "Dotsie," who was a member of the Smyrna High School Class of 1951. I really liked the Petty Pettet families. See *Sunset Avenue.*

Charles Petty married Sarah Hudson. He was born October 1, 1919, and died April 23, 19

"Jim" Petty, who was born November 28, 1920, married Myra Cassandra Turner. "Jim" worked for Dr. D.C. Landers at Landers Pharmacy, where he was the "soda jerk." The truth is tha really ran that fountain. (There is no doubt about it. "Jim" was in charge!) I remember that du World War II, after "Jim" had entered the Navy, Mrs. Petty hung a star in her window. Because "J kidded with me so much, I really missed him!

Myrtle Petty, who was born May 4, 1922, married Paul Copeland; they lived in Marie Later Myrtle married Edward C. Murry; they live in South Georgia.

Evelyn Petty, who was born July 4, 1925, married Norris William Hendrix, Jr. They live Houston, Texas. After Mr. Hendrix died, Evelyn moved back to Smyrna.

All three of Mrs. Petty's sons, in the United States Military during World War II, fough some of the major battles in the South Pacific.

The Pettys' early turn-of-the-century house was a pretty, white frame one with cottage st posts. It featured a long porch across the front and five French doors, each flanked with dark g shutters that matched the roof. The center door led to a foyer; the other doors entered each led to a the rooms, except the kitchen, which extended backwards on the west side of the house and forme "L" shape. Once inside the house, one would go from one room to get to another. The house feat two bathrooms. The Petty home site, surrounded by several large trees, was purchased by Spring Street Baptist Church; it was used as their first pastorium and, later, for Sunday School rooms. The house was razed to build the present pastorium.

NOTE: According to information from long-time residents, for a period of time, earlier in the Twentieth Century, the Petty House was used as a school; this probably was at the time the school burned; because of some damage unknown to us, the school could not be used.

SPRING STREET BAPTIST CHURCH

Spring Street Baptist Church was on the southwest corner of Spring and Foster streets. The church was chartered in the fall of 1933; Reverend J.W. Reeves was the founding pastor.

NOTE: The following information comes from W.F. Osburn. "The acreage for the Spring Street Church was donated by the W.J. Osburn Family to be used as long as a church is located on the property. My dad, W. J. Osburn, and two of my uncles, Claude and Ed Osburn, cut timber from their property on Elizabeth Street. At their sawmill on King Springs Road, the timber was cut into lumber and used to build Spring Street Church."

NOTE: Foster Street is a short street between Spring Street Church and the ninth house.

Ninth House

Claude T. Osburn and his wife, **Nina Sue**, known as "Sudie," lived on the southeast corner of Spring and Foster streets; their house faced Spring Street. Mr. Osburn owned the property beginning next door to the Petty house down to what became Foster Street, after he gave an easement for the City of Smyrna to cut Foster Street.

Mr. Osburn traveled as a salesman in his younger years; in his later years he made wooden venetian blinds. (According to information from the Osburn Family, the venetian blind business was started by Claude's brother, W.J. Osburn.) He owned and operated a business with his partner, Mr. Sam Jeffares. See *Jeffares, Fuller Street, Spring Street Church* and *Osburns, north side of Spring Street.*

Tenth House

Mr. and **Mrs. Charles Dobbs** were residents of this house. They had three children: **Eleanor**, **Madge**, and **Curtis**. Mrs. Dobbs was the former Blanche Groce, born in 1910. Having moved to Smyrna with her family in 1917, she grew up in the Groce House, it was the first house on the south side of Spring Street from the railroad.

When Mr. and Mrs. Dobbs bought the tenth house from C.T. Osburn, in 1944, it was a four-room rental house without a bathroom.

Mr. Charles Dobbs, known as "Charlie," founded Dobbs Roofing Company in 1950; before that he worked for Randall Brothers Building Supply Company, on Marietta Street in Atlanta. See *Groce, south side of Spring Street.*

Eleanor Dobbs married Slade H. Exley, Jr., of the Oakdale community, south of Smyrna. They had four children: Susan, Slade H. Exley III, Margaret, and Katrina. Slade's mother, Ruth Exley, a teacher at Fitzhugh Lee elementary and high schools, taught for more than forty years. Eleanor and Slade raised their family in Gainesville, where Slade is a doctor of veterinary medicine.

Madge Dobbs married Lamar Jackson of Buchanan and Austell. Madge and Lamar both worked for the Cobb County Government: She was in accounting, and he was an animal control officer. Lamar is deceased. Madge is currently living in the sixth house on the north side of Spring Street.

Curtis Dobbs married Margaret Hollifield of Rome. They had one son, John. Curtis Dobbs owns and operates Dobbs Roofing Company in Smyrna.

Eleventh House

Mr. and **Mrs. William A. "Mack" McAdams,** lived on the southwest corner of Spring and Elizabeth streets. They had a daughter, **Patsy**, and two older children from Mrs. McAdams' first marriage, **Alton Brown, Jr**., and **Katherine Brown**. Mrs. McAdams, a good paper customer, was one of the ladies who would give me something to drink when I stopped by to collect. See *Brown, south side of Concord Road.*

Mrs. McAdams, whose given name was Virginia, was known as "Ginny." She was a homemaker who later worked for many years at Puritan Chemical Company in Atlanta. Mr. McAdams, a master window trimmer for Jacobs Drug Company, traveled throughout the southeast and mid west, designing and setting up window displays.

Alton Brown, Jr. ., Mrs. McAdams' oldest child, graduated from Marietta High School and served in the United States Army during World War II.

Katherine Brown attended Reinhardt College in Waleska for two years. Afterwards, she became employed with the United States Government, Civil Service, in Washington, D.C. There she met her husband, Delbert Owen from Utah, who was in the United States Air Force. They had three sons, Jimmy, Gary, and David, and several grandchildren.

Patsy McAdams, known as "Pat," married Bill Barnett. They had three children: Debbie, Scott, and Anna. Bill Barnett died in 1995 in his middle years.

Pat and Bill Barnett were members of the Smyrna Historical and Genealogical Society. Bill, a faithful member of this organization, often volunteered at the Smyrna Museum until shortly before his death, in the mid 1990s.

Debbie Barnett married Don Vansant. She had one daughter, Courtenay Hicks.

Scott Barnett grew up with our son, Stephen; they played sports together, especially basketball and baseball.

Anna Barnett married Eddie Fulghum; they had a daughter, Sydney. Eddie and my wife, Lillie, are first cousins once removed.

NOTE: When I was a young child, Elizabeth Street was a short, narrow one that ran south off Spring Street between the McAdams' and Durhams' houses. Claude T. Osburn, who owned a parcel of land there, petitioned the City of Smyrna to pave the street. After the street was paved, on his property he built a house to sell. Also, at that time, the street was named for Elizabeth Durham, who grew up in the twelfth house.

Twelfth House

The following information about the Truman Durham Family was furnished by Priscilla Durham Gamwell.

Nathan Truman Durham

Nathan Truman Durham and **Lizzie Mary Etta Phagan Durham** raised their son, **John Phagan**, and two daughters, **Gloria** and **Mary Elizabeth,** in this house. They had another son, **Hugh**, who died as an infant. **Ruth Phagan**, Lizzie's sister, lived here with the Durhams. Nathan and Lizzie Durham purchased this house on June 27, 1925, from Sally Carter (Mrs. J.W. Magill), who had purchased it from C.M. Stanback June 14, 1919. Though the exact age of the house is not known, Cobb County records indicate it was built in 1917. This house was located on what was part of the Dempsey Farm.

Priscilla Durham shared, "It is reported that, during the Civil War days, the Union Army camped in this general vicinity while on their way through Smyrna. According to family information, opinion verbiage, by Lawyer's Title Insurance Company, in some of the ownership papers regarding one of the Dempsey Farm houses, included that records prior to the Civil War were burned by Sherman's Army during its march through Cobb County."

NOTE: It is a matter of historical record that Sherman's Army did, in fact, set up camp in the Smyrna area.

Lizzie, the epitome of hospitality, was well known for her caramel cakes, and she permitted the side yard of the Durham property to serve as the basketball court for Smyrna High School while Phagan attended there. Truman was a conductor for the NC&St.L Railroad and worked out of the old depot in Smyrna. Lizzie was very involved with the Eastern Star, and Truman was a Mason. They both passed away in 1949, within about six weeks of each other. Gloria continued to live in the house until Phagan bought it in 1950.

Lizzie's sister, **Ruth Phagan**, lived with the Durhams until her marriage to Jim Camp, after which, Ruth and Jim moved to a house on King Street. (Corrine Hosch purchased the King Street house, after Ruth's death, in 1971.) Ruth, a nurse in Dr. W.C. Mitchell's office for many years, was affectionately known as "Miss Ruth." All of the Durhams were members of First Baptist Church. See *Camp, east side of King Street.*

NOTE: Lizzie Phagan Durham and Ruth Phagan Camp were sisters of little Mary Phagan's father. Mary Phagan was the young girl who was murdered in the pencil factory in Atlanta during the early part of the Twentieth Century. Leo Frank was lynched in Marietta for her murder. (This information is a matter of public record.)

John Phagan Durham

John Phagan Durham and **Dorothy Williams Durham**, daughter of Harry and Wauda Williams, purchased this house January 2, 1950, from the estate of Lizzie Durham. They had one daughter, **Priscilla**, probably best known in Smyrna as "Prissy."

When Phagan Durham lived in this house as a child, Spring Street was not paved and the Durhams had an old crank telephone with a three-party telephone line; the telephone number was 15. Phagan played many sports at Smyrna High School.

Phagan and Dorothy met one day as she was walking past his house, from her house (later known as the Rutledge House, a little farther out Spring Street) to the bus stop, on her way to work. They later enjoyed each other's company while riding Phagan's horses all over the Smyrna area. (He owned several at that time.) They married in 1945. See *north side of Fleming Street.*

After Phagan and Dorothy moved to the twelfth house, they made many improvements; in 1963 they added a swimming pool, where they regularly entertained many Smyrna folks. Dorothy passed away in 1987.

Phagan was a lifelong member of First Baptist Church, where he served as an usher and greeter. Well known for his red coat and tremendous love for the Lord and the Church, Phagan had to be really sick to miss church services and hugs from the ladies. Phagan passed away in 1999. I really miss him!

Priscilla Durham, known as "Prissy," married Steve Gamwell. From a previous marriage, "Prissy" had one son, John Collier Ackerman, who is named after Phagan and John's paternal grandfather. John lives in Canton with his wife, Amy, and their three sons: Timothy John Ackerman, Cody Alston Ackerman, and Todd Garrett Ackerman. "Prissy" moved back to her family home in 1998, along with her husband, Steve, to assist her dad in taking care of the house and property. They still live here, but sold some of the property for redevelopment, in early 2005.

Tremendous changes have taken place in Smyrna since "Prissy" was raised in the twelfth house (1950-1969). "Prissy," like Phagan, had a love of horses and rode her horse, "Duke," all over Smyrna. Then Atlanta Road had just two lanes; Bobby Landers' Drug Store was still on the corner diagonally across from G.B.'s Place; houses were where Jonquil Plaza now is; and Colquitt's 5, 10, & 25 Cents store was a favorite place to shop.

NOTE: Dorothy's brother and sister-in-law, Ed and Martha Williams, owned and operated Williams' Day Care on Love Street, and later Dunn Street, and still later on Jones Shaw Road, which is now Windy Hill Road. See *Williams, north side of Love Street,* and *west side of Dunn Street.*

Gloria Ruth Durham married Carl T. Wheeler, a Southern Baptist preacher, in 1953. They had two children: Tommy and Miriam Ruth. Carl and Gloria live in North Charleston, South Carolina where Carl is retired. Gloria is the only surviving child of Nathan and Lizzie Durham.

Tommy Wheeler, having a Doctorate in Theology, is currently the pastor of a church in North Charleston, South Carolina. He and his wife, Becky, had two sons, Nathan (named after Nathan Truman Durham) and Daniell, and a daughter, Beth. Nathan and Daniell attended high school in North Charleston. Daniell is now a student at Bob Jones University.

Miriam Ruth Wheeler is a medical doctor and missionary in the Ukraine.

When Mrs. Corrine Hosch, a veteran teacher at Smyrna High School and Campbell High School respectively, died, Gloria Durham Wheeler gave a eulogy at her funeral service. Mrs. Corrine Hosch had taught Gloria at Smyrna High School. See *Hosch, west side of King Street.*

Mary Elizabeth Durham, who married Glen Rogers, moved to Doraville and later to Lilburn, where she passed away in 1999. Glen now resides in Gainesville. Mary Elizabeth and Glen had one daughter, Glenda, who is now married to Rich Gehri. Glenda and Rich live in Park City, Utah.

From a previous marriage, Glenda's daughter, Jennifer Schlenker, who is married and lives in Salt Lake City, Utah; had two children: Lily and Henry.

Truman Durham and Charles Durham, the father of Homer Durham, were first cousins. According to information from Patricia Durham Baldwin, the Charles Thomas Durham Family lived in this twelfth house before the Truman Durhams moved here. See *north side of Fleming Street* and *south side of Powder Springs Street.*

Thirteenth House

Mr. and **Mrs. Shelly Watson** and their daughter, **Peggy**, moved to this house in 1954. Mrs. Watson's given name was Nola. The Watsons, originally from Tennessee, had moved to Lithonia, where their daughter, Peggy, graduated from high school.

The Watson House, south side of Spring Street
Phagan Durham House to the left
Circa 1960s
Courtesy of Peggy Lynn Sheppard

Earl Sheppard, age 21
Circa 1951
Courtesy of Peggy Lynn Sheppard

Peggy Watson Sheppard (Whitfield)
Age 19
Circa 1951
Courtesy of Peggy Lynn Sheppard

Peggy Watson, a graduate of Georgia State College for Women, (GSCW) in Milledgeville began teaching at Campbell High School in the fall of 1954. She married Earl Sheppard from Oconee in Washington County, October 3, 1953. Earl Sheppard was employed by the Federal Aviation Administration for fifteen years as an air traffic controller at the Atlanta Airport, later known a Hartsfield/ Jackson International Airport.

After their marriage, Peggy and Earl lived with Mr. and Mrs. Watson in this house on Spring Street. They later moved to Gilbert Street, then to Concord Circle, where they were living when thei daughter, Peggy Lynn, was born. When development began off Cherokee Street, Peggy and Ear moved to Beaver Creek Road, where they were living when Earl died very suddenly, in 1968. See *wes side of Gilbert Street.*

After Mr. Watson's death, Peggy and Peggy Lynn, along with Mrs. Watson, moved t Marcia Drive, west of Concord Road, where they lived for the rest of Mrs. Watson's life.

<u>Peggy Lynn Sheppard</u>, a graphic artist, later purchased the house on Spring Street, where he grandparents, the Watsons, had lived. She and several other home owners in the area sold thei property for redevelopment in the early months of 2005. Peggy Lynn is employed by the City o Smyrna, at the Community Center on the Village Green.

In 1995 Peggy Watson Sheppard married Sam Whitfield, a Mason; they lived on Concor Road. Peggy and Sam were active in the Eastern Star. Peggy was an active member of Women o Mission at First Baptist Church, where she taught in the Church-sponsored English Language School (English is taught as a second language, mostly to foreign-born residents.) Peggy Sheppard Whitfiel died in November 2004.

Sam Whitfield
Cobb County Board of Education
1973-1985

Sam Whitfield and his first wife, the former Grace Garren, had two children: Bryan and Sally. Bryan is a professor at Mercer University in Macon; Sally, living in Dalton, is a teacher.

Sam, who had been a school teacher, was an insurance agent upon retiring. He was very active in the Masonic Order, the Eastern Star, and DeMolay (a youth organization associated with the Masons), in all of which he held local and state-wide positions of leadership. Sam is a deacon at First Baptist Church, where he was elected to the Board of Trustees in September 1967 and served as Church Treasurer for twelve years. Sam was elected to the Cobb County Board of Education and served for twelve years, during which time he was Chairman of the Board for two separate terms. He is a charter member of the Smyrna Rotary Club, which was chartered in the early 1960s.

Grace, who grew up in Morganton, taught in Cobb County's Belmont Hills, Milford, and Brown elementary schools, prior to becoming the Media Specialist at Brown Elementary School in Smyrna—the last position she held before her death in November 1993. In the Smyrna Chapter of the Order of the Eastern Star Grace held local and state-wide positions of leadership. She was a very effective leader of the Young Women's Auxiliary, a past part of the Woman's Missionary Union of the Church and the Southern Baptist Convention. At First Baptist Church, she also taught Sunday School, served as a Sunday School director, and worked in the Church media center.

<u>Fourteenth House</u>

Mr. and **Mrs. Dick Byrd** resided here. Mrs. Byrd's given name was Emma Lula. They had twins: **"Sonny"** and **"Tissy."** Mr. Irwin Beatty, a deacon at Bethel Baptist Church, lived here with the Byrds. (According to family information, Mr. Beatty and the Byrds were not related.)

Mr. Dick Byrd was a brother of Steve Byrd, who lived on Matthews Street. Mrs. Emma Lula Byrd was a school teacher. Dick, who died in 1965, and Emma Lula, who died in 1972, are both buried in Bethel Baptist Church Cemetery on Spring Road. See *Byrd, east side of Matthews Street.*

Fifteenth House

Mr. and **Mrs. Wilton R. Emmett,** who moved to Smyrna in the late 1940s, lived up the hill and across the creek, on the southwest corner of Spring Street and Corn Road about a block west of the beginning of the Chastain Property. Mrs. Emmett was formerly Frances Bennett from Augusta. The Emmetts had two children: John B. and Cheryl. See *Anderson Circle.*

Frances worked at Dobbins Air Force Base; Wilton was employed at Lockheed Aircraft Corporation before working for the State of Georgia Department of Revenue.

John B. Emmett never married.

Cheryl Emmett married Tom Bennett; they had two children: Perry and Jody.

Mr. Wilton Emmett was the son of John and Ruby Emmett. Mr. John Emmett died before the family moved to Smyrna. Wilton had three sisters: Betty, June, and Beatrice, who along with their mother, Ruby, later moved to Jonquil Drive. Mrs. Ruby Emmett had another son, George Emmett, who had earlier moved to Smyrna. See *Emmett, west side of Anderson Circle and west side of Walker Court.*

Betty Emmett married Bobby Lacy, and later a Wester. See *north side of Spring Street.*

June Emmett married Johnny Chesser from the Oakdale community, south of Smyrna. They had two daughters, Sheila and Beth. June, a member of the Smyrna High School Class of 1951, died October 10, 2004. See *Smyrna High School, north side of Church Street.*

Beth Chesser married Alan Holcombe.

Sheila Chesser (Hagermeyer) is the principal of Lewis Elementary School, in the Cobb County School System. Sheila has kept her maiden name in the teaching profession.

Beatrice Emmett married Clarence Nash. They had two sons: Emmett and Danny. Beatrice later married Charles Roberts, known as "Chuck"; they had a son, "Robbie."

NOTE: Sometime in the late 1940s or early 1950s, another street named Anderson Circle was cut off the south side of Spring Street, about a block east of, and running parallel with Corn Road. In the early 1960s, when the viaduct was built connecting Spring Road with Love Street, Corn Road was closed to through traffic on the north and south sides of the viaduct. At some point in time Corn Road entering Spring Street was named Anderson Circle, leaving a short section of Corn Road on the north side of the viaduct. Corn Road continued on the south side of the viaduct for about a mile. Most all the residents listed today on Anderson Circle lived in other parts of Smyrna.

NOTE: According to some long-time residents of the area, Mr. W.D Anderson, known as "Will," owned the property on Spring Street, between Corn Road and Anderson Circle, extending southward on the west side of Anderson Circle. There was an old home place, during the days of my youth, which stood about mid way between Corn Road and where Anderson Circle was later cut. Some long-time residents remember, at one time, an elderly lady, Mrs. White, used this house as summer home. We have no one who remembers either Mr. Anderson or Mrs. White living here. Paul Chastain, who grew up next door remembers Mr. "Slim" Gravely first moved to this house from Creatwood before he built his house on Corn Road. See *Gravely, Corn Road.*

Sixteenth House

Mr. and **Mrs. Emory W. Chastain, Sr.**, lived in this house. Mrs. Chastain was the former Donna York from Bells Ferry Road, in northwest Cobb County. They had eleven children: **Emory W. Jr.**, **Ruth**, **Jean**, **John**, **Edward**, **Ralph**, **Lavinia**, **Donna**, **Ann**, **Paul**, and **Sam**.

The Chastain Family is another one of the large Smyrna families that have been very influential in both the City of Smyrna and Cobb County over the years. Many of them continue to be leaders in Cobb County.

Emory W. Chastain, Jr.., married Louise McClure.

Ruth Chastain married "Bud" Hammond. Ruth and "Bud," who owned property for many years on Powder Springs Street in Smyrna, recently sold that property, which is now part of a new development of single-family homes in the Guthrie/Powder Springs streets area.

Jean Chastain married D. T. Darnell from Pickens County.

John Chastain
Councilman, City of Smyrna
1960-1961
Cobb County Tax Commissioner, Twelve Years
1970s and 1980s

John Chastain married Martha Segars, who taught home economics at Smyrna High School for several years, including the years when I was a student there. She also taught at Campbell High School after it opened in 1952. John and Martha had two children: "J.J." and Sheila.

John Chastain, in the 1970s and 1980s, served for about twelve years, as Cobb County Tax Commissioner. He served one term on the Smyrna City Council, 1960-1961; in fact, he defeated my dad, Roy Wood, for that position.

J. J. Chastain, the son of John and Martha, retired from the Cobb County Water Department.

Edward Chastain married Betty Gossa from Marietta.

Ralph Chastain died in 1966.

Lavinia Chastain married Tim Coker. They had three daughters: Debbie, Susan, and Gaye. Along with my son, Stephen, Gaye was a member of the Campbell High School Class of 1986. Lavinia and Tim are deceased.

Tim Coker was a brother of Blanche Ables, the wife of J. B. Ables, who served as Smyrna City Councilman, 1958-1961, and served as Mayor of Smyrna in 1962-1963. See *Lee Street*.

Donna Chastain married Olin Herndon from Hartwell.

Ann Chastain married Larry Merritt. They live in Marietta.

Paul Chastain married Vera Little od Smyrna. They had three children: Mark, Landra, and Keith.

Paul Chastain later married Pat Carden from Kentucky. They had no children. Pat Carden Chastain's mother worked at Atkins' Pharmacy when it was located on Atlanta Street.

Paul and I have been associated with each other through the years in the business and civic communities. I became reacquainted with him through the banking industry when BankSouth, where I was employed, opened a branch office at Town Center. We were closely connected through the Cobb County Convention and Visitors Bureau, where both of us served on the Board of Directors. I served as chair of the Cobb County Convention and Visitors Bureau from 1998 thru 2001; Paul followed me as chairman.

Paul also served as Vice-Chairman of the Gateway Welcome Center in Kennesaw for several years and as President of the Kennesaw Business Association. He is currently Chairman of the Southern Museum of Civil War and Locomotive History Foundation in Kennesaw. Over the years Paul has been an active member of the Cobb County Chamber of Commerce, and served as Chairman of the North Cobb Area Council.

Paul and Pat resided in the Pinetree Country Club area of Kennesaw. Paul, the owner of Chastain and Associates Real Estate Company, and his family are members of the Milford Church of God, on the corner of the East-West Connector and Hicks Road in South Cobb, where he was ordained as a minister. Pat Chastain passed away in 2004.

Sam Chastain married Cheryl McWhorter. They had three children: Sam, Whit, and Paula.

Mr. and Mrs. Emory Chastain, Sr., owned 160 acres of land that extended across the street from the corner of Spring and Matthews streets, behind King's Store, and connected with the Red Feather Farm property, in the proximity of the intersection of Village Parkway and Strathmoor Drive. Their property extended down Atlanta Road on both sides of the railroad and connected with the Crowe property, on Atlanta Street across from Brawner Sanitarium. The Chastain Family farmed this land from the late 1940s into the 1950s. Mr. Chastain and some of his sons developed part of this property and built houses on what became known as Emory Drive, named for Mr. Chastain. (Emory Drive was east of what we know today as the intersection of Spring Road and Jonquil Drive.)

Mr. Chastain sold a large portion of this land, including the area that later became Atlanta Terrace, to Rem Bennett, Sr., in the late 1940s, when Mr. Bennett first came to Smyrna and began building houses in the area.

The Chastains were from the Bells Ferry Road area, near the intersection of Chastain and Bells Ferry roads. Owning much land in that area before they came to Smyrna, they, later in life, moved from Smyrna back to their property on Chastain Road, bearing their family name.

King's Store

King's Store was located just past the Chastain property. The store was owned by Mr. and Mrs. Lester King and operated by Mrs. King, whose given name was Nellie. Mr. and Mrs. King lived across the street from the store, on the north side of Spring Street. They had two daughters: Marguerite and Evelyn. According to the memories of some of the local boys, Mr. and Mrs. King's daughters were "beautiful." The Kings were good customers on my paper route. See *north side of Spring Street.*

Seventeenth House

Mr. and **Mrs. W.A. Ransom** resided in this house. Mr. Ransom, known as "Bill," and his first wife, had two children: **Nema** and **Frances**.

Nema Ransom married Thomas Wright of Whitfield Street. See *Whitfield Street.*

Frances Ransom married Frank Davis.

W.A. Ransom, known as "Bill," later married **Angie Akins**, the daughter of Virgil Homer and Mary Dunn Akins. Their house stood on the southwest corner of Spring Street and Jonquil Drive,

King's Store, Route 2, Spring Street
Circa 1940s
Photo Courtesy of the King Family

Nellie King in front of King's Store
Route 2, Spring Street
Circa 1940s
Photo Courtesy of the King Family

just past King's Store. They had five children: **Billie Jean**, **Virginia**, **Lynn**, **W. A., Jr.**, known as "Bill," and **Max**. See *North Avenue.*

Billie Jean Ransom married Ivan Tatum. They had two children: Eric and Michelle.

Virginia Ransom married Thomas L. "Tom" Collins. They had three sons: Loren, Sean, and Todd.

Lynn Ransom, their first son, was stillborn.

W.A. "Bill" Ransom, Jr.., married Marge Dewar. They had two daughters: Mary Margaret and Elizabeth.

Max Ransom died when he was two years old.

"Bill" Ransom, Sr., and his wife, Angie, were members of Bethel Baptist Church. Angie Akins Ransom died when her youngest child was a baby.

Mr. W. A. Ransom, Sr., known as "Bill," later married **Lillie Thompson** from Atlanta. She had three grown children: two sons and a daughter. Fred Ransom and "Bill" Ransom, Sr. were brothers. Fred Ransom was the father of Mae Ransom Davenport. See *Davenport, east side of Matthews Street.*

Eighteenth House

Mr. and **Mrs. John W. Cameron** lived on the southeast corner of Spring Street and Jonquil Drive. Mrs. Cameron was the former Clessie Lee Hill. They had four children: **John H.**, **Mary Lee**, **Ollie**, known as "Buddy," and **Albert**, all older than I. Mr. and Mrs. Cameron came from Danville, Virginia, to Smyrna in the mid 1940s.

"Buddy" Cameron married Rayford Caldwell of Talladega, Alabama. They had five daughters: Cindy (Burton), Virginia (Mayes), Melissa, Phyllis (Kostas), and Rebecca (Aaron). Later on, "Buddy" and Rayford moved to Mimosa Circle, which runs off the north side of Spring Street, where they are currently living.

"Buddy" is a minister, as well as a retiree of Lockheed Aircraft Corporation. In the 1940s he pastored Bethel Baptist Church on Spring Road and, more recently, Providence Baptist Church in Cobb County. "Buddy" having been faithful to preach the Gospel of Jesus Christ through the years, served as Minister to Senior Adults at First Baptist Church of Kennesaw and currently is a Bible study teacher at Olive Springs Baptist Church in Marietta.

Nineteenth House

Mr. and **Mrs. Carl Marlowe** lived in the second house from the corner of the south side of Spring Street and Jonquil Drive. They had two daughters: **Margaret Ann** and **Jennie**. Mrs. Marlowe, formerly Margaret Harwell of Carrollton, worked at Lockheed Aircraft Corporation. Mr. Marlowe, a deacon at Bethel Baptist Church, retired from L&N Railroad as a conductor. The Marlowes currently live in Carrollton.

Margaret Ann Marlowe married Jerry Chalker from Rome. They had three sons, Courtney, Jeremy, and Kevin, and four grandsons. Jerry, a graduate of Southwestern Seminary, pastors a church in Ft. Worth, Texas.

Jennie Marlowe married Warren Thompson from Bremen. They had three children: Christopher, Russell, and Amy. They also had a grandson and two granddaughters. Warren is now deceased.

Twentieth House

Mr. and **Mrs. Murdock** were residents on the southeast corner of Emory Drive at Spring Road. They had four children: **Roy**, **Roger**, **Bobby**, and **Reba**. Mrs. Murdock was a sister of Mrs. G.L. Turner. See *south side of Spring Road.*

SPRING ROAD
The Country Road
North Side

Appreciation is extended to Helen Blackwell Hanson; Howard Gunn; Raymond Motter; Barbara Deaton Killingsworth; and Jean Deaton Bagley for their furnishing information about the residents of Spring Road. All of these contributors grew up on Spring Road in the middle of the Twentieth Century.

At that time Spring Road began near where Jonquil Drive and Spring Road intersect today. It ended at what is known today as Cumberland Parkway, at the intersection of Cobb Parkway and Akers Mill Road. In the days of my youth, Cobb Parkway was usually referred to as the Four Lane or U.S. Route 41.

NOTE: Prior to the building of the Four Lane, the Dixie Highway that ran through Smyrna was U.S. Route 41: the main north/south route from Atlanta to Chattanooga and points beyond. This route today is U.S. Highway 3 or, locally called, Atlanta Road.

I do not remember much about Spring Road from my young life. I knew some of the families who lived out that way because their children attended Smyrna School and/or they were faithful to attend the ball games. I also remember Bethel Baptist Church as always being there.

First House

Mr. and **Mrs. Cliff Haney** lived in this house. There was much open land between the Prater house, which is on the north side of Spring Street, and the Haney house. Howard Gunn shared, "Mr. Haney was a 'land baron' because he owned a large tract of land located all the way across Poplar Creek; on it he had cattle. Many of the kids in the area, among whom were Johnny Davenport, the Gunns, the Gibsons, and I, would swim in Poplar Creek. Mr. Haney did not appear to 'mind' our swimming there. He never stopped us."

Mr. R.M. Harper, Howard Gunn's grandfather, knew Mr. Haney well. Both of these men were in their senior years in the middle of the Twentieth Century.

Second House

The **Cook Family** house was located off the road in a grove of hardwood trees, which probably extended a thousand feet along the north side of Spring Road, almost directly across from where the SaveRite Grocery Store is today. This may have been the same Cook Family that earlier sold their house on the south side of Spring Road to the "Red" Hightower Family.

Third House

Mr. and **Mrs. Askew**, a middle-aged couple, lived east of the Cook Family.

Fourth House

Mr. Samuel Jones Adams resided on the west side of the Browns' home. He had twin sons: **Weyland Samuel**, known as "Buddy," and **Weyman Jones**, also known as "Buddy." Samuel Adams came to Smyrna from Elberton. See *Hawtorne Avenue.*

Weyland Samuel Adams married Margie Martin; they had three children: Sam, Weylene, and Mark. Margie, Weyland, and Mark are deceased. See *Walker Street.*

Weyman Jones Adams married Hilda Motter, the daughter of Mr. and Mrs. David Henry Motter, Sr. Weyman and Hilda had five children: Elise, Keith, Davy, Randy, and Melissa. See *Motter, north side of Spring Road* and *Anderson Circle.*

Fifth House

Mr. and **Mrs**. **Fred Brown** lived in the next house. Mrs. Brown was the former Landis Head from Griffin. They had four sons: **Freddie**, **George**, **Ray**, and **Jackie**. The Browns had about twenty acres of land, which covered most of the present Jonquil Park. This family had a very comfortable life style. Mr. Brown worked for Cleveland Electric Company. Mrs. Brown was employed by the Cobb County Board of Education as a lunchroom worker.

Freddie Brown is deceased.

George Brown married Linda Bailey Adams; they had no children. George and Linda still live in the Smyrna area.

Ray Brown married Linda Powell from Log Cabin Drive. They had two sons, Rusty and Sandy, and two granddaughters. Ray and Linda still live in Cobb County.

Jackie Brown married Angela Williams. They had two daughters, Hillary and Jessica, and two grandsons. Jackie and Angela still live in the area.

The Fred Brown Family were members of Bethel Baptist Church.

The Simpson Family

In the early part of the Twentieth Century, the Simpson property, located on the north side of Spring Road, extended from Poplar Creek, at the bottom of the hill, all the way to Bethel Baptist Church.

Mr. L.M. Simpson, known as "Mat," was born in 1835 and died in 1914. Mrs. Simpson's given name was **Katherine**. They had eight children: **John**, **William**, **Mack**, **Larkin**, **Charlie**, **Laura**, **Bertha**, and **Beulah O'Dessa**.

At one time the Simpson Family owned and operated a cotton gin on their estate. They also had a large warehouse where cotton was stored until time to market it. The Simpson Family began losing control of their property in the first part of the Twentieth Century. According to family information, several factors caused the demise of the Simpson Estate. World War I, raging in Europe, left the family without its young men; the boll weevil took its toll on the cotton crop; and, eventually, the "Great Depression" forced some members of the family to begin selling off portions of their land to pay taxes. Among the first to purchase land from the Simpsons in the early 1930s were the Blackwell, Cook, and Askew families.

From time to time, several members of the Simpson Family lived in different houses on their property. One Simpson granddaughter, Katherine Louise Harper, her husband, Robert Billy Gunn, and their children lived in a house that was located about where the third house was. The last Simpson Family members to live on the estate were Minnie Simpson, a daughter-in-law of the elder Simpsons, and her daughter, Mary.

The following members of the Simpson Family continued to reside in Smyrna, and many of their descendants are still in the area. Larkin Simpson raised his family on the north side of Spring

Street; Mrs. Bertha Simpson Davenport Byrd lived on the east side of Matthews Street; and Mrs. Beulah O'Dessa Simpson Harper, along with her husband, Roy Harper, lived on Spring Road.

John Simpson and his wife, Minnie, had four children: Cannon, Ethel, Maude, and Tom.

William Simpson and his wife, Ella, had five children: Tina, May, Rena, Ross, and Harold. Though he contracted polio when he was a child, Harold owned and operated a watch repair shop across the Chattahoochee River, in Atlanta's Bolton community.

Mack Simpson and his wife, Octie, had eight children: James, "Buck," Bob, Max, G.A., "Pinky," Geraldine, and Kathleen. Max Simpson at one time owned and operated the Raceway Speedway in Acworth.

Larkin Simpson and his wife, Nolar, had six children: Henry, Clarence, Vasser, Mary, Florence, and Margie.

Charlie Simpson married and moved to Atlanta.

Laura Simpson married Paul Coleman. They had three sons: Alfred, James, and Larry.

Bertha Simpson married John Davenport. They had two children: M.Y., known as "Sonny," and Agnes. Bertha was married the second time to Steve Byrd. "Sonny" Davenport died July 4, 2004. See *east side of Matthews Street.*

Beulah O'Dessa Simpson married Roy M. Harper. They had two daughters: Della Mae and Katherine Louise. Beulah O'Dessa and Roy owned and operated a neighborhood grocery store. See *south side of Spring Road.*

Sixth House

Mr. and **Mrs. Raymond Smith Blackwell** lived on the north side of Spring Road, next door to Bethel Baptist Church. They had four children: **Helen**, **Jerry**, **Neil**, and **Kenneth**. Mr. Blackwell worked for Atlantic Steel Company in Atlanta. Mrs. Blackwell, the former Arrie Florene Davenport, grew up in the New Hope community, located on what is now Wylie Road, east of Marietta.

Helen Blackwell Hanson provided the following information. "My family moved to Spring Road in 1934. Dad purchased a three-room house and fifteen acres for $750.00. We had lived through the Depression, when money was scarce. Dad expanded the house by three rooms, a bathroom, and two porches. It was country that far out Spring Road, which was dirt. When we finally got a phone, it was an eight-party line, and we had telephone operators to connect our calls! In the summers several families would get together and have a 'pot luck' supper. We children had plenty of room to play in the yard while the adults talked."

Helen Blackwell married Brumby H. Hanson, Jr., the son of Mr. and Mrs. Brumby H. Hanson, Sr. Helen and Brumby, Jr., members of First Baptist Church, in 1948 built a house on Bank Street, where they raised their three sons. Helen and Brumby, Jr., both graduated from Smyrna High School. See *Bank* and *Love streets.*

Neil Blackwell was a member of the Campbell High School Class of 1955. He married Judy Ball, who had moved, along with her family, from Toledo, Ohio, to the Belmont Hills area; she was also a member of the Campbell High School Class of 1955. Neil and Judy had two sons, Gregory Allen and Mark Douglas, and three grandchildren.

Jerry Blackwell is deceased.

Kenneth Blackwell now resides in Arivaca, Arizona.

Mr. Raymond Smith Blackwell grew up on Roswell Road, east of Marietta, near the Methodist Campground. (At that time, the area was known as the Blackwell community.)

After their children were grown, Mr. and Mrs. Blackwell purchased a large tract of property near where he grew up and built a house on the south side of Roswell Road, in the eastern part of Cobb County, where they lived the rest of their lives. (According to family information, part of the property that they purchased belonged to Mr. Raymond Blackwell's mother.) The Blackwell Farm is shown on Sherman's Civil War Map.

Seventh House

Mr. and **Mrs. Herbert Blackwell** lived in a small house on the dirt road off Spring Road between Bethel Baptist Church and Bethel Baptist Church Cemetery. Mrs. Blackwell's given name was Merzie. Herbert Blackwell was a first cousin of Raymond Smith Blackwell.

BETHEL BAPTIST CHURCH CEMETERY

Bethel Baptist Church Cemetery was located on a short road that ran between properties of the Blackwell and Williams families and to property of the Motters, which faced Hargrove Road. This road was between the old and new church buildings and between the cemetery and a section where Raymond Motter remembers some "colored" people being buried. He shared that, when he was growing up, there was a sign in the "Black section" of the cemetery that read, "Known only to God."

Eighth House

Mr. and **Mrs. Dub Williams** and their daughter, **Debbie**, lived just beyond the Blackwells. Mr. Williams owned and operated a service station near the Bolton community, across the Chattahoochee River, in Fulton County. Mrs. Williams, whose given name was Ruby, at one time worked for Southern Bell Telephone Company. In later years she worked for Betty Hightower Howard at the Kiddie Dude Ranch, a children's day care which Betty opened in her childhood home, on the south side of Spring Road. See *Hightower, south side of Spring Road, The Country Road.*

Ninth House

The **Columbus Brown Family** at one time resided in this house, which was located on the corner of Spring and Hargrove roads, just east of Bethel Baptist Church. This house was owned by Charlie Jones, who lived on the corner of Spring and Akers Mill roads. See *Charlie Jones, south side of Spring Road, The Country Road.*

Tenth House

The First Family of David Henry Motter

Mr. and **Mrs. David Henry Motter** came to Smyrna in the early part of the Twentieth Century. Mrs. Motter was the former Rebecca Mable Mapp. They had four children: **Robert Lee**, **Mable**, **Essie Mae**, and **Virginia**, known as "Jennie."

Immediately after their marriage, the Motters bought the farm located on Spring Road. Their house faced Hargrove Road, now known as Cumberland Parkway, just past the corner of Spring Road. Actually the road to their property, just east of the Blackwell property, veered northeast from Spring Road and ran behind Bethel Baptist Church and Cemetery. The Motter home was a large, white, one-story (colonial style) house, which was furnished with "ornately designed" furniture. Raymond Motter, one of David Henry's sons from his second marriage, especially remembers the roll-top desk (with a lock), which his dad used for studying and keeping his business papers. See *Flowers, Whitfield Street* and *Motter, Atlanta Street, from Miles Stop to the Motters.*

David Henry Motter, was born in Freeport, Pennsylvania, on March 16, 1869, and died October 12, 1932, at his home in Smyrna. He and his first wife, Rebecca Mable Mapp, are buried in Bethel Baptist Church Cemetery. (According to family information, Mr. Motter donated some land to Bethel Baptist Church for the cemetery.)

David Henry was the grandson of German immigrants who came to this country in the early part of the Nineteenth Century and settled in the Pennsylvania area. Mary Motter Fowler shared that when a direct family member of the Motter "clan" died in 1965, all the descendants of David Henry Motter were privy to an inheritance from a great-great aunt in McConnellsburg, Pennsylvania. Included in the inheritance was a family tree that showed almost every person in the family who was living in Pennsylvania at that time.

Mrs. David Henry Motter, the former Rebecca Mable Mapp, was a sister of Mr. Willie Mapp, who at that time was living on Atlanta Street near the Pinecrest Streetcar Stop. The Mapp home was on the northwest corner of Atlanta and Fleming streets. The Motters may have moved to Smyrna to be close to the family of Rebecca, who was in her early forties when she died. See *Atlanta Street, from Mapps to R & M Café.*

Mary Motter Fowler said that her dad, Robert Lee, remembered that his dad, David Henry Motter, was known to sit on his porch while rocking his baby and to say, "One of these days, Atlanta will be out here." If only he had lived to see it! Who would ever have believed the growth in Cobb County?

Mary Motter's aunt, Thelma Motter Goss, of the second family of David Henry Motter, said that her father helped to build bridges and railroads from Pennsylvania to Green County, where he may have met his first wife, Rebecca Mapp.

NOTE: Mary Motter Fowler and Robert Jones Motter were the children of Robert Lee Motter, the first-born child and only son of David Henry Motter and Rebecca Mable Mapp. They furnished the information about their grandparents. See *Motter, Atlanta Street, from Miles Stop to the Motters.*

The Second Family of David Henry Motter

NOTE: David Henry Motter has been referred to in the following section as "Senior" in regard to the birth of his and Bessie Cooper Motter's oldest son.

I want to thank Raymond Motter for sharing the following information about his family. Raymond was the fifth child of David Henry Motter, a widower with four children, who met and married his second wife, Bessie Cooper Motter of Gafney, South Carolina. David Henry Motter was working on the railroad in front of Bessie's mother's house in Gafney when they met. See *Flowers, south side of Spring Street.*

Mr. David Henry Motter, **Sr.**, and **Mrs. Motter**, the former Bessie Cooper, had six children: **Thelma**, **David Henry**, **Jr.**, **Hilda**, **William Oliver**, **Raymond**, and **Kelly**.

Thelma Motter married James Goss, who grew up in Smyrna. They had two children: Benny and Joan. Benny lives in Atlanta, and Joan lives in Florida. Thelma and James Goss are deceased.

David Henry Motter, Jr., married Louise Blackburn from North Carolina. They had one daughter, Peggy, who married Freddie Hayworth. Louise, whom I remember as a very nice lady, worked at the "new" Colonial Store, which was built on Bank Street in 1950. In earlier years Louise worked at Stop, Shop and Save on Atlanta Street, then at Atherton's Drug Store. She began working for A & P Super Market when it was located adjacent to Dickson Shopping Center, on South Cobb

David Henry Motter, Sr., holding **Raymond Motter**
Circa 1926
Courtesy of Raymond Motter

Raymond Motter, Christmas 2003. Raymond served in the United States Marines in World War II. He is a member of the "dwindling group" of veterans of that war who are still living.

drive, and at three different locations of A & P in Belmont Hills Shopping Center. She and David ar deceased.

David Henry Motter, Jr., was a member of the Civil Conservation Corps (CCC) in the 1930s David also served in the United States Army during World War II. His tour of duty included service i Europe under General George Patton. See *Motter, Anderson Circle.*

OTE: The CCC was a program that was set up by the administration of President Frankli Delano Roosevelt in the 1930s to put young men to work during the Depression years.

Hilda Motter married Weyman J. "Buddy" Adams, who also grew up on the north side o Spring Road and served in the United States Air Corps. They had five children: Keith, Elise, David Melissa, and Randy. Hilda was born September 2, 1922, and died January 9, 2005.See *Anderson Circle* and *fourth house, north side of Spring Road.*

William Oliver Motter, who died in the first year of his life, is buried in Bethel Baptis Church Cemetery.

Raymond Motter married Vivian Brasill. They had four children: Raymond Jr., known a "Ray," Deborah Ann, Alan Kent, and Jill. Vivian grew up on Atlanta Street, next door to the Robe Lee Motter Family and near the Pinecrest Streetcar Stop, at Fleming Street.

Raymond served with the United States Marine Corps in the Pacific during World War II. H received a Purple Heart for wounds he received in action. Raymond, who owned and operated vending machine company, and Vivian were members of Wilson Memorial Baptist Church o Oakdale Road, south of Smyrna. Vivian passed away April 9, 1999, due to congestive heart failure.

Kelly Motter married Laura Ann Jones, who grew up on Highland Avenue. They had fou children: Mike, Diane, Russell, and Kenneth. Kelly, who served in the United States Navy as a caree service man, was awarded for his service during the Cuban Missile Crisis. He passed away on April 8 1999, after a long illness due to a stroke. See *Jones, Highland Avenue.*

David Henry Motter, Sr., a Mason, was much older than his wife, Bessie. He died in 1932 a the age of sixty-three. Shortly after his death, Bessie and her family moved to Gafney, South Carolina to be near her parents. While Bessie and her children were there, the Motter house on Spring Road i Smyrna burned; however, a smokehouse on the property was not damaged by the fire. The members o the Masonic Order, building onto the smokehouse, made a four-room house, in which Bessie and he children came back to Smyrna to live.

With the stock market crash of 1929, the Depression in full force, and her husband's death i 1932, Mrs. Motter had a hard time making a living for the family. Raymond remembers her having t sell bits and pieces of the farm each year to pay the taxes. She never lost her home place; but, befor the Depression was over and her children were grown, she had sold the largest portion of it to mak ends meet. During the 1930s, Raymond remembers, his mother went to work in a sewing factor above Harbin's Grocery Store. (This was prior to "Shorty" Black's operating this grocery store, whic was on the east side of Atlanta Street.) This factory for making clothes was United States Governmen run as part of President Franklin Roosevelt's "New Deal" programs to put people back to work durin the "Great Depression." See *Bivins, south side of Spring Road, The Country Road*

Some of the children from both of Mr. Motter's families attended classes at old Bethe School. The Cumberland Parkway. Raymond Motter, born in 1925, remembers going to school ther when he was unpainted school building, not very large, was on the southwest corner of what is nov Spring Road and very small, prior to attending Smyrna School. Raymond thinks Bethel School close in the late 1920s or very early 1930s, perhaps because of the Great Depression.

Bethel School was located on the southwest corner of Spring Street, now known as Cumberland Parkway.

Top Row, L-R: Ella Mae Otwell, Lydia Spears, teacher; Georgia Otwell, and Florris Woodruff. **Second Row from top:** Thelma Motter, Mary Emory Simpson, Johnny Deaton, Mildred George, Florence Emory Anderson, and Horace Cochran. **Third Row from top, L-R:** Euvenia Cochran, Ralph George?, Hilda Motter, Herbert Emory, and David Motter who is barely visible. Raymond Motter is the little boy standing alone in front of picture

Circa Late 1920s
Photo Courtesy of Raymond Motter

It was at Bethel School that Zelma Motter, Robert's first wife, taught. Malinda Jolley Mor[t] tells that her parents, Lex and LeoDelle (Lassiter) Jolley, taught there in 1922; they boarded during t[he] week with Mr. and Mrs. Charlie Jones. Some older residents remember that classes may have be[en] held in Bethel Baptist Church. See *Jolley, west side of Lee Street.*

SPRING ROAD
The Country Road
South Side

Appreciation is extended to Howard Gunn; Betty Hightower Howard; Raymond Mott[er]; Nancy Jones Snipes; Barbara Alice Deaton Killingsworth; and Thelma Jean Deaton Bagley for shari[ng] their memories of growing up on Spring Road in the middle of the Twentieth Century.

Appreciation is also extended to the following: Connie Turner Kraemer for shari[ng] information about her family, the C.L. Turners, who moved to Spring Road in the early 1950s; Elai[ne] Scott Davis and Shirley Sentell Parsons for the information about the Sentell Family; and Erika Wrig[ht] Sams for the information about the Gus Jones Family.

In the days of my childhood, Spring Road was a long way off. My family did not have a c[ar] and, therefore, our travels were on the streetcar or in someone else's car. The people I remember fro[m] Spring Road were those I knew through my attending Smyrna School and/or ball games with them [or] their children. It was not an area I traveled by foot during my childhood.

R.M. HARPER NEIGHBORHOOD GROCERY STORE

Mr. and **Mrs. Roy M. Harper** operated the R.M. Harper Neighborhood Grocery Store a[nd] had living quarters in the rear of it. Mrs. Harper was the former Beulah O'Dessa Simpson. On t[he] south side of Spring Road, they owned a small tract of land, which was located west of the R[ed] Feather Farm. Mr. and Mrs. Harper had two daughters: **Katherine Louise**, born in Fulton Count[y] June 1, 1921, and **Della Mae**, who, named for her grandmother, died when she was a baby.

Beulah O'Dessa was one of the daughters of the Simpson Family who resided on the nor[th] side of Spring Road in the early part of the Twentieth Century. She was a sister of Mrs. Bert[h] Simpson Davenport Byrd, who lived on the east side of Matthews Street, and Mr. Larkin Simpso[n] who lived on the north side of Spring Street. See *Byrd, Matthews Street* and *north side of Spring Stre[et]* and *Simpson, north side of Spring Road.*

<u>First House</u>

Katherine Louise Harper married **Robert Billy Gunn**, who, known as "R.B.," was born [in] Newton County in 1910. They had eight children: **Howard**, **Frances**, **Leroy**, **Bonnie**, **Rand[y]**, **Carolyn**, **David**, and **Cathy**.

Mr. and Mrs. Roy M. Harper gave their daughter, Katherine, a small plot of land just east [of] the store. Katherine and "R.B." built this small house near her parents' store and moved here with the[ir] family in 1947. Katherine and "R.B." operated the Harper Neighborhood Grocery Store aft[er] Katherine's parents could no longer do so.

<u>Howard Gunn</u> was born on Akers Mill Road, near Smyrna. He married Peggy Driver of t[he] Oakdale community, south of Smyrna. She was the daughter of Mr. and Mrs. Walter Driver. Howa[rd] and Peggy were "sweethearts" at Campbell High School and married soon after graduating. They ha[d] four children: Becky, Dottie, Billy, and Sheri.

Having attended Georgia Institute of Technology, Howard worked for Fulton Coun[ty] Planning and Community Development as a civil engineer; he retired in 1991. Peggy Driver Gu[nn] attended Greenleaf Business College, in Atlanta; then worked for the Fulton National Bank and t[he]

Federal Reserve Bank, respectively. The Gunns, still living in Smyrna, are members of Wilson Memorial Baptist Church, in the Oakdale community.

Becky Gunn married Dan Adams, an executive with Equifax Company. He passed away in 2002. Becky is a secretary for an advertising firm.

Dottie Gunn married Steve Geiger. They had one daughter, Christie. Steve is President of Curtis 1000. Dottie, an RN, is currently employed by BellSouth in the Yellow Pages Department.

Sherri Gunn married Buff Olsen. They had one daughter, Amber. Later on, Sherrie married Michael Satterfield from White. They live in Woodstock and attend Goshen Baptist Church in Waleska.

Frances Gunn married Larry Youman. They had two daughters: Pat and Page. Frances later married Claude Coile. They live in Acworth.

Leroy Gunn married Barbara Power from Atlanta's Bolton community. They had one daughter, Sharon, and one son, Tony.

Bonnie Gunn married Dick Stewart; they had two daughters: Sandy and Robin. Bonnie later married Richard Tucker; they had a son, Ricky. Bonnie and Richard live on Nickajack Road in Mableton.

Randy Gunn married Nancy Cheek. They had one daughter, Randa.

Carolyn Gunn, married Kenneth Denson from Acworth. They had four children: Tony, Ronnie, Brian and Tracy, the latter two being twins; all of them live in the Metro Atlanta area. Carolyn and Kenneth live in Smyrna.

David Gunn married Virginia Holcomb from Smyrna. They had one daughter, Kimberly. David is a home builder. (In the days of my youth, most builders were referred to as carpenters.)

Cathy Gunn married Jerry Peppers of Cobb County. They had two children: Robert and Christie. Christie is married to a physician, Dr. Greg Ray; they live in Powder Springs.

Second House

Ben and **Janie Cochran** lived on the corner of Spring and Corn roads, probably in the 1940s.

Janie, previously married, had a son, James Day, who married Laura Harbin, a daughter of Mr. and Mrs. Harbin who owned and operated a grocery store on Sunset Avenue. James and Laura lived on Corn Road. See *Harbin, Sunset Avenue,* and *Day, Corn Road.*

Ben's first wife was "Teen" Osburn",; they had one son, Benjamin Bluford, known as "B.B." as well as "Jack," Cochran. "Teen" was a member of the large Osburn Family who lived on the north side of Spring Street. See *"Jack" Cochran, Elizabeth Street* and *Osburn, north side of Spring Street.*

Ben Cochran had two brothers, "Boots" Cochran and Will Cochran, who lived in Vinings, and a sister, Alice.

At one time "Teen" and Ben resided on King Springs Road, where Ben operated a sawmill. He provided lumber from his sawmill to help build Spring Street Baptist Church. See *Spring Street Baptist Church* and *Osburn, south side of Spring Street* and *Osburn, north side of Spring Street.*

THE RED FEATHER FARM

The Red Feather Farm was a large tract of land which extended from Harper's Neighborhoo Grocery Store to Poplar Creek and included, on the east side, a small rental house where mar different families lived through the years. The Red Feather Farm Restaurant was located in an ol house on the farm property, in the vicinity where the Highlands subdivision was built in the late 1950 According to long-time residents of Spring Road, the Spring Road property between the Red Feath Farm and Poplar Creek, was owned by Arthur Crowe, who lived on Atlanta Road, south of Smyrna.

I delivered newspapers to the Red Feather Farm Restaurant and would go by once a week collect my money from the restaurant personnel.

Past the small rental house was a large tract of land owned by **Luther Holcombe**. S *Alexander Street.*

Third House

Mr. and **Mrs**. **Charlie Freeman** and their daughter, **Nettie Ola**, were residents of th house. **Cecil**, who was related to them, lived there also, but I do not remember the family connectio There was also a small boy who lived with them. Mr. Freeman, an electrician, would frequent G.B. Place when I was working there.

NOTE: According to residents of the area, the McKenna Family owned the tract of land fro Poplar Creek to Campbell Road. Mrs. McKenna, a member of the Orme Campbell Family, sold son of the land on Campbell Road at South Atlanta Road to the Cobb County Board of Education in t early 1950s, with the stipulation that a school be built and named for Orme Campbell. Campbell Hig was completed in 1952 and was operated as a high school at that site until 1997, when Campbell Hig School and Wills High School were merged on Ward Street and named Smyrna High Schoo Diplomas from Smyrna High School were issued for one year. Afterwards, court action called for t name of the high school to revert to Campbell. At that time the Cobb County Board of Educatic relocated Nash Middle School (formerly next door to Wills High School) to this building on Sou Atlanta Road and it became known as Orme Campbell Middle School.

Fourth House

Mr. and **Mrs**. **Columbus Brown** were residents of the first house east of Campbell Driv located where Argyle Elementary School was later built. Mrs. Brown was the former Dorothy Timn from Canton. The Browns had six children: **Marvin**, **Sarah**, **Colleen**, **Jerry**, **Carl**, and **Don**. M Brown was a butcher at White Provision Company, a meat packing operation on Howell Mill Road i Atlanta.

Marvin Brown married Gloria Snyder. They had two daughters: Andrea and Kathy.

Marvin married again. He and the former Teresa Whitehead had two sons: Marvin, Jr., ar Mitchell. Marvin, Sr., played on Campbell's first football team which began in 1952, where he w known as "Bulldog."

Sarah Brown married Freeman Wallace. They had four children: Tony, Becky, Mike, ar Steve.

Colleen Brown married Albert Cartee. They had one son, Richard.

Jerry Brown married Harry Swartz. They had no children.

Carl Brown married Billy Jean Killingsworth. They had one daughter, Carman.

Don Brown married Linda Walker. They had two children: Mandy and Scott.

Fifth House

Mr. and **Mrs. Robert Carlton Loudermilk** moved to Smyrna in 1936. Mr. Loudermilk was nown as "Carl." Mrs. Loudermilk, the former Gertrude Daniels, was from Wrens, and Mr. oudermilk was from Demorest. They lived just past where Argyle School and the walkway over pring Road are located. The Loudermilks had four children: **Bobby**, **Geraldine**, known as "Gerry," **ouglas**, and **David**.

I well remember Mrs. Loudermilk as being a tall, stout lady and an avid fan when her laughter, "Gerry," played basketball at Campbell High School. It seemed as if she was always there. 'he Loudermilk Family was members of First Methodist Church.

Mrs. Loudermilk was the dietician at Campbell High School and Argyle Elementary School, espectively. She served for a time as hostess at First Methodist Church, where she directed and atered many weddings. Robert Carlton Loudermilk worked for Georgia Power Company for fifty ears.

William Robert Loudermilk, known as "Bobby," married Nancy Sanders. They had four hildren: William Anthony, Rebecca Lynn, Jennifer Carol, and Robert Jeffrey. They also had nine randchildren. Bobby is deceased.

Geraldine Loudermilk, known as, "Gerry," married Norman Douglas Brown from Corpus hristi, Texas. They had two children, Scott Lawrence and Clayton Hewett, and two grandchildren. Gerry" and Norman live in Acworth.

Douglas Loudermilk married Claudine Marshall. They had two children, Diana Gail and Aarshall Douglas, and three grandchildren. Douglas and Claudine live at Lake Oconee.

David Loudermilk married Patricia McCollum. They had one daughter, Amy Patrice. David ves in Acworth. Patricia, known as "Pat," is deceased.

Sixth House

Mr. and **Mrs. Homer Flowers** lived near the Loudermilk Family. Mrs. Flowers was ormerly Cassie Cooper, a sister of Raymond Motter's mother, Bessie Motter (Bivens). She was nown to the Motter children as "Aunt Cassie." The Flowers had two sons: **Homer, Jr.**, and **Edward**. ee *David Henry Motter's second family, north side of Spring Road.*

Edward Flowers, who served in the United States Navy, had one daughter, Susan.

Homer Flowers, Jr., served in the United States Army during World War II. He had one aughter, Linda, who retired from C.W. Matthews Contracting Company. Linda now lives in iedmont, Alabama.

Seventh House

Mr. and **Mrs. G.L. Turner** resided in this house, which stood on the southeast corner of pring Road and Woodruff Drive. Mrs. Turner was the former Louise Chitwood from Cartersville. 'hey had five daughters: **Barbara**, **Bonnie**, **Connie**, **Brenda**, and **Glenda**, the latter two of whom ere twins.

Barbara Turner, who graduated from Campbell High School, married Tom Dever, now eceased. Later she married Robert Brinson; they had one child, Robert, Jr., known as "Bobby," who ied in November 2004.

Bonnie Turner married Billy Watts; they had two children: Lisa and Mark. Bonnie, graduate of Campbell High School, and Billy are divorced.

Connie Turner married Ted Kraemer. They had three daughters: Paula, Angela, known a "Dawn," and Tammy Maria. Connie, who graduated from Campbell High School, and Ted still live i Smyrna.

"Dawn" Kraemer married Langley Rider. They had two sons: Hunter and Austin. Dawn i deceased.

Tammy Maria Kraemer married Barry William Lovern. See *Lovern, south side of Powde Springs Street.*

Paula Kraemer, not married, lives in Smyrna.

Brenda Turner married Danny Deaver (no relation to Barbara's first husband). They ha three daughters: Kim, Christy, and Susan. Brenda Turner graduated from McEachern High School i Powder Springs.

Glenda Turner married Everett Cox. Still living in Smyrna, they had no children. Glend Turner graduated from McEachern High School in Powder Springs.

Mr. G. L. Turner was from Dallas. Before moving to this house, he and Mrs. Turner, alon with their daughters, lived near the intersection of Akers Mill Road and U.S. Highway 41; later the lived in Vinings. On the north side of Spring Road Mr. Turner built a house in which they lived. In th late 1940s or early 1950s, Mr. Turner built behind the first house another one, just a short distanc north from Spring Road and facing Woodruff Drive. After the Turners moved to the newer house, th Spring Road house became rental property. Still later, Mr. and Mrs. Turner moved from Smyrna t Dallas Highway, in the area of its intersection with Barrett Parkway. There they lived for the rest o their lives.

A sawmiller, Mr. Turner owned and operated Turner Brothers Lumber Company, on Dalla Highway in Dallas. His brother Homer, who lived in Acworth, was in business with him. Mr. Turne had two other brothers, James and Dennis, who also lived in Acworth.

Mrs. Turner's sister, Mamie Murdock, lived on Spring Street where the foreign auto par place is currently located. The Murdocks had four children: Roger, Roy, Bobby Ray, and Reba. Se *twentieth house, south side of Spring Street.*

Eighth House

Ruth and **Vernon Cook** were residents of this house, located on the south side of Sprin Road, across the street from Bethel Baptist Church. They had two sons: **Hugh** and **Charles**, both o whom graduated from Woodward Academy, in College Park. Vernon owned and operated th cafeteria at Atlantic Steel Company in Atlanta.

The Robert Hightower Family

Mr. and **Mrs. Robert Hightower** purchased this house from Vernon and Ruth Cook. Rober known as "Red," moved his family from Atlanta where he grew up, to this house. Mrs. Hightowe formerly Mary Ruth Cross from Bessemer, Alabama, grew up in Birmingham, Alabama, an graduated from Brenau College, in Gainesville. "Red" and Mary Ruth had three children: **Bobby**, **Betty**, and **Tommy**.

During their lifetime, "Red" and Mary Ruth Hightower were members of St. Jude Episcopal Church on Jones Shaw Road, now Windy Hill Road.

Bobby Hightower married Barbara Tatum from Cartersille; they had three children: Vickie, Donna, and Robert, Jr. Bobby graduated from Marietta High School, where he played football for Coach James Pressley.

Betty Hightower married one of my friends, Dewey Lioneal Howard, who grew up on Lee Street. They had three children: Tracie, David, and Preston. Betty graduated from Campbell High School, where she was an outstanding player on the Campbell Girls' Varsity Basketball Team. The Howard Family attended St Jude's Episcopal Church on Jones Shaw Road, now Windy Hill Road. See *Howard, west side of Lee Street.*

Tracie Howard married Jeffrey Lanier from Kennesaw; they had two children: Haley and Conner. Tracie graduated from Campbell High School.

David Howard, a graduate of Campbell High School, married Cheri Conley from Mableton, a graduate of Georgia Institute of Technology. David and Sheri had two children: Kelsey and Parker. Lillie and I, David's godparents, have been very close to the Howard Family for more than forty years.)

Preston Howard, who graduated from Campbell High School in the Class of 1984, is unmarried.

Tommy Hightower, who graduated from Campbell High School, moved to Texas. There he married and had one child. Tommy, who died from a massive heart attack, is buried in Texas.

After her mother's death, in the mid 1960s, Betty Hightower Howard opened the Kiddie Dude Ranch, a day care center, in this house and operated it until the late 1970s. She then sold the business to Mrs. Kenneth ("Jerrie") Graham, who operated the day care for a long time before selling it to her niece. A day care business has been continually operated on this site, from the time Betty opened.

Ninth House

Mr. and **Mr. W. Dempsey Deaton** built this house near where the Bethel School once stood, on the south side of Spring and Hargrove roads, (Hargrove Road is currently known as Cumberland Parkway.) The Deatons had two sons: Carl Marion and John J. Deaton. See *Sentells, south side of Spring Road, The Country Road.*

Dempsey Deaton and his wife, the former Alice Sentell, moved to Cobb County in the late 1920s or early 1930s. Alice inherited twenty acres of land on Spring Road from the Power Family Estate; then Dempsey bought an additional twenty acres. Their property extended from where they built their home to the Four Lane Highway, known today as Cobb Parkway.

Carl Deaton married Mattie Doris Bivins, the daughter of Mr. W.H. Bivins. They had four children: William Terry, Barbara Alice, Thelma Jean, and Linda Marion. Carl worked for Lockheed Aircraft Corporation.

William Terry Deaton married Doris Day. They had two daughters: Tammy and Susan. Later on, William Terry married Sherrie Robati; they had two daughters: Jennifer and Tala.

Barbara Alice Deaton married Harold Killingsworth. They had one daughter, Kimberly Alice, who married Jeffrey Waldrip from Mableton. Barbara and Harold are members of Wilson Memorial Baptist Church, in the Oakdale community, south of Smyrna.

Kimberly and Jeffrey Waldrip had two sons, Harold Kyle and Jeremy, and a daughter, Kelly.

Thelma Jean Deaton married Donald R. Bagley from Cumming. They had three childre Donna Jean, Gary Scott, and Kasandra Doris. Donald and Jean live in Jasper and are members of Co Springs Baptist Church in Tate.

Donna Jean Bagley married James Culberson of Marietta. They had two children: Joshua ar Jessica.

Gary Scott Bagley married Linda Force from Louisana. Linda is a doctor of chiropract medicine with a practice on Highway 92 in Cherokee County. Gary and Linda, who live in Jaspe have no children.

Kasandra Bagley married Darrin Godwin from Albany. They had three children: Elizabet Elicia, and Kristopher.

Linda Marion Deaton married Harold Stewart. They had two children: Christopher and Ann Linda lives in Jasper. Harold is deceased.

John Deaton. married Edith Fouts from the Oakdale community, south of Smyrna. They ha two children: Joyce and Janice, known as "Jan." John served in the United States Army Air Cor during World War II and later worked for Lockheed Aircraft Corporation.

Joyce Deaton married Ronnie Jones from Smyrna. They had two daughters: Tracey ar Amy. See *Jones, Walker Court.*

Janice Deaton married Henry Hanson from Boston, Massachusetts. They had two childre Angie and Kevin, and one grandchild.

The Bivins

Mr. and Mrs. W. H. Bivins had three children: Howard, Mattie Doris, and Bill. Mrs. W. I Bivins died when her two younger children were ages four and two. Her older son, Howard, was young man at the time of her death.

Later on, when Doris and Bill were grown, their dad, W. H. Bivins, married Bessie Coop Motter, the widow of David Henry Motter, Sr., who lived on the north side of Spring Road. All Bessie's children were grown when she married Mr. Bivins.

Howard Bivins married and raised his family in Paulding County.

Mattie Doris Bivins married Carl Deaton. See *ninth house.*

Bill Bivins married Susie Cochran. They had two children: Jimmy and Diane. Jimmy liv in Smyrna. See *Bivins* and *Cochran families, south side of Spring Road, The Country Road, ar Cochran, Foster Street.*

Mr. W. H. Bivins ran a grocery store in the Elizabeth community of Marietta. Later on, the Georgia State Capitol, during the administration of Governor Herman Talmadge, he was a securi guard, a position in which he served until he was ninety years old. Mr. Bivins died at the age of ninet two.

The Sentells

Mr. Homer Sentell was a brother of Alice Sentell Deaton, who lived on Spring Road. Hom and his wife, the former Annie Dean Wood, had six children: Sarah Frances, Shirley, Albert, Rudolp Guy, and Jack. Homer and Annie raised their family on Oakdale Road in the Oakdale communit south of Smyrna. According to family information, Mr. Sentell inherited twenty acres of land from t 'ower Family estate, which he traded for property on Oakdale Road. See *Deaton, south side of Spring* *:oad, The Country Road.*

Albert Sentell married Alene Brown of the Oakdale community; they had two sons: Jack and)on Wayne. Albert and Alene were members of Locust Grove Baptist Church in the Oakdale ommunity, where Albert owned and operated a dry cleaning business for many years. He was known s "Sentell the Hatter." Alene was a member of the large Brown Family in the Oakdale community, vhere both Albert and Alene were leaders.

Jack Sentell died when he was two weeks old.

Asa Rudolph Sentell married Mildred Adams; they had no children.

Guy Lynn Sentell never married.

Sarah Frances Sentell married Leon Scott, known as "Scotty," from Riverdale, in Clayton ounty. They had two daughters: Elaine and Beth. The Scott Family were members of First Baptist hurch. "Scotty" passed away in 1986. Sarah is now a member of King Spring Baptist Church, and is urrently living in the Smyrna Towers retirement home.

Elaine Scott married Benny Davis; they had one son, Luke. Elaine and Benny are members f First Baptist Church. Elaine is a teacher at Russell Elementary School in Cobb County.

Beth Scott married Howard Thomas; they had one son, Bronson.

Sarah began losing her eyesight in her middle years and soon afterwards became an activist or the blind and visually impaired. Through her efforts, with the assistance of her husband, "Scotty," obb Services for The Blind & Low Vision was founded. The agency is now known as Blind and Low 'ision Services of North Georgia. It initially was housed in the Mitchell Building, on the corner of tlanta Street and Sunset Avenue; it later moved to South Cobb Drive, just north of Wade Ford.

Many of the people who receive assistance through this service lost their sight during their dult years. Because of Sarah's efforts, the blind and vision-impaired people north of Atlanta have ccess to training toward adjusting their lifestyle and continuing to live independently. Sarah's chievements are quite remarkable, including obtaining the funding for these services, an almost npossible hurdle to overcome. The agency has been providing these services for more than twenty ears. I have been privileged to serve on the Board of Directors of Blind and Low Vision of North ieorgia, along with Sarah, for many years.

Shirley Anne Sentell married Odell Parson. They had one son, Scott, who is a chiropractor in noxville, Tennessee. Shirley and Odell, members of First Baptist Church, live in Vinings.

Many Sentell descendants live in the Smyrna/Vinings/Oakdale areas.

The Jones Families

In the days of my youth, Mr. and Mrs. Gus Jones, Mr. and Mrs. Charlie Jones, and Walter ones lived in two houses within what is now known as the Cumberland Mall area. The men were rothers.

Spring Road in the middle of the Twentieth Century curved to the right, past the ook/Hightower house, and followed a route behind the present Cumberland Mall. It made almost a inety-degree curve to the left and ran east, past the south end of Cumberland Mall. There were two rge white houses located in that area. One was located on the south side of the road past the deep urve, and the other was on the north- east corner of today's intersection of Cobb Parkway and Akers Iill Road.

Tenth House

Mr. and **Mrs. Gus Jones** and their daughter, **Alice**, lived in the first large white hou located on Spring Road past the deep curve, in the vicinity of where Barnes and Noble Book Store presently located. Mr. and Mrs. Gus Jones were members of Vinings Methodist Church, located Paces Mill Road in the Vinings community.

Mrs. Gus Jones was the former Opal Ward. She graduated from the Normal School Athens, with a degree in home economics. The Normal School, an institution of higher learning f young ladies, was part of the University of Georgia. Mrs. Jones was employed for a time as Hon Extension Agent for Fulton County. In the Home Economics Department of the University of Georgi the Carman Wright Family of Smyrna maintains a scholarship in memory of Mrs. Opal Ward Jones.

Alice Jones married Carman Wright of Smyrna. They had four children: Allison, Erik Heather, and Robert. Alice, Carman, and all of their children graduated from Campbell High Schoo See *Hanson, south side of Love Street.*

Morris Reagin, the brother of my friend Lewis Reagin, both now deceased, rented land fro Mr. Gus Jones, 1959-1964. Morris, who raised hogs on the lower part of the property, had been quot as saying, "Mr. Jones was always nice to me and my family."

Eleventh House

Walter F. Jones, known as "Watt," a farmer who cultivated the land in this area for ma years, built this two-story house in 1883. (Mr. Jones was also the builder of the James Carmicha house on Log Cabin Drive. Both houses are built according to the same basic plan.) This house w the home place of **"Watt" Jones**, his wife, **Alice Power Jones**, and their three sons, **Charles Alfre Augustus P.**, and **Walter L. Jones**. Alice Power Jones was the granddaughter of James Power, f whom Powers Ferry Road was named. The house was situated on the northeast corner of what is no known as Cobb Parkway and Akers Mill Road, in the Cumberland Mall/Galleria area.

Alice Power grew up in the Power home place, which was located on a bluff overlooking t Chattahoochee River. Ray's on the River Restaurant is currently located on or near the home pla site. Alice Jane met her husband, "Watt," at Sandy Springs Methodist Church, where she taug Sunday School.

The Charles Alfred Jones Family

Charles Alfred and **Lucille Jones** resided in the eleventh house in the middle of t Twentieth Century. They had five children: **Rosemary**, **Beth**, **Charles A Jones, Jr.**, **Nancy Jane**, a **Lucy**, all of whom were raised at the home place, at the intersection of Akers Mill Road and the Fo Lane highway. Charles Jones' brother, **Walter**, also lived there.

Charles Alfred Jones, a professor at Georgia Institute of Technology, married Nancy Lucil McLain of Acworth in 1925. As a young lady, she had come to Vinings in 1923, to teach at Vinin School, where she taught until it was consolidated with Smyrna School in 1946. Mrs. Jones was al active in the Smyrna Woman's Club and Phillips Legion Chapter of the United Daughters of t Confederacy, located in Smyrna.

Both Mr. and Mrs. Jones were known for their strong leadership in their church and in t teaching profession. They were active, lifelong members of Vinings Methodist Church, where M Jones' parents, "Watt" and Alice, were founding members. Professor Jones taught at Georgia Institu of Technology for forty-seven years.

Rosemary Jones married Jim Cox of Cobb County; they had four children: Jim, Jr., Mary Beth, Sam, and Matthew. Jim and Rosemary live in Dunwoody.

Beth Jones (Crabill) , just out of college, taught at Smyrna Elementary School, along with Mrs. Mona Camp, for one year. She and her husband, Bill, are parents of three children: Betsy, Susan, and Steven. The Crabills now live at Sky Lake, near Helen.

Charles A. Jones, Jr.., married Ann Tygart of Nashville, a small town in South Georgia, where Charles and Ann lived. They had three daughters: Laura, Amy, and Julie. Charles A., Jr., died in April 2005.

Nancy Jane Jones married H.G. Snipes, who is a partner in the Cochran, Camp, and Snipes Law Firm on Atlanta Road in Smyrna. Nancy, who graduated in the Campbell High School Class of 1955, and H.G. live in East Cobb County. They had two children, John and Katherine, and two grandchildren.

Lucy Jones, who graduated in the Campbell High School Class of 1963, married Pem Cooley; they had two children: Brian and Laura. Lucy and Pem live in Marietta.

After Mr. Jones' death in 1969, Mrs. Jones moved to Smyrna, to be near her daughter and son-in-law, Nancy and H.G. Snipes, who lived on Spring Drive at that time. Mrs. Jones continued to live on Spring Drive until her death, in 1984.

Smyrna Schoolhouse about 60 years ago – children in grades one to four posed in front of the O
Masonic Hall on West Spring Street, which served as the town's school about 1905 or 1906 when t
picture was made. Teachers, Miss Margaret Mabel and Miss Payne are in the back of the group. T
principal, Mr. Turnell Hanson with dark hair is pictured on the right holding a buggy whip over h
shoulder, it is hardly visible. The original photo belonged to Mrs. Ida Henderson of Smyrna. (No
this picture appeared in the Smyrna Herald on the 1960s, it was made by F.L. Mangum.) Newspap
copy is the courtesy of Jeanette Hanson Taylor.)

CHAPTER FOUR

ALEXANDER STREET
East Side

<u>First House</u>

Alfred Slate, and his wife, the former **Rosa Adkins**, known as "Rose," lived here. "Rose" as from Cedartown and Alfred was from Bremen. They had eight children: **James T.**, **Jewel**, **Nita**, **etty**, **Bill**, **Edna**, **Ellen**, and **Jerry**. Betty and Bill were twins.

<u>Second House</u>

Mr. and **Mrs. Luther Holcombe** lived here. Mrs. Holcombe, the former Eva Cochran, and uther had four children: **Thelma**, **Bessie**, **Thomas**, **Luther**, and **Robert Franklin**. According to mily information, Mr. Holcombe at one time was employed by Glover Machine Works in Marietta, here he was paid in "scrip."

NOTE: "Scrip" is paper money in the amount less than one dollar or a certificate showing it's older is entitled to something. The Holcombe's daughter, Thelma, still has some of the "scrip" in her ossession.

<u>Thelma Holcombe</u> married James T. Slate. See *first house*.

<u>Bessie Holcombe</u> married Mr. Matthews. Bessie is deceased.

The other Holcombe siblings still live in the area.

Janet Brooks Brown shared the following story. "When I called Thelma Holcombe Slate to lk about her family for this book, Thelma asked, 'Do you still have Tom's Valentine?'

"Knowing immediately what she was talking about, I responded, 'Yes, in my baby book ere is a Valentine Tom gave me when I was an infant.' (My mother, Georgia Brooks, had written on e envelope: 'This Valentine is from Tom Holcombe, a little boy who used to live next door to us.' It as one of my first Valentines.)"

ALEXANDER STREET
West Side

Alexander Street is a short one, the first to the right off Spring Street, past the railroad ossing A small stream and the railroad run not far from the first house on the west side; this scouraged more building in the area.

Appreciation is extended to Janet Brooks Brown and Thelma Holcombe Slate, for the llowing information on the families who lived on Alexander Street, in the middle of the Twentieth entury.

<u>First House</u>

Clarence Brooks, and his wife, the former **Georgia Gilham**, in 1939 and 1940 lived in this use, built by Jim Ridley before the Brooks' oldest child, **Janet**, was born. This dwelling, the only e on the west side of the street, was used as rental property, where many different families lived rough the years. See *Brooks, south side of Walker Street, and Brooks, east side of Roswell Street.*

Alfred and **Dottie Coleman**

Alford and **Dottie Coleman** lived in this house at one time, as did the **Castleberry/ Gre** families. See *Castleberry, Elizabeth Street.*

FOSTER STREET
East Side

Foster Street, a short street, runs beside Spring Street Baptist Church, off Spring Street. W only a few houses, all on the east side, the street is basically the same as in the days of my youth.

Appreciation is extended to Linda Barfield, who grew up on Foster Street, where she s lives; to Janet Brooks Brown, Mildred Clayton Broyles, Ida Mae Clayton, and Mary Lou Re Cochran, who shared their memories of the Alfred Cochran family; and to Janet Brooks Brown a Willis Conn for information about the Conn Family.

NOTE: Claude Osburn, who lived on the southeast corner of Spring and Foster streets, a who was a maker of window blinds, had, behind his house, a workshop on Foster Street; it was locat on part of his property just before the first house. See *Osburn, south side of Spring Street.*

First House

Mr. and **Mrs**. **Virgil Lee Barnett** were residents of the first house on Foster Street. M Barnett was the former Vadie Rogers. They had three children: **Doyle**, **Thelma**, and **Becky**. T Barnett Family were active members of Spring Street Baptist Church.

Virgil Lee Barnett was a brother of Lorene, Adelaide, Evelyn, and Linton Barnett. Virgil L and Linton married sisters: Vadie and Sadie Rogers, respectively.

Vadie and Sadie Rogers were the daughters of Norma Jean and Ulysses Rogers of Oakdale community, south of Smyrna. They had seven siblings: Evelyn Rogers (Bennett), Aud Rogers (Groover), Margie Rogers (McKerley), Ruth Rogers (Loyd), Donald Rogers, Ralph Roge and Charles Rogers. Mr. and Mrs. Ulysses Rogers are buried in Collins Springs Cemetery, in Oakdale community, south of Smyrna,

Second House

Mr. and **Mrs**. **Herbert Wallace** resided in this house. Mrs. Wallace was the former Ed Wallace but not related to her husband's family. They had four children: **William**, **Joycelyn**, **Neal**, a **Fred**.

William Wallace married Betty Rogers of Rome. They had four children: Gwendol Daniel, Donald, and Johnny.

Joycelyn Wallace married Charles Whitener; they had one daughter, Rosilyn. After Joyce and Charles divorced, she married Wayne Fain; they had two children: Renea and Harold. Joyce was in the Smyrna High School Class of 1951; therefore, I see her occasionally, when we have cl reunions.

Neal Wallace and his wife, "Kit," had two children: Megan and Jason.

Fred Wallace, when he was fifteen years old, died because of complications from a ruptu appendix.

Edna Wallace was the daughter of Mr. and Mrs. Green Berry Wallace. She and her husband were regular attendees of Spring Street Baptist Church. See *Wallace, Gilbert Street*; *Akins, south side of Bank Street,* and *Conn, second house on Foster Street.*

Third House

Mr. and **Mrs. Ernest Ed Conn** lived in this house. Mr. Conn was known as "Ted"; Mrs. Conn was the former Mary Lillian Wood. They had five children: **Willis**, **Allen**, **Frank**, **Catherine**, and **Dickie**. Ted Conn was a deacon at Haney Grove Baptist Church in Marietta. See *Conns, west side of Matthews Street.*

Willis Conn, a graduate of Campbell High School Class of 1956, married Masako from Okinawa. They live in Mableton.

Allen Conn, who married Hazel Grantham, is deceased.

Frank Conn, who never married, is deceased.

Catherine Conn, who never married, still lives in this house.

Dickie Conn is married and lives in Illinois.

Mary Lillian Wood Conn was from Marietta. General Lucius Clay was her great uncle; Alexander Clay was a well-known relative.

Fourth House

Mr. and **Mrs. Howard Barfield** had two daughters: **Mary Ann** and **Linda**. Howard was a member of Spring Street Baptist Church, before joining First Baptist Church, where he has been a long-time, faithful member. After Lillie and I married, we attended First Baptist Church's Training Union classes with Howard and always enjoyed his company. He is a deep thinker and a good conversationalist. Mrs. Barfield, the former Irene Chaffin, was a sister of Hubert Chaffin, the father of my brother-in-law, Grady Chaffin.

Fifth House

Mr. and **Mrs. Alfred Cochran** lived in this house. Mrs. Cochran was the former Annie Black. They had eleven children: **Bonnie Susie**, **Allie Louise**, known as "Polly," **James Thomas**, known as "J.T.," **Vergile A.**, known as "V.A.," **Betty**, **Hubert Warren**, known as "Britches," **Mary Faye**, **Peggy**, **Jerry M.**, **Joanne**, and **Nettie Mae**.

Annie Black Cochran, the daughter of Mr. and Mrs. James Monroe Black, grew up in a log cabin on Terrell Mill Road, during the early part of the Twentieth Century. Annie was a sister of Ida Mae Black Clayton: their dads were brothers. According to information passed down in their family, Annie and Ida Mae probably spent their early years in the same log cabin, which belonged to their grandparents. See *Clayton, north side of Bank Street.*

Alfred and Annie began their marriage in Cobb County, in a small house located on a hill known then as the Carmichael Place. From there the Cochrans moved to Foster Street. Alfred worked for Atlanta Paper Company, which later became Sonoco Paper Company. Alfred and Annie Cochran were members of Haney Grove Baptist Church, on Franklin Road in Marietta. They are both buried in the church cemetery.

NOTE: The Carmichael Place, where the Cochrans first lived, is now the site of the Georgia Memorial Park Cemetery office.

Bonnie Susie Cochran, known as "Bonnie Sue," married William H. Bivins, known as "Bill." They had two children: James H., known as "Jimmy," and Diane. After their marriage, Bonnie Sue and "Bill" Bivins lived on Elmwood Drive, off Spring Road; from there, in 1955, they moved to Bank Street, where Susie still lives. "Bill" Bivins is deceased. See *Bivins, Elizabeth Street* and *south side of Spring Road, The Country Road.*

James H. Bivins, known as "Jimmy," and his wife, the former Carol Anders, of Alexandria, Louisiana, had two children: Michael and Jane. "Jimmy" retired as Assistant Fire Chief of the City of Smyrna.

Jane Bivins married Joel Criswell, who is retired from the Georgia Bureau of Investigation.

Michael Bivins married Laurie Mitchell.

Diane Bivins first married Felix Meadows; they had one daughter, Sue Ellen. Diane, who later married Marion Whitener, died in 2000.

Allie Louise Cochran, known as "Polly," married E.L. Cargile, known as "George," from Alabama. They had two sons, Kenneth and David, and also raised "Polly's" niece, Janice, as if she were their own daughter. "Polly" Cochran Cargile died September 5, 2004.

James Thomas Cochran, known as "J.T.," served in the United States Third Army, commanded by General George C. Patton. "J.T." had been discharged less than a month when he was killed in an automobile accident on Canton Highway in Cobb County on a bad, foggy evening. At the time of his death, he was in a "serious romantic relationship" with Maxie Martin, who lived on Walker Street.

Vergile A. Cochran, known as "V.A.," married Bettie May, who grew up in the area of Brawner Sanitarium, where her dad worked. Betty had two brothers whom I recall: Broughton May, who was at one time the City of Smyrna Police Chief, and Hudson May. Hudson's daughter, Tina May, graduated in the Campbell High School Class of 1984 with my daughter, Marilyn.

Betty Cochran married J.L. Anderson. They had two sons and a daughter: Michael, Chuck, and Maxie. See *Anderson, south side of Church Street*

Hubert Warren Cochran, known as "Britches," married Mary Faye Burns Smith of Talladega County, Alabama. Mary Faye, from a previous marriage, had two sons: Joey and Stacy Smith, who both graduated from Campbell High School. Joey Smith was killed in an automobile accident in Birmingham, Alabama, in 1964, at the age of twenty. Hubert and Mary Faye had one son, Mickey Cochran, in 1965. Hubert worked for the City of Smyrna Fire Department, where he served for several years as Deputy Chief and then for a year as Acting Chief. Having retired after thirty-five years with the Smyrna Fire Department, Hubert died October 30, 2004.

Mary Faye Cochran died when she was a young child.

Peggy Joyce Cochran married Bill Cheney. Peggy died while she was in her 30s.

Jerry Mayes Cochran married Dixie Camp. They had four children: three sons and a daughter.

Joanne Cochran married James Porter; they had one daughter. In 2004, Joanne Cochran Porter died, after the death of her sister, Allie Louise Cochran Cargile, known as "Polly," and her brother, Hubert Cochran. The three siblings died within a two month period, in the fall of 2004.

Nettie Mae Cochran married Everett Hopkins. They had six children, three sons and three daughters: Richard, Ronnie, Sharon, Judy, Janice, and Stevie. Nettie Mae Cochran is deceased.

Sixth House

Alfred and **Lottie Coleman** lived in this house. Alfred was the son of Paul and Laura Coleman, the former Laura SimpsonLaura's sisters were Bertha Simpson Byrd, Larkin Simpson, and Beulah O'Dessa Simpson Harper. See *Simpsons, north side of Spring Road, The Country Road.*

ELIZABETH STREET

East Side

Appreciation is extended to Barbara Bryson Blackburn, Frances Tippins Brooks, and Elizabeth Green for information about the Castleberry/Green families.

Elizabeth Street, like several other streets in Smyrna during the days of my youth, had some houses, which were rental properties, because the purchasing of a home before World War II was beyond the reach of many working families. During the War, the housing shortage increased because of the influx of people moving into the area to work at the Bell Bomber Plant. After the War, many veterans returning home were able to purchase their homes through the G.I. Bill. It was then that building in the area began to increase.

There was a pasture behind Phagan Durham's house, which faced Spring Street; thus the pasture was on Elizabeth Street.

First House

The **Pannell Family** lived in this house, just beyond the pasture.

Castleberry/Green Families

Mr. and **Mrs. D. P. Green** moved to this house after the Pannells had vacated. Both of the Greens, having been married before, had grown children and grandchildren. Mr. Green was known in the area as "Preacher Green." Mrs. Green was the former Luna Henderson.

Mrs. Green's First Family

Luna Henderson married **Dwight Castleberry**. They had two children: **Susie Ophelia** and **John Wallace**. Lula and Dwight also had another daughter, who died as a toddler from burns she received from playing in the fireplace.

Susie Castleberry married Robert T. Bryson of Bryson City, North Carolina. They had six children: Barbara, Nancy, Robert Thomas, known as "Tommy," John Thurman, known as "Johnny," Rebecca, known as "Becky," and Clifford. The Castleberrys had ten grandchildren.

John Wallace Castleberry married Lillian Crooke of Charleston, South Carolina. They had two children, Christopher, known as "Chris," and Jill *, and three grandchildren.

After Dwight Castleberry died, Luna married Mr. Milam, who died about a year after their marriage. Afterwards she married D. P. Green.

The First Family of "Preacher" D. P. Green

D.P. Green, known as "Paul," and first married to the former **Laura Wilson**, was a preacher. They had seven children: five sons, **John**, **Paul**, **Frankie**, **Arthur**, and **Howard**, and two daughters, **Jessie** and **Georgia**.

Paul Green, a son, married the former Elizabeth Lamine of Marietta. They had six daughters and one son: Mary Lou, Judy, Joyce, Peggy, Cindy, Rhonda, and Kenneth. Paul Green at one time was an electrician; Elizabeth worked at Holeproof Hosiery Company in Marietta.

After Laura Wilson Green died, "Preacher" Green married a widow, Laura Henderson Castlebery Milam Laura and D. P. lived on Alexander Street before moving here. They later moved to a Sunset Avenue duplex, owned by the Day Family. After Mrs. Green died, D. P. married a lady named Pearl.

Second House

The **Price Family** lived near the creek and across the street from the Sanders Family. Larry Yarbrough, who lived in the sixth house remembers, "Mr. and Mrs. Price were the oldest couple in Smyrna."

NOTE: A creek runs across Elizabeth Street on the north side of the Adrian Cochran House. It probably originates in the Whitfield/Walker Street area.

NOTE: There was a short lane that deviated from the main street on the north side of the Tippins house. The Adrian Cochran house was located down this lane past the Tippins' house and the Jeffares' where the lane dead-ended. Both the Cochran and Jeffares families had Elizabeth Street addresses.

Third House

Mr. and **Mrs. Adrian Cochran** were residents of the first house located on a small lane north of the Tippins' house. Mr. Cochran was in the United States Navy during World War II. During that time I delivered Mrs. Cochran's paper here, where she lived with her two small children: **Andrea** and **Billy**. Mrs Cochran, among my best paper customers in always being prompt with paying her bill, was the former Wylene Smith. See *Cochran, south side of Powder Springs Street* and *east side of Roswell Street*

The Cochran house was a small white frame one with a porch across the front. A wooden fence surrounded it, with a gate in front. I always had to go through the gate to deliver the paper to the porch. The Cochrans had a dog, but he never bit me; in fact, I remember him as being a nice pet.

Mr. and **Mrs. Dobbs**

Mr. and **Mrs. Dobbs** moved to this house after the Cochrans had vacated. Mrs. Dobbs was the mother of J.C. and Mary Ruth George. See *east side of Roswell Street.*

Fourth House

Mr. and **Mrs. Andrew Jeffares** and their family lived in this house. Andrew and his wife, Clara, and some of their children were deaf. Hard-working people, Andrew, Clara, and at least two of their children worked at First Baptist Church, where Andrew was the custodian and the others worked in the kitchen. The Jeffares Family were good people that made the best of what life had given them. Andrew and Clara Jeffares had five children: **Joe**, died when he was three months old, **Jane**, **Frances**, **Susan**, **Wanda**, and **Barbara**. Frances still lives in this house on Elizabeth Street.

Fifth House

Mr. and **Mrs. Clifford Tippens** lived in this house, facing the railroad; the side of their house abutted Elizabeth Street. They had six children: **Claudine**, **Louise**, **Frances**, **Harold**, **Brenda**, and **Linda**. Mrs. Tippins, the former Mamie Rutledge, and Mr. Tippins were both from Canton. Clifford was employed by Atlantic Steel Company in Atlanta and then by Cleveland Electric

Company, also in Atlanta. Later he worked on Atlanta Street in a garage located beneath Bill Scoggins' garage. Mrs. Tippins was an aunt of Wyolene Barnes, who lived next door to Lillie and me for thirty-two years; Wyolene died New Years Day, 2001. See *Barnes, east side of Roswell Street.*

Claudine Tippins married William Clark, known as "Bud." They had six children: Helen, William, known as "Buck," Ronald (now deceased), David, Chris, and Dean. Claudine died in 2000.

Louise Tippins married Clyde Jones. They had one son, Clyde, Jr.

Frances Tippins married Denward Brooks. They had two children: a daughter, Jackie, and a son, Denny. See *Brooks, east side of Roswell Street.*

Harold Tippins married Betty Clackum. They had three children: Robert, Vickie, and Linda. Harold's second marriage was to Mary. Harold died in 1998.

Brenda Tippins married Terry Washington; they had two children: Tina and Terry, Jr., known as "Bubba." Brenda is deceased.

Linda Tippins married William Hulsey, known as "Bill." They had no children. After they divorced, Linda married Larry Willoughby.

Sixth House

Reynold and **Eller DeBoard** were residents of this house. They had three children: Reynold Lee, Joseph, and Faye. Mr. DeBoard was a brother of Robert DeBoard, who lived on Atlanta Street, north of Smyrna. See *DeBoard, Atlanta Street, from Mapps to R & M Café.*

Faye DeBoard married Larry Yarbrough; they had a son, Larry. Faye later married Pete Jordan; they had five children: Sandra, Jimmy, Michael, David, and Mark.

ELIZABETH STREET
West Side

Appreciation is extended to Mary Lou Redd Cochran, Frances Tippins Brooks, and Janet Brooks Brown for their sharing of memories about residents on Elizabeth Street and to Linda Barfield for sharing the memories of her grandmother living on Elizabeth Street.

First House

Mr. and **Mrs. Benjamin Bluford Cochran** lived here with their four children: **Betty**, **Bobby**, **Mack**, and **Donnie**. Mr. Cochran, named for Benjamin Bluford Osburn, his maternal grandfather, was known both as "B.B." and "Jack." Mrs. Cochran was the former Dessie Brooks, a member of the large Brooks Family on Roswell Street. See *Cochran, east side of Roswell Street and Osburn, north side of Spring Street.*

Betty Cochran married Kenneth Wiggs; they had four daughters: Sherrol, Juanita, Susan, and Dianne. Kenneth served with the United States Army in the European Theater, where he lost a leg in combat. See *Brooks, east side of Roswell Street.*

Bobby Cochran married Mary Lou Redd, who grew up on both Concord and King Springs roads. They had three children: Steve, Donna, and Charles. See *Chadwick, west side of Concord Road, Redd, west side of King Springs Road, and north side of Concord Road, The Country Road.*

Mack Cochran married Linda Buttram from the Fair Oaks community. They had three children: Karen, Gary, and Mickey.

Donnie Cochran married Kathy Pyren. They had two children: Nick and Wendy.

When Dessie died, at the end of the Twentieth Century, Smyrna lost one of its most colorful citizens. After the Smyrna Community Center and Village Green were built downtown and the City started having concerts, Dessie was always there, having a good time. Loving to dance, she always managed to find a partner with whom to dance at the concerts. A sharp-minded person with a gift of wit, she loved everybody, especially the Mayor of Smyrna, Max Bacon, and was often heard saying, " He is my little boy."

Second House

Mr. and **Mrs. James Burton Parks**, who moved from Ellijay in 1944, resided in this house with their two sons: **Donald** and **Hansel**. Mrs. Parks was the former Gladys Allen. Mr. Parks was a tall, friendly gentleman. On my paper route, the Parks were always nice to me. Mr. and Mrs. Parks were members of First Methodist Church.

Donald Parks married Joyce Hamby, the daughter of Mayes and Lola Hamby, who lived on the west side of Concord Road. Donald played basketball at Smyrna High School. He and Joyce had three children, Jennifer, James D., Jr., and Joy, and one granddaughter. See *Hamby, west side of Concord Road.*

.

Hansel Parks married Eleanor Garner, who grew up on Dixie Avenue. They had two daughters: Sherrie and Debbie, both of whom are graduates of Campbell High School, as were their parents. The Parks Family are members of First Methodist Church. See *Garner, Dixie Avenue.*

Third House

Susie and **Bill Bivins** lived in this house, on the west side of Elizabeth Street. They had two children: **James H..**, known as "**Jimmy**," and **Diane**. Susie and Bill Bivins later moved to Elmwood Drive and then to Bank Street. See *Bivins, north side of Bank Street, and Cochran on Foster Street.*

James H. "Jimmy" Bivins married Carol Anders of Louisiana. They had two children: Michael, who married Laurie Mitchell, and Jane, who married Joel Criswell.

Diane Bivins married Felix Meadows; they had one daughter, Sue Ellen. Later on, Diane married Marion Whitener. Diane passed away in 2000.

Bill Bivins and Raymond Motter are stepbrothers: Bill's dad and Raymond's mother married late in life, after all of their children were grown. See *Bivins, south side of Spring Road, The Country Road.*

NOTE: After the Bivins vacated, the third house became a rental dwelling and the following families, in the order listed, resided here.

Mr. and **Mrs. Curry**.

Mr. and **Mrs. McDowell**—See *Dixie Avenue.*

Mr. and **Mrs. Homer Butler**. See *May, north side of Church Road, The Country Road.*

Lem and **Mattie Lou Priest**, along with Lem's parents, lived here. See *Reed Hawthorne Avenue.*

Mr. and **Mrs. Yarbrough** still live in this house.

Fourth House

Mrs. Sarah Elizabeth Murner Barfield, known as "Sally," and her husband, Timothy, had five children: **Hollis**, **Howard**, **Roy**, **Ralph**, and **Louise**. After Timothy died, "Sally" moved from the Sardis community to this house.

Mr. Timothy Bryant Barfield was a Mason. For many years there was a plaque, bearing his name, in front of the Masonic Hall on West Spring Street. When the Market Village was built, the marker was removed. (The Barfield Family has lost track of it.)

Hollis Barfield married Ada Priest; they had two children: Michael and Carol. Mr. Barfield served in the United States Army during World War II.

Michael Barfield married and had two children. He died when he was about forty years old.

Carol Barfield, an employee of Lockheed Aircraft Corporation, married Martin O'Toole, an attorney in Marietta. Carol and Martin, active members of First Baptist Church, live in Marietta. They had no children.

Howard Barfield married Irene Chaffin; they had two daughters: Linda and Mary Ann. Irene was a sister of Hubert Chaffin, the father of my brother-in-law, Grady Chaffin. Howard who worked for Colonial Stores, served in New Guinea during World War II, after the War he worked at Ft. McPherson. Later on, after completing studies at Georgia State University, in Atlanta, he was a substitute teacher qualified to teach Spanish and French. Active in First Baptist Church, he played an important role in Discipleship Training, where he was also the pianist.

Roy Barfield married Agnes Yarbrough; they had two children: Dwight and Brenda. Roy was ordained to the Baptist ministry. A barber, Mr. Barfield operated his barber shop in Dickson Shopping Center; from there he retired.

Ralph Barfield married Billie McClain. She had one son, Neal, from a previous marriage. She and Ralph had three children: Larry, Wayne, and Marion Fay. Mr. Barfield served in the United States Army during World War II and later on worked for the Atlantic Steel Company in Atlanta.

Louise Barfield married Ansley McDonald. They had three sons: Steve, David, and Mark.

Fifth House

Mr. and **Mrs. Lawrence Butler** were residents here at one time. The Butlers had more than one child. One of their daughters, **Mary**, was a member of the Smyrna High School Class of 1951; therefore, I see her occasionally, when we have reunions. While Mr. Butler was working for Brawner Sanitarium, the family moved to the Brawner campus, where they lived in one of the houses provided for employees of the hospital. (It was a practice in the days of my youth for employees to be able to live on the campus.)

Between the fifth and sixth houses, there was an open field.

Sixth House

One of the elder **Conn** couples lived in this house, at one time.

Seventh House

The **Samples Family** lived here. Mrs. Samples was the former Agnes Conn, whose parents lived in the sixth house.

Mr. and **Mrs. Roy Barfield** lived here at one time. She was the former Agnes Yarbrough.

Luther and **Cordy Dickerson** were also residents of this house. Luther was a nephew to Mrs. Tippins, whose house was directly across the street.

The **Sanders Family** was one of several ones remembered by neighbors who lived in this house. They had two sons: **Henry** and **Harry**, who attended Spring Street Baptist Church. Janet Brown remembers that her mother, Georgia Brooks, taught the two Sanders boys in her Sunday School class there.

There was a creek that ran between the seventh and eighth houses, and across the street, which prevented the building of houses there.

Eighth House

Mr. and **Mrs. Kenneth Wiggs** lived in this house with their four children: **Sherrol, Juanita, Susan**, and **Dianne**. Mrs. Wiggs was the former Betty Cochran. Kenneth was injured during World War II where he lost one of his legs. He worked at Lockheed Aircraft Corporation. Betty and Kenneth are deceased. See *Brooks, east side of Roswell Street*, and *first house, on Elizabeth Street*

Mr. and Mrs. Bobby Cochran

Later Betty Wiggs' brother, **Bobby Cochran**, and his wife, the former **Mary Lou Redd**, bought this house and lived here with their two children until a train derailed at the end of Elizabeth Street. At that time, Mary Lou and Bobby had a toddler and a two-week old daughter. According to Mary Lou, she never slept another "wink" in this house. They bought themselves another house away from the railroad. The street dead-ended at the railroad.

CORN ROAD
West Side

Corn Road runs south from Spring Street and up the hill before the southwest corner of Anderson Circle. A desolate area, it was little more than a pig trail when Mr. William Boyd Gravely bought this property from Glenn Lewis. The Gravely Family is the only one I am certain about, as living on Corn Road during the days of my youth.

Gratitude is extended to Richard Gravely, Robert Gravely, and their sister, June Gravely Duke, who shared their memories of living on Corn Road in the middle of the Twentieth Century. Appreciation also goes to Paul Chastain, Howard Gunn, and Bill Scoggins, for their memories about the residents of Corn Road.

First House

Mr. and **Mrs. William Boyd Gravely** resided in this house on Corn Road. Mr. Gravely was known as "Slim" and Mrs. Gravely was the former Bessie Jane Weaver. They had seven children: **June, Evelyn, Richard, Robert, Raymond, Virginia**, and **Michael**.

Mr. and Mrs. Gravely moved from the Talking Rock/Hinton communities of North Georgia to the Creatwood area of Smyrna, for Mr. Gravely to work for Creatwood Dairy Farm. They moved from there to the south side of Spring Street, until their house on Corn Road was ready for occupancy. (During World War II, building materials were hard to obtain, thus Mr. Gravely used lumber and other materials from a house that was razed in Talking Rock to build this house on Corn Road.)

After working for Creatwood Dairy Farm, Mr. Gravely drove a taxi, picked up garbage, worked in a grocery store, and was a policeman for the City of Smyrna. Later he was employed at Atlantic Steel Company, in Atlanta; from there he retired.

June Gravely married Wayne Duke. They had a son, Eric, and a daughter, Cynthia.

Evelyn Gravely married Ed Medlin. They had three children: Frank, Harry, and Teri. See *Medlin, south side of Concord Road* and *Hann, west side of Roswell Street.*

Richard Gravely married Betty Payne; they had three children: Ann, Aletha, and Richard, Jr. Betty and Richard, who retired from Georgia Power Company, are divorced.

Robert Gravely, Sr., married Bobbie Mann. They had three children: Robert, Jr., Tria Sheree, and John Robert. After Robert, Sr., and Bobbie divorced, he married Linda Owen.

Raymond Gravely married Pat McMinn; they had three children: Tamara, Trent, and Travis. Raymond and Pat live in Pennsylvania.

Virginia Gravely married Donzel Pendley. They had three children: Kera, Kristi, and Brad.

Michael Gravely married Susan Hopkins of the Smyrna area. They had two children: Michael Thomas, Jr., and Amanda.

Members of the Gravely Family, through the years, have been members of Spring Street Baptist Church.

Second House

The **Barker Family** lived in this house.

Third House

Mr. and **Mrs. James Lovern,** in the late 1940s, on the southeast corner of Corn Road and Jonquil Drive, built a house for themselves and moved from Powder Springs Street to Corn Road. The Loverns had two children: **Joyce** and **Jimmy**. It was to this property that James relocated J. E. Lovern Construction Company and Cobb County Products; here he also had room for his equipment. See *Lovern, south side of Powder Springs Street.*

CORN ROAD
East Side

First House

According to area residents, living in this house, was a lady whose name no one was has been able to recall.

Second House

Sometime later, **J. D.** and **Ruby Gunter** built a small house across the road from the Gravelys house.

Third House

Joe and **Mae Anderson** and their family at one time lived in this house, which was located on the corner of Corn Road and Anderson Circle. Through the years, several other families resided here. See *Anderson west side of Old Roswell Road.*

NOTE: There was an expanse of land between the Anderson and the Day houses.

Fourth House

James Day and his wife, **Laura Harbin Day**, lived on the opposite end of Corn Road from the Andersons. The rear of their property at that juncture on Corn Road abutted the property of James' mother and stepfather, Janie and Ben Cochran, whose house faced Spring Road, the Country Road. James Day was Janie Cochran's son from a previous marriage, and Laura Day was the daughter of Mr. and Mrs. Harbin, who owned and operated Harbin's Grocery Store. See *Harbin, south side of Sunset Avenue* and *Cochran, south side of Spring Road, the Country Road.*

Corn Road, which originated at the south side of Spring Street, on its northern end, intersected with Spring Road, the Country Road near the home of Janie and Ben Cochran, on the south end.

ANDERSON CIRCLE
East Side

Appreciation is extended to Betty Jean Ridling, Vida Lou Spearman Poor, Elise Adams Rowland, and Helen Emmett Massey Stymest, all of whom shared their memories of the residents on Anderson Circle in the middle of the Twentieth Century.

First house

The Clark Family

The **Clark Family** were the first residents of this house.

The Palmer Family

Later the **Palmer Family** resided here. Mrs. Palmer was a sister of Wilma Cook, who was a resident on the opposite side of Anderson Circle.

The Blackwell Family

Earl and **Anna Blackwell**, lived in this house, together with their children until they moved to Kentucky in the late 1960s.

Second House

James Webb
Smyrna City Councilman
1961-1964

Mr. and **Mrs. James Webb** and their family were the first ones to live in this new house. Mrs. Webb was the former Florine Jarrett. Mr. Webb, known as "Jim," was from Kentucky, but he and Florine met in Adairsville. They had four children: **Betty Jean**, **Jimmy**, **Robert**, and **Cheryl**. Florine died in 1964.

Betty Jean Webb married Stephen Ridling of Atlanta. They had no children. While in Smyrna, Betty Jean and her brothers attended Spring Street Baptist Church. Betty graduated from Campbell High School in 1961 and began work for the United States Government, from which she retired with twenty-nine years service. Betty Jean lives in Douglasville; Stephen is deceased.

James William Webb and
Florine Jarrett Webb
March 29, 1944
Courtesy of Betty Webb Ridling

James William Webb, Jr. and **Betty Jean Webb**
In Front of Anderson Circle House
Circa 1950
Courtesy of Betty Webb Ridling

Home of James and **Florine Webb**
133 Anderson Circle
Circa 1950
Courtesy of Betty Webb Ridling

James Webb, Jr., known as "Jimmy," graduated from Hapeville High School and married Cathy Poltzer; they had one daughter, Lisa. "Jimmy" later married Pam Nantz and they had two daughters, Melanie and Ashley, and two grandchildren. Jimmy and Pam live in McDonough.

Robert Webb, a graduate of Hapeville High School, married Dianne Campbell. They had one daughter, Stephanie, and a son, Jeremy, and four grandchildren. Dianne and Robert lived in Conyers. Robert is deceased. Betty Ridling, Robert's sister, shared: "At the time of his death, Robert was a fireman for Rockdale County, where he was buried with full military honors. The service was awesome!"

Cheryl Webb, who graduated from Hapeville High School, has two sons: Michael and Matthew. She lives in Marietta.

"Jim" Webb served with the United States Army in Germany during World War II. Afterwards he worked for NC&St.L Railroad (Nashville Chattanooga & St Louis Railroad) which later became L&N Railroad (Louisville & Nashville Railroad) and, still later, CSX, from which he retired.

"Jim" served on the Smyrna City Council, 1961-1964. Other titles he held included membership within Nelms Lodge # 323, 32nd Degree Mason Knights Templar, (at the Yaraab Temple Shrine in Atlanta), and Past Patron of the Chapter of the Order of the Eastern Star, in Hapeville.

NOTE: After Florine's death, in 1964, "Jim" married again and moved to Hapeville, where he ran unsuccessfully for a seat on the Hapeville City Council. In Hapeville he became a member of American Legion Post # 50 and continued to be involved as a Mason and a Shriner.

Third House

Warren and **Vicky Beckley** lived here with their seven children: **Dorothy Ann**, **Alan**, **Clyde**, **Rhoda**, **Karen**, **Gary**, and **Sandra**.

The Beckley Family members were very active in First Baptist Church, where Vicky served as director of Vacation Bible School in 1951 and for many years taught a Sunday School class for young women. Warren, a deacon, served as Training Union Director, 1951-1955, Parliamentarian, and Church pianist. He served on the building committee for the present-day sanctuary and later served as Chairman of the Budget and Finance Committee, and the Pulpit Committee. (This latter information was extracted from *A Beacon For Christ,* A Centennial History of First Baptist Church of Smyrna.)

Fourth House

Mr. and **Mrs**. **David Motter** and their daughter, **Peggy Ann,** resided here. Mrs. Motter, the former Louise Blackburn from North Carolina, and David met while he was serving in the United States Army at Fort Bragg, in Fayetteville, North Carolina. Louise Motter worked for Colonial Stores and later for A & P, from which she retired. David Motter was a civil service employee at Dobbins Air Force Base, where he retired. He and Louise are deceased. See *Motter, north side of Spring Road, The Country Road, and North Avenue.*

Peggy Ann Motter, who graduated from Campbell High School, married Freddie Hayworth, also a Campbell High School graduate. They had three sons: Joe, Doug, and Ray, all of whom are graduates of Sprayberry High School. Peggy and Freddie had four grandchildren.

Joe Hayworth married Lynn Erwin. They had one son, Jesse.

Doug Hayworth married Gina Searcy. They had no children.

Ray Hayworth married Tammy Butterworth. They had three children: Tiffany, Randa, and Travis.

Freddie Hayworth had a brother, Johnny, and a sister, Pat, who married Larry Cobb, a member of the Marion Cobb Family on Old Concord Road. See *Marion Cobb, Old Concord Road.*

Freddie Hayworth is deceased; Peggy now lives in Cartersville.

Fifth House

George Morris Emmett and his wife, the former Minnie Lee Rich, moved in the early 1950s from Lula, in Banks County, to Roswell Street in Smyrna. There they rented rooms from Mr. and Mrs. Richard Brooks while this house on Anderson Circle was being built. Mr. and Mrs. Emmett had three children: **George Herman**, known as "Herman," **Helen**, and **Rachel**.

George Morris Emmett's father, John Emmett, was a resident of Banks County; his mother's given name was Ruby. George Morris had three sisters and one brother. See *Emmett, south side of Spring Street, and Walker Court.*

After moving to Smyrna, Mr. Emmett worked for the City of Smyrna in charge of the maintenance and automotive equipment department. Mrs. Emmett worked in one of the Cobb County School lunchrooms as well as in Bethel Baptist Church Nursery.

George Herman Emmett graduated from Lula High School. After moving to Smyrna, he married Barbara Bryant, a graduate in the Smyrna High School Class of 1951. They had two sons, Darrel and Derrick, and five grandchildren. Herman is deceased. See *Bryant, Pickens Street.*

Rachel Emmett married Alan Richards; they had two sons: David and Mark. Rachel, who later married Fred Brooks, is currently living in Florida.

Helen Emmett married Terrell Massey; they had one son, Donnie, and three grandchildren. After Terrell's death, Helen married Jimmy Stymest of Louisville Kentucky; they had one son, John. Now divorced, Helen lives on Anderson Circle, where the Spearman Family once lived.

NOTE: Anderson Circle has since been extended to encompass what was a section of Corn Road.

Sixth House

Mr. and **Mrs. Weyman Adams** built this house in the early 1950s. Mr. Adams was known as "Buddy"; his wife was the former Hilda Motter. They had five children: **Elise**, **Keith**, **David**, known as "Davy," **Randy**, and **Melissa**. See *Motter, north side of Spring Road, The Country Road.*

Elise Adams, who graduated from Campbell High School, married Jon Rowland, also a graduate of Campbell High School. They had two children, "Buzz" and Lori, and three grandchildren.

Keith Adams married Marsha Todd. They had two children, Katie and Andy, and five grandchildren.

"Davy" Adams first married Suzanne Davis; they had two children, Julie and Tommy, and two grandchildren. "Davy" is now married to Glenda Williams; they live in Canton.

Randy Adams married Cathy Stow, daughter of Mr. and Mrs. Everett Stow of Oakdale Drive. Randy and Cathy had one son, Josh. They live in Hiram.

Melissa Adams married Keith Collis. They had two children: a daughter, Ashley, and a son, Cameron. They live in Powder Springs.

The Adams House was the last dwelling on the east side of Anderson Circle before it intersected with Corn Road.

NOTE: In the more recent past, Corn Road from Spring Street to Anderson Circle was renamed Anderson Circle; which is really a semi-circle. When this change was made, a small section of Corn Road was left on the north side of the Spring Road viaduct. No houses were located in that area.

ANDERSON CIRCLE

West Side

First House

Mr. and **Mrs**. **Moore** lived here with their four children: **Cathy**, **Diane**, **Wayne**, and **Janet**.

Second House

The **Walravens** lived in this house, which had a living area upstairs and a garage apartment downstairs. Mary Lee Walraven an active member of First Baptist Church, and her husband are deceased. The Walravens were Martha Moore's parents. See *Moore, first house.*

NOTE: There was an open field between the Walraven and the Spearman houses.

Third House

Mr. and **Mrs**. **Garland Brady Spearman** resided here. Mrs. Spearman, an artist, was the former Betty Crowder of Marietta. They had two children: Allan and Vida Lou, both graduated from Campbell High School. Mr. Spearman worked at Atlantic Steel Company, in Atlanta, for forty-two years before his retirement. Mr. and Mrs. Spearman were members of First Baptist Church.

Allan Spearman married Laura Watkins, a graduate of Campbell High School and a resident of the Log Cabin community, south of Smyrna. They had four children: Doug, Cathy, Bryan, and Roger. Allan and all of his family live in Texas.

Vida Lou Spearman married Charles A. Poor, a graduate of Campbell High School and a resident of the Kenwood community, south of Smyrna. They had a daughter and a son: Dana and Scott. The Poors are members of First Baptist Church of Atlanta.

Dana Poor, a graduate of Berry College in Rome, married Mark Hannah, a producer for Fox 5 Television in Atlanta. They had four children: Madeleine, Katie Faith, Peter, and Ethan. Prior to his marriage to Dana, Mark was missionary to Casablanca, Morocco.

Scott Poor, who lives in Smyrna, is not married.

Fourth House

Wilma and **Bill Cook** lived here. They had no children. See *Palmer, east side of Anderson Circle.*

MIMOSA CIRCLE

North Side

Appreciation is extended to Rayford Cameron and Lucretia Monroe for sharing their memories about the residents of Mimosa Circle.

A newer street, Mimosa Circle, was developed in the late 1940s, off the north side of Spring Street from the railroad. One side of the circle will be referred to as the north side and the other one, the south side.

NOTE: On the north side of the circle, the first, second, and third houses were demolished in the 1960s for the construction of the Southern Bell Telephone building (now the BellSouth).

<u>First House</u>

Hershel and **Media McClure**, together with their son, **Billy**, were residents here.

Mr. and **Mrs. Edge**

Mr. and **Mrs. Edge** moved here with their daughter, **Janice**, after the McClures vacated. Mr. Edge, at one time, was a policeman in Smyrna.

<u>Second House</u>

Mr. and **Mrs. Cooper** lived here.

<u>Third House</u>

Mr. and **Mrs. Charles Pickelsimmer** lived in this small house that was located much farther from the street than the other dwellings.

<u>Fourth House</u>

Mr. and **Mrs. George McEntyre** were residents here.

<u>Fifth House</u>

Mr. and **Mrs. Roy Dobson** resided here with their children: **Karen**, **Billy**, and **Lori**. Mrs. Dobson's given name was Gerry.

<u>Sixth House</u>

Mr. and **Mrs. Ray Donaldson** and their daughter, Gloria, were residents of this house. Mrs. Donaldson, whose given name was Gladys, was a faithful member of First Baptist Church.

<u>Seventh House</u>

Mr. and **Mrs. John Collier** lived at 1437 Mimosa Circle. Mrs. Collier was the former Emaline Hamby, a member of the Tommie Lee Hamby Family, whose home place is still located on the north side of Spring Street. See *Hamby, north side of Spring Street*, and *Collier, Atlanta Street, Marlowe's to Creatwood.*

Mr. and **Mrs. H.K. Irish**

Mr. and **Mrs. H. K. Irish** and their granddaughter lived here after Mr. and Mrs. Collier had moved.

<u>Eighth House</u>

Mr. and **Mrs. Ted Kiger** and their son, **Tim**, resided here. Mrs. Kiger's given name was Ann. Ted and Ann Kiger are deceased.

When Tim was seven years old, the Kigers moved to the southwest end of Concord Road so that Tim would have room to have a horse. Now a mortgage broker, Tim is married to the former Joan Biggers of Fitzgerald. They had two children: Meagan and Andrew.

Mr. and **Mrs. Charles Swindell**

Mr. and **Mrs. Charles Swindell** and their daughter, **Cathy**, moved to this house after the Kigers had vacated. Afterwards **Mrs. Cooper** moved here.

Ninth House

Mr. and **Mrs. Bayshore** and their two sons lived here.

Mr. and **Mrs. Wallace Knighton**

Mr. and **Mrs. Wallace Knighton** lived at 1449 Mimosa Circle. They had three children: **Van**, **Melody**, and **Chris**. In 1959 the Knighton Family moved from Smyrna to Powder Springs, where all their children graduated from McEachern High School. Mr. and Mrs. Knighton retired from Lockheed Aircraft Corporation in 1986.

Van Knighton, a graduate of the University of Georgia, retired from Cobb County Government.

Melody Knighton, a graduate of Kennesaw College (now Kennesaw State University), in her younger years, entered beauty contests. She won "Miss Georgia Posture," "Miss Southern Tech," and third runner-up position in the "Miss Georgia" Pageant. (Her talent competition was based upon gymnastics.) In recent years Melody has been traveling throughout the United States with others as a look-a-like star—Dolly Partan and a make-up artist for Hollywood stars.

From early childhood, Melody remembers Mimosa Circle as lined with mimosa trees. She vividly recalls that every yard had a different kind of tree: a next-door neighbor's yard had a black walnut tree; a plum tree was in her yard.

Chris Knighton was born while the family lived on Mimosa Circle, six months before they moved to Powder Springs.

Tenth House

Mr. and **Mrs. Smalley** lived here with their children: **JoLynn**, **Jerry**, and **Eddie**. They later moved to the Forest Hills community.

Ruby and **Virginia Carmichael**

Mrs. Ruby Hamby Carmichael and her daughter, **Virginia**, resided at 1455 Mimosa Circle. Ruby was a member of the Tommie Lee Hamby Family, who lived on the north side of Spring Street. Ruby's family home is still standing. See *Hamby, north side of Spring Street.*

Eleventh House

Mr. and **Mrs. Beckett** lived here. They had a daughter, Marie Beckett Forman, who lived next door with her family. A neighbor remembers that Mr. Beckett was a golf instructor. See *twelfth house.*

Twelfth House

Mr. and **Mrs**. **Fred Forman** resided here with their four children: **Sudi**, **Ted**, **Ruthie**, and **ecky**. Mrs. Forman was the former Marie Beckett. See *eleventh house.*

NOTE: Mimosa Street re-enters Spring Street in front of Spring Street Baptist Church.

MIMOSA CIRCLE
South Side

The south side of Mimosa Circle begins across the street from Southern Bell Telephone ompany (now BellSouth) property. There are only four houses on this side of the circle.

First House

Mr. and **Mrs**. **Gordon Morgan** resided at 1408 Mimosa Circle, together with their five ildren: **Jeff**, **Eddie**, **Pat**, **Brenda**, and another child whose name we do not recall. Mrs. Morgan's ven name was Edna.

The Harp Family

Mr. and **Mrs**. **Harp** and their son, "**Butch**," were residents of this house. Mrs. Harp's given me was Molly.

The Vess Family

Mr. and **Mrs**. **Gene Vess** lived here with their son, **Martin**, known as "Marty." Mrs. Vess, e former Betty Martin of LaFayette, was a substitute teacher for the Cobb County Board of lucation. The Vess Family were active members of Welcome All Baptist Church. Betty is deceased.

"Marty" Vess married Sharon Blankenship. They had four children: Joshua, known as osh," Heather, Jacob, known as "Jake," and Jesse. They live in LaFayette. Sharon, in her youth, was nember of First Baptist Church, where her parents, Twila and "Bill" Blankenship, are still members. aron had a sister Kathy, and a brother Bryan.

Second House

Mr. and **Mrs**. **Ollie F**. **Cameron** are still residing at 1426 Mimosa Circle, where they moved the late 1940s. Mr. Cameron, known as "Buddy," and his wife, Rayford, had five daughters, **Cindy**, **nnie**, **Melissa**, **Phyllis**, and **Rebecca**, twenty-two grandchildren, and ten great-grandchildren. They ve been married over 60 years.

"Buddy," an ordained Baptist minister, has preached and taught in many churches throughout bb County, including Bethel Baptist, First Baptist of Smyrna, Locust Grove Baptist, Olive Springs ptist, and Providence Baptist. He was for a while minister of Senior Adults at First Baptist of nnesaw. "Buddy" retired from Lockheed Aircraft Corporation. See *Cameron, south side of Spring reet.*

Third House

"**Shorty**" and **Dorothy Palmer** and their daughter, **Belva**, lived at 1444 Mimosa Circle.

The Monroe Family

Mr. and **Mrs**. **George Harold Monroe** resided here after the Palmer Family had moved. Mr. onroe of Forsyth County, retired from Lockheed Aircraft Corporation, where he was a research echanic. Mrs. Monroe, the former Leo Wilson, of Cherokee County retired from Six Flags Over

Georgia, where according to her daughter, Lucretia, "Mother was Head of Live Show Wardrobe." Harold and Leo had had three children: **Lucretia**, **Michael**, and **Ronda**. The Monroe Family were members of Spring Street Baptist Church, and later, Sharon Baptist.

Lucretia Monroe, who graduated from Campbell High School; retired from Allstate Insurance Company with forty-two years of service. She still lives in this house.

Michael Monroe graduated from Campbell High School and owns his own business. He married Valerie Puckett of Powder Springs. They had one daughter, DeeDee, who married Bre Sleight; they have two children.

Ronda Monroe graduated from Wills High School. She married William Swords of Tifton. They had three children: Robin, Sarah, and Matthew. Ronda and William live in Atlanta.

NOTE: Leo Wilson Monroe's mother, Bertha Segars, earlier in the Twentieth Century, lived with her family on Atlanta Road near Second Baptist Church. Bertha married William Wilson and moved to Cherokee County, where Leo Wilson (Monroe) grew up.

Fourth House

These are the four families known to us that lived in this house.

Mr. and **Mrs. Tingle** were the first ones to live at 1458 Mimosa Circle.

The **Lescault Family** was the second ones to live here. They had two daughters: Cecile and Peggy. Mr. Lescault was in the United States Military. They moved from here to Winston Salem North Carolina.

Mr. and **Mrs. Carmichael** were the third residents of this house. Mr. Carmichael was barber in Belmont Hills Shopping Center.

Mrs. Gladys Wright was the fourth resident of 1458 Mimosa Circle.

WALKER COURT

East Side

Walker Court is a short street, running from the north side of Spring Street to Walker Street.

Appreciation is extended to Edna Sparks for sharing her memories of the residents on Walker Court, where she and her family lived before moving to Whitfield Street in the middle of the Twentieth Century.

First House

Mrs. Ruby Emmett and her three daughters, **June**, **Betty**, and **Beatrice**, lived here. This house was on the northeast corner of Spring Street and Walker Court, facing Walker Court. See *Emmett, east side of Anderson Circle, and Emmett, south side of Spring Street.*

Second House

Mr. and **Mrs. Eugene Sparks** moved to this house in 1950. Mr. Sparks, known as "Red," was from Indiana; and his wife, the former Edna Price, was from Marietta. They had a daughter **Candace**, known as "Candy."

Candace Sparks married Bill Chumley; they had one son, Billy Eugene, and one grandson Bill is deceased.

"Red" Sparks served in the United States Army Air Corps (now United State Air Force), ıring World War II, where he was a combat photographer. He worked for radio station WFOM in arietta, where he broadcast the Marietta High School football games. Later, he worked for the nited States Post Office, and still later for Lockheed Aircraft Corporation, from which he retired.

Edna worked first at Southern Bell Telephone Company (now BellSouth) and then for ɔckheed Aircraft Corporation, from which she retired after thirty-seven years. Eugene and Edna later oved to Whitfield Street.

Third House

Mr. and **Mrs. James L. Bloodworth** lived here. James, known as "Jimmy," and his wife, ıogene, had a daughter, Barbara. Imogene was a sister of Edna Price Sparks. See *second house.*

Fourth House

"Red" Ergle and his wife, **Lee**, were residents here. Lee was a beautician in Oakdale.

Later on **Mr.** and **Mrs. Bodiford** lived in this house.

Fifth House

James and **Jackie Rainey** and their daughters, **Vickie** and **Sharon**, resided in this house

Later on **Bill** and **Betty Wallace** moved to this fifth house. See *Wallace, Foster Street.*

Sixth House

Mr. and **Mrs. Leon Owens,** along with their daughter, **Gail**, lived in this house, which is on e southeast corner of Walker Street and Walker Court, facing Walker Court. Mrs. Owens' given ıme was Faye.

WALKER COURT
West Side

First House

Mr. Fain and his wife, **Margaret**, and their two daughters resided here.

Mr. and **Mrs. Milton Jones**

Milton and **Ruby Nell Jones** and their children, **Ronnie** and **Sharon**, moved to this house ter the Fain Family had vacated.

Ronnie Jones married Joyce Deaton; they had two daughters: Tracy and Amy. See *Deaton, uth side of Spring Road, The Country Road.*

Sharon Jones married John Leavins; they live in Houston, Texas. They had three children: ephen, Christy, and Cathy.

Ruby Nell Jones worked in the Cobb County School Lunchroom Program, from where she tired. Milton Jones retired from Lockheed Aircraft Corporation, in Marietta.

Second House

The **McDougal Family** lived here first.

Robert and **Mary Wood** were later residents here.

Third House

Mr. **Childs**, a barber, and his wife lived here with their children: **David**, **Byron**, and **Nancy**.

Fourth House

Mrs. **Manley** and her daughter, **Mrs**. **Whitaker**, lived in this house.

CHAPTER FIVE

ROSWELL STREET

East Side

Appreciation is extended to the following long-time Roswell Street citizens for sharing their .owledge of the people who lived on Roswell Street in the years between 1938 and 1951: Sara iderson Gentry; Evelyn Edwards Pressley; William H. "Bill" Scoggins; James "Jim" Barnes; Lucille ooks Barnett; Arvil Hicks, Jr.; Marge Cochran Maloney; Lee Maloney; Sarah Hensley Miles; mmy Hamby; Quinton Hamby; Elizabeth Black Davis and the Bennett twins, Jean and Joan. ammy Hamby is still lives in the Hamby house on Roswell Street, where he grew up.) Appreciation also extended Janet Brooks Brown for information about her grandparents, Mr. and Mrs. Richard ooks, Sr., and to Frances Tippins Brooks, who married the youngest Brooks' son, Denward, for ntributing her knowledge of the Brooks Family. Appreciation is further extended to Juanita Bruce d Eleanor Reed Bruce for the information about the Ellis/George families, who lived on Roswell reet from the early 1940s until 1959.

Roswell Street in the days of my youth was very much as it is today, except that some houses ve been demolished and new ones built. The houses I miss most were immediately across the ilroad at the beginning of the street. They were beautiful, imposing homes that shaped my opinion of : entire street. Some of Smyrna's "finest families" lived there in the early part of the Twentieth ntury. Many of them were still living there in the days of my youth.

First House

Mr. and **Mrs. Virgil Brooke** lived in the first house, since demolished, on the east side of oswell Street. Mrs. Brooke was the former Myrtle Crowe. They had three children: **Betty**, **Thomas igene**, known as "Gene," and **Robert Lamar**, known as "Bobby."

Aunt Myrtle Brooke was my mother's sister. Her dad, Ed Crowe, had lived with Aunt yrtle since his wife, Callie Brewer Crowe, died in 1934. I visited Aunt Myrtle often in the 1940s, ien she and her family lived there.

When the Bell Bomber Plant opened in Marietta in the 1940s, my mother went to work there. :cause my brother, Sammy, was under three years old at that time, Aunt Myrtle would keep him iile Mother was at work, and I would go to her house after school. I remember she lived in this use throughout World War II years and beyond.

Uncle Virgil was a carpenter, and during the World War II years he worked in Oak Ridge, nnessee, where there was much construction in support of the War effort. The United States ovemment established there the Atomic Energy Commission, which was involved with the velopment of the atomic bomb. My understanding was that the Atomic Energy Commission ntrolled all aspects of this program. At the time, there was not much talk about what was being done cause the nation was involved in World War II.

In the days of her youth, Aunt Myrtle was a member of Olive Springs Baptist Church in arietta, where she, along with my mother and their sister, Lula, were members from their childhood. ter she moved to Smyrna, Aunt Myrtle had become a member of First Baptist Church.

Betty Brooke married J. Calvin Johnson, Jr., who grew up on Fleming Street. See *south side Bank Street* and *south side of Fleming Street.*

Thomas Eugene Brooke, known as "Gene," was a United States Navy career man. He irried Opal Robinson; they had three daughters: Amy, Iris, and Peggy.

Bobby Brooke
United States Air Force
Circa, early 1950's
Photo courtesy of Pete Wood

Robert Brooke, known as "Bobby," married Vida Haws , the daughter of Aletha and urence Haws, who lived in the Fair Oaks community. Vida graduated from R.L. Osborne High hool on Barber Road, in the Fair Oaks community. She taught at R.L. Osborne High School after it as relocated to Favor Road. "Bobby" Brooke, an accountant, served in the United States Air Force in e early 1950s.

"Bobby" Brooke had two daughters from a previous marriage: Kathy and Bobbie Jean.

Mr. and Mrs. Laurence Haws had two other daughters: Earline, who married Jimmy Cook, d Jenny, married Larry Franklin, who later became a Baptist minister. Earline and Jenny graduated om Campbell High School. See *west side of King Street.*

The Haws Family moved to Lee Street, in the Forest Hills community, in the late 1940s or rly 1950s.They were active members of First Baptist Church, where Mr. Haws was a deacon; Mrs. aws, deeply involved in the Sunday School and Women's Missionary Union, also served as director the Vacation Bible School in 1974.

Second House

The next house was the home of **Mrs. Beatrice Lowe**, who had three grown children: **ubert**, **Agnes**, and **Lillian**. A widow, Mrs. Lowe worked as a seamstress in her home, even making othes for Lillie after we married, in 1960. A very nice lady, she was on my paper route. At one time e Lowe Family lived north of Smyrna; they relocated when their land was purchased for the Bell mber Plant to be built. Mrs. Lowe's son, Hubert, was a member of the Smyrna High School Class 1931.

The Virgil Cobb Family

When **Mr.** and **Mrs. Virgil Cobb** returned to Smyrna early in the Twentieth Century, they sided in this house for a short time: Then they moved to the corner of Church Street and what is now emorial Place, which runs in front of the Smyrna Memorial Cemetery. It was from that house they oved to Old Concord Road, where they lived the rest of their lives. See *Cobb, north side of Church reet.*

The Joseph Anderson Family

Some time in the 1930s **Mr.** and **Mrs. Joseph Power Anderson** lived in this house with eir family. Known as "Joe," he and Mrs. Anderson, the former Homer Davis, had four children: **atherine**, **Anna Bell**, known as "Ann," **Florence**, and **Frank**.

Catherine Anderson married Horace Rogers.

Anna Bell Anderson, known as "Ann," married Robert Haney. They had one daughter, rena. See *Anderson, west side of Roswell Street.*

Florence Anderson married Arthur Simpson. They had no children.

Frank Anderson died in an automobile/bicycle accident when he was thirteen years old.

Anna Bell Anderson Haney and her daughter, Serena, are the only survivors of this family.

Third House

The Edwards/Shipp House

Mr. and **Mrs**. **Pat Edwards** moved their family here in 1918. Their daughter, Evelyn, wh married Coach James Pressley, was a year old at that time. The Edwards lived here until the mi 1930s, when they moved to Love Street.

After they moved to this house, Mr. Edwards installed an inside bathroom. According t long-time family residents of Roswell Street, this was the first inside bathroom in Smyrna. It was als said that the bathroom inside the Reed House on Atlanta Street at Reed's Alley was close behind. Se *south side of Love Street.*

NOTE: Long-time residents of Roswell Street remember that the short street from Roswel Street across the railroad to Atlanta Street, between the B.F. Reed, Sr., and Mrs. Mazie Whitfiel Nelson houses, was known as "Reed's Alley." Later named Nelson Street, was ordered closed by th City of Smyrna in the latter part of the Twentieth Century when Atlanta Street was widened.

Mr. and **Mrs. George Miller**

Mr. and **Mrs**. **George Miller** and **Nell** and **King Davis**, along with their son, **Miller**, move into the Edwards House, as it was known at that time. (This was after The Edwards Family had move to Love Street.) Mr. and Mrs. George Miller were Nell Davis' parents. Mr. and Mrs. Davis' younges son, **Clark**, was born in this house, April 28, 1937. See *Pace, east side of Atlanta Street, from Mrs Mazie's to Creatwood,* and *south side of Church Street, and seventh house, west side of Roswe Street.*

Mr. and **Mrs. Shipp**

Mr. and **Mrs**. **Shipp** moved here in the late 1930s, after the Miller/Davis families moved t Church Street. Several generations of the Shipp Family lived here for the next twenty-five or mor years, with the house becoming known as the Shipp House. Mr. and Mrs. Shipp had two daughters **Ovalene** and **Jewell**.

Jewell Shipp married Richard, known as "Dick" Williams. Here they lived with her parents Jewell worked at Atherton Drug Store, later named Atkins Pharmacy upon Bill Atkins' purchasing th business, located on the west side of Atlanta Street. Jewell, who worked there for many years, was faithful member of First Methodist Church. See *Atkins, south side of Bank Street, Williams, north* an *south sides of Church Street.*

"Dick" Williams, who served in the United States Navy, during World War II; later worke for Atlantic Steel Company, on 14th Street in Atlanta.

Ovalene Shipp and her son, Tommy,_ lived here with Mr. and Mrs. Shipp. Ovalene worke for Lockheed Aircraft Corporation.

Fourth House

Mr. and **Mrs**. **Clayton Belk Hamby**, **Sr**., lived in this house. Mrs. Hamby was the forme Mary Elliott from Commerce. Clayton Hamby grew up in this house, which he acquired after hi parents died. In this house he and Mary raised three sons: **Clayton B.**, **Jr**., known as "Sonny, **Quinton**, and **Sammy**.

"Sonny" Hamby was very active in the Boy Scouts when he was growing up.

Quinton Hamby married Annette Bell, who grew up on Fleming Street. See *north side of* *ming Street.*

Sammy Hamby and his wife, Sandra, known as "Sandy," are the current occupants of the mby House. Sammy's children are the fourth generation of Hambys to live here.

Family members from each Hamby generation attended First Methodist Church.

Sammy Hamby tells a story of his growing up in this house. He says that he, using a BB gun, uld shoot the diamond-shaped panes out of the windows on the front of the house. The irony is s: Sammy was the one who bought the house. He had to pay dearly to have the diamond-shaped ndowpanes restored.

The Hamby House, built in 1907, was bought by Mr. and Mrs. David C. Hamby in 1917. s. Hamby was the former Jinnie L. Gable, whose father was the Reverend J.L. Gable, a large downer in Cobb County. According to information from the Hamby Family, Reverend Gable nated land for the Marietta Square.

NOTE: There is a Reverend J.M. Gable in Sarah Blackwell Gober Temple's book, *The First* *ndred Years: A Short History of Cobb County, In Georgia,* published in 1935. I could not establish this is the same Reverend Gable. According to my information from the Hamby Family, their ndfather's initials were J.L. Reverend J.M. Gable was born on June 5, 1826, and died on September 1911.

Mr. and Mrs. David C. Hamby had eleven children. One child, David Ladell, died from eumonia when he was six months old. Ten of their children grew into adulthood in this house: **ve H.**, **Littie H.**, **Howard H., Sr.**, **Joseph J.**, **David Otis**, **Jenny Lou**, **Quillian**, **Alta**, **Clayton** **lk, Sr.**, and **Danny Banks**.

Quinton Hamby, son of Clayton Belk Hamby, Sr., who grew up in this house on Roswell eet, relates that he can remember the "chain gang," wearing striped uniforms and working on swell Street, which was still unpaved. (The "Chain Gang" was a group of convicts chained together, rking as a group on a special assignment.) They raked and picked up leaves, pine straw, and debris then swept the street. He also remembers when the sidewalks were built on Roswell Street. He d that his dad, figuratively speaking, went into a tailspin when the City assessed him for a hundred t across the front of his house. But he paid!

1940s NEIGHBORHOOD WATCH

Anonymous

Roswell Street, like the other Smyrna streets, had many residents that planted jonquil bulbs. the springtime there would be a beautiful sea of yellow flowers growing in their yards.

"There was a certain resident of Roswell Street who went all out when it came to jonquils, her yard was beautiful in the spring. One day during World War II, a group of us boys from the ghborhood decided to 'pick' some of her flowers. She called our efforts 'stealing.' While we were cking,' we found in her flower garden two German medals. We ran away fast because we decided nt then and there that she was a German spy. (The medals were for pinning onto a uniform lapel.)

"We kids had a committee meeting and decided that it was our 'patriotic duty' to catch her ing out secrets to the German Army. We took turns watching her house for about two weeks. thing happened, and nobody was able to prove she was doing anything wrong. We boys buried the rman medals in a back yard, for we could not take a chance on getting caught with those medals. could have been sent, so we thought, to one of the prison camps we had heard about on the radio.

"Another boy, who thought he had a more logical explanation, responded, 'It might be th someone in the 'War Over There' (World War I) may have taken them off a dead soldier and broug them home to Smyrna. One of us surmised, 'Do you think they fell out of a German War Plane?'

"Some of us 'boys,' to this day, wonder how two German medals could have turned up in sea of jonquils on Roswell Street."

Fifth House

In the early 1940s **Alma Ellis** and **Arvie Ellis George** bought this house, located between th Austin and Hamby families and directly across the street from the ice plant. Arvie's son, **J.C. Georg** and Alma's dad, **Reverend "Jim" Ellis**, moved here with them. Soon after the house was bought, tw grandsons of "Jim," **Lake** and **Wayne Ellis**, came to live here for a few months. **Herbert C. Ellis**, son of Jim and his wife, Bertha Neely Ellis, rented the upstairs living area.

Herbert and **Bertha Ellis** had four children: **Gerald**, **Lamar**, **Jimmy**, and **Shelby**, who als lived in the fifth house. Herbert and Wayne were both Smyrna policemen.

Reverend "Jim" Ellis and Lavada had ten children, only four of whom lived in Smyrn Alma, Arvie, Herbert, and Grace, who married Thomas Lewallen Bruce and lived on Camp Highlan Road in the Oakdale community, south of Smyrna. Grace and Thomas had two children: Robert Ty Bruce, known as "Bobby," and Juanita. "Bobby" Bruce married Eleanor Reed, the daughter of Mr. an Mrs. B.F. Reed, Jr. See *Reed, south side of Bank Street*

"Jim" Ellis was a member of Spring Street Baptist Church, where he led the singing. sacred harp singer, he had taught singing schools in what was then known as the "Old Blue Ridg Revival Circuit." Sometimes the extended family and friends would gather on Sunday afternoons sing gospel songs into the evening. There would be, at times, forty to fifty people in attendance.

Arvie Ellis George worked at the Bell Bomber Plant, in Marietta and later at Atlanta Pap Company. She rode the streetcar to work.

Alma Ellis worked for the Lovable Bra Company and would do home assignments. Th neighbors remember seeing Alma and other members of the family sitting on the porch in the ear evenings, threading bra straps through the adjustable slides and rings.

Arvie's son, J.C. George, who grew up in this house, attended elementary and high school Smyrna. He was employed at J.D. Daniel's Grocery Store and later as manager of the Colonial Stor He also worked at Big Apple.

Arvie Ellis George died in 1955; her sister, Alma Ellis, died in 1958. After their dad, "Jim Ellis, died in 1959, the house on Roswell Street was sold.

Reverend James Walter Ellis

In the late 1930s Reverend James Walter Ellis, known as "Jim," and two of his daughter Alma Ellis and Arvie George, together with Arvie's son, J.C. George, moved from Blue Ridge to rental house near Six Points on Roswell Street, next door to the Anderson Family. The wife of "Jim Lavada Roper Ellis, had been killed in a car wreck as she and "Jim" were returning from church Blue Ridge, in 1936.

Eleanor Reed Bruce, a granddaughter-in-law of Reverend and Mrs. "Jim" Ellis, remembe hearing her mother, Jessie Cook Reed, tell how devastated her grandparents, Reverend and Mrs. Joh E. Cook of Morganton, were when Mrs. Ellis was killed. (Reverend Cook, a Methodist minister in th North Georgia area, would preach at revivals, and Reverend Ellis would lead the singing.) Elean learned about this accident shortly before she married her beloved husband, "Bobby" Bruce, who die

The Clayton Belk Hamby House on Roswell Street

Built in 1907
Currently owned and occupied by Sammy and Sandy Hamby
Great-grandson of the original owners

The Ellis / George House
Circa 1960s
Courtesy of Juanita Bruce

in 2004. It was at that time she realized it was the same accident her mother remembered from h grandparents' telling.

Sixth House

Mr. and **Mrs. Loren Joseph Austin, Sr.**, lived in this house. He was known as "Bearcat." See *Austin, west side of Walker Street* and *McCollum, south side of Bank Street.*

Seventh House

Mr. and **Mrs. Monroe Adams** from Dunwoody moved to this house. Mrs. Adams was th former Eula Reed from Roswell (not related to the Reeds in Smyrna). Mr. and Mrs. Adams had thre children: **Ruth**, **Myrtle**, and **Gene**.

Ruth Adams married Hubert Hancock from Atlanta. They had three children: Gary, Davi and Nancy. See *south side of Bank Street.*

Myrtle Adams married Fletcher Donaldson. They had four children: Fletcher, Jr., Ra Ronnie, and Martha, all of whom they raised in Chamblee.

Gene Adams married Sarah Bagwell from the New Hope area of Cherokee County. They ha two children: Michael and Kelly. Michael lives in Alpharetta, and Kelly lives in Peachtree City.

Mr. Monroe Adams and his first wife, Pavie Wade, had four children: Horace, Ellen, Grad and Ruth. See *south side of Bank Street.*

Mrs. Eula Adams, who had milk cows, sold milk and butter. Sometimes she would trade mil and butter for Mrs. Clayton Hamby's eggs. Trading consumables was a common practice amon neighbors in the days of my youth.

Eighth House

Mr. and **Mrs. Brackett** resided in this house. They had two sons whose names I do n recall. Native American Indians, they were very fascinating people, for whom I had much respec They were both short people, very cordial and self-sufficient. They did not take the paper.

I never knew Mr. Brackett to work away from home; nor do I ever remember the Bracket going to the store. He had a small plot of land where he grew a garden and raised chickens. Many litt things around his house, such as the windmill, birdhouses, beehives, fruit trees, and strawber patches, fascinated me. His livelihood was derived from many of the aforementioned.

Sometimes, when I was at my Grandmother Tucker's house, I would go to Mrs. Brackett house, which was nearby. I remember one time, when I went there, she was cooking cornbread on th top of the stove. This fascinated me because my mother cooked her cornbread in the oven. I rememb adults remarking about the Bracketts, "They know how to maximize what they have." While th country was feeling the effects of the Great Depression, the Bracketts seemed to live well.

The Bracketts' yard and house were always neat and orderly. It is impossible for me to thin of Roswell Street and its residents without thinking of Mr. and Mrs. Brackett. They were always ver nice to me, and I remember them fondly.

Ninth House

Dr. Milton L. Collins
Smyrna City Councilman
Elected January 1948

Dr. and **Mrs**. **Milton Collins**' house was in the triangle at Walker and Whitfield streets. The llins Family lived there as far back as I can remember. Dr. Collins and his first wife had three ldren, twin daughters, **Frances** and **Ruth**, and a son, **Joseph**, known as "Joe." Their mother was a y young woman when she died.

Frances Collins married Colin Osborne; they had four children, Colin III, Pamela, Rebecca, 1 Elizabeth, and seven grandchildren. Frances and Colin live in North Carolina.

Ruth Collins married M.J. Hensley, who grew up on the west side of Roswell Street. They 1 four children, Carol, Sandra, Kathy, and John, and eight grandchildren. Ruth and M.J. live in attanooga, Tennessee. See *Hensley, west side of Roswell Street.*

Joseph M. Collins, known as "Joe," became a dentist and practiced in Smyrna from 1950 til his retirement in 1980. "Joe" and his wife, Joyce had three children: Diana, Joseph Milton, Jr., Celia, six grandchildren, and eleven great-grandchildren. They lived on Pretty Branch Drive, in Forest Hills community until they moved to Forest Drive, also in the Forest Hills community. m there they relocated to Fairmount. Dr. "Joe" Collins died December 5, 2004.

Dr. Milton Collins was a pharmacist who operated a drug store in downtown Smyrna, where and his second wife, Gladys Collins, a first cousin of the first Mrs. Collins, worked together. Gladys ght school for forty years in Waleska. Members of First Methodist Church, they were active in the nmunity. I always liked Dr. and Mrs. Collins, who, on my paper route, were always nice to me.

Gladys Collins was born October 7, 1896. When she was a hundred years old, she was living this house, which is still standing on Roswell Street. Upon her 100th birthday, the Smyrna Mayor City Council honored her. She died September 28, 2000, nine days short of her 104th birthday.

Tenth House

Mr. and **Mrs**. **Arvil Hicks**, **Sr**. lived in this house. Mrs. Hicks, the former Lorene Barnett, s the daughter of Mr. and Mrs. Jesse Sanford Barnett. Mr. and Mrs. Hicks had four children: **Arvil cks**, **Jr**., **Joyce**, **Brenda**, and **Patsy**. The Hicks Family were members of Spring Street Baptist urch.

Arvil Hicks, Jr., married Judy Booseler of Marietta. They had three children, Carole, David, 1 Kent, three grandchildren, and one great-grandchild.

Joyce Hicks married Don Cochran; they had two children: Debbie and Jason, and two ndchildren. Joyce later married Frank Weber.

Brenda Hicks married Rod Townsend; they had three daughters, Angie, Kelly, and Sherry, seven grandchildren.

Patsy Hicks married Aaron Sexton; they had two children, Luann and Tim, and five ndchildren.

When Lorene's dad, Mr. Barnett, died, her mother, **Mrs**. **Cleo Adams Barnett**, and Lorene's er, **Adelaide**, came to live with the Hicks in this house on Roswell Street. Then, during World War Lorene's sister, **Evelyn Barnett Fridell**, came to live here also.

Arvil Hicks, Sr. whose parents had died when he was about four years old, was from t Dawsonville/Cumming area. One day, as he was plowing, he decided, "I don't want plow and look the rear end of a mule the rest of my life." He took the mule to the barn and set out for Smyrna. Ar had lived with, or known, the Reese Family of Juno. One of their sons, Milton Reese, had married daughter of Mr. and Mrs. Harbin, who owned and operated Harbin's Neighborhood Grocery Store Atlanta Road, and later on Sunset Avenue. After coming to Smyrna, Arvil, whose nickname w "Kaiser Bill," drove Mr. Harbin's delivery truck, a red Ford pickup; later, he worked at Simmo Mattress Company.

Remembering, Arvil Hicks, Jr., said, "When I was a small child, our house, in Smyrn burned. We had made our weekly family trip to a grocery store in the Bellwood community of Atlan in 1940, to buy groceries. On our way home, we were crossing the bridge over the railroad tracks South Atlanta Road, in a sharp curve near the Chattahoochee River, when we met a car coming towa us; people hanging out of the car were 'hollering' and waving their hands. When Dad pulled off t road, he was told our house was on fire. We hurried home and found three or four rooms burned. M family rebuilt the house."

Mr. and **Mrs. Jesse Sanford Barnett**

Lorene Barnett Hicks' parents, Mr. Jesse Sanford Barnett and Mrs. Cleo Adams Barne were originally from South Carolina; they moved to Norcross before moving to Smyrna. Mr. Barne and later his sons, worked at Dahl's Florist/Nursery, located on south Atlanta Road near t Cobb/Fulton County line. Between the railroad and the Chattahoochee River bank, they grew flowe which florists bought from them at wholesale prices.

Mr. and Mrs. Barnett had three daughters, Lorene, Adelaide, and Evelyn, and two sor Virgil Lee and Linton L.

Lorene Barnett married Arvil Hicks, Sr.; they had four children. See *Arvil Hicks, Sr., ten house, east side of Roswell Street.*

Adelaide Barnett, married John Watson; they had two children: John and Amy.

Evelyn Barnett married Edward Fridell; they had one daughter, Elizabeth.

Virgil Lee Barnett married Vadie Rogers; they had three children: Doyle, Thelma, a Becky. See *Foster Street.*

Linton L. Barnett married Sadie Rogers; they had six children: Kenneth, Shirley, Melvi Nancy, Nathan, and David. Linton and Sadie lived in the Oakdale community.

Eleventh House

Mr. and **Mrs. Richard Brooks** lived in this house. Known as "Mom" and "Pop" Brook Richard and his wife, the former Adeline Fuller, were blessed with a large family of twelve childre **Wadeus**, **Russell**, **Patricia**, **O'Dessa**, **Clarence**, **Lucille**, **Mary**, **Luther**, **Pauline**, **Homer**, **Richar Jr.**, and **Denward**.

Richard Brooks and Adeline Fuller married in Cherokee County in 1904, and came Smyrna in 1922 from Pickens and Cherokee counties, respectively. The Brooks Family were membe of Spring Street Baptist Church.

Mrs. Brooks and her sister, Mary Fuller Ruddell, were raised in Jasper by relatives after the parents died in Oklahoma Territory. See *Family of Mary Fuller Ruddell at the end of Brooks Fami.* and *Cole, west side of Access Road.*

Picture amd Newspaper Article appeared in the Atlanta Journal "Smyrna's Baseball Team of Brothers in Service."
Richard and **Adeline Brooks**
Circa 1944
Photo Courtesy of Janet Brooks Brown.

December 4, 1954, 50th Anniversary of Mr. and **Mrs. Richard R. Brooks**
nt Row, L-R: Mr. and Mrs. Richard Brooks (Adeline) **Second Row, L-R:** Russell C. Brooks, Mrs.
t Page, Mrs. Odessa Cochran (Dessie), and Clarence Brooks **Third Row, L-R:** Denward Brooks,
Richard Brooks, Jr., Homer Brooks, Mrs. Mary Black, and Mrs. Lucille Barnett
One son, Luther Brooks, not in picture, lives in California
Photo Courtesy of Janet Brooks Brown

"Pop" Brooks ran a blacksmith shop and gristmill on West Spring Street. After he closed th blacksmith shop, he moved his equipment to his back yard on Roswell Street and continued to d some blacksmith work there. In 1948 he renewed his business license for the last time.

During World War II, Mr. and Mrs. Brooks had six sons serving our country: Seaman Fir Class Russell C. Brooks, United States Navy; Private Clarence Allen Brooks, with the Army A Corps; Corporal Homer C. Brooks, United States Army; Private First Class Luther F. Brooks, Unite States Army; Private First Class Richard Brooks, Jr., with the Army Corps of Engineers in the Pacifi and Denward, who entered the United States Army. I remember seeing in Mrs. Brooks' window th hanging stars, showing she had sons serving in the military.

In 1944 Mr. and Mrs. Brooks were featured in *The Atlanta Journal*. This picture shows fiv of their sons, ranging in age, at the time, from twenty to thirty-eight. (Not pictured is Denward, wh entered the United States Military later in 1944 because of his age.)

In addition to their six sons, Mr. and Mrs. Brooks had two sons-in-law, Hubert Black ar William Duke, and two grandsons-in-law, Kenneth Wiggs and Corporal William A. Hayes. Th brought the total in the military to ten, thus making a perfect baseball team plus one. When they we home, all the sons played baseball together. Homer, known as "Joby," was a regular player on t Smyrna Amateur Baseball Team before and after the War.

NOTE: The Brooks' son, Richard, Jr., was taken as Prisoner of War; son-in-law Hube Black, was badly injured; son-in-law, "Al" Duke, was taken as Prisoner of War; and grand-son-in-la Kenneth Wiggs, lost a leg.

Wadeus Brooks, the oldest of the Brooks' children, was killed when he was eighteen yea old. He was on an elevator in the 101 Building, on the east side of Marietta Street (between Cone ar Spring streets), in Atlanta, when something went wrong with the elevator, and it fell with him in The family never learned what caused the elevator to fall.

Russell Brooks married Pauline Gunter of Marietta; they had one son, Lewis, and tw grandsons, Jock and Mark. Russell served as Seaman First Class in the United States Navy duri World War II. He later married Lillian Duckett of Marietta.

Patricia Brooks, known as "Pat," married "Edd" Thompson. They had a daughter, Evely who married William A. Hayes. Evelyn later married Mel Lebow; they had two children: Gail a Ricky. Evelyn and her family lived in Tennessee.

"Al" Duke
Prisoner of War
World War II

Patricia Brooks Thompson later married William A. "Al" Duke, a Sergeant in the Unit States Army. He served in the Pacific, where he was captured and held as a Prisoner of War. Mu later, Patricia married "Stoney" Page.

O'Dessa Brooks, known as "Dessie," married B.B. "Jack" Cochran.. See *Elizabeth Stre* and *Cochran, south side of Spring Road, The Country Road.*

Clarence Allen Brooks married Georgia Gillham, who also grew up in Smyrna. He was Private in the United States Air Corps during World War II. See *Walker Street, Dixie Avenue, Bro Street,* and *Gillham, north side of* Fleming Street.

Lucille Brooks married Milton Barnett, a member of the large Barnett Family in Oakda They had three children: Martha, Harry, and Peggy. Lucille lives on Reed Road.

Martha Barnett married Billy Akins, who grew up on Bank Street. They had one son, Mark, and two daughters, Jane and Lynn. Grandparents of two boys, David and Joshua Akins and a girl, Audrey Bowles, Martha and Billy live in the Bennett Woods subdivision. See *Akins, south side of Bank Street.*

Harry Barnett and his wife, Martha, live in North Georgia. They had one daughter, Beja.

Peggy Barnett is married to Ronald Gibson; they live in Alabama. They had a daughter, Meg, two sons, Mil and Michael, and five grandchildren.

Mary Brooks married Hubert Black, who lived on Terrell Mill Road, in the vicinity of where Interstate 75 crosses over Terrell Mill Road. Hubert's dad, Roy Black, owned much acreage in that area. Hubert served in the United States Army during World War II and was badly injured while on active duty in France. See *Black, third house, north side of Walker Street.*

Luther Brooks married Inez; they had a son, Rodger. Luther later married Louise; they had two daughters: Janet and Priscilla. A Private First Class in the United States Army during World War II, Luther as an adult, has lived in California.

Pauline Brooks died when she was six months old.

Homer Brooks married Nina Gillham, who, along with her sister, Georgia Gillham Brooks, grew up in Smyrna. Nina and Homer had two children, John and Carolyn, two grandsons, and three great-grandsons. Homer, known as "Joby," was a bookbinder and coach of Little League Baseball. In the United States Army during World War II, he was a Corporal. See *Brooks, south side of Walker Street, Brooks, Dixie Avenue,* and *Gillham, north* side of Fleming Street

Richard Brooks, Jr.
Prisoner of War
World War II

Richard Brooks, Jr., known as "Junior," married Mildred DeBoard. They had three children: Barbara, Ricky, and Tommy. They also had six grandchildren and ten great-grandchildren. Richard, a Private First Class in the United States Army Corps of Engineers, during World War II, served in the Pacific; in 1944 he was taken Prisoner of War in Okinawa and held captive for eighteen months. After Mildred DeBoard Brooks died, "Junior" remarried.

Denward Brooks, who served in the United States Army during World War II, married Frances Tippens of Smyrna. They had two children: a son, Denny, and a daughter, Jackie. Frances Tippins and her family lived on Elizabeth Street. Frances' mother, Mrs. Mamie Tippins, was a paternal aunt of Wyolene Barnes; Wyolene and Mrs. Tippins were from Canton. (Wyolene lived next door to Lillie and me on Havilon Way for thirty-two years.)

Jackie Brooks married Donnie Shaw from Alabama. They had one son, Koby. Jackie lives in Smyrna and is involved with the Campbell High School baseball program.

Koby Shaw was a 2004 graduate of Campbell High School.

Denny Brooks married Betty Godby. They had two sons, a daughter, and a granddaughter.

Family of Mary Fuller and Mathis Ruddell

Mary Fuller, the sister of Adeline Brooks, married Mathis Ruddell. They had five children: Grace, Myrtle, Mae, Roger, and Cleo.

Grace Ruddell married Lewis Roland.

Myrtle Ruddell married Lonzo Smith.

Mae Ruddell married Curtis Jackson.

Roger Ruddell married Lula Mathis.

Cleo Ruddell married Wylie Cole, known as "Buddy." They had two daughters: Pat and Debbie. See *Cole, west side of Access Highway.*

Twelfth House

Mr. and **Mrs. Paul Cochran** resided in this house. They had two sons, **Adrian** and **Crafton,** who were in the produce business; I remember the big trucks in their back yard; I also recall that they maintained a nice house. The Cochrans, who were on my paper route, always paid their paper bill promptly. Crafton Cochran still lives in this house. The Paul Cochran Family were members of Spring Street Baptist Church. Mr. Cochran wrote and published many religious songs. He also taught classes at singing schools, teaching shape notes, as opposed to Fa Sol La singing. See *Cochran, east side of Elizabeth Street,* and *south side of Powder Springs Street*

PACE NEIGHBORHOOD GROCERY STORE

According to some residents on Roswell Street, Mr. and Mrs. Carl Pace built a neighborhood grocery store next door to the Cochran house. I am not sure when it was built, but it was probably in the late 1940s or early 1950s. Because Mr. Pace was a railroad man, Mrs. Pace ran the grocery store. At some point in time, she was robbed and beaten very badly; she never went back to the store. Mr. Posey took over the operation of the store; after him, the Paul Cochran Family ran the store. The building is still there.

Thirteenth House

Mr. and **Mrs. Carl Pace** lived in this house.

Fourteenth House

In the days of my childhood, this house on Roswell Street was referred to as the **Elmer Anderson** home. **Sara Anderson** (Gentry), and **Lewis Anderson**, along with siblings **Jay, Tom, Leila,** and **Clara,** grew up in this house. But, in the days of my youth, the Elmer Anderson Family had moved to a larger house on the west side of Roswell Street. The larger house today belongs to Elizabeth Black Davis, a granddaughter of Mr. and Mrs. Elmer Anderson. She and her husband, Ron, reside there. See *Andersons* on *Roswell Street, west and east sides of Roswell Street,* and *Andersons of Roswell Street.*

The Pritchetts

During my teenage years **Mr.** and **Mrs. Lewis Pritchett** lived in this house, always referred to as the "Anderson House." Lewis and Laura Pritchett had three daughters and a son: **Louise Rosalee, Carolyn**, and **Charles**.

Mr. Pritchett was a barber in a shop on Cone Street near Davison-Paxon Department Store in downtown Atlanta. He rode the streetcar to and from Atlanta each day. Mrs. Pritchett at one time used some of the rooms in this house for boarders. Later on she and Mr. Pritchett ran The Corner Grill on Smyrna's Atlanta Street.

Louise Pritchett married Harold Griskat and had one son, George, known as "Sonny."

Rosalee Pritchett married H.H. Partain, Jr., known as "Junior."

Carolyn Pritchett married Jack Holcomb. They had four children: Doris, Jean, Scotty, and Tony.

Charles Pritchett graduated from Campbell High School in 1954 and joined the Georgia National Guard for three years. He worked at Lockheed Aircraft Corporation before enlisting in the United States Marine Corps for three years. He went back into the Guard in 1975 and stayed in until 1994, during which time he served in Desert Storm.

Charles and his first wife had three children: a son, Paul (named after Paul Hensley), and two daughters, Robin and Randi.

Charles Pritchett later married the former Kristie Tomlin, the daughter of Philip and Ann Tomlin, who came to Smyrna in 1951 to work for Lockheed Aircraft Corporation. Philip and Ann resided on Quarles Avenue. The Tomlins, and Charles and Kristie were members of First Baptist Church, where Charles and Christy are still regular members. See *Dalton, south side of Hill Street.*

The following story about a special person in Charles' life during the years he was growing up on Roswell Street was shared with me. Charles said, "Mr. Paul Hensley, who lived across the street from me on Roswell Street, was my mentor and my friend. Mr. Hensley hired me to work in his construction business and paid me $7.00 a week, when I was seven and eight years old. This was good for me because my own dad, who was a barber in Atlanta, had to leave early and return late every day."

Stated Charles, "Many of the things I learned from Mr. Hensley have stayed with me all of my life: things such as character building and honest work. I also credit Mr. Hensley for so many good things that I have enjoyed throughout my life. There were so many people in Smyrna in that day that took the time to be a friend and mentor to young men in the area. I am sure there were women were also doing the same for girls."

NOTE: For the last twenty-five or more years of the Twentieth Century until the present, the Anderson/Pritchett House has been the home of Smyrna City Councilman "Bill" Scoggins and his wife, Gerrye. "Bill" has represented this area on the Smyrna City Council since the mid 1980s. See *south side of Bank Street.*

Fifteenth House

Tom Anderson, son of Mr. and Mrs. Elmer Anderson, lived here with his family at one time. Mrs. Anderson was the former Eexie Arzona Tuck. See *Andersons of Roswell Street.*

Sixteenth House

Mr. and **Mrs. Walter Morris** resided next door to the Andersons. Uprooted by the Bell Bomber Plant expansion, they relocated here. They had two daughters, **LaVerne** and **Gwendolyn**, known as "Gwen," and a son, **Winton**.

LaVerne Morris married "Tubby" Turley; they had one daughter, Angela. "Tubby" was killed in an automobile accident. LaVerne later married Jay Harkins; they had a daughter, Yvonne.

Gwendolyn Morris married Lamar Whitener. They had three sons, Barry, Rick, and Bruce, nine grandchildren and one great grandchild. After "Gwen" and Lamar divorced, "Gwen" married Ty Woods of Carrollton. They are currently living in Centre, Alabama.

Winton Morris married Dot Cabe; they had two sons and one daughter. One of the sons is deceased.

Seventeenth House

Mr. and **Mrs**. **Ware**, residents of this house, had two daughters, **Peggy Jo** and **Polly**. I liked Peggy Jo, who was in my class in school, because she was always nice to me.

Eighteenth House

Mr. and **Mrs**. **Harmon Ellis** resided here with their four children: **Ovilene**, **Betty Jo**, **Peggy Jean**, and **Charles**. Prior to living on Roswell Street, Mr. and Mrs. Ellis lived on Pickens Street. See *Pickens* and *Hughes streets.*

Ovilene Ellis married Dallas Gibson; they had three children: Ronnie, Donnie, and Mike.

Betty Jo Ellis married "Turk" Murphy; they had three daughters: Janet, June, and Joan.

Peggy Jean Ellis married Joe Harris; they had two children: Darrell and Donna. Peggy Jean is deceased.

Charles Ellis married Edith Jacqueline Crews, known as "Jackie," who was born in Daytona Beach, Florida, and grew up in Euharlee. Charles was 18 and "Jackie" 16, when they eloped. They had three children: Brenda Jean, Charles, Jr., known as "Chuck," and Rebecca, known as "Becky." "Jackie" Ellis died at age 54, in 1990. Charles Ellis and his second wife, Dona, currently live in Marietta. Dona, from a previous marriage had two sons: Chad and Brannon Rickmon. Chad and his wife, Alissa, and Brannon, and his wife Kellye, live in East Cobb County.

Brenda Jean Ellis married Randy Bugg; they had two daughters: Anna and Katie. Anna Bugg married Jared Swafford.

Charles Ellis, Jr., known as "Chuck," married Donna Guchian; they had two children: a daughter, Jackie, and a son, Charles Ellis III, known as "Chas." Charles Ellis, Jr., known as "Chuck," is a doctor of pharmacology and director of the pharmacy at Kennestone Hospital in Marietta.

Rebecca Ellis, known as "Becky," married Charles Robert Lallerstedt, known as "Sonny." They had two children: Bethany Lynn and Charles Andrew.

Bethany Lynn Lallerstedt, a Campbell High School graduate, married Gene Foran of Mableton. They had one son, Christian.

Charles Andrew Lallerstedt, a Campbell graduate, married Shanda Cole. They had a daughter, Savannah.

The Stevenson Family

B.O.and **Helen Stevenson** bought this house from Lewis Anderson in 1944, and lived here until 1965. They had four children: **Grady**, **Glenn**, **Margaret**, and **Sandra**.

B.O. was from Little Rock, Arkansas and Mrs. Stevenson, the former Helen Montgomery, was from Concord.

Mr. Stevenson owned his own business. It was door to door merchandising, (selling merchandise like blankets, etc.).

Nineteenth House

Mr. and **Mrs. Homer Barnes, Sr.**, lived in this house. Mrs. Barnes was the former Jessie Dennis. They had eleven children: **Carl**, **Alice**, **Charlie**, **Homer**, **Jr.**, **Jessie**, **Horace**, **Elizabeth**, **Joseph P.**, known as "Joe," **Clifford**, **James**, known as "Jim," and **Donald**, known as "Bugger." Mrs. Barnes' brother, "**Shorty**" **Dennis**, lived with them. Mr. Barnes was from Cherokee County, and Mrs. Barnes was from northwest Atlanta, where they lived early in their marriage and where nine of their children were born. In 1924 they moved from northwest Atlanta to Smyrna, here their sons Cliff and Jim were born in 1926 and 1927, respectively. They moved back to Atlanta; there their youngest child, Donald, was born in 1931. Returning again from Atlanta, they moved to this house on Roswell Street, where they resided the rest of their lives.

Carl Barnes married LaRue Gardner from Clarkston.

Alice Barnes married James Leslie Mills from Rome. They had one daughter, Kay.

Charlie Barnes married Johnnie Block, known as "Hazel." They had one daughter, Betty.

Homer Barnes, Jr., married Carolyn Cook from Atlanta.

Jessie Barnes died in 1918 during the great influenza epidemic.

Horace Barnes married Eliza Mae Gussie from South Carolina.

Elizabeth Barnes married "Ed" Livesey from Clarkston. After "Ed" died, Elizabeth married Bill Love from South Georgia. Mr. Livesey was general manager over all the Beuhler Markets in Atlanta.

Joseph P. Barnes, known as "Joe," married Elizabeth Hethcock of Smyrna; they had two children, Michael and Dennis. "Joe" later married Montez Reese Matthews, who had two sons, Ronnie and Richard Matthews, the latter currently serving as organist at First Baptist Church. Montez had two brothers, Marvin and Huey Reese, who also lived in the Smyrna area. " Joe" was store manager for the Beuhler Market on Broad Street in Atlanta. Born July 17, 1922, "Joe" died December 30, 2004; he is buried in Crestlawn Cemetery in Atlanta.

Clifford Barnes married Edith Guest from North Carolina.

"Jim" Barnes married Wyolene Rutledge from Cherokee County. They had two sons: Gary and Greg. In 1969 "Jim" and Wyolene and Lillie and I built houses next door to each other on Havilon Way, in the Bennett Woods subdivision. We moved in on Labor Day of that year and have been next door neighbors since. Wyolene died very suddenly on New Year's Eve, 2001. "Jim" is still our next door neighbor.

Gary Barnes and his wife, Debbie, and their daughter, Samantha, live in Florida.

Greg Barnes and his wife, Cindy, and daughter, Shannon, live with "Jim" on Havilon Way.

"Jim," who served in the United States Navy in the 1940s and later in the United States Army during peace time, was stationed in Germany and at Fort McPherson, in Atlanta, where he was a dental technician. After his discharge, he, along with some partners, opened Cascade Dental Lab, from which he retired.

FIREMAN FOR A DAY

"Jim" Barnes related this experience from his youth, when Smyrna only had a Volunteer Fire Department; some of the men in town who were volunteer firemen at that time were George Groce,

B.F. Reed, Jr., and Paul Clayton. "When I was a teenager, the two-story house across the street from First Baptist Church (now First Baptist Chapel), on the southeast corner of Church and King streets, was on fire, and the volunteer firemen were summoned. To the firemen's dismay, the fire truck, housed in an old tin building on Roswell Street, would not crank, mainly because the engine had not been started on a regular basis. Alton Langley and I, along with some other boys, were called to push the fire truck to the blazing house. But the house burned to the ground before we could get it pushed there." NOTE: The tin building was located where the ice plant was later built.

Donald Barnes, known as "Don," married Regina Wheeler from Cherokee County. They had one daughter, Donna. "Don" later married Frances Daniel Black from East Cobb; she had two sons: Jimmy and Wesley.

Frances Daniel Black Barnes' father in the late 1950s donated land on Lower Roswell Road in East Cobb for the building of Eastside Baptist Church. Frances is a sister of J.D. Daniel, who lived on Bank Street and built Jonquil Plaza Shopping Center in the 1950s. (J.D. still owns and operates the Center but now lives on Pinetree Drive in the Forest Hills community, next door to his son, Steve.) See *Bank Street.*

Twentieth House

Mr. and **Mrs. William David Anderson**, known as "Will," married Lily Idele White from Marietta. They had ten children: **Maude**, **Power**, **Joe**, **James**, known as "Jim," **Frey**, **Arrie Gertrude**, **Bill**, **Jeanette**, **Crafton**, and **Louise**.

Maude Anderson married H.P. Green of Marietta. He worked for the railroad.

Arrie Gertrude Anderson never married.

"Jim"Anderson married Curtis Hill of Marietta. They had three children: Herlene, Jim, and Fred. "Jim" died while he was a young man and his children were small. Fred was a member of the Smyrna High School Class of 1951. See *east side of Matthews Street, Smyrna School, north side of Church Street, and Andersons of Roswell Street.*

Jeanette Anderson, who married Robert Upchurch, lives in Doraville.

Louise Anderson, graduated from Smyrna High School in the Class of 1947, married Albert Valliere and lives in Florida. She is a member of The Smyrna Historical and Genealogical Society. See *Anderson, Matthews Street* and *Andersons of Roswell Street.*

Twenty-first House

Mr. and **Mrs. Anderson Harris** resided here with their son, **Bobby**, and a daughter, whose name I do not recall.

The Martin Family

Long-time neighbors in the area remember a **Martin Family** living in this house after the Harris Family moved. They had three children: a son, **Almarine**, was known as "Al," and two daughters, Barbara and Delores. See *Davis, Nichols Street.*

NOTE: Between the Harris/Martin families and the Collins Family, there was a big white house which in the days of my youth was a rental house. It was located in an alley, or a private road, later named Crumbley Drive. The alley connected with Roswell Street on the north end and Whitfied Street on the south end. Many different families lived in this house through the years.

Twenty-second House

Mr. and **Mrs. Larson Collins** lived in this house. Larson and Mary, the former Mary Pritchard, had three daughters: **Betty**, **Regina**, and **Mary Jane**. Mr. Collins, who was a union representative for the railroad, had a brother, "Happy" Collins, who later married Margie Hiatt. See *twenty-fifth house on Roswell Street*, and *Hiatt, south side of Concord Road.*

Regina Collins married Ira Richards, a union representative for Atlantic Steel Company, in Atlanta.

Twenty-third House

Mrs. Beatrice Cochran was a widow when she moved to this house on Roswell Street. Her husband, William Jesse, known as "Will," was hit and killed by a troop train that was traveling from Chattanooga to Atlanta on January 28, 1942. He was killed at Richardson's Crossing, just north of Smyrna, near the entrance to Naval Air Station Atlanta. According to family information, the report shows that the train was traveling without lights and that it had already struck and killed two other men before it hit Mr. Cochran. Reportedly, because the troops were rowdy, the train personnel were instructed to proceed to Atlanta.

Mr. Cochran, who had been a horse trader, had a horse barn at the Atlanta Stockyards, located in Atlanta, just north of Howell Mill Road on the right side of Marietta Street. (The Atlanta Stockyards encompassed all the land between Marietta Street and the railroad across from the Exposition Cotton Mill that was located on the south side of Marietta Street.)

Mrs. Cochran, a "pillar" in First Baptist Church, bought this house on Roswell Street from Scott Edwards, Sr., in April 1942. She resided here until her death, thirty-three years later. Forty-two years old when she was widowed, she lived to be eighty-three.

Mr. and Mrs. Cochran had six children: **Duvelle**, **Lois**, **Jimmy**, **Catherine**, **Marge**, and **Faustine** known as "Sam."

Duvelle Cochran married George Pearson. They had four children: Peggy, Neal, Harold, and Joyce. Duvelle and George are deceased.

Lois Cochran married Ezell Hood. They had a son, Bill Hood, who was the principal of Griffin Middle School while my children, Marilyn and Stephen, were students there. Lois Cochran died August 27, 2005.

Jimmy Cochran married Gay Nell Bowman, who grew up on Powder Springs Street. See *Powder Springs Street* and *Stephens Street.*

Catherine Cochran had one daughter, Melissa. Catherine is deceased.

Marge Cochran married Lee Maloney from the Oakdale community. They had three daughters and a son: Jane, Bonnie, Sandra, and Jeff, who died from leukemia when he was seven. They also raised Melissa, Catherine's daughter. Marge and Lee are long-time, active members of First Baptist Church, where Lee is a deacon. Marge has been an active "greeter" at the church for many years.

Faustine Cochran, known as "Sam," married Martha Wright. They had three children: Claudia, Mark, and Karen

Faustine and Martha are deceased. See *north side of Bank Street.*

Twenty-fourth House

Mr. and **Mrs**. **Charlie Pritchard** lived on the southwest corner of Roswell and Matthews streets. They had one son, **Carl**, and a daughter, **Mary**.

Mrs. Pritchard, the former Fanny Matthews, was the daughter of Mr. and Mrs. John Matthews. When she was young, she and her family lived on Spring Street. The Matthews had several children: Fannie, Lucy, Hattie, Lena, Sadie, and three sons, whose names I do not know.

After Fanny Matthews Pritchard's mother died, her dad, Mr. John Matthews, married Mary Lester. John and Mary had one daughter, Margaret, who married Tom Tucker, a half-brother of Roy Wood. The Tuckers had one son, Guy. See *Blount, Highland Avenue*.

Carl Pritchard lived on Matthews Street with his wife and son, Carl, Jr.

Mary Pritchard married one of the Collins men. See "*Old Collins' Home Place.*"

Twenty-fifth House

"Old Collins' Home Place"

The Collins Family at one time lived just past Six Points. Though they owned all the land to the corner, they did not live at the corner. Since Mr. and Mrs. Collins died before my time, I only remember hearing about them; I did, however, know two of their children, "**Happy**" and **Betty Collins**.

The Harris Family

The Collins Family sold their property to **Herbert** and **Irene Harris**, who had two sons: **Fred** and **Jimmy**. Herbert Harris worked for Atlanta Dental Laboratory.

Fred Harris, who also worked for Atlanta Dental Laboratory, lives with his wife in North Georgia.

Jimmy Harris is a pilot for Continental Airlines.

Twenty-sixth House

The next house was the home of the **Cowart Family**. They had two sons: **Harold** and **Calvin**.

Calvin married Margaret Wheeler; they had two sons. See *Waters, north side of Spring Street.*

NOTE: Roswell Street ended at Six Points; from there Roswell Road extended outward into the county.

POSEY NEIGHBORHOOD GROCERY STORE

Mr. and Mrs. Posey owned and operated a grocery store in the triangle at Roswell and Hawthorne streets. Mrs. Posey was the sister of LeRoy Martin. See *east side of Old Concord Road.*

Twenty-seventh House

Mr. and **Mrs**. **Lester Bennett** lived farther out Roswell Street, past Six Points. I remember that Mr. and Mrs. Bennett had both served in World War I: he, in the Army and she, in the Women's

Army Corps (WAC), as a nurse. They had five children: **Lester**, **Lorraine**, **Peggy**, **Joan**, and **Jean**, the latter two being twins.

Lester Bennett, Jr., and his wife, Frances, raised their three children on Roswell Street, next door to Lester's parents. Frances and Lillie worked together in the Preschool Department at First Baptist Church.

Lorraine Bennett married Joseph C. Bowen, known as "Joe." They had no children.

Peggy Bennett, a registered nurse, never married.

Jean and Joan Bennett, with me, were members of the Smyrna High School Class of 1951. In high school they played on the girls' basketball team. They also sang at school often with Doris Bailey, Joan McDowell, and Phillip Walker, all of whom were vocally talented. Jean and Joan retired from Troutman, Sanders, Attorneys at Law, in Atlanta, and live in the Covered Bridge area, near Smyrna. Lillie and I have been associated with them through the years, both in First Baptist Church and in the community. Jean and Joan, both married but divorced, had no children.

In the 1960s Mr. and Mrs. Bennett moved to the Bennett Woods subdivision; in fact, they lived on the same street with Lillie and me until their deaths. (They were not related to Rem Bennett, who developed Bennett Woods.) After Mr. and Mrs. Bennett died, their daughters, Loraine and Peggy, lived in the house on Havilon Way the rest of their lives. After Lorraine died, Jean resided in the house for a short time, until they sold the house. Later on, First Baptist Church purchased the house to be used as a furlough home for Southern Baptist international missionaries.

Just past the Bennett house was the United States Government fence, encircling a large tract of land, where the following government installations were built: the Bell Bomber Plant, during World War II, and Dobbins Air Force Base. Later on, Naval Air Station Atlanta was moved from Chamblee to this location.

The following was written by Joan and Jean Bennett as a tribute to their family and to the influence the Smyrna community had on their lives and the lives of their family.

THE SMYRNA OF OUR YOUTH

by
Joan and Jean Bennett
Written by Joan M. Bennett
Smyrna, Georgia 30082
July 12, 2003

When we were about nine or ten, all skinny-armed and bony-kneed, Dr. Cousins, our family doctor in Atlanta, Georgia, where we resided at that time, told Mother and Daddy, Mr. and Mrs. Andrew Lester Bennett, Sr., that they needed to "get the twins in the country for their health." We were living at 367 West Lake Avenue, in beautiful Grove Park. We had a wonderfully big house, complete with three large bedrooms, a sleeping porch, a huge living room, a dining room (from which ceiling hung an authentic Tiffany lamp), a somewhat small kitchen area, and beautiful hardwood floors. We had a nice, long sidewalk directly in front of our home, and we walked everywhere on pavement.

Shortly after World War II all of that changed for us. One day we were attending Lena H. Cox Elementary School and the next day, Smyrna Elementary School; we had very little say-so in the matter. And, thus, for the better part of our now-70 years, Smyrna has been our home. Our parents, both of them living well into their eighties, spent more than half their lives in Smyrna.

Our eldest sister, Lorraine, and her husband, Joe, lived most of their married life alongside our home on Route 2, Roswell Road. Our middle sister, Peggy, who graduated from Georgia Baptist

Mr. and **Mrs. A.L. Bennett, Sr**.
In front of their house on Roswell Street in 1959
Photo courtesy of Jean and Joan Bennett.

L-R: Jean Bennett, Pete Wood, and **Joan Bennett**
In their 70th year, 2004 – at the 70th birthday luau
for Doris Bailey Fowler, a former classmate at
Smyrna High School.

Hospital School of Nursing in 1950, actually did not live at the Smyrna home place for any length of time. Our brother, Lester, and his wife and children lived next door to our house. All three of their children graduated from Smyrna schools. The year was 1945.

The people who reside in Smyrna today and enjoy the amenities of the Village Green, the lush parks, and the more elaborate homes which we see up and down Atlanta Road would probably find it difficult to believe that some of us, now in our sixth and seventh decades, actually lived on streets that were not paved. While most of the downtown city streets were paved, ours, of course, held that dubious distinction of not being paved. As newcomers drive around any area in Smyrna and its environs now and see the huge schools, they perhaps cannot imagine the diminutive high school, which we attended. But it still stands today on the property of First Baptist Church—a silent and empty monument to those sweet times of yesteryear!

Those were the days! Yet, in looking back on those yesteryears, I can still see my Mother, standing in the kitchen of that old dilapidated farmhouse, gazing out of the window as the rain was pelting the glass panes, looking at all the red mud we would have to slush through, and saying to herself, "Dear Lord in Heaven, what have we done?" Daddy, like most men, did not buy the house; he bought the land, all 46 acres of it. At a later time, he subdivided two acres, one each to Lester and Lorraine for their homes. He worked at Georgia Power Company during the day; but, before and after work during the seasons for so doing, he plowed and he sowed. He fed chickens and the hogs and milked old Bessie. And Mother washed and scrubbed that red mud and dust from that old oak floor almost every day. We had moved from a two-bathroom home to a home with a view: an outhouse. We moved from a warm and "toasty" home into a drafty barn of a house, with no underpinning and no furnace. We bathed in washtubs in the kitchen, using water Mother heated on the potbellied stove. Truth! This was in 1945, dear Reader, 1945 and into 1946. Mother was an absolute saint through it all.

But, our parents were tough folk. Each of them had served our country during World War I. While Daddy was shipped by the United States Army to France to fight in a skirmish known as the "Battle of Argonne Forest," our mother was serving in Washington, D.C., in the United States Navy as a Yeomanette, 2nd Class. His name was Andrew Lester Bennett, and her name was Marie Delona Jones. Having met one Sunday evening at church on Ashby Street in Atlanta, they were engaged prior to Daddy's departure to France. Daddy, one of nine children, was born in Cumming, and Mother, one of five children, was born in Atlanta. They were married in 1920. Lorraine came along in 1921, Lester in 1924, and Peggy in 1929. We were born in 1934.

The world stood still during the late 20s and early 30s, as the Great Depression deepened, maimed, starved . . . and humbled this nation. Daddy was the man on our street to keep a job during the Depression. He and Mother kept their neighbors supplied with butter, fresh vegetables, and eggs. Yes, even in Atlanta, my Daddy had his garden. He was born to it.

Then, in 1941, came Pearl Harbor and World War II. My parents sent Lester, a fresh-faced, skinny boy off to War. He returned whole—and a man. Yes, they were a tough stock of folk, my parents . . . they, and so many of the parents of our school chums we knew and loved in Smyrna . . . and we can only pray that we inherited that character, that type of sacrifice, that tenacity for endurance and going the distance.

So, a little mud, lots of cold nights, and many a scary visit to the outhouse would not defeat the Bennett Family. Gradually, as we entered the teen years, none of that really mattered. Daddy eventually put all the pieces together in that rambling house, and just about the time Joan drove out of the semi-circled, thrift-laden driveway, heading to Carson-Newman College in 1954, it had become what is the most precious word any child knows: Home! It is, though it no longer stands except in our memories, the home of our youth.

Growing up in Smyrna during those years was nothing short of special. For spending money we Bennett girls would clean the residence of Dr. Fred Dowda, whose house was across the street (and is still standing) or collect from neighbors used coat hangers to sell to Smyrna Cleaners for $1.00 per what today would be a garbage bag full. Downtown Smyrna boasted many hangouts for teenagers: G.B.'s Place was at the top of the list; Chat N' Nibble was another hangout; Landers Drugstore was another; and on and on. The owners knew all of us. Of course, there was the Jonquil Theatre, where Saturday matinees were the ticket.

And there was basketball in that wonderful, old, low-ceilinged gym at Smyrna High School. The lofty 3-pointers of today's games could not have been accomplished in that gym. But both boys' and girls' teams played many an exciting game on those floors. I wouldn't change a thing. I see Pete Wood, scurrying after a handoff from Phillip Walker... I see Doris Bailey, thief that she was (while positioned on the court), steal a ball from one of the Fitzhugh Lee girls, dribble it down to that center line, and pass it to me. I toss it to Jean Scoggins. Lurking down court underneath a sweet prize is my twin sister, Jean; and then Jean Scoggins dribbles her way around a stealthy guard and rifles that ball to Jean Bennett, who pivots to the right, then to the left, and tosses the ball into the gaping mouth of that basket. Swish! Game over. Victory! That old gym bellows for joy.

Afterwards, the boys would walk their sweethearts home, for very few boys had cars in those days. The walk to our house was about two miles. The ones who would "walk the two of us" home would have that same distance to return to their homes. Sweetheart walks ended when Daddy would just flip the porch light on and off several times. The boys got the message.

Time moved slowly in those days. It seemed an eternity from the time we moved to Smyrna in 1945 until we graduated in 1951. But graduation finally came. We believe it's safe to say we were probably the only graduating class anywhere, before or since, in which most of the graduates cried on their graduation night. We loved and would miss all 50 classmates.

Time moves more quickly now. And with that quickening has come change in the Smyrna of my youth. But change is good. Oh, if looking here and there, one can still find remnants of the Smyrna of my youth: First Baptist rock chapel, for one. Jean and I gave our hearts to the Lord and were baptized in that old chapel over 50 years ago.

NOTE: On many Sunday evenings in those days, an opportunity was given for those in attendance to go to the altar to pray. Many of the youth of that day took advantage of this opportunity. (This is again a practice at First Baptist Church during the Sunday morning services, and many people go forward to pray.)

And some of the homes just across the railroad, while we are winding our way toward our old home place, still are familiar sights. The Bailey home is still there; Laura Ann Jones' home is next to it. Down the way on the left is the old Hensley home place. And, very familiar to us, is Davenport Town. Our pasture abutted that area, and some of my fondest memories include playing with some of the children from Davenport Town in my Daddy's pasture. (Davenport Town was the Black section of Smyrna in that era.) Several of the homes down on Powder Springs and Bank streets are familiar as well. Of course, we still have the Covered Bridge, which was, for lack of a better description, a "Smooching Place" for boys who had cars in those days and drove their dates there.

Though we lived in Atlanta for a season between college and marriage and divorce, our parents were still here and our visits were so frequent that we never really left Smyrna folks. With rapid movement of time, we inevitably have had our good-byes to say. So many of us who were at the altar almost every Sunday evening during our high school years have stood there beside loved ones and, ultimately, at the grave sides too. We twins have buried our parents and two sisters up on the hill of Georgia Memorial Park, just a few yards down the road from where we grew up and overlooking what we called the Four-Lane Highway, now Cobb Parkway. We will lie there, too, one day. That thought gives us comfort in a way, which many people might not understand. Some call it "roots."

This essay will occupy a place in the memoirs of Pete Wood. Jean and I are both honored to be included in such an undertaking by him and his wife, Lillie. As our classmate and a member of our Smyrna High School Class of 1951, Pete is our generation. He has exemplified all of his life the essence of the upbringing he, too, enjoyed in Smyrna. He has, first and foremost, honored his Lord in an exemplary Christian manner. He has honored the name his parents gave him, as well as their legacy. He has honored his wife and family with integrity and faithfulness. He has brought honor and pride to his country during his stellar military career. He brings honor and character to his city. His life is one well lived...and blessed. We are not surprised by any of his church, political, and civic accomplishments, and we rejoice with him and his family in all of them.

In the years ahead, as others read these memoirs, perhaps they can gain through some form of osmosis the essence that Smyrna is still that small town of yesteryear.

Living here has been part and parcel of who we are today. Still just small-town girls!

ROSWELL STREET
West Side

Appreciation is extended to Nancy McGee for sharing memories of her family, the Terrells, and their close neighbors who lived on the west side of Roswell Street. Thanks to Sara Hensley Miles, and Sam Hensley, Sr., for memories of their family, the Paul Hensley Family. Thanks also, to Sara Anderson Gentry for information about the Andersons and Blacks of Roswell Street, and to Serena Haney for information about the Haney Family. Appreciation to Miller Davis for information regarding the Judson Davis Family, to Johnny Black for information about the Black Family, to Don Carroll about the Carroll Family. Thanks to Jean Goodwin McMillan for information on her family, the Goodwins, to Jeanne Tinsley, for information on her husband's family, the Tinsleys; and to Hugh Lee McDaniell, whose dad, Dudley Houston McDaniell, built Six Points Grocery Store in the 1940s.

NOTE: G.V. Cochran told me that he was born, March 8, 1927, in a house that stood where the "ice plant" was later built.

THE ICE PLANT

Southland Ice and Cold Storage, or the "ice plant," as it was called in those days, was the first building on the left side of Roswell Street past the railroad from G.B.'s Place. It was a cement block building with wood trim, a one-story building but two stories in height to accommodate the cranes and machinery necessary for the operation of the business. In later years the building was painted blue, but during the days of my childhood, I seem to remember that it was composed of raw wood and unpainted cement blocks. It was a very large structure standing there across the railroad and towering over the houses in the area, or at least that is the way I remember it. The building was divided into two sections: the upper part was for making ice for future delivery, and the lower section was for storage of the machinery and equipment.

The ice was made in this way. Steel rectangular shaped canisters were filled with water and lowered into a large tank that had been filled with water and a heavy concentration of salt. This was called a brine tank. An overhead crane was used to lower and raise the steel canisters. The ice would be emptied out of the canisters into the cold storage area, where the three-hundred-pound blocks of ice would then be cut by an electric saw into twenty-five, fifty, and hundred-pound blocks. As a kid I would go to the "ice plant" just to watch the operation. I especially liked to watch the workers cut the ice, but it was also cool in there.

The front of the building, facing Roswell Street, had a long loading dock. At the most southern end of the loading dock was a small office. There was parking room at the dock for several delivery vehicles, (pickup trucks and horse-drawn wagons), all painted yellow with *Southland Ice Company* on their sides. Because there were no new cars, trucks, or tires available, as all materials for the manufacturing of new vehicles and tires were being used for the World War II effort, and because gasoline was rationed, one would often see a horse-drawn wagon loaded with ice for customers. The company delivered all over the area: to homes, businesses, schools, churches, and to Brawner

Sanitarium, on South Atlanta Road. When the ice reached its destinations, it was clean and covered with a heavy tarpaulin to keep the ice from melting while on the truck or wagon.

On the opposite end of the loading dock from the office was the storage portion of the plant. There was a chute that opened onto the saw area on the platform. The workers would pull those three-hundred-pound blocks of ice into the chute. The multiple saw blades, powered by electricity, were configured to cut the three-hundred-pound blocks into six fifty-pound blocks. That was typical, but if someone wanted more or less, the saws could be reset for the size the customer wanted. Most family iceboxes could accommodate fifty pounds.

We did not buy ice for our house because, from my earliest memories, we had a refrigerator. But I knew many people in the area, before and during World War II, who still used iceboxes that required commercial ice.

NOTE: **Southland Ice** and **Cold Storage** business was owned and operated by the **Hancock Family** from Marietta, where they operated a plant in addition to the "ice plant" in Smyrna.

When I was a kid, I spent much time at the "ice plant" in Smyrna because my Uncle Alton Langley managed it before and during World War II. We saved lard cans, among other things, for further use. (This was before Tupperware.) My friends and I would fill a lard can with a mix of milk, eggs, and sugar, take it to the "ice plant," and lower it into the brine tank. It would not be long until we had ice cream.

During World War II, sugar was rationed and thus limited in purchase amounts. Therefore, since my family raised a lot of chickens, I would trade eggs to neighbors for sugar. Thus, between my friends and me, we could put our eggs, milk, and sugar together to make ice cream. I remember how much fun it was to make ice cream and take it to Uncle Alton and have him freeze it for us!

In the summertime, when my friends and I were out of school, we would gather empty drink bottles, such as Coke, RC, and Pepsi, and take them to the store, where we would be paid two cents per bottle. Also, we were paid for tin cans after we had cut out both ends and flattened the cans. We were paid a few cents per pound. These were good sources of income for me in those days. I had neighbors, like Mrs. Pressley, who would regularly give me lard cans. I was always looking for something to do to make a little money in those days to support my wants, usually not much more than a hot dog and a drink from G.B.'s Place, which was very close to the "ice plant." A big drink and a hot dog, along with ice cream, would make for a good lunch!

The term *recycling* is not a new idea because we recycled everything we could during World War II, but for different reasons than we do now. I must add that my mother saved used cooking grease and newspapers. These items were taken to designated centers and recycled for the War effort.

NOTE: The G.B. Williams Park, built on the property where the "ice plant" stood, was dedicated April 24, 2004.

NOTE: Long-time residents of Roswell Street remember when the short street running from Gilbert Street to Atlanta Street, between the B.F. Reed, Sr., house and the Mazie Nelson house, was called "Reed's Alley." Eventually the street, which had been re-named Nelson Street, was closed at the railroad, due to the widening of Atlanta Street late in the Twentieth Century.

Mrs. Fanny Crawford's house was located between the "ice plant" and the railroad. It is one of the four houses that faced Atlanta Street.

The mailboxes for the Crawfords and Reeds were located on Roswell Street, side by side. I can picture seeing the mailman, walking on Roswell Street and delivering mail to those boxes. I guess the postal employees thought it was better for the two families to walk to Roswell Street each day than it was for the mailman to walk to their houses. In any event, whatever they were thinking, I saw the mailman deliver the mail to those boxes, and I remember seeing Mr. Crawford and Mr. Reed walking out to get their mail.

When I was a kid, I spent many hours at my Aunt Myrtle Brooke's house, across the street from the mailboxes, and at Ma-Ma Tucker's house, which was up the street, and at the "ice plant," where my Uncle Alton Langley worked. I knew what those neighbors were doing every day!

First House

Mr. and **Mrs. Reuben Haney** owned and occupied this house. They had six children: **Frank, Morris, Earl, Mary, Ruby**, and **Robert**. Earl and Ruby are the only survivors of this family.

According to information from family members, **Robert Haney** also lived in this house, on the west side of Roswell Street. He married Anna Belle Anderson; they had one daughter, Serena Haney, who currently lives in Smyrna. See *Joe Anderson Family, east side of Roswell Street.*

The James Elmer Anderson Family

James Elmer and **Dovie Thomas Anderson** resided in this house, located on the west side of Roswell Street just beyond Gilbert Street. Elmer and Dovie had six children: **Lewis**, born in 1905; **Tommie Lee**, known as "Tom," born in 1908; **James William**, known as "Jay," born in 1910; **Leila**, born in 1912; **Sara**, born in 1915; and **Clara**, born in 1918. See *Andersons of Roswell Street* and *thirteenth house on east side of Roswell Street and Andersons of Roswell Street.*

Having married January 1, 1905, Elmer and Dovie, as newlyweds, moved into their first home, which was located on a farm on Roswell Road, now Windy Hill Road. The house was a large two-story, white framed one, located in the vicinity of the current site of WellStar Windy Hill Hospital. The house stood in that location until the "big building boom" started in the mid 1950s.

Dovie and Elmer first moved to Roswell Street in 1920, to the house on the east side of Roswell Street, currently known as the home of Councilman "Bill" Scoggins and his wife, Gerrye. In 1938 they moved to this first house on the west side of Roswell Street and were living here when all of their daughters married. They lived here the rest of their lives. Elmer died January 31, 1958, and Dovie died May 28, 1967.

Sara Anderson Gentry shared, "When my family first moved to the house on the west side of Roswell Street, we had an area about fifty feet wide, between our garage and Gilbert Street, that was filled with jonquils. For many years a photographer from *The Atlanta Georgian*, which was one of the two major afternoon newspapers in Atlanta, came to take pictures. My mother, Mrs. Anderson, would permit some of the young boys in the neighborhood to help her pick the jonquils and arrange them in bouquets. The boys would go to different areas along Atlanta Road, including streetcar stops, where they would sell the bouquets for ten cents each. Mother allowed them to keep a nickel per sale."

Mr. and **Mrs. William L. Black, Jr.**

Leila Mae Anderson and her husband, William L. Black, Jr., and their daughter, Clara Elizabeth, known as "Liz," lived in this house with Dovie and Elmer in their senior years. Leila Mae died January 21,1965, and William L. Black, Jr., died March 11, 1980.

The current owners and occupants of this house are Clara Elizabeth Black Davis, known as "Liz," and her husband, James Ronald Davis, known as "Ron." Elizabeth is a granddaughter of Dovie and Elmer Anderson and the daughter of Leila Anderson Black and William L. Black, Jr. "Liz" was born in the house next door, on the north side, where her parents were living at that time. See *Andersons of Roswell Street.*

James Elmer and **Dovie Lee (Thomas) Anderson**
Children, **L-R:** Jay W., Lewis, infant; Leila Mae; and Tom Anderson.
NOTE: The Anderson's two younger children, Sara and Clara, had not been born.
Circa 1913
Courtesy of Elizabeth ("Liz") Black Davis.

James Elmer Anderson and **Dovie Lee Anderson** at their 1371 Roswell Street home. Circa 1940s
Courtesy "Liz" (Black) Davis

L-R: Cousins **Sara** (Anderson) **Gentry**, **Ethel** (Thomas) **Pharr**, **Frances Thomas**, and **Leila** (Anderson) **Black** Circa late 1920s Courtesy "Liz" (Black) Davis

Sara (Anderson) and **"Jim" Gentry**
60th Wedding Anniversary First Methodist Church Circa 2001
Courtesy "Liz" (Black) Davis

"Ron" and **"Liz" (Black) Davis**
Circa 1980s Latest Anderson Family member to reside at the 1351 Roswell Street
Courtesy "Liz" (Black) Davis

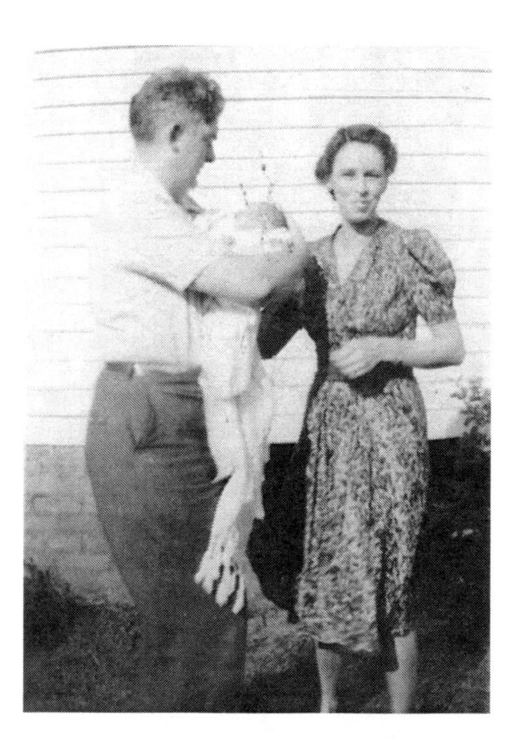

William L. Black, Sr., holding **Elizabeth Black** (infant), known as "Liz", and **Leila Anderson Black**, in front of their 1371 Roswell Street home.
Circa 1943
Courtesy "Liz" (Black) Davis
NOTE: See Haney, Anderson Black house (next door).

William L. "Bill" Black and **Leila Ande**
At their home, 1351 Roswell Str
Circa 1960
Photo Courtesy of Elizabeth Black I

L-R: Haney Brothers and Sisters, **Frank, Earl, Mary Haney, Maurice, Ruby Haney** (Riggs), and **Robert Haney**, at home at 1351 Roswell Street .
Circa late 1930s or early 1940s.
Courtesy Sabrina Haney

Mr. and Mrs. Ronald Davis

Mr. and **Mrs. Ronald Davis**, known as "Liz" and "Ron," met at North Georgia College and married after "Ron" graduated. He served in the United States Army from east coast to west coast, and in between, with service also in Vietnam and two different locations in Germany. Kirk, their only child, was born at Kennestone Hospital in Marietta while "Ron" was in Vietnam.

While "Liz" and "Ron" were at Fort Hood, Texas, Kirk graduated from high school and entered college in Texas; he still lives in the Greater Austin, Texas area. Kirk married Colene McCormack; they had one daughter, Keely Elizabeth Davis, born January 28, 1995. She is the pride and joy of "Ron" and "Liz."

Having attained the rank of Colonel, "Ron" retired from the military. He and "Liz" now spend much time in Texas with their children.

"Ron" served as Treasurer throughout the planning and building stages of the Twentieth Century Veterans Memorial, which was dedicated in 2002. He continues as Treasurer of the Veterans Memorial Association, and is active in the Golden K Kiwanis Club in Smyrna, where he is the in-coming President.

Second House

Mr. and **Mrs. Sam Morris** lived in the house next door to the Andersons. They were the parents of Sally Morris Adams, who lived across the street from my family on Bank Street. Later on, Mr. and Mrs. Morris lived farther out Roswell Street. See *eighth house, east side of Roswell Street* and *Adams, south side of Bank Street.*

Mr. and Mrs. Morris had two sons: **Pinkney**, known as **"Pinky,"** and **Harley**. During World War II, I remember the star in Mrs. Morris' window represented Harley's serving his country. I also remember going to my grandmother's on Roswell Street when Mr. and Mrs. Morris lived there. I liked Mr. and Morris, for they were always nice to me. They probably moved from this house in the early 1940s.

Pinkney Morris never married.

Harley Morris married Betty Poteet. They had three children.

Mr. and Mrs. William L. Black, Jr.

Later on, **Leila Anderson Black** and **William L. Black, Jr**., lived here. Their daughter, **Clara Elizabeth**, was born in this house on September 1, 1942. Elizabeth currently lives next door. See *First House.*

Third House

Carl C. Terrell
Smyrna City Councilman
Elected January 21, 1952

Mr. and **Mrs. Carl Terrell** and their two children, **Helen**, and **Robert**, resided in this house. Mrs. Terrell was known as "Bess." I recall that Mr. Terrell was Smyrna's City Clerk for several years, June 1938-July 31, 1942. His beginning salary was $60.00 a month; his ending salary was $110.00. Mr. Terrell was elected January 21, 1952, to finish the term of Mr. C.W. Jones on the Smyrna City Council.

Robert Terrell married Dorothy Benson. They had three sons: Bruce, Dennis, and Richard.

Helen Terrell married Marion McGee, who was also known as "Fibber." They had thre children: Suzanne, Nancy, and David.

Jack Shinall
Smyrna City Councilman
1978-1991

Suzanne McGee married Jack Shinall. They had two children: Brian and Kristin. Bria married Donna Moody; they had one daughter, Emma. Kristin, a school teacher, is not married at thi time. Jack served on the Smyrna City Council, 1978-1991. Suzanne is a registered nurse.

Nancy McGee

Nancy McGee lives on Roswell Street in the Terrell House, which was and still is a ver nice home. She once worked for the Federal Reserve Bank in Atlanta. Nancy, active in man organizations in the area, is currently serving as secretary of the Taylor-Brawner House Foundatior Inc. (This group is working to restore the structure and preserve the history of the house, which i located on the Brawner Hospital campus.)

David McGee, who resided for ten years in Asia, where he worked with the Diebol Corporation, now lives in Ohio.

Helen Terrell McGee lives on South Atlanta Road in the house where she and "Fibber raised their children; their house is across the street from the Brawner Hospital property. I remembe "Fibber" well. He was a very active member of American Legion Post #160, where he was Commander. Helen for many years taught eighth graders at Griffin Middle School, from which sh retired.

NOTE: Nancy McGee shared the following story. "When Granddaddy Terrell was eightee years old, he helped to build, in 1906, the house on Roswell Street for his mother. She moved to thi house from the East Cobb family farm on Terrell Mill Road, which is named for the Terrell Family and lived here until her death, in 1926. One of Granddaddy's sisters also lived here part of that time 'Mimi' and Granddaddy (Bess and Carl) met in Omaha, Nebraska, where 'Mimi' grew up. The married there and came to live permanently in Smyrna in 1927, after Granddaddy's mother, Grandm Terrell, died."

Fourth House

My paternal grandparents, **Mr.** and **Mrs. R.G. Tucker**, lived in the house next door to th Terrells when I was a small boy. We called them "Ma-Ma" and "Pa-Pa." She was the former Mami Langley Wood and a sister of Alton Langley, who managed the Southland Ice Company ("ice plant" on Roswell Street in the days of my childhood. "Ma-Ma" Tucker's daughter and grandson, **Mardell Wood Farmer** and **Bobby Farmer**, also resided here. "Ma-Ma" and "Pa-Pa" Tucker had two grow sons, **Harold** and **Tom**, who also lived here. "Pa-Pa" Tucker died in this house in 1939. See *north sid of Bank Street.*

In the early 1940s, before the bombing of Pearl Harbor, "Ma-Ma" and Mardelle moved t Lucille Avenue, in the West End section of Atlanta, to be closer to Mardelle's work. Her son, Bobby graduated from Joseph Brown High School in Atlanta in the early 1950s.

"Ma-Ma" Tucker and Mardelle were both members of First Baptist Church, where remember going to church with them.

Hilda and **"Pete"Wood** with their Grandmother "Ma-Ma" Tucker on Roswell Street
Circa 1936

Thomas Guy Tucker known as "Tom"
United Stated Navy, World War II
Picture Courtesy of Pete Wood

Tom Tucker and Cousin, **Jack Langley**
Circa 1943
Courtesy Roy Wood Family

Tom and **Margaret Tucker** in Murphy, N.C.
Smyrna Amateur Baseball game
Circa 1947
Courtesy Roy Wood Family

Center: Mamie Langley Wood Tucker Back Row: Tom Tucker and **Roy Wood**
Front Row: Harold Tucker and **Bill Davis**
Circa mid-1940s on Lucille Avenue in Atlanta
Picture Courtesy "Pete" Wood

Mr. and Mrs. Leon Bizzell

Mr. and **Mrs. Leon Bizzell** moved to this house in 1942. They had four children: **Leon, Jr.**, nown as "Bubba," **Mary**, **Nan**, and **Sybil**. The Bizzells continued to own this property until 1999.

Leon Bizzell, Jr., who served in the United States Navy during World War II and the Korean onflict, had a daughter, Suzanne. Leon Bizzell, Jr., died in 1999.

Mary Bizzell worked for the Telephone Exchange. She married Sid Davis, who grew up on hurch Street. See *north side of Church Street.*

Nan Bizzell married Hugh Hall; they had no children. However, Nan had two children, arry and Lisa, from a previous marriage.

Sybil Bizzell married Al Cantrell. They had one daughter, Kristin.

Fifth House

Jim and **Jewell Goss** lived in this house, next door to my grandmother; they had one aughter, **Henrietta**, also known as "Sara." She married Ronnie Waddell; they had one son, also amed Ronnie, who grew up with our children and is the same age as my daughter, Marilyn. Ronnie, a etective, has more than fifteen years service with the Smyrna Police Department.

Later on Mr. Goss opened a radiator repair business in Smyrna. I really liked Jim and Jewell, r they were very nice people, to whom I enjoyed delivering their paper.

Mr. and Mrs. Emmett Cox

Emmett and **Lena Cox** moved from the Howell Mill Road area in Atlanta, into this house, in 942. Mr. Cox worked at the Bell Bomber Plant and later at Lockheed Aircraft Corporation. Mrs. Cox as from Emerson, and Mr. Cox was from Cass Station, near Cartersville. They had two children, **ennis** and **Sandra**, both of whom graduated from Campbell High School.

Dennis Cox married Beverly Padgett. They had two sons, Richard, Jr., and Glenn, and four randsons.

Sandra Cox married Carl Biddy. They had four children: Michael, David, Michelle, and anielle. Sandra and Carl live in Cartersville.

Sixth House

Mr. and **Mrs. Jesse Bailey** and their two children, **Doris** and **Roger**, lived in this house on e west side of Roswell Street; the last City street light was located in front of their house.

Beulah Morgan, mother of Mrs. Bailey, the former Lois Murphy of Dacula, was the ostmistress in Auburn; there she met and married Carl Murphy. As a young man, Carl died from neumonia; this left Beulah with six children, the youngest of whom were six-year-old twins, Ceylon nd Leylon, who are now 82 years old. All of Lois' brothers (G.W., Carl, Ceylon, and Leylon) served the United States Military; fighting during World War II, each one safely returned home.

Hardy Bailey, Jesse Bailey's oldest brother, who owned much property on Medlin and ickens streets, in the early 1940s encouraged Jesse and Lois to move from Flowery Branch to Smyrna work at the "new" Bell Bomber Plant in Marietta, built for the War effort. The family moved to a ouse, owned by Hardy, on the west side of Pickens Street; there they lived for their first year in myrna.

In 1944, when the owner of the sixth house and some adjoining land on the west side Roswell Street decided to sell, Jesse bought it and moved his family here. In the early 1950s, Jes built a home on Pretty Branch Drive, where he and Lois resided for twenty years. In the early 1970 Jesse bought much acreage in the Lost Mountain community, in West Cobb County, where he a Lois lived the remainder of their lives.

Jesse's mother, a young widow with six children, moved from Sand Mountain, Alabama, in wagon. Jesse, the youngest child, was six months old when his father, Moses (a twin brother Aaron), died. Jesse's mother never remarried.

In the 30 years they were residents of Smyrna and the Smyrna area of Cobb County, Jes and Lois Bailey were active members of First Baptist Church, where he was a Deacon and she was Sunday School teacher. Lois was also involved in Smyrna School P.T.A.

Personally, I remember that Jesse Bailey and Jim White, working together, had the reputatic of being excellent brick masons. Later both of them became developers and builders in Smyrna. Wh I was a lad growing up in Smyrna, I thought how easy they made brick laying look!

As a building contractor, Jesse constructed many buildings in Smyrna. Doris Bailey Fowl recalls, "Dad's building the following: Smyrna City Hall and Jail on Bank Street; the Masonic Ha building on West Spring Street, and Castellaw Funeral Home on Church Street. Dad also built ma homes in the Forest Hills area; Pretty Branch Drive, Pinetree Drive, and Forest Drive, where he bu the First Baptist Church parsonage. He also helped with the building of First Methodist Church Concord Road, completed in 1967." Jesse served one term as building inspector for the City Smyrna.

Doris Bailey, a graduate in the Smyrna High School Class of 1951 had been a member of t high school's Girl's Basketball Team. Later she played semi-professional basketball for Atlanta "Sports Arena Blues," attended the Atlanta Division of the University of Georgia (now Georgia Sta University), and worked as a secretary. Doris married Bobby Fowler in 1954. They had thr daughters: Leesa, Leslie, and Lauren. Doris and Bobby built a house on Pretty Branch Drive next do to her parents, Jesse and Lois Bailey. In 1973 they built a house in the Lost Mountain community West Cobb County, on property adjoining that of her parents.

Bobby Fowler, the son of Mr. and Mrs. Gordon Fowler, who lived on King Springs Roa served four years in the United States Navy, during the Korean Conflict. After his discharge, became a real estate agent and insurance underwriter at Poston, Guthrie, and Fowler Insuran Agency. While living in Smyrna, Bobby served as President of the Smyrna Chamber of Commer was twice named "Smyrna's Outstanding Young Man of the Year." He later became a homebuilder West Cobb County.

Leesa Fowler was an art major in college; in the early 1970s, she owned and operated Dow to Earth Arts and Crafts Shop, located in Dickson Shopping Center. A fire at the shopping cent destroyed the back of the craft shop and Fowler Insurance Agency. Leesa married Bill English Peachtree City; they built their home on her family's property in the Lost Mountain community West Cobb County.

Leslie Fowler married Jim Bowes of Dunwoody. They had a daughter, Grace, and a s Cameron. Leslie and Jim live in Roswell, where she owns and operates an interior design business.

Lauren Fowler married Randy Shepherd of Smyrna. Lauren had two daughters: Michelle a Rachel. Lauren and Randy also built their home on her family's property in the Lost Mounta community. Lauren owns and operates a custom design drapery and decorating business.

Roger Bailey married Anne Florence of Marietta. They had four sons: Dale, who died as infant, Chris, Scott, and Shawn.

Chris Bailey and his wife, Tina, had a daughter, Savannah, and a son, Christopher.

Scott Bailey and his wife, Laura, had a son, Andrew, and a daughter, Katelyn.

Roger Bailey worked in the building business and later owned and operated a music shop in owder Springs. Roger lives in Yorkville.

MEMORIES
by Doris Bailey Fowler

Doris has shared the following memories of her growing up in Smyrna in the middle of the wentieth Century: "I remember living on Roswell Street and all the kids in the neighborhood athering on the paved sidewalk wearing metal clamp-on skates that pulled the soles off their shoes.

"I remember that my dad, Jesse, had hunting dogs, chickens, pigs, and a calf named 'Buster,' hich my brother, Roger, and I would not eat when he was slaughtered and canned. Dad loved ardening and had a huge cornfield on the land behind our house.

"Our garage, which was apart from our house, had a center post as a divider for two cars. long with Laura Ann Jones in the front seat, I decided at age thirteen, that I would learn to drive; istead I tore out that center post of the garage. Mom and Dad were not at home. At age fourteen, I rove the same car (without permission), with Joan Bennett in the front seat. While I was trying to turn round at the railroad near the Reed House, I backed off into a ditch. A Stranger came along and ulled us out.

"I remember my Uncle Hardy Bailey and his wife, Aunt Leonie, who lived in a large log ouse on the north side of Medlin Street near the creek in the middle of the woods off Medlin Street. hurch groups often would go to their house on Sunday afternoons for 'sing-a-longs' down by the reek. Uncle Hardy had built on both sides of the creek, long benches for people to sit on. He also had vo rental houses on Pickens Street, at the top of the hill, just off Medlin Street. Here he encouraged y parents to move in the early 1940s. See *Bailey west side of Pickens Street* and *north side of Medlin treet.*

"Reminiscing my past, I recall all the fun we had dancing at the 'Teen Canteen' in the myrna American Legion Post # 160; roller skating and bowling at the old 'B&H' Skating Rink on outh Cobb Drive; eating Hamburgers at G.B.'s Place by the railroad after basketball games or driving the Varsity in Atlanta with a car packed full of guys and girls; riding the 'streetcar trolley' to larietta to swim at Brumby's swimming pool, the only one around; movies at the 'Jonquil Theatre' here the smoke curled up all over the theater from the cigarettes and you could barely see the movie times.

"I remember singing with twins, Jean and Joan Bennett, throughout our high school years, on larietta's radio station WFOM; Gene 'Red' Sparks was the station DJ. See *Sparks, Whitfield Street.*

"As young people, we walked, ran, and or rode bicycles on dirt roads all over Smyrna —even the Concord Covered Bridge.

"Riding bicycles, Joan Bennett and I, after basketball practice, would ride from Smyrna's oswell Street across the 'new' Four Lane Highway (Now U.S. Highway 41), to Windy Hill Road hen a dirt road), with everything thereafter totally country, then to Powers Ferry Road, and across the ld bridge over the Chattahoochee River to Buckhead; there we would visit Susan Bradley (now oward), a former classmate. On our return trip to Smyrna, caught in the dark (no street lights nywhere), we rode across the river and through miles of woods. Then came the hills on Powers Ferry nd Windy Hill roads (which were dirt), where we would push our bikes. But those were times of true eedom—and safety!

Mattie Maude Davis and **Judson Clement Davis**
Great-Granddaughter, **Dana Davis**
Circa early 1960s
Photo Courtesy of Miller Davis

King Davis
Downtown Atlanta
Middle of the Twentieth Centu
Photo Courtesy of Miller Davi

Willard Graham Davis
Circa 1940s
Courtesy of Miller Davis

"These are memories of laughter, singing, and respect and honor for each other. Blessed ere those years, growing up, with plenty of chores to perform and no television to watch."

"Pete, how about our 1951 Senior Class Trip to Florida with the girls on one bus and all the ys on another?"

Seventh House

The Judson Clement Davis Family

According to Davis Family information, **Mr. Judson Clement Davis** and his wife, the rmer **Mattie Maude King**, both from Floyd Springs, in Floyd County, moved to this house in 1928. dson Clement and Mattie Maude had seven children: **King**, **Willard Graham**, **Hubbard**, known as Iub," **Florence**, **Tom**, **Wallace**, and **Betty**. For the most part, Judson Clement and Mattie Maude ised their children in the Allgood Road area in Cobb County.

King Davis married Nell Miller of Powder Springs. They were the parents of Miller and lark Davis, who grew up on the south side of Church Street in Smyrna. Miller and I were both embers of the Smyrna High School Class of 1951. See *south side of Church Street.*

Willard Graham Davis married Martha Manning of Marietta. They had two children, anning and Madeline, and three granddaughters. Graham was a graduate of Marietta High School d Emory University. After graduating from the Candler School of Theology, Graham was ordained. everend Davis also studied at Baliol College, of Oxford University in Oxford, England. As a ethodist minister he was a member of the North Georgia Conference of the Methodist Church.

Prior to World War II, he served the following churches in the Atlanta area: Mt. Gilead, Owl ck, Union Point, and Peachtree Road Methodist Church in Atlanta. In the late1930s, he served as aplain in the Civilian Conservation Corp (CCC). During World War II Graham served as Staff aplain of the 8th Army Air Corps in England and of the occupation forces of Germany and Japan. mong his many decorations is the Air Force Commendation Medal for Meritorious Service. After enty-seven years as Chaplain, he retired from the United States Air Force with the rank of eutenant Colonel. Following his retirement, Graham taught at Emory University at Oxford in ewton County. Among Graham's many activities was membership in the Masons, the British Legion, d a lifetime supporter of the Boy Scouts of America.

Born in Floyd County, November 1, 1906, Graham died November 15, 2004, at 98 years of e. He is buried at the Oxford Historical Cemetery in Newton County.

Hubbard Davis, known as "Hub," played football at Marietta High School.

Florence Davis married John Chapman; and they had four children. John had a farm in ula, north of Tifton, they lived there and worked the farm for many years, before retiring. terwards, they moved to Albany, to be close to their daughter.

Tom Davis was a member of the Smyrna High School Class of 1933.

Wallace Davis died in 1924 at one year and nine months of age.

Betty Davis, in the 1940s, worked at the Fulton National Bank, Candler Building office, ong with my mother, Dora Wood. They rode the streetcar together.

Mr. and Mrs. Judson C. Davis, in the early 1930s, moved from Roswell Street to Atlanta's lton community, across the Chattahoochee River, in Fulton County.

The Paul Hensley Family

Mr. and **Mrs. Paul Hensley** were residents of this house, which was located just past t deep curve. Mrs. Hensley was the former Ober Penland. They had five children: **Marble Jo Hensley, Charles, Sarah, Greta,** and **Sam**. The Hensleys bought this house from the Judson Cleme Davis Family in the early 1930s.

Mrs. Ober Hensley, who was from Ellijay, had a twin sister named Opal. They were born 1900 to Mr. and Mrs. Thomas Young Penland; their dad was 50 years old when they were born. Sar Hensley Miles shared, "My mother, Ober, remembered her dad talking to her and her sister a lot abo his memories of the Civil War, which began when he was eleven years old."

Mr. Paul Hensley, from Ballground, in Cherokee County, was the son of Mr. and M Marble John Hensley. His sister, Clementine, known as "Aunt Tiny," was married to Jim Barnes, first cousin of Mr. Richard Barnes, Sr., who lived on the east side of Roswell Street.

Marble John Hensley, known as "M.J.," was named for his grandfather. He married Ru Collins, one of the twin daughters of Dr. and Mrs. Collins, who also lived on Roswell Street. "M. and Ruth had three daughters and one son: Carol Hasty, Sandra Wise, M.J., Jr., Kathy McFarla "M.J." and Ruth live in Chattanooga, Tennessee.

Sarah Hensley married Bill Miles in 1951. They had four children: Paul Miles, Sarah Panf Mary Miles, and Greta Gantt.

Bill Miles published *The Smyrna Herald,* 1952-1961. He also worked in Austell with S Williams, the publisher of *The Austell Enterprise*, and he helped publish *The Sweetwater News.* addition, Bill wrote the book *People of Smyrna* for the Smyrna Centennial, 1972.

Sarah stated, "When my brother, Sam, was playing on *The Marietta Journal*/Americ Legion baseball team, I went with Mother and Dad to see him play. Between innings, Mother an went to the restroom; Mother said, 'Sarah, that is a nice- looking young man sitting next to me on th bench; you need to be sitting by him.'"

Sarah further related, "When we went back, Mother sat down so that I had to sit by B Miles. Bill and I started talking, and before the year was over, we were married. That was 1951. I w the last one at home, and I think my mother was set on getting me out of the house."

Sarah and Bill Miles and their family were members of First Baptist Church, where Sarah still active in Sunday School and church attendance. Bill died many years ago.

NOTE: The Marietta American Legion Post # 29 sponsored a baseball team of young m seventeen and younger, who played at Brown's Park, adjacent to Marietta School. I played on th team along with a number of other guys from Smyrna, including: Sam Hensley, Pat Edwards, Dan a Bud Theodocian, "Buddy" Jones, and Tommy Oglesby. I remember that we took a trip all the way Jacksonville, Florida, playing in Macon, Millen, Savannah, and Jacksonville, Florida. The Americ Legion chartered a bus and we were gone for a week. I seem to recall that, when we played our l road game in Jacksonville, Evelyn and James Pressley were there.

Charles Hensley died as an infant.

Greta Hensley married Charles McMillan; they had three children: Laura Lavin, David, a Beth Long. Charles' dad was a member of the McMillan Family that lived on the east side of So Atlanta Road, a short distance from Brawner Sanitarium; his mother was a member of the Wor Family that lived on Church Street. Charles McMillan was a graduate of Smyrna High School, No Georgia College, in Dahlonega and Mercer University in Macon. Charles entered Southeast Seminary in Wake Forest, North Carolina. After completing his studies at the Seminary, he w dained as a minister at First Baptist Church. His first pastorate was at First Baptist Church of 'oodstock in Cherokee County. Retired, he and his wife, Greta, now live in North Carolina. See *cMillan, south side of Church Street; north side of Spring Street;* and *Atlanta Street, from Mrs. azie's to Pearce Matthews.*

Sam Hensley married Iris Antley, the daughter of Mr. and Mrs. Shuler Antley. Shuler served the Superintendent of the Marietta School System. Sam and Iris had three children: Sam, Jr., evanne Thomas, and Shuler.

Iris Antley Hensley was the Director of Georgia Ballet. She left quite a legacy in the arts of bb County when she passed away in 2003.

Sam and his brother, "M.J.," were in business together at Hensley and Associates.

Sam Hensley remembers that his dad, Paul Hensley, Cobb County Surveyor, was hired by City of Smyrna to draw the City Limits, a half-mile circle from the center which was the Masonic ilding on West Spring Street. He remembers helping his dad with the survey.

Sam also remembers the subdivision of white, frame homes of Concord Road, built by Rem nnett as the first annexation into the City; these broke the circle. J.Y. Wooten was the primary altor that sold these homes. These houses are still located on both sides of Concord Road from nton Street to McLinden Avenue on the north side and McCauley Road to Ridgecrest Drive on the uth side, extending through to South Cobb Drive.

Mrs. Ober Hensley, who worked at the Bell Bomber Plant during World War II, became a al estate agent and sold houses in the Belmont Hills subdivision, on Cherokee Street; and in the '50s she served as City Clerk of Smyrna. Ober, a very intelligent businesswoman, was also a member the Cobb County Board of Registrars. See *Ober Hensley, north side of Spring Street.*

Mr. Paul Hensley, both of his sons, and one of his grandsons graduated from Georgia stitute of Technology.

NOTE: Just past his family's house Mr. Hensley built three houses, which he sold.

Eighth House

Mr. and **Mrs. Carroll** lived in the first of the new houses. This was not the Johnny Carroll mily.

Ninth House

Mr. and **Mrs. Ralph Goodwin** moved from Atlanta to the second of the new houses, for ich they paid $6,000.00. She was the former Virginia Elliott. They had four children: **Jean**, **Steven**, own as "Steve," **Kim**, and **Robin**. Mr. Goodwin, self-employed, sold mops, brooms, and cotton rn.

Jean Goodwin, who graduated from Campbell High School, married Larry McMillan of ring Street. Larry played football at Marietta High School, from which he graduated. (This was fore Campbell High School had a football team.) Jean and Larry had three children, Christopher, own as "Chris," Lisa, and Kent, and nine grandchildren. See *McMillan, north side of Spring Street, lanta Road, from Mrs. Mazie's to Pearce Matthews;* and *south side of Church Street.*

"Steve" Goodwin and his wife, Diane, had two daughters: Gigi and Leeann.

Kim Goodwin married Joel Tomlin; they had one daughter, Stephanie. Kim and Joel are now vorced.

Robin Goodwin married Luke Davenport; they had one daughter, Merridy.

Tenth House

The **Williams Family** lived in this house.

Eleventh House

Mr. and **Mrs**. **Bill Miles** and their young son, **Paul**, lived here. Mrs. Miles was the former Sara Hensley. See *Hensleys, seventh house.*

Twelfth House

Mr. and **Mrs**. **Sam Morris** were residents in this house, on the west side of Roswell Stre They were the parents of Sally Adams, who lived on Bank Street. They had two sons that I rememb Harley and "Pinky." This is the same Sam Morris Family who lived at one time in the second house the west side of Roswell Street, next door to the Elmer Andersons. See *second house on Roswell Str* and *south side of Bank Street.*

Thirteenth House

Harley Morris lived in this house next door to his parents. Harley served in the Unit States Military during World War II. When he came home from military service, he married, Bet They had children, whose names I do not recall.

Fourteenth House

Mr. and **Mrs**. **Tom Black** resided in this house, on the site of the present-day feed sto Mrs. Black was the former Sophia Ophelia Frisbee. They had three children: **Hershel**, known "Pete," **Evelyn**, and **Harold**. One of Mrs. Black's brothers married Ada Black, Tom's sister. The To Black Family were members of Haney Grove Baptist Church, where Tom at one time was song lead See *Black* and *Stephens families, Walker Street.*

Hershel Black
Prisioner of War
World War II

Hershel Black, known as "Pete," served in the United States Army during World War After fighting in the battle at Cherbourg, France, "Pete" was captured in the Battle of Bastogne Belgium), in January 1945 and held until June 1945. Hershel and his wife, Jessie, had three childre Johnny, Cheryl, and Richard.

Evelyn Black married Floyd Clayton. They had three children: Thomas, Doris, and Jimmy.

Harold Black married Mary Lou Brand. They had six children: Harold Dean, Patricia, Elai Sharon, Debra, and David.

NOTE: According to information from the Black Family, Hershel Black, known as "Pet owned land from Roswell Street through to Hawthorne Avenue. He built four houses on the west si of Roswell Street past the fourteenth house, (owned and occupied by his father, Tom Black), to the S Points Grocery Store.

Fifteenth House

The **Clayton Family**, in the upholstery business, lived here.

Sixteenth House

Mr. and **Mrs. Henry Tinsley** built this house on the west side of Roswell Street. Mrs. nsley was the former Evelyn Wheeler (Matthews). While having this house built, Mr. and Mrs. nsley lived in the house with Mr. and Mrs. R.R. Brooks on the east side of Roswell Street.

Henry Tinsley worked at Atlanta Metallic Casket Company, from which he retired; Evelyn nsley worked for the United States Department of Agriculture.

Evelyn Wheeler (Matthews) Tinsley, previously married, had one sister, Katherine Wheeler, d three brothers, Rogers Wheeler, who bore their mother's maiden name, William Wheeler, who ed in Florida, and Roy Wheeler, who lived in South Carolina.

Henry Tinsley, previously married to Fannie Lou Anderson, was one of 14 children; grew up what is now Windy Hill Road, near Windy Hill Hospital's current location. Fannie Lou had orked at Brumby Chair Company in Marietta.

Henry and Fannie Lou had one son, Clifford, who married Jeanne Pruitt of the Oakdale mmunity. Clifford and Jeanne had two sons: Jeffrey, known as "Jeff," and Douglas, known as oug," who married Mary Preuit.

Clifford Tinsley was in the Air National Guard when his unit was activated, and served in ance during the Korean Conflict, in the 1950s. He retired from the United States Postal Service.

Henry Edward Tinsley had three brothers: Joe T., Hubert, and William Guy Tinsley.

Seventeenth House

Hershel Black, known as "Pete," lived in this house, before moving to the eighteenth house, ich was brick. He then used this house as a rental one. There was also a rental house to the rear of s house.

Eighteenth House

Herschel Black, known as "Pete," moved to this dwelling from the seventeenth house. See *urteenth house.*

Nineteenth House

Mr. and **Mrs. Johnnie Lee Carroll**, in the early 1940s, moved from Marietta to the last use on the west side of Roswell Street before the Six Points Grocery Store. Mr. Carroll, from atsworth, married Margie Atkinson, from Atlanta's Riverside community. They had three children: **nald Lee**, known as "Don," **Janice**, and **James Stephen**, then known as "Butch," now known as m."

Johnnie Carroll was first employed by General Motors and later as a wholesale grocery esman. Margie Carroll first worked for Montag's Blue Horse Stationery Company, which made iting tablets and composition books, then at the Bell Bomber Plant during World War II, and later Pfarner Counter Company, located on Concord Road past Dickson Shopping Center. Much later er Twelve Oaks Restaurant opened near the corner of Cherokee Street and Atlanta Road (in front of lmont Hills Shopping Center, circa 1954); Mrs. Carroll worked there. The restaurant later became own as Weems Restaurant. (Janet Brooks Brown seems to remember the wallpaper mural in the staurant was scenes of Belmont Farm.)

The Carroll Family, minus "Butch,"(he was not born), was a gospel-singing group, known as he Carroll Family." They sang at many churches and auditoriums and, along with the Smith

Brothers, sang on *WSB Barn Dance*, on early television, at the *Tennessee National Barn Dance* Knoxville, Tennessee and on Capitol Records.

"Don" Carroll married Mary Ann Otwell, who lived on Concord Road, The Country Road, the rear of Dickson Shopping Center. They had three children: Lee Ann, Steven, and John. See *Otw south side of Concord Road, The Country Road.*

"Don" and Mary Ann, both Campbell High School graduates, live in Dallas, where "Don' semi-retired but still writing songs and producing records.

Janice Carroll married James Rhodes, known as "Dusty." They had four children, Don Randy, Mike, and Brent, and nine grandchildren. Janice and "Dusty" both were graduates of Campb High School, as were all of their children.

After Janice and "Dusty" divorced, She married Gene Elmore, who is now deceased, as "Dusty." Janice, retired, after 37 years at Lockheed Aircraft Corporation, is currently living Marietta. She has nine grandchildren.

Donna Rhodes married Mike Raines of Marietta.

Randy Rhodes married Allison Lindsey. They are active members of First Baptist Church.

Mike Rhodes married Kari Winness of Buford.

Brent Rhodes married Sheri Drake.

"Butch" Carroll was the mascot for the Campbell High School Class of 1959. He f married Renee Leonard and they had three children: Stacy, Jason, and Patrick. "Butch," now known "Jim," and his second wife, Tammy, had two sons: Casey and Drew; they live in Murfreesbo Tennessee.

SIX POINTS GROCERY

Mr. and **Mrs. Dudley Houston McDaniell**, in 1946 had a farm in West Cobb County wh they mortgaged for $4,500.00 to purchase, from the McManus Family, Six Points Grocery Sto located in the triangle at Hawthorne Avenue and Roswell Street. The store, built after World War began, had in the back part two-story living quarters for themselves and their three children: **Hu Lee**, **Marvena**, and **Inez**.

Hugh Lee McDaniell—See below.

Marvena McDaniell married Cecil Metcalf. They live in Vinings.

Inez McDaniell married Hansel Bruce. Inez lives in Daytona Shores, Florida.

Hugh Lee McDaniell

Georgia State Representative
1963-1974

Hugh Lee McDaniell, a 6 feet-tall basketball player at McEachern High School, rememb playing at Fitzhugh Lee High School. During World War II, Hugh Lee served in the United Sta Army Air Corps (now United States Air Force) for 14 months, in the China Burma India Theater War. In 1943, for two weeks, he was stationed in Black River Falls, Wisconsin, where he met Mar Thompson; they married after the War had ended. After living in Wisconsin from 1948-1952, th moved to Smyrna. Hugh Lee and Marion had three daughters, (Marsha, Nancy, and Gail), se grandchildren, and one great-grandchild. (The last grandchild recently graduated from college.)

Marsha married Charlie Crowder.

Nancy married Sam Hester.

Gail married Harold Barton, who recently retired as a Colonel in the United States Air Force.

Hugh Lee shared some of his memories of living in Smyrna, both during the days his dad ran Six Points Grocery Store and afterwards: the beginning of his own career as a businessman in Smyrna and his years in the insurance and real estate business on Atlanta Street.

Hugh Lee relates, "I fondly recall the McColloughs, who lived on the northwest corner of North Matthews Street and Hawthorne Avenue, and Harley Morris, who lived on Hawthorne Avenue, near the railroad. I also remember the Carroll Family, rented from dad the last house before Six Points Grocery Store, on Roswell Street. Six Points Grocery Store, owned and operated by my dad, was a type of business from prior years. Dad delivered groceries and also extended credit—with most customers having a 'running tab.'

"I remember that the basement of American Legion Post #160 building was constructed in 1948, followed by the construction of the upper story.

"Early in my career, for National Life Insurance Company I ran a debit route, from Pat Mell Road, in Cobb County near Smyrna, to Inman Yards in Atlanta.

"In 1952 on Jonquil Drive, Marion and I purchased a house by assuming the $8,250.00 loan. I bought my parents' store— in 1955, the same year that I founded McDaniell's Insurance and Real Estate Company within the store building.

"I remember Al Cochran's Atlanta Street office, leaking from the ceiling's. Afterwards Al and I, together, bought property and built Cochran & McDaniell office building at its current location, next door to the Huddle House (now Ken's Corner Grill) on Atlanta Street. I also bought and demolished the old house on Love Street for the construction of First Methodist Church.

Hugh Lee shared, "I developed Creatwood subdivision, south of Smyrna, across Atlanta Road from Campbell High School (now Campbell Middle School), and through to Ridge Road; I was also involved in the development of several other communities around Smyrna.

"Bill Ward and I teamed together to build and sell new houses on Cherokee Road (now Windy Hill Road). Some buyers would have two G. I. Loans, one on the house and one on the lot; the two loans would later be combined into one.

"I remember that a group of us men would meet every Friday afternoon, above Belmont Hills Theater, and 'settle the business of Smyrna.' I served 10 years in the Georgia Legislature and was President of the Smyrna Chamber of Commerce before its being combined with the Cobb County Chamber of Commerce.

"In 1961, I bought James Pressley's Real Estate business and merged it with my business. Howard Scoggins, who was working for James Pressley at that time, became Sales Manager of McDaniell Realty Company, Inc.

"In 1962, from W.D. Anderson, Marion and I bought two lots, one on Anderson Circle and one on Spring Street. On one of the Anderson Circle lots we built a house; where we lived for several years."

Later on, Hugh Lee McDaniell developed Terrell Mill Estates in East Cobb County, where he and Marion located their family. Al and Leila Cochran, along with their family, moved there also.

Smyrna was a town "on the move" from the late 1940s, when there was a large increase in the building of new homes and establishment of businesses. After Lockheed Aircraft Corporation opened in 1952, the building pace increased even more. In the middle of the Twentieth Century Hugh Lee McDaniell, along with Bill Ward, Al Cochran, Rem Bennett, Sr., Gardner Potter, Hobart Early and others, were involved in shaping the growth of Smyrna. (This growth trend has continued into the Twenty-first Century.)

Later in the Twentieth Century, Marion and Hugh developed Cohutta Lodge and Restaurant outside Chatsworth. There many Smyrna residents enjoyed themselves.

Hugh Lee related, "Through the years, I was able to keep 12 acres out of the the 98 ½ acres of my parents' farm in West Cobb County. I recently sold this property for the development of McDaniell Farms, a very upscale subdivision near Frank Kirk Road, which was named for my maternal grandfather and grandmother, Mr. and Mrs. Frank Kirk."

NOTE: Hugh Lee McDaniell served as Georgia State Representative from 1963-1974, during the administration of Carl Sanders, Lester Maddox, and Jimmy Carter. After having served 10 years in the Georgia Legislature and being Chairman of the Parks Committee, Hugh Lee purchased 320 acres atop Fort Mountain State Park, near Chatsworth. There he developed a village consisting of a restaurant and the 60-room Cohutta Lodge, and a conference center, which was used by church and civic groups; he also developed a 111-lot subdivision at 2,800 feet elevation. He sold the Lodge and conference center in 2002. Having also built a shopping center in Ellijay, Hugh Lee is now retired to Barrett Knoll subdivision in Cobb County.

Twentieth House

Mr. and **Mrs. Claude Hann** were residents in this house, on the northeast corner of Roswell and North Matthews streets. Mrs. Hann, the former Ruby Scoggins, and her husband had four children: **Venard**, **Betty**, **Marion**, and **Neal**. The Hann house was a large two-story country-style structure, which had a large porch on the front and sides. The Hanns owned a large tract of land in this area.

Mrs. Ruby Hann, a seamstress, also ran a boarding house in Marietta. She was a sister of Howard Scoggins and an aunt of "Bill" Scoggins, Smyrna City Councilman.

Betty Hann married "Buckles" Graham.

Marion Hann married Billy Williams. They had three children: Connie, Steve, and Billy Williams, Jr. Marion Hann Williams later married Ed Medlin, a widower who had three children: Harry, Frank, and Terri. His first wife, Evelyn Gravely Medlin, died from cancer. Ed grew up on Cooper Lake Road, which is now King Springs Road, in the second house on the west side from Concord Road. Some of the property on the west side of King Springs Road at one time was part of the Medlin Farm.

Connie Williams Gravitt had three children: Sammy, Amy, and Melissa.

Steve Williams had two children: Steve Williams, Jr., and Tiffany.

Billy Williams, Jr., had two children: Nathan and James.

Venard Hann
World War II
MIA

Venard Hann was a belly gunner on a B24 bomber during World War II. Shown as "Missing in Action," his name is on the Twentieth Century Veterans Memorial in Smyrna.

Neal Hann lived in Smyrna and never married.

Twenty-first House

Dr. and **Mrs. Fred Dowda** lived in an imposing two-story dwelling that is still standing. They had one son, **Dr. Bill Dowda**, a general practitioner in Atlanta. He was my Aunt Mardelle Wood Farmer's doctor. Dr. Fred Dowda was a surgeon who also practiced in Atlanta. Mrs. Fred Dowda, a member of the Jonquil Garden Club, and Dr. Dowda were members of First Baptist Church.

Beyond the Dowda House was the United States Government fence, referred to by the locals as the "Bomber Plant fence." This property beyond the Dowda estate was acquired by the United States Government sometime in the early 1940s. It included what is now Fox Creek and Legacy Golf courses and Dobbins Air Force Base

THE ANDERSONS OF ROSWELL STREET

Appreciation is extended to Sara Anderson Gentry for the many hours she spent compiling the following information about her family in Smyrna and Cobb County. The Power, Johnston, and Anderson families helped to settle Cobb County. Here before the Indians left, their ancestors date back to the early 1800s in Cobb County. The Anderson Family on Roswell Street dates back to the earliest part of the Twentieth Century in Smyrna.

Powers Ferry Road was named for James Power, Sara Anderson Gentry's paternal great-grandfather. He was born in the Laurens District, now a county in South Carolina, on April 15, 1790. He fought in the War of 1812, between the United States and Great Britain. James came to the Chattahoochee River in 1826, while the Cherokee Indians were still on the north side of the river. The Indians at that time would ford the Chattahoochee River on horseback. Having learned that James Power could repair wagons and guns and shoe horses and respecting his abilities, they sought his services and became friendly with him. They began to visit back and forth across the river and accepted his presence.

For transportation across the Chattahoochee River, James Power built a "boat-like vessel." It was large enough for a two-horse wagon with mules or horses to ride across the river. Made of heavy lumber; it was hand pulled by heavy wire stretched across the river and securely fastened to big trees on the banks. One or two men could manage the vessel, but many times others would help, especially if it were heavily loaded. They never called it a boat or a ferry. It was called a flat.

Later on, after the Indians left, James Power acquired seven hundred acres of land on the north side of the Chattahoochee River. In 1835 he built a ferry that would provide transportation across the Chattahoochee River between Fulton and Cobb counties. (Note the improvement in river crossing equipment within just a few years.) According to family information, he was the first person to operate a ferry in Georgia.

Also, according to family information, James, Justice of the Peace in Cobb County for many years, and two other men rode horse back to Milledgeville, which at that time was the Capital of Georgia, to secure the Charter for the City of Marietta.

James Power married the daughter of Mr. and Mrs. Solomon Hopkins. Though his wife's given name is not known, she was born November 22, 1805, and was fifteen years younger than James. They had one daughter, Samantha Elizabeth, born December 8, 1847.

Samantha Elizabeth Power married James Louis Anderson on December 31, 1872. They had six children: James Elmer, Ada, William David, known as "Will," Joseph Power, Sallie, and Gertrude.

In 1882 they moved to a farm overlooking the Chattahoochee River. (Interstate 285 now runs through the area where their home was located.) Theirs was a lovely home, built on a rock foundation, with a nice porch across the front. It was a two-story home, painted white and decorated with green shutters. In 1889 James Louis bought, at auction, 554 acres of the Hargrove property, which today is part of the Interstate 75 corridor. In 1893 James Louis and Elizabeth bought a two-story house in Waleska in order for their children to attend Reinhardt College, which at that time was a two-year college.

When they returned from Waleska in 1902, James and Elizabeth bought a house at 209 Atlanta Street in Marietta, about a block from the Marietta Square. They lived there until James Louis died in 1905.

Sallie Anderson married Jack Miller. After their marriage, they also lived at 209 Atlanta Street, in Marietta, until the 1950s. In the meantime, the family still owned the farm land near Smyrna, on Roswell Road, now known as Windy Hill Road, and kept tenants on the farm through the years.

Ada Anderson married Joe Thomas .

Gertrude Anderson married Ernest Titshaw, known as "Rip." After attending Reinhardt College, she attended nursing school at Piedmont Hospital, where she was a member of the school's second graduation class. Gertrude and Ernest had no children.

William David Anderson, known as "Will," was a farmer. After graduating from Reinhardt College, he married Lily White from Marietta; they had ten children. See *east side of Matthews Street* and *nineteenth house, east side of Roswell Street*

Joseph Power Anderson married Homer Davis. She and Joseph had four children: Catherine, Anna Belle, known as "Ann," Frank, and Florence. The Joseph Power Anderson Family lived on Roswell Street in the dwelling that later became known as the Lowe House.

When he lived in Smyrna, Joseph Power Anderson was the station agent for Georgia Power Company. He worked at the sub-station, which was located on Atlanta Street, in a large brick building having office space for ticket sales and two waiting rooms marked "White" and "Colored." Joe was promoted to the company's Davis Street Headquarters in Atlanta, and the family moved to Atlanta's West End area in1937.

Anna Belle Anderson, known as "Ann," was a member of the Smyrna High School Class of 1931, along with Sara Anderson Gentry and Leila Anderson Black. Ann married Robert Haney; they had one daughter, Serena. Anna Belle currently lives in Dunwoody, and Serena is currently residing in the Bennett Woods subdivision in Smyrna. See *High School Class*, listed at the end of this section, and *Andersons, west side of Roswell Street.*

Florence Anderson married Arthur Simpson. They lived in Atlanta's West End area for many years. After Arthur's death and in her senior years, Florence moved back to Smyrna, where she passed away in 2003.

James Elmer Anderson married Dovie Thomas on January 1,1905. They had six children: Lewis Elmer, born October 9, 1905; Tommie Lee, born February 27, 1908; James William, known as "Jay," born in 1910; Leila Mae, born in 1912; Sara Elizabeth, born in 1915; and Clara Bell, born in 1918.

Dovie Thomas was the great-granddaughter of Mr. and Mrs. William Marion Johnston. Mr. Johnston built the Johnston Ferry that provided transportation across the Chattahoochee River and operated it for many years. The road to the ferry was known as Johnston Ferry Road. According to information from family members, Cobb and Fulton counties at some point removed the "t" from the name of the road. The Thomas Family lobbied through the political structure of the day to get the name corrected, but officials of the counties told them it would be too costly for the businesses and the counties to correct the mistake. Therefore, according to information from the Anderson Family, "A name in history was officially changed for political reasons."

After finishing school at Reinhardt College, in Waleska, James Elmer worked for Georgia Railway Express, which later became Georgia Power Company. He operated a two-horse-drawn streetcar in downtown Atlanta. After the first electric streetcar arrived in Marietta in 1905 and his dad had died, Elmer did some bookkeeping at Georgia Power. Missing being outside, he returned to the farm on Roswell Road near Smyrna.

James Elmer and Dovie Thomas Anderson moved into their first home, on a farm on Roswell Road, now known as Windy Hill Road. At that time this road was connected to Roswell Street coming out of Smyrna. This house, where their two oldest children were born, was a two-story white frame one, very imposing! It stood there well into the middle of the Twentieth Century, when the "big building boom" started in East Cobb County. The property is now the site of WellStar Windy Hill Hospital.

In 1909 Elmer and Dovie built a house on Old Canton Road, near Robinson Road, in East Cobb County, where three of Elmer's and Dovie's children (James William, Leila Mae, and Sara Elizabeth) were born.

NOTE: Robinson Road is named for the family of Harry Robinson, a friend Elmer met at Reinhardt College, in Waleska, while they were both students. They remained friends as long as they lived.

The Anderson Farm on Old Canton Road had two other houses: one for a tenant and one for a school for the boys from the neighborhood as well as the Anderson sons. The school's tuition was five cents per day; the teacher was Miss Addie Howard, an older sister of Paul Howard, who later became the conductor on the Marietta-Atlanta streetcar line. ("The Howards were also an old Cobb County Family.")

Still pursuing an education for their children, Elmer and Dovie, in 1917, built on the farm a house, facing Roswell Road. Their youngest child, Clara, was born here. The Andersons chose this site so they could be near Bold Springs School, where one teacher taught six grades. This house was built on land that was part of the Hargrove Farm, where some of the Anderson ancestors are buried in the Hargrove Cemetery. (This cemetery is in a fenced in area located on the south side of Windy Hill Road, just west of what is currently known as WellStar Hospital at Windy Hill.)

NOTE: Elmer's family still owned the 554-acre farm out Roswell Road (now Windy Hill Road) at Rottenwood Creek.

After about two years the older boys drove a buggy to Smyrna School, where there were nine grades and nine teachers; Mrs. Nollie Barrett was the principal.

In 1920 James Elmer and Dovie moved their family to Roswell Street in Smyrna to be closer to Smyrna School. Their new residence, located on the southeast side of the street just after Roswell Street makes a ninety-degree curve, was on a rural route at that time. Elmer and Dovie Anderson lived in this house for eighteen years. In 1938 they moved to the west side of Roswell Street. See *Andersons, first house, west side of Roswell Street.*

NOTE: This house is now the home of Councilman "Bill" Scoggins and his wife, Gerrye, who have lived here for over twenty-five years.

<u>Lewis Anderson</u> married Rhoda Opal Baldwin on March 10, 1927. They spent their wedding night in the family home on the east side of Roswell Street. Establishing their own home on Church Street, there they raised their only child, James Larkin Anderson. Lewis and Opal were very active members of First Methodist Church. Lewis died January 20, 1983. See *south side of Church Street.*

"Tom" Anderson married Eexie Arzona Tuck July 4, 1933. They had four children: Beverl Ann, Jerrilyn Gay, Tommie Lee, Jr., and Terry James. Tommie Lee and Eexie raised their family i Atlanta's West End area. They were in the produce business at the Farmers Market, located in thos days on Murphy Avenue in Atlanta. "Tom" Anderson died December 13, 1990.

Beverly Ann Anderson married William Cooper Craig. They had two children: Cheree an Scarlett. Beverly Ann later married Lou James; they had two children: Lisa and Louis.

Jerrilyn Gay Anderson married James Taylor Braswell. They had two sons: Harold an James.

Tommie Lee Anderson, Jr., married Sandra Lee Opal. They had one daughter, Christina Jean

Terry James Anderson married Glenda Jean Knight. They had one son, Terry Marcu Anderson.

James W. Anderson, known as "Jay," married Ruth Slate April 1, 1933. They had twc children: Barbara Jeanneen and Brenda Shaw.

Barbara Jeanneen Anderson married Jackson Stonewall Cowart III. They had two children Melanie and Jackson Stonewall Cowart IV.

Brenda Shaw Anderson married Roger William Michel. They had no children.

Leila Mae Anderson married William L. Black, Jr., February 22, 1940. They had one daughter, Elizabeth. Leila died January 21, 1965. See *first house, west side of Roswell Street.*

Sara Elizabeth Anderson married James Floyd Gentry, known as "Jim," April 24, 1943. She and Jim had two daughters, Janet and Ellen, and three grandchildren. Sara and "Jim" live on Pinetree Drive in the Forest Hills community, an area developed in the late 1940s and early 1950s.

Janet Gentry married Patrick James Kelly, known as "Jim." They had three children: Rachael Marie, Rebecca Elizabeth, and Scott. "Jim" and Janet live on Pinetree Drive.

Sara Ellen Gentry married Gary Alan Smith. Ellen and Gary, who had no children are permanent residents of Kekaha, Kauai, Hawaii.

Clara Bell Anderson married Hugh McCollum March 10, 1940. They had two daughters: Patricia Ann and Andrea Lee. Clara Bell McCollum died August 6, 1991.See *east side of Gilbert Street.*

Patricia McCollum married Robert Elling.

Andrea Lee McCollum married John Linster.

Sara Anderson Gentry shared the following story about her dad, Elmer Anderson. "Elmer and Joe Anderson owned a farm together; but, to my knowledge, Joe never farmed. When Elmer moved to Smyrna, he sold his livestock and farm equipment but kept his favorite horse, Dixie. At that time the house on Roswell Street had a large barn, chicken house, hog pen, and smokehouse, plus cover for a wagon and the family car.

"Dixie, his riding horse, was settled in the barn before the family unpacked. Dixie remained in the fenced backyard and seemed always at the back door, waiting for sugar, apples, or any treat, which she always received, and followed whoever was there. Living to be very old and feeble, she had to be helped up. Later on, because she was not able to stand, about a dozen friends came, helped tear the boards off the barn, and lifted Dixie out into the side yard, near a field of blooming jonquils; there she went to sleep in a light snow storm.

"Many years later I told my daddy how much I appreciated his moving to Smyrna, where we did not have to ride in a buggy to school. He answered, I did not want my horse standing out in the weather.' This reflected a lifetime of his love of horses!

"Dad always told the boys: 'You should stay on the farm and not move to town; the time will come when the town will come to you.'

"He would be pleased to see hotels, restaurants, hospitals, office buildings, and gas stations today where the farm was. If he were here today, he would say. 'See, I told you!'"

All three of Dovie and Elmer Anderson's daughters graduated from Smyrna High School, located on the north side of Church Street. It was a two-story brick building that was razed in the last half of the Twentieth Century. The former school property now belongs to First Baptist Church. See *north side of Church Street.*

Sara Anderson Gentry, after graduating from Smyrna High School in 1931, taught for a year at Mt. Bethel School in East Cobb County, which was really "country" in those days. (The roads were unpaved, there was no running water or electricity, and a potbellied stove was used for heat. The toilets were outhouses, separated from the main building. Such were the early 1930s, during the Great Depression years.) Later on, Sara worked for Georgia Power Company.

The Andersons and Gentrys have been long-time members of First Methodist Church. Leila and Sara joined the church in 1923, when the Rev. V.L. Bray was the pastor. Leila and Clara married in the church in 1940, and Sara married in the church in 1943; Rev. J.W. Stephens performed all three of the ceremonies. Sara, the only surviving member of her family, and her husband, "Jim" Gentry, are Honorary Lifetime Members of the Administrative Board at the Church, where they are both still regular in attendance.

In the early months of 2004 six members of the Class of 1931 at Smyrna High School are still living:

Sara Anderson Gentry
J.C. Bankston, who became a Baptist preacher
Sadie Matthews Scarborough
Anna Belle Anderson Haney
Thelma Wright Walker
Octa Mitchell Bacon

NOTE: J.C. Bankston died in 2004

Some of the people who taught school at Smyrna School when Sara Anderson Gentry was a student are as follows:

John Self, Principal

Mazie Whitfield Nelson
Annie Mae Brown
Ruth Hanson
Mrs. Wells
Mrs. Breland

Mrs. Agnes Baldwin Faucett Feely
Maude Baldwin Paris
Vickie Reed Griggers
Mrs. Lena Mae Gann Green
Mary Hudson Perkins

Reverend Clary, the Presbyterian minister

The following are graduates of the class of 1931

Anna Bell Anderson Haney
Leila Anderson Black
Sara Anderson Gentry
Annie Grace Austin Epperson
Reverend J.C. Bankston
Hazel Cantrell Franklin
Sidney Davis
Phagan Durham
Hubert Lowe
Irvin McBrayer
Frances Massey Pressley
Sadie Matthews Scarborough
Octa Mitchell Bacon
Billy Quarles
Catherine Reed Rutherford
Sherrill T. Wills
Thelma Wright Walker

At one time three of the Anderson brothers, Elmer, "Will," and Joe, lived on Roswell Street. Joe and his family lived in the second house on the right, across the street from the railroad crossing, which is now the parking lot for BellSouth. Later on, this house was the home of the Lowe Family. Elmer lived at 209 Roswell Street, just past the ninety-degree curve, and William David, known as "Will," lived farther out Roswell Street, on the southeast side. See *nineteenth house, east side of Roswell Street.*

According to information from Sara Anderson Gentry, Elizabeth Black Davis is the only Anderson descendant living on Roswell Street at the present time. See *first house, west side of Roswell Street.*

NOTE: Smyrna School was opened for classes in 1925. See *north side of Church Street.*

DAVENPORT STREET

Davenport Street was one of the five streets that intersected at Six Points. The other four were Roswell Street, a pass-through street, Hawthorne Avenue, Matthews Street, and North Matthews Street, which ended at Roswell Street. This intersection is basically the same as it was in the days of my youth with the exception that the streets are wider. "Davenport Town," a "colored" community in mid Twentieth Century Smyrna, was/is located on Davenport Street. Now a part of Smyrna's Third Ward, it was not in Smyrna's City Limits in the days of my youth.

Davenport Town is about a mile and a half from the center of Smyrna. "Bill" Scoggins and I delivered papers to this area. Or, I should say, most days "Bill" delivered the papers to Davenport Town the first year because he had a bicycle; I helped the second year because, by that time, I also had a bicycle.

From the days of my youth, I remember several families who lived in Davenport Town: the Kings, Bedfords, Burtons, Ezzards, Clowers, Coopers, and the Ike Thorntons.

Mrs. Missouri Davenport Burton

NOTE: The following information was taken from a memorial of Mrs. Burton's life story distributed at her funeral service, Saturday, September 4, 2004.

" 'Mother' Missouri Davenport Burton, known as 'Ma Zoot' and 'Miss Zootie,' was born in Smyrna on March 10, 1912, to the late Henry and Priscilla Davenport. She was the fifth child of eight siblings. 'Ma Zoot' was called to her reward on Saturday, August 28, 2004, at 11:59 P.M., while in WellStar Cobb Hospital in Austell.

" 'Ma Zoot' was educated in the Cobb County School System. She worked diligently with her hands as a caretaker for Mr. Lewis Anderson for twenty-two years. She also worked as a caretaker for Ms. Opal Byrd, Ms. Charlotte Theodocian, and Mrs. Martha Theodocian for many years.

"She was a faithful member of Mount Zion First Baptist Church in Smyrna, which was founded by her father, the late Reverend Henry Davenport. She remained a faithful member at Mount Zion for ninety-two years, including the years under her beloved pastor, Reverend John C. Hurst. 'Ma Zoot' served on the Mothers' Board. She was also a member of the Willing Workers Club and the Mission Club.

"In 1932, she was united in Holy Matrimony with John H. Burton. She was the mother of eight beautiful children: Carrie, known as 'Betty,' Claude, Gladys Mae, Lewis, known as 'Butchie,' Bernice, and Loretta, known as 'Pat,' Theodore, and Lamar.

" 'Ma Zoot' also raised her nephews, Paul Moss and Troy, and a niece, Annette Florence, all of whom she loved and treated as her very own children.

"Mother was preceded in death by her parents, Henry and Priscilla Davenport; her children, Theodore Burton and Lamar Burton; her siblings, Carrie Lou Davenport, Marie Davenport, Gertrude Davenport Wallington, James Davenport, H.D. Davenport, Jr., and Jessie Davenport; and a very special nephew, Lavon Harris.

"Her survivors are as follows: Carrie, known as 'Betty' Burton, who married Guy Hammond, Sr., of Marietta; Claude Burton and his wife, Dolly, of Stockbridge. Miss Gladys Mae Burton, of Smyrna; Mr. Lewis Burton, known as 'Butchie'; his wife, Willie Mae, of Marietta; Miss Bernice Burton, of Forest Park; and Miss Loretta Burton, of Smyrna.

"She is also survived by two sisters: Ms. Lizzie Mae Weathersx, of Smyrna, and Mrs. Roberta Earl, of Syracuse, New York and two brothers-in-law: Mr. Jimmy Wallington of Detroit, Michigan, and Mr. John Childs, of Cleveland, Ohio."

Mr. and Mrs. Paul King

Appreciation is extended to Gloria King Aaron Summerour for sharing the following memories of growing up in Davenport Town in the middle of the Twentieth Century.

Gloria was the daughter of Mr. and Mrs. Paul King. Mr. King supported his family by working at First Baptist Church and for Mr. Paul Hensley, who was the Cobb County Surveyor. Mr. King also worked at the Bell Bomber Plant during World War II and until its closing. Gloria shared her memories of her dad. "My daddy was a hard-working survivor. He worked long hours to support and care for his family. To supplement the family income, my mama, Hattie, took in laundry. She would wash and iron for many white families in Smyrna. This is how we met the Roy Wood Family.

"My parents insisted on and encouraged all of their children to attend school. Initially we attended school at Mount Zion Baptist Church, just up the road, on Hawthorne Avenue, at what we called Six Points. Later on, a one-room schoolhouse was built to the rear of the Church. We attended school there until the schoolhouse was burned down during what was called 'Smyrna's race riot.' After that, a school was built in the neighborhood, on Davenport Street. That school was for grades one through seven. After seventh grade we had to ride the streetcar to go to Perkinson High School in Marietta. (That school was later renamed Lemon Street School.)

"When we moved to Davenport Town, there were only a few families living there: the Davenport Family, for whom the street was named, and 'Uncle Bud' Bates and his wife.

"After living there for several years, my mama wanted to get a Methodist church for children to attend. In order to raise funds for the church, she sold ice cream, candied apples, strawberries, etc. Until the church was built, we had services in our living room. The new church became Kings Chapel AME Church. The Sameltons, the Mosses, and, of course, the Kings became the first members of the church, which still stands today, more than sixty-five years later, on Davenport Street.

"Some of the children we played and socialized with outside the neighborhood were the Hensley and Bennett children. When Mr. Bennett could not find his girls, he would call for them from across the pasture to our house. They loved my mama's cornbread and often ran off from their house to ours to sit on the back porch and eat Mama's cornbread. Some of my fondest memories are of us kids playing stickball (with sticks and old mashed-up cans) in the field."

At the time of this writing there are several vibrant churches in the Davenport Town community. One minister that I know well, Reverend John Hurst, the current pastor of Mount Zion First Baptist Church, facing Hawthorne Avenue on the corner of Davenport Street, also works for the City of Smyrna. I am grateful to the leaders in the Davenport community, the Kings and others, who saw a need for a spiritual influence in the community. They worked hard during very trying times, such as the Great Depression and World War II years, to establish a strong Christian and educational environment there."

Mrs. Mattie Clowers

Mattie Clowers, who died in March 2005 at age 99, was Rose Garden Hills' oldest resident. Never having married until age 35, Mattie and her husband, Willie, bought a $8,000.00 new house on a shady lot at the end of Gordon Circle. (This purchase was in the early 1950s, when Rose Garden Hills, adjacent to Davenport Town, was being developed.)

The Rose Garden Hills/Davenport Town area has been an enclave, with a strong sense of community—even including "looking after" Mrs. Clowers just prior to her entering a nursing home, a year before her death.

A native of Chattanooga, Tennessee and a 50-year resident of Davenport Street Smyrna's all-Black community, Mattie was a living history as well as a treasured historian. Mattie's family Bible contains the names of some of the oldest Black families in Cobb County.

At age 14, she taught herself how to drive—just by reading a book; then she would drive her family's car, a model-T Ford, to Marietta and back. Three years before her death she quit driving. She had maintained a "spanking clean" record: no accidents, no tickets. Other of Mattie's "historical" feats include her teaching eight grades in a one-room schoolhouse, selling eggs from the chicken house in her back yard, and making "spiced hog meat" for her Rose Garden/Davenport Town neighbors. A native of Chattanooga, Tennessee and a 50-year resident of Smyrna's all-Black community, Mattie was living history, as well as a treasured historian. Mattie's family Bible contains the names of some of the oldest Black families in Cobb County.

As a storyteller, Mattie participated in the festival at the Mable House, in Mableton. On other occasions, she would sing songs about cornbread and write poems about collard greens.

NOTE: The previous information about Mattie Clowers, who had a brother, Luther Bennett, and two stepdaughters, Jean and Laura Clowers, was extracted from her obituary as set forth in a March 2005 issue of *The Atlanta Journal-Constitution.*

CHAPTER SIX

SUNSET AVENUE

North Side

Appreciation is extended to Frances Skelton; Rebekah Austin Walker; Joyce Lovern Davis, and her husband, Miller Davis, for sharing their invaluable knowledge about the residents of Sunset Avenue in the days of my youth. Frances, Rebekah, and Miller were all born in Smyrna; Joyce moved to Powder Springs Street in 1943, as a small child, their property extended through to Sunset Avenue. Appreciation is also extended to Warren Day and Carol Day Harris, for information about the Day Family; and to Mrs. Ella Cook McBrayer, who shared her memories about the McBrayer Family.

Sunset Avenue was one of the streets that had to be sacrificed during the City of Smyrna's great renovation period of the 1980s and 1990s. The entrance off Atlanta Street into the Village Green is a little north of the Sunset Avenue entrance during the days of my youth. A pretty street with a pretty name, nice homes, and stable families, Sunset Avenue was one of the first streets in Smyrna to get sidewalks. Some residents of Sunset Avenue with whom I have talked remember the street before it was paved and the sidewalks were poured.

The information that I have been able to obtain regarding the sidewalks is a matter of public record. The procedure was that the City would pour the sidewalks and then assess the property owners by the foot for the cost of the sidewalks in front of their property. Some people wanted them; some did not. There have been reports that it was not a popular political move; of course, every house did not get a sidewalk.

First House

Southern's Store/Home

Mr. and **Mrs. Southern** owned and operated a small grocery store, in one side, of the first house on the northwest corner of Sunset Avenue and Atlanta Street, across from the Jonquil Theatre. This was a building with a narrow, street-level seating area, like a porch and two entrances: one into their living quarters and the other into the store. The store side was closest to Atlanta Street. In addition to the property where their store was located, the Southern Family also owned the property from Sunset Avenue through to Powder Springs Street, which included the property where Mr. and Mrs. James Lovern later lived. (The Lovern house faced Powder Springs Street.)

Whittington Antique Shop

Mr. and **Mrs. Whittington** bought the above-mentioned property from the Southern Family. While the Whittingtons lived there, they operated a successful antique shop from the front part of their house.

Dr. W.C. Mitchell purchased the property where the Southern, Whittington, and Lovern families had lived, on the north side of Sunset Avenue extending to Atlanta Street. There he constructed a medical office, known as the Mitchell Building. This facility housed his medical practice until his retirement. Later on, probably in the mid 1950s, Dr. Mitchell purchased the Ed Skelton property and used it as a parking lot for the Mitchell Building. After Dr. Mitchell retired, the Mitchell Building was used as the first home of Cobb Services for the Blind and Low Vision. Still later, the Mitchell Building and all of the houses on Sunset Avenue and Powder Springs Street, from Atlanta Street to Hamby Street, were sold to the City of Smyrna for the construction of the Smyrna Public Library, Community Center, and Village Green.

Second House

Mr. and **Mrs. Ed Skelton** lived in the next house. They had two daughters: **Jeanne** and **Frances**. Mrs. Skelton was the former Irene Hill from Kennesaw. The family moved from Kennesaw to Smyrna in 1922 to be closer to Ed's work on the railroad, rented a house on the corner of Church Street and what is now Memorial Drive. Their daughter, Frances, was two months old at the time. In 1924 they moved to Sunset Avenue. (Ed was a brother of Mrs. Leila Arrington, who also lived on Sunset Avenue.)

Jeanne Skelton moved to Athens after she graduated from Smyrna High School in the late 1930s. While there she met and married her husband, Sam Davis, from Athens, and worked for the United States Government. Later on Jeanne and Sam moved to Dunn Street in Smyrna. They had one daughter, Dianne. Sam Davis died in 1962; Jeanne died in 1996. See *west side of Dunn Street.*

Dianne Davis married Ronnie Ingram. They had three children: Scott, Sandra, and Stephanie.

Dianne's son, Scott Ingram, became employed with the hotel industry after college. His office is currently located in the Galleria Center in Cobb County.

Dianne later married Neil Berger; they had one daughter, Sabra. Dianne and Neil live off Concord Road.

Frances Skelton related that, when she was growing up on Sunset Avenue, there was a vacant lot across the street, east of the Austin house. She shared with me that she and Rebekah Austin, who also grew up on Sunset Avenue, could remember seeing the Ku Klux Klan members assemble on that vacant lot. Frances said that her dad instructed her that, when the Klan was there, she was to go inside the house. She remembers how afraid she was to see the Klan members.

Frances was a long-time employee of Lawyers Title Insurance Company of Atlanta, from which she retired. A lifelong member of First Methodist Church, she was a member of the adult choir and the Susannah Wesley Sunday School Class.

In 1952 Frances and her dad moved from Sunset Avenue to Memory Lane, off Collier Drive, where they lived the rest of their lives. After they moved, they rented their house on Sunset Avenue to Vickers Funeral Home, which opened in 1953 and remained there about two years. When the funeral home closed, the Skeltons sold their property to Dr. Mitchell, who used it as a parking lot for his medical building. Frances, who never married, died very suddenly on June 10, 2004.

Third House

Mr. and **Mrs. Bob Arrington** resided next door to the Skeltons. They had one daughter, Joyce. Mrs. Arrington, the former Lessel McBrayer, was the daughter of Mr. and Mrs. W.A. McBrayer. Bob was the son of Mrs. Leila Arrington, who lived on the opposite side of Sunset Avenue.

Joyce Arrington married John Gregorie, who served in the United States Military during World War II. Janet Brooks Brown shared that Mrs. John Gregorie was her teacher at Smyrna Elementary School in the early 1950s. See *McBrayer, seventh house* and *Arrington, south side of Sunset Avenue.*

Fourth House

Mr. and **Mrs. McLarty** lived in this house, where they raised their two sons: **Harold** and **Roy**. The elder McLartys operated a small restaurant in Smyrna at one time.

One of their sons, **Roy McLarty**, his wife **Nell**, and their daughter, **Doris**, were residents here with Roy's parents until the elder McLartys died. Afterwards Roy and Nell moved to King Street. See *east side of King Street.*

Fifth House

Mr. and **Mrs. W.W. Day**, affectionately known in the community as "Mama" and "Papa" Day, lived in the next house. Mrs. Day was the former **Elizabeth Myers** of Buford. They had three children: **Levi**, **Robert**, and **Clara**.

"Papa" Day owned and operated Day's Taxi Service on Atlanta Street until he began working at Lockheed Aircraft Corporation when it opened in 1951. Later on, "Papa" Day opened Day's Used Cars on the lot where the taxi business had previously been located. See *Robert Day, west side of Gilbert Street.*

Spending much time in Atherton's Drug Store (which later became Atkin's Pharmacy), "Papa" Day was jokingly known as "The Mayor of Atlanta Street." He loved ice cream and "Bill" Atkins.

"Mama" Day opened a beauty shop in a garage behind their house on Sunset Avenue in 1945. Eva Lee Day, also a hairdresser, worked in the shop with "Mama" Day. According to Day Family information, Levi and Eva Lee built a new house next door to "Mama" and "Papa" in 1950; the beauty shop was then moved from "Mama" Day's garage to the basement of their new home.

In 1958, when "Mama" could no longer manage the shop, Eva Lee took over the business. In 1989 she moved the shop to Roswell Street, where it is now owned and operated by Eva Lee's daughter, Carol Day Harris. Carol's daughter, Cheryl, who is currently working there, is the fourth generation Day lady to work in Day's Beauty Shop.

Prior to Eva Lee's being in the hair styling profession, my mother had her hair styled by Mrs. Cano, on Atlanta Street. Afterwards, Eva Lee styled Mother's hair until Mother moved to the Smyrna Towers, where she began using the beauty shop there. To my mother a "hairdo" was a big thing, for she always felt it was important to look nice. Dad said that hair was her first priority and after that, food.

Levi Day *see next house.*

Robert Day, in the early 1950s, owned and operated Day's Taxi and Day's Grading Company, a county-wide business. See *sixth house, north side of Sunset Avenue* and *Day, west side of Gilbert Street.*

Clara Day married Andy Anderson; they had one daughter, Carmelita, known as "Lita." Andy, a World War II soldier, died following treatment of a brain tumor.

Clara Day later married Bob Lee. They had two sons: Bobby and Lester. Bob is deceased. Clara moved to Elberton.

Sixth House

Mr. and **Mrs. Levi Day** lived here with their two daughters: **Rebecca**, known as "Becky," and **Carol Sue**. Mrs. Day was the former Eva Lee Dollar of Buford.

"Becky" Day married Jack Diemer. They had two sons, Alvin and Calvin, and four grandchildren. See *Dixie Avenue.*

Carol Sue Day married Larry Harris. They had three children: Cindy (Cumbie), Sid, and Cheryl (Raines), and five grandchildren. Larry Harris works for Wal-Mart.

Levi and Eva Lee came from Ohio, where Levi worked in a defense plant during World War II, to Smyrna where Levi began for General Motors. In early1950, Levi began working for Lockheed Aircraft Corporation where he worked for ten years.

In the late 1950s Levi Day opened Day's Chevrolet dealership, in Acworth, and operated this business for the rest of his life. Levi's daughter, Becky, and her husband, Jack Diemer, were both involved with the business from the beginning. The Diemer sons, Alvin and Calvin, continued to operate Day's Chevrolet dealership after their parents retired. Alvin has since retired; Calvin continues to operate the dealership, which is still owned by the Diemer Family.

Levi Day was an active Mason; Eva Lee became an Eastern Star member when the Smyrna Chapter was organized, in 1950. Together they were advisors for the Smyrna Rainbow Assembly, a Masonic organization for teenage girls. They were loved by and greatly influenced many young girls in Smyrna in the late 1950s and early 1960s.

NOTE: The Day property on Sunset Avenue was sold to the City of Smyrna for the development of the Village Green.

Seventh House

Mr. and **Mrs. Phillip Vern McBrayer, Sr.**, lived here. Mr. McBrayer, known as "Vern," and Mrs. McBrayer, the former Velma Nichols, had two children: **Phillip Vern, Jr.**, and **Joanne**. Mr. McBrayer was an umpire for the Smyrna Amateur Baseball Team; he and my dad, Roy Wood, were big "buddies." Vern, Sr., served in the United States Army during World War I, and Vern, Jr., served in the United States Army during World War II.

Eighth House

Mr. and **Mrs. William Alonzo McBrayer** resided here. Mr. McBrayer was known as "W.A." They had eight children: **William Carlos**, **Phillip Vern.**, **Flora**, **Lessel**, **Brener**, **Coleman**, **Leland,** and **Murphy McClelland.** See *Vern McBrayer, Sr., seventh house.*

W. A. McBrayer and Etta Rowena Coleman, were married in Carroll County on February 11, 1893, by Reverend Rooper. They came from Carroll County to Smyrna in the early part of the Twentieth Century, sometime about 1912, where he served as Justice of the Peace. Mrs. McBrayer died in Smyrna on March 6, 1939.

Three of the McBrayers' sons, William Carlos, Brener, Coleman, and a daughter, Leland, died either in infancy or early childhood.

Phillip Vern McBrayer.. See *seventh house.*

E. E. Jackson
Smyrna City Councilman
1947

Flora McBrayer married E.E. Jackson, who was a very large man. They lived with the elder Mr. and Mrs. McBrayer in this house. (Mr. Jackson was not related to the Jackson Family on Bank Street.)

Lessel McBrayer married Bob Arrington. See *third house, north side of Sunset Avenue* and *Arrington, south side of Sunset Avenue.*

The Vern McBrayer House
North side of Sunset Avenue
Early-to-mid 1900s
Courtesy of Ella McBrayer

The W.A. McBrayer Home
North side of Sunset Avenue
Early-to-mid 1900s
Courtesy of Ella McBrayer

Mr. and **Mrs. W.A. McBrayer** on the right
Mrs. McBrayer's sister and brother-in-law on the left
Circa early 1930
Courtesy of Ela McBrayer

W.A. McBrayer
Justice of the Peace
In his Smyrna Office
Circa 1931
Courtesy of Ella McBrayer

Ella and **"Murph" McBrayer**
Just married 1942
Courtesy of Ella McBrayer

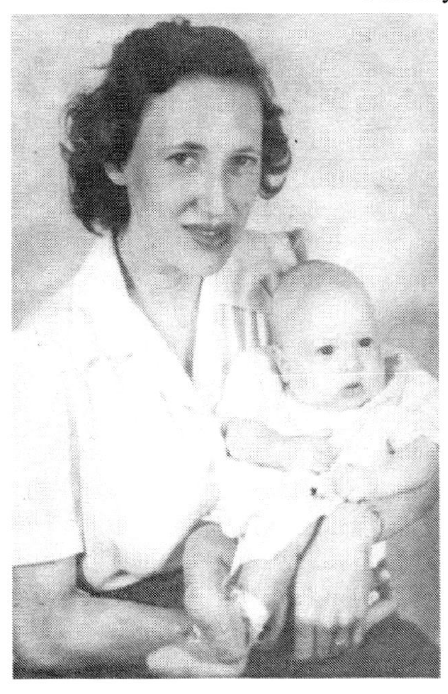

L-R: **Ella McBrayer** and son, **"Mac"**
Circa 1943
Courtesy of Ella McBrayer

"Murph" Mc Brayer
United States Army
Stationed with Mountain Climbers –
West Virginia Circa 1942
Courtesy of Ella Mc Brayer

Murphy McClelland McBrayer, known as "Murph," and Miss Ella Cook were married o September 11, 1942, at First Methodist Church by Reverend James W. Stephens, the pastor. Mrs. D.J Ray was their witness. After their marriage, Ella and "Murph" lived with the McBrayers for a whil and then moved to the Wooten House, which is known in this book as the Westbrook House on Ban Street. They had one son, Murphy McBrayer, Jr., known as "Mac." Ella was a sister of Mrs. B.F Reed, Jr., who lived on the south side of Bank Street.

Ella Cook McBrayer, the youngest child of John and Emma Cook, attended Fannin Count High School, where she earned fifteen units. In her freshman year at Piedmont College, she enrolled i a history course at the local high school and thus completed the sixteen units required for graduation After two years at Piedmont College, Ella taught school in Fannin County for one year. Having move to Smyrna from Fannin County in 1938, she became employed by the Cobb County Board o Education. Ella earned her Bachelor of Science degree at Oglethorpe University in 1953. She taught i the Cobb County School System for forty-three years as a first grade teacher: at Smyrna Elementar School until it closed and then at Belmont Hills Elementary School until her retirement. She is livin on Pinetree Drive in the Forest Hills community.

Murphy McBrayer, Sr., known as "Murph," born December 11, 1909, was educated in th Smyrna schools. He owned and operated the Gulf Service Station on Atlanta Street until he wa inducted into the United States Army at the beginning of World War II; he served overseas for th better part of four years. After the War, he went back into business. Murphy McBrayer, Sr., died Apri 26, 1980.

Known as "Mac," Murphy McBrayer, Jr. married Sheila Diane Wood. They had one son Brian, a student at West Georgia State University in Carrollton, in 2005.

"Mac," having graduated from Campbell High School, attended South Georgia Junio College, in Douglas. He served more than twenty years in the Georgia Air National Guard at Dobbin Air Force Base, in Marietta. "Mac" was employed at Atlantic Steel Company for 27 years, until i closed in 1998.

Ninth House

Mr. and **Mrs. Rex Pruitt** were residents of this house, on the corner of Sunset Avenue an Hamby Street.

Mr. and **Mrs. Harold Pettet**

Harold and **Woody Pettet** later resided in this house. They had one daughter, **Dorothy Ellen**, known as "**Dotsy**." Mr. and Mrs. Pettet moved from Spring Street to Sunset Avenue. Woody, a member of the Homemaker's Sunday School Class at First Baptist Church, and my mother were friends. Harold, a preacher, at one time was the pastor of a small church in Marietta. "Dotsy" and I, the same age, were in the Smyrna High School Class of 1951. See *south side of Spring Street*.

"Dotsy" Pettet married Tommy Cranford from the Oakdale community, south of Smyrna They had five children: David, Hal, Connie, Allen, and Mary Jean. My daughter, Marilyn, and Mary Jean, the same age, were associated with each other in Sunday School and Vacation Bible School at First Baptist Church. "Dotsy" passed away in the 1990s.

Woody, after selling this property on Sunset Avenue to the City of Smyrna for development of the Village Green and Community Center complexes, moved to Creatwood Trail, off South Atlanta Street.

R & M Cafe' on Atlanta Street above.
The Jouquil Theater on Sunset Avenue below.
This Scene is on the southwest corner of Atlanta Street
and Sunset Avenue.
Photo Courtesy of Smyrna Museum.
Circa 1940s.

Photo, courtesy of "Millie" Broyles, circa 1940s.

SMYRNA LIONS CLUB
CHARTERED
DECEMBER 18, 1946

Charter Officers

Leonard Branscome, President

Robert Bacon, First Vice-President
Dr. W.C. Mitchell, Second Vice-President
J.Y. Wooten, Third Vice-President

W.F. Stewart, Secretary & Treasurer
John Nakos, Lion Tamer
C.C. Black, Tail Twister

Directors

Dr. D.C. Landers
W.C. Patterson
B.F. Reed, Jr.
C.J. Huggins

Charter Members

Arthur T. Bacon
R.H. Bacon, Jr.
Charles Bereferd
Clarence C. Black
W.A. Blan
Leonard Branscome
David P. Cano
Paul K. Clayton
M.L. Collins
Frank C. Dabney, Jr.
Charles Pittner
Henry L. Duncan
Jasper Griffin
D.A. Hamby, Jr.
Eugene F. Herndon
C.J. Huggins
E.E. Jackson
Guy Lackey
Dr. D.C. Landers
Dr. W.C. Mitchell
Joe McCurry
John Nakos
W.C. Patterson
Charles T. Poss
Jimmy Quarles
B.F. Reed, Jr.
Bill M. Reed
S.M. Slaughter
W.F. Stewart
Fred G. Swain
Zelan T. Wills
J.Y. Wooten
Thomas G. Young
T.C. Young, Jr.

The Charter Night Committee

J.Y. Wooten
Dr. W.C. Mitchell
Zelan T. Wills

Some of the Smyrna Lions Club members who have served in Smyrna, Cobb County, or Georgia Government are as follows:

Rem Bennett, Smyrna City Councilman
Hoot Gibson, Mayor of Smyrna
George Kreeger, Smyrna City Councilman and Mayor
Homer Kuhl, Smyrna City Councilman
Stanley McCalla, Smyrna City Councilman
Forster Puffe, Smyrna City Councilman
Hugh Ragan, Smyrna City Councilman and State Senator
Bill Sanders, Smyrna City Councilman
Jack Shinall, Smyrna City Councilman
Joe Thompson, State Senator and County Commissioner
Pete Wood, Smyrna City Councilman

The Smyrna Lions Club met for the last time on Thursday, June 1, 2000, when the Club was fifty-three years old. It was another passing of Old Smyrna: the people, places, and groups that had shaped my life as a young person growing up in Smyrna.

The above information was provided by Harold Smith, Director of the Smyrna Museum.

SUNSET AVENUE
South Side

Appreciation is extended to Rebekah Austin Walker, who shared her memories of growing up on the south side of Sunset Avenue in the 1930s and 1940s. Appreciation is also extended to Patricia Arrington Reeves, whose grandmother lived on Sunset Avenue.

The Jonquil Theatre

The first building on the south side of Sunset Avenue from Atlanta Street was the **Jonquil Theatre**. Mr. **Leonard Branscome** built the theatre after World War II and owned and operated it for several years. Jeanice and "Wit" Carson, Jr., managed the theatre. When I was a kid, I distributed coming attraction posters to store owners for their windows and tacked posters to telephone poles. My pay for this job was free admission to the theatre.

Leonard was a leader in the community. I recall that he was involved in organizing the Smyrna Lions Club. One of the Lions' first fundraising projects was a play, *The Womanless Wedding,* which was performed in the Jonquil Theatre and in which Mr. Branscome was one of the actors. I also remember that B.F. Reed, Jr., played the role of the bride; a huge man, he was perfect for that role. The play was a big success and is still remembered by many Smyrnans who attended. I was a teenager when the play was held and remember well the fun those guys had while acting.

<u>First House</u>

Mr. and **Mrs. Chester Austin** lived in the first house past the theatre. They had five children: **Annie Grace**, **Katherine**, **Frances**, **Adair**, known as "Chet," and **Rebekah**. The Austin family were active members of First Methodist Church. Chester Austin was employed by Simmons Mattress Company in Atlanta. He was a brother of Paul Austin, and Mrs. Chester Austin was a sister of Mrs. Paul Austin. See *Austin, North Cooper Lake Road.*

<u>Annie Grace Austin</u> married and moved to Canton.

<u>Katherine Austin</u> married and moved to South Georgia.

<u>Frances Austin</u> married and moved to South Georgia.

<u>Adair Austin</u>, known as "Chet," married Hazel Stanfield from Jasper. They had three children: Sharon, Lori, and David. They raised their family on North Cooper Lake Road, west of Smyrna, and were faithful members of Tillman Methodist Church, on Concord Road. "Chet" and Hazel later moved to Marietta, where they are living.

NOTE: The new development on North Cooper Lake Road, "Austin Grove," is located where the "Chet" Austin House stood. This area was annexed into the City Limits of Smyrna several years ago.

"Chet" was a partner with Al Burruss in Tip Top Poultry, in Marietta. This is a very successful business that is now operated by second generation members of the Austin and Burruss families.

I have been associated with "Chet" through the years. He and I have both been members of the Hospital Authority of Cobb County and also the WellStar Health System Board.

<u>Rebekah Austin</u> married Mickey Walker, the son of Buna and Julia Worley Walker. They had four children: Lewis Austin, known as "Bo," Joey, Greg, and Rebekah Ann. Mickey and Rebekah graduated from Smyrna High School, where Rebekah was the scorekeeper for the boys' and girls' basketball teams, in the mid-to-late 1940s. They lived on Northview Place in Forest Hills, where they

raised their family, until 2005, when they moved to Kennesaw. The Walkers are faithful members of First Methodist Church. See *Walker, south side of Spring Street* and *Atlanta Street, from the Mapps to R & M Café.*

Second House

Harry Arrington
Mayor of Smyrna
January 1933-February 1937

Harry and **Bell Arrington** were residents of the next house. Mrs. Arrington, was the former Bell Estes. They had one daughter, Doris. Harry was Mayor of Smyrna from January 1933 until February 1937.

Bell Arrington lived in this house until she married Harry Mitchell, who grew up on the south side of Church Street. Bell was a young woman when her mother died, and her younger sister, **Alice Estes**, was only nine years old at that time. After her mother's death, Alice came to live with Bell and Harry. See *Mitchell, south side of Church Street.*

Between the Austin and Arrington houses there was a walking trail that passed by Harry and Bell Arrington's tennis court, behind their house, and Mrs. J.J. Hill's property on Bank Street. Mrs. Hill had a rooster that had a reputation of being "mean." Rebekah Austin Walker shared that, as she was walking home from school on that trail, Mrs. Hill's rooster started chasing her. She threw her book bag at him, but she missed. When she tried to retrieve the bag, the rooster would not let her; thus she went home, terrified of that rooster. Rebekah's mother told her that she would have to go back and get her book bag. The rooster had Rebekah so scared that she does not really remember what happened to her book bag but seems to recall that she did go back to get it.

Miss Dorris Arrington was my teacher in the fourth grade at Smyrna School. I really liked Miss Arrington, a nice lady and a very pretty one. Doris married Jimmy Quarles, who was Mayor of Smyrna, 1955-1957. See *Quarles, Atlanta Street, from Marlowe's to Creatwood.*

Third House

Mr. and **Mrs**. **Willie Adair** were occupants of this house. Mrs. Adair's given name was **Mildred**. They had two children: **Allyn** and **Faye**. Mr. Adair was a barber. I do not remember where his shop was located, but I am sure it was not in Atlanta. The Adairs were very active members of First Baptist Church, where Mrs. Adair sang in the choir.

Allyn Adair was a year or two younger than I, and Faye Adair was in the same class with my sister, Hilda in school.

Fourth House

Mr. and **Mrs**. **Augustus Basil Ware** lived here. Mr. Ware, known as "A.B.," was married to the former Carrie Belle Kemp. Their house was just past a vacant lot and directly behind our house. They had five children**: Lorene**, **Melda Jo**, **A.B.**, **Jr**., **Helen**, and **Spurgeon**. I remember seeing stars hanging in Mrs. Ware's window, indicating that her sons, A. B. Jr., and Spurgeon, were serving in the United States Navy and the United States Army, respectively.

Mr. and Mrs. Ware were both native Cobb County residents, who grew up in the Macland/Lost Mountain area. Mr. Ware attended Macland A&M College, which later became what is known today as McEachern High School. Mr. Ware was a tool designer for the Bell Bomber Plant; afterwards he owned and operated a small insulation company.

Mr. and **Mrs. Augustus Basil Ware**
(Former Carrie Belle Kemp)
Circa mid 1960s
Photo Courtesy of Corrine Austin Ware Cates

Mrs. Ware was the daughter of Mr. and Mrs. Kemp, who owned and operated a dairy farm i the Lost Mountain area. Mrs. Ware's brother, Hayden Kemp, continued to maintain that farm unti recent times. In 2002 the Cobb County Board of Education acquired part of the Kemp property i West Cobb County, near the intersection of the southwest corner of Lost Mountain and Corner road and built Kemp Elementary School, which bears the Kemp Family name.

Spurgeon Ware married Corrine Austin, who was born on Sunset Avenue in the house wher the Adairs later lived but grew up on North Cooper Lake Road. Her dad was a brother of Mr. Cheste Austin, who lived in the first house on Sunset Avenue; her mother was a sister of Mr. Chester Austin' wife. See *third house on Sunset Avenue* and *Austin, North Cooper Lake Road.*

Spurgeon, who played baseball for my dad on the Smyrna Amateur Baseball Team, was Staff Sergeant in the United States Army in the European Theater during World War II. After the Wa Spurgeon worked for Ford Motor Company, where he retired as an executive. See *North Cooper Lak Road*

Lorene Ware married John Bowden Ellis, Jr. They had one son, John Bowden Ellis III.

Melda Jo Ware married John Harrison. They had three daughters: Joan, Sarah Carolyn, an Louise.

A.B. Ware, Jr. ., married Cecile Willis. They had two daughters: Sheila and Cherial. A.B Jr., served in the United States Navy during World War II, then worked for Georgia Power Company First climbing poles, he then advanced to the position of overseeing the construction of power pole throughout Georgia. A.B., Jr., would travel from job to job in a small aircraft to check on the work i progress.

Helen Ware married Edward Maner. They adopted two children: Meldarene and Edwar known as "Eddie."

Fifth House

Mrs. Leila Arrington, the former Leila Skelton and a widow, resided in this house. She ha four sons: **Harry**, **Bob**, **Emmett**, and **Wallace**, all grown men during my youth. Mrs. Arrington, sister of Ed Skelton, who also lived on Sunset Avenue, was a member of First Methodist Church. Se *Skelton, north side of Sunset Avenue.*

Harry Arrington and his wife, Bell, lived on Sunset Avenue, next door to the Austins. Se *second house, south side of Sunset Avenue.*

Wallace Arrington
Smyrna City Councilman
Dates Unknown

Wallace Arrington and his wife, Leola, at one time lived in the fifth house with Mrs. Lei Arrington. Wallace Arrington served on the Smyrna City Council.

Emmett Arrington married Evelyn Herndon from Atlanta. They had one daughter, Patrici known as "Pat." Emmett enlisted in the United States Army Air Corps during World War II but late served in the United States Army Infantry for three years. After World War II, Emmett worked f Simmons Mattress Company in Atlanta. Evelyn was the secretary to Reverend York Chambless, past of First Baptist Church for many years. I knew Evelyn well, as we were closely associated on man occasions in my young and middle adult years at First Baptist Church, where Emmett, Evelyn, an Patricia were active members. Emmett died in 1987 and Evelyn in 1988.

Patricia Arrington, known as "Pat," graduated from Campbell High School and married andy Holden; they had two sons, Rob and Sid, and one granddaughter. After she and Randy ivorced, "Pat" married Reuben Reeves, who is now deceased. "Pat" lives in Marietta. See *Holden, outh side of Church Street.*

Bob Arrington married Lessel McBrayer, the daughter of the elder McBrayers, who lived on e opposite side of Sunset Avenue. Lessel's brothers were Vern, Sr. ., and Murphy. Her sister, Flora, arried Mr. Jackson. See *McBrayer, north side of Sunset Avenue.*

Sixth House

Just past the Arrington house and before the Farrar house, there was a garage apartment that as set back from the street, near the back of the Bank Street property. It was almost as if someone ad left the front area open to build a house. I do not know who owned this garage apartment, but I member **Everhart** and **Herman Hulsey** lived there for a long time when I was a kid in the 1940s. ee *J. C. Johnson, south side of Fleming Street.*

Seventh House

Mrs. Farrar lived in the house next door to Mrs. Leila Arrington. She had a daughter named eggy.

There is one particular thing I remember about Mrs. Farrar, whose given name I do not now. She had a DeSoto automobile, a very shiny, fancy car—a rarity in Smyrna in the days of my outh. A kid like me could not help noticing it. An older woman in those days and very private, Mrs. arrar appeared to me to want to be left alone. My parents said we needed to respect that; therefore, I ever had any interaction with her. Though I did not know anything about her or what she did, I ways thought she seemed to be very intelligent.

HARBINS' NEIGHBORHOOD GROCERY STORE

Eighth House

The Harbins lived next door to Mrs. Farrar. They owned and operated a neighborhood ocery store, which was located on the corner of Sunset Avenue and Hamby Street, next door to their ouse. (The house and store faced Sunset Avenue.) The Harbins had children who were grown when I as growing up.

I did not frequent Harbin's Store because I lived closer to the stores on Atlanta Street. hough I did, however, go there on occasion, I did not know the Harbins very well. People would say at Mr. Harbin's Store was always open, except on Sundays. I think Mr. Harbin must have worked ere most of the time.

Marvin Stephens, who grew up on the north side of Powder Springs Street, shared his emories of Harbin's Store. It was a two-room wooden building with a small porch in front and arious signs (i.e. *Drink Coca-Cola, Smoke Lucky Strikes, Chew Brown Mule*) posted onto the front. oviding light, two or three bare bulbs hung from the ceiling. The front room included the store oper; a refrigerated meat case was in back. There were no pre-packaged meats or cheese. In some spects it was like a deli and butcher shop combined. On the counter tops were hoops of cheese, along ith a large roll of brown butcher paper for wrapping the purchases. After weighing and wrapping a archase, Mr. Harbin, using a crayon, would carefully mark the contents and price on the paper.

"Also in the front of the store were rows of canned food and boxes and bags of staples. In ason were baskets of apples, pears, corn in husks, watermelons, potatoes, and other fruits and getables. There were jars of cookies and candy and a cooler of sodas in glass bottles. Mr. Harbin ould take a customer's order and pull the items from the shelves.

"The side room had a large butcher block and sawdust on the floor. Various meat cleaver saws, and knives adorned the walls and tables. Mr. Harbin would take large portions of meat to th side room to cut them to his customer's specifications. Outside he had a tank and pump for dispensin kerosene for lamps and lanterns.

"The front porch of the store was a gathering place for children on their way home fro school. The lucky ones would each buy a Grape or Orange Nehi, or an RC with his or her nickel. Th they would sit on the porch, swapping tales and jokes. Sometimes they would laugh so hard, whi drinking, that the soda would come out their noses. At other times they shook their bottles and squirte each other until Mr. Harbin ran them off. Adult men, while drinking Coca- Cola, also sat on the porc to discuss the weather and politics. Girls usually only stopped in to buy something and then left.

"It was common for my mother, Gladys, to send me to Harbin's Store to buy groceries. Mo of the time I would walk; other times I would ride my big Roadmaster bicycle with a basket on th handlebars.

"On one occasion Mr. Harbin took me into his house. Mrs. Harbin and several other wome were in one of the second floor rooms, having a 'sewing bee.' With needles and thread, whi gossiping, they were busy working on a patchwork quilt. It was a scene seldom seen today, except historical reenactments.

"Later on, Mr. Harbin retired and sold the store to Mr. Reese. Over a number of years it ve slowly evolved into a convenience store, eventually forced out by the arrival of Colonial Stores, supermarket on Bank Street." See *Janie and Ben Cochran, south side of Spring Road, The Count Road.*

CHAPTER SEVEN

POWDER SPRINGS STREET

North Side

The following residents of Smyrna have been very generous in providing me with formation about the families that lived on the north side of Powder Springs Street between 1938 and 951. Appreciation is extended to Joyce Lovern Davis, Dorene Dunn, Gay Nell Bowman Cochran, 'irginia Gann McDaniel, Marvin Stephens, and Estelene Hammondtree Biddle, all of whom lived on owder Springs Street. Thanks to "Jenny Ruth" Bacon, who grew up on Bank Street, and was very enerous in sharing information about her grandparents, Mr. and Mrs. R.H. Bacon, Sr.; to Ruby angley Hunter, who having grown up in Smyrna, related knowledge about her relatives, the Bells, nd to Laurentine Brannon, whose husband, Fain, grew up on Powder Springs Street.

Thanks also to Frances Skelton and Rebekah Walker who grew up on Sunset Avenue. rances, who lived on Sunset Avenue until 1953, when she moved to the Forest Hills community, off ollier Drive, died in April 2004. Rebekah Austin Walker married Mickey Walker; they raised their mily on Northview Drive, which is also off Collier Drive. (Recently they moved to West Cobb ounty, to be near their daughter.)

Powder Springs Street was reconfigured northward for the building of the Community enter, developing the Arboretum, and enhancing the pond area during Smyrna's redevelopment eriod of the late 1980s and early 1990s.

First House

Guye Duncan
Mayor of Smyrna
1953-1954

Guye and **Thelma Duncan** resided in the first house on the north side of Powder Springs reet. They had one son, **Bill**.

Second House

Mr. and **Mrs. Robert Howard Bacon, Sr.**, lived in this house, next door to the Duncans. frs. Bacon was the former Nina Elizabeth Turner. Mr. and Mrs. Bacon, affectionately called "Mama" d "Papa" Bacon, had eight children: **Eugenia**, **Richard**, **Robert H.**, **Jr.**, **Louise**, **Arthur**, **Ruth**, **lizabeth**, and **E.I.**; seven of these were born while the Bacons were residents of the Salem mmunity of Oglethorpe County. Their youngest child, E.I., was born on November 16, 1924, after ey moved to Smyrna. According to family information, the Bacons lived on Roswell Street before ey moved to this house on Powder Springs Street. But it is here that I remember their living in the ys of my youth.

Mr. Robert Howard Bacon, Sr., was the oldest of the five children of Richard Morgan Bacon d Cleo Freeman Bacon. Born December 7, 1882, in Oglethorpe County, he had three brothers, Joel, ed, and Gibson, and one sister, Eugenia.

Robert Howard Bacon, Sr., attended North Georgia College, in Dahlonega, for two years. He as then a farmer. The Bacons moved to Decatur in 1921 in order for the family to be near Richard, ho was a patient at Scottish Rite Hospital. While living in Decatur, "Papa" Bacon was employed by room Construction Company as a carpenter. In 1923, he became employed by NC & St. L Railroad d moved his family to Smyrna.

Eugenia Bacon was sick for some time and lost her eyesight. She died July 13, 1928.

Mr. and **Mrs. Robert Howard Bacon, Sr.**
(Nee Nina Elizabeth Turner)
Circa mid 1940s
Courtesy of "Dot" Bacon

L-R: Robert, Louise, Arthur, "Libba," Ruth, and **E.I. Bacon**
Aunt Fanny's Cabin
January 6, 1978
Photo Courtesy of "Dot" Bacon

Richard Bacon was eight years old when he contracted osteomyelitis, an infection, which as the result of an injury from the buckle on a saddle stirrup while riding the family horse, Peter. ichard was admitted to Scottish Rite Convalescent Hospital for Crippled Children in Decatur for eatment and was there for several months. (This hospital opened in 1915.)

Two thirds of Richard's life was spent in hospitals. As a patient in Georgia Baptist Hospital, Atlanta, he had part of the bone removed from his hip, contracted pneumonia, and died March 27, 931.

Robert Bacon was the oldest of Mr. and Mrs. Robert Howard Bacon's children. He married ctavia Mitchell, known as "Octa." They had four children: Mitchell, Freddie, Mike and Nancy. See acon, *Reed* and *King streets*.

Louise Bacon married Woodrow Langford, who was in the United States Army during World ar II. They live in Gainesville.

Arthur Bacon married Dorothy Moseley, known as "Dot," from Sumter, South Carolina. ney had four children: Linda, Max, David, and Virginia Ruth, known as "Jenny Ruth." "Dot," a nurse the United States Army Nurse Corps, and Arthur knew each other before World War II, but they d to wait until they were discharged from the United States Army to marry. (Nurses were officer nk, and the military rule was that officers and enlisted personnel could not fraternize.) They married 1946. See *Arthur Bacon Family, south side of Bank Street.*

Ruth Bacon married Lewis Davies from Florida. He was a paratrooper in the United States rmy during World War II.

Elizabeth Bacon, known as "Libba," married Harold Chandler from the Smyrna area. He was the United States Army during World War II.

E.I. Bacon, who married Mary Roberts from the Atlanta area, was in the United States Navy ring World War II. He and Mary had four children: Kenneth, Doug, Rebecca, and Judy.

It is interesting to note that Mr. and Mrs. Robert Howard Bacon, Sr., had two sons, three ns-in-law, and one future daughter-in-law, all of whom served in the United States Military during orld War II. I remember seeing, during World War II, a star in Mrs. Bacon's window, indicating at someone in her family was serving in the military. Because the Bacon Family had already lost two their children to death, it is obvious they were survivors. This story of the Bacon Family is heart arming and shows how people can withstand so much and survive.

"Mama" Bacon suffered a cerebral hemorrhage and died on October 25, 1950. After "Papa" con married Sarah Whitley, December 24, 1953, he lived on Sandtown Road in Marietta. He died bruary 3, 1970.

Third House

Mr. and **Mrs. Jimmy Pierce** resided on the northwest corner of Powder Springs and Fuller eets. Mrs. Pierce was the former Mary Esther Campbell from Augusta. Their children were born in following order: **Jimmy, Jr.**, **Richard**, known as "Dick," **Sherwood**, known as "Cotton," **Robert**, own as "Bob," **Mary Jean**, **John**, known as "Jack," and **Frank**. The Pierce Family attended Saint mes Episcopal Church in Marietta, where they were members.

Mr. Pierce was my coach on the sandlot baseball team; our games were played in Brinkley rk. Mr. Pierce also ran the poolroom on Atlanta Street.

Jimmy Pierce, Jr., married Mary Frankie Gann of Smyrna. Her dad was Smyrna Police Chi while I was growing up. The family lived on Powder Springs Street, across the Access Highwa which is now South Cobb Drive. See *Powder Springs Road, The Country Road.*

Richard Pierce married Dorothy Shelor, known as "Dot," from Calhoun. They had thr children: Linda, Nancy, and David. I had a long and enjoyable association with Richard Pierce: he a I were both in the 425th Transportation Group, a United States Army Reserve unit, from the 1950s un the 1970s, when he retired. Richard worked for L & N (now CSX) Railroad at Hill's Park Termin located near Atlanta's Bolton community.

Linda Pierce married Charles Orr.

Nancy Pierce married Ralph Stewart.

David Pierce, not married, lives in California.

Robert Pierce, known as "Bob," married June O'Neal from Norfolk, Virginia.

Frank Pierce married Sara from Georgia.

Mary Jean Pierce married Andy Anderson from Georgia. She later married Silas Bobo.

John Pierce, known as "Jack," married Linda from Georgia.

Sherwood Pierce, known as "Cotton," married Sarah Anderson from Tennessee. They h one son, Woody.

Woody Pierce, still living in Smyrna, in 2002 built a new home on Powder Springs Street, the location where Mr. and Mrs. Charlie Clayton lived when I was growing up. See *Clayton, south si of Powder Springs Street.*

Fourth House

Mr. and **Mrs.Ted Bowman** were the residents of this house. Ted and his wife, the form Viola Vance, were from western North Carolina. I remember the Bowmans had two daughters: **Joy** and **Gay Nell.**

Ted Bowman was a supervisor at the main United States Post Office in Atlanta. Trained the Art Institute in New York City, he was an artist. Dr. Claude Mitchell had three of Ted's paintin hanging in his home on Atlanta Street. According to information from his daughter, Gay Nell, "T Atlanta History Center commissioned dad to paint several scenes from Old Atlanta photographs; th hang in the Atlanta History Center. The Syrian Orthodox Church in Atlanta commissioned him paint life-size icons that were on the walls of both sides of the sanctuary. (This church burned.) T United States Post Office in Atlanta commissioned him to paint a portrait of Postmaster Sanders up his retirement. Such are a few of Dad's artistic accomplishments."

The Bowman Family had almost four acres on Powder Springs Street. Over the driveway the street, there was a trellis bearing the name of the Bowmans' home place, called "Overbrook." Af parking, just before the footbridge, one walked up a long driveway to the house. The engineers w designed the Community Center did a nice job of incorporating the pond from the Bowmans' fr yard into the Arboretum area by the Community Center. Gay Nell shared that her dad kept their pla like a park. "More than a few people thought it was a spot where they would stop and have a picni (The Bowmans were the first to sell to the City for redevelopment.)

Joyce Bowman married Jack Demshock from Washington, D.C. They had three daughte Donna, Melanie, and Rebecca. Joyce, now widowed, lives in Knoxville, Tennessee.

Gay Nell Bowman married Jimmy Cochran, a member of the large Cochran Family that ved on Roswell Street. They had seven children: Ted, Shawn, Van, Bronwyn, Casey, Cathryn, and evin. See *Stephens Street* and *east side of Roswell Street.*

After Jimmy and Gay Nell Cochran married, their first home was on the corner of Bank and amby streets, directly across the street from Mrs. Grace Evans. They moved from that house to ephens Street, and later to Pretty Branch Drive in the Forest Hills community, off Collier Drive. mmy worked for Myers-Dickson Furniture Company in Atlanta, as did Sam Cochran, his brother.

Jimmy, very active in the youth baseball program in Smyrna, died when he was still a young an. Regarding her husband, Gay Nell related, "When our children, their spouses, our grandchildren, d great-grandchildren are counted, we have fifty-two members in our family." Gay Nell said, "Joe ttanzi once remarked to Jimmy, 'The world is going to know you were here.' Gay Nell concluded, mmy was a wonderful husband and father."

I have had a close relationship with Gay Nell throughout my life. In more recent years, she d I served together on the Board of Blind and Low Vision Services of North Georgia. Gay Nell is rrently living in Alpharetta, near one of her daughters.

Ted Cochran married Cheryl Chambers, who grew up on Anderson Drive. Ted and Cheryl aduated from Campbell High School.

Shawn Cochran married Barbara Barnett of Smyrna. Shawn and Barbara, both of whom aduated from Campbell High School, had two sons.

Van Cochran married Marilyn Moore from Atlanta.

Bronwyn Cochran married Mike Randall from Florida.

Casey Cochran married Linda Matheson from Hawaii.

Cathryn Cochran married Nick Oympiodes from Greece.

Kevin Cochran, not married, is currently living in Colorado.

Fifth House

Mr. and **Mrs. Lawrence Hill** lived in the fifth house. Mrs. Hill's given name was Bessie. ey had four daughters: **Ruth**, **Inez**, **Edna**, and **Jeanie**, all of whom were older than I.

Jeanie worked at the Telephone Exchange when I was a kid. She married Charles Poss of nyrna, the son of Mrs. and Mrs. Horace G. Poss, who lived on Lee Street, where Jeanie and Charles er lived. Jeanie and Charles had two daughters: Patty and Cathy, and a son, Charles, known as huck." Charles preceded Jeanie in death. She died in the summer of 2004. See *Poss, east side of Lee reet.*

Sixth House

In the early days of my childhood, this was a three-room house, occupied by **Mrs. Leila odges**, who worked at Brawner Sanitarium. A lady who lived on Sunset Avenue had this house, as ll as some of the other houses, built in the area.

Mr. and **Mrs. Chris Dunn**

Mr. and **Mrs. Chris Dunn** later moved here. Mrs. Dunn was the former Dorene Copelan m Siloam, in Green County. They had two sons, **Chris** and **Jimmy**, and five grandchildren. Powder

Springs Street was reconfigured in the late 1980s and early 1990s, when Smyrna began the gr renovation of the City. The beautiful Dunn home place is still standing across from the City's gazet on the northwest corner of Powder Springs Street, which curves around the pond. It is a pretty wh frame house with a well-established yard; in the spring the yard, filled with jonquils and azaleas, is blaze of color. Because the flowers appear each year without her effort, Dorene gives God the praise.

When Chris and Dorene Dunn first moved to Smyrna, they lived in a small apartment in t Oakdale area. In 1949 Chris and Dorene bought this house on Powder Springs Street from M Hodges, through the J.Y. Wooten Real Estate Agency. They built an addition to their house, whi made it the size it is today.

Dorene Dunn has been a long-time faithful member of First Baptist Church, where she is st active in the Friendship Sunday School Class. Chris Dunn, a Catholic from childhood, was a good man. Shortly before his and Dorene's 50th wedding anniversary, at age 80, Chris joined First Baptist Church and was baptized by Dr. Steven Kimmel, pastor. Chris lived into his late 80s.

Chris Dunn, serving with the United States Navy, was in the convoy where General Dougl McArthur signed the peace agreement ending World War II. After he was discharged, Chris went work with the United States Post Office (1948) and retired after thirty-six years. (Prior to 1948, m of Smyrna was on a general delivery route.)

Janet Brooks Brown shared, "Because the people on his route were like family, they want to show their appreciation for his years of outstanding service—above and beyond the call of duty. T Oakdale community, part of Chris's rural route, gave a party for him when he retired. Held at Loc Grove Baptist Church, it was quite a celebration."

Chris Dunn, Jr., was married and had two children: a daughter, Shannon, and a so Christopher III. Chris, Jr., retired as chief forester at Fort Benning. Having remarried, he and his wi Sylvia, live in Columbus.

Jimmy Dunn married Brenda Bounique from Indianapolis, Indiana. They had three childre two sons, Patrick and Jonathan, and a daughter, Casey. Jimmy and Brenda live in West Lafaye Indiana, where Jimmy works with Campus Crusade for Christ at Perdue University. He also wor with college faculties in nine mid-western states.

Seventh House

George Langston, Jr., and his wife, **Lena**, lived in this house from at least 1941 or earlier about 1947. (It is not family knowledge if George Langston, Sr., built or bought this house.) Alma Langston Stephens and her children resided here for a short time during World War II. George, Jr., was the manager at Georgia Power Company's Plant Atkinson, located on Access Road, now called South Cobb Drive.

Marvin Stephens shared: "My grandfather, George Langston, Sr., whom we called 'Papa,' was a carpenter by trade; he used his carpentry skill, one of the many he had, while raising a large family during hard times." George, Sr., and his wife, Lena, had four sons: George, Jr., Ed, James Donald, and Mace. He also had five daughters: Alma Gladys, Evelyn, Delores, Jean, and Joan. See *Marvin Clifford Stephens, Sr., eighth house.*

Mr. and **Mrs. Harold Dison**

Margaret and **Harold Dison** moved to this house after the Langstons vacated. They had o daughter, **Charlotte**, who was a member of the Smyrna High School Class of 1951. The Disons we members of First Baptist Church, where Mrs. Dison is still a very faithful member.

I remember that Harold Dison refereed high school basketball games at Smyrna High Scho

The Paschal Hopkins Family

Harry Hopkins
Casualty of War
Vietnam 1969

Paschal Hopkins and his wife, **Marion**, and their three children**:** **Vickie**, and twins, **Harry** and **Harriett**, lived here. As head of security, Mr. Hopkins worked at Lockheed Aircraft Corporation. Marion Hopkins, who had worked at Lockheed, was later employed at Rich's Cobb Center, where she was working at the time of her death.

Vickie Hopkins married Jerry Brown. They lived for a long time on the corner of Dunn Street and Collier Drive before moving to Florida.

Harry Hopkins served in the United States Army in Vietnam, and was a casualty of war.

Harriett Hopkins lives in California. All three Hopkins children graduated from Wills High School.

NOTE: Marvin Stephens referred to the aforementioned house as the Langston/Dison/Hopkins House.

Eighth House

Mr. and **Mrs**. **Marvin Clifford Stephens**, **Sr**., resided in this house from 1944 to 1963. Mrs. Stephens was the former Alma Gladys Langston. They had five children: **Marvin**, **Jr**., **Marian Claire**, **Betty Jean**, **Rosemary Grace**, known as "Teeny," and **Russell Thomas**, known as "Rusty." The Stephens adopted a baby boy in the 1960s. See *seventh house*.

Marvin Stephens, Sr., grew up in Atlanta and was employed as a machinist, by National Biscuit Company. During World War II he served with the United States Navy on a PT boat in the Pacific.

Gladys Langston Stephens grew up in Piedmont, Alabama, and Atlanta. Also employed at National Biscuit Company at one time, she later worked for the Atlanta Parks and Recreation Department. Alma Gladys Stephens died in the autumn of 2004.

Marvin Stephens, Jr., first married Carolyn Marie Fountain. They had three children: Randy J., Holly Rebekah, and Jennifer Lynn. After Marvin and Carolyn divorced, he married Dianne Marie Austin, who had two children from a previous marriage. Marvin and Dianne live in Florida.

Marian Claire Stephens married Bill Cantrell; they divorced several years later. They had no children. Marian died October 13, 1997.

Betty Jean Stephens married Bill Birney; they had three children: Tammy Lynn, Nick and Jason. After Betty Jean and Bill divorced, Betty Jean married Ken Best; they live in Loganville.

Rosemary Grace Stephens, known as "Teeny," married Mr. Mercer. They live in Canton.

Russell Thomas Stephens, known as "Rusty," lives in Woodstock.

Marvin Stephens, Jr., said, "Sometime in 1944 or 1945, during World War II, my mother, Alma Gladys Langston Stephens, arranged to get a loan to build a house at 314 Powder Springs Street. She, along with her father, George Langston, Sr., (whom we called "Papa") and brother, George Langston, Jr., built this house for our family while we were living with Uncle George and Aunt Lena.it is not known if George, Jr., gave or sold the lot to Mother. Her brother-in-law, Jimmy Gaddy, installe the plumbing. The work on the construction of the house most likely began in 1944.

"Over a period of several months, they erected a modest four-room house, which by today' standards would be very small. It was a large rectangle, almost square in structure, with a gable roo and a bathroom attached to the back (almost like an afterthought). If you looked at a floor plan of th main part of the house, it was divided into four rooms, all the same size. The four main rooms wer squares, each connected by a door leading into the next room. Imagine a rectangle that was almos square! Draw a line down the middle; then draw another perpendicular line to divide it in half.

"Through the front door we entered the 'front room' (as we called it). It was essentially screened porch that served as a living area in good weather. (This room was later closed in; b installing windows instead of screens, a living area was created for the entire year.) From there a doo led into the children's bedroom. A door from the children's room opened into an eat-in-kitchen, wher there were other doors: one for entrance to the rear yard; another leading to the the parents' bedroom which doubled as a nursery, for a couple of years at a time, for each of Marvin and Gladys' children The bathroom was reached by way of the parents' bedroom. All the floors were wood.

"Mother made this house a home for her family. Life was easier for her than in her growing up years in a rural area. This house had electricity, running water, and an indoor bathroom. But fo years she did not have a washing machine, and it would be even longer before she had a clothes dryer essentials of today. We did have a gas furnace, which eliminated the need for gathering wood and coal For a short time we had a ice box, but later we were able to get a refrigerator.

"When I was about four and a half years old and the weather was warm, my grandfather Papa (George Langston, Sr.), and Uncle George (George Langston, Jr.) were working on the house. have earlier bits and pieces of memories, i.e. Papa's working on the rafters before the roof went on, bu this memory is much clearer than those: I was given jobs, such as picking up pieces of boards or trash to keep me out of the way, and I remember playing with a block of wood—as my bulldozer—in som sand near the house. With the house almost finished, from leftover lumber Papa had even made 'corner cabinet' to go into the 'front' room.

"Sometime after that—I am not sure if it was a few days or weeks—I remember a specia morning. I woke up in a bed at my Uncle George's house, and Daddy was in the room, back from th War; I cannot remember when I had last seen him. In fact, I do not have any earlier memories of hin except his going into the Navy when I was younger. However, that was of the troop train, not him. Bu I knew he was my father, I do not know if Mom (Gladys) told me he was my dad or if I had seen photo or what. Nonetheless, I was very happy to see him."

Marvin continued, "I remember one of the toolboxes 'Papa' used when building this house a 314 (later 228) Powder Springs Street, where we lived for many years. It was a simple, open wooden box with a couple of dividers. About 30 inches long and 8 inches wide and tall, it had a round wooden rod for a handle. In it were all kinds of hand tools: saws, hammers, planes, brace and bits (drill) pinches, nail sets, files, chisels, and a tool for setting the teeth on the saws when he sharpened them Even as a young boy, I was impressed at the care he gave these tools. And I knew not to play witl them! As a young boy, I also got to straighten bent nails for Papa and later my father— a job that kep me busy and out of the way."

Marvin also shared a story about life with his mother, Gladys. "Mother loved animated stories and shared these stories with us children—stories such as *Uncle Remus Tales* and *Aesop's Fables*. One of the good lines from one of the animated movies she took us to see was 'Everybody's got to have a laughing place.' She apparently adopted this literally and instilled it into each of us children as well.

"We often went down Powder Springs Street, to a pasture owned by Mr. Guthrie. We migh have taken a small picnic lunch or some cookies. Or we might have cracked some hickory nuts from the trees at the edge of the pasture. We would walk or skip down the street, singing, '*Zip a dee do dah, zip a dee eh, my oh my, what a wonderful day….*'

"I can see Uncle Remus walking down the road, holding the hand of a small boy. As he is singing, brightly colored cartoon butterflies, birds, and other creatures are darting about. A bluebird lands on his shoulder in perfect synchronization with the lyrics.

"Mother called this pasture our 'secret laughing place.' For her as well as us children it was a place of joy, peace, and solace. It was a place to run and be carefree and childlike, to fall down and roll in the grass. I am sure it was a place for her to relieve stress. She would tell us children stories and fairy tales. She would also recount memories from her childhood. It was a place of bonding for her and her children. Today the pasture is gone and has been replaced by houses. But it was and is a special place! Sometimes I go there in my memory just to visit, and I can hear my mother say, 'Everybody's got to have a laughing place!'

"On occasion, Mother and Dad took us children on outings to see such structures as Dodgen's Mill, near Cooper Lake Road, about where it crossed Nickajack Creek. I remember large sections of the dam, covered with moss that littered the waterway; the water from the creek had been slowly eroding the large stones. Still standing on either side of Nickajack Creek were large stone walls, solemn reminders of the past, when a mill once used the water stored by the dam upstream. Mom and Dad took us children many times to wade and swim in Nickajack Creek. From the time I was eight years old until I was about thirteen, alone, I rode my horse, Patsy, from our house (and later from Mr. Guthrie's or Mr. Fraser's pasture) on Powder Springs Street to Nickajack Creek. On numerous occasions, with my horse, I went swimming in the creek.

"My mother was a compassionate woman who felt the pain of others. One time she and I rode the streetcar to Marietta. As we were walking by the Cobb County Courthouse on the Square, an old Black man was sitting on the sidewalk with some pencils. Mom gave me a dollar and said, 'He needs this more than we do. Go, give it to him!' And I did—while learning a lesson as well. (A dollar was a lot of money then.)

"On several occasions an old Black man came through our neighborhood, offering to plow people's yards. For several years we had a garden even though we hadn't planned to have one. When the man would work for my mother, she always had something for him to eat and drink, as well as water for his mule. One year after he stopped coming, I often thought about what might have happened to him. Growing up in the 'often intolerant' South where grown Black men were called 'boy,' my mother used words such as 'please' and 'sir.' She gave him meaningful work and yet allowed him to have dignity. Her actions spoke volumes! I learned from her.

"Another place I enjoyed going to when I was growing up was George Waites' Barber Shop. He had two barber chairs and large fans hanging from the ceiling, slowly circulating the air. The men gossiped and bragged about politics, sports, weather, other people, and almost any subject you can imagine. Some of the men were there every time I got a haircut. George Waites and the other barber would join in the lively conversations, especially if the topic involved haircuts going from 25¢ to 50¢. No matter what the topic, someone would chime in to make his opinion known. On occasion, some of the men would play checkers. George made sharpening his straight razor an impressive ritual; he would strop the razor up and down the wide leather strops until he could split a hair. The customers usually quieted down as he sharpened his instrument. Sometimes he would test the razor on the hair on his arm. It was best not to have him engaged in animated conversation while he was shaving around the ears and/or the back of the neck.

"In 1947 our family bought some horses. Dad brought them home on an old flatbed truck that he had borrowed from one of my uncles, James Coleman Stephens. The horses were Dan, a large pinto (probably a Quarter Horse), Patsy, my "Indian Pony," and her colt, Mary Legs. Patsy was black except for a small white patch on her forehead; she was smaller than a horse but much larger than a Shetland pony. I felt so grown as I rode 'my pony.' On September 1, 1947, Mom and Dad led Patsy, with me proudly atop, to Smyrna Elementary School for my first day of school. As Mom recorde later, 'He was thrilled to death!' As I grew older, I was able to ride that horse all around Smyrna.

"I recall the following story from my mother. 'I received a phone call from Mike Williams mother, on Brown Circle. Mrs. Williams told me that "Buck" (Marvin, Jr.) and Mike were playin Cowboys and Indians in her back yard behind our house; 'Buck,' a second grader, didn't have on an clothing except a saddle blanket. The boys are having a good 'ole' time, 'Buck' is dressed like he ha seen some Indians in the movies and like some Boy Scouts that gave a war dance at the scout hut a Brinkley Park. Anyhow I showed him how to put the blanket over and under the belt and told him t wear some shorts.'

"Our neighbors, Mr. and Mrs. Hill, had some chickens in a pen and a cow in their back yard my family had the horses. Mother said, 'One day Dad brought home a pig for us and two other pigs fo his friends; he built a pen for them in our back yard. Dad could not feed the pigs until he got hom from work, about midnight. Therefore, because the pigs would squeal when they got hungry, I had t feed them. That fall, when the pigs were killed, Mom made Dad tear down the pen."

Romulus Nester Hughes

Virginia Gann McDaniel shared the following information. "Grandfather Romulus Neste Hughes owned and farmed all the tract of land bounded by Grady, Fleming, Hughes, and Powde Springs streets. After he stopped farming and went to work for Georgia Power Company, he decide to sell part of his land for development. But before that time, he gave each of his children a lot fo building a house. All but one of them did build. Therefore, the area became a type of 'Hughes Famil Compound.'" Virginia added, "Naturally, Hughes Street was named for him."

"While working for the Georgia Power Company, Grandfather Hughes was foreman of th men that laid the streetcar line from Atlanta to Marietta in the early 1900s. I know my grandparent moved to Smyrna prior to 1905 because my mother, Irene, was born in Smyrna that year."

Virginia continued, "While the tracks were being laid, my grandfather one night found a littl Black boy who was about six years old. Because he had no home, my grandfather took him home wit him. This was not an accepted practice in those days. Grandfather only knew the boy's name wa Frank; therefore, he became known as 'Frank' to the family, who treated him like the other kids in th household except that he had to sleep in the tool house in the back yard. Frank was a playmate t everyone, but he was especially 'big buddies' with my Uncle Bill. He lived with my grandparents unti he was grown, could get a job, and be on his own. The boys in the family kept in touch with Frank fo many years."

Romulus Nester Hughes from his first marriage had two children: Erby and Pearl. His firs wife died when Pearl was a baby. Afterwards Romulus married Fronie Ester; they had six children Emma, Ethel, James, William, known as "Bill," Irene, and Robert, known as "Bob."

Erby Hughes. See *eleventh house.*

Pearl Hughes married Jack Hufstutler. See *tenth house.*

Emma Hughes married Albert Hammond.

Ethel Hughes married Mr. Noah Reeves.

James Hughes married Leila Croft.

William Hughes, known as "Bill," married Millie Shaw.

Irene Hughes married Ed Gann. See *ninth house.*

Robert Hughes, known as "Bob," married Mary Alice Lord.

"Although Uncle Erby and Aunt Pearl were from my grandfather's first marriage, there was never any difference shown between the two of them and the other children. No one was ever 'step-child,' and the siblings never made a difference among any of the eight children. Erby and Pearl considered Fronie as their mother," Virginia related.

Ninth House

Mr. and **Mrs. Ed Gann** resided in this house, which was located on the northwest corner of Powder Springs and Hughes streets. They had one daughter, **Virginia**. Mrs. Gann was the former Irene Hughes. Also living with them was Irene's sister, **Ethel Hughes**, known to Virginia as "Aunt Ethel," and Irene's mother, **Fronie Ester Hughes**, known to Virginia as "Granny." The husband of Mrs. Ester Hughes, the former Fronie Ester Hestely, died before Virginia was born.

Irene and Ed Gann never owned a house of their own. Once they planned to buy one, on the corner of King and Bank streets, near where the new houses are now located on the Village Green. The house was $900.00, with $100.00 down and $25.00 per month house payments. They could swing the $25.00 monthly payments but could not put together the $100.00 down payment even though they were both working. This shows how little people's income was in those days. Later Howard and Ruby Akins bought that house. See *south side of Bank Street.*

In the 1930s Mr. Ed Gann was burned badly from starting a fire at home. He could not be moved to the hospital and was thus kept in bed for several weeks with only a sheet, not touching him but over him. The doctor had to come every day to cut off dead skin and put ointment on him. Virginia stated that she was born soon after her dad's accident and only knows what she was told.

Mr. and Mrs. Ed Gann were members of First Baptist Church, where Irene Gann was an active member of the Homemaker's Sunday School Class.

Virginia Gann, a member of the Smyrna High School Class of 1949, married J.R. McDaniel, known as "Bob." They had five children: "Butch," Joni, Ricky, Melanie, and Robin.

"Bob," who is musically talented, sings with the Vintage Barber Shop Quartet. They perform at different functions; the most recent of which I know was the "Senior Day" luncheon at First Baptist Church.

Robin McDaniel, who has a beautiful voice, was in church music ministry for a time. She is very generous in sharing her talent at her church.

Bob's mother was Mrs. Estelle Addison McDaniel, who lived on Dunn Street. She and her husband also had another son, Travis, and a daughter, Latrelle.

Estelle McDaniel later married W.J. Pennington, known as "Bill." They had a daughter, Sandra. See *McDaniel-Pennington east side of Dunn Street*

Tenth House

T.W. Hufstutler
Mayor of Smyrna
April 1937-June 1938
City Councilman
1927-1928, 1933

Mr. and **Mrs. T.W. Hufstutler** lived in the next house. Mrs. Hufstutler was the former Pearl Hughes. Mr. and Mrs. Hufstutler, who did not have children, were active members of First Baptist

Church, where he was a deacon and she taught Sunday School. The Hufstutlers were Virginia Gann McDaniel's aunt and uncle. "Uncle Jack," as he was known to Virginia was a native of Alabama. H served in the United States Army in France during World War I.

Virginia stated, "We had the first and only sidewalk in Smyrna for a long time. It extende from the front of our house, on the corner, to the driveway in front of Aunt Pearl's and Uncle Jack' house. Thinking back now, I suppose its length was because Uncle Jack was Mayor and had been o the Smyrna City Council. Whatever the reason, we all got skates every year for Christmas because w wore them out from one year to the next on that sidewalk. I especially remember that not only all o my cousins and I would skate, but also Calvin Johnson, from Fleming Street, would come and skat with us all the time, too."

NOTE: When my family lived on Grady Street, I can recall, I went down to Powder Spring Street to watch the workmen pour the cement for the sidewalks. I wonder if they were the sam sidewalks that Virginia is remembering in the story above.

T.W. Hufstutler was Smyrna City Councilman, 1927-1928, and again in 1933. He wa Mayor of Smyrna, April 1937- June 1938.

Virginia Gann McDaniel remembers that, between the houses of the Hufstutlers and Uncl Erby Hughes, there was a vacant lot where she and all her cousins played when they were children (Later on Guye and Thelma Duncan built a house on this lot.)

<u>Eleventh House</u>

The **Erby Hughes** home was past the vacant lot. He and his first wife had three children **Harold Melvin**, **Gladys**, and **Rae**. When Rae was only a few months old, "Uncle Erby's" first wif died. Then he married "**Aunt Alice**," whose maiden name Virginia McDaniel does not remember they had one child, **E.B. Hughes**.

Virginia shared, "'Uncle Erby, a godly man,' was burned in an electrical fire while workin for Georgia Power Company. He had a long but complete recovery. An active member of First Baptis Church, he served as a trustee and deacon.

"It seems 'Uncle Erby' had so many troubles," remarked Virginia. "I think it was in the lat 1950s when so many of our family died. They seemed to die all at once: E.B., his son, died one month his wife, Aunt Alice, died the next month; and his mother, who was my Grandmother Fronie, died th following month."

<u>Harold Hughes</u> married Velma Norton from another "old Smyrna" family. Harold and Velm are currently living in Christian City, a senior retirement complex south of Atlanta. See *North Cooper Lake Road.*

<u>Gladys Hughes</u> married Raymond Francis from Nashville, Tennessee. They had two sons, Paul and Greg. Raymond served with the Seabees during World War II. After Raymond died, Gladys remarried

Harry Jordan
Prisoner of War
World War II

<u>Rae Hughes</u> married Harry Jordan from Marietta, who served in the United States Military during World War II and was taken Prisoner of War. They had one daughter, Beverly Ann, who is married and lives in Conyers. Both Rae and Harry died from cancer.

<u>E.B. Hughes</u> married and had two daughters, Brenda and Connie, who live in Texas. E.B. died in his thirties.

T. W. Hufstutler, Mayor | H. E. Fawcett, Clerk

Town of Smyrna

Smyrna, Georgia

May 2, 1938

HONORABLE COUNCIL OF THE TOWN OF SMYRNA.

Gentlemen:

Please accept this as my resignation as Mayor of the Town of Smyrna, Georgia.

Due to my physical condition I find that it will be impossible for me to continue serving as Mayor, as it seems that I will have to get all the rest possible for me to continue my work.

I have enjoyed being Mayor and also serving with practically all of you as a Member of the Council, it is with regret that I find it impossible for me to continue serving as Mayor for the rest of my term.

May you all accept my best wishes for the continuance of the work to be done for the good of the people of the Town of Smyrna.

Very truly yours,

T. W. Hufstutler

The Erby Hughes Home
North side of Powder Springs Street
More Recent Picture

The Ernest Brannon Home
North side of Powder Springs Street

Twelfth House

Estelle and **Bud Fortner** resided in the next house on Powder Springs Street. Set back from the street and facing Powder Springs Street, the house was on the northeast corner of Powder Springs and Grady streets. Later on Ruby and Jack Hunter bought this house for her parents, Alton and Ethel Langley, who ran a neighborhood grocery store there for a short time. Due to the Langleys' declining health, Ruby and Jack sold the store to Mr. and Mrs. Raymond Myers, who operated the neighborhood grocery store for the next twenty-five years. "The Little Store" (as it was called by the local people) was in operation until the late 1980s. See *Langley, Old Roswell Street.*

In the days of my youth there was a vacant lot on the northwest corner of Grady and Powder Springs streets.

Thirteenth House

The **Smith Family** occupied the house just past the vacant lot.

Fourteenth House

Mr. and **Mrs. Jim Bell** lived just west of the Smiths when I was a small boy living on Grady Street. A short while after we moved from Grady Street, the Bells moved to Fleming Street. Some members of that family resided on Fleming Street continually after Mr. Jim Bell, the patriarch of that large family, first moved there. The last member, Mildred, their daughter-in-law, moved in 2004. See *Bell, Fleming Street.*

Mr. and **Mrs. Hammontree**

Mr. and **Mrs. Paul Webb Hammontree** lived in this house. The Hammontrees had five children: **Lee**, **Estelene**, **Cleave**, **Retha Jean**, known as Jean, and **Peggy Sue**. Lee, a big healthy baby, died of diphtheria at age six months.

Paul and Alice Hammontree, having moved from Tennessee to Marietta, where they lived for two years, bought this house in 1946. At that time, Paul, doing the work himself, rewired the house for electricity, added siding, installed sheet rock, rebuilt the porches, and added a bath and half. Mr. Hammontree, from McClain Mountain in Jasper, was a cement finisher and a master carpenter; he was known for building beautiful stairways. During World War II he worked at Bell Bomber Plant. He died in 1996 at 90 years of age.

Mrs. Hammontree was the former Alice Reece of Ellijay. She worked at the Bell Bomber Plant during World War II. Though only 4' 11'' tall, she was a "Rosie the Riviter." She died in 1994.

Estelene shared, "My parents, each with only a grade school education, were self-taught people who worked hard to provide for a better education for us children. Though needing to move, Alice insisted they not go back to Jasper. She was determined that her children have an opportunity to attend better schools and not have to do laborious work, as she and her husband did because of the lack of higher education. All four of us children graduated from high school: I from Smyrna and the others from Campbell. After high school, all four of us attended classes for further educational training. We will be forever grateful to loving parents who cared!"

After their children were grown, Paul and Alice, for twelve years, were foster parents. Through those years, they kept five children at different times. On two different occasions, the children were siblings.

Estelene Hammontree, a graduate of Smyrna High School, married Robert Earl Coleman, known as "Bobby." They had three children, Denise, Rita, and Robert Alan, and six grandchildren.

After twenty-eight years, Estelene and Bob divorced. Bob died in 1995. Later Estelene was married to William Biddle for eleven years. William died in 1996.

Estelene was an employee of Crowe, Shipley, and Martin, Attorneys at Law, in Marietta, for five years; afterwards she worked nine years for Crisp County School Superintendent Ray Darley. After working sixteen years for Lee County School Superintendent, Robert Clay, she retired in 1998.

Cleave Hammontree worked at G.B.'s Restaurant and Jonquil Theatre while a student at Campbell. After he graduated from Campbell High School in 1955, Cleave became employed at Lockheed Aircraft Corporation; then he enlisted into the United States Army, where he served three years. He later bought four houses from G.B. Williams: (the one in which G.B. lived and others that G.B. built on the south side of Powder Springs Street as rental houses). After G.B. retired from the restaurant, Cleave bought the café and operated it until the Georgia State Highway Department bought the property for the widening of Atlanta Road. Later Cleave worked for Republic Airlines (which became Northwest Airlines) as chief mechanic; from there he retired.

Cleave married Carol Brown of Vinings, who from a previous marriage had a son, Doug, whom Cleave adopted. Then they had four children: Vickie, Gina, Patrick, and Amanda.

After his divorce from Carol, Cleave married Jacquelyn McMichael, known as "Jackie," who had a son, Nat, from a previous marriage. Cleave and "Jackie" had a son, Cleave Jefferson Hammontree, Jr. "Jackie" and Cleave, Sr., are divorced.

Later Cleave married Eva Braswell of Riverdale. From a previous marriage, Eva had a son, Michael Christopher, whom Cleave adopted. Cleave and Eva had two daughters: Heather Ashley and Brittany Nicole. Cleave had ten grandchildren.

Retha Jean Hammontree, known as Jean, graduated from Campbell High School and worked for Lockheed Aircraft Corporation for eighteen years. She married Frank Richardson and they had two sons: Steve and Derek. Steve, at age nineteen, died in an accident.

After her divorce from Frank, Jean married Bob Tyson; they had a daughter, Donna Jean. Still later Retha Jean married Glenn Ellis, now deceased. Retha Jean had three grandchildren.

Peggy Hammontree, a Campbell High School graduate, married Darrel Harmon, They had two daughters, Alicia Gay and Kimberly, and four grandchildren. Peggy and Darrel divorced. Peggy died in car accident in 1989. Darrel is also deceased.

This property remained in the Hammontree Family until Paul and Alice were deceased, at which time the house was sold to Maria Zygmunt. At the present time the house is still standing.

Fifteenth House

Mrs. Belle Parks' home was the next one that I remember. Here she raised her two nieces: **Sara** and **Edna Nabors**. This house was on the east side of the creek from the Campbell High School property, formerly F.T. Wills High School.

Sara Nabors married Jack Herndon, whom I recall, served in the United States Navy during World War II. I remember that the Herndons were good friends with my "Ma-Ma" Tucker and one of her sons, Tom. Mrs. Mamie Fleming, who had no children, lived with the Herndons after she sold her house to Mr. and Mrs. John Richards.

NOTE: I did not establish if Mrs. Fleming was related to the Fleming Family of Fleming Street.

Sixteenth House

Mrs. Mamie Fleming, an older lady, resided here when I was a small child living on Grady Street.

Mr. and Mrs. John Jacob Richards

Mr. and **Mrs. John Jacob Richards** lived here. Mrs. Richards was the former Georgia Ann Hasty. They moved to Powder Springs Street around 1943 from Davis Road because the Dobbins Air Force Base runway was built too close to their home. This house on Powder Springs Street was located between the home of Mrs. Belle Parks and the creek. Across the creek was the Sinyard property, which later became the site of F.T. Wills High School, now Campbell High School. The Community Church currently stands on part of the property.

Patricia Durham Baldwin provided this interesting information about her grandfather Richards, "Grandfather, for a number of years, worked for the United States Postal Service as a mail carrier in Smyrna. He knew everyone! Strangers trying to find someone frequently went to his house to ask directions. He was known to the rural folk as 'Friend.' Roads were not paved, ruts were many, but somehow he would get the mail delivered, sometimes along with needed medicine or other items." See *Davis Road* and *south side of Powder Springs Street.*

The Richards' were the parents of Mrs. Allene Durham and the grandparents of Patricia Durham Baldwin and Richard Durham. Mr. Richards died December 2, 1950; Mrs. Richards died March 26, 1968.

Seventeenth House

Mr. and **Mrs. Sinyard** resided in this house, which was across the creek and up the hill from the Richards' home. The Sinyard house was some distance from the street. In the 1960s the Cobb County Board of Education built F.T. Wills High School and Nash Middle School on part of the Sinyard property. F.T. Wills and Campbell high schools were merged in the early 1990s and became known as Campbell High School. Nash Middle School, relocated to the former Campbell High School campus on South Atlanta Road, is known as Campbell Middle School. I remember Mr. and Mrs. Sinyard had a son, Grady.

NOTE: Part of the land behind the Sinyard property, where Wills and Nash schools were built, belonged at one time to Mrs. Helen Pace Thompson. See *Pace, Atlanta Street, from Mrs. Mazie's to Creatwood.*

Eighteenth House

Mr. and Mrs. Duncan Johnson

Mr. and **Mrs. Duncan Johnson** were living in this house in 1939 when the Ben O'Bryant Family moved to this property. See *Johnson, north side of Stephens Street, and Benny Lou O'Bryant Tackett's memories below Mr. and Mrs. Ernest Brannon*

Mr. and Mrs. Ernest Brannon

Mr. and **Mrs. Ernest Brannon** and their son, **Fain**, lived in this house, which is still standing. Large, with a front porch and asbestos siding, it is just east of Rosalyn Lane, a street that did not exist in the days of my youth. Mrs. Brannon was the former Effie Elliott. A plumber, Mr. Brannon owned and operated his own business, Brannon Plumbing Company. This property was not within the City Limits when the Brannons moved here, I believe the Smyrna City Limits ended at Guthrie Street at that time.

Mrs. Effie Brannon was a member of the Homemaker's Sunday School Class at First Baptis Church. She and my mother were good friends, and I was always aware that my parents had much respect for the Brannons. Mr. Brannon, a deacon at First Baptist Church, was one of those men like Mr. Hughes and others, who, I thought, God had appointed to be deacons, for they always seemed to be at the church.

Fain Brannon graduated from Smyrna High School in the Class of 1949. In 1950, Fain entered the United States Navy. He married Laurentine Aiken of Covington. They had two sons: James and Timothy, which they raised in Atlanta.

After graduating from high school, Fain played on the Smyrna Amateur Baseball Team, and again after his tour in the United States Navy. After being discharged from the Navy, Fain attended Georgia Institute of Technology, and established a mechanical contracting business, then later a min storage business. Laurentine, among the first teachers of Campbell High School, taught there from 1953-1959.

James Brannon graduated from Rhodes College and the Medical College of Georgia. He married Carmen Thorn of Atlanta. They live in Myrtle Beach, South Carolina, where he is an anesthesiologist.

Timothy Brannon lives in Atlanta, where he is a certified chef. He married and had two sons: Timothy and John.

Laurentine Brannon remembers her mother-in-law, Effie Brannon, saying, "When we first moved to this house, we could see, looking toward Smyrna, one other house in the distance.

Ernest Brannon was an uncle of Ethel O'Bryant, who lived on this property, and later moved to Concord Road near the Covered Bridge. Benny Lou O'Bryant, a member of the Smyrna High School Class of 1951, I knew well and remember the Brannons were related to her.

Mr. and Mrs Joseph Benjamin O'Bryant

Mr. and **Mrs. Joseph Benjamin O'Bryant** in 1939 moved to this house, which was located on the same property with the Ernest Brannon home.

The following memories of moving to Smyrna are shared by Benny Lou O'Bryant Tackett.

A New Beginning for A Young Farm Family

"The first thing I remember about Smyrna, Georgia, was the day we moved here in 1939. I was five years old. Daddy had no vehicle except a farm wagon and an old mule so he hired a friend of his with a truck to move our sparse household belongings from Forsyth County to Smyrna. That first memory of Smyrna was our crossing the railroad track on Roswell Street at Atlanta Street. It was noon, and Daddy had his friend stop the truck on the street in front of G.B.'s Place; Daddy went in and brought back hamburgers for us. I thought my hamburger, the first I had ever eaten, was the best thing I'd ever put into my mouth! Until this day, I can remember how good that hamburger tasted, and I loved G.B.'s hamburgers as long as he was in business on that corner.

"My Mother's uncle was Ernest Brannon. In the 1930s he was a pipe fitter (plumber) with the Tennessee Valley Authority. Because TVA projects in North Carolina and Tennessee were coming to an end, Uncle Ernest looked around for a home back in Georgia. He bought a farm on Powder Springs Road. My father, a farmer, at that time was a sharecropper on property in Forsyth County that belonged to my mother's grandmother (Uncle Ernest's mother). After Grandma Brannon had died in the fall of 1939, her property was sold. The new owner asked all the Brannon family members to vacate the property. With that, Uncle Ernest bought the place on Powder Springs Street and asked Daddy if he would move to Smyrna and farm the land for him.

"There were two houses on the property. One was the big white farmhouse, which still stands on Powder Springs Street just west of Campbell High School. To the north and down behind the white house was a barn, and just beyond the barn was a very small, unpainted three- room house. That was our new home. We moved in December; somehow I seem to remember that it was late in the month. I remember it was a clear, sunny day but cold.

"Upon arrival at our new home, Daddy immediately began to build a fire in the fireplace of the front room of the little house. About that time, a young man came to the door and said his mother sent him to invite us to come to their house until our house was warm. I believe the young man was Amos Johnson. The kind woman was his mother, Mrs. Duncan Johnson. She and my mother remained friends and shared telephone visits from time to time as long as Mr. Johnson lived. The Johnsons had several children: Virginia, Robert, Evelyn, Amos, and Gene. See *Johnson, eighteenth house.*

"Gene, my age, and I entered first grade at the same time. First grade was dismissed at 12:00 noon each day because the school bus didn't come to take us home until 2:00 p.m. Gene and I walked home together every day. The walk from Smyrna School took us down King Street, then Bank Street before our cutting through Harbin Street (now Hamby Street) to Powder Springs Street, and on to home. The city pavement and sidewalk ended about where the Guthrie Place stood on Powder Springs Street. (The City of Smyrna took pride in the fact that every main street within the City Limits was paved and had a sidewalk.) The city limits extended one-half mile in all directions from the Masonic Lodge on West Spring Street. Our house was not in the City limits"

NOTE: (The above information about the City Limits was according to the survey by Mr. Paul Hensley, Cobb County Surveyor.)

"From the end of the pavement to our house on Powder Springs Street was red clay on dry days and red mud on wet days! The distance from school to our homes was well over a mile, and we were just six years old! No one worried that we might be molested, for we knew everyone in every house along the way. We didn't have to worry about traffic either: very few people owned automobiles, and those that did were at work at that time of day. (Who today would allow a first grader to walk that route?)

"Today I can remember many of the houses and residents on Powder Springs Street in those days. At the end of the pavement, on the south side, was the Guthrie home: it was the biggest house there. On the right side lived Mrs. Ray, who worked in the school lunchroom. (Later the Hammontrees bought that place and made extensive renovations to the house, still standing.) There was a "Fleming" house in there somewhere, but I can't remember which side of the road it was on! I know that the Richards' home was the last house on the north side, next to the woods and a little creek that ran through a culvert underneath the street. Mrs. Richards' name was "Georgia." Mr. Richards was a mail carrier in Smyrna at one time; but, as I recall, he retired shortly after we moved to Smyrna. Mr. and Mrs. Richards were the parents of Allene Durham and the grandparents of Patricia and Richard Durham. Richard started first grade in Smyrna School the day I did, and we graduated in the Smyrna High School Class of 1951.

"From the Richards' home to our house was open farm land, but there was a beautiful home place about where Campbell High School is now located. Not easily seen from the road, it was surrounded by a beautiful grove of trees and was owned by the Sinyard Family. Daddy got to be friends with the family, and I remember visiting them from time to time. I also remember that Mr. Sinyard raised syrup cane. Daddy would take us over there in the fall to watch the syrup-making process. The owner of the syrup mill would come and set up the mill. Consisting first of an apparatus to squeeze the juice from the cane, this mechanism was pulled by a mule, which spent the entire day just going around and around, tugging that extractor while a person or persons kept feeding the cane into it. The juice, caught in some kind of vessel, was poured into a huge, flat, metal pan that sat atop a big log fire. The juice was cooked in that pan until it was thick and the syrup was just the right consistency. It was hot and meticulous work! One had to be careful that the fire didn't get too hot, for the juice would burn. Also, if cooked too long, the syrup would be dark and have a strong flavor.

Therefore, it took a highly experienced person to make cane syrup. I don't think there were any recipes written for the process!

"On the south side of the street, opposite the Sinyard farm, was a pretty place with a neat rock house. The George Howard Family lived there. Their son, Lioneal, now known as "Dewey," was about a year younger than I. He attended kindergarten on the first floor of the Old Masonic Hall. On many days, he walked home from school with Gene Johnson and me.

"The next house, past the Howards and on the south side of the street, was occupied by the Sanfords. I can't remember Mr. Sanford's given name, but Mrs. Sanford's name was 'Izzie.' They had two children at the time: Sammy and Jeannie. Izzie Sanford was a sister of Nettie Kelly. See *Kelly, Brown Circle.*

"Daddy raised cotton on the Powder Springs Street property next to the Sinyards. On the back side of the property he raised corn and hay to feed his cattle; on the other side of the house was the pasture, which butted right up to the yard. The livestock (cow, mule, and hogs) would come up to the fence and beg for food, whenever someone was out there. Mother and Daddy also had a vegetable garden, where they grew about everything we ate. On a ridge in the cotton field and to the right of the house were two or three long grape arbors. Those vines were just loaded with grapes in the summertime. Because my mother was a person who could never stand to see anything wasted, she made grape jelly and grape juice by the gallons—it seemed like!

"Across from Daddy's cotton field was a big farm owned by a Mr. Cheney and leased to the John Jackson Family. Mr. Jackson, a World War I veteran, would tell us grim stories of his experiences as a young soldier in France during World War I. I believe he was wounded in France and received a government pension for his service. The Jacksons later moved out to Roswell Road, across from where the Dobbins Radar Station now stands. (He lived to be a very old man, and I happened to be standing at his bedside when he died.) Mrs. Jackson, whose given name was Pearl, and John had four children: James, Becky, Ellen, and Johnny. All the children were teenagers when my family moved near them.

My mother, then 28 years old, had never been outside Forsyth County or spent time away from her family. Thus Cobb County must have seemed like a foreign land to her. The Jacksons, having become close friends, were always there to help Mother and Daddy with any problem or chore. Becky especially loved taking care of my brother, Reginald, who was six months old at the time. The Cheney property stretched all the way back to Church Street and what is now South Cobb Drive, from which you could see a little creek, across from the present location of Blockbusters, a video store. Mother would take us there on a summer morning so that she could pick blackberries by the creek, where my brother, Lamar and I would wade. (Those were the biggest and sweetest blackberries I have ever seen and what delicious jelly and cobblers they made!)

"I don't remember what year it was, but I remember the surveyors coming through that property and putting in grading stakes for the construction of a new highway. (Now South Cobb Drive, at the time it was simply known as the "Access Road.") Unknown to us, the road was to afford a direct route to a highly secretive military installation that we came to be know as Dobbins Air Force Base and Bell Aircraft Corporation. The year must have been about 1942. See, *Johnson, north side of Stephens Street.*

"Our neighbor, Mr. Duncan Johnson, was a carpenter. During the War, he got a job with a contractor that was building military installations all around Georgia and recommended Daddy for a job with them. During the rest of World War II Daddy and Mr. Johnson worked at one military installation and then another. It seemed Daddy was gone more than he was at home!

"In 1942, Uncle Ernest's job with the Tennessee Valley Authority ended. He and Aunt Effie and their son, Fain, moved into the house on Powder Springs Street. (I don't remember where the Johnsons moved to, but they stayed in Smyrna.) We moved to North Cooper Lake Road (referred to as

Cooper Lake Road then); Daddy worked for a construction company building the Bell Bomber Plant, where he later went to work. He became one of the thousands of people who took pride in having had a part in building the B-29 airplane that dropped the A-Bomb on Hiroshima, Japan, and thus ended the War.

"Uncle Ernest and Aunt Effie's house was on Powder Springs Street. They had a little white goat that, I assume, was a pet for Fain. That goat terrorized the place! He would butt us children and push us down, almost scaring us to death. He also pulled Mother's clean laundry off the clothesline, causing her to have to retrieve and re-wash it. She was constantly chasing that goat with the garden hoe, a rake, or a piece of stove wood, threatening to kill that goat if she ever caught it—but she never did! I remember a funny event that happened just after Aunt Effie, an immaculate housekeeper, had finished cleaning and waxing the most beautifully polished wooden floors that you can imagine. One day she had just finished cleaning and waxing the floors when, as she started out the front door to allow the floors to dry, the goat ran in, hit that wet wax, and slid on all four legs all the way across the living room. Although Aunt Effie later laughed when she told the story, I expect she was furious with that goat. I don't know what happened to that goat, but I don't remember seeing him after that."

Nineteenth House

"**Mr.** and **Mrs. Logan Nichols** and their two daughters, **Shirley** and **Ellen** lived here I do not recall who lived in the house to the west of Uncle Ernest and Aunt Effie. Shirley, a little younger, and I enjoyed playing together. On Sunday afternoon, December 7, 1941, I was at the Nichols' home when the news came over the radio that the Japanese had bombed Pearl Harbor. I was too young to know the full impact of what that meant, but I knew from my parents' and neighbors' reactions it was pretty serious, and I was afraid of what it meant. Surely enough, it meant pretty much the end of life as we knew it in Smyrna at that time. So many young men went off to war; several of them never returned. Our neighbor, Robert Johnson, went into the United States Army Air Corps (now known as United States Air Force) and was killed. I also remember that the son of Mr. McIntosh, the barber, was killed, as was Adolph Turley. I don't know how many other young Smyrna men were killed in that war, but those are the ones whose deaths impacted me, for they were the ones I knew personally." See *Johnson, south side of Stephens Street; McIntosh, south side of Bank Street;* and *Turley, west side of North Cooper Lake Road.*

Twentieth House

Henry Fortner married **Ruth McFall**; they had four children: **Alton**, **Diane**, **Sandra**, and **Mike**. Henry was self employed. See *next house.*

Twenty-first House

Mr. and **Mrs. George Fortner** were residents of this house. They had five sons and two daughters: **Robert**, known as "Hoofie," **Truman, Henry**, **William Tatum**, known as "W.T.," and **James E.**, known as "Bud," **Betty Lou**, and **Evelyn**. Mrs. Fortner was the former Ollie Susan Hamby. See *Fortner, both sides of Access Road, Hamby, north side of Love Street,* and *Redd, south side of Medlin Street.*

POWDER SPRINGS STREET
South Side

The following residents of Smyrna have been very generous in furnishing information about their families, who lived on the south side of Powder Springs Street in the middle of the Twentieth Century: Patricia Durham Baldwin; Joyce Lovern Davis; Dewey Lioneal Howard; Mildred Gann Hudlow; Chad Williams; and Ruby Langley Hunter.

NOTE: The Smyrna Woman's Club, which was on the southwest corner of Powder Springs and Atlanta streets, faced Atlanta Street.

First House

Mr. and **Mrs. James Lovern**, who had two children, **Joyce** and **Jimmy**, lived in this house, on the south side of Powder Springs Street, just behind the Smyrna Woman's Club. Mrs. Lovern was the former Johnnie Reynolds of Jackson County. Mr. Lovern, from Oconee County, owned and operated Lovern Construction Company.

When Johnnie Reynolds Lovern was in the eighth grade, her family moved from Jackson County to Bishop, in Oconee County. Due to the lack of transportation to the nearest high school, Johnnie was unable to continue her education. Because it bothered her that she did not get a high school education, she, after her two children were in school, enrolled at Patricia Stephens Finishing School in Atlanta, where she received her diploma.

James Lovern came to Smyrna in the spring of 1942. He left his job at Hannah Manufacturing Company in Athens and his family farm in Bishop to work for a construction company that was grading for the Bell Bomber Plant. He lived with his sister-in-law, Clara Parsons, on Walker Street, until he rented living quarters in a house on Roswell Street that had been divided into four apartments. Located on the north side of the street, this dwelling was next door to the Hamby House. James, Johnnie, and their young daughter, Joyce, lived there for a short time.

Learning that he could make more money at a shipyard in Savannah than he was making at the Bell Bomber Plant, James departed for Savannah—only to find there was a housing shortage. Though he boarded with Mrs. Helms, in a house for men, Johnnie and Joyce were allowed. A short time later, Johnnie found for the three of them, an upstairs apartment, in the home of Mr. and Mrs. Alfonso, on Oglethorpe Street. There they became lasting friends with Mr. and Mrs.Wings, who lived in the second upstairs apartment.

The major problem was that the Loverns had earlier had a taste of Smyrna, which had lingered. Thus James and his family moved back to Smyrna in the summer of 1943. Having sold his car, James bought a truck; then he established the Lovern Construction Company, a utility/construction contracting company, active through the years, building sewer and water systems throughout the north Georgia area. After returning to Smyrna, Mr. and Mrs. Lovern joined First Methodist Church, where they were faithful members for the rest of their lives.

NOTE: It is reported that Jim Barnes said he and some others (at ages 16/17) worked for James Lovern when he had his first business—hauling.

The Loverns, upon their return to Smyrna, rented an apartment from the Lawrence Butler Family. The apartment was in the Atlanta Street house, where the Lemon Sisters later lived. James and Johnnie were living there when their son, Jimmy, was born. They moved again to Concord Road into a rental house owned by Mr. Dunton; this house was "way out" toward the Covered Bridge. Johnnie would get very upset when something would happen to Joyce or Jimmy; therefore, Dr. Mitchell told James that he needed to "get Johnnie closer to town." When James explained that he could not find housing, Dr. Mitchell told him that his rental house on Powder Springs Street was available; James immediately rented the house. He and his family lived there until Dr. Mitchell made plans to build a parking lot and erect the Mitchell Building on the corner of Sunset Avenue and Powder Springs Street.

The Lovern House was the only one in this block that faced Powder Springs Street. The other houses, which faced the north side of Sunset Avenue, had property that extended all the way through to Powder Springs Street. The Sunset Avenue residents grew gardens and/or had livestock and chickens on their property.

Then James bought, from Emory Chastain, some land at the intersection of Jonquil Drive and Corn Road. (The property's mailing address was Jonquil Drive.) There James built his home and, later, his office for the J.E. Lovern Construction Company and Cobb County Concrete Products.

When James was relocating his family to Corn Road, Dr. Mitchell asked James to move the magnolia tree from the property on Powder Springs Street/Sunset Avenue to Dr. Mitchell's home on South Atlanta Street. That tree, which James dug up and replanted, is still living in the front yard of the Mitchell House. See Lovern,*south west side of Corn Road, and Mitchell, Atlanta Street from Marlowe's to Creatwood.*

Joyce Lovern Davis, who was in the fifth grade when her family moved from Powder Springs Street, shared her memories about some of the people that were their neighbors while she was growing up there. Joyce remembers fondly the Ed Skelton Family, who had two grown daughters, Jean and Frances, the latter working with John Matthews in Atlanta. She recalls going to church at First Methodist and seeing the Skeltons and the Chester Austin Family, who, along with the Guye Duncan Family across the street, were all great neighbors: with the Smyrna Library, located in the Woman's Club building, being next door to her house. Joyce fondly remembers Mrs. Williams, the librarian, who would call Joyce and Jimmy in and read to them. See *Williams, west side of Lee Street.*

The Loverns lived on Corn Road until 1987, when they built a house on the corner of Lakeshore Drive and Hurt Road. Because of his failing health, James liquidated Lovern Construction Company.

James Lovern was born November 20, 1916, and died February 12, 1997. Mrs. Johnnie Reynolds Lovern was born November 29, 1918, and died December 21, 2004. Both are buried in the Georgia Memorial Cemetery in Marietta.

Joyce Lovern, a graduate of the Campbell High School Class of 1955, married Miller Davis, a graduate of the Smyrna High School Class of 1951; they had four children: Dana, Mike, Bobby, and Brent. Joyce, Miller, and all of their children are members of First Methodist Church. Miller is a lifelong member; and Joyce, along with her family, joined in 1943. See *Davis Family, south side of Church Street* and *west side of Roswell Street.*

Dana Davis married; Alan Lamb they had two daughters: Janna and Kayla. Dana is a graduate of Campbell High School and West College College; her daughters are graduates of South Cobb High School.

Later on Dana Davis (Lamb) married Andy DeSandro of Florida. They live in Marietta.

Mike Davis married Karen Mize of Marietta. Karen and her family are very active in the M.U.S.T. Ministries organization in Marietta and Cobb County, where Karen is employed as an accountant; she also volunteers at the homeless shelter and soup kitchen on Elizabeth Street in Marietta. Mike, a graduate of Campbell High School and West Georgia College, in Carrollton, and Karen live in East Cobb County.

NOTE: There is also a very active M.U.S.T. Ministry in Smyrna. I was chairman of the Capital Campaign in 1998, to assist in raising money for M.U.S.T Ministries to purchase a permanent home. First they were located in Dr. Mainor's former office building on West Spring Street, next door to Smyrna Fire Station #1, with Dr. Bud Abbott leading the prayer of dedication; later they moved to the shopping center complex on the northwest corner of South Cobb Drive and Concord Road. When the monetary goal had been reached, property was bought at the southeast corner of Pat Mell and Old Concord roads; the existing building was razed; and a new one was erected in 1999. Susan Williams is the senior person in charge of Smyrna M.U.S.T.

Bobby Davis married Tina Rogers of Smyrna. They had two sons: James Rogers, known as "Jamie," and Luke Michael. Bobby, a graduate of Campbell High School, and Tina, a graduate of Wills High School, live in Smyrna.

Brent Davis, also a graduate of Campbell High School, is not married. He lives in Smyrna.

Miller Davis and I, members of the Smyrna High School Class of 1951, started and finished school together. We are the same age: my birthday is November 29, 1933, and his is December 5, 1933. We have lived within two to three blocks of each other most all of our lives. We still do!

Lillie and I moved to Havilon Way in 1969; Joyce and Miller had moved onto the street two years earlier. We two couples, who raised our children together, still live on Havilon Way and are good friends.

Jimmy Lovern married Donna Evans of Smyrna. They had three sons: James David, known as David, Daniel Edward, known as "Dan," and Barry William, known as Barry. Jimmy, Donna, and all three sons are graduates of Campbell High School. Jimmy died in 1979.

David Lovern married Lisa Brackett of Smyrna. They had two daughters: Laura Mayne and Jessica Nicole. Lisa Lovern graduated in the Campbell High School Class of 1984.

"Dan" Lovern married Cory Lively of Smyrna. They had one daughter, Kristin Ashley. Cory Lovern graduated in the Campbell High School Class of 1984.

Barry William Lovern married Tammy Maria Kraemer, a graduate of Campbell High School. They had one son and two daughters. Their first child, Jordan Hunter Lovern, died at birth, December 4, 1997. Their daughters are Angela Brooke and Abbigail Marie, known as "Abby." See *Turner, south side of Spring Road, The Country Road.*

Second House

The **Knox Family** lived in the this house, still on the south side of Powder Springs and Hamby streets, in a grove of trees off the road. Three of their children are **Nancy**, **Terry**, and **Gail**.

Third House

Mr. and **Mrs. Adrian Cochran** in the late 1940s built this nice brick house on the south side of Powder Springs Street, between the house in the grove and the Durham house. They had two children: Andrea and Billy. Mrs. Cochran, the former Wylene Smith, had a brother, Bill Smith.

Adrian and his brother, Crafton, who lived on the east side of Roswell Street, had a produce business; they used a large truck to haul produce to and from the Atlanta Farmer's Market, which was on Murphy Avenue. Wylene, who had been active in the Eastern Star, as well as Rainbows and DeMolays, died of cancer in her middle years. See *east side of Roswell Street* and *east side of Elizabeth Street.*

Andrea Cochran married Riston Smith (no relation to her mother) of the Grove Park community in Northwest Fulton County. They had four children: Rusty, Lisa, Susie, and Jeff. They also had five grandchildren.

Billy Cochran married and had three children, Angela, Todd, and Stephanie, and two grandchildren.

Fourth House

Homer Durham
Smyrna City Councilman
1947-1948

Mr. and **Mrs. Homer Durham** lived in the house next door to the Cochrans. Mrs. Durham was the former Allene Richards. The Durhams had two children: **Patricia** and **Richard**. Mr. Durham died in 1994 at age eighty-six; Mrs. Durham died in 2000 at age eighty-eight.

The following information was shared by Patricia Durham Baldwin: "My parents, moved to this house from Davis Road in 1943 when the runway at Dobbins Air Force Base was built too close for comfort to the our house on Davis Road. While our house on Powder Springs Street was being built, we moved in with my mother's parents, Mr. and Mrs. John Jacob Richards, on the north side of Powder Springs Street, located between Mrs. Belle Park's property and the creek. Across the creek the former Sinyard property was used to build F.T. Wills High School, which is now Campbell High School. At the present time, the Community Church sits on what was the Richards' property. See *north side of Powder Springs Street.*

"We moved into our new home on New Year's Eve, 1943. Powder Springs Street was not paved; and after much rain and traffic, the street was a quagmire of red mud and ruts. A truck couldn't get through, but the move had to be made that day in order for my parents to claim homestead exemption. Grandfather Richards hitched his horse, Dolly, to a wagon and moved the family to our new residence, where only the four-room basement was complete at that time. (Because of World War II, building materials were scarce.) My father retired from the railroad, where he was a pipe fitter and sheet metal worker."

Patricia Durham Baldwin also related the following story about her dad, Homer Durham, serving on the Smyrna City Council under Mayor Lorena Pruitt, who was Smyrna's only woman mayor and one of the first women mayors in Georgia. "He was instrumental in getting Smyrna's first fire truck and was generally on duty as a councilman during the day because he worked at night for the railroad. For example, when the City could not get anyone to climb up and inspect the inside of the Smyrna water tank, which had been unused for some time, Mrs. Pruitt got Daddy to do it. Because of these inspections, the City had to take out some extra hazard insurance. My mother was very nervous about this job, as I recall. Afterwards, I believe, the City again used the tank."

Patricia Durham graduated in 1948 from Smyrna High School, where she had played on the girls' basketball team. See *fifth house.*

Richard Durham and I were the same age. The two of us were members of the Smyrna High School Class of 1951, and both of us played basketball on the Smyrna High School "winning team" throughout our high school years. Richard and I had association through church as well.

After graduating from North Georgia College in Dahlonega, Richard married Margaret Kelly and lived much of his life in Florida and Tupelo, Mississippi. I did not see him very often after high school. In the mid 1990s, while his parents were still living, Richard's sister, Patricia, invited Lillie and me over to her home one evening to visit with him; on this nice occasion it was good to see him again. I am glad we had that time together, for Richard died in September 1999. (In Tupelo Richard was Vice President of Operations for Savings Oil Company when he died.) He is buried in the Cheatham Hill Cemetery in West Cobb County. Richard's widow still lives in Tupelo, and his only son lives on Lake Lanier in Cumming.

Mr. and Mrs. Homer Durham and their family were active members of First Baptist Church, where Mrs. Durham and my mother were both in the Homemaker's Sunday School Class for as long as I can remember; also they were friends who talked to each other often. Mr. Durham was a deacon at First Baptist Church. I miss them!

Fifth House

Patricia Durham married a hometown boy, **Bill Waldron**, who grew up on Concord Road They had two children: **Beverly** and **John**. Following their divorce, Patricia raised their children on Powder Springs Street in the house next door to her parents. The Waldrons were members of First Baptist Church. See *east side of Concord Road.*

Beverly Waldron married Philip Johnson, whose parents, George and Evelyn Johnson, were also members of First Baptist Church, where Beverly was the pianist for many years. Philip is a soloist and member of a quartet at First Baptist Church, where he sings in the choir. Beverly and Philip had three daughters: Melissa, Lara, and Nicole, reared on Powder Springs Street until they moved to East Cobb because of the transition that was taking place in Smyrna at the time.

John Waldron is a very talented young man who served First Baptist Church for many years by performing drama roles and helping to produce musical programs. He married Darlene Whatley of Douglasville, where they now live. They have one son, Bryant Wesley Waldron.

Patricia, in July 1975, married Chris Keisling, who passed away in October 2000. They lived throughout their married life on Powder Springs Street and Forest Drive, in the Forest Hills community, off Collier Drive. Chris also was a faithful member of First Baptist Church.

Patricia is now married to "Bob" Baldwin, who grew up on Concord Road. Bob and Patricia both joined First Baptist Church during a revival that was held from June 10-24, 1944, and were baptized on Sunday evening July 2, 1944. They attended Smyrna Elementary School and Smyrna High School, where they both enjoyed playing basketball. Bob is an active member of Lost Mountain Baptist Church in West Cobb County, where he has served as a trustee and is a deacon. Patricia and Bob currently live off Dallas Highway in West Cobb County. See *Baldwin west side of Concord Road.*

Sixth House

"T" and **Ethel McRae**, along with their son, **Richard P. McRae**, and Ethel's mother, **Mrs Emma Parker**, resided just beyond the Durham house. Mrs. Parker was a sister of Mrs. Austin, who lived on Bank Street with her daughter and son-in-law, Mary and Reed McCollum. See *south side of Bank Street.*

NOTE: In 1946 G.B. Williams built four houses past the McRae house: one for him and his family, one for Vonceil's mother and grandmother, and the next two for rent or sale.

Seventh House

Mr. and **Mrs. G.B. Williams** were residents of the house next door to the McRaes. They had three children: Mary Diane, James Daniel, known as "Danny," and Terry Dwayne. Mrs. Williams was the former Vonceil Curtis, whose grandparents, the Thompsons, owned much property off Davis Road, north of Smyrna. The first home of G.B. and Vonceil was an apartment in the Atlanta Street house where the Lemon Sisters later lived. "Buddy" and Virginia Weems resided in the other side of the house. From Atlanta Street Vonceil and G.B. moved to this house that G. B. built on Powder Springs Street. The Williams Family later moved to Hurt Road, where G.B. established a horse farm and a lake and where Vonceil still lives. G. B. passed away in 2002. See *Lemon Sisters, sixth house on Atlanta Street, from Mapps to R & M Café.*

Mary Diane Williams was born September 28, 1944. She married Johnnie Rae Acree; they had three children, John, Kevin, and Mark, and two grandchildren. Diane worked for the Cobb County Tax Commissioner's Office, and Johnnie worked for General Motors. Now retired, they live in Ellijay.

James Daniel Williams, known as "Danny," was born December 30, 1949. Never married, he was employed for many years at Coca-Cola Company; now he manages G.B.'s Lake, a fishing lake on Hurt Road near the Williams' home.

Terry Dwayne Williams was born June 20,1958. He and his wife, the former Karen Jane Glosson, had two children: Chad Spencer Williams, born November 6, 1984, and Kadie Elise Williams, born February 27, 1991. Since they married in 1979, Terry and Karen have lived on Hurt Road, next door to his parents. Terry worked at Georgia Tech for over twenty-six years; Karen works at Cobb County's Norton Park Elementary School. Along with Vonceil, Terry and his family attend Milford Baptist Church.

Chad Williams attends Kennesaw State University, where he is majoring in banking and finance. He has two related responsibilities: working at his grandmother's brokerage firm part-time and managing his grandparents' horse stables and other business enterprises his grandfather started.

Kadie Elise Williams, who attends Floyd Middle School, has been active in softball since the age of five.

Vonceil Curtis Williams was born to James Brady Curtis and Mary Thompson Curtis August 18, 1923, while they lived on Davis Road, north of Smyrna. When Vonceil was three years old, her parents' house burned; the family then moved to Canton, where her father had previously lived. After James Brady Curtis' death, in May 1940, Vonceil and her mother moved back to Smyrna, where her grandmother, Emma Thompson, lived. Her grandparents, Emma and Ephraim Thompson, had settled in Cobb County around 1918. Their farm was sold as part of the property that was bought by the United States Government for the building of the Bell Bomber Plant and surrounding facilities. After the sale of the home on Davis Road, Vonceil's grandmother, Emma, moved the family to Matthews Street, near Six Points. See *Thompson on Davis Road.*

Because Vonceil always loved to ride horses and her Aunt Viola Dean knew G.B. Williams, Vonceil's aunt arranged for Vonceil and G.B. to go horseback riding in August 1942. Vonceil was late getting home from work; while G.B. waited, the horses "got loose." G.B. was mad and said to Vonceil, "I am going to divorce you before we get married." Vonceil was not looking for a date; she was simply looking for a way to ride horses. Well, ride horses she did! For a month Vonceil and G.B. rode horses all over Smyrna—even on the dirt road that was being transformed into Cobb Parkway.

Vonceil and G.B. had known each other just that thirty-day period when he proposed. The couple was married October 22, 1942, by the Reverend E.B. Awtry, pastor of First Baptist Church, in his home on Love Street. Though G.B. and Vonceil had only known each other two months prior to being wed, their marriage lasted just three months short of sixty years.

Doug Stoner
Georgia State Representative
2002-2004
Georgia State Senator 2005-

G.B. and Vonceil's friends, Virginia and John Sargent, "stood up" with them at their wedding. The Sargents had two daughters: Dale and Judy. Virginia and John later opened the Dairy Queen on North Atlanta Road, near Turner Drive, which was a thriving business, they later moved to the present location on South Cobb Drive. It is owned and operated at the present time by one of the Sargent's daughters, Dale, and her husband, "Bogey" Stoner, and their son, Doug Stoner, a Georgia State Senator. Virginia and John Sargent, both deceased, had lived south of the Oakdale community, near the Chattahoochee River, before they later built a house on Pinetree Drive, in the Forest Hills community, where they resided the rest of their lives.

Once they were married, Vonceil and G.B. for about six months shared a home with the Weems Family on the north side of Powder Springs Street, across from the Woman's Club building.

Afterwards, G.B. and Vonceil moved to one of the houses which G.B. built, on the south side c
Powder Springs Street; there they remained until 1949, when they moved to Hurt Road. G.B. died a
his home on Hurt Road July 8, 2002.

Their grandson, Chad Williams, stated: "Without Grandmother much of Granddad's succes
would not have been possible, as she supported him through 'thick and thin.' She stood by his side n
matter what Granddad said. One night he brought home sixteen horses he had bought. He related t
me: 'Your grandmother didn't say a word; she just came out and helped me unload them. I could hav
brought home a pink elephant, and she would have been just as willing to help without questionin
me.' There was between them a trust, which was unlike any I had ever seen. They depended on eac
other, as a couple should. Grandmother probably didn't realize how much she was needed and wa
depended upon by Granddad.

"Grandmother is still actively involved in her community, serving in numerous positions i
civic organizations as well as having been a devoted member of Milford Baptist Church since 1950
She is the most active eighty-year-old I have ever seen: she is regularly seen working around her lak
and her yard or traveling with friends and family. Her work for the Lord to this day is her top priority
along with being the matriarch of the Williams Clan, which consists of three children, fiv
grandchildren, and two great-grandchildren."

The following stories furnished by Chad Williams, G.B.'s grandson, as a tribute to hi
grandfather, reflect the way G.B. lived his life. Many people in town could have shared these stories
which will be of interest to the people who knew and respected the unique personality of G.B
Williams, known to many people in Smyrna and Cobb County.

"Granddad always prided himself on being the gun salesman to the Smyrna Polic
Department. He said that whenever a new police officer was hired, the Chief would send him to G.B
because he had a larger selection of guns than that of the Police Department. To make sure it was
good gun, G.B. and the new deputy would test it in the middle of the café. Granddad said there wer
hundreds of rounds of bullet shells found in the building when G.B.'s Place was being demolished i
1989, for the widening of Atlanta Road.

"Once some neighbors called the police because there were some men shooting guns in th
pasture below G.B.'s home on Powder Springs Street. It ended up being the police and G.B. targe
shooting.

"One of my favorite stories of Granddad was that of the time he built a chicken house on hi
property on Hurt Road. Someone who had a disagreement with him had a relative that was a clerk a
the County Commissioner's office. The man reported to his relative that, because Granddad wa
building a structure without a permit, Granddad's property should be rezoned. As Granddad said, '
didn't want the property rezoned so I went to the office of Commissioner Herbert McCollum, the onl
county commissioner at this time. When Mr. McCollum asked me how far along I was with th
building, I told him it was already finished. 'Herbert came out and looked at the building and wen
back to his office.'

"Commissioner McCollum told that clerk (the same clerk who was related to the man wit
whom he had a disagreement), 'Write Mr. Williams out a permit.'

"The clerk said, 'Mr. McCollum, that is a big chicken house that needs to be rezoned.'

"Mr. McCollum responded, 'G.B. eats a lot of eggs.'
"G.B. said, 'If I were to try something like that now, they would have probably put the jai
on top of me.'

"I once asked Granddad why they didn't have any pets in his family when he was a child. H
responded, 'We didn't have anything to feed them.'

"Grandmother said, 'Well, we always fed our pets the scraps.'

"To that he remarked, 'Vonceil, we ate the scraps.'

"Granddad said he wished he had spent more time with his children, but he had also wished that his dad had, had some money; thus he tried to give his children what he didn't have. Everything he did was to make his children have it better than he did."

The following involves a conversation Chad Williams had with his granddad one Christmas. "Every Christmas Granddad would get some white lightning from different bootleggers and give it to the 'old timers' when they would come into the café. He said it was far more than he could handle. Granddad did mention one time that the police broke up a moonshine still down Spring Road (I believe near present-day Carolyn Drive). He said, the police chief called him to come to see it; and when he arrived, the police were loading up their cars with liquor to take home.

"I asked Granddad if the Depression hurt him and his family. He remarked, 'We never did know it. We were so poor we never did know the difference.'

Prior to 1936, Granddad was in charge of the City water pump. Because of a lack of wells in the City, a pump had to be run on an on/off hourly schedule. He also kept horses at Mr. Anderson's place on Roswell Street prior to the time he opened his café.

"Granddad went to Mrs. D.A. Ray to see about renting her little building next to the railroad track for his café, which later became G.B.'s Place. She said, it had been so long since anyone expressed interest in the building she did not know what to think. At the time there was an old wallpaper hanger who was staying there free of charge because Mrs. Ray felt sorry for him, for he couldn't afford to pay the rent. She didn't charge Granddad rent until he was able to pay, and when she did, she asked him if $5.00 was fair. He said that if he couldn't pay it, he shouldn't be in business.

"Granddad borrowed $50.00 from his dad to open the café. He had to pay $35.00 to have some electrical work done, leaving him $15.00 to buy things to make the building a café. He bought an icebox and six stools on credit (only time in his life). Paying 80¢ a case for drinks, he said he got rich selling them for 5¢ per bottle, which brought in $1.20 per case. After the purchase of ice to keep the drinks cool, he would make about 25¢ per case. He had a few customers for the first few days, but sometimes he wouldn't have more than $5.00 to $6.00 in the register after an entire day. The milkman made Granddad a sink to go under the water faucet that hung from the wall. When it was full of water, he had to dump in into a ditch outside. He said, 'Today they (the County Health Department) would never let me stay open.'

"Later Mrs. Ray wanted Granddad to buy the place for $350.00, but he didn't have the money at the time. After he did feel he was able to afford the price, he went to her. She said she would have to go up to $400.00 because of the improvements he had made. Granddad said, 'When I went to pay Mrs. Ray, I felt I needed the state militia for protection because I was carrying such big money.'

"At this time, there was no bank in Smyrna. There had been a bank located on the corner of Atlanta and Bank streets, which failed during the Great Depression. When Granddad was saving the money, he was storing it in the post office where it was a common practice to store money because it was not convenient to travel to a bank in Marietta. That is why Granddad and some of the other men in the community started the Bank of Smyrna.

NOTE: The bank referred to here was originally named the Bank of Smyrna; it is presently the Wachovia Bank.

"Granddad opened a second restaurant next door to Dr. Milton Collins' Drug Store. Gladys Collins, Dr. Milton Collins' wife, asked him to name it 'Blue Bird Café'; he did. At this café he had full meals that were served; on Sundays he had chicken dinners. Due to the fact that chicken wasn't sold in the grocery stores then, he had to go to a chicken farmer on Bells Ferry Road (after he closed midnight on Saturdays) and buy a load of chickens. He would then take them back to the kitchen of th restaurant to prepare them for cooking the next morning. Afterwards he would go into the little roo in the back of the café, where he had a small bed, and get some sleep. He hired Mrs. Jackson, a elderly Black lady who was a good cook, to be the manager of the Blue Bird Café.

"During World War II, when sugar and many other items were being rationed, Granddad went to the agency in charge of rationing at Coca-Cola to complain that he needed more drinks. The told him that he was already getting five cases more than the other merchants in Smyrna. He cam back home and did not push the issue any further.

"Local boys would stand along the railroad tracks whenever the trains with the serviceme would pass through. As the train slowed, the boys would collect money from soldiers, run into th café to buy cigarettes, soft drinks, hot dogs, etc., and then run back to the train with the merchandis for the troops before the train departed.

"Granddad bought land on Powder Springs Street from Mr. Guthrie for $600.00. It consiste of two lots, where he built four houses. He later bought the land that adjoined the back of his propert thus giving him frontage on Bank Street, where he built two houses. The Criders lived in one of thes houses; Granddad's sister, Edith Williams Hunton, her husband, Roy, and their children, Sammie an Betty, resided in the other one.

"Smyrna's first female Mayor, Lorena Pruitt, was soliciting money to put a fence aroun what is known today as the Smyrna Memorial Cemetery. Granddad told her, 'those people aren't goin to get out of there'; but he finally did give her a donation, and she eventually raised enough money t put up the fence."

G.B. Williams was one of the most genuine, down-to-earth people I have known througho my lifetime. I always knew without a doubt that, if I needed help, he would be there for me. He wa also this kind of friend to many people in Smyrna. G.B. went about his daily life, working hard an being himself. G.B. Williams died July 8, 2002.

NOTE: In addition to his horse farm and bank involvement, the business he was most note for was G.B.'s Place. See *G.B.'s Place* and an *interview by Chad Williams, north side of Spring Stree*

Eighth House

Mary Thompson Curtis and her mother, **Emma Thompson**, resided in this house, built fo them in 1946 by Mary's son-in-law, G.B. Williams. They remained here until Emma died, in 195 after which Mary moved to Hurt Road to live with her daughter and son-in-law, Vonceil and G.B until her death. See *seventh house*.

Ninth House

Mr. Randolph E. Weems, known as "Buddy," and his wife, the former Virginia Kitchens o Covington, had a son, **Lynn**, and a daughter, **Ann**. They were residents of this house, one of the fou that G.B. Williams built in the 1940s. Virginia died in an automobile accident in the autumn of 2004.

"Buddy" and Virginia together with G.B. and Vonceil earlier shared a house on Atlant Street

Tenth House

Raymond and **Vivian Motter** lived in this house, which they bought from G. B. William who built it. Raymond worked at G.B.'s Place as a young man, before he joined the United State Marines early in World War II. Vivian is deceased. See *Brasill Family, Atlanta Street, from Mile Streetcar Stop to the Motters* and *Spring Road, The Country Road.*

The Shumakes

Wayne and **Nelda Shumake** bought this house after Raymond and Vivian Motter had vacated. Virginia Gann McDaniel shared, "When I lived with my family on the north side of Powder Springs Street, Wayne and Nelda would walk down Powder Springs Street in the evenings on their way home from work. They would wave and speak to our family, on the corner of Hughes and Powder Springs streets. Soon they became like one of our family. They would come many nights and sit with us on our porch. When we would have vegetables out of the garden, they would help us shell peas, string beans, or shuck corn; whatever we were doing, they would join right in.

"They later said they were so jealous of our big family because they lived so far away from their own families: Nelda's, in Murphy, North Carolina, and Wayne's, in Roopville. Nelda, a hairdresser, in later years would go to my Aunt Emma's on Hughes Street and do her hair when she was not able to go to have it done."

Nelda retired after thirty-five years in hairdressing; Wayne retired after thirty-seven years in the Parts Division of General Motors. The Shumakes are faithful members of First Baptist Church.

Eleventh House

Mr. and **Mrs**. **Charley Clayton** raised their family in the next house. She, the former Maude Fraser, was the daughter of Mr. and Mrs. William Earnest Fraser, Sr., who lived farther out Powder Springs Street. Charley and Maude Clayton had four children, three daughters and a son: **Martha**, **Edna**, **Betty**, and **Johnny**. All three daughters married brothers.

Martha Clayton married Bill Hawkins, a plumber. They had three daughters and one son: Gail, Donna, Shantay, and Lynn. They lived off Roswell Street, on a short dirt street, now named Windy Hill Place, across from the Anderson and Barnes families. Later on they moved to Powder Springs Street, where they resided until Martha's early death.

Edna Clayton married Thomas Hawkins, a house painter and a Baptist minister. They had two daughters: Marilyn and Lorie.

Betty Clayton married Jimmy Hawkins, a pipe fitter. They had a daughter, Carol, and a son, Jimmy, Jr.

Johnny Clayton married Pat Terrell from Marietta. They had two daughters, Kelly and Melonie, and two sons, Rickie and Tony. Johnny, who owned an electrical company, later on built beautiful homes in Paulding County and around Lake Weiss in Cedar Bluff, Alabama, before his death on his sixty-seventh birthday, June 14, 2000.

Twelfth House

Mr. and **Mrs**. **Beverly Guthrie** lived next door to the Claytons. Mrs. Guthrie was the former Anna Corley of Gwinnett County. They were the parents of **Theron**, **Dallis**, and **Alice**, who were in my parents' generation. See *Atlanta Street, from Marlowe's to Creatwood.*

Theron Guthrie married Thelma Winter from Virginia. They had three children: Beverly, Patrick, and Theron, Jr.

Beverly and Patrick Guthrie were killed in an automobile accident in Tennessee when they were very small.

Theron Guthrie, Jr., is married and lives in Tennessee.

Dallis Guthrie married Colene Reed, a member of the B.F. Reed, Sr., Family, who lived c the east side of Atlanta Street in downtown Smyrna. See *Atlanta Street, from Mrs. Mazies Creatwood.*

Alice Guthrie married George Howard. They had two children: Dewey Lioneal and Jud See *George Howard Family, west side of Lee Street.*

I remember hearing my dad and Alice Guthrie Howard speak of their attending scho together and walking from this area on Powder Springs Street to Smyrna School. (This was when th school was in the Masonic Lodge Building on West Spring Street.) When my dad's family first can to Smyrna, in 1918, they lived for a while on the north side of Powder Springs Street, across from th Guthrie Family. My dad's family later moved to Roswell Street. See *Tucker, west side of Roswe Street.*

Thirteenth House

Mr. and **Mrs. William Earnest Fraser, Sr.**, resided next door to the Guthrie Famil Actually, Mr. Fraser's full name was William David Joseph George Reuben Sanford Jackson Fo Earnest Fraser, Sr. His grandfather was Simon Fraser, who came to this country from Scotland ar settled in Liberty County, near Savannah. Mr. Simon Fraser was an accountant and a minister. H accepted a job from Mr. Roswell King as the head bookkeeper at Roswell Mills in Roswell. His havi persuaded his son and daughter-in-law to name their oldest son after the past Kings of Scotland, is th reason for Mr. Fraser's many names. However, Mr. Fraser officially and commonly used only his fir and last given names, William Earnest.

Mr. William Earnest Fraser, Sr., was married to the former Nanni Bell from Kennesaw. M Fraser was a sister of Mr. Jim Bell, who lived on Fleming Street, where some of his descendan resided until early 2004, when their daughter-in-law, Mildred R. Bell, sold her property and moved a retirement home. Mr. and Mrs. Fraser had five daughters and one son: **Ethel**, **Maude**, **Willia Earnest, Jr.**, known as "Bill," **Sara Nell**, and **Leatha**. They had two other children who died infancy. See *north side of Fleming Street.*

Ruby Langley (Hunter), the granddaughter of William Earnest Fraser, Sr., shared th following information: "My grandfather owned ten acres of land that he farmed. It lay from his hou through to what is now Bank Street. In addition to farming, my grandfather raised livestock ar chickens. The Guthries, who lived next door, also owned ten acres, and the lay of the land was th same. Guthrie and Fraser streets, named for these two families, were cut on part of the Fraser a Guthrie farms when new developments began in the late 1940s and early 1950s.

Ethel Fraser was their oldest daughter. She worked at Davison-Paxon department store, Atlanta. When she married Alton Langley from Marietta, there was a home wedding, with Alton father, Reverend James Thomas Langley, my great-grandfather, officiating. Ethel had been a memb of First Methodist Church before she married; afterwards, she joined First Baptist Church, where all her family attended. She and Alton had five daughters and one son. See *Alton Langley, Old Roswe Road.*

In the early 1920s Mr. Fraser built a small house next to the creek for Ethel and her husban Alton. The three oldest Langley children, Mary, Sue, and Ruby, were born there.

When Ethel became pregnant with her fourth child, she thought the house was too small for anoth person; thus the family moved to a house on the north side of Fleming Street, next door to the Arch Tedder home. Their only son, Alton, Jr., was born in this house on October 22, 1929. Six weeks late while the Langleys were visiting with their across-the-street neighbors, the Gillhams, their residen on Fleming Street burned. They lost everything they had except their four children. With their alrea having had a hard time, the stock market crash occurring the same month and the Great Depressi setting in, life was very difficult for them.

Maude Fraser, listed previously, married Charlie Clayton. See *eleventh house.*

William Earnest Fraser, Jr., known as "Bill," married Mildred Parker from Gordon. They had two daughters, Nancy and Elizabeth, both of whom married ministers. "Bill," in the United States Army, served in Burma during World War II.

Nancy Fraser married Richard Hemphill. They had two sons, Allen and Tim, and one daughter, Renae. Richard, a Southern Baptist minister, was Pastor at Trinity Baptist Church in Smyrna, which was located on Atlanta Street, across from the Brawner Hospital. (Later the name was changed to Brawner Psychiatric Institute.) When the downtown redevelopment began on Atlanta Street, the Church sold its property and relocated to Pair Road in West Cobb County where Richard is still the pastor.

Elizabeth Fraser married Jimmy Owens from the Oakdale community, south of Smyrna. They had two sons, Doyle and Mark, both of whom are ministers. Jimmy Owens is deceased. Elizabeth is now married to Dewain Seese; they reside in Lakeland, Florida.

Sara Nell Fraser married Henry Foster from Marietta. They had three sons: Jim, Wayne, and Harry.

Leatha Fraser married Andrew Hembree. They had two children: Andrea and Bill.

Fourteenth House

Mr. and **Mrs. Guy Lackey** lived in the next house, beyond the creek from the Frasers. They had two children: Bobby and Betty. Mrs. Lackey was the former Irene Edwards from Jersey (ten miles from both Monroe and Covington). Mrs. Lackey had a brother, J.B. Edwards, who lived in Marietta.

The Lackeys moved from this house to Concord Road, in the vicinity of where Vickery Hardware and Sherwin Williams Paint stores are currently located.

Guy Lackey grew up on Neal Street in Atlanta and graduated from Georgia Institute of Technology. His sister, Grace, married Ernest Disharoon, who worked for Western Electric Company in New York.

Mr. Lackey, a civil service worker, was employed at Bell Aircraft Corporation, in Marietta, and later at Fort McPherson for about two years. In the early 1950s, he was transferred to Ft. Walton Beach, Florida. The Lackey Family were members of First Baptist Church, where Mr. Lackey was a member of the choir.

Bobby Lackey and his wife, Carolyn, live in Lawrenceville. They had one son, Brian. Bobby remembers, "When I lived in Smyrna, I had a summer job, delivering milk from door to door."

Betty Lackey married John B. George; they had one son, Sean. Betty and John reside in Melbourne, Florida.

Betty Lackey was in the fourth grade with Janet Brooks (Brown). Betty would take banana nut bread to school with her lunch and would share it. She took the recipe so that Janet's mother could use it. Janet, who still uses that same recipe, said: "The banana nut bread is delicious! Every time I make it, I remember Betty."

Mr. and Mrs. Warren Berry Lackey

Mr. and **Mrs. Warren Berry Lackey**, the parents of Guy Lackey, were residents of another house located on the property as Guy and his family. Mrs. Lackey's given name was Elizabeth.

Fifteenth House

The **Johnson Family**, Bobby Lackey remembers, lived in the house just west of his family.

NOTE: These were the last houses that I remember being on the south side of Powde Springs Street before it crossed the Access Road, known today as South Cobb Drive.

POWDER SPRINGS ROAD
The Country Road
South Side

Appreciation is extended to Mildred Gann Hudlow for sharing information about her famil who lived on Powder Springs Road, "The Country Road."

First House

Mr. and **Mrs. William Henry Gann** lived on the south side of Powder Springs Road. Mr Gann was the former Bertha Reynolds. They had ten children: **Rilla Mae**, **Annie Lou**, **Mary Franki** **William Henry**, **Jr.**, **Margaret**, **Tom Hicks**, **Mildred**, known as "Millie," **Lamar**, **Jimmy**, an **Virginia**.

The Gann house was located on Powder Springs Road, about midway between the Acces Road and Old Concord Road. Powder Springs Road beyond the Access Road (now South Cobb Driv was not in the Smyrna City Limits. In the days of my youth Mr. Henry Gann was Smyrna's Chief Police. I remember that he would patrol the area in a pickup truck.

Rilla Mae Gann died at the age of sixteen.

Annie Lou Gann married Edward Holbrook, a native of England. They had three children.

Mary Frankie Gann married Jimmy Pierce of Smyrna. They had three children.

William Henry Gann, Jr. ., married Rose Mankin from West Virginia. They had thre children. One son died as an infant in a hospital.

Margaret Gann married Henry Payton. They had three children.

Tom Hicks Gann married Geraldine Fain, known as "Gerry," from the Fair Oaks communit They had two children.

Mildred Gann,, known as "Millie," married Robert G. Hudlow, known as "Bobby," Smyrna. They had two children: Kenneth, known as "Kenny," and Donna Jean, who died at ag fourteen in 1974. "Bobby" Hudlow, 74 years old, died July 28, 2005.

Robert G. Hudlow was known as "Bobby." In 1945 along with his parents, Elsie and Fre Hudlow, and younger sister, Joy, moved from Marietta to Campbell Road, located near Aunt Fanny' Cabin. Joy married Earnest Earwood of Atlanta; they had two children.

Elsie and Fred had two older sons, Cecil and Edward, who lived in Columbus.

While in high school, "Bobby" worked for Rust Cheese Company. Later he retired fro Lockheed Aircraft Corporation in Marietta.

Fred Hudlow worked for Creatwood Dairies. Working at Aunt Fanny's Cabin for twent seven years, Elsie Hudlow took reservations in the mornings and cashiered in the evenings.

NOTE: Located on Campbell Road, south of Smyrna, Aunt Fanny's Cabin was known throughout the Atlanta area and the southeast. Harvey Hester was the owner and operator of Aunt Fanny's Cabin in those days. With a unique and colorful atmosphere, the Cabin enticed many celebrities from different parts of the country to dine there. When the Cabin closed in the 1990s, the City of Smyrna purchased the Cabin during the Smyrna renovation period, and had it moved to Atlanta Street next door to the Smyrna Museum. Today it serves as the Smyrna Welcome Center and is a much-visited location.

Lamar Gann married Joanne Metcalf from Vermont. They had three children. Their daughter, Karen, is married to Ron Lomax; together they serve as Southern Baptist missionaries in Cape Town, South Africa.

Jimmy Gann married Joyce Gayton. They had two children.

Virginia Gann married Phillip Turner of Austell. They had three children.

FULLER STREET

Fuller Street, about a block long, turned off the north side of Powder Springs Street a short distance from Atlanta Street. Jeanie recalls that there were only three houses on this street.

Appreciation is extended to Jeanie Harrelson Jeffares for sharing information about her husband's family, who lived on Fuller Street. Her mother-in-law was still living there when the City of Smyrna bought the property for the Community Center and Village Green.

According to long-time resident Ida Mae Clayton, who came to this street as a bride in 1931, Fuller Street was called "Sally's Alley" at that time. She still calls it that.

First House

Mr. and **Mrs. Forrest Jeffares** lived on the west side of Fuller Street. Mrs. Jeffares was the former Annie Lee Bagwell from Marietta; Mr. Jeffares grew up in Atlanta. They had six children: **Edward, Harold**, **Jean**, **Dan**, **Mildred**, and **Richard**.

Edward Jeffares
United States Marine Corps
World War II Casualty

Edward Jeffares, in the United States Marine Corps, was killed on Iwo Jima during World War II.

Harold Jeffares married Jeanie Harrelson of the Oakdale community. They had four children: Diane, Edward, Greg, and Russell.

Harold, who served in the United States Marine Corps during World War II, was active in American Legion Post #160, in Smyrna. Employed by Cowan Supply Company, Harold died while he was still a young man.

Jeanie Harrelson Jeffares graduated from Fitzhugh Lee High School in Oakdale, south of Smyrna. She and her children were active members of First Baptist Church, where she is a faithful member of the Friendship Sunday School Class.

Dan Jeffares, who was in the United States Marine Corps, served in the Korean Conflict during the early 1950s. He is deceased.

Richard Jeffares. served in the United States Air Force in Vietnam. He is deceased.

Jean Jeffares was a member of the Smyrna High School Class of 1951. Jean, who died i 1974, had never married. Harold's sister, Jean, and I graduated in the Smyrna High School Class c 1951. I would see Jean often when she worked at Fulton National Bank, in Atlanta. Jean, only in h early thirties, when she died in 1974, was the first member of the Smyrna High School Class of 195 to pass away. She was forty-one years old. See *Jeffares, Fuller Street.*

Mildred Jeffares, married Gilbert Hoffman; they live in San Antonio, Texas.

The Jeffares' house on Fuller Street was demolished in the late 1980s for the building of th Smyrna Community Center. A creek behind the Jeffares house on Fuller Street was redirected int what is now the lake beside the Community Center.

Jeanie shared with me that her mother-in-law, Mrs. Annie Lee Jeffares, had a well at the sid of her house on Fuller Street. The well had been inactive since the house was piped for City wat many years earlier; however, when "little Jessica" fell into the well in Texas (a high profile rescue th the entire country watched on national television), Mrs. Jeffares was reminded of her well. She went the City of Smyrna and asked that her well be covered. Her house was one of several in this are bought by the City of Smyrna in the late 1980s for the building of the Smyrna Community Cente built in front of Mrs. Jeffares' well, which is still there—but covered.

Second House

Mr. and **Mrs**. **Duncan** resided here. They were the parents of Guye Duncan, who served Mayor of Smyrna, 1953-1954. Guye and his family lived on Powder Springs Street, around the corn from his parents. See *north side of Powder Springs Street.*

Third House

The **"Buck" Pope Family**, according to "Bill" Scoggins, lived here. "Buck" was a barber George Waites' shop on Atlanta Street. George acquired ownership of the barber shop that w formerly run by Ralph Argo and Roy McLarty.

CHAPTER EIGHT

FLEMING STREET

North Side

Appreciation is extended to Ruby Langley Hunter, Virginia Gann McDaniel, Carolyn Bell Sanders, Beverly Cobb Amacker and her mother, Edna Ledbetter Cobb, for sharing their memories of the residents on Fleming Street, and to Patricia Durham Baldwin and Charles Mobley for furnishing information on their grandparents, Mr. and Mrs. Charles Thomas Durham.

Carolyn Bell Sanders' family moved to Fleming Street in 1942. Her grandfather, Jim Bell, and her dad, Hugh, built a number of houses in Smyrna in the 1940s and 1950s. One of the finer homes they built was the Wyckoff House, on the southeast corner of Hughes and Fleming streets. Carolyn remembers playing in this house when it was under construction and going up and down the stairs. Her mother, Mildred R. Bell, the last member of the Bell Family to live on Fleming Street, sold the family dwelling in 2004 and moved to a retirement home.

Appreciation is extended to Janet Brooks Brown, a Fleming descendant, who furnished the following information about the Fleming and Gillham families in Smyrna. Elijah Fleming was her great-great-great-grandfather; his tombstone is the oldest dated marker in the Smyrna Memorial Cemetery. Fleming Street was named for the Fleming Family.

The Fleming/Gillham Families

Fleming Street begins at the Pinecrest Streetcar Stop, on Atlanta Street, and currently runs to the parking lot entrance of Campbell High School. The Fleming Plantation House was located on the site of the present Campbell High School. Gay Nell Bowman Cochran, who grew up on Powder Springs Street and remembers the Fleming Estate, said "the entrance to the plantation began about where Fleming Street ends in front of Campbell High School." The road to the plantation house was a beautiful tree-lined driveway, about a quarter of a mile long. A large portion of the Smyrna area of that day was farm land; this farm belonged to **John N. Fleming**; and later his son, **William Richard Fleming**, who lived elsewhere on the farm land. Still later, the farm was divided among John N. Fleming's children.

NOTE: John N. Fleming fought with the Confederate Army, in the Civil War. See *Brooks, south side of Walker Street.*

William Richard Fleming, the son of Huldy A. and John N. Fleming, married Emily Albertina Brown, known as "Emmer," in 1886. William Richard and Emmer had six children: two daughters, Marrie and Willie, and four sons, Arthur, Gene, Tom, and Weaver. They raised their children on part of the Fleming farm located on land where Fleming and where Powder Springs streets were later cut. According to information from the neighborhood, the Jimmy Pierce Family afterwards bought William Richard and "Emmer Fleming's" house on the north side of Powder Springs Street.

The lake in the Smyrna Community Center complex area was created from a spring the Fleming Family used for drinking water. See *Bowman, north side of Powder Springs Street.*

Marrie Catherine Fleming, the only Fleming child to marry and have a family, became the wife of William Pierce Gillham of Cobb County. They had eight children: **Georgia**, **Emmer**, **Virginia**, known as "Jennie," **Nina**, **Pierce**, **Jr.**, **Billy**, **Gene**, and **Gwen**. The Gillhams raised their family on both Fleming and Powder Springs streets.

Pierce Gillham was a well-known builder and stone mason. Edgar Anderson contracted him to do masonry construction at Stonewall Court, now just a memory. This tourist court, a fine one, with one room cabins and a stone exterior, was located on the west side of South Atlanta Road across from Paces Ferry Road. Stonewall Tourist Court was one of many which were built on the old Dixie

The William Pierce Gillham Family
Back Row L-R: Marrie Gillham, holding Son, Billy, George Gillham, and William Pierce Gillham, Sr.
Front Row L-R: Emmer Gillham, Jennie Gillham, William Pierce Gillham, Jr., and Nina Gillham.
Circa 1930
Courtesy of Janet Brooks Brown.

Highway, the main north/south route to Florida, in the early-to-mid Twentieth Century. See *Stonewall Court, Atlanta Street, from Marlowe's to Creatwood.*

Georgia Gillham married Clarence Brooks. See *Walker Street* and *east side of Roswell Street.*

Emmer Gillham married Carl Cohran of Atlanta; they had one son, Frank. Emmer later married Ben Jones of Atlanta. After Ben's death, she married Harold Dunn, a long-time resident of Smyrna.

Frank Cohran, an artist, married Darthy Richardson of Camp Highland Road in the Oakdale community. They had two sons: Kenny and Kyle. Kenny died from leukemia as a child. Frank and Darthy live in Bowden.

Virginia Gillham, known as "Jennie," was a self-taught artist. She married Clemon Richards; they had two children: Joyce and James. "Jennie" later married Dewey Powell.

Nina Gillham married Homer Brooks, known as "Joby." He was a member of the large Brooks Family on Roswell Street. *See Brooks, east side of Roswell Street.*

William Pierce Gillham, Jr. , married Madon Holmes, a member of the Smyrna High School Class of 1948. They had two children: David and Carol. The Holmes Family lived in the Guernsey Jug at Creatwood Dairy Farm, where Madon's dad was the dairyman. Pierce died July 27, 2005.

David Gillham married Harriett, a teacher with the Cobb County Board of Education. They had no children.

Carol Gillham married Danny Tadlock; they had three children: Sherel, Christina, and Jason David, and two grandchildren.

Gene Gillham died when he was a small child.

For Billy Gillham, we have no further information.

Gwen Gillham, who graduated from Osborne High School in 1959, married Carl Hughes. They had three children: Vickie, Mac, and Tim, and several grandchildren.

Marrie and Pierce Gillham, having raised their family on Fleming and Powder Springs streets, later moved to Broad Street, which was formerly Pat Mell Road. In the early 1940s, the Gillhams, along with Marrie's brothers (Arthur, Tom, and Weaver) moved to a farm on Favor Road in Marietta.

Arthur Fleming worked for King Plow Company in Atlanta and drove a "T Model" Ford as late as the 1960s, and Tom and Weaver worked the farm.

William Pierce Gillham had two sisters, Leila Martin and Irene McLarty, and a brother, Mayes Gillham.

First House

The **Cobb Family** and the **Roy Wood Family** lived in this duplex, located on the north side of the street, behind the Willie Mapp House, where my sister, Hilda, and I were born, September 1, 1931, and November 29, 1933, respectively. (The Mapp house faced Atlanta Street.)

Mr. and **Mrs. Cobb** lived in the other side of the duplex. "Miss Gertie," which was what my family called her, lived here for the rest of her life; I never knew what Mr. Cobb's given name was. I seem to remember that "Miss Gertie" was a mid-wife and assisted in delivering babies in Smyrna. If she helped deliver me no one ever talked about, for adults did not talk about things of that nature when I was a child. The Cobbs were good friends with my parents.

The Phagan Durham Family

At a later time **Phagan** and **Dorothy Williams Durham** and their daughter, **Priscilla,** known as "Prissy," were residents of this house See *Durham, south side of Spring Street.*

Mr. and **Mrs. Ed Tinsley**

Louise and **Ed Tinsley** also lived in this house before they built a new one across the street, and moved there. Louise shared with me that she and Ed moved to this house after my family moved to Hill Street. See *south side of Fleming Street* and *west side of Gilbert Street.*

Second House

The Charles Thomas Durham Family

Mr. Charles Thomas Durham, a railroad engineer, and his wife **Bessie**, purchased this property, along with the property where the first house was located; they moved here from Kennesaw, in 1925, to be closer to Mr. Durham's work. The last few years of his employment, Mr. Durham engineered a passenger train. Mr. and Mrs. Durham had six children, who were in my parents' generation: **Hiram**, **Charlie**, **Homer**, **Mary Lou**, **Delia**, and **Wylie**. See *Durham, south side of Spring Street.*

Hiram and Charlie Durham, who moved from Smyrna when they were young men, now live in California.

Homer Durham married Allene Richards. See *Durham, on the south side of Powder Springs Street* and *Richards on the north side Powder Springs Street*, and *Davis Road.*

Mary Lou Durham, who never married, lived on Fleming Street until 1971.

Delia Durham, married Ralph Mobley; they had two sons: Charles and Ralph. Mr. Mobley worked for Cotton States Producers Association, later known as Gold Kist.

Mary Lou and Delia, who had attended high school in Marietta, worked at Fort McPherson in East Point.

Wylie Durham married Wyonna; they had two children: June and Jerry. Sometime 1950s they built a house in the garden area of his mother's property.

Third House

Mr. and **Mrs. Edgar Brantley Spratlin, Sr.**, resided here, Mrs. Spratlin was the former Cynthia Naomi Varner. They had four children: Floy, Edgar, Jr., Sybil, and Robert Martin. Mr. Spratlin worked for Simmons Mattress Company.

Floy Spratlin married James Robert Harris; they had two children.

Edgar Brantley Spratlin, Jr., married Daisey Mae Puckett; they had five children.

Sybil Spratlin was one year old when she died.

Mr. and **Mrs. Edgar Spratlin, Sr.**
Fleming Street
Early 1940s

Bob Spratlin
Smyrna High School
1940

L-R: **Bob Spratlin** and **Wylie Durham**
Next Door Neighbors on Fleming Street
During World War II

Robert Martin Spratlin married Virginia Ann Dempsey. They had two children: Suzanne and Lynn. Robert, known as "Bob" was a member of the United States Merchant Marines during World War II. Afterwards, he was the head buyer for Colonial Stores.

Suzanne Spratlin married Dan Scoggins. They had two children: Michele and Michael. Suzanne later married Sid Walker, they live in Smyrna. Sid worked for Federal Reserve Bank in Atlanta for 39 years; he is retired. Suzanne worked in the legal profession for 30 years; she is retired.

Lynn Spratlin married Robert Leon Ash, Jr, known as "Bob." They had four children: twin daughters, Laurie and Julie, and Andrew and Emily. Lynn and "Bob" live in Acworth. "Bob" Ash, Jr., is the son of "Bob" and Carolyn Ash. "Bob" Ash, Sr. was the basketball and baseball coach at Fitzhugh Lee High School in the early 1950s, and later the Principal of Campbell High School. They live in Smyrna. "Bob" Ash, Jr. is an Agency Director for the Cobb County Government.

Fourth House

Mr. and **Mrs. Will Ledbetter** moved to this house about 1930. They had five children, who were in my parents' generation: **Bill, Madeline, Ed, Edna,** and **Bob**. Mrs. Ledbetter was the former Reba Carter.

When they first moved to Smyrna, the Ledbetter Family lived in a two-story house farther down the north side of Fleming Street. Their neighbors were the Luther Tedders.

Bob Ledbetter played football for Boys High and Brown High schools in Atlanta. One of his teammates was Sid Williams, founder of Life University in Marietta. Bob currently lives in Americus.

Edna Ledbetter married Ralph Cobb, who was a member of the William Virgil Cobb Family on Church Street and, later, Old Concord Road. See *Church Street* and *Old Concord Road.*

The Black Family

A family named **Black** moved here, after the Ledbetters had vacated.

The Willis/ Evans Families

The **Willis/Evans families** moved from Highland Avenue to this house on Fleming Street. Mrs. Evans given name was Grace. Their son, **Wayne Evans**, was born while they lived here. Mrs. Evans moved from Fleming to the Bank Street house, where the Howard Scoggins Family had lived. I seem to recall that they moved to Bank Street after I had finished high school in 1951. Because I never knew Mr. Evans, I believe he must have died while they lived on Fleming Street. Mrs. Evans had two children, Miles and Dorothy, by a previous marriage; Mr. Evans, formerly married, had three young sons: Harold, Kenneth, and Harry.

Miles Willis married Eleanor Eaton, who grew up on King Springs Road. They live in Marietta.

Dorothy Willis married Martin Ruff, a member of the Ruff Family on Concord Road. They had one daughter, Paula.

Harry Evans married Lucy Mitchell, the daughter of Dr. and Mrs. W.C. Mitchell.

Wayne Evans, a graduate of the Campbell High School Class of 1960 is deceased.

Mrs. Grace Evans, Harry Evans, Miles, and Dorothy were all members of First Baptist Church. See *King Street, King Springs Road, Highland Avenue,* and *Bank Street.*

Fifth House

Mr. and **Mrs**. **Archie Tedder**, from my earliest memories, lived here; they had two children: **Lamar** and **Janet**. Lamar, and I started and finished school together; Lamar was president of our senior class.

I remember Mr. Archie Tedder, a kind and gentle man, as being rather large. He owned and operated the Pinecrest Pottery Shop on the east side of his house, which along with the house, is still standing. I believe the name of the shop, was derived from the streetcar stop located on Atlanta Street at Fleming Street. I remember going to the Tedders house to watch Mr. Tedder work with the clay; I thought it was fun to watch him mold the clay into items of many shapes. Because clay molding looked hard, I never tried to mold clay myself.

I know that Mr. Tedder was employed at Georgia Institute of Technology. Though I am not sure, I believe he worked with ceramics there.

I liked going to the Tedder home to visit; Mrs. Tedder was a kind lady who always made me feel welcomed. The Tedders had one of the nicest houses on Fleming Street—that is, unless one looked closely at Mrs. Bradley's house. They both lived here for the rest of their lives.

Lamar Tedder married Sara Page Camp, the daughter of Mr. and Mrs. Leslie Camp, who lived on the east side of South Atlanta Road. (Their house stood in the area across from Brawner Hospital.) Lamar and Sara Page had two children: Kellie and Charlie. Lamar died at the age of 50 due to heart problems. He was my friend, and I still miss him! Sara Page died several years after Lamar. See *Atlanta Street from Mrs. Mazie's to Creatwood Farm.*

Janet Tedder was a very special person to her family, the neighborhood, and her church. After their parents had died, Lamar very lovingly cared for her and saw that her needs were met.

Sixth House

Mr. and **Mrs**. **Hugh Bell** built this house in 1942 on property previously a part of the Jim Bell property. Hugh and Mildred had three children at the time; their fourth child, Tony, was born in this house. After Hugh died, in 1989, Mildred continued to live here until the fall of 2004, when she sold the property for redevelopment.

Mildred, the former Mildred Roberts of Marietta, and Hugh Bell had nine children: **Annette**, **Carolyn**, **Charles**, **Tony**, **Diane**, **Joe**, **Neil**, **Jimmy**, and **Susan**. Hugh, a carpenter and brick mason, served in the United States Army during World War II. Mildred is a member of First Baptist Church.

Annette Bell married Quinton Hamby, who grew up on Roswell Street. They had two sons: Kenneth and Michael. When Lillie and I first married, we moved into the Southern Manor Apartment complex, the first one on Davis street off Church Street. Annette and Quinton lived in the first unit of this building; Lillie and I resided in the second one.

Carolyn Bell married Larry Joe Sanders, who grew up in Smyrna and at one time, attended school with me. In his mid life, Larry passed away a few years ago after a long illness. Carolyn and Larry had one son, Alan. Carolyn Sanders is a member of First Baptist Church, where she has been teaching in the Children's Sunday School Department for more than thirty-five years.

Alan Sanders married Marcia Marez; they had two children: Annie and Dylan.

Dylan Sanders married Rondi Shelton; they had one son, Hayden. Later on, Dylan married Amanda Filliat; they had one son, Logan.

Charles Bell married Patricia Reeves of North Carolina. They had two sons, Chuck and Nathan, and a daughter, Selena. Charles died in 1995.

Tony Bell married Janet Black, known as "Dolly," of Marietta. They had three children: Jerry, Wende, and Robin. "Dolly" died in 1989.

Diane Bell married Robert Young of Atlanta. They had a daughter, Dana, and a son, Rob.

Joe Bell married Joann Vaughn of Smyrna; they had one son, Joey.

Neil Bell married Jane from Florida; they had one daughter, Natalie.

Jimmy Bell married Joan Porter; they had a daughter, Shanda, and a son, Ben.

Susan Bell married Tommy Stokely; they had a daughter, Kayla.

NOTE: Mildred Bell, a daughter-in-law of Mr. and Mrs. Jim Bell sold her property on Fleming Street in 2005 and moved to Delmar Gardens Retirement Center. She was the last member of the Bell Family to live on Fleming Street after more than sixty years.

Seventh House

Mr. James (Jim) Bell and **Pearl Gentry** met on Christmas Eve, 1904, when he had to carry her groceries home from his uncle's store, where Jim worked. "She could have carried them herself, but my uncle was trying to fix us up," said Mr. Bell with a chuckle. "And it worked too! From then until October, I didn't stay away." On October 1, 1905, they "ran away" to get married. (She was sixteen, and he was seventeen.) Having celebrated their 70th wedding anniversary in 1975, Mr. Bell died February 25, 1976. Mrs. Bell is also deceased.

The Bells had four daughters and five sons: **Geneva**, **Emmaline**, **C.J.**, **Hugh**, **Earl**, **Stella Mae**, **Frank** and **Frances**, (the latter were twins), and **Bobby**. When I was a small boy living on Grady Street, I remember Mr. and Mrs. Bell were residents on the north side of Powder Springs Street. They moved from there to the seventh house on the north side of Fleming Street in the late 1930s. In 1951 they moved from Fleming Street to Macland Road in Marietta.

Jim Bell was a native of Cobb County and a charter member of Nelms Lodge #323 F&AM. He and Pearl were members of First Methodist Church.

Mr. Bell was a carpenter. He and his sons built several houses in Smyrna, in addition to remodeling many others. He and his son, Hugh, built the house where the Hugh Bell Family lived on Fleming Street.

During World War II Mr. and Mrs. Bell had four sons and a son-in-law serving in the United States Military at the same time.

Geneva Bell married King Story of Powder Springs. They had two children: Dorothy and Marvin. King and Geneva, having lived most of their married years in Charleston, South Carolina, later moved to Dallas, Texas, where King worked for a few years as a glazer for a large manufacturing company. Then they returned to Cobb County, where they resided the rest of their lives. Dorothy, Marvin, and their families currently live in Cobb County.

Emmaline Bell married Oscar Turner of Marietta, where they lived and Oscar worked many years for Saul's Department Store. They had two daughters: Joann and Charlotte.

Joann Turner married Charles Perry. Joann is now deceased.

Pearl Gentry and **James S. Bell**
Sixty-fifth Wedding Anniversary. October 1, 1970
Courtesy of Carolyn Bell Sanders

James S. and **Pearl Bell** in 1970
With their children
L-R: Earl Bell, Frances Bell Newton, Geneva Bell Story, Stella Bell Evans, Hugh Bell, Bobby Bell, C.J. Bell, Frank Bell, and Emmaline Bell Hogan.
Courtesy of Carolyn Bell Sanders

Over One Hundred Bell Family Members
Pearl Gentry and James S. Bell
Sixty-fifth Wedding Anniversary, October 1, 1970.
Courtesy of Carolyn Bell Sanders

The Archie Tedder Home
North Side of Fleming Street

Charlotte Turner married Morris Frey.

C. J. Bell. see *eighth house*.

Hugh Bell married Mildred Roberts of Marietta. They had nine children. See *sixth house*.

Earl Bell, who served in the United States Marines during World War II, married Mildred Bearden, known as "Mimi," from Dalton. They had two children; Rex and Brenda. Earl and "Mimi" lived on Macland Road, next door to his parents. Many years after "Mimi's" death, Earl married his second wife, Sara; they live on Shallowford Road in Marietta. Earl retired from the Cobb County Land Acquisition Department

Frank Bell married Gladys; they had four children: Donald, Linda, Cindy, and Tommy. After Gladys' death, Frank remarried; he and his second wife, Lillian, lived in East Cobb. Frank who served in the United States Navy during World War II, was employed at Lockheed Aircraft Corporation, from which he retired.

Frances Bell, a twin of Frank, married Clarence Newton of Marietta. They had two children: Harold and Gail. Frances and Clarence lived on Sandy Plains Road in Marietta. Clarence, who served in the United States Military during World War II, was a butcher.

Stella Mae Bell married Raymond Evans from Douglas County. They had two sons and a daughter: Ray, Jimmy, and Donna. They lived in Charleston, South Carolina, where Raymond was employed at the Naval Yard. Their son, Ray, had a career at Cape Canaveral, (now John F. Kennedy Space Center named for President John F. Kennedy after his death in 1963). Ray still lives in Florida. Jimmy is a resident of Charleston, as is his mother, Stella; Donna lives in North Carolina.

Bobby Bell married Mary Ledbetter from Ballground; they had two children: David and Elaine. Bobby worked at Simmons Mattress Company for many years but later went into the upholstery business. Mary is deceased; Bobby still lives on Macland Road.

Eighth House

C. J. Bell and his wife, the former **Louise Foster** of Dalton, built this house on Fleming Street in the 1940s, after C. J. returned home from serving in the United States Navy, during World War II, here they lived for many years. They had one son, **Douglas**, known as "Doug." C. J. retired from Simmons Mattress Company in Atlanta, and Louise Bell worked in the Cobb County School Lunchroom Program. C. J. and Louise later built a house on the east side of Dunn Street, south of Collier Drive.

Douglas Bell, known as "Doug," is a graduate of the Campbell High School Class of 1960; he married Janice Alverson of the Oakdale community, south of Smyrna. They had three children, two daughters, Stacy and Kelly, and a son, Jeff, and six grandchildren. After Janice and Doug divorced, he married Jean Ray Chitwood, who from a previous marriage had a daughter, Shelley, and two grandchildren.

FLEMING STREET
South Side

Appreciation is extended to Carolyn Bell Sanders and Susan Bradley Howard for their help in remembering the residents of Fleming Street.

NOTE: In 1948 the following property owners petitioned the Smyrna City Council to pave Fleming Street: H.N. Dorris, E.W. Tinsley, James C. Hardy, Dorothy Camp, J.C. Johnson, Sr., and Mrs. W.H. Mapp.

The first house on the south side of Fleming Street was referred to by the locals as the Fleming House. See *Fleming/Gillham Family, north side of Fleming Street.*

First House

The **Camp Family** resided in the first house on the south side of Fleming Street during the days of my childhood and youth. Mrs. Camp's given name was Dorothy. They had a daughter named **Faye**. My cousin, Betty Brooke Johnson, and Faye, (the same age) were good friends.

Second House

Mr. and **Mrs**. **H.N. Dorris** lived here with their family when I was a child. See *Dorris, Access Road*

Third House

Mr. and **Mrs**. **Ed W**. **Tinsley**, together with their daughter, **Winifred**, were residents of this house. Mrs. Tinsley, the former Louise Brown, was the daughter of Millie Matthews Brown and Robert Rankin Brown. Louise was born in Atlanta but spent her earliest years in Calhoun, in Gordon County. When Louise was two years old, her family moved to the Kennesaw Mountain area of Cobb County; Louise was in the fourth grade when they moved to Smyrna.

For many years, Ed and Louise operated an upholstery business on South Atlanta Road, across from Campbell High School (now Campbell Middle School). See *Tinsley, Gilbert Street.*

Fourth House

Mr. and **Mrs**. **J.P. Hardy** lived here. They had three daughters, Judy, Louise, and Theresa, and one son, "Jimmy." J.P. was Smyrna Chief of Police in the early 1950s.

Fifth House

Mr. J.C. Johnson
Smyrna City Councilman
1939

Mr. and **Mrs**. **J**. **Calvin Johnson**, **Sr**., resided here. They were the parents of a son, **J. Calvin Johnson**, **Jr**., and daughter, **Everhart**.

J. Calvin Johnson, Jr., married Betty Brooke, my first cousin. They built a house on Bank Street after it was extended from Hamby Street in the early 1950s; there they raised their two children, John III and Susan. See *Brooke, east side of Roswell Street, Calvin Johnson, south side of Bank Street, and the Masonic Order, north side of Concord Road, The Country Road.*

Everhart Johnson married Herman Hulsey. They had three children: Lynn, born in 1946; Douglas, born in 1948; and Carol, who was about fifteen years younger than Douglas.

The Senior Johnsons were active members of Spring Street Baptist Church. Janet Brooks Brown remembers Mr. J. Calvin Johnson, Sr., as the Sunday School Director there when she was a little girl, or—as she says— "a long time ago

Sixth House

Mr. and **Mrs**. **Dorough** were residents of this house. Mrs. Dorough was the former Bessie Mae Weems. They had three children: **Bill**, **Peggy**, and **Lamar**.

Seventh House

Mr. William Grady Baldwin, known as "Billy," and his wife, the former Helen Williams lived here. They had two children: **Lamar** and **Rose Anne**. See *Baldwin, east side of Concord Road.*

Herbert Baldwin, the father of "Billy," was born in 1879, and died in 1922. His mother, Liddell Hill Baldwin, who was born 1886, died in 1959. "Billy," a member of the large Baldwin Clan, grew up in Smyrna. He was a first cousin of Robert and Voss Baldwin and their siblings, who grew up on Concord Road.

From Acworth, Helen was the daughter of Johnson Green Williams, known as "J.G.," and Effie Lee Harrison Williams. "J. G." worked for Louisville and Nashville Railroad (L&N). Helen, Smyrna's City Clerk for many years; was a member of the Business and Professional Women's Club. Helen and Rose Anne moved from Fleming Street to Cherokee Street. Rose Anne later moved to Roswell Street.

Lamar Baldwin, a graduate of Acworth High School, married Susan Howell of Athens. They had one daughter, Clara Elizabeth.

Rose Anne Baldwin, a graduate of Campbell High School, lives in Marietta. She never married.

Eighth House

Mr. and **Mrs. E.T. Bradley, Sr.** resided here. Mrs. Bradley's given name was Floy. They had a daughter, **Susan**. Mr. Bradley, an attorney in Atlanta, moved his family there after school started in 1950. The Bradleys were members of First Baptist Church, where Mr. Bradley was elected as a trustee in 1947.

Susan Bradley married Harry Howard, who grew up in the Fair Oaks community and graduated from Osborne High School. Susan, a member of the Smyrna High School Class of 1951, moved to Atlanta, where she finished her senior year.

Ninth House

Mrs. Rachel Bradley, a widow, whose house faced Fleming Street, lived on the southeast corner of Fleming and Grady streets. She was the mother of E.T. Bradley, Sr. ., who lived next door. When my family and I lived on Grady Street and I was a small child, we would ride to church with Mrs. Rachel Bradley. I remember her car was a very nice, shiny black sedan, very impressive to me as a child.

Mrs. Bradley, a good neighbor, was a long-time member of First Baptist Church. I remember her as a very dedicated Christian lady who was always nice to children.

HILL STREET
North Side

The next six houses were on the north side of Hill Street, beginning at Atlanta Street. Appreciation is extended to Charles Gustafson, Jr., for the information about his parents, Mr. and Mrs. Charles Gustafson, Sr.

Gustafon House
1223 Hill Street
Circa 1950
Courtesy of Charles Gustafon

The Gustafon House on Hill Street
(with corn growing beside)
Circa 1950
Courtesy of Ann Bramblett Fowler

First House

Mr. and **Mrs**. **Charles Anton Gustafson**, **Sr**., lived in this house, #130 Hill Street; their phone number was 86J. They had two children: **Charles Gustafson**, **Jr**., and **Carol**. Previously, for about ten years, they lived with Mrs. Gustafson's mother, next door, on the corner of Hill and Atlanta streets, in a brick house that faced Atlanta Street. See *Sprayberry* and *Gustafson, Atlanta Street, from Mapps to R & M Café*.

Charles Gustafon, Sr., was from McKeesport, Pennsylvania. He attended Theil College in Pennsylvania. In 1949 he received a Wartime Emergency Teachers Certificate from the State of Georgia's Department of Education where he taught veterans of World War II, and subsequently, veterans of the Korean Conflict. These classes were held in Canton, under the G.I. Bill of Rights. He later was manager of Piedmont and Georgian Terrace hotels in Atlanta and an active member of Our Savior Lutheran Church on South Cobb Drive.

Mae Sprayberry Gustafson, with six semesters, graduated from A & M College (later McEachern) in Powder Springs in 1922 and then attended Young Harris College. In 1932 Mae was presented a General Elementary Class Teachers Certificate from the State of Georgia. After teaching at Osborne High School for many years, she became employed at Lockheed Aircraft Corporation in Marietta, from which she retired. Mae and her children, along with her mother, Julia Sprayberry, were members of First Methodist Church.

Charles Anton Gustafson, Jr., graduated from Campbell High School in the Class of 1958. He furthered his education at Young Harris College, where he received an associate degree, and at the University of Georgia, where he earned a Bachelor of Science degree. Charles lettered in varsity track and field in shotput and discus. Serving in the United States Air Force, he spent four years in Northern Italy and throughout Europe. Charles married Diana Carney of Rome, Georgia; they had no children. Now living in Lawrenceville, he is in sales and marketing at *The Atlanta Journal Constitution*.

Carol Ann Gustafson was born with Down's Syndrome but learned to read and participated well in Special Olympics. Her parents, Mae and Charles, were very involved in preparing for Carol's life after their deaths. They enrolled her in a private school for exceptional children, in Atlanta: where Mae and Charles took turns driving Carol to and from school each day. At the school, Carol learned many life skills that enhanced her quality of life. Later on, Carol was enrolled at Happiness Hill, on Cherokee Street, in a program for handicapped people, many of whom, including Carol, were given work opportunities; thus she earned some money, which contributed to her upkeep. Before her mother's death, Carol lived as an adult in a group home in Douglas County, along with four or five others with whom she could relate. Carol outlived both of her parents: her brother, Charles, became her guardian. Carol Ann died in 2000.

Second House

Bill Ross
Casualty of War
Vietnam

Mr. and **Mrs**. **Ross** and their children, **Bill** and **Rachel**, were residents here. Bill was killed in Vietnam.

Third House

Mr. and **Mrs**. **"Rube" Leonard** and their daughter, **Wylene**, resided here. The Leonards were active members of First Baptist Church, where Mrs. Leonard, whose given name was Martha, worked for more than a quarter of a century in the Church nursery. She loved being around children.

The Rube and Martha Leonard House
Hill Street
Circa 1940s
Courtesy of Ann Bramblett Fowler

The Bill Stewart House
North side of Hill Street

"Rube" Leonard worked for the North Carolina and St. Louis Railroad (NC&St.L). I recall that Mr. Leonard, relatively young, died not long before Wylene graduated from high school.

Wylene Leonard married Gary Sisson, who grew up on Dixie Avenue, across the railroad from Belmont Streetcar Stop. Later Gary's parents moved to Hughes Street, where they lived the rest of their lives. Gary's mother, Ann Sisson, was a hairdresser. She later owned and operated an antique shop in Smyrna. See *Sisson, west side of Hughes Street.*

Wylene and Gary, each of them an only child, had four children: Cindy, Garen, Brett, and Jeff, and eight grandchildren.

Both Wylene and Gary graduated from Campbell High School, as did their children, except Jeff, who died as a child.

In 1954, Wylene Leonard, holding the title of "Miss Smyrna," participated in the "Miss Georgia" pageant in which she placed as one of the five finalists.

Gary, Wylene, Lillie, and I were associated very closely in the days when we were active in the Smyrna Jaycees and Jaycettes organizations. Gary is deceased.

Fourth House

The **James Waters Family** lived in this house, on the northeast corner of Hill and Hughes streets. They had two children: **Jimmy** and **Frances**.

Fifth House

The **Henry Family** were residents in the fifth house on the north side of the street. They had two daughters: **Sandra** and **Lucy**. The Henrys moved from Smyrna to Athens.

Mr. and **Mrs. Williams**

Mr. and **Mrs. Alton Williams** and **Family** moved into this house after the Henrys vacated. Mrs. Williams was the former, Wayne Stewart. They had two daughters: **Mary** and **Flora Ann**. Mr. Williams was the manager of the Sears Warehouse, on Marietta Street in Atlanta. The Williams moved from Roswell to Smyrna.

Note: No relation to the Leland Williams Family.

Sixth House

Nell and **Leland Williams** moved from Church Street to this house, which backed up to the home of Mr. and Mrs. J. Calvin Johnson, Sr., residents on Fleming Street. Nell's brother, Ralph Cobb, and his wife, Edna, bought the Williams' house on Church Street, where Ralph and Edna raised their family. Later Leland and Nell built a house on Old Concord Road, across from Nells' parents, the Cobbs. Leland is deceased. See *Cobb, north side of Church Street.*

Seventh House

Bert and **Evelyn Alexander** resided on Hill Street near Hughes Street. Evelyn was a cousin of Virginia Gann McDaniel; Bert, and his family, from the Fair Oaks area, were members of Olive Springs Baptist Church. Bert and Evelyn had two daughters, **Judy** and **June**, nine grandchildren, and two great-grandchildren. Since moving from Hill Street, they have lived in Germany, Idaho, and the North Georgia Mountains; now they reside in Apopka, Florida. Bert Alexander was an usher when my sister, Hilda, wed Grady Chaffin, in 1951.

Eighth House

Mr. and **Mrs. Bill Stewart**, along with their young son, Bill, lived on the northeast corner of Hill and Hughes streets; their house faced Hill Street. Mr. Stewart owned and operated Bill Stewart Insurance and Realty Company in downtown Smyrna prior to his untimely death in late 1949 or early 1950. The Stewarts moved from Hill Street to Brown Circle, where they were living when Bill died. Betty Burruss Brown worked for Bill Stewart.

Mr. and **Mrs. Jewell**

Mr. and **Mrs. A.D**. **Jewell** resided here after the Stewarts moved to Brown Circle. They had two sons that I knew: **Frank** and **Sam**.

After I had graduated from college and entered the United States Army in (1955), I was stationed at Fort Eustis, Virginia, where I met Frank Jewell. He was the Captain and Commanding Officer of the 544th Transportation Company (LT), to which I was assigned. When he learned that I was from Smyrna, he told me that his family was living in the eighth house on Hill Street.

HILL STREET
South Side

Hill Street is a short street that runs from Atlanta Street to Hughes Street, just north of the current location of Smyrna Fire Station #1.

Appreciation is extended to Beverly Amacker, Ruby Langley Hunter, Hilda Wood, and Virginia McDaniel, who shared their memories of Hill Street residents.

After Hilda and I were born, Mother and Daddy moved from Fleming Street to Hill Street, on the north side, about mid way between Atlanta and Hughes streets. While I do not remember living on Hill Street, my sister, Hilda, does. Having vivid memories, she recalls a bad storm, causing a tree to fall onto our house on Hill Street. Hilda, though only five years old at the time, can also remember the events surrounding the birth and death of our brother, Willie Ellison, on Hill Street, August 18, 1936. A full-term baby but stillborn, he is buried in the New Smyrna Cemetery on Hawthorne Street.

Neither Hilda nor I can remember when we moved from Hill Street to Grady Street. However, we both have many memories of living on Grady Street, including Hilda's starting to school, in 1937.

Ruby Langley Hunter remembers that my grandfather and grandmother, Guy and Mamie Tucker lived on Hill Street at one time. Though she does not remember their house, she vividly recalls visiting them when she was a child. In his later years, when he was very ill, my dad, Roy Wood, wandered away from home. When we found him on Hill Street, he said that he was going to see his mother

Though I remember families who lived on Hill Street, I may not necessarily have the houses listed in the order in which they stood.

First House

Mr. and **Mrs. Elder Bramblett** lived in the first house on the south side of Hill Street from Atlanta Street. Mrs. Bramblett, the former Willie Mae Garrison, was from Marietta. They had two children: **Jerry** and **Ann**. The Brambletts moved to Hill Street around 1930. They moved from this house to Marietta, in 1964.

Mr. Bramblett, originally from Cuba, moved from Cumming (Forsyth County) to Smyrna. When I was a child, he was the general secretary of First Baptist Church Sunday School. I thought he

Elder and **Willie Mae Bramblett**
Hill Street
Circa 1930s
Courtesy of Ann Bramblett Fowler

Elder Bramblett Home
125 Hill Street
Circa 1940s
Courtesy of Ann Bramblett Fowler

Side view, Elder Bramblett Home
125 Hill Street
(notice unpaved street)
Circa 1930s
Courtesy of Ann Bramblett Fowler

Jerry and **Ann Bramblett**
Circa 1944
Courtesy of Ann Bramblett Fowler

Jerry Bramblett
Skelton House, on Atlanta Street, in the background. Circa 1950
Courtesy of Ann Bramblett Fowler

was one of those people appointed to hold that position forever. Mr. Bramblett worked for Perfection Stove Company at one time; later he worked for Thomas S. Perry: who owned an auto parts business. During the War, he worked at Bell Aircraft Corporation in Marietta, from 1943-1945.

Jerry Bramblett, a graduate of Grady High School, in Atlanta, was a very talented pianist, whose playing I remember at First Baptist Church.

Ann Bramblett graduated from Westminster High School in Atlanta. She married Robert Fowler, known as "Bobby," from Marietta. They had two children: Angie and Robert.

Ann shared, "I remember well the Gustafson Family, who lived in the first house across the street. They had a son, Charles, and a daughter, Carol Ann."

Angie Fowler married Alan Sheldon from Buffalo, New York. They had two daughters.

Robert Fowler married Angie Stephens from Cumming. They had three daughters.

Second House

Boyce and **Addie Davis** moved to this house in 1954. She was the former Addie Horton from Ranger (Gordon County). They had three children: **Larry**, **Dwight**, and **Patricia**.

Larry Davis married Carole Glover. They had no children.

Dwight Davis married Alice Moseley. They had two children, Dwight, Jr., and Renee.

Dwight Davis, Jr., a Major in the United States Air Force, served during the Iraq War.

Third House

Mr. and **Mrs**. **Walter Beecher Dalton** lived in this house, on the corner of Hill Street, facing Hughes Street. Mr. Dalton was known as "Beecher" They had three daughters: **Mildred**, **Catherine**, and **Annabelle**, known as "Ann." The Daltons moved from Ashville, North Carolina to Smyrna.

"Ann Dalton" married Philip Tomlin. They lived on Quarles Avenue until they built a house on Lee Street after its extension from Collier Drive in the early-to-mid 1950s. They had three children: Phyllis, Kristina, known as "Kristie", and Joel.

Phyllis married Richard Wallace. They had a daughter, Sherrie. Phyllis' second marriage was to George Haskins. They had two daughters: Georgeanne and Regina.

Kristie married Charles Pritchett, who grew up on Roswell Street in Smyrna. *See Pritchett, east side Roswell Street.*

Joel, first married Ann Young, the daughter of Dr. George Young, who was an ophthalmologist in Smyrna; They had a son, Dustin. Joel's second marriage was to Kim Goodwin; they had a daughter, Stephanie.

BROWN CIRCLE
East Side

Brown Circle is a short street that runs from Hughes Street on the south end to Hill Street on the north end. In reality, it is really a semi-circle with two sides.

Appreciation is extended to Cecil Haralson, Louise Crowder Logan, Virginia Gann McDaniel, and Hilda Wood for their help in recalling the residents of Brown Circle in the middle of the Twentieth Century.

In the days of my childhood, all the land on the east side of Brown Circle was vacant except for the Turley and the Millwood homes. Later on, in the days of my youth, Ham Dabney, a builder, bought some of the property on the east side of the circle and built several houses, including his own.

First House

Mr. and **Mrs. Ham Dabney** and their daughter, **Marian Elizabeth**, lived on the south corner of Hughes Street and Brown Circle. Mrs. Dabney was the former Rachel Fishburne. Mr. Dabney bought property on Brown Circle, in the mid-to-late 1940s, from the Tatum Estate and built three houses here. The Dabneys, who were members of Smyrna Presbyterian Church, later moved to Colby Court, in the Forest Hills community. The Dabneys later moved to Forest Drive, also in the Forest Hills community. Mr. and Mrs. Dabney are both deceased. Their daughter, Marion Elizabeth lives on Forest Drive, in Forest Hills.

Ham, the son of Mr. and Mrs. Frank Dabney, grew up on the southwest corner of Atlanta and Westwood roads, in a large country cottage style house, accented with stone. It featured a large car or carriage port on the north side and a screened porch on the front. The house, now demolished, was owned and occupied in later years by Mr. and Mrs. Chess Burruss. See *Burruss, Atlanta Street from Miles Stop to the Motters* and *Morris, Atlanta Street, from Marlowe's to Creatwood.*

Marshall and **Polly Brand**

Marshall and **Pauline Brand**, known as "Polly," had two daughters: Paulette and Patricia, known as "Pat." They moved to this house after the Dabneys vacated. Part of this property included an extra lot, on the corner of Brown Circle and Hughes Street; there Mr. Dabney had built a utility house, which he sold, along with the house, to "Polly" and Marshall. "Polly" is still living here; Marshall is deceased.

"Polly" Brand is a sister of Elsie Smith, who, along with her family, was a neighbor of Lillie and me, when we first moved to Havilon Way. Elsie and her family lived on Richland Circle, a cul-de-sac near the end of our street. Elsie's daughter, Sandy, along with her husband, Howard Betts, and their children, still live on Richland Circle. Howard is employed with the City of Smyrna Fire Department

Second House

Mr. and **Mrs. J.O. Cobb** had this brick house built early in the 1950s. Her given name was Annabell. They had two children: a daughter, Martha, and a son, whose name we do not recall. The Cobb Family moved here from East Atlanta. To our knowledge, this family was not related to the large Cobb Family in Smyrna. The Cobbs were members of Smyrna Presbyterian Church.

Martha Cobb married Mac McKinder. See *McKinder, third house.*

Third House

Mr. and **Mrs. Millwood** and their family lived on the east side of Brown Circle. Mrs Millwood's given name was Charlotte. They had two children: "**Buddy**" and **Jane**. The Millwood Family attended First Baptist Church.

Dr. and Mrs. Charlie Garland

Dr. and **Mrs. Charlie Garland** moved to this house after the Millwoods vacated. They had wo children. Dr. Garland was in practice with Dr. Claude Mitchell, in his medical practice.

The McKinders

Mr. and **Mrs. Mac McKinder** moved here after the Garland Family vacated. They had two :hildren: **Marilyn** and **Jim**. Martha McKinder was the former Martha Cobb. Mrs. McKinder still lives n this house. See *second house.*

<u>Fourth House</u>

Mr. and **Mrs. Douglas Turley** were residents here. They had a son, "**Sonny**." I seem to ecall that "Sonny" Turley and "Buddy" Millwood were cousins. Both families moved away from 3rown Circle at the same time. The Turley Family attended First Baptist Church.

"Sonny" Turley, became Chaplain at Milledgeville State Hospital in Milledgeville.

Virginia Gann McDaniel remembers there was a "trolley-type swing" that extended from a ree on a hill behind the Turley house and over the creek to a tree at the top of the hill behind /irginia's house on Powder Springs Street. "It was a thrill to ride!" Virginia exclaimed.

NOTE: The swing mentioned was actually a rope tied from one tree on a small hill to a tree n another hill; another rope was attached to a pulley, which would slide down the rope. The rider vould hold onto the hanging rope and ride from one hill to the lowest.

The Williams

Later **Mr.** and **Mrs. Williams** and their son, **Mike**, were residents here after the Turleys had 'acated.

Mr. and Mrs. Harold Hancock

The **Hancock Family** moved here after the Williams Family vacated. They had two sons: ,eslie and David. David married Sheila Brewer of Smyrna.

<u>Fifth House</u>

Mr. and Mrs. Harold Chandler

Elizabeth Bacon, known as "Libba" married Harold Chandler, they lived in this house. They ιad one daughter. See *Bacon, south side of Powder Springs Street.*

'he Hudson Family

The **Hudson Family**, who lived here, had several children. Mr. Hudson worked for either *'he Marietta Journal* or *The Cobb County Times*, a weekly newspaper, both edited by Otis Brumby, ;r.

Sixth House

Bill and **Claudia Stewart**

Bill and **Claudia Stewart** and their son, **Billy**, moved from Hill Street to this house in the late 1940s. They were living here when Bill, the owner of Bill Stewart Insurance and Real Estate Company on Atlanta Street, died in the early 1950s.

Claudia Stewart died from cancer about three years after Bill's death. Her sister and brother-in-law, Mr. and Mrs. Marvin Leathers, moved to this house with Billy Stewart, who was still a child when his mother died. They lived here until Billy had graduated from high school. Afterwards Mr. and Mrs. Leathers, who had a daughter, moved to the Chastain Park area of Atlanta.

Seventh House

Harold and **"Lil" Davis** lived in this small two-story house, near the northeast corner of Brown Circle and Hill Street. They had two children: **Leroy** and **Dottie Sue**. Mr. Davis owned and operated Davis Clothing Store, on the east side of Atlanta Street, in front of Landers Drug Store. Afterwards, Harold Davis was a Cobb County Policeman. Harold and "Lil" Davis were active members of Smyrna Presbyterian Church.

NOTE: Many years later, after this house had burned, a friend of my mother, **Nettie Kelly**, built a new house on this property. She moved here from her house on North Cooper Lake Road, which she had shared for many years with her beloved husband, Jimmy Kelly. See *Sanford, south side of Powder Springs Street.*

BROWN CIRCLE
West Side

Brown Circle was one of the streets sub-divided by Virginia Gann McDaniel's grandfather, Romulus Nester Hughes, who lived on Powder Springs Street in the early part of the Twentieth Century. According to family information, he owned and farmed all that tract of land bounded by Grady, Fleming, Hughes, and Powder Springs streets. After he stopped farming and began working for Georgia Power Company, he decided to sell part of his property for development. Hughes Street is named for him.

In the days of my youth, Ralph and Willie Argo and their son, Alan, lived in the house on the corner facing Hughes Street. The Haralson House at that time was the first house on Brown Circle. See *Hughes Street* and *north side of Powder Springs Street.*

First House

In my earliest remembrances, **Mr.** and **Mrs. R.C. Haralson,** and their son, **Cecil**, lived in the first house on the west side of Brown Circle from Hughes Street. Cecil Haralson was employed for over thirty years with Trust Company of Georgia in Atlanta, which is now SunTrust Bank. He was a charter member of the Smyrna Jaycees, which was organized in 1959. Cecil remained a member of the Jaycees until he retired at the mandatory age of thirty-six. He is a long-time, active member of the Smyrna Kiwanis Club and First Methodist Church.

Cecil Haralson married Gennie Valentine, the daughter of Mr. and Mrs. B.H. Valentine of the Log Cabin community. The Valentine house was across the street from the Log Cabin Community Sunday School. Gennie attended Fitzhugh Lee High School in Oakdale, where she played on the girls' basketball team. Because Gennie's years in school overlapped mine, I remember seeing her play many games; she was an excellent player

The Log Cabin community, about five or six miles from Smyrna, was on the streetcar line, bout ten miles north of Five Points. A community of very attractive upscale homes that had much to ffer people with growing families, Log Cabin Drive was easily accessible to Atlanta. The Log Cabin unday School was an asset, offering a spiritual and social connection for the people in the ommunity. Scouting and other community-related activities were also held there. The Log Cabin unday School today, in the early part of the Twenty-first Century, is still a vibrant congregation of elievers. See *Mitchell, Atlanta Street, Marlowe's to Creatwood.*

An important fact to remember is that Boy Scout Troop #1 was the first Boy Scout Troop rganized in the Atlanta Area Council. The troop still meets in the scout building located on the Log abin Sunday School property.

Gennie, active in the Smyrna Jaycettes, where she served as President, and Cecil have been ery active throughout their married life in First Methodist Church, where she teaches Sunday School nd serves on the Altar Guild. She was a member of the adult choir for many years.

When Lillie and I were newly married, we moved to Pinehurst Drive off King Springs Road; ennie and Cecil, who lived on Oakview Drive, in the same community, later moved to Highview rive; in the area off North Cooper Lake Road where Rem Bennett, Sr., built houses in the 1960s. ecause Lillie and I later moved to the same general area, we have been privileged to live very near to em all of our married life.

Gennie Valentine Haralson shared the following information about her family. "My family ways identified where we lived by using the Log Cabin community as the location of their home, but ey always considered themselves 'Smyrnans.' Our address was Valentine, Rural Route 1, Smyrna, eorgia; the people in our community were very supportive of Smyrna and its environs."

Bob and **Louise Logan**

"Bob" Logan
Smyrna City Councilman
1948-1949

Mr. and **Mrs. Robert Logan**, moved to this house, in 1946, after the Haralsons vacated. obert was known as "Bob". Mrs. Logan was the former Louise Crowder of the Oakdale community, outh of Smyrna. "Bob" and Louise had one daughter, Connie. "Bob" Logan, who grew up on Log abin Drive, is a graduate of Marietta High School, where he was the "First Class Benchwarmer," hen he was not playing in the band. Louise Logan is a graduate of Fitzhugh Lee High School, where ne played center guard on the basketball team, throughout her high school years. The Logans are ng-standing members of Smyrna Presbyterian Church, where "Bob" was elected a Deacon in 1967, nd also served as church treasurer and Sunday School teacher. In more recent years, he is serving as resident of his Sunday School Class.

Connie Logan married Danny Martin; they had four children: Brent Logan, Peter Shane, and vins, Ashleigh Danielle, and Courteney Marie. Connie Logan is a graduate of Campbell High School, nd Danny graduated from Marietta High School. They were members of Smyrna Presbyterian hurch.

Louise's parents, were James Buford Crowder, known as "Buford" and the former Daisy rgo, a sister of Ralph Argo. After their marriage, they moved from Atlanta to a 'dirt' road in akdale, where they raised their six children: Esther, Mary, James, Frances, Louise, and Ruth. Two of e Crowder sisters were named "Miss Cobb County," during the days of my youth. Mary Crowder as "Miss Cobb County" and "Miss Georgia," in the mid to late 1930s. Frances was also "Miss Cobb ounty," in the late 1930s and her daughter, Trina, was also "Miss Cobb County" in 1960. See *oepner, on Hughes Street* and *Argo, east side of Hughes Street.*

"Bob" Logan grew up on Log Cabin Drive, (a paved road) south of Smyrna, the son of M and Mrs. Orrin Brown Logan. "Bob's" mother was the former Ruth Boynton of Newnan, and hi father was from Opelika, Alabama. They had three other sons: Brown, Edgar Peyton, known as "Pete, and William, known as "Billy."

"Bob" Logan served during World War II, in the United States Army Air Corps, (now know as United States Air Force). He flew "the Hump" (a chain of mountains in China), in a plane known a a C-47 in the military, and also known as a DC-3. After the War "Bob" worked at Georgia Institute c Technology. Elected to the Smyrna City Council in 1948, he served one term. See *Logan, on Ol Concord Road.*

In 1945, while "Bob" was overseas, a small plane crashed to the ground in flames on Lo Cabin Drive, near his parents' home. The trees caught fire and, in turn, set his parents' house on fir At the time of the crash, "Bob's" mother was upstairs in bed when the plane's engine penetrated a wa and landed against a bedpost. She was rescued without injury; the house was repaired.

In the downstairs section of the house, rented to a young family, a mother and her baby gi were at home when the plane crashed. Though injured, the baby, along with her mother was rescue The pilot was killed, but the two other crew members escaped.

After the crash, Louise sent "Bob" a letter stating his mother was okay. She later se newspaper clippings of the crash, but due to poor mail service during the War, he received th newspaper clippings first and thought his mother was dead.

Second House

Mr. U.S. Worley, the Smyrna School principal, and his wife lived in this house. It had bee said that at least one schoolteacher lived there with them.

Mr. and Mrs. Jim Burruss

Mr. and **Mrs. Jim Burruss** lived in this house after the Worleys moved. Mrs. Burruss wa the former Polly Keck. They had a son, **Donnie**, and a daughter, **Kay**. Mr. Burruss worked for a airline.

NOTE: There was a vacant lot between the Jim Burruss house and the George Wood hous When the Burruss family moved, Hilda and George Wood bought the vacant lot.

Mr. and Mrs. Howard Scoggins

Mr. and **Mrs. Howard Scoggins** moved to this house in later years. She was the forme Victoria Dean Crowe. Having moved from Bank Street, they lived here the rest of their lives. See *Ba Street.*

Third House

George and **Hilda Wood** and their son, **Larry**, moved to this house in 1948. They are n related to my family, although George and my dad were very good friends. George and Hilda we active members of First Baptist Church, where he was a deacon. In the late 1950s, Dad was chairm of the building committee for the new sanctuary at First Baptist Church, and George was extreme active and supportive of that project. Dad always said, "George Wood and Jesse Cook were my rig hand men." George, very handy with tools, was always doing what he could to work on the buildin His dedication to the Church was invaluable in those days.

George Wood was employed at Lockheed Aircraft Corporation. Before the Woods we married, and for a while afterwards, Hilda, a registered nurse, worked at the Old Marietta Hospital, large red brick building, about a block from the square, on Cherokee Street in Marietta. The docto ad their offices downstairs, and the nurses "tended" patients upstairs. After leaving Marietta Hospital, Iilda worked at Kennestone Hospital many years. Later, for seventeen years, she was employed at the ,eventh Day Adventist Hospital in Smyrna, which is now Emory-Adventist Hospital. George is eceased. Hilda, still active in First Baptist Church is in the Friendship Sunday School Class, with ,illie.

Larry Wood graduated from Campbell High School and attended Georgia Southern College 1 Stateboro, now known as Georgia Southern State University. He married Christina Hull of College 'ark; they have two daughters: Kerry and Paige. Kerry married Brian Bardorf. A lovely person, Kerry ied in 2005 after an extended illness.

GRADY STREET
East Side

First House

Mrs. Estelle Ray lived in the only house on the east side of Grady Street.

GRADY STREET
West Side

My family and I moved to Grady Street from Hill Street, where I do not remember living; ıerefore, my earliest memories are of our house on Grady Street. In 1940 we moved to Bank Street; I tarted to school in September of that year.

We were living on Grady Street when my dad began managing the Smyrna Amateur Baseball 'eam. Though I am not sure when he began, I remember going with him to the games. I was about .ve years old when I became the water boy for the team. I felt very important, for Dad said, "The layers need a lot of water and, as water boy, it is your job to make sure it is there for them between ınings." I took this job seriously.

I became very close to the men who played ball and also to their families. These people ecame role models for me at a very early age. I remember their traits, their personalities, and their ·ay of thinking (I would know when they wanted water even before they asked for it). Other than my ımily, these closest people around me at that time helped to shape my life. See *Smyrna Amateur 'aseball Team* for the names of the players.

Some of the players whom I remember best at this time were Ralph Cobb, J.C. Austin, Sonny avenport, Woodrow Lutz, Spurgeon Ware, Homer Brooks, O.L. Pinson, Harry Mitchell, Alvin .ustin, Aubrey and Clyde Herren, and my uncle, Tom Tucker.

I also remember some of the team sponsors who furnished money for the uniforms: Black nd Webb Grocery Store, Smyrna Drug Store, Collins Pharmacy, Saul's Department Store, and W.F. Bill" Stewart Insurance and Real Estate Company. I am sure there were others, but these are the ones remember from those early years.

There was also a large group of people who always went to the games. Many of the families f the players were always in attendance; my Mother and sister never missed.

First House

Dora and **Roy Wood** (my Parents), my sister, Hilda, and I lived in the first house on the 'est side of Grady Street from Powder Springs Street. My brother, Sammy, was not born until we ıoved to Bank Street. *See Bank Street.*

"Pete" Wood on Easter Sunday at the Wood home on Grady Street. The house in the background was the home of Ora and Sam Turman.
Circa 1938

Roy and Dora Wood moved from this house on Grady Street, to Bank Street in 1940.

<u>Second House</u>

Sam and **Ora Turman** were residents of this house next door to us. They did not have any ildren. Sam was employed with a family real estate business in Atlanta. I am reasonably certain that ra worked for Southern Bell Telephone Company in Atlanta. The Turmans were wonderful ighbors.

<u>Third House</u>

The **Hubert Decker Family** resided in this house. I do not recall anything about them.

<u>Fourth House</u>

The Hester Family

The **Hester family** lived in this house. The only thing I recall is that they were older people.

The Ledbetter Family

Beverly Cobb Amacker shared the following information about her mother's family, the dbetters, who were residents on Grady Street in the early 1930s.

Mr. and **Mrs. Will Ledbetter**, according to their daughter, Edna Ledbetter Cobb, moved m Fleming Street to Grady Street sometime in the early 1930s, probably to the second house where m and Ora Turman later resided. This is where the Ledbetters were living, when Edna Ledbetter met lph Cobb, whom she later married. Edna remembers the house they lived in was next door to the y Wood Family.

The Avery Family

Mr. and **Mrs. Avery**, later in the 1940s, lived on Grady Street. They had several children, o of whom were **Eugene** and **Shirley**.

Mr. Avery, who worked for the railroad, also managed the Jonquil Theatre at one time. The eatre opened in Smyrna in 1946 or early 1947. Beverly Cobb Amacker remembers going there on a ld trip with her first grade class to see "Song of the South." (She had started to school in the fall of 46.)

HICKORY HILL STREET

I remember when this street was cut off Hill Street. On it a developer built small but very ce frame homes—probably a response to the opening of Lockheed Aircraft Corporation, in 1951.

Appreciation is extended to Jeannie Jeffares for sharing the information, on her family, who ed on Hickory Hill Street when the neighborhood was first developed.

The **Harold Jeffares Family** was the only family I knew who lived on this street. I am not re if they moved to this house when it was first built, but I know they have been here a long time. rold Jeffares married Jeanie Harrelson of the Oakdale community, a graduate of Fitzhugh Lee hool. Jeanie and Harold had four children: **Diane**, **Edward**, **Greg**, and **Russell**.

Harold Jeffares, who served with the Marines during World War II, was active in American gion Post #160. He was employed by Cowan Supply Company, there he was accidentally killed ile on the job.

Jeanie Harrelson Jeffares was employed at Fulton National Bank when I worked there. Sh and her children attended First Baptist Church, where she is still an active member of the Friendshi Sunday School Class. Thus Lillie and I have had the privilege of knowing Jeanie through the year After Harold's death, Jeanie continued to raise her children in this house, where she has maintained home base for them. See *Jeffares, Fuller Street.*

HUGHES STREET
East Side

Appreciation is extended to Virginia Gann McDaniel, Ruby Langley Hunter, Beverly Cob Amacker, and Hilda Wood for sharing their memories of the residents of Hughes Street.

Virginia Gann McDaniel, who grew up on Powder Springs Street in the middle of th Twentieth Century, furnished the following information. Her grandfather, Romelus Nester Hughe owned and farmed all the tract of land bounded by Grady Street, Fleming Street, Hughes Street, an Powder Springs Street. See *Hughes* and *Gann, north side of Powder Springs Street.*

Virginia related, "After Grandfather stopped farming and went to work for Georgia Powe Company, he decided to sell his land for development. At that time he gave each of his children a lo from the farm before he sold the remainder of his land. Hughes Street was, naturally, named for hi family.

"The only one of Grandfather Hughes' children who did not build a house on the lot that wa given him by his dad was W.M. Hughes, known to me as "Uncle Bill." "Uncle Bill" married Milli Shaw, of the Fair Oaks area; they had two children: W.M. and Evelyn. Millie Shaw had two sister Annie Mae Shaw, who married "Slim" Davenport and lived on the west side of Hughes Street; an Willie Shaw, who married Roy Howard and lived on Bank Street. See *Howard, south side of Ban Street* and *Davenport, west side of Hughes Street.*

"W.M. Hughes, the son of 'Uncle Bill,' married Martha Hartness of Marietta; they had thre children and several grandchildren. W.M. and his sister Evelyn live in Marietta. (W. M. is nin months younger than I.)

"When W.M. was very small, his family moved to Miami, Florida, where 'Uncle Bill' starte working for Eastern Airlines. (W.M. is the one who got Bill and Bud Hammond their jobs wit Eastern Airlines.) Bill and Bud, not married at the time, lived with 'Uncle Bill' and 'Aunt Millie' unt they could get settled.

"Evelyn Hughes married Bert Alexander from the Fair Oaks area. They had two daughter Judy and June, and several grandchildren. They live in Florida.

"During World War II blackouts were frequent, especially in airports and related areas. On night during a blackout in the area, there were not supposed to be any planes with engines running. B one was. Uncle Bill, on patrol in the airfield, and not seeing the plane, walked into the engine that wa running. He was killed instantly. After his burial and Aunt Millie could sell the house, she, W.M., an Evelyn moved back to Smyrna to live with us until 'Aunt Millie' was able to buy a house. They the moved to a house on Maple Avenue in Marietta; later 'Aunt Millie' married Kelly Spiller of Mariett 'Aunt Millie' died in the early 2000s at the age of ninety-five.

"The first two lots on the east side of Hughes Street at Powder Springs Street were vacant f a long time. My family had three huge apple trees on these lots. The creek (or branch, as it was calle ran through the lower section and under Powder Springs Street.

"Frances Johnson, who had two sons, Amos and Gene, and two daughters Virginia an Evelyn, built a house on these lots in the early 1960s. Virginia married "Bud" Fortner and Evely married "Butch" Brooks. My husband, Bobby McDaniel, and I were neighbors to the Brook Famil hen we lived on Stephens Street and they lived on Pinehill Drive. Evelyn and "Butch" had two iildren: Phyllis and Tony.

"Before the aforementioned house was built, we had a large garden, cows, pigs, and chickens n those lots. I guess you might have called this area a mini farm. My Aunt Ethel had a garage in this ea. Other than Uncle Erby, she was the only one in the family who had a car. The outhouse, which rved our house, was also in this area; this meant that we had to cross Hughes Street to get to it. In is area, during the winter, we also killed hogs in this area, an all-day affair, with everyone in the mily working; it was a fun time, I guess, especially at the end of the day. The first part of the day as messy and smelly, but by six o'clock, or so, when the biscuits, tenderloin, gravy, and eggs were one, and everybody gathered in the kitchen, it was a delicious and fun time. As you can see, our tire family did everything together. From hog killing time to canning time, to eating and playing me, we did it all together.

"I remember once, when Bill and Beth Hammond came up from Florida, we acquired fifty ozen ears of corn from some source. We dumped the corn in the back yard of the house where I lived d started shucking corn. (There were probably 20 or so of us.) We shucked it, cut it off the cob, oked it, and canned it. We ate quite a bit of it for supper that night and worked until about eleven or elve o'clock, but nobody went home until the tasks were done."

The following residents lived on the east side of Hughes Street from Powder Springs Street.

First House

Ralph and **Willie Argo** lived on the northeast corner of Hughes Street and Brown Circle, ith their house facing Hughes Street. Willie Argo was the former Willie Black, a sister of Homer lack, who lived on Concord Road, toward the Covered Bridge. Ralph Argo, a barber, and Roy cLarty owned and operated Argo and McLarty Barber Shop, located on Atlanta Street, next door to e Telephone Exchange. Ralph Argo was the only policeman in Smyrna at one time in the late 1930s.

Ralph and Willie had plans to build a house on Concord Road where they owned property. ne evening while visiting there, Ralph had a heart attack and died. At the time of his death, in late 39 or early 1940, after eighteen years of marriage, Willie was pregnant with their first child. After alph's death, and their son, Alan was born, Willie chose to continue living in this house on Hughes reet. She never built on the Concord Road property, but her son, Alan, did. There he lived for many ars with his family. See *Black, north side of Concord* Road, *The Country Road.*

Second House

Mr. and **Mrs**. **Robert Lewis**, known as "Bob," lived in this house, which was built sometime the 1940s. They had two children: **Billy** and **Barbara**. "Bob" Lewis owned a tavern/billiard parlor downtown Smyrna. See *Bob's Pool Room, Atlanta Road, from Marlowe's to Creatwood.*

Third House

Dr. and **Mrs**. **Hugh A. Wyckoff** lived on the southeast corner of Fleming and Hughes eets, facing Hughes Street. Mr. Jim Bell, who lived on Fleming Street, built this house for the yckoffs in the 1940s. Dr. Wyckoff, a professor at Georgia Institute of Technology, was involved in th the Cobb-Marietta Water Authority.

NOTE: The following is a facility of the Cobb-Marietta Water Authority.

The Hugh A. Wyckoff
Water Treatment Plant
3728 Mars Hill Road
Acworth, Georgia 30101

The Albert Hammonds Home
West Side of Hughes Street

HUGHES STREET
West Side

The families named in the following paragraphs lived on the west side of Hughes Street from owder Springs Street.

Appreciation is extended to Virginia Gann McDaniel, who grew up on the northwest corner Powder Springs and Hughes streets in the middle of the Twentieth Century, for her sharing the llowing information about her family on Hughes Street.

Bob and **Virginia McDaniel**

Facing Hughes Street was a vacant lot behind the house on Powder Springs Street where irginia Gann McDaniel grew up. Romelus Nester Hughes gave this lot to his daughter, Irene Hughes ann, when he sold his farm. Irene and her husband, Ed Gann, never building on the lot, gave it to eir only child, **Virginia Gann**, and her husband, **Bob McDaniel**, when they married in 1949. Bob d Virginia built their first house here. Virginia remembers this tract of land as originally being the weet potato patch." She also remembers walking behind the mule and a plow and picking up freshly owed sweet potatoes when her family was farming this land.

"When Bob and I planned to have our first house built, we had 'our hearts set on a stone replace.' Ham Dabney, who built the house, said he could have built another bedroom for what the replace cost. 'But that fireplace was so beautiful!'" Virginia remarked. "The lot stood for the down yment on the house. The total cost of the house was $7,500.00, and the payments were $53.80 a onth. You have to remember this was in 1950; Bob was making $35.00 a week and I was earning 2.50 per week. At that time, Bob was working for Southern Bell Telephone Company, from which retired with thirty-seven years of service."

<u>First House</u>

Mr. and **Mrs. Albert Hammonds** were residents of the first house on the west side of ughes Street; directly behind the Gann house. Mrs. Hammond's given name was Emma. They, irginia Gann McDaniel's "Aunt Emma" and "Uncle Albert," had two sons: **Herbert**, known as Bud", and **W.A., Jr.**, known first as "June" and later as "Bill." Virginia Gann McDaniel shared, Next door to the Hammonds was another vacant lot, where we played." Aunt Emma and Uncle Albert ould make ice cream every Sunday afternoon. The entire family, thirty to thirty-five from around the ock, would be there. When out-of-town relatives came (who knows how many we would have?), we ways had a good time."

"Bill" and "Bud," later working for Eastern Airlines, moved to Florida. "Bill" married Beth udson from Dade City, Florida, where they still live. They had four children and six grandchildren. Bud" married Ruth Chastain, of Smyrna, the daughter of Mr. and Mrs. Emory Chastain, who lived on ring Street; they also had two sons: Mike and David. "Bud" died a few years ago; David, in the nited States Air Force, was killed while flying. Ruth and Mike live in Canton.

Beverly Cobb Amacker said that her Uncle Ed Ledbetter told her that he played with the ammond children. He seemed to remember that "Bud's" birth name was Herbert.

<u>Second House</u>

Mr. and **Mrs. Bill Stewart**, after residing in this house, moved to Brown Circle.

Leila and **Wallace Arrington**

Later, **Leila** and **Wallace Arrington** moved to this house.

<u>Third House</u>

The **Henry Swain Family** lived next door to the Hammonds. Mrs. Swain, whose given nam was Edwina, was known as "Wanna." They had two daughters: Elaine and Jane. Mr. and Mrs. Swai previously lived on Church Street, next door to First Baptist Church. After they sold their property First Baptist Church, of which the Swains were members, the Church built an educational buildin there in the late 1940s. (I believe the building began there in 1947.)

After Mrs. Swain's death, Henry married Mrs. Dobbins, who worked for Southern Be Telephone office on Atlanta Street. Henry Swain worked for the railroad.

<u>Elaine Swain</u> married Foster Rolfe.

<u>Jane Swain</u> married Ed Poss.

<u>Fourth House</u>

Etta Nix, her son **David**, and her **mother** were residents of this house. Virginia Gan McDaniel remembers being a few years older David.

<u>Fifth House</u>

Robert N. Hughes, known as "Bob, (also known to Virginia Gann McDaniel as "Unc Bob") married **"Teeny" Lord** of Atlanta. While living in Smyrna, they had two children: **Robert** an **Carol**. After moving from this house, they had another daughter, **Candace**, known as "Candy Virginia Gann McDaniel shared that "Uncle Bob" built for his family, this house on the lot that wa given to given him by his father, Romelus Nester Hughes.

Uncle "Bob" and "Aunt Teeny" moved to Florida, where Uncle "Bob" went to work f Eastern Airlines.

<u>Carol Hughes</u> married Hugh Smith, known as "Buddy" of the Smyrna area, where they live a long time before moving to Hapeville and later to Alabama, where they still live. They had tw children and two grandchildren.

<u>Robert Hughes</u> is married and lives in Florida.

<u>Candace Hughes</u>, known as "Candy," is married and also lives in Florida.

John and **Martha Colston**

John and **Martha Colston** and their two children, **David** and **Edith**, lived in this hous which they bought from "Bob" and Teeny Hughes.

Mrs. Colston, the former Martha McCleskey of Marietta, worked at Cobb Federal Ban which later became Fulton Federal Savings and Loan Association. Martha had a younger brother wh died as a result of electric shock from a fence.

John Colston, employed by the United States National Park Service, was working Kennesaw when he and Martha met. John, who later worked as a maintenance engineer Westinghouse, served on the Cobb County School Board in 1961. John Colston, from Virginia, ha two brothers: Newton and Edward.

David Colston married Brenda Garner from Soperton. They had three daughters, Sandi, Jamie, and Michelle, and four grandchildren. David Colston, who graduated from Campbell High School, is deceased.

Edith Colston, who graduated from Campbell High School, married Martin Stanger from Denver, Colorado. They had two children, John Kenneth, known as "Jake," and Amanda.

Sixth House

Mr. and **Mrs.** **"Slim" Davenport** resided here. Mrs. Davenport, the former Annie Mae Shaw, was a sister of Virginia McDaniel's Aunt Millie. "Slim," who must have had another name was from Smyrna. He was killed in a riot in Davenport Town, probably in the late 1930s or early 1940s.

Ernest and **Frances Hoepner**

Ernest and **Frances Hoepner**, with their two daughters, **Trina** and **Lisa**, moved to this house, which they bought from the Davenport Family after "Slim" had died.

Ernest Hoepner, from Attalla, Alabama (the Gadsden area), worked for Southern Bell Telephone Company for thirty-three years. From injuries received in an automobile accident, Ernest died in 1969.

Frances Hoepner, the former Frances Crowder, grew up in the Oakdale Community, south of Smyrna. Her parents were Daisy Argo Crowder and James Buford Crowder, who had four other daughters: Mary, Esther, Ruth, and Louise, and a son, James. In the early 1970s, Frances moved to the Colston House, where she still lives.

Mary Crowder married Jack Bagwell. They had one son, Morgan. Morgan, Mary, and Jack are deceased.

Esther Crowder first married Carl Lester; they had two sons: Robert and Donald. Esther later married George Crosby. Both Edith and George are deceased.

Ruth Crowder married Harold Brinkley. They had a daughter, Becky, and a son, Stanley. Stanley is deceased. Ruth and Harold reside in Danville Virginia. See *Brinkley, north side of Love Street.*

Louise Crowder married Bob Logan from the Log Cabin community. See *Logan, west side of Brown Circle.*

Frances Crowder Hoepner, as well as her sister, Mary, held the title of "Miss Cobb County" in the late 1930s. Frances' daughter, Trina, carried on the tradition when she was named "Miss Cobb County" in 1961.

Trina Hoepner, a graduate of Campbell High School, married Earl Reed of the Oakdale community. She was "Miss Cobb County" in 1961. They had one daughter, Amanda. Trina is now married to Wallace Gardner; they are retired. In retirement, Trina's hobby is stained glass; "Wally's" pastime is woodworking and fly fishing.

Amanda Reed married Jody Wise; they had two daughters: Nicole and Micayla.

Lisa Hoepner married and had one son, Brian Roach, and one grandson, Cole.

NOTE: There was a vacant lot between the fifth and Sixth houses.

Seventh House

Mr. and **Mrs**. **Jimmy Hughes** were residents of this house, located on the corner of Hughe Street and Brown Circle. Mrs. Hughes was the former Leila Croft of Atlanta. The lot where this hous was built was given to Jimmy Hughes by his dad, Romelus Nester Hughes. Jimmy and Leila had tw daughters: **Barbara Ann** and **Betty Jo**. Jimmy Hughes, working for Eastern Airlines, moved t Florida.

Barbara Ann Hughes married Billy Barlow from Eatonton, Florida, an employee of Easter Airlines. They had two children: Debra and Darrell. The Hughes later moved to Baltimore, Maryland where Barbara still lives. Because of heart problems, Billy died about eight years ago.

Debra Hughes married and had two children and two grandchildren. Darrell Hughes, wh lives in West Virginia, had no children.

Betty Jo Hughes, who had one child, moved to Baltimore, Maryland, after her parents died Widowed twice, Betty Jo Hughes died about ten years ago.

While Jimmy and Leila Hughes were living in this house, on the corner of Hughes an Fleming Street, it burned. Afterwards they built a house on the vacant lot. Here the **Bradley Famil** later resided. The Bradleys had one child. See *Fleming Street.*

CHAPTER NINE

KING STREET

East Side

Appreciation for information shared about their families is extended to Parker Lowry and John Fulton, Sr., known as "Johnny," both of whom grew up on King Street in the middle of the Twentieth Century.

First House

Mr. and **Mrs**. **Ray Fulton** lived in the first house, built by Ham Dabney on King Street, in a northward direction from Love Street. They had two children: **John**, known as "Johnny," and **Marion Amy**. Mrs. Fulton, the former Margaret Davis, was the daughter of Mr. and Mrs. Grover Warren Davis, who lived on the northwest corner of Church and Davis streets. The Fulton Family were active members of Smyrna Presbyterian Church, where Ray was an elder and a deacon. Ray worked for First National Bank of Atlanta. See *north side of Church Street.*

Ray Fulton, originally from Weymouth, Massachusetts, graduated from Northeastern University. He met Margaret when she was visiting a relative on "Martha's Vineyard Island" for the summer.

Marion Amy Fulton married Richard Chester Lillie, Jr., known as "Rick," of Duxbury, Massachusetts. They had three children, Richard III, Katherine Amy, and Elizabeth Ann, and five grandchildren.

John Kent Fulton, Sr., known as "Johnny," married Darlene Pederson from the Chicago, Illinois, area. They had three children: John Kent, Jr., Jennifer Rae, and James Kyle Fulton. They also had one granddaughter.

The following information was provided by John Fulton, Sr., remembering his "growing up" years in Smyrna. "My first recollections of Smyrna filter into my conscious memory at/or about the age of three or four. I had a tricycle that I rode almost everywhere, from my grandparents' house on Church Street (the Grover Davis' house). I could ride the sidewalks all the way to the downtown area. I do not recall what happened to the tricycle, but it was replaced with a bicycle; then I could really get around town. The remarkable thing about that time was having the run of the town without any fear of strangers or being in danger.

"One of the most interesting things about the middle of the Twentieth Century was the innocence of the era. Children were allowed to do things that would be unthinkable today. For the most part, it was a safe time in the South; people trusted and looked out for each other.

"As a nine year old, I remember, I was allowed to ride the bus alone to downtown Atlanta. I remember adventuring all around downtown before going to my dad's office.

"Our house on Stephens Street has lots of memories, which are not all good. The first time I remember being afraid had to do with a gas (it could have been kerosene) stove that had a habit of exploding, not with a force that would cause much damage but one quite unsettling to a young kid. Consequently, I do not like open flame stoves.

"When we lived on Stephens Street, I got my first 'pet,' (a female cat). I fondly remember the milkman's delivering milk in glass bottles to our house. When I was rather small. On occasions, I even got to ride with the milkman on his delivery route.

"My dad, Ray Fulton, was Vice-President of First National Bank, located in a multi-storied building at Five Points, in downtown Atlanta. Even in the early 1950s, some of the buildings still did not have air-conditioning. Because there were no screens, when the windows were open, people could literally lean out the windows. I specifically remember a ticker tape parade for Dwight Eisenhower in downtown Atlanta. We watched the parade from the bank building windows, which were open. Also we threw every kind of paper we could find out the windows that day; the streets, as well as tops of the electric trolley busses, soon were covered with paper.

"Dad, who always drove a station wagon, had a carpool for years. He would pick up the riders on the way to town, or they would come to our house. For many years the crew consisted of Ferd Brown, John Matthews, Henry Konigsmark, Frances Skelton, and Mrs. Duncan. Another rider, Joe Abrams, was added years later, after their route took them down Northside Drive and crossed Howell Mill Road where he was picked up.

"When I would go downtown, if I timed my day in Atlanta right, I could meet with the riders in the underground parking lot around 5:00 PM and catch a ride home. (This was long before Underground Atlanta was built. In those day there were many places underground where downtown workers could park their cars.)

"In Smyrna in those days no one had air-conditioning. I remember very well when we got our first window fan, which dad bought from someone he worked with at the bank. Church was even hotter than our home in those days. Without the funeral home fans, I think we might have all perished. It was amazing how much air could be moved with one of those fans! We spent many hot summer evenings in revival service in the little brown building of Smyrna Presbyterian Church. The musical portion of the program was always enjoyable; for several years we had the same couple; with the husband taking the lead and playing the trumpet while his wife was singing along with the rest of us. Everyone was there; and it wasn't a question of going or not going—members were expected to be there. Generally the revival lasted a week, and then things got back to normal.

"Vacation Bible School was also a 'must.' My mother and her friends always helped with the food and the program. I remember one memorable VBS when somehow a single windowpane cut the neck of Mike Bacon (I think). There was a lot of blood and confusion. I don't remember if Mike went to see Dr. Mitchell, or if Dr. Mitchell came to the church. Mike did survive!

"Dr. Mitchell delivered me at Crawford Long Hospital in Atlanta on Valentine's Day, 1943. I can still remember his nurse, Mrs. Ruth Camp. She was a no-nonsense nurse and never took 'no' for an answer. Back then the needles used for shots seemed the size of pencil lead and as dull as an eraser. They had a funny square twist hub for a connection to the syringe and were used over and over again. The syringes were made of glass and had to be autoclaved or sterilized, along with the needles, before and after each use. Dr. Mitchell maintained his practice in an upstairs office in downtown Smyrna. As a kid, I spent a lot of time going there.

"Johnny" Fulton further shared: "Doug Nally, who lived on the other side of King Street, and I, were very good friends. Doug helped me memorize the Boy Scout Oath. Many of our days were spent around the school, which was just behind Doug's house. It was always easy to gain entry into the school after hours, and we became familiar with every 'nook and cranny' of the place; from the furnace room to the top of the roof, we explored every part of the building. Our birthdays were the same and our bond was so great that we even cut our arms and let our blood flow together to become 'blood brothers,' just as we had seen done in the movies. Not what you would want your child to do today!

"One day as Doug, his brother, Don, and I were headed back to their house from downtown Smyrna, we took a short cut through what is known today as the Smyrna Memorial Cemetery. While jumping from one tombstone to another, one headstone became unstable and fell from its perch onto Don's leg—breaking a bone. Doug and I made a makeshift saddle pack and carried Don home. We stayed clear of the cemetery after that."

NOTE: The Ray Fulton Family were residents of several houses in Smyrna: the home of Margaret's parents, Mr. and Mrs. G.W. Davis, on the corner of Church and Davis streets; a dwelling on the corner of Davis and Stephens streets; a house on Atlanta Terrace; the former Presbyterian Manse on Love Street; this small house on King Street; and finally, in 1956, their new home on Dogwood Circle in the Forest Hills community, where Ray and Margaret resided the rest of their lives

Mrs. Blanche Rice Brawner

Mrs. Blanche Rice Brawner, after the Fulton Family had vacated, moved into this King Street house, where she lived the rest of her life. Mrs. Brawner was married to **Dr. Albert Brawner**, who was a psychiatrist at Brawner Sanitarium. They had three children: **Albert F. Brawner, Jr., Mary,** and **Harriette**. Blanche Rice Brawner, who died in 1987, is buried in New Smyrna Cemetery. See *Taylor House, Atlanta Road, from Marlowe's to Creatwood.*

Albert Brawner, Jr., was born in 1923. He died in 1939 from his spleen's having been ruptured during a football game at Marietta High School.

Mary Brawner married Albert L. Rambo. They live in Marietta. See *Taylor-Brawner House, Atlanta Street, from Marlowe's to Creatwood.*

Harriette Brawner married George Mathews after she graduated from the University of Georgia. They moved to Cuthbert, then to Birmingham, Alabama, and later to Florida. Harriette died in 1980.

Mrs. Blanche Brawner was a sister of Mrs. Judith Rice Lowery. See *west side of King Street.*

NOTE: This house, along with the McLarty House and the Kreeger House on the corner of Love and King streets, was razed to accommodate the building of the First Methodist Church parking lot.

Second House

Mr. and **Mrs. Roy McLarty** lived here. Mrs. McLarty's given name was Nell. They had one daughter, **Doris**, who graduated from Smyrna High School in the Class of 1947. Roy and Ralph Argo were partners in a barber shop they owned. Ralph was the first person to cut my hair at the Argo and McLarty Barber Shop. In later years, Roy was a Deputy Sheriff in Cobb County.

Doris McLarty married and moved to Virginia. Johnny Fulton remembers that after she graduated from college, Doris worked on top secret projects in White Plains, New Mexico.

Nell McLarty worked for Western Union, which was located on the west side of Marietta Street at Henry Grady Square in Atlanta, across the street from Fulton National Bank, where I worked. She rode the streetcar and, later, the bus to work when I was attending the Atlanta Division of the University of Georgia; many mornings Mrs. McLarty and I would ride the same bus. The McLarty Family previously lived on Sunset Avenue. See *McLarty, north side of Sunset Avenue.*

A member and loyal supporter of the Smyrna Historical Society, Nell would ride occasionally with Lillie and me to the meetings. An intelligent lady, Nell always taught me something when I talked with her. She was also a staunch Christian lady with strong opinions. I liked her very much!

The McLartys were members of First Baptist Church, where Mrs. McLarty, in her upper years, taught the Joy Sunday School Class. (This was the same class that Lillie taught, 1992-2002; most of the ladies that Mrs. McLarty taught were still in the class when Lillie taught.) Due to "age and declining health," Mrs. McLarty moved to Virginia to be near her daughter. The ladies of the Joy Sunday School Class gave her a farewell party at Lake Laurel Clubhouse on Cooper Lake Road; she was very sad to leave her friends in Smyrna. After Nell passed away, Doris had her mother's body brought back to First Baptist Church for her funeral service.

Third House

Mr. and **Mrs. Jim Camp** resided here. The former Ruth Phagan, Mrs. Camp was a sister of Lizzie Mary Etta Phagan Durham, who lived on Spring Street; Ruth was also Dr. Mitchell's nurse. See *Durham, south side of Spring Street.*

Parker Lowry shared, "I have always been told that Ruth Phagan (Camp) helped deliver me, but she did not live in this house at the time. She and Mr. Camp married later in life and moved here. Mr. Camp had the largest collection of Civil War relics I had ever seen."

Mrs. Corrine Hosch

Later on **Mrs. Corrine Hosch** moved from the north side of Love Street, where she had shared a house with Miss Eunice Padgett, to this house on King Street, where she lived into the early 1990s. See *west side of King Street* and *north side of Love Street.*

First Baptist Church

In the days of my youth First Baptist Church was located on the northeast corner of Church and King Streets. Then it was commonly referred to as "the rock church"; today that building, with beautiful stained glass windows, is known as First Baptist Church Chapel. (The church dedicated the present-day sanctuary in 1962.) Parker Lowry remembers, "First Baptist Church had the only smooth sidewalks fit for skating, and the window pits in the church were also fun places to play." See *north side of Church Street.*

NOTE: It is hard to imagine children in today's world being allowed to play in the church's window areas around that stained glass. Amazingly, the children of that era were allowed to play there, and yet the stained glass windows were never broken.

Fourth House

John L. Pollock
Mayor, City of Smyrna
1923-1924
Smyrna City Councilman
1914-15, 1917-1918

Mr. and **Mrs. John L. Pollock** lived in this house, located on the north side of First Baptist Church. They had two daughters: Mary Sue and Nancy Lee. Mr. Pollock owned a coal yard on the west side of the railroad, off Atlanta Street, at the rear of Jonquil Plaza.

Mary Sue Pollock married Mr. Torbert; they had two children: Duke and Johnny. Mr. Torbert, who died in 1940, was buried in New Smyrna Cemetery. Mary Sue re-married and moved to one of the Carolinas.

Nancy Lee Pollock married P.M. Rice, Jr. After his death, she married L. B. Suther. Nancy never had children.

Parker Lowry related, "Earlier in the century the Pollock Family lived near the corner of Atlanta and Love streets, where they owned much property."

The Robert H. Bacon, Jr., Family

R.H. Bacon, Jr.
Smyrna City Councilman
1946

Mr. and **Mrs. Robert H. Bacon, Jr.**, were residents of the fourth house in the days of my youth. Mrs. Bacon, the former **Octavia Mitchell**, known as "Octa," grew up on Church Street. The Bacons had four children: **Mitchell**, **Freddie**, **Mike**, and **Nancy**. See *Mitchell, south side of Church Street; Bacon, west side of King Street* and *east side of Reed Street.*

Mrs. "Octa" Bacon was a member of the Mitchell Family that lived on the south side of Church Street in the "Mitchell House."

Parker Lowry remembers that when the Bacon's children were small, Robert and "Octa" Bacon lived in the apartment in Mrs. Rice's house, on the southwest corner of King and Church streets, and that from there they moved to Reed Street and then to King Street.

Mitchell Bacon attended Marietta High School, where he played baseball. He also played baseball at North Georgia College, in Dahlonega. He married Carol Hulsey; they had three children: Vickie; a son, Chris; and Beverly.

Freddie Bacon married Jane Tatum from the Oakdale community. They had three children: Greg, Gary, and Sherri. Jane, whose dad owned and operated Tatum Lumber Company, had two brothers: Gene and Harold Tatum.

Nancy Bacon married Philip Stanley of Gainesville. They had two children: Michelle and Scott.

Michelle Stanley married Lee Batson of Atlanta; they had two sons, Christopher and Ben, and a daughter, Madison.

Scott Stanley married Jennifer Hale of Canton. They had a son, Wright, and a daughter, Ellie.

Mike Bacon, a graduate of Campbell High School, married and had a daughter, Debbie. Debbie married and had two children. Later Mike married Ann Williams; they had a son, Travis. Mike and Ann live in Ormond Beach, Florida.

Memories
by Mitchell Bacon

"I remember the old city jail, at the foot of the town water tower and next to the blacksmith shop and feed mill. I used to go down and watch the blacksmith shoe and treat horses and repair wagons.

"The Goat Man would come through Smyrna every so often, and rest up, and stock up with supplies and be on his way again. You could hear him coming from quite a ways off and, when he got close, you could smell him. He had six or eight goats (I can't remember) pulling his wagon. A heavy-set man with a long white beard, he would send me up to Mr. Pressley's to buy a couple of chickens. After wringing the chickens' necks, he would clean, and cook the chickens in a big pot. I never did sample his cooking!

"We used to play baseball behind the Presbyterian Church on Church Street (before it was rebuilt and extended). We were coached by our seniors at the time: Pat Edwards, Tommy Oglesby, Buddy Jones, Mickey Walker, and Fain Brannon. Players included: Sammy Mitchell, Phillip Walker, Don Walker, Miller Davis, Pete Wood, Parker Lowry, Bill Pavlovsky, Larry McMillan, and myself.

We would treasure a baseball until the cover came off; then we'd tape it with any tape we could find; we could fix broken bats with small nails and tape. Our mothers, calling us to dinner would scream our names—we were not late for supper. We all lived within screaming distance.

"Pete, were you a party to this one? (Remember the Greasy Spoon diner at the traffic light across from Landers Drug Store?) We would get on the roof of the diner and throw torpedoes onto the pavement when cars were stopped at the red light. The fireworks we had access to back then were much more powerful than those sold today. There was one elderly policeman on duty at night, and he could never find out where those torpedoes were coming from."

Mr. and **Mrs. C.D. Stricklin**

Mr. and **Mrs. C.D. Stricklin**, when I was in high school, lived in the basement apartment of the Bacon home. Mr. Stricklin was my social studies teacher and the assistant principal of Smyrna High School during my senior year.

On the east side of King Street, there were no other houses between the Pollock House and Bank Street. The City of Smyrna water tank, located about a half block between King Street and the cemetery, had been a landmark in Smyrna all of my life until it was dismantled in the early 1980s to make way for progress.

Mrs. McKinney

Mrs. McKinney, her son **Akridge**, and daughter, **Sue**, lived in the basement apartment after the Sticklins had vacated.

Mr. and **Mrs. Phillip Walker**

Phillip Walker and his bride, the former **Peggy Jo Addison** of the Oakdale community, moved to this apartment. See *Walker, south side of Spring Street* and *south side of Church Street.*

The Bacons, after selling this house on King Street to First Baptist Church in the middle-to-late 1950s, moved to Memory Lane, where Robert lived the rest of his life.

NOTE: The Bacon/Pollock House was the only house that faced King Street between First Baptist Church and Bank Street. The sanctuary of First Baptist Church is now located on the property where the Bacon/Pollock house stood.

KING STREET
West Side

Appreciation is extended to Gerald Eaton, Harold Flynn, John Fulton, Sr., and Parker Lowry for sharing their memories of growing up on King Street. Appreciation is also extended to Jack Nally and Laura Helen Jones Allgood for their memories of the Nally and Jones families.

<u>First House</u>

Mr. and **Mrs. William Frank Flynn** moved from Sommers Street in Kennesaw to this residence, on the northwest corner of King and Love streets. They had two children: **Harold** and **Kathryn**. Mrs. Flynn, the former Agnes Brown, was raised in the Lost Mountain community of West Cobb County. According to family history, this house on King Street was built in 1917.

Mr. Flynn worked for the railroad for thirty-seven plus years. He was one of those fortunate people that had a secure job during "The Great Depression," years beginning in 1929 and extending into the late 1930s.

According to her son, Harold, Mrs. Flynn went to the Washington, D.C. area in 1945 to be near her sister. While she was there, she worked at the Immigration and Naturalization Service (INS) for twelve years. She then returned to her home on King Street, where she lived until she died, in 1993 at age ninety-seven.

Mrs. Flynn, who often worked in her yard, was also an active member of First Baptist Church. I remember seeing a star hanging in her window to show that she had a son serving in the United States Navy during World War II. I was always told, "The Flynns are very nice people."

Harold Flynn married Kathryn Poynter from Virginia. See *north side of Love Street.*

Kathryn Flynn married Paul Miller. They had three children: Paula, Richard K., and Donna. Kathryn Flynn Miller died in 1985 from complications due to a brain tumor.

Paula Miller lives in Myrtle Beach, South Carolina.

Richard K. Miller resides in Stafford, Virginia.

Donna Miller lives in Highpoint, North Carolina.

Mr. and Mrs. Russell Hosch

Mr. and **Mrs. Russell Hosch** and their daughter, **Mary Ellen**, lived in an apartment in the Flynn home. Mr. Hosch was a farmer before coming to Smyrna. As a student in elementary school when he died, I seem to remember that he was in ill health for a long time. Mrs. Hosch (Corrine) was the senior homeroom teacher at Smyrna High School and taught English literature. I studied under her for four years.

Mrs. Hosch was a wonderful Christian lady who had so much influence on many people over the years. After Smyrna High School closed and the Campbell High School building was opened, she began teaching there. After retiring from Campbell High School in the late 1960s or early 1970s, she volunteered at First Baptist Church as a counselor to high school and college students for at least fifteen years. She was still counseling at First Baptist when my two children were in high school and college in the 1980s. Mrs. Hosch was faithful to assimilate the names of the high school and college graduates for recognition at the end of each school year; her ministry in that arena touched many lives. To my knowledge she was never paid for this service. With her true talent used effectively Mrs. Hosch was, to me, a "God-appointed teacher."

Smyrna was lucky to have teachers like Mrs. Hosch. Those of us who knew her were richer because she touched our lives. I say that sincerely—even though *Macbeth* almost killed me; in fact, I thought there were times that I would not live through the required learning experiences. It wouldn't surprise me at all if she isn't teaching English Literature to the angels in heaven. If she is, I assure you that some of them are not making passing grades. Rest in peace, Mrs. Hosch!

Mrs. Hosch lived into her mid-nineties. By forty years, she outlived her daughter, Mary Ellen, who died as a young woman, not long after she had graduated from high school, married, and had a son, Jimmy. Mrs. Hosch was always very close to her grandson and his family, who lived in Cartersville. When she became unable to live alone, Jimmy and his family took her to their home and cared for her in her final months.

Second House

Mr. and **Mrs. Jesse J. Cook** were residents in this house, next door to the Flynns. Mrs. Cook's given name was Ruby. They had four sons: **Richard**, **Jimmy**, **Charles**, and **Curtis**. The Cooks, active in First Baptist Church, brought their sons up in the programs of the church, where Jesse was a deacon and Ruby sang in the choir. In the late1940s Ruby and Jesse moved from this house to the east side of Lee Street, where they lived the rest of their lives.

My dad was especially close to Jesse, a carpenter, who, Dad thought, was one of the best. I remember that, when the First Baptist Church sanctuary was being built in the late 1950s, Dad relied on Jesse's building knowledge and advice.

Many years later Jesse, while crossing Concord Road one night on his way to church, was struck by an automobile and killed. It was just like Jesse to be going to church, for he was a faithful member. His death was a great loss both to the church and the community.

Parker Lowry shared that Jimmy told him one time why his dad always attended church. "When we boys were small, he was playing horseshoes with us when either Charles or Curtis was hit in the head, near the eye. Though not much damage was determined, Jimmy said his dad attended church almost every service, day and night, thereafter." According to information from the Cook Family, Mr. Jesse Cook did not attend church before the horseshoe accident. After that, he hardly missed a service!

<u>Richard Cook</u> married Dot Sanders of Cumming. They had two sons, Leslie and Tommy, and two grandchildren. Richard, with his dad and brother, Charles, did construction work. Dot had worked at Atherton's Drug Store before she and Richard married. Formerly members of First Baptist Church, they are currently members of Smyrna Christian Fellowship, off Favor Road in Marietta, near Osborne High School.

Dot Cook shared with Janet Brown this unusual story of how she and Richard became acquainted. "We met as pen pals through *The Southern Farmer* magazine which had a pen pal column. I wrote to the publisher and said my hobbies were 'hillbilly music' and 'going to church.' Richard's dad subscribed to the magazine, thus Richard saw the ad, also liking 'hillbilly music,' he wrote to me. We corresponded with each other for a long time.

"My great aunt, Sallie Jones, told me that the Buices (my second cousins I had never met) were looking for someone to keep their children because Ruby Buice was working at Lockheed Aircraft Corporation. I was in my nineteenth year when the Buices brought me from Cumming to live with them on Dunn Street, where I kept their children for two years.

"One day I asked Linda Buice (Smith), who was about ten years old, if she knew where Lee Street was. 'Yes' she said, 'it is the next street over.'

"We walked around the block and found where the Cooks lived. I wrote Richard and told him where I was.

"He wrote me back and said, 'I would ask you out for a date, but I am sure you will not go.' (He was seven and a half years older than I.) My reply was, 'You'll never know 'til you ask!' He did ask, and I said, 'Yes.' After dating for about two years, we married in 1956 and are still married—forty-eight years later."

<u>Jimmy Cook</u> married Earline Haws; they had six children: Larry, Keith, Carolyn, Teresa, Russell, and Michael; nine grandchildren and five great-grandchildren. For many years they resided in the South Cobb area, near Austell.

Earline was the daughter of Mr. and Mrs. Laurence Haws, who lived on Lee Street, in the Forest Hills community. Mr. and Mrs. Haws were members of First Baptist Church, where they were both involved in the church programs. Mr. Haws worked for Lockheed Aircraft Corporation.

Earline and Jimmy, along with their family, were also In the Baptist Training Union (now called Discipleship Training), which was designed to teach students leadership skills, Jimmy served as

First Baptist Director, as well as District Director in Noonday Baptist Association. For many years Jimmy was the Sunday Bible teacher at Delmar Gardens Retirement and Nursing Home on King Springs Road, He remained faithful to the Church and its programs and all phases of Southern Baptist endeavors. Jimmy, who worked for Lockheed Aircraft Corporation until his retirement, passed away December 28, 2003.

Earline Cook was employed at First Baptist Church Kindergarten, from which she retired. Teresa, one of her daughters, still works in the Kindergarten.

Charles Cook married Patsy Ramsey from Marietta. Like Charles' parents, they also had four sons: Chip, Andy, Lee, and Doug. Charles, a builder, was the contractor for the Smyrna Museum, built in 1999. Charles and Patsy are currently living in Ellijay.

Charles Cook was very active in sports activities in Smyrna all of his adult life. In fact, a Little League Baseball field at Brinkley Park is named "The Charles Cook Field" in his honor because of his extensive involvement with baseball. Two of Charles' and Patsy's sons, Lee and Doug, for many years, worked for the City of Smyrna Department of Recreation.

Curtis Cook married but had no children. He was a Smyrna policeman for more than twenty-five years.

Reverend and **Mrs. York Chambless**

In 1946, First Baptist Church purchased this second house from Jesse and Ruby Cook to be used as the first pastorium. **Pastor Charles Drake** and his family were the first to live here. **Reverend** and **Mrs. York Chambless** were the second residents to occupy the pastorium. They had three children: twins, **Brenda** and **Glenda**, and son, **David**. Reverend Chambless, pastor of First Baptist Church, 1949-1973, is now deceased.

The Gilbert Sisters

In 1957 Reverend and Mrs. Chambless moved to the new church pastorium, in Forest Hills community. Afterwards the Gilbert sisters (Alma, Leila, and Lula), who had sold their home place on Gilbert Street moved here. Parker Lowry, who lived next door, stated that they were wonderful neighbors. See *Gilbert Street.*

Third House

Mr. and **Mrs. A.B.S. "Brooke" Lowry** were the residents of this house. Mr. Lowry, known as "Brooke," and Mrs. Lowry, the former Judith Rice, had one son, Parker Lowry, who now lives in Acworth.

A.B.S. "Brooke" Lowry
Smyrna City Councilman
May 1941-May 1942

Mr. "Brooke" Lowry worked for Sears Roebuck and Company on Ponce de Leon Avenue in Atlanta, then for Rich's Department Store, and later for Davison-Paxon on Peachtree Street. I remember that Mr. Lowry was Scoutmaster at First Methodist Church. Though I was not in his troop, I was aware of his dedication and liked him very much. His untimely death was a loss to both his family and the community.

Mrs. Judith Rice Lowry first taught at Sylvan Hills School in southwest Atlanta, where Miss Ira Jarrell was the principal. When Miss Jarrell transferred to W.F. Slaton Elementary School, Mrs. Lowry also transferred there, where Colene Reed Guthrie and Miss Martha Quarles also taught. After Mrs. Lowry became the principal of Bolton Elementary School, Mrs. Guthrie and Miss Quarles

Mike Bacon and **Betty Griffin**
Bank Street, 1949
Courtesy of "Dot" Bacon

The home of A.B.S., Judith, and Parker Lowry on King Street. The house was built in 1910 and demolished in 2005. Photo courtesy of Mike Terry.

transferred to Bolton, from which the three of them retired. Mrs. Lowry, born in 1905, passed away in 1996 and is buried in New Smyrna Cemetery.

NOTE: Miss Ira Jarrell (later, Dr. Ira Jarrell) was Superintendent of the Atlanta Public Schools.

Parker attended first grade at Smyrna Elementary School before transferring to W.F. Slaton Elementary School, where he attended three years; then he returned to attend three more years in Smyrna Elementary School. He attended high school two years in Marietta and one year at St. Andrews, near Sewanee, Tennessee, from which he graduated. He attended North Georgia College, in Dahlonega, for three years before tranferring to the University of Georgia in Athens, where he received his degree.

Parker Lowry married Frances Roach Ledford from Anderson, South Carlolina. She had two children, Rhonda Jan and James A. Ledford, Jr., who were twelve and seven, respectively, when Frances and Parker married. Parker remarked, "We, as a family, do not use the word 'step' anymore. Frances and I live in West Cobb County; Rhonda and James reside in East Paulding County."

Sharing with me how much his relationship with Rhonda and "Jimmy" means to him, Parker related, "The affection they show me and their giving of a gift almost always brings tears to my eyes. I cannot imagine life without the memories of watching them grow up and mature into fine young adults."

Mr. and Mrs. "Brooke" Lowry were long-time members of First Methodist Church. Mrs. Judith Lowry, a very intelligent lady, greatly contributed to the writing of *But Thou Art Rich,* A History of Smyrna Methodist Church, written in 1990. In her later years Mrs. Lowry was an active member of the Smyrna Historical and Genealogical Society.

Fourth House

Mr. and **Mrs**. **Parker M**. **Rice**, **Sr**., lived on the southwest corner of King and Church streets, at the location where Carmichael Funeral Home now stands, but their house faced King Street. They had four children: **P.M.**, **Jr.**, **Henry**, **Blanche**, and **Judith**, all of whom are buried in New Smyrna Cemetery. One child, who died in infancy, is buried in the Ruff Cemetery, on Concord Road. The Rice children were in my parents' generation. The tombstone dates shown for Mr. Parker M. Rice, Sr., are 1859-1929; Mrs. Blanche Ruff Rice's tombstone dates are 1872-1964. See *east side of King Street.*

The Rice home was a beautiful, white wood house with a large front porch. I can still see Mrs. Rice in her rocking chair. In my mind's eye, such was a usual scene on a pretty day in my young life: people sitting in their chairs on their front porches in Smyrna, "getting fresh air." (As I have said before, kids in the days of my youth could rest assured that an adult somewhere had an eye on them. I never thought much about that, but I now believe it added to the security which kids felt then.)

Another thing I remember about Mrs. Rice was that the Church Street side of her yard was always filled with jonquils. In the early spring, beginning in early March, that property was a sea of yellow. The jonquils were the "old-fashioned" ones, which would bloom year after year. We had some blooming at the corner of our house on Bank Street, and I always thought they were so pretty. I still think so. In the days of my youth, most people in Smyrna had jonquils blooming in their yards. Hardly a yard was seen without at least a few. After all, Smyrna was/is "The Jonquil City."

In the six months (October 1960–April 1961) that Lillie and I lived at the corner of Church and Davis streets, in the Southern Manor Apartments, Lillie came to know Mrs. Rice, who by that time, was a very aged lady. Many days Lillie would ride the bus from work and then walk past Mrs. Rice's house. Mrs. Rice would be on her porch, and Lillie would stop and talk with her—especially after the jonquils started to bloom that spring.

Harriette Brawner
Picture made in the yard of Mrs. P.M. Rice on the corner of King and Church streets – Harriette's grandmother.
Circa mid – 1940s – in an *Atlanta Newspaper*
Courtesy of Mary Lee and Doug Jones

I am not sure how long Mrs. Rice lived after that, but I do know that Bill and Juanita Sanders bought her property and converted her house into their funeral home. The Sanders had been in business with B.C. Castellaw and Bill's brother, Warren Sanders. I assume that partnership dissolved. B.C. Castellaw and his family built Castellaw Funeral Home on Church Street and began operation there in 1966.

In November 1970, when my dad died, we used Sanders Funeral Home, which at that time was still located in the Rice House. (Mother was in the Eastern Star in those days with Bill and Juanita Sanders.) In the early 1970s, Randy Carmichael began working for Sanders Funeral home. At a later date he acquired ownership of the funeral home and had constructed that which we know today as Carmichael Funeral Home.

NOTE: According to public records, Carmichael Funeral Home (the former Rice House) burned, and the present structure was built.

Parker Lowry shared the following information about his maternal grandfather. "My grandfather, Parker M. Rice, Sr., who was from a well-to-do Atlanta family, as a young man came to Porter, Love and Rice Woolen Mill to keep books. There he met and married a "country girl," Blanche Ida Ruff. His father, Major Z.A. Rice, who served in T.R.R., Cobb's Calvary Legion during the Civil War, was buried in the family plot in Atlanta's Oakland Cemetery. When Parker M. Rice, Sr., died in 1929, he was buried in New Smyrna Cemetery. It is reported that some of his Atlanta family became upset because they expected him, along with the rest of his family, to be buried in Oakland Cemetery.

"My grandmother was Mrs. Parker M. Rice, Sr., the daughter of Mr. and Mrs. Henry Clay Ruff, who had twelve children. Mr. Ruff owned and operated the grist mill which was located near the Concord Covered Bridge. I remember my mother, Julia Rice Lowry, talking about going to the covered bridge area as a child to visit with her grandparents; her grandfather had much to do with the running of Ruff's Mill. The Ruffs were very prominent people in and around the Smyrna and the Mableton area of that day. In fact, the Ruff Family name still lingers in Smyrna and the South Cobb County area."

NOTE: In the Smyrna Museum there are many records regarding the Covered Bridge and Ruff's Mill area and the Ruff, Rice, and Lowry families.

Fifth House

Appreciation is extended to Gerald Eaton for furnishing information about his grandparents, who resided on King Street in the days of my youth.

Mr. and **Mrs. John Fletcher Parnell's** home, on the southwest corner of King and Church streets, faced King Street. When I knew the Parnells, they had four adult children: **Myrtis**, **Edna**, **Jeanette**, and **John Chesley**, known as "J.C." Mrs. Parnell was the former Ida Smith, the daughter of J.E. and Mittie Smith of Cherokee County. (J.E. Smith was a Confederate Army Veteran.)

Myrtis Parnell married R.A. Eaton. When I was a young boy, I remember, Mr. and Mrs. R.A. Eaton and their family lived here with the Parnells for a while. See *west side of King Springs Road.*

Edna Parnell married Sam Lewis. See *Highland Avenue.*

Jeanette Parnell married Kary Jackson. See *south side of Bank Street.*

John Chesley Parnell, known as "J.C.," married Sarah Lewis, a sister of Sam Lewis, who lived on Highland Avenue. See *Highland Avenue*.

At one time Max Parnell lived here with the Fletcher Parnells, who were his grandparents.

Sixth House

Mr. and **Mrs**. **Robert Bacon** moved to this house from Reed Street. From here they moved to the east side of King Street. See *Bacon, east side of Reed Street, and east side of King Street.*

Mr. and **Mrs. W. W. Nally**

Mr. and **Mrs**. **W.W**. **Nally**, who moved from Bartow County to Smyrna, lived here after the Bacons vacated. They had two sons: **Phillip Douglas** and **Donald Roger**. Mr. Nally, known as "Ben," was a member of a family of nine boys and one girl. Mrs. Nally was the former Ruby Fouts, an aunt of the Fouts brothers: C. J., Jerry, Charles, and Alvin; their father was Mrs. Nally's brother. "Ben's" brother, Jack Nally, owns Oakdale Hardware. See *Hardage, west side of Concord Road* and *Fouts, Atlanta Street, from Mrs. Mazie's to Pearce Matthews.*

W.W. Nally wrote and published a book about his family: *Footprints of the Nally Family along Little Pine Log Creek*. (A copy is in the Smyrna Library.) Having joined the United States Army Air Corps, which later became the United States Air Force, he spent three years in the Southwest Pacific during World War II. After that he worked for the United States Post Office (Railway Mail Services Department), from which he is now retired. Having worked on the northbound train that picked up mail from the Smyrna Depot, Mr. Nally told, "The mail car was set up like a post office."

About 1950 the Nallys built this King Street house, where they lived until about 1969. At that time they moved to the house they had built on Pretty Branch Drive in the Forest Hills community.

Seventh House

Mr. and **Mrs**. **Ernest Jones** were residents of the house on the southwest corner of King and Stephens streets. They had two children: **Ernest Olin** and **Laura Helen**. Mrs. Jones was the former Annie Jane Bryan of the Blackwell community in North Cobb County; the oldest of four sisters, all of whom she outlived, she died in April 2003 at the age of 100, almost 101. Mr. Jones, who grew up on Gilbert Street, was the son of Bertie Johnson Jones and Bedford Jones; he had one brother.

The Jones Family were active members of First Methodist Church, where Mr. Jones served as Sunday School Superintendent and Chairman of the Board of Trustees; Mrs. Jones was a member of the Lovejoy Sunday School Class.

According to family information, Mr. Ernest Jones served with the United States Army in France during World War I. He retired from Western Union before working as a tax assessor in Smyrna and Cobb County. He was Commander of American Legion Post #160 when the present building was constructed in 1948. Mrs. Jones served as President of American Legion Post # 160 Auxiliary.

NOTE: As recorded in *The People of Smyrna, 1972*, American Legion Post #160 was organized in 1941 in a meeting held at the drug store of M.L. Collins, its first Adjutant and third Commander. Ernest Jones was the first Commander.

During World War II Mrs. Ernest Jones, Martha Theodocian, and Hester Edwards ran a "nursery school" on Stephens Street for children whose mothers worked at the Bell Bomber Plant. After her youngest child, Laura Helen, started to school, Mrs. Jones began working in Smyrna School's lunchroom. When Campbell High School was opened in 1952, she became the dietician there, where she retired with twenty-five years of service. See *north side of Stephens Street.*

Ernest Olin Jones, after retiring from the United States Army, taught at the University of Nebraska. He married Dottie from Minnesota. They had two children: a son, Michael, and a daughter, Jackie. Now living in Pagosa Springs, Colorado, they have five grandchildren, one step-grandchild, and three great-grandchildren.

Laura Helen Jones graduated from Campbell High School in 1956 and entered the University of Georgia. After graduation from the University, she taught in Cartersville. She met Charles Allgood, who had graduated from Emory University and was teaching in Rockmart, his home town. After their marriage they moved to Birmingham, Alabama, where Charles entered the banking business. Laura Helen and Charles had a son, Lee, a daughter, Sloan, and four grandchildren. They now live in Dalton.

NOTE: There were four parcels of land in the block between Church Street and Stephens Street. This included the Parnell, Nally, and Jones properties, and a vacant lot. First Baptist Church purchased the Nally property in 1968 and subsequently purchased the other three parcels. (This entire block, including the Smyrna School property, now belongs to First Baptist Church.)

After selling their property to First Baptist Church, the Jones Family moved to Northview Place, in the Forest Hills community.

The rest of King Street was the setting of Mr. Pressley's pasture, barn, and house. Though Mr. Pressley's house faced King Street, everybody always associated him and his family with Bank Street. See *south side of Bank Street.*

STEPHENS STREET
North Side

Appreciation is extended to Rebecca McLean for sharing her memories of growing up on Stephens Street and to Betty Burruss Brown for information regarding the Johnson Family. Also, appreciation is extended to Gay Nell Bowman Cochran who, along with her husband, Jimmy, lived with their young family on Stephens Street.

Stephens Street in the days of my youth was a short street, only about three blocks long. It ran west from King Street, between Mr.William Pressley's pasture and the Smyrna School property. I remember only a few houses being on this street in my early life. Later on, in the late 1940s and early 1950s, more houses were built, and Stephens Street was eventually extended all the way to Church Street, as it is today.

First House

Mr. and **Mrs. Andrew Q. McLean** (pronounced McLane) lived in the first house on the north side of the street. Mrs. McLean's given name was Linnie. They had three children: **A.Q., Jr.**, known as "Buddy," **Rebecca**, known as "Becky," and **Elizabeth**, known as "Betty." Becky shared, "My dad was a widower with three older children when he married my mother. We younger children did not see the older ones very often, as they were married and involved with fighting a war while we were growing up."

"Becky," a very smart girl was in the Beta Club. She and I, the same age, graduated in the Smyrna High School Class of 1951. I have seen her only a couple of times since high school. When she finished college, she married a guy who was in the United States Military. Never moving back to Smyrna, Rebecca settled in California, where she raised her family.

She returned for our 50th Class Reunion, held in May 2001 at Howards's Restaurant. "Becky" updated information about her siblings: "My brother, Andrew Jr., who became a CPA, is now retired in Huntsville, Alabama. Elizabeth, known as 'Betty,' and her husband, Jack, a retired Air Force officer, now live in Ormond Beach, Florida. Like me, they both have children and grandchildren of which they're proud."

The following four paragraphs are from a letter I received from "Becky."

"I don't think we really appreciated how good we had it while growing up. After hearing about all the progress around there, I feel fortunate to have memories of Smyrna as it was, back when Gypsies camped at the blacksmith shop on their way to Florida; convicts in striped uniforms paved Stephens Street; and the Civil War trenches and cannonball holes in the tree trunks across the street, west of the school, could be seen. In my mind, I can still see all of our classmates as they were when we graduated from Smyrna High School."

NOTE: The blacksmith shop, to which she refers, was on West Spring Street, now where the Market Village is currently located.

Continuing, she shared, "I can still visualize our big brick house that Daddy built and all the land we had as a 'playground,' including the school grounds across the street. Our three-story garage had a room for cars on the middle level, a stall for the cow on the basement level, and Daddy's woodworking shop (with fancy saws) on the upper level. (When we were there after Mother died, some people told us their kitchens still had the cabinets Daddy made for them.)

"Later on Daddy built a house on each side of our brick one; plus, he built a 'temporary' house in the back of what was to be our permanent home. During World War II, the Draft Board ordered him to rent to families of men serving in the military—and I remember one nice family, the Bivins, who were close-knit cousins of the Cochrans.

"The Moore Family, who lived way down the street, had three kids: Zane, Arvis and Jean. I remember they built an 'ice-cold' swimming pool that was fed by a little branch that ran behind our house. Anyhow, they later moved to Rabun Gap. My sister and I went up to visit for a couple of summers afterwards."

One of the houses that Mr. McLean built is still standing, just west of where their house stood, across the street from the rear of the high school building that is now part of the First Baptist Church property. After Mrs. McLean's death, First Baptist Church bought her home place and the two adjacent houses, which were used for several years as Sunday School space. When the City of Smyrna started the downtown development, the City and Church traded lands, to the advantage of both. The McLean house was razed to accommodate much needed parking space behind City Hall.

Mrs. McLean, an active member of First Baptist Church, worked in the Church nursery for a long time, well up into her advanced years. She was one of five people with whom Lillie would leave our children. The other trusted people we used for childcare were Alice Howard and Florence Johnson, who lived in an apartment at the Howard home, and two teenage girls who lived in our neighborhood, Rhonda Reagin (Hydrick) and Jill Brissey.

It is my understanding that Mrs. McLean sold and/or traded buttermilk to the neighbors. (Many people in Smyrna traded their consumables during that period of time.)

Second House

The Moore Family resided in this house, on the north side of Stephens Street and down the hill past the McLeans. Rebecca McLean remembers **Zane**, **Arvis**, and **Jean Moore**. I do not remember their parents' given names.

Zane Moore was in the United States Army Air Corps during World War II, during which time he flew a few bombing missions. He married a girl from Ohio.

Arvis Moore also served in the United States Military during World War II. (I remember seeing the stars in Mrs. Moore's window, indicating that she had sons serving our country.) Arvis married Madge Parnell, who was a sister of Max Parnell, a Prisoner of War during World War II. See *Parnells, Highland Avenue.*

Jimmy and **Gay Nell Cochran**

Sometime in the late 1940s or early 1950s the Moore Family moved from this house, after which **Jimmy** and **Gay Nell Cochran**, the former Gay Nell Bowman, relocated here. They had seven children: **Ted**, **Shawn**, **Van**, **Bronwyn**, **Casey**, **Cathryn**, and **Kevin**. My dad and Jimmy Cochran were close friends; I remember going with Dad to this house. Jimmy, a furniture salesman, worked for Myers-Dickson Furniture Company at one time. Later Jimmy Cochran and Lee Maloney owned and operated Maco Table Company on South Atlanta Road. See *Bowman, north side of Powder Springs Street.*

Third House

Doug and **Ethel Westbrook** were residents here. She was the former Ethel Eldridge, who grew up on North Atlanta Road near the Parnells.

In the days of my youth, Stephens Street did not go all the way through to Church Street as it does today. It was a fragmented street, stopping and starting at least two times. One of the sections branched off Mann Street, which ran off Church Street. Two families lived in that area.

Nursery School

Down in the hollow of Stephens Street, in a house somewhat like a cabin, three ladies in our community, Mrs. Hester Edwards, Mrs. Martha Theodocian, and Mrs. Annie Jones, operated a nursery school. In the early 1940s, when our country was involved in World War II, most of the young men in the community had volunteered or been drafted to go into the Armed Forces. President Franklin D. Roosevelt had called for the citizens to become involved in defense work to support the War effort. The Bell Bomber Plant had been built in Marietta, and women had begun leaving their home to work there. A need for childcare arose. Thus this nursery school was organized for the purpose of caring for the children of those mothers, although there were some exceptions. The nursery school was part of the Cobb County School System and the Cobb County Government, which paid the employees' salaries. (Mr. Paul Sprayberry was the Superintendent of Cobb County Schools.)

Mrs. Hester Edmonds was the lead teacher, Mrs. Martha Theodocian was the assistant teacher, and Mrs. Annie Jones was the dietician. Later on Mrs. Edmonds was promoted to another job in the school system, and Mrs. Theodocian became the lead teacher of the nursery school. Some of the children that were cared for in this nursery school are these: Peggy Spradley, Bennie Theodocian, and Bobby Brewer.

In January 2005, Martha Theodocian related, "My son, Bennie, and I walked from our home on Old Concord Road to the nursery school (a good mile) and back each week day." Most people walked from their homes to Smyrna in the days of my youth.

STEPHENS STREET
South Side

There were no houses on the south side of Stephens Street from King Street to Reed Street. This entire block was Smyrna School property, except for the back yards of the residents whose houses faced King Street.

First House

Robert Johnson
Casualty
World War II

Mr. and **Mrs**. **Duncan Johnson** lived in the first house past Reed Street. They had five children: **Robert**, **Amos**, **Gene**, **Evelyn**, and **Virginia**. Gene Johnson, my age, was my classmate at Smyrna School. Mrs. Johnson was the former Frances Westbrook, a sister of Talmadge Westbrook, who lived on Bank Street. See *Westbrook, north side of Bank Street, and Johnson, east side of Hughes Street, and north side of Powder Springs Street.*

Robert Johnson was killed in action during World War II. Rebecca McLean shared, "I remember when Robert was killed, my family received an appropriate phone call because the Johnsons did not have a telephone." (Telephones were difficult to get during the War.) I remember the gold star hanging in Mrs. Johnson's window, indicating she had lost a son serving in the War. Later on Mrs. Johnson moved to Brown Circle.

Virginia Johnson married Truman Fortner. Virginia and my cousin, Betty Brooke, who married J. Calvin Johnson, were classmates and good friends. See *Johnson, south side of Bank Street.*

Second House

Nell and **Harris Burruss** resided in this house, (Mr. Burruss, known as "Red," was related to the large Burruss Family on Atlanta Street). They had two sons: **Stanley** and **David**. For many years "Red" worked for the Cobb County Police Department. Nell was employed for many years by Rich's at Cobb Center, from which she retired. Nell and "Red" moved from Stephens Street to Collier Drive, in the Forest Hills community, and then to Kennesaw. See *Burruss, Atlanta Street, from Miles Stop to Creatwood.*

Stanley Burruss, who lives in Albany, is with the United States Secret Service. Stanley lived in Washington, where he was a part of the Secret Service detail for Jimmy Carter, when Jimmy was President of the United States.

David Burruss, in the insurance business, lives in Atlanta.

Third House

Mr. and **Mrs**. **John Bradfield** lived in this area of Stephens Street. They had two children: **Wendell** and **Norma**. In a way, this family would be more associated with the north side of Church Street, for one had to go up to Church Street and turn north on Mann Street to get to this house: this small section of Stephens Street was not connected to the Stephens Street that intersected with King Street. Later on, Stephens Street was cut through to Church Street, near the present location of the Smyrna Senior Center and the Senior Aquatic Center. See *Bradfield, Atlanta Street, from Motters to R & M Café.*

Fourth House

Mr. and **Mrs**. **Judson Still** were residents here. They had a son, **Ronnie**.

CHAPTER TEN

CHURCH STREET
North Side

Appreciation is extended to Beverly Cobb Amacker, who grew up on Church Street in the 1940s and 1950s, for sharing information about her family (the Cobbs, Crowes, and Williams), residents of Church Street in the middle of the Twentieth Century. Gratitude is also extended to Lucile Cobb Crowe, who furnished information about her parents-in-law, Mr. and Mrs. Samuel Jefferson Crowe. (Affectionately known in my family as "Uncle Jeff," Mr. Crowe and my grandfather, George Crowe, were brothers. George was the father of Dora Crowe Wood.) Appreciation also goes to Diane Tatum Carter for providing information about the Tatum Family; to "Johnny" Fulton for sharing his memories about his grandparents, Mr. and Mrs. G.W. Davis; to Henry Konigsmark III for information regarding his parents, Elizabeth Davis and Henry Konigsmark, Jr.; and to Earline Dunton Pettit, for sharing information about the Dunton families on Church Street. See *Davis, seventh house on Church Street,* and *Cobb, west side of Old Concord Road.*

First Methodist Church, facing Atlanta Street, stood on the northwest corner of Atlanta and Church streets. It was a beautiful red brick building with stained glass windows. The pulpit and choir were on the Atlanta Street side of this building; thus the congregation would face Atlanta Street.

Smyrna Presbyterian Church was located on a small street that we know today as Memorial Place, between the First Baptist Church and the Smyrna Cemetery. The rear of the Presbyterian Church backed up to Church Street. The Presbyterian Church property was sold to Smyrna Assembly of God Church in 1964; the Presbyterian Church was relocated on Atlanta Road in early 1965. The Smyrna Assembly of God Church, after selling this building and grounds to First Baptist Church in 1983, erected their current sanctuary on King Springs Road. See *Smyrna Assembly of God Church, Hawthorne Avenue.*

NOTE: U.S. Highway 41 inside the Smyrna City Limits was referred to as Atlanta Street; north and south of the Smyrna City Limits, it was Atlanta Road.

First House

Beverly Cobb Amacker told that her grandparents, **William Virgil** and **Rubie Cobb** moved from the Shipp House, on Roswell Street, to this house on Church Street; from here, in 1918, they relocated to a farm on Old Concord Road. Beverly related, "As a child, even though my grandparents no longer lived in the Swain House, I was fascinated by the iron fence, about three feet high, along the sidewalk in the front of and on the side of this house." See *Old Concord Road.*

Mr. and Mrs. Henry Swain

Mr. and **Mrs. Henry Swain** and their family, in the days of my youth, lived in this house, which was located on the northwest corner of Memorial Place and Church Street. It was the only dwelling between Memorial Drive and First Baptist Church. According to First Baptist Church records, the Church, in October 1947, voted to purchase the Swain property for $7,500.00. On this property, adjoining the Church property, First Baptist Church's educational facility was built. See *Swain, Hughes Street* and *north side of Concord Road.*

First Baptist Church

The **First Baptist Church** congregation, after moving into the rock church building on the northeast corner of Church and King streets, held their first service on August 10, 1924 (now known as the First Baptist Church Chapel). Earlier First Baptist Church had been located on Atlanta Street, just north of Powder Springs Street.

First Baptist Church on the corner of Church and King streets. Many people in Smyrna have pictures of the Church made at different times. This photo made in the early years of the Church was the courtesy of Mike Terry. Note: The grass lawn in front of the Church. Circa 1926.

Hilda Wood and **Grady Chaffin** married December 16, 1950
Smyrna First Baptist Church
Reverend York Chambless and **Reverend E.B. Awtry**
Mr. and **Mrs. Grady Chaffin**

L-R: Sue Carol Miller, Ruth Haygood Chaffin, Bobbie Ruth Chaffin, Mildred Gann Hudlow, Sue Ingle Lewis, Hilda Wood Chaffin, Grady Griffin, J.E. Chaffin, Tom Tucker, Robert Lewis, Bert Alexander and "Pete" Wood

I think it is obvious how Church Street got its name. The nice thing about this arrangement (sanctuaries was that on Sunday mornings the congregations of all the churches could see each othe going to and/or from the services.

Smyrna Elementary School and **Smyrna High School**

The first school building on this site was constructed by the Smyrna School District an opened for classes in 1925. It was a large two-story building with a basement. The cafeteria was in th basement when I started to school in 1940. Each school lunch cost ten cents. (Prior to 1938, when separate high school building was erected, this building was called Smyrna School; it was the locatio of the elementary school, (grades 1 through 7) and the high school, grades 8 through 11).

NOTE: In the 1970s, when First Baptist Church was having the elementary school buildin razed, "Buddy" Mason, the building superintendent of First Baptist Church, called me and said, "Pet they are wrecking the old school building. Do you want the cornerstone? Because I really wanted th historical part of Smyrna, I made arrangements to have some friends remove the cornerstone and brir it to my house. The cornerstone will become the property of the Smyrna Museum when space available.

The Class of 1951 was the last one to graduate from Smyrna High School. Because th facilities for Orme Campbell High School (except for the 8th Grade hall) had not been completed f the Class of 1952, the senior students from both Smyrna and Fitzhugh Lee high schools, along wi grades 9 through 11 attended classes in their respective school. However, seniors from each scho received diplomas issued by Campbell High School; therefore, together they became the Class 1952. Gene Atkins, of Dixie Avenue, was handed the first diploma issued by Campbell High School the new gym. The 1951-1952 seniors attending school in the Smyrna High School Building that ye were known as North Smyrna, and those who attended school in the Fitzhugh Lee High Scho building were known as South Smyrna.

NOTE: The 8th Graders who started school in the fall of 1952 were the first ones to comple five years of education in the Campbell High School building. Laura Helen Jones (Allgoo remembers that first year having to take her lunch from home, and Mary Faith Manning (Williams another of those students, remembers that the milk truck would drive up daily to supply milk to g with their lunches.

NOTE: The Smyrna School property covers the entire block bordered by Church, Kin Stephens, and Reed streets. The Smyrna High School building was constructed in 1938 as a project the Works Progress Authority, known as the WPA. To my knowledge, in Smyrna this was the on building constructed by the WPA. First Baptist Church owns this building and all of the adjoinin property, which they purchased from the Cobb County Board of Education in1974. (Glad that th building is still standing, I would like to see my Church, First Baptist, consider restoring this buildi for use as an arts or drama facility—or something else that would benefit both the Church ar community.) Later on, Boy Scout Troop 88 constructed a Scout Hut on part of the former scho property; the Hut was dedicated in 1984.

Smyrna Elementary School built in 1925
Picture courtesy of Mildred Clayton Broyles

Smyrna High School built in 1938
Picture courtesy of Mildred Clayton Broyles

Smyrna Elementary School First Grade 1940 Miss Fannie B. McClure, Teacher

Back Row L-R: Mary Motter, Jimmie Lacy, Dorothy Ellen Pettet, Charles Campbell, Miss Fannie B. McClure, H.D. Gibson?, Barbara Ann Hughes, Elvery Hasty, Grace Jefferies, Bobby Tanner, Joe Davis. **Middle Row L-R:** Carrie Jean Black, Dewey Petty, Mary Lois Anderson, Bud Theodocian, Eleanor Swain, Lamar Akins, Rebecca McLean, and Emma Jean Faucett. **Front Row L-R:** Hubert Ward, "Pete" Wood, Johnnie Clayton, Charles Wade, Ernest Metters.

Smyrna Elementary School Mrs. Bonnie Keller Smith's Fifth Grade Circa 1942-1943 School Year
Bottom Row L-R: Billy Akins, Clarence Crother, Amos Johnson, Tommie Humphrey and Billy Wilson. **Second Row L-R:** Betty Joe Ellis, Lois Vaughan, Hilda Wood, Edna Earle Moon, Patricia Durham, Mary Nell Godfrey, Margaret Anderson. **Third Row L-R:** Marcelleus Hamby, Sue Ingle, Bessie Holcombe, Mrs. W. F. Smith, Martha Voss, June Wagoner, Margaret Tanner. **Back Row L-R:** Roy Bowling, Eugene Humphrey, John Parson, James Stephens, Edward Puckett, Henry Jenkins, Edgar Medlin, Douglas Turley and Earl Conn.

Smyrna High School Seventh Grade 1947 Teacher, Mrs. Curtis

Front Row L-R: Gene Barrett, Milton White, Bill Pavlovsky, Eugene Crow, Bobby Fortner, Bobby Carson, Hal Shields and Charles "Pete" Wood. **Second Row L-R:** Ruth Wilson, Mary June Quarles, Becky McLean, Mary Motter, Joyce Goodson, Susan Bradley, Dotsey Pettet, Charlotte Dison and Joann McDowell. **Third Row L-R:** Martha Sue Wilson, Mildred Hethcock, Mildred Clayton, Peggy Ann Lutz, Charlene Clark, Patsy Ferguson, Joan Bennett, Gwen McDuffee, Doris Bailey, Jean Bennett, Louise Akins and Mrs. Curtis, Teacher. **Top Row L-R:** Gene Johnson, Lamar Tedder, Calvin Calvert, Hugh Dunn, Jimmy Barrett, Bobby Shetter, Trudy McCook, Edwin Eaton, Roy Murdock, George O'Neil and Claude Gibson. Photo Courtesy of Mildred Clayton Broyles

Smyrna Girls Basketball Team Circa 1942
Front Row L-R: Ann Howard, Juanita Barfield, Ruth Chastain, Evelyn Petty, Margaret Hanson and Imojean Chastain. **Second Row L-R:** Polly Ware, Hazel Austin, Mary Cantrell and Katherine Manders **Back Row L-R:** Helen Blackwell, Mary Diemer, Jean Bobo, Joyce Bowman, Dorothy Shetter and Teacher/Coach Ella McBrayer. Courtesy of Ella McBrayer

Smyrna High School Class of 1943-1944 Girls Basketball Team
Front Row L-R: Jean Chastain, Margaret Hanson, Dorothy Shetter, and Mary Diemer. **Back Row L-R:** Betty Black, Elizabeth Hethcock, Phyllis Jones, Celia Craig, Coach, Greta Hensley and Willie Martin. Photo Courtesy of Jeanette Hanson Taylor.

Smyrna High School Girls Basketball Team 1950-1951
L-R: Jean Bennett, Jean Scoggins, Doris Bailey, Gwen Duffee, Bobbie Dean Martin, Joyce Scogin and Joan Bennett. Picture courtesy of Mildred Clayton Broyles.

Smyrna High School Boys Basketball Team 1948-1949
Front Row L-R: Jack Diemer, Buddy Scoggins, J.O. Davis, John Porterfield and Raymond Martin. **Back Row L-R:** Coach C.D. Strickland, John Leonard, Mickey Walker, Lamar Dickson, Ed Medlin, Cecil Haralson and Jimmie Guthrie.

Smyrna High School Boys Basketball Team 1950-1951
Back Row L-R: Lioneal Howard, Forward; Buddy Burgess, Guard; Wilson McEntyre, Guard; Lamar Tedder, Center; Lamar Akins, Forward; Milton White, Forward. **Front Row L-R:** Phillip Walker, Guard; Hoyt Dorris, Forward; Jimmie Guthrie, Captain-Center; Richard Durham, Guard; "Pete" Wood, Co-Captain Forward; and Lamar Gann, Guard.
Picture copied from Smyrna High School Yearbook, *The Talisman*, 1951.

Smyrna High School, 1950-1951 Senior Class
Assembled on the west side of the building. Lamar Tedder, class President presiding
Original Picture belonged to Jeanette Hanson Taylor.

Class of 1951 Smyrna High School, in front of First Baptist Church.

Front Row L-R: Joycelyn Wallace, Jean Black, Peggy Ann Lutz, Lois Anderson, June Emmett, Peggy Duncan, Charlotte Dison, Mary Motter, Dido Christian, and Shirley Martin. **Second Row L-R:** Rebecca McLean, Bobbie Dean Martin, Jean Faucett, Mildred Clayton, Gwen Duffee, Dotsey Pettett, Joan Bennett, Jean Scoggins, Jean Bennett and Lois Akins. **Third Row L-R:** Joann McDowell, Charlene Clark, Mary Butler, Jean Jeffares, Barbara Bryant, Glenton Allen, Hazel Grant, Benny Lou O'Bryant, Doris Bailey, Mary June Quarles and Ella Scogin. **Forth Row L-R:** Hugh Dunn, Bobby (R.D.) Carson, Milton White, "Pete" Wood, Bobby Fortner, Hoyt Dorris, Fred Anderson, Grady Swafford and Donald Merritt. **Back Row L-R:** Phillip Walker, Jimmie Guthrie, Buddy Burgess, Wilson McEntyre, Miller Davis, Lamar Tedder and Lamar Akins. **Graduates not pictured:** Emialee Whitener, Richard Durham, Jill Quarles and Air Force student Jerle Hernandez. **Mascots:** Nancy Strickland and David Lutz. Not pictured Mac McBrayer who was sick. Picture courtesy of Mildred Clayton Broyles.

SMYRNA HIGH SCHOOL
CLASS OF 1951

Lamar Akins
Louise Akins
Glenton Allen
Emialee Anderson
Fred Anderson
Lois Anderson
Doris Bailey
Jean Bennett
Joan Bennett
Jean Black
Barbara Bryant
Buddy Burgess
Mary Butler
Bobby Carson
Dido Christian
Charlene Clark
Mildred Clayton

Miller Davis
Charlotte Dison
Hoyt Dorris
GwenDuffee
Peggy Duncan
Hugh Dunn
Richard Durham
June Emmett
Emma Jean Faucett
Bobby Fortner
HazelGrant
Jimmie Guthrie
Doris Hulsey
Jean Jeffares
Peggy Lutz
Bobby Dean Martin
Shirley Martin

Joann McDowell
Donald Merritt
Mary Motter
Wilson McEntyre
Rebecca McLean
Benny Lou O'Bryant
Dotsy Pettett
Jill Quarles Poss
Mary June Quarles
Jean Scoggins
Ella Scogin
Grady Swafford
Lamar Tedder
Phillip Walker
Jocelyn Wallace
Milton White
Pete Wood

Mascots
Nancy Stricklin
David Lutz

Class Officers
Lamar Tedder, President
Lamar Akins, Vice President
Charlotte Dison, Secretary
Joan McDowell, Treasurer

Jean Scoggins, Miss Smyrna High School

PRINCIPAL
Jasper Griffin

ASSISTANT PRINCIPAL AND **COACH**
Mr. C.D. Stricklin

TEACHERS
Mrs. Russell (Corrine) Hosch, Counselor
Mrs G.C. (Lena Mae) Green, Latin and Librarian
Miss Eunice Padgett, Mathematics
Mrs. John (Martha) Chastain, Home Economics
Mr. Claude H. Walker, Social Science
Mrs. Leslie (Mona) Camp, English
Mr. H.B. McClure, Commercial
Mr. Robert Alford, Science
Mrs. Jasper (Bess) Griffin, Music and Dancing
Ken Stanton, Band

Mr. Jasper Griffin Smyrna Elementary and High School Principal
Picture copied from *The Talisman* Smyrna High School Annual, 1949-1950

Mrs. Corrine Hosch English and Homeroom Teacher
Counselor
Picture copied from *The Talisman*
Smyrna High School Annual, 1949-1950

Smyrna High School Class of 1951, First reunion held June 1, 1968
(At Squires Steak House U.S. 41 Four Lane Highway)
Standing L-R: Lamar Akins, Grady Swafford, Lamar Tedder, Hoyt Dorris, Miller Davis, "Pete" Wood, Phillip Walker, Joann McDowell, Fred Anderson, Jean Scoggins Zimmerman, Donald Merritt, Joan Bennett, Hugh Dunn, Jean Bennett, Bobby Fortner, Jasper Griffin, Principal and Doris Bailey Fowler. **Seated L-R:** Peggy Lutz, Barbara Bryant Emmett, Joycelyn Wallace Fain, Benny Lou O'Bryant Tackett, Peggy Duncan Dickson, Dido Christian, Mrs. Corrine Hosch, Teacher, Louise Akins, Emma Jean Faucett Barden, Mildred Clayton Broyles and Mary Motter Fowler.

Councilman "Bill" Scoggins, Martin Cantrell and **Councilman "Pete" Wood**
Shown just before the Smyrna Elementary School was razed in 1994
The school opened in 1925
Photo courtesy of "Pete" Wood

Second House

Mary Crowe and her sons, **Jerry** and **Ronald**, resided in this house, between Reed and Davis Streets. The Crowe house was located on part of the property that at one time belonged to Mr. Virgil Cobb.

NOTE: B.F. Reed Construction Company purchased the Crowe property, as well as other tracts of land bordered by Church, Reed, Stephens, and Davis streets.

Southern Manor Apartments

Southern Manor Apartments were built on the aforementioned properties by B.F. Reed Construction Company. B.F.'s, brother, Raymond Reed, purchased the apartments sometime in the 1950s and sold them near the end of the Twentieth Century. The purchaser converted them into condominiums; they are now called Madison Manor. After Lillie and I married, in 1960, we rented from Raymond the second unit in the first building on Davis Street; having lived there six months, we moved to our first house, on Pinehurst Drive, off King Springs Road.

Third House

Mr. and **Mrs. Grover Warren Davis** lived on the northwest corner of Church and Davis streets. They had seven children: **Sidney**, **Warren**, **James**, **Julius**, known as "Jule," **Margaret**, **Elizabeth**, and **Dorothy**. Mrs. Davis, the former Amy Hughes, was from South Carolina. Mr. Davis, known as "G.W.," was a railroad engineer whose run was from Atlanta to South Carolina. "Having worked for the railroad for fifty years, he claimed he never injured a passenger or the train while working for the railroad," his grandson, Johnny Fulton, related. Beverly Amacker remarked, "When Mr. Davis walked by the school, he always had candy or gum that he would pass out to the students on the playground." The Davis Family were members of Smyrna Presbyterian Church.

Sidney Davis married Mary Bizzell, who grew up on Roswell Street, in the house where my grandmother Tucker had lived when I was a small boy. See *west side of Roswell Street.*

Warren Davis and his wife, Joyce, who was from Cobb County, had two sons: Bobby and Buddy. Joyce and Warren lived in Moultrie, where Warren died a few years ago. Bobby Davis and his wife, Shirley, live in Moultrie. Buddy Davis and his wife, Tina, live in Dothan, Alabama.

James Davis and his wife, Sue, live in Myrtle Beach, South Carolina.

Julius Davis, known as "Jule," and his wife, Maurice, live in Vinings. "Jule," 90 plus years of age, still plays golf regularly!

Margaret Catherine Davis married Ray Fulton. I was first acquainted with Mr. Fulton when he was employed at First National Bank in Atlanta, where he worked a long time. My career at Fulton National Bank spanned many of the years while he was still working downtown. The Fulton Family were members of Smyrna Presbyterian Church. See *east side of King Street.*

Elizabeth Davis married Henry Konigsmark, Jr., in the late 1930s. They had two sons: Henry Konigsmark III, known as "Hank," and Reed.

Soon after their marriage, Henry constructed a house on Atlanta Terrace, where he and Elizabeth lived until he entered the United States Army during World War II. After the War, he built a house on Dunn Street, where he and Elizabeth lived until 1952. At that time, they bought another house on Atlanta Terrace, where they were residing when Henry died. Elizabeth continued living there until the area was sold for redevelopment. At that time, she moved back to Dunn Street but to a different house from that where she raised her familySee *Konigsmark, east side of Dunn Street,* and *Atlanta Street, from Mrs. Mazie's to Pearce Matthews.*

NOTE: Atlanta Terrace is part of the property where Montclair subdivision was developed during the great renaissance period of the 1990s.)

Elizabeth, a floral designer, along with her sister-in-law, Louise Osborn Konigsmark, known as "Bill," owned and operated a florist on Atlanta Street. Henry Konigsmark, Jr., who worked in downtown Atlanta, was also one of the developers of Jonquil Plaza Shopping Center, on Atlanta Street. The Konigsmarks were members of First Methodist Church. Elizabeth, who was a member of the Smyrna Social Club, founded in 1908, died suddenly in the early part of the Twenty-first Century. See *Osborn, Atlanta Street, from Marlowe's to Creatwood.*

Dorothy Davis married Everett Lee; they had one son, Allen. Dorothy and Everett lived in Rome. Everett died many years ago.

Fourth House

Mr. and **Mrs. Leland Williams** lived here before the Cobbs. They had one daughter, **Virginia Lenell**. Leland served in the United States Merchant Marines during World War II. Afterwards, he worked for Atlantic Steel Company, in Atlanta, where he retired. See *Leland Williams, north side of Hill Street,* and *east side of Old Concord Road,* and *Virgil Cobb, west side of Old Concord Road.*

Mr. and **Mrs. Ralph Cobb**

Ralph and **Edna Ledbetter Cobb** resided next door to the Davis Family. They had three daughters: **Beverly**, **Ann**, and **Nancy**. Beverly Cobb (Amacker) said that her mother and dad purchased this house on Church Street from Ralph's dad, Virgil Cobb. Prior to relocating to this house, the Ralph Cobb Family lived with Ralph's parents, on Old Concord Road. Their second daughter, Ann, was born after they moved to this house. The Cobb Family were members of First Methodist Church. See *Ledbetter, south side of Fleming Street* and *Williams, east side of Old Concord Road and Cobb, west side of Old Concord Road.*

Ralph Cobb who worked for the railroad, played on the Smyrna Amateur Baseball Team that my dad managed. Probably one of the best friends my dad ever had, Ralph and Dad were close! Ralph died of cancer in the 1950s, when his daughters were young. Cobb Park on Bank Street was named in memory of Ralph. Beverly Cobb Amacker remembers, "For years, during the ball season, we spent every Saturday at a baseball game."

Edna Ledbetter Cobb, whose parents earlier had lived on Fleming Street, was a homemaker during the years their daughters were growing up. While her daughter, Beverly, was a student at Campbell High School, Edna worked in the lunchroom there; afterwards, she managed the cafeteria at King Springs Elementary School, where Lillie and I saw her often during the years our children were students there.

Edna and her brothers grew up in Atlanta, where one of her brothers, Bob Ledbetter, played football at Boys High School, from which he graduated.

Beverly Cobb married Gerald Amacker, known as "Jerry." They had two children: Alicia Michelle and Scott Allen.

Alicia Michelle Amacker (Duncan) had one daughter, Ashton Elizabeth.

Scott Allen Amacker married Nancy Buese from New Jersey. They had no childen.

Ann Cobb married Jimmy Pressley from Cobb County. They had one daughter, Kelli Ann. Jimmy was the son of Gaines Pressley and grandson of Mr. and Mrs. William Pressley, who lived on the corner of King and Bank streets, where the City Hall is currently located. Jimmy is deceased. See *south side of Bank Street.*

Nancy Cobb married Charles Griffin; they had no children. They live in Sharpsburg.

Beverly Amacker shared, "When my family moved to Church Street in 1942, the street in front of our house was still a dirt road; the portion from Atlanta Street to the front of Mr. and Mrs. Davis' house had been paved. I remember the section in front of our house being paved later but I do not remember the year." She stated that the fifth and sixth houses were built between the Cobb and the Leonard homes after she and her family had moved into the fourth one.

Fifth House

Claude and **Frances Nunnally** and their son, **Ronnie**, resided in the first new house, which was next door to the Cobbs. Mrs. Nunnally, the former Frances McDonald, moved from Roswell to Atlanta Road at Gilmore Streetcar Stop, in the Oakdale Community. Frances worked for Rich's in the accounting department downtown, and later she worked in the ladies sportswear department at the Cobb Center store in Smyrna. Claude first worked for Hub Ford and later at Wade Ford, from which he retired in 1993. For the last forty years, the Nunnallys have lived in the Bennett Woods subdivision. See *Whitfield on Dixie Avenue.*

Ronnie Nunnally married Lynn Hicks of Atlanta. They had one son, Christopher.

Sixth House

Gaston and **Opal Tatum** and their daughters, **Dianne** and **Deborah**, known as "**Debbie**," lived in the second new house, next door to the Nunnallys.

Dianne Tatum married Edward Carter. They had two daughters, Margie and Ginna, and two grandsons. Dianne retired from the Cobb County School Board of Education.

Deborah Tatum married but divorced. They had one daughter, Stacy.

Gaston was from Pickens County, where he and Opal met while attending Pickens County High School. They moved to Smyrna in 1951 for Gaston to work at Lockheed Aircraft Corporation.

Mrs. Tatum, the former Opal Holmes from Cherokee County, is a sister of Madon Holmes Gillham and Carolyn Weikert. Their dad, Mr. Elmer H. Holmes, was the dairyman at Creatwood Dairies.

NOTE: Mann Street is a short street that separated the Tatum and Leonard homes. See *Mann Street.*

Seventh House

Mr. and **Mrs. Frank Leonard** were residents of the next house. Mrs. Leonard was the former Rebecca Hilda Reed. They had five sons: **John Franklin, Jr.**, **Robert William**, known as "Bobby," **Raymond Patrick**, known as "Pat," **Charles Edward**, and **Thomas Claude**, known as "Tommy." Frank Leonard worked at Fisher Body Company in Atlanta.

Rebecca Reed Leonard was the daughter of Mr. and Mrs. B.F. Reed, Sr., who lived on the corner of Atlanta and Nelson streets in downtown Smyrna. See *Atlanta Street, from Mrs. Mazie's to Creatwood.*

John Franklin Leonard, Jr., married Laura Carol Hood.

Robert William Leonard married Charlotte Jean Alldread.

Raymond Patrick Leonard married Siromi Desaram.

Charles Edward Leonard married Susan Oldham.

Thomas Claude Leonard married Lane Kelley; later he married Margie McGee.

Eighth House

Mr. and **Mrs**. **Edward Branch** and their son, **Bobby**, lived down the hill, west of the Leonards' house.

NOTE: The Branch house was razed, and the Riveria Apartments were built there in the 1960s.

Ninth House

Mr. and **Mrs**. **Mulkey**, who had grown children, lived farther down the hill from the Edward Branch Family. Mrs. Mulkey worked at Regenstein's Department Store in Atlanta; Mr. Mulkey was retired. The Mulkey house was later moved to Old Concord Road, where it still exists, old and weathered looking, on the west side of Old Concord Road, near Nickajack Creek and about three blocks north of the intersection of Church and Old Concord roads.

Mr. and **Mrs. Dunton**

Later on **Mr**. and **Mrs**. **James Raymond Dunton** lived here with their five children: **Joe**, **Earline**, **Judy**, **James Robert**, and **Margaret Joan**. (Margaret Joan was born after the family moved from Church Street to Concord Road.) Mr. Dunton, known to his friends as "J. R." and his wife, Martha, moved to this newly built house just beyond the curve where Flagler Circle currently connects with Church Street, but nearer the intersection of Church Street and South Cobb Drive. Mr. Dunton bought this property and built this house himself, even molding the cement blocks he used in construction. When finished, this house was totally constructed from hand-made cement blocks. Raymond Dunton was a cement contractor. The Dunton Family were members of First Methodist Church.

Joe Thomas Dunton married Ellen Nichols; they had three children: Thomas Anthony, Jo Ellen, and Jamie Lynn.

Earline Dunton married Clyde Pettet. They had one daughter, Kelly, who married Gary Gray. They had two children: Ansley Rachel and Zachary Robert.

Judy Dunton married Quenton Thomas Lewallen; they had three children, Michael, Jason and John. Judy and Quenton divorced. Judy then married Robert Bartram; they had two children Erin Diane and Ryan Michael.

James Robert Dunton married Nanci Fredrick of Sandy Springs.

Margaret Joan Dunton married Winston Clyde Burger III; they had one daughter, Kathryn Rachel. Margaret and Winston Clyde are divorced. See *Dunton, north side of Bank Street, south side of Church Street, south side of Church Road, The Country Road, South* and *north sides of Concord Road,* and *south side of Concord Road, The Country Road.*

CHURCH STREET
South Side

Appreciation is extended to Miller Davis and his brother, Clark, for their help in remembering the families that lived on the south side of Church Street, where Miller and Clark grew up; to Joyce Hill Harper and Polly Harper Webb for information about the Harper Family; to Betty Henderson Davies, for relating about her family, the Hendersons; to Athlene Mitchell Paulk for data about her family, the Mitchells; and to Sue Sargent Cantrell for information about the Kinard Family. I thank Beverly Cobb Amacker for sharing her knowledge about some of the other residents of the south side of Church Street, and to Kenneth Williams, for sharing about his family, the Williams.

First House

Mr. and **Mrs. H.B. Mitchell** raised their family in the first house, on the south side of Church Street, a large green one that was known locally as the "H.B. Mitchell House." They had seven children: **Sam, Virginia, Octavia,** known as "Octa," **Willie, Alexander Mable, Harry**, and **Athlene**. Mrs. Mitchell was a Mable, a member of the family on Floyd Road, in Mableton, that lived in what is now known as the "Mable House." See *note at end of Mitchell Family information.*

Sam Mitchell married Grace Worley. They had two sons: Sammy and Richard. After their marriage Sam and Grace lived in the Mitchell House.

Virginia Mitchell married Gene Rice, who operated the Rice Furniture Store on Atlanta Street in Smyrna. They had two children. See *west side of Lee Street.*

Octavia Mitchell, known as "Octa," married Robert Bacon. They had four children: Mitchell, Freddie, Mike, and Nancy. The Bacon Family have been members of Smyrna Presbyterian Church. Later on, Robert and "Octa" built a house on Memory Lane off Collier Drive, where Robert lived until his death. See *Bacon, east side of King Street.*

Willie Mitchell married Harlan Watkins and lived in Cartersville. They had two children: Daniel Eugene and Janice Athlene. Willie died in 1984.

Daniel Eugene Watkins, who had two sons, is retired from the Boy Scouts of America and lives in Washington, D.C.

Janice Athlene Mitchell married Reverend Jim Clifford. They had two daughters, who live in Birmingham, Alabama.

Alexander Mable Mitchell married Mary Otwell of Roswell. They had one daughter, Sue Lane, who married Erwin Thompson. The Thompsons had three sons and a daughter.

Harry Mitchell
Smyrna City councilman
1952-1953

Harry Mitchell married Alice Estes, who was a sister of Belle Arrington. Alice lived with the Arringtons on Sunset Avenue before her marriage to Harry, who served on the Smyrna City Council, 1952-1953. Later on Alice and Harry built a house on Northview Place, off Collier Drive, where they lived until his death. See *south side of Sunset Avenue.*

Athlene Mitchell, *Miss Smyrna* in 1941, married Ed Hiles, Executive Director of the Georgia Savings and Loan League. Later on, after Mr. Hiles' death, Athlene married Willis D. Paulk; they lived in Atlanta.

When I was a young man, I knew Mr. Ed. Hiles, a nice man. I remember the time he gave me two patriotic prints, which Lillie had framed; these hung in our home for many years.

Athlene remembers the tennis courts on Love Street: "As a teenager, a group of us proceeded to play on this court. We knew it was private, but what could it hurt if we enjoyed playing there for a while? Mrs. Manning—with hands on her hips—reminded us this was a private court and ran us off. The next time we teenagers had a watermelon cutting, the remnants were disposed of privately—onto those courts.

"My group of teenagers included Mary Brawner," continued Athlene. "I remember we would go to visit Mary, and she would take us to Brawner Sanitarium, where the residents always had ice cream on Sunday afternoons. If we teenagers went to the back door, Max, a friendly Black employee there, would hand out dishes of delicious ice cream to us."

NOTE: The historical Mable House, along with the Mableton Cultural Arts Center and the Barnes Amphitheater, both located on Floyd Road in Mableton, are part of the Cobb County Parks and Recreation Department. The Amphitheater is named for the well-known Barnes Family, in Mableton, in regard to their many contributions to the area. Roy Barnes, a native son of Mableton, and an attorney in Marietta, served as State Representative, State Senator, and Governor of the State of Georgia. He was instrumental in obtaining funds for the building of the Amphitheater.

The Worley Family

Mr. and **Mrs. Gordon Worley** moved to this first house after the Mitchells had vacated. (Very large, the Mitchell House could accommodate many people). Mrs. Worley was the former Emma Potter. Mr. and Mrs. Worley had five children: **Julia**, **Harriett**, **Nell**, **Grace**, and **Ben**, all in my parents' generation.

Julia Worley married Buna Walker; they had four children: Mickey, Phillip, Donald, and Beverly Jane, known as "Jane." According to information from the family, Buna Walker bought the Mitchell House sometime in the late 1940s. See *south side of Spring Street* and *Atlanta Street, from Mapps to R & M Café, Austin, south side of Sunset Avenue,* and *Wood, north side of Bank Street.*

Harriett Worley, known as "Hattie," married Kenneth Rice. They had one daughter, Nancye, who married John Glenn. "Hattie" and Kenneth owned and operated a furniture store in Marietta.

Nell Worley married Charles McMillan, known as "Red." They had three children: Dorothy Jean, known as "Dot," Charles, known as "Hike," and Larry. At one time the McMillan Family lived with the Worleys in the Mitchell House. The McMillans were members of First Baptist Church, where "Red," with a beautiful bass voice, was active in the music ministry.

Dorothy Jean McMillan married Harry Peacock from Atlanta. They had three children: Stephen, known as "Steve," Barbara, and Linda.

"Hike" McMillan married Greta Hensley, who grew up on Roswell Street. They had three children: Laura, David, and Beth. "Hike" McMillan was ordained a Baptist Minister at First Baptist Church. His first pastorate was at First Baptist Church of Woodstock; afterwards, he was pastor of several churches in North Carolina. See *Hensley, west side of Roswell Street.*

Larry McMillan married Jean Goodwin of Smyrna. They had three children: Christopher, known as "Chris," Lisa, and Kent. Larry and Jean live in Dalton. See Goodwin, *West Side of Roswell Street, and McMillan, north side of Spring Street.*

Grace Worley married Sam Mitchell, who grew up in the Mitchell House. They had two children: Samuel, known as "Sammy," and Richard.

"Sammy" Mitchell married Margaret Voyles of Oakdale. They had three children: Sammy, Carolyn, and Billy.

Richard Mitchell married Rose Marie Bradshaw of Smyrna. They had two children: Tammy and Ricky. Richard and Rose Marie live in Marietta.

Ben Worley lived in the Mitchell House with his parents. A bachelor, he drove a taxi for his livelihood. One day on his way to pick up a passenger, he suffered a heart attack. When his taxi hit a utility pole, Ben was killed.

NOTE: The Potter Family listed below who lived in the Smyrna area, were related to Mrs. Gordon Worley. The Potters never lived in this house on Church Street.

The Potters

Mrs. Gordon Worley was the former Emma Potter, a sister of Miss Hattie Potter and Miss Henrietta Potter, both of whom lived on the south side of Atlanta Road, just north of the Chattahoochee River. (Their house stood near the overhead bridge at the railroad.) Gardner Potter was their nephew.

The Gardner Potter Family

Gardner Potter, a nephew to Mrs. Gordon Worley and his family moved to Smyrna in 1954 He and his wife, Emily, had four children: Allen, Elizabeth, Johnny, and Bobby, all of whom graduated from Campbell High School and Mercer University. Gardner and Emily lived on Hillside Drive, in the Cheney Woods subdivision, which was developed in the 1950s. As a real estate broker and developer, Mr. Potter built and sold many houses in the Smyrna area in the 1950s and 1960s.

In 1960 Gardner Potter founded Potter and Company, a real estate and insurance business. Later he established Central Mortgage Corporation, which his sons, Allen and Johnny, now operate on South Cobb Drive, in the Potter Building, which Gardner Potter constructed in 1966. Gardner was a long-time member of First United Methodist Church, a 32nd degree Mason and a member of the Smyrna Lions Club until it was disbanded. He was the first president of the Smyrna Rotary Club, and later elected District Governor of Rotary. He also served as Chairman of Smyrna's first Civil Services Board and director on the Board of the Bank of Smyrna. Mr. Potter died September 19, 2005.

The Potters have been an integral part of the business and civic life of Smyrna for a half century. Allen, Johnny, and their families are active members of First Methodist Church, where Allen is a member of the adult choir. Allen is also a long-time member of the Smyrna Optimist Club. Both Allen and Johnny have been involved with West Smyrna Swim and Tennis Club from its inception; instrumental in its being built, they have assisted in maintaining it through the years.

Allen Potter married Susan Safran from Portsmouth, Ohio, and Narrows, Virginia. They had two daughters, Emily Clare, known as "Mimi," and Leslie, two granddaughters, and a grandson.

"Mimi" Potter, a graduate of Campbell High School and Georgia Institute of Technology, married Victor Rodriguez of Vero Beach, Florida. They had two daughters: Carmen Clare, known as "CiCi," and Liliana Isabel, known as "Lili."

Leslie Potter married Tom Lawley of Atlanta; they had a son, Thomas Joseph Lawley IV. Leslie Potter Lawley, a graduate of Campbell High School, Vanderbilt University, and Emory University School of Medicine, is a dermatologist.

Elizabeth Ann Potter, known as "Liz," married Charles Merrell of Charlotte, North Carolina. They had a daughter, Kristy, who married Chris Morley of Charlotte, North Carolina. They had two sons, Corban and Zane. "Liz," now divorced, lives in Charlotte.

John W. Potter, known as "Johnny," was married to Betty Cavallo of Marietta; they had one son, John Andrew, known as "Andy." Johnny is now married to the former Dianne Shirley Newman of Smyrna, who had two children from her first marriage: a son, Brett Newman, and a daughter, Amanda Newman, both of whom are graduates of Campbell High School. Amanda, a graduate of North Georgia College, in Dahlonega, teaches in an elementary school in Smyrna.

Robert Randall Potter, known as "Bobby," married Ann Pope of Atlanta. They had two sons: William Randall, known as "Will," and Robert Mark. "Bobby," an attorney, lives in Atlanta.

Second House

Mr. and **Mrs. George Miller**, who moved from Powder Springs to Smyrna in the early part of the Twentieth Century to be near the streetcar line, lived in the next house. Mrs. Miller was the former Eula Smith. They had six grown children: **Mamie**, **Florence**, **Nell**, **Corine**, **George Miller II**, known as "Buck," and **James**.

Clark Davis recalls that his Granddaddy Miller had a chicken house along the property line by the Mitchell House; he also had a mule he used to plow his garden, and, sometimes he raised pigs. After the mule died, Clark remembers he and Miller had to pull the plow to till the garden.

Mamie Miller married Speigal Huey from Calhoun. They had no children.

Florence Miller married Clyde Wheeler from Austell.

Corine Miller married Glenn Bearden from Marietta. They had a daughter, Barbara Ann, who married Burgess Williams. See *west side of Lee Street.*

"Buck" Miller was married to Evelyn from Redan, Georgia. They had two children: George and Patricia. "Buck," Evelyn, and their children lived here with the George Millers for a few years.

James Miller was stricken with infantile paralysis when he was three years old. Progressing with his walking, he was stricken at the age of four with spinal meningitis. From that time on he was unable to walk or care for himself. With tender loving care, the Millers kept him in their home his entire life.

Nell Miller married King Davis from Smyrna. They had two sons, Clark and Miller. Nell and King lived in this house with Mr. and Mrs. George Miller. (Miller Davis and I started and finished school together in the Smyrna High School Class of 1951 and have been friends all of our lives. We were both born in 1933, six days apart: I was born on November 29th; Miller was born on December 5th. That makes me older.)

King Davis was a professional man. He worked in the bond department at Citizens and Southern National Bank in Atlanta; his office was on the southeast corner of Broad and Marietta Streets, one block south of Henry Grady Square. He later worked as comptroller at Abernathy Publishing Company. King Davis died May 7, 1955, in his middle years, just before Clark graduated from Campbell High School. See *Davis, east side of Roswell Street.*

Miller Davis married Joyce Lovern, who grew up on the south side of Powder Springs Street; she was the daughter of Mr. and Mrs. James Lovern. Mr. Lovern owned and operated Lovern Construction Company, in Smyrna, for many years. Miller and Joyce had four children: Dana, Mike, Bobby, and Brent. See *Lovern, south side of Powder Springs Street.*

The George Miller House on Church Street at the end of Dunn's Alley was built by Mr. John Baldwin in 1908, and razed in the 1980s. Photo courtesy of Mike Terry.

Clark Davis, a graduate of the Campbell High School Class of 1955, married Sandra Teasley, a member of the Campbell High School Class of 1959, from the Log Cabin Community, south of Smyrna. They had three children: Lynn, Steve, and Allen. Sandra died from cancer in the 1980s.

Several years after Sandra's death, Clark Davis married Ellen Roundtree of Jacksonville, Florida. Ellen had three children from a previous marriage.

The Teasleys

Sandra Teasley Davis was one of three daughters of Mr. and Mrs. Roy A. Teasley; the other two were Glenda and Jan. Mrs. Teasley, the former Lenora Henderson and known as "Nokey," was the daughter of Mr. and Mrs. D.A. Henderson, Sr., of Cornelia. Mrs. Teasley had four sisters (Austell, Ruth, Kathleen, and Martha) and two brothers (William and D.A, Jr.). Mrs. Teasley taught for many years at Fitzhugh Lee School.

Glenda Teasley, from a previous marriage, had a son, David. Glenda's second marriage was to Frank Downs, known as "Sandy"; they had a son, Scott.

Jan Teasley married Bill Firmery; they live in Florida.

NOTE: Mr. Roy Teasley was the principal of both Fitzhugh Lee (elementary and high schools) during the 1940s and 1950s. Teasley Elementary School, in Vinings, is named for Mr. Teasley. The Teasleys lived on Log Cabin Drive near Carmichael's Store and Log Cabin Sunday School until plans were made for 1-285 to encompass their house; then they moved to Northview Place in Smyrna.

HOT PANTS
by Miller Davis

Miller Davis tells a story of his growing up in Smyrna. "When I was six or seven years old, most of the streets in Smyrna were still unpaved. The City Fathers at that time decided that it was time to have the streets paved. The weather was cold; thus the pavers, using diesel oil, would build fires to keep warm. One day, in particular, in the fall of the year, the workmen did not completely extinguish a fire.

"As kids would do, some of my buddies and I were playing around the fire those men had started at the back of First Methodist Church parking lot, across the street from my home. All of a sudden, one of the kids hollered: 'Miller, your pants are on fire.' I looked down to see the bottom of my pants' leg in a blaze. I took off, running to my house with my pants burning. My mother was mopping the floor in the kitchen; when she saw me with my pants on fire, she jerked me up, stuck my leg into the mop water, and put out the fire! The bottom of my pants' leg was really burned, but Mother was able to patch it. I kept on wearing the pants as if nothing had happened. That shows how frugal people were in those days: they did not throw away anything that could be salvaged and used again."

GUARDIAN ANGEL
by Miller Davis

"One day when I was six years old, some other little boys and I were playing ball in the front yard of my house on Church Street. I was eating a banana. Somehow that banana became lodged in my throat; I was choking to death, or 'literally dying.' The banana wouldn't come up, and it wouldn't go down.

"George Groce, a big man, lived on Bank Street. For some reason, he happened to be walking down Church Street toward the coal yard by the railroad. He saw my plight and took the matter into his own hands. Taking me by the waist, he turned my head down and shook me. The banana came out of my mouth, and I was able to breathe—I was okay! From that day on, every time I saw George Groce, I thought of him as my guardian angel even though he didn't look like one."

Dunn's Alley

Between the George Miller home and the next house was a walking path called "Dunn's Alley." It ran from Church Street to Love Street, which is now Concord Road. That alley today would go along the west side of First United Methodist Church. If a person in this section of Smyrna were going to Brinkley Park, he would walk through "Dunn's Alley," a good short cut from the north side of town to the park. (Most people did not have cars in those days; a little short cut helped so much.)

Third House

Mr. and **Mrs. Jackson Kinard** were residents of the next house. They had two children: **Gene** and **Effie**. Mr. and Mrs. Kinard were members of First Methodist Church.

Effie Kinard married Duff Cantrell. See *Cantrell, Reed Street.*

NOTE: The Kinnard House was razed, a dental office, still standing, was built on this site.

Fourth House

Dr. and **Mrs. D.C. Landers** lived in the nice brick house, still standing on the southeast corner of King Street and facing Church Street. They had one son, **Robert**, known as "Bobby." Mrs. Landers was the former Julia McCleskey from Acworth. Dr. Landers, who owned and operated Smyrna Drug Company, was a pharmacist. The Landers were members of First Methodist Church; Mrs. Landers was a member of the Smyrna Social Club, founded in 1908.

Dr. Robert Landers, known as "Bobby," married Jacqueline Hyde, known as "Jacque." They had two children, Wayne and Connie, and one grandson, Dayton Allen Landers.

"Jacque" Hyde Landers grew up on DeFoors Ferry Road in northwest Atlanta. (In that area is Hyde Park, named for her family.) "Jacque," a long-time member and former president of the Jonquil Garden Club, is also a member of the Smyrna Social Club.

After his father died, Dr. Robert Landers, known as "Bobby," continued to own and operate Smyrna Drug Store on Atlanta Street, even handling the pharmaceutical needs for the patients at Brawner Hospital, until he closed the drug store, at the beginning of the City renovation period in the late 1980s. Afterwards he became Chief Pharmacist for Saint Joseph's Hospital in Atlanta. After Windy Hill Hospital was built, Dr. "Bobby" Landers opened the hospital pharmacy, where he worked until he retired. "Bobby" died in the fall of 2002. I miss him!

Fifth House

The "Dodd House" was the next dwelling on Church Street. The only thing I remember about the **Dodd Family** is their dog! One time when I was delivering the Dodds' paper, their dog bit me. The dog was under their house, which did not have underpinning. I did not see him; thus when I started up the steps to put the paper onto the porch, he bit my leg. That was the first time I was ever bitten by a dog, but it was not the last. (This happened before the Southern Manor Apartments were built.)

Sixth House

Mr. and **Mrs. Samuel Jefferson Crowe** lived in the house between the homes of the Dodds and Mrs. Ida Harper. Mrs. Crowe was the former Effie Lenora McWaters. Mr. Crowe, whom we called "Uncle Jeff," rode the first streetcar that ran between Marietta and Atlanta in 1905; in February

1947 he rode the last streetcar that ran this route. (The aforementioned information was furnished by Lucile Cobb Crowe.) See *Crowe, Old Roswell Road.*

Seventh House

Mrs. Ida Viola Hamby Harper resided in the next house. The widow of **Roy Harry Harper**, she had five sons: **Thomas James**, known as "T.J.," **Sam**, **William Ray**, **Harry**, and **Henry**, the latter two being twins. See *Hamby, south side of Love Street.*

Thomas James Harper, known as "T.J.," married Irene Towns. They had three children: Thomas Ervin, known as "Tommy," James Leroy, and Frances Pauline, known as "Polly." Thomas James, known as "T.J." was killed in a sawmill accident in March 1940, when his children were young. Thus his children and their mother lived with Mrs. Ida Harper on Church Street and later on Love Street. Irene Towns Harper attended Smyrna Elementary and High schools.

Tommy Erwin Harper, known as "Tommy," married Joyce Hill of Smyrna. They had two children: Lori and Kenny. On Havilon Way, Joyce and "Tommy" have been neighbors of Lillie and me for thirty-five years; they moved to this street when Rem Bennett, Sr., began developing the subdivision in the early 1960s. "Tommy," a fireman, was employed with the City of Smyrna Fire Department for twenty-seven years before retiring. Both he and Joyce had worked for many years for John and Virginia Sargent at the Dairy Queen on South Cobb Drive in Smyrna. "Tommy" died in the summer of 2004.

Lori Harper married but divorced.

Kenny Harper and his wife, Sandra, had one son, Justin, and one granddaughter, Ashley.

Frances Pauline Harper, known as "Polly," was the daughter of Thomas J. and Irene Towns Harper. She married Hubert Lindsey Webb; they had three children: Ricky Ray, Cheryl Anne, and Angela Renee.

Ricky Ray Webb married Ramona Padgett; they had a son, Kyle Lindsey. Ricky Ray later married Debbie Diekfuss.

Cheryl Anne Webb married Glen Leslie Ross; they had one daughter, Cassie Nicole.

Angela Renee Webb married Roderick Tolbert. They had two children: Ashley Renee and Tyler Madison.

James Leroy Harper married Carolyn Nunnually and had one daughter, Saundria, known as "Sandy." Leroy and Carolyn divorced.

Sam Harper. See *Sam Harper Family* below.

William Ray Harper married Margaret Green from the Marietta area. They had two children: William, known as "Billy," and Beverly, who lived in Marietta.

Harry Harper, one of the twin sons of Mr. and Mrs. Roy Harper, died when he was eleven years old.

Henry Harper, the other twin son, who never married, is now deceased.

The Sam Harper Family

Sam Harper married **Louise Lindley**, who grew up north of Belmont Hills, near Smyrna. They had three children: **Henry**, **Harry**, and **Sue**, who also lived in the seventh house, where Mrs. Ida

Harper had previously lived. After Sam's death, Louise continued to reside here until near the end c her life, when she needed assisted living.

Henry Harper married and had two children: Hudson and Angela. Henry is deceased.

Harry Harper married but had no children.

Sue Harper married Ben Turner from the Oakdale community, south of Smyrna; they ha one daughter, Cherie. Sue, now married to Mr. Wallace, lives in Marietta.

Louise Lindley Harper, a member of the, Phillips Legion Chapter, of the United Daughters c the Confederacy, was very active in both Smyrna and Cobb County. She was also a member of Fir Baptist Church, where she was active in the Friendship Sunday School Class. A family genealogis Louise contributed extensive information to The Smyrna Historical Society and the Smyrna Museun Much is recorded in each place about her and the Lindley and Harper families.

Louise Lindley Harper had a brother, Sam Lindley, Sr., whose son, Sam Lindley, Jr., raise his family in Smyrna. When I was a member of the Board of Directors of the West Smyrna Swim an Tennis Club, so was Sara, the wife of Sam Lindley, Jr.

Both Mr. and Mrs. Roy Harper and Mr. and Mrs. Sam Harper had sons named Henry an Harry. Unlike his parents' sons, Sam's sons were not twins.

Eighth House

The Noble Family

The **Noble Family** lived here. According to neighbors, he was a graduate of Georgia Institut of Technolgy.

The Verbille Family

Mr. and **Mrs**. **Verbille** lived in this house, where Mrs. Verbille is still residing.

Ninth House

Lillard and **Bernice Williams** and their children, **Kenneth** and **Linda,** resided in this house Mrs. Williams, the former Bernice Hendricks, was born in Whitesburg but graduated from Campbe High School in Fairburn. Bernice had five brothers and sisters: Leola, Clifford, Bertha, Woodrow, an Margaret.

Lillard, inducted into the United States Army in 1944, at the age of 29, received his basi training at Camp Blanding, in Starke, Florida. He was being transferred to the West Coast, on his wa to the Phillippine Islands, when World War II ended. He was then reassigned to Japan, where h served with the Occupation Forces. Later Lillard worked for Simmons Mattress Company.

Kenneth Williams, a graduate in the Campbell High School Class of 1955 (in Smyrna) an Georgia Institute of Technology, married Camille Nappier, a graduate of Sprayberry High School They had one daughter, Kimberly, known as "Kayce."

Kayce married Jim Hollingsworth; they had two daughters: Kathryn and Mallory. "Kayce," now divorced, lives in Dallas, Texas.

Kenneth, now known as "Ken," is retired as a sales representative for Holophane Company as a sales representative. "Ken" and Camille now own their own company, C.W. Sales and Marketing.

Kenneth Williams remembers that the telephone number for his parents was 516R, a four-party line. He also remembers that "Arthur Bacon, who ran a laundry route, would stop along the route and play marbles or ball with the neighborhood children."

<u>Linda Williams</u>, a graduate of Wills High School, married Mike Hillhouse. They had one son, Clark. After Linda and Mike divorced, Linda married Bruce Thompson.

Mr. and **Mrs. Henry Howard Williams**

Henry Howard Williams and his wife, Mary Alice, Lillard Williams' parents, had five other children: Merrill, Homer, Richard, Leland (a twin of Lillard), and Mary Alice. According to family information, Henry and Alice, in the late 1930s or very early 1940s, lived on the north side of Powder Springs Street; from there they moved to Fairburn.

Merrill Williams, Sr., graduated from Brown High School in Atlanta, where he lived most of his life. Being the oldest of the Williams' children, Merrill was beyond draft age during World War II. He married and had two children: Merrill Jr., and Howard. Merrill, Sr., retired from Delta Airlines.

Homer Williams married and had two children. He worked for National Biscuit Company and lived in Union City.

Richard Williams, known as "Dick," who married Jewell Shipp, served in the United States Navy during World War II. Kenneth Williams remembers the Shipps, who lived on the east side of Roswell Street as a very fun-loving family who took in boarders.

Kenneth related, "It was an ordinary occurrence for "hobos" to leap from the train as it slowed at the crossing, which was near the Shipps' house. Invariably someone in the Shipp Family would befriend them with food or drink. One time the Shipp Family had what they referred to as some 'proper folks' visiting with them. Ovalene Shipp and one of the boarders, slipped out of the room and dressed up like "hobos." They appeared at the front door, where 'Dick' Williams invited them in. Ovalene sat on the sofa next to one of the 'proper visitors' and kept sliding closer—thus making that person very uncomfortable—but all done in fun!"

Leland Williams. See *Williams, north side of Hill Street* and *east side of Old Concord Road.*

Mary Alice Williams married Robert Ford of Miami, Florida. They had one child, Karen.

<u>Tenth House</u>

Mr. and **Mrs. Humphrey** were residents directly across the street from Mr. and Mrs. Sidney Davis' house, which stood on the corner of Davis and Church streets. They had six children: **Harold**, **Louise**, **Ona Mae**, **Dorothy**, **Ann**, and **Tommy**. Harold served in the United States Navy during World War II; Betty Henderson, their next door neighbor, remembers that, when Harold came home from military service, how glad he was to be back. Ona Mae Humphrey worked for the Federal Reserve Bank in Atlanta, where she was in charge of the vault.

The Young Family

Tom and **Jean Young** and their two daughters, **Nancy** and **Patricia**, known as "Pat," lived in the ninth house after the Humphreys had moved. Neighbors remember Mrs. Young as working for an insurance company.

Kenneth Williams, who lived next door, remembers Tom Young owned and operated Young Neon Company, in Atlanta, where he manufactured neon signs. He also remembers that the Young's daughters, Nancy and Patricia, graduated from Emory University. Nancy became a librarian and Patricia an elementary school teacher.

Eleventh House

`**Mr.** and **Mrs. Jesse D. Henderson** resided here. Mrs. Henderson, the former Johnnie Be Murphy, and Mr. Henderson had two children: **Jesse Murphy** and **Betty**. Mr. and Mrs. Hendersc were members of First Baptist Church, where he was ordained a deacon October 6, 1948, and serve as Sunday School Superintendent, 1950-1952. Mr. Henderson worked for the United States Post Service in Atlanta; Mrs. Henderson worked in the Smyrna School lunchroom for several years.

Jesse Murphy Henderson married Betty Jane Gates from Porterdale. They had thre daughters: Janie, Joann, and Jeanine. Before and after his marriage, Jesse was very active at Fir Baptist Church, which he joined June 15, 1941, and where he was elected Church Treasurer in Jur 1950. In September 1950, Jesse was drafted into the United States military; he served stateside i Louisiana during the Korean Conflict. After returning from military service, Jesse worked as Assista Postmaster to Smyrna Postmaster Zelan Wills; later he worked with the United States Regional Po Office in Memphis, Tennessee. Jesse and his wife lived in Woodstock, where Betty Jane Henderso died in January 2005.

Janie Henderson married Mr. McGinty of Smyrna; they had a daughter, Shannon. Janie, wh later married Dave Krocker, retired as a United States Government employee.

Joann Henderson married Dr. Angel Garcia, a medical doctor from Macon. They had a so and a daughter.

Jeanine Henderson married Dan Bartlett of Smyrna. They had one son, Tyler. Jeanine work for the Center for Disease Control and Prevention; Dan is in the air-conditioning business in Cob County.

Betty Henderson married Kenneth C. Davey; they had two sons: Kenneth, C., Jr., and Joh Betty and Kenneth live in the Bennett Woods subdivision. Kenneth was an auditor for Fireman's Fun Insurance Company, from which he retired. Betty, who worked in the Bond Division of Feder Reserve Bank throughout her life, attended First Baptist Church, where she was a member. Both sh and Kenneth are currently members of Locust Grove Baptist Church in Mableton. Betty and Kennet who grew up in Pennsylvania, married on "Bride and Groom," a television show that was aired fro New York City in 1953. Kenneth Davey served with the United States Merchant Marine Corps i England, New Guinea, and India during World War II.

Kenneth Davey, Jr., graduated from Campbell High School and attended technical schoo where he selected welding as his chosen field, in which he worked for twenty years. Kenneth marrie Sheron Harkins; they had two children: Kenneth III and Nicholas. Kenneth, Jr., who lives i Adairsville, and Sheron divorced. Sheron Harkins Davey died December 3, 2004.

John Davey graduated from Campbell High School, where he was awarded a Rotary Clu Scholarship to study music for one year in Florence, Italy. Afterwards he earned a Bachelor of Ar degree from Shorter College in Rome and a Masters degree from the University of Michigan in An Arbor. John is a law librarian for Cromwell and Sullivan Law Firm in New York City. A lover c music, John has pursued his passion as a soloist, particularly singing at weddings, but he also sing with groups in church services.

NOTE: First Baptist Church information about the Hendersons is recorded in *A Beacon fo Christ,* A Centennial History of First Baptist Church of Smyrna, Georgia.

Twelfth House

Mr. and **Mrs. W.R. Mountcastle** lived in this house. They had two children: Betty an Billy, both of whom graduated from college. Mr. Mountcastle was a pharmacist in Smyrna in th arlier part of the Twentieth Century. Betty Mountcastle married Dr. James Skinner, a pediatric hysician who practiced south of Atlanta.

The Adair Family

Willie and **Mildred Adair** later were residents in this house for a short while. They had two hildren: **Faye** and **Allen**.

Mrs. Thelma Frady

Mrs. Thelma Frady moved to this house after the Adair Family had vacated. She had a son, **Iarvin Frady**, who graduated from Fitzhugh Lee School. He was older than I. A Baptist preacher, he vas pastor of several churches in Cobb County, including Calvary Baptist Church in Smyrna, before ecoming pastor of First Baptist Church of Clarkdale and Chaplain at the Cobb County Jail. Mrs. 'rady later married O.L. Pinson. See *north side of Spring Street.*

Thirteenth House

Robert and **Anita Paris** lived here with their two sons: **Bobby** and **Jimmy**.

The Tom Prickett Family

Later on **Mr.** and **Mrs. Tom Prickett** and their daughter, **Carolyn**, were residents f this house. Carolyn, a graduate of Campbell High School, attended North Georgia College, in)ahlonega. She married Hanes Hill, who graduated from North Georgia College and served in the Jnited States Army.

Fourteenth House

Johnny and **Ovalene Pettitt** moved to this house, which was built later than most of the ouses on Church Street in the days of my youth. They had one daughter, Janice. The Pettitts moved rom here to Canton.

Fifteenth House

Mr. and **Mrs. Still** lived in the fourteenth house.

The William Holden Family

Mr. and **Mrs. William Holden** moved here after the Still Family had vacated. Mrs. Holden, ormerly Caroline Green, and William, known as "Bill," had two children: **Randy** and **Libby**.

Libby Holden married Charles Chandler from Kansas. They had two children: Caroline and ustin. Libby, a registered nurse, works for WellStar Tranquility Hospice at Cobb Hospital. Charles is leceased.

Randy Holden married Patricia Arrington. They had two sons: Rob and Sid. Patricia and Randy divorced. See *Arrington, south side of Sunset Avenue.*

Sixteenth House

Mr. and **Mrs. Lewis Anderson** and their son, J.L., lived here. I knew them well. The ndersons were members of First Methodist Church, where Lewis was a member of the Pearce Iatthews Sunday School Class. The oldest child of the large Elmer Anderson Family on Roswell treet, Lewis was active in the Masons; he was also a Shriner. Lewis was in the produce business, as vere several of the other Anderson men. See *eighteenth house.*

Mrs. Anderson was the former Opal Baldwin, a sister of Mrs. Agnes Baldwin Faucett Feel who lived on Medlin Street. See *Roswell Street, the Andersons on Roswell Street,* and *Faucett, c Medlin Street.*

Seventeenth House

Mrs. Embrey, a widow, resided next door to the Andersons. Her house was barely visib from the street.

Eighteenth House

J.L. Anderson and his wife, **Connie**, lived in the house west of Mrs. Embrey. J.L., the son Lewis and Opal Anderson, worked with his dad in the produce business. See *Fifteenth House, Churc Street* and *Andersons of Roswell Street.*

NOTE: Houses 15-17 were razed in the 1990s. The properties are now part of the Glen Ros subdivision.

Nineteenth House

Later on **Mr.** and **Mrs. Herbert Peeler** built this house, which was a large, beautiful whi house located on a hill, where they lived with their family. Beverly Cobb Amacker stated that h family shared a telephone party line with the Peelers.

NOTE: Castellaw Funeral Home is located on the Herbert Peeler property.

Twentieth House

Mr. and **Mrs. Earl Lingo Dunton**, known as "Doc," lived in this house. They had on daughter, Linda. Earl was one of the children of "Joby" and Elizabeth Dunton. See *north side of Bar Street, north side of Church Street, south side Church Road, The Country Road, north* and *south side of Concord Road,* and *south side of Concord Road, The Country Road.*

CHURCH ROAD

The Country Road

North Side

Church Road runs from the Access Road, now known as South Cobb Drive, out into th countryside.

Appreciation is extended to Peggy Norton Cochran, Betty Norton Cox, and Odelia Norto Rogers for sharing information about the Norton Family on Church Road, Dunn Street, and Nort Cooper Lake Road; to Bettie May Cochran for sharing memories about her family on Church Road i the middle of the Twentieth Century.

First House

Mr. and **Mrs. Fonzie May** in the 1930s, lived in this house, just west of the intersection c Church and Old Concord roads, with their three children: **Fonzie William**, known as "Jack," **Clyd Broughton**, and **Bettie**. Mr. Fonzie May was from Cedartown; Mrs. May, the former Minnie Hudso was from Vienna.

During the Depression years, Fonzie May was employed by the Works Progres Administration (WPA), a government program instituted during the administration of Preside Franklin Delano Roosevelt. Afterwards, for the next thirty years, Fonzie worked for Brawn Sanitarium on Atlanta Road, where the May Family lived when their fourth child, **James Hudson**, wa orn. Bettie May Cochran recalls there were four houses, behind the Hospital building, for Brawner mployees. Some of the people she remembers living there included Floyd and Fannie Mae Wilson; Ir. and Mrs. Lawrence Butler and their two daughters, Mary and Vivian; Lawrence's brother and his ife, Homer and Aletha Butler, who had no children; Fonzie May's sister, Billy Manders, and her usband; Willie Mae Manders, and her husband, Bill Manders.

Fonzie and Minnie May, active members of Spring Street Baptist Church, later became harter members of Second Baptist Church, which still stands on Atlanta Street near the Smyrna ommunity Center.

Fonzie William May, known as "Jack," married Inez Jones. They had two children: William, nown as "Butch," and Frank. "Jack" later married Stella Weaver. They had six children, two aughters, Brenda and Gwendolyn, and four sons, Jackie, Bobby, Jimmy and Michael

Clyde Broughton May, known as "Broughton," married Elvis Legg. They had four children: David, Diane, Cindy, and Donald. Broughton who was Smyrna's Chief of Police in the 1950s, later etired from Lockheed Aircraft Corporation.

Bettie May married Vergile A. Cochran, known as "V.A.," from a large family who lived on 'oster Street. They had three children, Gail, Vergile, Jr., and Bonita, six grandchildren, and four great-randchildren. Bettie was employed by International Service Systems (earlier known as Oxford Building Service). See *Cochran, on Foster Street.*

James Hudson May, known as "Hudson," married Margit Tosch from Munich, Germany. Bettie shared that she and her husband, "V.A.," sponsored Margit; thus she was permitted to enter the Jnited States. Hudson and Margit had two daughters: Yvonne and Bettina, known as "Tina." Both aughters graduated from Campbell High School; "Tina," along with my daughter, Marilyn, was in the Class of 1984,

NOTE: In the early-to-mid Twentieth Century, the Norton families owned much land from Church Road through to Hurt Road, including the property where the May Family lived. In the days of ny youth, it was the Charles Norton Family, who I remember, lived in the second house.

Mr. and Mrs. Phillip Norton

Mr. Philip Norton and his wife, **Martha**, in 1894 moved their family from Paulding County o a brick house, which they rented, near the Concord Covered Bridge. They had two sons: **Oliver** and **Coby Norton**.

Mr. and Mrs. Coby Norton

Mr. and Mrs. Coby Norton, the son of Philip and Martha, owned a farm on North Cooper Lake Road, where they raised six children. See *North Cooper Lake Road.*

Mr. and Mrs. Oliver Norton

Mr. Oliver Norton, the son of Philip and Martha, and his wife, Linnie, and their six children, Mattie Lou, Otho, Luther, Henry, Charles and Odelia, lived on Church Road, west of Smyrna. They had a farm approximately two miles from South Cobb Drive; it was west of Nickajack Creek and where the Norton Park community is today. The Norton Park subdivision and Norton Park Baptist Church are named for this family.

Peggy Norton Cochran stated, "According to family information, Mrs. Linnie Norton was a member of First Baptist Church from the time she was twelve years old until her death, at the age of ighty-two. When she joined the Church, it was located on Atlanta Road. From Nickajack Creek,

Grandfather Norton and his sons hauled rocks and sand in a horse-drawn wagon to help with t building of the rock church, now known as First Baptist Church Chapel."

Mattie Lou Norton married Luther Gann, a member of the Gann Family whose cemetery located on North Cooper Lake Road.

Otho Norton married Ethel Harris, who grew up in the Harris Road area, west of the Nort Farm. See *west side of Dunn Street.*

Luther Norton, who had never married, died at the age of twenty-five.

Henry Norton married Mildred Lamb of Marietta. See *Medlin Street.*

Odelia Norton married Bryson Rogers. They lived in the Oakdale community before movi to the Grant Park area of Atlanta.

Second House

Mr. and Mrs. Charles Norton

Mr. and **Mrs. Charles Norton** and their daughters, **Elizabeth** and **Virginia**, resided on t north side of the road. Their house, still standing, was a nice, white frame one, located on a hill west Nickajack Creek. The property is the site of Norton Park Baptist Church.

Mrs. Norton, whose given name was Idelle, died November 28, 2004, and was buried Georgia Memorial Park Cemetery.

Elizabeth Norton, who married Mr. Rudolph, lives in Heflin, Alabama.

Virginia Norton married Milton White, who grew up on Highland Avenue and was graduate in the Smyrna High School Class of 1951. Virginia, a graduate of the first Campbell Hi School Class, in 1952, and Milton had three sons: Keith, Kregg, and Kenneth. See *White, Highla Avenue*

CHURCH ROAD
The Country Road
South Side

First House

Mr. and **Mrs. Hollis Jewel Dunton**, known as "H.J.," lived in this house, located on t southwest corner of South Cobb Drive and Church Road, The Country Road. Mrs. Dunton's giv name was Vera. He owned much property here. Mr. "H.J." Dunton drove one of the buses wh Beverly Cobb Amacker attended Smyrna Elementary School. See *Dunton, north side of Bank Stre Church Street, north* and *south sides, Concord Road, north* and *south sides* and *south side of Conco Road, The Country Road.*

Second House

Mrs. Burton resided here at one time.

Mr. and Mrs. Roy Martin

Later on **Mr.** and **Mrs. Roy Martin** became residents next door to the Duntons. The Mart children are **Laura**, **Estelle**, **Bobbie**, **Clara**, **Mary Jo**, **Leroy**, and **Ed**. Leroy married Lenell William the daughter of Mr. and Mrs. Leland Williams and a cousin of Beverly Amacker. One of the Mart daughters married Mr. Posey; they ran a neighborhood grocery store on the east side of Roswell Street. See *east side of Old Concord Road* and *east side of Roswell Street.*

Mr. and **Mrs. Tommy Self**

Still later, **Tommy Self** and his wife, the former **Clara Martin**, lived here with their family.

NOTE: The Surrey Park Townhouses have been built where the second house once stood.

<u>Third House</u>

The **Waid Family** were residents of the next house, not visible from the road. Some of their children are **Jim**, **Marvin**, **Evelyn**, and **J.W**.

<u>Fourth House</u>

Mr. and **Mrs. Hubert H. Head** resided in the last house on the south side of Church Road. **Hubert**, **George**, **Jimmy**, and **Eula** are some of their children that I remember. Mr. and Mrs. Head maintained on their property some stables where, I seem to recall, people boarded their horses.

<u>Fifth House</u>

<u>Eula Head</u> married Mr. Browning. They built a house on the west side of her parents' home. Mr. Browning worked at Georgia Power Company.

NOTE: The Head and Browning houses were razed for the building of Ennisbrook subdivision.

<u>George Head</u> married Eloise Williams, the daughter of Mr. and Mrs. Foy Williams, who lived on Lee Street. George and Eloise built a home on Cooper Lake Road, east of the railroad, where they raised their two daughters, Patricia and Joni. Many years after George's death, Eloise moved to Cloudland Drive, in the Bennett Woods subdivision, where she lived until she moved to North Georgia. The Heads were members of First Methodist Church. George and Eloise are deceased. See *Williams on Lee Street.*

NOTE: Cash Farms on Cooper Lake Road now covers all of the property once owned by George and Eloise Head. The East-West Connector and The Silver Comet Trail have been constructed southwesterly from the Head's home place.

MANN STREET
East Side

Mann Street is a short street that runs north off Church Street, between the Tatum and Leonard houses. For many years there were no houses on this short street. Eventually two houses were built on the east side of the street.

Beverly Cobb Amacker shared the following information about the residents of Mann Street in the 1940s and early 1950s, while she was growing up on Church Street.

<u>First House</u>

Mr. and **Mrs. Lawrence Brasington** were residents of this house for a while.

<u>Second House</u>

Mr. and **Mrs. W.T. Shackelford** and their daughters, **Nancy** and **Judy**, lived here.

MANN STREET
West Side

First House

For their son and daughter-in-law, **Johnny** and **Carol Leonard**, Mr. and Mrs. Frank Leona built a house on the west side of Mann Street. This house was immediately behind the Frank Leonard house.

Second House

The **Yanceys** resided in the house next door to the Johnny Leonards.

REED STREET
East Side

First House

Mr. and **Mrs**. **Wright**, who lived in this house, had one daughter, **Anna Felice**. The Wright had a place at Cloudland Canyon, in Summerville, where they spent much time.

Mr. and **Mrs. Robert Bacon**

Mr. and **Mrs**. **Robert Bacon** moved to this house after the Wrights vacated. Afterward Robert and Octa moved to the east side of King Street, where they were living when they sold the property to First Baptist Church. (The First Baptist Church sanctuary now stands there.) See *Baco east side of King Street.*

Mr. and **Mrs. Homer Bell**

Mr. and **Mrs**. **Homer Bell** and their daughters, **Mary Vaughn** and **Rosalyn**, moved from apartment in Mrs. Judith Lowry's house, on King Street, to this one after the Bacons had vacate From here they relocated to the Pace/Pruitt House, on Atlanta Street, where they were living when M Bell, the principal of Smyrna School, died. See *south side of Love Street.*

Mrs. Agnes Flynn, who owned all of the land behind her house, sold two lots to "Re Hamby in the 1940s. Here he built the following two houses, near the northeast corner of Reed a Love streets.

Second House

A young man named **Wheeler** moved to this house when it was new.

Third House

Mr. and **Mrs**. **Ottis Cheatham** (**Ann**) resided here with their son, **Tommy**. In the 1950 they bought this house, which was the second one built by "Red" Hamby. The Cheathams, members First Baptist Church, recently moved to West Cobb County.

Tommy Cheatham, a graduate of Wills High School and Kennesaw State University, is accountant. He is married to the former Jill Kennedy, who graduated from Osborne High School a Kennesaw State University. They had two daughters, Carolynn and Katie, who are both Campbe High School International Baccalaureate students. Jill is the daughter of Frank and Ann Kenned Minister of Music and Organist, respectively, of First Baptist Church prior to moving the membership to First Baptist Church of Powder Springs, where Ann is the organist.

REED STREET
West Side

Reed Street runs north and south from Church Street to Love Street. Appreciation is extended o Sue Sargent Cantrell for sharing her memories of the Cantrell Family, who lived on Reed Street in he days of my youth.

In the late 1940s B.F. Reed built the Southern Manor Apartments, known today as Madison tation condominiums. They encompass properties on Church, Davis, Reed, and Stephens streets.

<u>First House</u>

Mr. and **Mrs. Duff Edward Cantrell** resided on the northwest corner of Love and Reed treets. Mrs. Cantrell was the former Effie Kinard. They had five children: **Hazel, Henry, Olin ackson, Mary Edna,** and **Martin,** all of whom were all older than I. The Cantrells were members of 'irst Baptist Church. See *Kinard, south side of Church Street.*

<u>Hazel Cantrell</u> married Harold Franklin, a member of the Franklin Family who owned the 'ranklin Pottery Company on Franklin Road in Marietta, where Hazel and Harold once lived.

<u>Henry Cantrell</u> married Elizabeth Noel, known as "Betty," who came to Smyrna from Saint ohns, Newfoundland. They met while Henry was stationed in Newfoundland during World War II.

<u>Olin Jackson Cantrell</u> married Minnie Sue Sargent, who grew up on Pickens Street. They had ne son, Kenneth Edward Cantrell, who married Judy Sly. Kenneth and Judy had two daughters: 1issie Evette and Carli. Both daughters graduated from college. See *Sargent,Pickens Street.*

Sue Cantrell has shared the story of how she and Olin met. Sue and her girlfriend were on the ame streetcar with Travis H. Gann, also known as "T.H.," whom Sue knew quite well. He invited iem to go that evening to the graduation ceremony at Smyrna High School, where they saw Olin; 'ravis introduced the girls to him. The four of them began double dating, and before long Sue and)lin were serious in their relationship. When Olin returned from World War II, he and Sue married.

Olin was employed at Bauer Pottery Works, across the street from Fort McPherson. He was ater employed at Lockheed Aircraft Corporation, from which he retired.

Olin and Sue Cantrell lived on the east side of South Cobb Drive, just south of King Springs .oad, on property that is adjacent to Ridgeview Institute. This area was part of the property owned by)lin's dad, Duff Cantrell, whose property extended across South Cobb Drive and down King Springs .oad; this encompassed what is known today as Rhyne Park, on which site was the house where Olin vas born. (According to information from the Cantrell Family, Duff sold the property to the Rhynes.)

<u>Mary Edna Cantrell</u> married Richard Leffew from the Oakdale community, south of Smyrna.

<u>Martin Cantrell</u> married Marie Fondanaut, from Stinton, Louisiana. They met while he was tationed with the United States Navy in Louisiana. Marie is deceased. Martin and his second wife, lell, are members of the Smyrna Historical and Genealogical Society.

CHAPTER ELEVEN

LOVE STREET
North Side

Appreciation is extended to Harold Flynn, who grew up on Love Street, where he still lives, r his help in identifying the residents who resided on the north side of Love Street from about 1938 1950; to Evelyn Edwards Pressley who, grew up on Roswell Street, moved with her family to the orth side of Love Street in the mid 1930s, when she was still in high school. Evelyn's memories bout the residents of Love Street and Roswell Street during this era have been very helpful; to Lee ubanks, known as "Butch," who, along with his family were long-time residents of Love Street; to lary Knight Hamby and Claudia Hamrick Adams, each of whom has shared their memories of rowing up on Love Street in the early 1950s; to Melvin Holleman who was born on Love Street and, xcept for his time in the United States Navy during World War II, has resided here his entire life; and Sara Dunn Corley, who in her early life, also lived on Love Street.

Love Street in the days of my youth ran from Atlanta Street past the street that we know day as Concord Road. The road name was changed when the viaduct over the railroad was built in e 1960s connecting Spring Road with Atlanta Street.

Mr. S.B. Love, for whom Love Street was named, was a partner in the Love, Pope, and Rice oncord Woolen Mills, near the Covered Bridge. Mr. Rice was the grandfather of Mrs. Julia Rice owery and Mrs. Blanche Rice Brawner, who lived on King Street. Personally I do not recall having nown anyone related to Mr. Love or to Mr. Pope. According to information from long-time residents, Ir. Love was the first husband of Mrs. D.J. Ray.

First House

Mr. and **Mrs. Ed Williams** were residents of the first house that faced Love Street. They had wo daughters: **Jane** and **Vickie**. Mrs. Williams, whose given name was Martha, owned and operated Villiams Day Care, on Dunn Street which backed up to Brinkley Park. In the 1950s, she opened Villiams Daycare and Nursery School on Jones Shaw Road, now called Windy Hill Road.

Martha Williams, the former Martha Hicks, grew up on Hicks Road in Marietta. She had ree brothers, John A. Hicks, "Rip" Hicks, and J.N. Hicks, and one sister, Mary Hicks Bearden, who ill lives on Hicks Road. Ed Williams had one sister, Dorothy Williams Durham, who married Phagan urham. See *Durham, south side of Spring Street.*

Jane Williams, a graduate of Campbell High School Class of 1959, married Edward Stabell, dentist. They had four children, Kim, Edward III, Kristy, and Paige, and eight grandchildren. Edward tabell is deceased.

Kim Stabell married Greg McNulty.

Edward Stabell III married Robin Hill.

Kristy Stabell married Doug Hubbard.

Paige Stabell married Scott Payne.

Vickie Williams married Mike Reagan. They had two sons: Sean and Zac.

Second House

Still there, this house is a small, white frame house that was owned by Dr. and Mrs. G. Green. At least two of their three daughters, Sara Green Farrar and Laura Alice Hamrick, lived he after their marriages.

Laura Alice Green and her husband, **Claude Hamrick**, began their married life in th house. They had two daughters: **Claudia** and **Laura Ellen**. In the early 1950s Laura Alice and Clau moved to the southeast corner of Love and Lee Street. See *Dr. G.C. Green* and *Claude Hamrick, sou side of Love Street.*

Corrine Hosch

After her husband and daughter died, **Mrs. Corrine Hosch**, a teacher at Smyrna a Campbell High schools, shared this house with another teacher, **Miss Eunice Padgett**. Mrs. Hos moved from this house to the east side of King Street, where she lived into her nineties. See *west si of King Street.*

Third House

Reverend and **Mrs. John Knight were** residents here. They had two daughters, **Mary a Grace.** Reverend Knight, the Presbyterian pastor from 1951-1961, and his family occupied this mans a small brick house with a screened front porch, large enough for two to three rocking chairs. The fro door opened into the living room; then came the dining room off which was a small eating nook; t kitchen, very small, was next. The house had three bedrooms: one for Reverend and Mrs. Knight, o for their two daughters, and one for Reverend Knight's mother, Eva, who also lived here. The proper included a small garage and a large place for a garden.

John Henry Knight was educated at Andover Newton Theological Seminary in Bosto Massachusetts. He also studied and received degrees from Mercer University in Macon and Columb Seminary in Decatur. He preached in Presbyterian churches for over forty years.

John Knight married Bonnie Hale, from LaFayette and Rome, whose dad was in the lumb business. Bonnie graduated from LaGrange College, in LaGrange, which at that time was a girl school; she also graduated from Andover Newton Theological Seminary in Boston, Massachuset where she received a Masters degree in Christian Education.

Mary Knight married Arnold Hamby from the Oakdale Community, south of Smyrna. Ma and Arnold, both graduates of Campbell High School, had two sons: Carl Ray and John Russell.

Carl Ray Hamby married Michelle Morgan; they had two sons: Josh and Ryan. Josh is in th United States Navy; Ryan Hamby is still in school.

Carl Ray Hamby's second marriage was to Shirley Carroll from Mississippi. She had tw children: Tyler and Carley Carroll.

John Russell Hamby married but had no children.

Grace Knight married Lloyd George Deen of Johnson City, Tennessee; they had no childre They curently reside in Las Vegas, Nevada.

Fourth House

Mr. Pat Edwards
Mayor of Smyrna
1927-1930

Mr. and **Mrs. Pat Edwards, Sr.**, lived in the fourth house. They had two daughters and a on: **Nan, Evelyn** and **Pat, Jr.**

Mr. and Mrs. Edwards in 1936 moved from Roswell Street, to this house, a large red brick, vo-story structure, one of the fine homes in Smyrna, in the days of my youth. Eventually it was razed or the building of the present day First Methodist Church. Mr. Edwards, who was always rofessionally dressed, often traveled. He served as Mayor of Smyrna, 1927-1930. The Edwards amily were active members of First Methodist Church.

Nan Edwards married Glenn Yarbrough of Smyrna. See *Yarbrough, south side of Love treet.*

Evelyn Edwards married James Pressley. James was the son of Mr. and Mrs. William ressley, who lived across the street from my family on Bank Street. During the building boom of the arly 1950s, James and Evelyn built a home on Collier Drive in the Forest Hills community, where ey have lived since. Many new homes were built in Smyrna during that era. See *Pressley, south side f Bank Street.*

James and Evelyn had three children: James Jr., Melda, and Mary. James Jr., lives in larietta; Mary lives in Durham, North Carolina. Melda married Charles Collins of Smyrna; they aised their family in Marietta. Melda died in January 2004.

Evelyn Edwards Pressley shared a neat story about her younger days. "James Pressley, rthur Bacon, and Glynn Byrd came by my house every Monday night after attending National Guard eeting in Marietta. They gave my mother fits because they ate everything they could find there. One ight Mother and I made chocolate fudge, using Castoria (a laxative), instead of vanilla flavoring. hey enjoyed the candy till the next day."

Pat Edwards, Jr., married Carolyn, a very nice person who was from Powder Springs. Pat, r., in my generation, attended Smyrna School during his early years and was recruited by James ressley to play football for Marietta High School, from which he graduated. Pat also attended Vofford College in Spartanburg, South Carolina, where he played football. When the Jaycee Chapter 'as organized in Smyrna in 1959, Pat and I were members; therefore we had much association with ach other.

Fifth House

Mr. and **Mrs. Henry Hunter Dunn** lived here. The former Pauline Brinkley, Mrs. Dunn was e daughter of Mr. and Mrs. P.F. Brinkley. The Dunns had three children: **Henry**, **Sara Jane**, and **eorgia Rilla**. Pauline Dunn, who worked for Dr. Mitchell in his medical office, was also a member f the Smyrna Social Club, founded in 1908.

When their children were small, Pauline and Hunter Dunn lived in Florida for several years. 'hile they were there, Georgia Rilla, at the age of six, was hit by an automobile and killed. Pauline ade a decision to return to Smyrna, where she lived again in the house with her mother, Mrs. inkley. See *seventh house.*

The Dunn Family were active members of First Baptist Church, where Pauline served as esident of the Alathean Sunday School Class in 1953. She also served on the Missions Committee at brought to the church a recommendation to purchase property for what would become King

Spring Baptist Church. The above church information is from A *Beacon for Christ*, A Centenn History of The First Baptist Church.

NOTE: This house was built by Hunter Dunn's dad, who lived on Spring Street, east of t railroad, in the earlier part of the Twentieth Century.

Henry Hunter Dunn, Jr., married Patricia Uri of Seattle, Washington. Henry died at age for four.

Sara Jane Dunn married W.C. Corley, ordained as a minister at First Baptist Church Octob 6, 1940. Sara is a second-generation member of the Smyrna Social Club. Sara remembers assisti with the preparations for her mother and Mrs. LeoDelle Jolley to host the Social Club when she w growing up. She also remembers that Mr. and Mrs. Lex Jolley lived in this house while their house Lee Street was being built. (This was during the time when Sara's family was living in Florida.)

NOTE: Rev. W.C. Corley is a long-standing prominent minister, in the Lawrenceville area.

Mrs. P.F. Brinkley

According to family information, after Mr. and Mrs. Hunter Dunn had moved to Flori Pauline's mother, **Mrs. P.F. Brinkley**, moved to this house.

While Mrs. Brinkley was living here, her daughter-in-law, **Millie Valentine Brinkley**, a her children, **Mickey** and **Patsy**, lived in Mrs. Brinkley's garage apartment. In 1950 Millie married I W.C. Mitchell, at which time Millie and her children moved to Dr. Mitchell's home, on Atlanta Stre See *Mitchell, Atlanta Street, from Marlowe's to Creatwood.*

NOTE: Dunn's Alley, a walking trail that ran from Church Street to Love Street, between t Dunn and Holahan houses, was used as a short cut from the churches and downtown to Brinkley Pa and to Lee and Dunn streets.

Sixth House

The **Butch Holahan Family** lived next door to the Dunns. They had one daughter, **Pegg** she attended high school in Marietta.

Mr. Holahan was the commander of American Legion Post #160, in which he was ve involved for many years. I never knew Mrs. Holahan.

Mr. and Mrs. T.P. Holleman

Melvin Holloman, who has lived on Love Street all of his life, was born in this house 1925. His family lived here for a short time while their house on the south side of Love Street w being built.

The Eubanks Family

Dyer and **Caroline Eubanks** lived here with their son, **Lee Eubanks**, known as "Butch "Butch" shared, "My parents moved to Smyrna in 1942 for Dad, to work at the Bell Bomber Pla they resided here for about two years, or until Dad was transferred, they returned to Smyrna, in about 1947, and lived in the seventh house. "Butch" added, "The sixth house burned completely dov during the 'ice storm' of 1961. Due to the conditions of the streets, the fire department could not g there in time to save the house." See *Eubanks Family, seventh House.*

Seventh House

P.F. Brinkley
Smyrna City Councilman
1926-1929
Mayor of Smyrna
1931-1932
January-April 1941

Mr. and **Mrs**. **P.F**. **Brinkley** (P.F. standing for Pomp Fowler) lived here. They had five children who were in my parents' generation: **Edgar**, **Pauline**, **Ben Hoyt**, **Jessie Leigh**, and **Julius Eugene**, known as "Gene." Mr. Brinkley was a native of Cobb County. Mrs. Brinkley, the former Rilla Stanley, was from Kennesaw; she lived to be ninety-five years old.

Mr. Brinkley served as Smyrna City Councilman, 1926-1929, and was Mayor of Smyrna first, 1931-1932, and again January-April 1941. He left office because of declining health. It was P.F. who donated to the City of Smyrna the land for the building of Brinkley Park, which is bounded by Dunn Street on the east side, Concord Road on the west side, Hunter Street on the north side, and Legion Drive on the south side.

The Brinkleys were active members of First Baptist Church where he served as treasurer, October 1933-October 1938 and again, October 1940-March 1941. He also served as a trustee of First Baptist Church in 1940. The above church information is from *A Beacon for Christ,* The Centennial History of The First Baptist Church.

I do not have any information about Edgar or Jessie Leigh Brinkley.

Pauline Brinkley married Hunter Dunn. See *fifth house, north side of Love Street.*

Ben Hoyt Brinkley and his wife, Marie, had two sons: Ben and Harold. See *west side of Dunn Street.*

Julius Eugene Brinkley, known as "Gene," married Mildred Valentine, known as "Millie," of the Log Cabin community, south of Oakdale. She was the daughter of Benjamin Henry and Ludie Mae Valentine. "Millie" and "Gene" had two children: Patricia Ann, known as "Pat," and Milton Scott, known as "Mickey." When their children were small and Gene had died, Millie and their children lived in a garage apartment on the Brinkley property. See *fifth house, north side of Love Street.*

Patricia Ann Brinkley, known as "Pat," married Johnny Sims from Nevada. They had five children: Cheryl Sims Anderson, Susan Sims Mele, Bart Sims, Pam Sims Upson, and Gayle Sims Stewart. Johnny Sims is now deceased; Patricia still lives in Nevada.

Milton Scott, known as "Mickey" married Barbara Joan Rose of Harriman, Tennessee. "Mickey" had two daughters from a previous marriage: Michelle Leigh Brinkley Cottingham and Lisa Marie Brinkley Brownlee.

Barbara Joan Rose Brinkley had two children from a previous marriage: a daughter, Melissa Joan Shacklett, and a son, James Shannon Loy.

The Eubanks Family

Dyer and **Caroline Eubanks** moved to this house after the Brinkleys had vacated. They had one son, **Lee**, known as "Butch." Mr. and Mrs. Eubanks first moved to Smyrna, to the sixth house in 1942, for Mr. Eubanks to work in the Bell Bomber Plant. The Eubanks were active members of Smyrna Presbyterian Church, where Caroline, an accomplished musician, played the piano for the church services for many years.

"Butch" shared, "When my parents bought this house, in or about 1947, it had been used as two apartments. I remember that Miss Eunice Padgett, a teacher at Smyrna School, and her dad had lived in one of them. My parents both lived here until their deaths, in the 1990s.

"After my parents had died, I sold this property, along with the property I had purchased from the Kreegers, to First Methodist Church. These properties are now used as a church parking area."

Dyer Eubanks, for many years, was active around the community and was extremely interested in the history of the area. He was a member of the Civil War Roundtable.

I remember that Mrs. Eubanks had arthritis that crippled her so badly that she was not able to be active. I was always impressed as to the faithfulness and attentiveness of Mr. Eubanks, whom I liked very much, during those hard times.

Eighth House

George Kreeger, Sr.
Mayor of Smyrna
1960-1961, 1964-1969
Councilman-at-Large
1958-1959

Mr. and **Mrs. George Kreeger, Sr.**, in 1954 moved from the Oakdale community, south of Smyrna, into this house, on the northeast corner of Love and King streets. George, Sr., came from Greenville, South Carolina; Mrs. Kreeger, the former Laura Hyde (Wilson), from Oakdale, Tennessee, from a previous marriage, had a daughter, Audrey Wilson. She and George had one son, George Kreeger, Jr. The Kreegers were members of First Methodist Church. Laura Kreeger died July 3, 1954.

Audrey Wilson married Stanley Pair of the Oakdale community. Both graduated from Fitzhugh Lee High School in 1946. George Kreeger, Jr., was the senior class mascot. Audrey and Stanley had one daughter, Linda, who was killed in an automobile accident during the Olympics in Atlanta, July 1996. Audrey and Stanley live at Lake Oconee, in Greensboro.

George Kreeger, Jr.
Georgia State Representative
1969-1976
Cobb County State Court Judge
1979-1984
Cobb County Superior Court Judge
1984-

George Kreeger, Jr., a graduate of Campbell High School, married and had a daughter, Christa.

Christa Kreeger married Nathan Bowden. They had a son, Zachary.

George, Jr., is married to Helen Pruitt (Mallett), who was from a large family in Atlanta's Bolton community. Previously married, Helen had two daughters: Paige and Holly Mallett.

Paige Mallett married Warren Shiver. They had two daughters: Avery and Morgan.

Holly Mallett married Stavros Leocaucus.

An attorney in Marietta, George, Jr., is currently a Superior Court Judge. He has served on the bench in Marietta for the larger part of the last quarter of the Twentieth Century. Former classmate, "Babe" Atkins Byrne has been his Judicial Administrative Assistant for more than 25 years.

George Kreeger, Sr., served as Mayor of Smyrna, 1960-1961, and again 1964-1969, during which time, my dad, Roy Wood, served on the City Council with him. As Mayor, George was a driving force in the building of the King Street Library in 1961. Until that time Smyrna's only library space was in a room in the Smyrna Woman's Club, on the corner of Atlanta and Powder Springs streets. Even that library was a result of the efforts of many people, in the 1930s, who were desirous to offer some kind of library service for the children of Smyrna. As a child I remember going to the library in the Woman's Club on many occasions to study. In the days of my youth, the only public library in Cobb County, to my knowledge, was in Marietta.

I had always thought we were fortunate to have the library in the Smyrna Woman's Club building. But I also had an appreciation for George Kreeger, Sr., and his efforts to insure that the citizens of Smyrna would continue to have their own library.

I know that along the way there was much pressure to merge the library in Smyrna with the Cobb County Library system. George and the City Council of those days, after being adamant about maintaining a library for Smyrna—then in 1961 the King Street Library was dedicated. That building served Smyrna well until the present library was built in 1991.

I regret that George, Sr., was never sufficiently honored for the work that he did in this arena. One of the distinctions that Smyrna holds today is that our library is the only city-owned library in the State of Georgia: all the others are either county or regionally operated. Today, an average of 22,000 people a month, use the Smyrna Public Library. George Kreeger, Sr., would be very proud of these facts, and maybe they themselves would be honor enough for him.

NOTE: Harold Flynn's parents' house stood on the northwest corner between his house and the Kreegers, facing King Street.

Ninth House

Mr. and **Mrs. Harold Flynn** resided here with their three children: **Linda**, **Bonnie** and **Edward**. Mrs. Flynn was the former Kathryn Poynter from Aylett, Virginia (King William County). After the first portion of Love Street was renamed Concord Road, Harold and Kathryn Flynn thus became the first residents on the north side on Love Street. (In the days of my childhood Love Street began at Atlanta Road, and continued along the current Love Street. Concord Road began in the curve where the Love Street Antiques and Gift Shop is now located.) See *west side of King Street.*

Bonnie Flynn married Kenneth Rountree of Atlanta. They had two daughters: Amanda and Pamela. Bonnie and her second husband, Gary Cohoon, live in Woodstock.

Linda Flynn married Mr. Scarbrough from Alabama. They had four children: Leslie, Jason, Jarred, and Kendall. They live in Smith Station, Alabama.

Edward Flynn married Cynthia Wampler, the daughter of Mr. and Mrs. Mars Wampler. Edward and Cynthia live in Norcross.

Harold and Kathryn Flynn had two great-grandchildren: Timothy and Kayla. See *Flynn, west side of King Street.*

Tenth House

Mr. and **Mrs. Groover** lived in this house, located on the northeast corner of Love Street where it connects with Reed Street.

NOTE: Mr. and Mrs. Henry Cantrell's House stood on the northwest corner of Reed and Love Street, facing Reed Street.

Eleventh House

Mr. and **Mrs**. **Martin Cantrell's** house, immediately past Reed Street, faced Love Street. Martin and his wife Marie, of Louisiana, met while he was serving in the United States Army.

Twelfth House

Mrs. **Jackson,** moved from Bank Street to this house which she had built. Living with her, were her daughter, Muriel Jackson Evans, whose son, Cliff, still lives here.

Thirteenth House

Alfred Carson and his wife, **Frances Matthews Carson,** in the late 1940s, had this house built near the end of Love Street. Alfred was the son of Mr. and Mrs. A. H. (Hery) Carson, who lived on South Atlanta Road across the street from the Spring Hill Streetcar Stop. Mrs. Hery Carson was the former Mary Camp, known as "Mary B." Alfred had a sister, Annette Carson, who married Bev Jones. Frances Carson was a niece of Mr. Pearce Matthews. See *west side of Concord Road* and *Atlanta Road, from Mrs. Mazie's to Creatwood* and *Camp* and *Hardage, west side of Concord Road.*

LOVE STREET
South Side

Appreciation is extended to Melvin Holleman, who grew up on Love Street, where he has lived all of his life; he and his wife, Mary Ruth still reside there. Appreciation is also extended to "Dot" Cranshaw Petty, Bobby Carson, and Mary Knight Hamby, all of whom grew up on Love Street; to Arnold Hamby, who growing up in the Oakdale community, had grandparents, the Hambys, who lived on Love Street; and to Claudia Hamrick Adams, who as a child lived on both sides of Love Street.

NOTE: Parker Lowry shared these historical notes about some of the people that lived on Love Street prior to the time frame of this book. "Mr. P.M. Rice, Jr., married Nancy Lee Pollock, who, after Mr. Rice's death, was married to L.B. Suther. The Pollock homestead was on the southwest corner of Love and Atlanta streets. In that era, the Pollocks were large landowners in this area." Parker added, "Mrs. Pollock and Mrs. W.A. Quarles, who lived next door, but on Atlanta Street, were sisters, Nancy Lee Pollock Rice inherited, from the Pollack Estate, the fourth house on the west side of King Street." See *Quarles, Atlanta Street, from Marlowes to Creatwood* and *Rice, west side of King Street.*

NOTE: Mrs. Marion Coppenger owned all the land that bordered the corner of Love and Atlanta streets. Her house, facing Atlanta Street, covered a large part of that block in the days of my youth.

First House

Mr. and **Mrs**. **Paul Gresham** lived in the first house, a pretty, brick one with a well-kept yard, on the south side of Love Street from Atlanta Street. Mrs. Gresham's name was Erma. They had one daughter, **Martha**. Mr. Gresham worked for the railroad; though I never knew what kind of position he held. I know he must have been a well-paid man. Later on he was the first President of the Cobb Federal Savings and Loan Association in Marietta.

Second House

Dr. G. C. Green
Smyrna City Councilman
1913-1917

Dr. and **Mrs. G. C. Green** lived next door to the Greshams. They had three daughters: **Sara,** **aura Alice**, and **Mary Russell**. Dr. Green, whose full name was Grover Cleveland Green, was an ptometrist in the Peachtree Arcade in Atlanta. (I recall hearing Dr. Green comment from time to time hat he rode the first streetcar from Smyrna to Atlanta and the last one, in 1948, from Atlanta back to myrna.) Mrs. Green was the former Lena May Gann, whose ancestors were among the earliest ettlers in Cobb County. A teacher at Smyrna High School, she also taught at Campbell High School, hich opened in 1952.

G.C. and Lena Mae Green were active members of the First Baptist Church, where they had nany responsibilities. Together, they were the Church Historians for the first half of the Twentieth entury. (Numerous church records have been preserved because of their efforts.) Dr. Green served as hurch Clerk in 1913, was named a life member of the Board of Deacons April 6, 1949, and was amed a Church trustee in 1956; at one time he was Chairman of the Budget and Finance Committee; r. Green served as Smyrna City Councilman, 1913-1917.

Lena Mae Green was a member of the Smyrna Social Club, founded in 1908. She, in 1936 vas instrumental in helping to organize the first library in Smyrna, located in the Smyrna Woman's lub building. The City of Smyrna honored Mrs. Green for her work in the library by dedicating the esearch room in the new library building, the Lena Mae Green Room, constructed on King Street in 961. Her framed picture was displayed in that room until the library moved in 1991 to its new home n the Village Green; it now hangs in the Smyrna Museum. The Greens were definitely leading nembers of their church and the community. See *Atlanta Street, from Mapps to R &M Café.*

Sara Green married Dr. Virgil Farrar, a pharmacist. They had two children: Sally and Virgil. ally Farrar married Jack Daniel of Thomaston; they live in Milledgeville.

Laura Alice Green married Claude Hamrick. They had two daughters: Laura Ellen and laudia. Claude, born in Carrollton, moved with his family to Sebring, Florida, where he attended the niversity of Florida. Claude was a Certified Public Accountant and a partner in the CPA firm Napier nd Hamrick in Atlanta.

Harris Adams
Assistant District Attorney
1971-1973
Judge, State Court of Cobb County
1984-2002
Chief Judge, Georgia Court of Appeals
2002-

Claudia Hamrick married Harris Adams. They had three children: Lanier, Elizabeth, and achary.

Lanier Adams married Philip Ivester. They live in the Ruff House on Concord Road in the overed Bridge area. Philip, the son of Mr. and Mrs. Harold Ivester, grew up in the Ruff house in the 970s and 1980s. (This historic house dates back to 1851.) See *Ruff, Concord Road, The Country oad.*

Elizabeth Adams married David Marshall Jones in 2004; their wedding reception was held in beautiful Greek Revival house on Church Street, in Marietta, the home of her grandparents, Claude nd Laura Alice Green Hamrick.

Zachary Adams, a graduate of Georgia Institute of Technology, is a chemical engineer, living in Marietta, is currently not married.

Laura Ellen Hamrick married Richard Cambron and had a lovely daughter, Laura, who is married to Mr. McCullough.

Mary Russell Green married Bill Carter; they lived in Atlanta. They had three children: Nancy, Bill, and Bob. Mary Russell Green died in 1971.

Third House

Mrs. Ada Gann Kent, a cousin of Mrs. G.C. Green, lived alone in the third house, which was located next door to the Greens. She had a very small lawn because most of her yard was filled with shrubs and flowers. (According to family information, this house had a room with a dirt floor on the rear of the house.)

Fourth House

Mr. and **Mrs**. **Cedar Gause** resided in this house, located on the southeast corner of Love and Lee streets, facing Love Street. Mr. Gause was the science teacher at Smyrna High School, where he also coached the school's baseball team.

Mr. and **Mrs. Claude Hamrick**

Later **Mr**. and **Mrs**. **Claude Hamrick** and their daughters, **Laura Ellen**and **Claudia**, lived, in this house, on the southeast corner of Love and Lee streets. They moved from here to Forest Drive in the Forest Hills community during the 1950s. See *Dr. G.C. Green, second house.*

Fifth House

Mr. and **Mrs**. **Tolleson**, an elderly couple, resided in the fifth house on Love Street. Neighborhood children referred to Mr. Tolleson as "Pop" Tolleson. According to long-time residents of the street, Mrs. Cannan, Mr. Tolleson's daughter, lived here also.

Sixth House

Fred and **Mary Swain** were residents of this house, facing Love Street at the southwest corner of Lee Street. They had two daughters: **Mary** and **Rosalyn**. Mrs. Swain taught at Marietta High School, where she became principal in the 1950s. The Swain Family were active members of First Baptist Church, where Mary taught the Homemaker's Sunday School Class.

Seventh House

Mr. and **Mrs**. **Wilton B**. **Carson**, **Sr**., lived in the next house. They had three children: **Wilton B**. **Carson**, **Jr**., known as "Wit," **Betty**, and **Bobby**. Mr. Carson passed away in June 1943. The Carson Family were members of Smyrna Presbyterian Church.

Wilton B."Wit" Carson III
Cobb County Commissioner
1980s

Wilton B. Carson, Jr. ., known as "Wit," and his wife, Jeanice, managed the Jonquil Theater in the late 1940s. Their son, Wit Carson III, served as a Cobb County Commissioner in the late 1980s.

Betty Carson married Fred Fritch, who worked with Delta Airlines. Due to a transfer by Delta, Fred and Betty, with their two sons, moved to California.

Betty Carson and Melvin Holleman, were Mr. and Miss Smyrna, at Smyrna High School in 942.

Bobby Carson married and lives with his family in Cherokee County, near Woodstock. ecause Bobby was a graduate of the Smyrna High School Class of 1951, I have been privileged to e him through the years at our class reunions.

NOTE: Mr. Wilton B. Carson, Sr., was a brother of Mr. Hery Carson who married the former lary Camp, known as "Mary B"; they lived on South Atlanta Road, near the Spring Hill Streetcar top. Mr. and Mrs. Hery Carson had two children: Alford and Annette. Alford married Frances latthews, and Annette married Beverly Jones, known as "Bev." Mr. A. H. (Hery) was one of the top fficials at the Southern Freight Association in Atlanta. He was accidentally killed near the Spring Hill treetcar Stop sometime in the late 1960s or early 1970s. Mr. Carson was a leader in First Baptist hurch, serving as a Sunday School Superintendent and deacon, he was elected as a trustee of the hurch in 1941. See *Carson, north side of Love Street,* and *Camp, west side of Concord Road.*

Eighth House

Lex and **LeoDelle Jolley** rented this house, located on the southeast corner of Love and unn streets, and lived here until they built their house on Lee Street in 1935. See *Jolley, west side of ee Street.*

The Eaton Family

Ed and **Sue Eaton** lived in the eighth house for a short time in the 1940s.

Glenn Yarbrough
Smyrna City Councilman
1954-1956

Mr. and **Mrs. Glenn Yarbrough** were residents of this house, located on the southeast orner of Love and Dunn streets, facing Love Street. Mrs.Yarbrough was the former Nan Edwards, ho grew up on Roswell and Love streets; she was the daughter of Mr. and Mrs. Pat Edwards. Nan nd Glenn had four children: **Sue, Johnny, Cathy**, and **Cindy**. Glenn was a real estate agent; he serve n the Smyrna City Council from 1954-1956. (I believe that Glenn Yarbrough's parents lived here efore Nan and Glenn moved into this house.)

Ninth House

Reverend and **Mrs. E.B. Awtry** resided on the southwest corner of Love and Dunn streets. hey had no children. Reverend Awtry was the beloved pastor of First Baptist Church for thirteen ears, December 1934-May 1946. As pastor, he baptized many people during his ministry at First aptist Church. A picture of Reverend Awtry in full Georgia State Militia uniform is in the First aptist Church History, *A Beacon for Christ.*

Tenth House

Mr. and **Mrs. D.A. Hamby, Sr.**, lived next door to the Awtrys. They had three sons: **D.A.**, **r., Judson**, and **Marcellus**. Mrs. Hamby, was the former Emma Lou Barrett, daughter of Carrie lamby Barrett. D.A Hamby, Sr., and his wife, Emmalou Barrett, were step siblings. Mr. Hamby, who orked for the railroad, was at work, when he was crushed and killed, by a train in Atlanta. See *mmett Marcellus Hamby, south side of Concord Road.*

D.A. Hamby, Jr. , was the oldest child. He married Mary Vaughn Bell, the daughter of omer Bell, who was the principal of Smyrna School at one time.

Judson Hamby married Gale Peek, the daughter of Mr. and Mrs. Ed Peek. Mr. Peek served as Smyrna Chief of Police at one time. See *Atlanta Street, from Miles Stop to the* Motters.

Marcellus Hamby married Betty Waldron. They had two daughters: **Marsha** and **Frances**. Betty was a member of the large Waldron Family who lived on Concord Road. See *Waldron, east side of Concord Road.*

Marsha Hamby was first married to Max Bacon, who, having served as City Councilman, is now Mayor of Smyrna. They had two children: Ashley and Ty. See *Bacon, south side of Bank Street.*

Marsha is now married to Haywood Savage. They live in the North Georgia mountains. Marsha is a renowned artist; her paintings are signed "Marsha Bacon" or "Marsha Savage."

Eleventh House

Roy Fowler and his sister **Leila Fowler** resided in the next house. I recall that, at one time, it was Mrs. Baldwin's home and for many years was called the Baldwin House. It was after Mrs. Baldwin had vacated, or died, that Roy and Leila bought this house and moved here.

Roy Fowler was a barber. He and Leila, both hairdressers, operated Fowler's Beauty and Barber Shop on Atlanta Street. In the 1950s Leila opened Leila's Beauty Shop on Bank Street, next door to the Roy Wood House. The mother of Leila and Lee (twins), and Roy, was a sister of Emma Brown Fleming. See *Fleming, on Fleming Street, Atlanta Road from Marlowe's to Creatwood* and *north side of Bank Street.*

NOTE: Leila Fowler, late in her life, married Harry Black, who was a partner in the Black and Webb Grocery Store on Atlanta Street in the days of my childhood and youth. By the time he and Leila married, Harry was a Deputy Sheriff of Cobb County.

Twelfth House

Mr. and **Mrs. James Pervis Cranshaw** were residents of this house. They had three daughters: **Dorothy,** known as "Dot," **Catherine**, and **Marion**.

"Dot" Cranshaw married Watson Petty, who grew up on his father's farm, located on the east side of King Springs Road. They had two children: Patsy and Ronald.

Watson was one of the Smyrna men captured and held as Prisoner of War during World War II. He spoke during the first Veterans Memorial Day observance that was held at the Twentieth Century Veterans Memorial, May 26, 2003. See *Petty, King Springs Road.*

Catherine Cranshaw married Charles Walker. They had three daughters: Ann, Jane, and Nancy.

Marion Cranshaw is deceased.

Mr. and Mrs. Cranshaw were members of First Methodist Church, where he was in the Pearce Matthews Men's Class and she sang in the choir. Mr. Cranshaw was a member of Nelms Lodge; both Mr. and Mrs. Cranshaw were in the Eastern Star.

Mr. Cranshaw owned and operated the J.P. Cranshaw Company, an office supply business. A short man, with stooped shoulders in his latter years, he often walked. I can still picture him, always dressed in a business suit, walking around Smyrna.

Thirteenth House

Mr. and **Mrs. Charlie Turner** resided in the house on the southwest corner of Love Street nd Concord Road. Still standing, the house is a nice brick structure that currently houses Love Street Antiques. Mrs. Turner's given name was Lena. They had two sons and a daughter: **Claude**, **Lawrence**, and **Viola**. The Turners were active members of First Baptist Church. Mr. Turner worked or the railroad.

Claude Turner married Louise Emory. They had two sons and a daughter: Billy, Kenny, and Connie. Connie Turner (Denny) still lives in Smyrna and sings in the First Baptist Church Choir.

Connie Denny stated, "We called our grandfather 'Dad Ah.' My brother Kenny's children picked up on that and now they affectionately call Kenny, 'Dad Ah' also." Connie spoke very lovingly of her grandparents.

Lawrence Turner was married twice. His first wife died when his first son was a small child. He and his second wife, Louise, had a son, Charles.

Viola Turner married Earlie Cooper. They had one son, "Buddy," who still lives in Smyrna.

NOTE: The Turner house still stands at the intersection of Love Street and Concord Road. This house is also listed in these memoirs as the first house on the west side of Concord Road. I was ever sure if the house was on Love Street or Concord Road. Love Street Gift Shop is currently ocated here.

Fourteenth House

Claude Turner, along with his **Family**, lived in a small house that faced Love Street, just ehind his mother's house.

Fifteenth House

Melvin and **Mary Ruth Holleman** lived in this house. They had two daughters: **Dianne** and **Charlotte**. I remember when Mary Ruth came to Smyrna. According to my wife, Lillie, the Holleman ourtship and marriage make a beautiful love story. After they met in college, Melvin enlisted into the United States Navy during World War II. When he came home for a weekend leave, he and Mary Ruth married. They celebrated their sixtieth wedding anniversary June 26, 2004, at the home of their aughter and son-in-law, Dianne and George Spears.

Before Melvin and Mary Ruth began attending First Baptist Church, Melvin served as an lder in Smyrna Presbyterian Church and in Calvary Presbyterian Church, located on what is now Windy Hill Road (formerly Jones Shaw Road) at the intersection of Favor Road.

Melvin is a life-long resident of Love Street. He graduated from Smyrna High School, where e was named "Mr. Smyrna High" in 1942. (Betty Carson was Miss Smyrna.) His two daughters ttended Smyrna Elementary School, and both of them graduated from Campbell High School. On anuary 29, 2004, the Smyrna Moose Lodge named Melvin "Mr. Smyrna," for his many years of utstanding community service. He is also a long-time volunteer at the Smyrna Museum, where he erves weekly.

Melvin and Mary Ruth have been active in many areas of First Baptist Church life, where he as ordained a deacon September 15, 1968. In the 1970s, Melvin served as Chairman of the Board of eacons for several terms. (He also served on the Board of Deacons for many years when he was not hairman.) For many years Melvin taught a Sunday School class and served as Sunday School epartment Director. He and Mary Ruth have been members of the adult choir of First Baptist Church r more than thirty years. Melvin, having a beautiful voice has often sung at weddings, funerals, and church services, (both alone, and with his daughter, Charlotte). When my sister and brother-in-law, Hilda Wood and Grady Chaffin, married in 1950, Melvin Holleman sang at their wedding, held in what is now the First Baptist Church Chapel.

After World War II, Melvin worked for The Atlanta Newspapers. He later worked for the Veterans Administration, from which he retired.

Dianne Holleman a graduate of Campbell High School, married George Spears, who also graduated from Campbell High School. Having grown up on Jonquil Drive, George was the son of Mr. and Mrs. James Spears, who grew up in Atlanta. Mrs. Spears was the former Marguerite George. Marguerite and James had three other children: Donnie, Pat, and Jimmy.

Charlotte Holleman, a graduate of Campbell High School married Charles Winkles. They had two children: Christie and Joshua. Christie married Bryan Blankenship; the two had been associated many years in First Baptist Church, where both were members. Bryan is the son of Bill and Twila (Travis) Blankenship, long time members of First Baptist Church.

Sixteenth House

Mr. and **Mrs**. **T.P. Holleman** were residents of this nice brick house, still standing. They had three children: **Irene**, **Harold**, and **Melvin**. **(**Harold died accidentally in 1938 while he was a student at Berry High School in Rome.) Mr. and Mrs. Holleman were both very distinguished people; she, the former Kate Brown, was an attractive, statuesque lady. See *Irene McRae, Medlin Street,* and *Holleman, fifteenth house on Love Street.*

During my early life Kate and T.P. Holleman were members of Smyrna Presbyterian Church. Mr. Holleman was ordained a deacon in First Baptist Church in 1948. After Mr. Holleman died, Mrs. Holleman served as a "greeter" in the sanctuary foyer of First Baptist Church for many years, as well as a Sunday School teacher in the Junior Department, a faithful and dedicated church member. I miss her!

Mr. T.P. Holleman worked at the Chevrolet Plant on McDonough Boulevard in Atlanta. Mrs. Holleman worked in Clarkdale, along with Nina Chaffin (the mother of my brother-in-law, Grady Chaffin) at Clark Thread Mill, owned and operated by Coats and Clark Company; Mrs. Chaffin rode to work with Mrs. Holleman. Mrs. Holleman's dad, Mr. "Jim" Brown, was the first night watchman at Clark Thread Mill, even while it was being built (in/or about 1925). The Brown and Holleman families were long-time residents of the Clarkdale and Powder Springs areas. See *Chaffin under Wood, north side of Bank Street.*

NOTE: Early in the Twenty-first Century, the Austell Mayor and City Council voted to purchase the Clarkdale Thread Mill building and grounds, creating a complex, where the City offices are now located .

There was a vacant lot next door to the Holleman House in the days of my youth.

Seventeenth House

Mr. and **Mrs**. **L.P. Jones** resided in this house. They had four children: **Billy**, **Barry**, **Sarah Frances**, and another daughter whose name I do not recall.

Sarah Frances Jones married Mr. Flowers, who led the singing at Hurt Road Baptist Church. Mr. Flowers is deceased.

The Bobo Family

After the Jones Family moved, the **Bobo Family** lived in this house. They had a daughter, **Jean,** and a son, **Jack.**

Eighteenth House

B.H. Hanson
Smyrna City Councilman
1946-1947

Mr. and **Mrs**. **B.H**. **Hanson** were residents of this house. Mrs. Hanson was the former Curtis Edwards. They had five children: **Helen**, **Lucille**, **B.H**., **Jr**., **Margaret**, and **Jeanette**. The Hansons were members of First Methodist Church.

Curtis Hanson was an active member of the Smyrna Woman's Club and a member of the Methodist Woman's Society of Christian Service, which is currently known as the United Methodist Women. During World War II, years 1944-45, she was employed at the Bell Bomber Plant; this was the only time she ever worked outside the home.

B.H. and Curtis Hanson came to Smyrna from Walton County in 1924. They resided in a couple of houses a short time before moving to Love Street, where they lived the rest of their lives. Mr. Hanson was one of eighteen children; Mrs. Hanson was an only child. After moving to Smyrna, Mr. Hanson worked at a dairy farm located in the vicinity of what is known today as the Concord and Old Concord roads, which was owned by his brother, W.T. Hanson. During World War II B. H. Hanson worked at the Bell Bomber Plant until it closed. Having been in retirement for few for years, he began working for Lockheed Aircraft Corporation in 1961; from there he retired, in 1971.

NOTE: W.T. Hanson was Chairman of the Board of Trustees when Smyrna Elementary School was built on Church Street, in 1925. His wife, Ruth, taught there. They lived in a large brick house on the east side of Atlanta Road, in the vicinity of the Spring Hill Streetcar Stop.

B.H. Hanson, Jr.. married Helen Blackwell, who grew up on Spring Road. During World War II, he served with the United States Navy aboard the U.S.S. Biloxi in the Pacific. See *south side of Bank Street* and *the north side of Spring Road, The Country Road.*

Lucille Hanson married Robert Austin, known as "Bob," who grew up on North Cooper Lake Road. They had two children: Karen and Wayne. Karen married Bill Kelly. Wayne, who never married, is currently living in his family home on Bank Street. "Bob" and Lucille are both deceased. See *Austin, south side of Bank Street.*

Helen Hanson married Robert Wright. They had four children: Harriett, Carman, Hanson, and Selina. Robert served in the United States Army during World War II. The Wright Family were members at First Methodist Church. Mrs. Wright died in May 2004.

Harriett Wright married Gene Atkins of Smyrna. They had three daughters: Kim, Jill, and Hope. See *Atkins, south side of Bank Street.*

Carman Wright married Alice Jones of Vinings. They had four children: Allison, Erika, Robert, and Heather. Alice Jones Wright grew up in the area where Cumberland Mall is today. The Carman Wright Family are members of First Methodist Church. See *Jones, Spring Road, The Country Road.*

Several years after Alice's death, Carman married Judy Whaley, who taught at Campbell High School for many years, including the years my children were students there. She later became principal of Campbell, where she retired. Carman and Judy still live in Smyrna.

Home of Mr. and Mrs. B.H. Hanson, Sr., 307 Love Street, Smyrna, Georgia.
House built in 1929, by Mr. Duncan Johnson. The Johnsons lived in an old barn on the property for one year until Mr. Johnson completed the house. They then moved into the house, living in it one year, before selling it to the Hanson Family. The house was sold after the death of Mr. Hanson in 1973.

Photo courtesy of Jeanettte Hanson Taylor.

Allison Wright married David Warren from Selma, Alabama. They had four children: Claire Alice, Catherine Helen, Anna Grace, and Augustus David, known as "Gus." (Anna and "Gus" are twins.) The Warren Family, though living in West Cobb County, are still members of First Methodist Church.

Erika Wright married Jason Sams of Smyrna. They had two daughters: Lily Caroline and Charlotte Opal. The Sams Family, members of First Methodist Church, live in Smyrna.

Heather Wright married Andy Andersen. They had one son, William James, known as "Will." Heather and Andy live in Atlanta.

Robert Power Wright is married to Sara Elizabeth Whaley, daughter of Judy Whaley Wright. Robert and Sara live in Eugene, Oregon.

Hanson Wright married Sheryl Bettenbaugh of Fayette County. They had one son, Garrett. Hanson, who retired from CSX Transportation as a sales executive, and Sheryl are residing in Hillsboro, Oregon.

Selina Wright married Jerry Wengard from Ellijay. They had two sons: Casey and Thomas. Selina and Jerry live in Cherokee County, where Selina teaches school. Both sons are students at Georgia Southern University in Statesboro.

Margaret Hanson, who never married, has been a very active member of the First Methodist Church all of her life. In 1952 she helped to organize the first Girl Scout Troop in Smyrna. Due in part through her influence, a Girl Scout hut was built off the southeast corner of Legion Drive and Concord Road. According to local information, the City of Smyrna and American Legion Post # 160 had some kind of agreement concerning this scout hut, at one time was named "The Mary Wills Scout Hut." Margaret worked with the Girl Scouts for a number of years. For forty years she was employed by Fireman's Fund Insurance Company in Atlanta, from which she retired. See *Zelan* and *Mary Wills, west side of Lee Street.*

Jeanette Hanson married Jerry Taylor; they had four children: Kathy, Ronnie, David, and Mark. The Taylors are members of First Methodist Church, where Jerry served for many years on the Governing Board and he and Jeanette are members of the Roland Walker Sunday School Class. Jerry, from Gallatin, Tennessee, retired from Lockheed Aircraft Corporation in 1994, after forty years of service. Serving stateside, Jerry was in the United States Air Force during the Korean Conflict.

Jerry is a graduate of Gallatin High School, in Gallatin, Tennessee, and Jeanette graduated from the Smyrna High School Class of 1950; their children graduated from Campbell High School.

Kathy Taylor married Roy Kindel from Marietta. They had two sons: Bryan and Jeff. Kathy, who graduated from Middle Georgia College in Millegeville, is a teacher. She is currently teaching at Hayes Elementary School, in Northwest Cobb County, which was named for Harold Hayes, the principal of Brown Elementary School, in Smyrna, for many years.

Ronnie Taylor married Sandra McDaniel from South Cobb County. They had three children: a daughter, Casey, and two sons, Jeremy and Jacob.

David Taylor, and his wife, Paige, had two children: Krissey and Kedrick.

Mark Taylor married Cher Mosley, who graduated from Wills High School. They had one son, Colt.

Nineteenth House

Mr. and Mrs. Wylie Gibson

Mr. and **Mrs**. **Wylie Gibson** resided in this house. Mrs. Gibson was the former Carrie Mae Hamby, a sister of Carl Hamby and Giles Thomas Hamby, known as "Red."

NOTE: According to information from the neighborhood, Mr. and Mrs. Wylie Gibson willed this house to Mr. and Mrs. Carl Hamby. Giles Thomas Hamby, known as "Red," also lived here but never owned the house.

The Carl Hamby Family

Mr. and **Mrs**. **Carl Hamby** lived with their three children: **Carla**, **Arnold**, and **Eunice**. On Atlanta Road, south of Fitzhugh Lee School, Carl owned and operated a neighborhood grocery store. (The store was located just before crossing the railroad at Collins Springs Primitive Baptist Church.)

Carla Hamby married Johnny Sweatt, who lived on Gilmore Road in the Oakdale community, south of Smyrna. They had two children: Gloria and David.

Arnold Hamby married Mary Knight, the daughter of the Reverend and Mrs. John H. Knight. In the days of my youth, Reverend Knight was the pastor of Smyrna Presbyterian Church. Most of my life, I have been privileged to know Mary and Arnold, who are very faithful members of Smyrna Presbyterian Church. Arnold retired from the United States Post Office after thirty-eight years of service. Under Postmaster Zelan Wills, he had a walking route that took him all over Smyrna to deliver mail; later he drove a little mail bus. See *Knight, north side of Love Street.*

Eunice Hamby married Bobby Lumpkin from Columbus. They had two children: Kathy and Dwayne. Kathy married Mr. Hall.

Mr. and Mrs. Truman Hamby

Mr. and Mrs. Truman Hamby, the parents of Carl and Carrie Mae Hamby, raised their children (who were in my parents' generation) on the west side of Concord Road in the area where Mr. Robert Baldwin later built the Rock House.

Truman Hamby and his wife, the former Vannie Eidson, had eight children: Robert T., known as "Robbie," Vannie Ida, Carrie Mae, a son Ada, Edward Waddell, known as "Waddie," Ollie, Giles Thomas, known as "Red," and Carl Judson.

Robert T. Hamby never married.

Vannie Ida Hamby married Robert Harry Harper. See *Harper, south side of Church Street.*

Carrie Mae Hamby married Wylie Gibson. See *eighteenth house, south side of Love Street.*

Ada Hamby, the second son, never married.

Edward Waddell Hamby, known as "Waddie," married Elton O'Dell Hammond in 1923. They had two children: Edward Waddell Hamby, Jr., and Edith Jackie Hamby. "Waddie," was born July 12, 1894, died November 9, 1947; he is buried in the Daniell Cemetery, located in the Bennett Woods subdivision.

NOTE: Later on, O'Dell Hamby worked for Poston Realty Company, on Atlanta Street.

Edward Waddell Hamby, Jr. ., married Debra Joy Hamby, the daughter of Mr. and Mrs. Carl Mayes Hamby. See *Mayes Hamby, west side of Concord Road.*

Edith Jackie Hamby never married.

Ollie Hamby married George Fortner. They had several children, among whom were: Truman, Robert, "Bud," and Henry. They also had some daughters. The George Fortner Family lived on the northeast corner of the Access Road, now South Cobb Drive, and Powder Springs Street. See *Fortner, east side of Access Road* and *north side of Powder Springs Street.*

Giles Thomas Hamby, known as "Red," and Carlton Chambers were in an automobile accident, Carlton Chambers was killed. After the automobile accident, Giles Thomas Hamby, known as "Red," and Carlton's widow, Sadie Peeples Chambers married; they had one daughter, Vannie. Sadie and Carlton Chambers had one son, Weldon Chambers. See *Whitfield Street.*

Carl Judson Hamby married Eunice Hite. See *Hamby, eighteenth house. south side of Love Street* and *Knight, north side of Love Street.*

CHAPTER TWELVE

LEE STREET

East Side

Appreciation is extended to Jane Steppe Chastain for furnishing information on her family: the Steppes on Lee Street and the McMillans on Atlanta Street. Appreciation is also extended to Betty McNelley Sager for sharing memories of her family on Lee Street.

First House

In the late 1940s or very early 1950s, "Gene" Rice entered into a contract with Don Pair to build a small house for his children's grandmother. The property site was near the southwest corner of Love Street; the house was to face Lee Street.

Mrs. English later lived in this house.

Second House

Mr. and **Mrs. Paul Crump** and their daughters, **Judy** and **Jean,** were residents here. After Jasper Griffin had transferred to become Principal of Campbell High School, Mr. Crump became the principal of Smyrna Elementary School, in 1952. Janet Brooks Brown shared with me that she has report cards, which Mr. Crump signed, for the 1951-1954 school years

Third House

Mr. and **Mrs. Robert David McNelley** lived here with their two children: **Betty** and **Robert, Jr.**, known as "Junior." Mrs. McNelley was the former Willie Mae Hood of Copper Hill, Tennessee. The McNelleys moved from Walker Street, in 1948, to this house which was built for them by Mr. Coppenger; the house has been occupied by members of the McNelley Family ever since. The McNelley Family were members of First Baptist Church, where Mr. McNelley served as President of the Men's Brotherhood. Mrs. McNelley, originally from Germany, died in 1973. See *McNelley, north side of Walker Street.*

After his children were grown and his wife had died, Mr. McNelley remarried and moved to Portland, Oregon.

<u>Betty McNelley</u> married Jack Wayne Harris of the Oakdale community, south of Smyrna. They had five children: Michael, David, Paul, Richard, and Betty. Jack Wayne Harris, employed by Rust Cheese, delivered ice cream mix.

Betty McNelly, a 1949 graduate of Smyrna High School, where she was the Sweetheart of the Senior Class, a cheerleader, and Editor of *The Hornet*, the school's paper. In 1946, while she was still in school, Betty worked for Harry Black's Grocery Store and The Smyrna Telephone Exchange, on Atlanta Street.

Michael Harris married Ann Frost; they had one child. Michael, now divorced, lives in Smyrna.

David Harris married Diane Bryant; they had two children.

Paul Harris married Sherrie Lynn Dunn; they had one daughter. Amanda, who is divorced, lives in Kennesaw.

Richard Harris married Michelle Yoxon from England. They had one child.

Betty Harris married and had three children. After Betty divorced, she married Eddie Sager; they live in Dallas.

Robert McNelley, Jr., a graduate of Campbell High School, married Frances Bennett, known as "Frankie," of Tampa, Florida. They had two children, Roberta Ann and Douglas Scott, and four grandchildren. Now divorced, Robert is currently living in this family house on Lee Street. Robert first worked for Motor Convoy, later for Commercial Carriers, and still later for Fouts Brothers, as a truck salesman; he is now selling used trucks for U-Haul.

MEMORIES

by Betty McNelley

"I remember the first time I saw Smyrna. In the middle of the night, confused, I asked, 'What's that red light in the middle of the road?' It was the lone traffic light.

"My dad, Robert McNelley, who grew up in the Atlanta area, moved his young family to New Orleans, where he worked on a banana boat during the Great Depression years; it was the only work he was able to find during that time. Because housing was scarce, we lived on Desire Street in a two-room apartment, over what was called a 'Honkey Tonk.' When it rained, the streets would fill with water; there children would swim. Later on we moved to Hope, which was in the Baton Rouge area. While we were living there, on Canal Street, my little brother died.

"My family's life improved in 1942, when we moved to Florence, Alabama, where my brother, Robert McNelly, was born. We moved from Alabama to Oak Ridge, Tennessee, for Dad, a welder and steamfitter, to work for the Atomic Energy Commission. There my family purchased a house trailer, in which we lived during the World War II years. Afterwards, we moved from Kingston, Tennessee, to a trailer park in the Fair Oaks community; there I began my freshman year at Osborne High School. From Fair Oaks we moved to Smyrna's Walker Street into the house with my grandparents; here we used a tin wash tub for bathing. It was from this house that I started to Smyrna High School. From Walker Street, we moved to this house on Lee Street, which was built for us by Mr. Coppenger. When we settled here, I thought 'We are rich.' By this time I had attended a Catholic kindergarten, 16 different elementary schools and 2 high schools.

"The living conditions for my family improved tremendously after we moved to Smyrna. I have many fond memories of residing here—including ordering groceries from 'Shorty' Black's store which were delivered to our house by Sammy Waldron and 'Hamburger' Westbrook.

"During my growing-up years in Smyrna I always managed to get some kind of job. (It was the only way I could have any spending money.) During my high school years, I worked for Harry Black at Black and Webb's Grocery Store. Not yet 16, I applied for a job with Southern Bell Telephone Exchange on Atlanta Street. I bugged Mrs. Dobbins, the chief operator, for a job; she told me I could not work there until I was 16. 'If you still want a job when you are 16, come back then, and I will hire you.' I did go back, and she hired me in 1946, and Jeanie Hill, who married Charles Poss, trained me; there I worked until 1951. (I still have all the pay "stubbs" from the checks I received.) In those years at the Telephone Exchange I earned seniority, trained trainees, and worked up to supervisor and chief operator. In 1951 the phone system changed from operator service to the dial system, and I had to leave the Smyrna office.

"Another fond memory I have is that of working on a horse farm, on Hawthorne Avenue, for a man whose name I do not recall. I do remember that 'Bearcat' Austin and 'Britches' Cochran also worked there. Loving to ride horses, I learned to ride well. The owner of the farm noticed and gave me a job taking care of the horses. I also accompanied the young females who were there to learn the basics of horseback riding. I remember well how excited I was when I was assigned to 'Prince,' the best horse. (I believe the guys who worked there were jealous.) When the farm was sold, each employee was allowed to buy the horse he or she was taking care of, I gave my only $25.00 War bond

The F.T. Wills Home on Lee Street
Picture made in 2004
Current Resident is Paula Weekes

as a down payment for 'Prince' and moved him to my back yard on Walker Street. After the passing of an ordinance requiring an acre per house, I moved 'Prince' to a pasture on Fraser Street."

Fourth House

J.B. Ables
Smyrna City Councilman,
1958-1963
Mayor of Smyrna
1962-1963

J. B. and **Blanche Ables** moved from Toccoa to Lee Street in 1951 for J.B. to become employed at the newly opened Lockheed Aircraft Corporation; there he worked for the next 25 years. Blanche, the former Blanche Coker, and J.B. had two children: **Diane** and **Quinton**.

Diane Ables married Jerry Rand; they live in Marietta. Diane works for Austin Byrd, Attorneys at Law in Atlanta; Jerry is self-employed as a home repairman.

Quinton Ables married Ann Groschuesch. They live in Bluffton, South Carolina, where Quinton owns and operates Ables Stock Market Exchange.

Quinton and Diane Ables, both graduates of Campbell High School, are also college graduates: Diane, from Georgia State University in Atlanta, and Quinton, from Middle Georgia University, near Milledgeville, and from Louisiana State University School of Business, where he majored in investment management.

Fifth House

Mr. F. T. Wills
Smyrna City Councilman
1926-1927

Mr. and **Mrs. F.T. Wills** from my earliest memories, were residents in this house on Lee Street. They were the parents of **Sherrill**, **Zelan**, **Fanny**, and **Elizabeth Wills**. Elizabeth, who never married, taught third grade at Smyrna School for as long as I can remember; in fact, she taught me, my sister (Hilda), and brother (Sammy) in the third grade. See *Wills west side of Lee Street.*

Mr. F.T. Wills was the Superintendent of the Cobb County School System before I started to school. (The superintendent that I remember in my school years was Mr. Paul Sprayberry.)

The Wills Family was very active members of First Baptist Church.

Sixth House

Mr. and **Mrs. Jesse Cook** lived here. Mrs. Cook's given name was Ruby. Jesse Cook, along with the help of his oldest son, Richard, in the mid 1940s constructed this house for his family. I remember well when this house was built and the Cook Family moved here. The Cooks sold their house on the west side of King Street to First Baptist Church for use as a pastorium; Reverend Charles Drake, after he became pastor of the church in 1946, was the first to reside there. See *Cook, west side of King Street.*

Seventh House

Mr. and **Mrs. Ben Morris** and their two children, **Richard** and **Ronald**, lived in this house, a white frame one. Directly across the street from the George Howard Family, the Morris house was set much farther back from the street than the others.

Eighth House

Mr. and **Mrs**. **Horace G**. **Poss** and their son, **Charles**, resided in this house, which was a nice brick one located on a large tract of land. The Poss Family were members of First Methodist Church. Horace owned a business, Horace G. Poss and Son, on Howell Mill Road in Atlanta, at Fourteenth Street; there steam engines, rail cars, and boilers were repaired.

In the 1960s, I remember, Horace and Charles were coin collectors. Doing some collecting myself, one time I helped them obtain some coins they wanted. Because of my efforts, Horace and Charles, whom I really liked, gave me a nice briefcase. (I still have that briefcase in my possession.)

Charles Poss married Jeanie Hill, who grew up on the north side of Powder Springs Street. They had three children: Patty, Cathy, and Charles known as "Chuck." After the elder Mr. and Mrs. Poss died, Charles and Jeanie were residents of this house the rest of their lives. Jeanie died in 2004. Charles had preceded Jeanie in death. See *Hill, north side of Powder Springs Street.*

NOTE: In 2005, the Poss house was razed after it and the large tract of land had been sold to a developer for the building of a small subdivision, Stonegate.

Ninth House

There was a house here, but I do not remember its residents. During the days of my youth, the property on the northeast corner of Lee Street and Collier Drive was vacant.

Several families, whom I had known well over the years, moved to Lee Street early on after the street was extended beyond Collier Drive.

Tenth House

Mr. and **Mrs**. **Quinton Steppe** moved, with their only child, **Jane**, to this house from Blairsville in 1950. On the southeast corner of Lee Street and Collier Drive, this house was a newly built brick one. In Blairsville Quinton Steppe had worked as a funeral director for his brother's funeral home; after moving to Smyrna, he became employed as a mechanic with Georgia Power Company. Mrs. Steppe, the former Lina Abernathy, was a medical assistant in Atlanta.

Lina Abernathy Steppe's family home was the McMillan House, located on the east side of Atlanta Road, north of where Campbell High School (now known as Campbell Middle School) was built in 1952. Lina was the daughter of Mr. and Mrs. Luther Abernathy; her mother was the former Bertha McMillan, who owned and operated a millinery shop in Copperhill, Tennessee. ("She was famous for her hats, which were worn by the 'best dressed' women of the area," remarked Jane Steppe.) Bertha died in the flu epidemic of 1918, when Lina was a little girl. See *McMillan, Atlanta Street, from Mrs. Mazie's to Pearce Matthews.*

Quinton Steppe was a cousin of the Reverend J.T. McHann, a well-known Baptist minister, serving at one time as pastor of Sharon Baptist Church on South Cobb Drive. Quinten and Lina are deceased.

Jane Steppe has been married to Roger Chastain for 38 years. They had one son, Blayne Chastain, who is a minister. Roger, an industrial designer from South Georgia, and Jane met while he was working at Georgia Institute of Technology. Jane and Roger live in southern California, where Roger is an industrial design engineer. Both Jane and Roger, private pilots with multi instrument ratings, enjoy flying airplanes as their joint hobby.

"After graduating from Campbell High School, Jane Steppe became known as the nation's first female sportscaster, she was known as "Coach Friday" (on WAGA-TV in Atlanta), predicting football games. Though now best known for her news and political commentaries, Jane will always be remembered as this nation's first woman sportscaster. During her 17 years as a television sports reporter and anchor in Atlanta, Raleigh, Miami, and Los Angeles via the CBS network, she broke many journalistic barriers for women. CBS made her the nation's first woman network sportscaster in 1974. While with CBS and traveling throughout North America, she covered some of the world's most exciting sporting events: The Pan American Games, NFL Football, NBA Basketball, the Sun Bowl, the Cotton Bowl, pro golf, tennis, and a variety of other sports—from cycling to surfing. She was the first woman allowed on a major league baseball playing field and the first woman admitted to the NASCAR pits and garage area."

"Following the birth of their son, in 1975, Jane returned to WTVJ, where she claimed an anchor spot for the evening news.

"In more recent years, Jane has been a southern California-based broadcaster, author, and political commentator. Her outspoken commentaries on the political, social, and moral issues of the day can be read at *WorldNetDaily.com,* the most popular independent news site on the World Wide Web. Her radio programs have been syndicated to some of the largest radio markets in the country for more than a decade.

"Based in California, Jane served as a commissioner on Women's Progress Commemoration Commission, which was created by an act of Congress in 1998. She also served on the advisory boards of the Family Research Council, the Christian Television and Film Commission, and ChildCare International.

"Jane is the author of *I'd Speak on the Issues If I Only Knew What to Say* and the hostess of such documentary videos as *Freedom Held Hostage, The Feminine Mistake, Conceived in Liberty*, and *The Incredible Power of Prayer.*

"Jane Chastain lives with her husband, Roger, on a private runway in the mountains above Palm Springs, California. Roger, an eminent industrial designer is recognized for his innovative contributions to the automotive and mode aviation industries."

NOTE: The above information in quotes on Jane Steppe Chastain and her family is from Jane's Biographical Profile, which she furnished.

Angelina Shaw Abercrombie

This house later became the home of **Angelina Abercromie**, who was a writer for *The Marietta Journal*. See *Shaw, west side of Dunn Street.*

Emmett and **Evelyn Arrington**

Evelyn and **Emmett Arrington** and their daughter, **Patricia**, known as "Pat," in 1950 moved from Sunset Avenue to Lee Street, which was unpaved at the time. Their new house was constructed on the seventh lot from Collier Drive; at that time, their house was the second one built south of Collier Drive—the first being that of the Steppes.

"Pat" shared with me that her parents bought this house on Lee Street while it was under construction. For the house and lot they paid $8,000.00, with payments being $52.00 a month for the next 30 years. Emmett and Evelyn, who resided in this house the rest of their lives, were privileged to live several years without a house payment. After having leased the house to tenants for 10 years, Pat sold it in 1998 for $114,500.00. See *Arrington, south side of Sunset Avenue.*

LEE STREET
West Side

Appreciation is extended to Janet Jones Brown, Jane Steppe Chastain, Dewey Lioneal Ioward, Malinda Jolley Mortin, "Buddy" Rice, and Marilyn Rice, for sharing their memories of rowing up on Lee Street in the 1940s and 1950s. Appreciation also goes to Andy Anderson, who noved to Lee Street in 1940 and has lived there for 60 years.

First House

Mrs. Foy Williams and her three children, **Burgess**, **Eloise**, and **Rita**, all older than I, esided in this house. Mrs. William's husband, Garner, had deceased; thus I never knew him.

Burgess Williams married Barbara Ann Bearden from Rome. She was a first cousin of my riend Miller Davis.

Eloise Williams married George Head. The Heads raised their family on Cooper Lake Road. Both the lake and some of the houses at Cash Farms are located on the former Head property. See *Head, Church Road, The Country Road.*

Rita Williams married Hubert Head.

Mrs. Foy Williams, whose picture is hanging in the lobby of the library on the Village Green, served as Librarian for the Smyrna Public Library. The Williams Family were active members of First Methodist Church.

NOTE: The Smyrna Public Library is the only city owned library in the State of Georgia at the time of this writing. The others are county or regional.

Second House

Eugene Rice
Smyrna City Councilman
Elected January 21, 1952

Mr. and **Mrs. Eugene Alton Rice, Sr.**, known as "Gene," lived in the second house on the west side of the street. They had two children: **Eugene A. Rice, Jr.**, known as "Buddy," and **Marilyn**. Mrs. Rice was the former Virginia Mitchell, the daughter of Mr. and Mrs. H.B. Mitchell. The Rice Family attended Smyrna Presbyterian Church. See *Mitchell, south side of Church Street.*

"Gene" Rice was from Midlothian, Texas, southwest of Dallas. His family moved from Texas to Cobb County's Macland area, in Powder Springs. He had two brothers, Kenneth and Jack Rice, who lived in Atlanta, and two sisters, Polly Rice Wheatley and Marybell Rice, who remained in Texas. Jack Rice, along with the help of "Gene," owned and operated Hotel Bel Air in Atlanta.

"Gene" owned and operated a furniture store on Atlanta Street in downtown Smyrna; later on, he opened a furniture store on the Four-Lane Highway (now U.S. Highway 41). "Gene" also owned the property where the Corner Grill, Johnson's Shoe Shop, and Chat N'Nibble were located. (Chat N' Nibble was opened and operated and by "Butch" Alexander, the former butcher at Rogers Store.) According to family information, Mr. Rice could not obtain insurance on Johnson's Shoe Shop because it was "too cluttered." Gene Rice was elected to fill the unexpired term of John Collier on the Smyrna City Council January 21, 1952.

Marilyn Rice shared that her mother, Virginia, was active in the community: rolling bandages for the Red Cross and hosting garden club meetings in their home. She also remembers the magnolia trees in front of their house. Her dad kept them trimmed so that the kids would not run into them. Leaves from those trees were used in decorations for many weddings and other social functions in the community.

"'Gene" Rice, Sr., contracted Don Pair to build, a house behind the Hambrick home, (across the street), for his children's grandmother, said "Buddy" Rice.

Marilyn Rice shared, "Our house had asbestos siding, which dad replaced with bricks from a Civil War era house that he had torn down somewhere out Concord Road."

NOTE: The house alluded to could have been the P.F. Daniell House.

Eugene A Rice, Jr., known as "Buddy," married Brenda Kathy McMahan from Asheville, North Carolina. They had three children: two daughters, Christy, and Kelly, and a son, David.

"Buddy" Rice remembers that, during the "Cuban Crisis" in 1962, his dad built a fallout shelter, complete with a steel door. Though covered up, it is still there. When the house was being sold, the buyers were informed about it.

NOTE: Many people during this period of time built fallout shelters. I am sure there are others still around town.

Marilyn Rice married and had a son, Mark Gamel. Marilyn, who now lives in Marietta, was born when her dad was 44 years old and her mother was 35. Though Marilyn was often thought of as "Gene's" granddaughter, Gene was very proud to say, "No this is my baby!" Marilyn, whose memories included Girl Scouts as being a part of her "growing-up life" in Smyrna, also recalls an archery range to which many of the children went.

NOTE: This archery range was probably on what is now known as Pinetree Drive, in the Forest Hills community

Marilyn related the following story about a camping trip before the days of their having a "store-bought" camper. "My dad had a camper built onto the back of a two-ton truck. We took that camper on a five-week vacation through the New England states. When we drove up to the Drake Hotel, quite fancy, the bell hop took our luggage from the back of the camper; he must have thought we looked like the 'Beverly Hillbillies.'"

Third House

Robert Taylor, known as "Bob," his wife, Marilyn, and their daughter, **Margo**, were residents here. According to information from the Taylor Family, Mr. and Mrs. Howard Taylor, parents of "Bob," had this house built for their daughter-in-law, Marilyn, and granddaughter, Marguerite, known as "Margo," while "Bob" was in the military. When "Bob" returned home, he attended Georgia Institute of Technology to pursue an architectural degree. He built an addition to this house to include a workroom and a place for his architectural drawings.

This house, farther off the street than the "Gene" Rice house, backed up to the Pavlovsky house on Dunn Street. "Bob" Taylor was a brother of Louise Pavlovsky. *See Pavlovsky, east side of Dunn Street* and *Taylor on Atlanta Street, from Mrs. Mazie's to Pearce Matthews.*

"Bob" Taylor was the building inspector for the City of Smyrna while he was enrolled in the School of Architecture at Georgia Institute of Technology. While working for the City, "Bob" developed a map of the City of Smyrna. (It is part of the public record of the City of Smyrna.)

Margo Taylor, a teacher in Philadelphia, Pennsylvania, will soon retire.

The John Pennington Family

Later on, **John** and **Marilyn Pennington** moved to this house, which became known as the 'aylor/Pennington House. They had three children, **Gail**, **Stuart**, and **Jeffrey**. Mr. Pennington was a olumnist for *The Atlanta Journal.*

Fourth House

Mrs. Louise Richardson and her son, **Tommy**, lived in the fourth house on the west side of ,ee Street. Louise's sister, Mrs. Ruth Giles, was a reporter for *The Atlanta Journal* and *Constitution,* nd later for *The Marietta Daily Journal.*

Fifth House

Mr. and **Mrs. Lex Jolley** were residents of the fifth house on the west side of Lee Street. 'hey had two children: **Fleming** and **Malinda**. Having had this house built, they moved here from ,ove Street. This house backed up to the Koningsmark house, located on Dunn Street. In 1954 Mr. nd Mrs. Jolley had a house built on Pretty Branch Drive, in the Forest Hills community. After their noving during the summer, Malinda started high school in the eighth grade. "It was a hot summer," aid Malinda. Their new home was just a few blocks from the Jolley's Lee Street house. See *north side f Love Street and Bethel School on the south side of Spring Road, the Country Road.*

NOTE: Development began in the Forest Hills community during the early 1950s.

I first became acquainted with Mr. and Mrs. Lex Jolley when I was a kid, working at Rogers tore, where I would service them. (In those days the customer would come in or call the store with a rocery order. Rogers Store would hire students to put up stock and to fill orders for the customers. I vas an employee that was hired for those purposes.) Going throughout the store, I would fill Mrs. olley's order and take her groceries to the car. I always liked to service her; very nice to me, she vould always give me a good tip.

After I had finished college and begun work at Fulton National Bank, I saw Mr. Jolley requently in downtown Atlanta. He began work for the Citizens and Southern Company in 1929 in Atlanta. (At that time "bank" was not a part of the company name.) After the change by The Securities Exchange Commission in 1934 (separating banks from brokerage firms accounts), Mr. Jolley went to vork for Johnson Lane Space Smith, a spin off of the Citizens and Southern Company. He worked here until 1954. When he became associated with Robinson and Humphrey Company. He worked here until 1963; then he and his daughter, Malinda, established a brokerage firm.

Still later, Mr. Jolley started his own business, Lex Jolley and Company, Inc., a municipal ond company. He operated that business for many years before selling it to Bank South, formerly 'ulton National Bank. I was with Fulton National Bank and Bank South in those years and came to now Mr. Jolley well; we had much association with each other in the business arena. I have been rivileged to enjoy a good business relationship with the Jolley Family throughout my adult life.

Mrs. Jolley was the former LeoDelle Lassiter, a native of Cobb County. Her father, Leamond ,assiter, Sr., served as Superintendent of the Cobb County School System; Lassiter High School was amed in his memory. Lex and LeoDelle Jolley were faithful members of First Methodist Church, ntil their deaths.

At the time of her death, Mrs. LeoDelle Jolley was the oldest living member of the Smyrna Social Club. I believe it would be safe to say she was a member longer in her lifetime than any other erson that ever belonged to the club. Her daughter, Malinda, is a current member of the Smyrna Social Club, which was organized in 1908.

Mrs. Lex (LeoDelle) **Jolley** in front of he
Style" home, 130 Lee Street, in 1944. Not
number on the porch post and the rock wa
Photo courtesy of Malinda Jolley (Mortin)

Kids on Lee Street, early 1950s. In front of the Jolley Home, 130 Lee Street L-R: Back Row: **Malinda Jolley**, **Elaine Eskew**. L-R: Front Row: **Margo Taylor**, "eating ice" and **Marilyn Rice**.
Photo courtesy of Malinda Jolley (Mortin).

Malinda Jolley at the wheel with her dog
basket. **Marilyn Rice** on the back. Next to
the Rice house on Lee Street, 1952
Photo courtesy of Malinda Jolley (Mortin)

The Jolley Lodge at Kennesaw State University is named in honor of Lex and LeoDelle olley. They were long-time, faithful benefactors of Kennesaw State University.

Fleming Jolley lettered in football, basketball, tennis, track, and golf at Marietta High School. Ie was named Mr. MHS at Marietta High School in 1941, the year of his graduation. Having studied iedicine at Emory University, he received his neurological surgery degree at Columbia University Iedical School in New York City. Serving in the United States Navy, he was a Lieutenant ommander, 1949-1951. A renowned neurosurgeon, Dr. Jolley practiced medicine at Emory niversity Hospital, where he trained many neurosurgeons; he later practiced at Sea Island, where he as living at the time of his death, November 4, 2004.

Malinda Jolley married Gordon Mortin. She attended Smyrna Elementary School, graduated om Campbell High School, and earned a BBA degree from the University of Miami in 1963. She stablished a brokerage firm with her dad in 1964. Gordon was a senior official with Lex Jolley and ompany, Inc. and later Knox-Wall Division of Morgan Keegan Company, a municipal bond ompany. He and I, through business relationships, have had much association over the years.

Malinda and Gordon Mortin live in Kennesaw, in the vicinity of the Marietta Country Club. Ir. and Mrs. Jolley moved to that area in 1987 to be near Malinda and Gordon.

The Truesdale Moseley Family

The **Truesdale Moseley Family** resided here after the Jolley Family moved to Pretty Branch rive. They had two daughters: **Elizabeth**, known as "Betty," and **Mary Ellen**. Mr. Moseley was nown as "True"; Mrs. Moseley was the former Elizabeth Cuttino. Elizabeth had a brother, Harold attino, known as "Happy," who lived in Lithia Springs. Al of her other family lived outside Georgia.

Elizabeth Moseley, known as "Betty," married Jack Edwards. They had three daughters: Iary Elizabeth, Cynthia, and Vickie. Elizabeth and Jack live in Montrose, Arkansas.

Mary Ellen Moseley married Dick Hagman from Marietta. They had two daughters, Jeanne nd Katherine. Jeanne has two children.

"True' and Elizabeth Moseley later moved to Campbell Road, south of Smyrna, where lizabeth lived until her death.

Mr. "True" Moseley's sisters are: Dorothy Moseley Bacon, known as "Dot," Ruby Moseley pradley Atkins, Irene Moseley Ferguson Dow, who lived in Vinings and New York before moving ack to Smyrna; Annell Moseley McCook, whose husband, Sam, was a preacher. See *Bacon, south ide of Bank Street* and *Spradley, west side of Matthews Street.*

Mr. "True" Moseley's brothers are: Julius Moseley, who with his wife, Helen, stayed in outh Carolina, where the Moseley clan grew up, later moving to Dothan, Alabama and Andrew Villiam Moseley, known as "Billy," who with his wife, Carman, lived in Vinings.

Sixth House

Mr. and **Mrs. Vivan Cobb** lived in the sixth house. Mrs. Cobb was the former Fanny Mae Vills. They had two children: a son, **Mark**, and a daughter, **Margie**. See *F.T. Wills, east side of Lee treet.*

Margie Cobb married Mr. Leveque. She taught at King Springs Elementary School when my hildren were there in the 1970s.

Mrs. Cobb, an artist, has many of her paintings gracing the home of Smyrna people. I remember that Judy Howard Hawkins, when operating the Concord Gallery in the latter part of the Twentieth Century, featured some of Mrs. Cobb's paintings in her shop.

Seventh House

Zelan and **Mary Wills** and their son, **Ted**, resided next door to the Cobbs. Ted lives in Dalton, Georgia, where he is a pharmacist. After Zelan's death, Mary moved to Dalton to be near Ted and his family. Zelan was the son of Mr. and Mrs. F.T. Wills. See *east side of Lee Street.*

Mary Wills was from Conyers, east of Atlanta. I remember when she and Zelan married. Mary was a lovely lady, for whom I always had a deep respect.

Zelan Wills, who grew up on Lee Street, across from where he and Mary lived, served in the United States Army during World War II. When he came home from his tour of duty, he worked for the United States Postal Service, where he later became Postmaster in Smyrna. (I believe he succeeded Mr. M.V. Cobb.)

After Lillie and I married, I taught a young adult Bible Class at First Baptist Church. Mary was the director of the department, and Zelan was the secretary. Zelan, Treasurer of First Baptist Church for many years, was also on the Board of Deacons. He was a faithful member of the Church throughout his lifetime.

Eighth House

Mr. and **Mrs. Sherrill Wills** lived in the house just south of Zelan and Mary. Sherrill was a son of Mr. and Mrs. F.T. Wills, who lived on the east side of Lee Street. Mr. and Mrs. Sherrill Wills attended First Baptist Church. See *Wills, east side of Lee Street.*

NOTE: One might say this section of Lee Street, in the days of my youth, could be called the Wills Family Compound.

Ninth House

Mr. and **Mrs. Harry Timmerman** and their daughter, **Marlene**, lived in this house. They were active members of First Baptist Church, where Mr. Timmerman was ordained a Deacon May 5, 1946. The Timmermans were a very nice Christian family.

I do not remember how Mr. Timmerman earned a living, but I know that he must have been a professional man, for he always wore a suit to work.

Tenth House

Mr. and **Mrs. George Howard** lived here. Mrs. Howard was the former, Alice Guthrie, a member of the Guthrie Family on Powder Springs Street. The Howards had two children: **Dewey Lioneal** and **Judy**. Lioneal, as I called him, was a year younger than I. While we were growing up, Dewey and I saw a lot of each other at school and at First Baptist Church. See *Guthrie, south side of Powder Springs Street.*

In her senior years, Mrs. Alice Howard was on the staff of First Baptist Church's Pre-school Division. She and Lillie, very close, enjoyed a good relationship until the end of Mrs. Howard's life. She was one of the few people with whom Lillie would leave our children when they were small.

George Howard at one time ran a hardware store in downtown Smyrna.

Dewey Lioneal Howard married Betty Hightower, who grew up on Spring Street, close to the ur Lane Highway (now known as Cobb Parkway). Lillie and I have had a close relationship with tty and Dewey through the years. They had three children, Tracie, David, and Preston.

Dewey Howard, also known as Lioneal, attended Smyrna School through the 1951 school ar—after which the Cobb County School System built Campbell High School. With the Campbell ilding not finished for the beginning of the 1951-1952 school year, Dewey's class continued to end Smyrna High School. Although Dewey received his diploma from Campbell High School, he ver attended classes in the new building. The school building was not completed until time for the 52-1953 classes. Dewey, a Captain in the United States Army Reserves in the 1960s, and I both rved in the same unit in those days.

Tracie Howard married Jeff Lanier; and they had two children: Conner and Haley. The niers live in Acworth.

David Howard married the former Cheri Conley; they had two children: Kelsey and Parker. avid and his family live in West Cobb County. He runs his own business, Compass Display, located Marietta. Lillie and I have been privileged to be David's godparents.

Preston Howard lives in Smyrna and is employed with David's company, Compass Display Marietta.

Jim Hawkins
Smyrna City Council
1978-2003
Mayor Protem
1985-2003

Judy Howard married Jim Hawkins from the Oakdale community, south of Smyrna. Jim ended elementary school at Fitzhugh Lee and graduated from Campbell High School. He was the ngest serving elected official in Cobb County when he retired in 2003. He served on the Smyrna City uncil, 1978-2003. I had the pleasure of serving with him from 1991, when I became a member of nyrna City Council, until he retired in 2003. Judy died suddenly from a heart attack on March 1, 01.

Both Jim and Judy were very active members First Baptist Church. He taught Sunday hool, and she was active in the Women's Ministry. Judy, a very talented person, only referred to rself as a painter, but she was really an artist.

Judy operated an art and gift shop, Concord Gallery, on Concord Road. After the first office d retail business buildings were constructed on Atlanta Street at the Village Green, she and Jim oved the Concord Gallery to that building. They were still operating it when she died. After her ath, Jim sold the business to Sue and Wendell Dean, who moved the shop to Concord Road. It is w known as The Flashy Frog.

Jim and Judy had one son, Brad Hawkins, who is married to the former Donna Longdin, the ughter of Betty and Howard Longdin. They had two children: a daughter, Taylor, and a son, Cory. rad and Donna, life-long attendees of First Baptist Church, reside in Smyrna off North Cooper Lake oad.

NOTE: Later on in the 1950s, the Howards built a brick ranch house just on the north side of e aforementioned house, where they lived the rest of their lives

BEING A GOOD NEIGHBOR

by Dewey Lioneal Howard

"One cold morning, when I was about sixteen years old, Mrs. Poss came running across the street to our house and exclaimed, 'Some dogs were killing my chickens!' She then screamed, 'Get your shotgun and come over and stop the killing!' I did; I shot the dogs! Very soon afterwards, I found out they were the prized bird dogs of Gene Rice who, also lived on Lee Street. He was a little upset with me—to say the least. But I had Mrs. Poss on my side."

Eleventh House

Houston and **Edna Jones** and their daughter, **Janet**, were residents of this house. Earlier they had lived out in the country, on Cooper Lake Road, and from there they moved, in 1948, to this house on Lee Street, unpaved at that time. Their property, extending all the way through to Dunn Street, included a vacant lot they used as a garden. (In 1984 Janet built a house on her parents' garden spot, where she still lives. She shared that the deed to the property read, "no hooved animals.") At first the Jones Family were members of Second Baptist Church; later they moved their membership to First Baptist Church because Janet's friends attended there.

Houston Jones was employed, as an inspector for Atlantic Steel Company in Atlanta. Edna Jones, who worked for Davis Department Store, was also an accomplished seamstress; LeoDelle Jolley was one of her neighbors for whom she made clothing.

Janet remembers her mother's flowers were so pretty that people would stop and ask for a bouquet to take to someone in the hospital. Mrs. Jones would cut them, and always refused payment. Jane said that her mother and Mrs. Anderson would share with each other cuttings and seeds for their flower gardens; now Jane and Mrs. Anderson do this.

Janet Jones married Glenn Green of Marietta. They had two children: a daughter, Glenda and a son, Shannon.

Glenda Green married Jerry House from McDonough. They had two children: Harold and Cassie. Glenda and Jerry live in Jackson.

Shannon Green married Billie Jo Aultman of Stockbridge. They had two children: Shelby and Tanner. Shannon and Billy Jo live in Jackson.

Janet Jones later married Steve Brown, who had two children from a previous marriage: Troy and Mandy.

Troy Brown and his wife, Jeanie, had two sons: Michael and Alex.

Mandy Brown, a school teacher, married Adam Pollock. They had two children: Drew and Courtney.

In sharing her memories, Janet related, "One time two boys drove their tractors to my house and parked them in the driveway. (It was okay at that time to drive tractors on a road without a license.) My dad had a 'fit.' He didn't want tractors parked in his driveway."

Steve and Janet attended a Campbell High School reunion. Regarding that event, Janet shared, Some guys who knew about the tractor incident, asked Steve, how he got along with Janet's dad?

Steve replied, "Fine."

The boys told Steve, "He sure did not like us because we drove a tractor in his driveway."

Twelfth House

Mr. and **Mrs. Hubert Anderson**, lived in this house, on the northwest corner of Lee Street ɹ Collier Drive. Mr. Anderson, known as "Andy" and his wife, Ozelle, had two children: **Yvonne** ɹ **Hubert Stanley**.

When the Andersons moved to this house, which they had built, the street was dirt. Because neighbors wanted to have the street paved. "Andy" had to sell his car to pay his share of the cost. did without a car for six months. Not long afterwards county workers came and paved the rest of street. "Andy," is now 85 years old, has lived in this house for 60 years, longer than any other ident has ever lived on Lee Street.

DUNN STREET
East Side

Appreciation is extended to Jack Taylor for the information he shared regarding his family, o lived on Dunn and Atlanta streets, and to Henry Konigsmark III, known as "Hank," for ormation about his family on Dunn Street. Appreciation also goes to Jean Brannon, who, having ved to Dunn Street in the 1950s, shared her memories of the longer-time residents on the street.

First House

Mr. and **Mrs. Glenn Yarbrough**, who lived here, had this house built, probably in the early 50s. I do not recall this house being here while I was growing up. Mrs.Yarbrough was the former n Edwards. She and Glenn had three children. See *Yarbrough, south side of Love Street* and *wards, north side of Love Street.*

Second House

Mr. and **Mrs. Howard L. McEntyre, Sr.**, moved from the west side of Dunn Street to this use in the early 1950s. Here they lived the rest of their lives. See *west side of Dunn Street.*

Third House

"Jimmy" Quarles
Mayor of Smyrna
1955-1957

James Quarles, Sr., known as "Jimmy," and his wife, Doris, moved to this house in the 50s. They had two sons, **James, Jr.**, also known as "Jimmy," and **Harry**. Mrs. Quarles, the former ris Arrington, who grew up on Sunset Avenue, was my fourth grade teacher at Smyrna Elementary hool. "Jimmy" Quarles, the son of Mr. and Mrs. W.A. Quarles, grew up on Atlanta Road. See *rington, south side of Sunset Avenue* and *Quarles, Atlanta Street, from Marlowe's to Creatwood.*

Fourth House

Mr. and **Mrs. Howard Taylor**, having had this house built, moved here from Atlanta Street. ey were the parents of Louise Pavlovsky, who lived next door. See *Taylors, Atlanta Street, from s. Mazie's to Pearce Matthews* and *Reed, Atlanta Street, from Marlowe's to Creatwood.*

Fifth House

Mr. and **Mrs. Max Pavlovsky**, who lived in this house, had one son, **Bill**. Mrs. Pavlovsky, former Louise Taylor, grew up on Atlanta Street. Louise was the first lady to serve as City of yrna Clerk; her employment was during the mayoral term of Guye Duncan. Ralph Argo was the only policeman in the City of Smyrna at that time. See *fourth house, east side of Dunn Street* and *Taylor, Atlanta Street, from Mrs. Mazie's to Pearce Matthews.*

NOTE: After development began farther down the street, the Pavlovskys moved from this house to the west side of Dunn Street.

Mr. and **Mrs. Bryant Paul Eskew**

Mr. and **Mrs**. **Bryant Paul Eskew** resided here. Mr. Eskew was known as Paul, and Mrs. Eskew, the former Evelyn Lane, was known as "Lane." Paul and "Lane" had one daughter, **Elaine**.

Paul Eskew was the son of Mr. and Mrs. Lawrence Thomas (L.T.) Eskew; his mother's given name was Bertha Pauline. Paul, born in Toccoa, grew up in Atlanta. His family, having moved to Smyrna in the 1930s, lived on and farmed land on the west side of Campbell Road near its intersection with Spring Road. Paul, a Captain in the United States Army, was stationed at Camp Blanding, Florida who trained soldiers there. There Paul met his future wife, Lane, who was from West Virginia.

A Second Lieutenant in the United States Army, Evelyn Lane, known as "Lane" (military personnel being known by their surnames) was a nurse. Forever after her military service, Evelyn was called "Lane."

After their discharges and marriage, the Eskews moved to an apartment in Marietta, where "Lane" worked first at Bell Bomber Plant and later at Marietta Hospital, on Kennesaw Avenue. When they moved in 1945 to this fifth house, "Lane" was a nurse at Brawner Psychiatric Hospital. Afterwards, she worked at Lockheed for a short time after it was opened but then returned to Brawner, where she retired.

Elaine Eskew married Ron Coker from the Oakdale community, south of Smyrna, in 1964. They had two children, Ron, Jr., and Rhonda. Elaine and Ron, Sr., lived on Ridge Road while their children were growing up. Elaine, Ron, Sr., Ron, Jr., and Rhonda all graduated from Campbell High School. Elaine and Ron, Sr. had six grandchildren. See, *Stone, north side of Concord Road, The Country Road.*

Elaine Eskew Coker, having graduated from Piedmont Nursing School, followed her mother's profession. Ron Coker, Sr., for many years has been the business of building swimming pools.

First owned by Brawner Sanitarium, this house was bought by the Eskews, who resided here into the 1960s.

Sixth House

Mr. and **Mrs**. **Henry Konigsmark, Jr**., had two sons: **Henry Konigsmark III**, known as "Hank," and **Reed Konigsmark**. Mrs. Konigsmark was the former Elizabeth Davis, who grew up on the north side of Church Street. The Konigsmark's house backed up to the Jolley house, which was located on the west side of Lee Street. See *Davis, north side of Church Street.*

Immediately after World War II, Henry, Jr., built this house on Dunn Street for his family, who lived here until 1952. At that time they bought another house on Atlanta Terrace (different from the one where they lived before the War). In the early 2000s, many years after Henry's death, Elizabeth sold the Atlanta Terrace house. NOTE: The Montclair subdivision is now located in that area.

After World War II, Henry, Jr., owned and operated Smyrna Feed and Seed Store for several years, located diagonally across the railroad tracks from G.B.'s Place, on Spring Street. Henry, Jr., one of the developers of Jonquil Plaza Shopping Center, on Atlanta Street, also worked in downtown Atlanta. See *south side of Spring Street* and *Atlanta Street, from Mrs. Mazie's to Pearce Matthews.*

Elizabeth Davis Konigsmark, a floral designer, and her sister-in-law, Louise Osborn Konigsmark, known as "Bill," owned and operated a florist on Atlanta Street. ("Bill" Konigsmark's husband, Reed, was a twin brother of Henry, Jr.) Later on, Elizabeth worked many years as a floral designer for Owens Florist in Marietta.

James and **Jean Brannon**

Jean and **James Brannon** became residents of this house after the Konigsmarks moved to Atlanta Terrace in 1952. They had one son, "Chuck." James, known as "Jim," worked at Lockheed Aircraft Corporation; Jean taught first at Smyrna Elementary School and later at Griffin Middle School. Jim and Jean lived in this house 43 years before moving to Hickory Mill Drive in West Smyrna. Through the years, the Brannons have been very active Smyrna citizens and members of King Spring Baptist Church.

"Chuck" Brannon and his wife, Tammy, had two daughters: Allison and Erin.

Seventh House

Mr. and **Mrs**. **J.C. Hethcock**, who reside here, had four children: **Eunice**, **Dean**, **Elizabeth**, and **Mildred**. Mr. Hethcock worked the Transit Division of Georgia Power Company; he was first a streetcar conductor and then a bus driver.

Dean Hethcock. See *eighth house.*

Elizabeth Hethcock married Joe Barnes. They had two sons: Joseph Michael and Dennis Martin. Joe was a member of the large Barnes Family on the east side of Roswell Street. One of his brothers, Jim, has lived next door to Lillie and me since 1969; Jim's wife, Wyolene, passed away in 2001. See *Barnes east side of Roswell Street.*

Mildred Hethcock and I were the same age.

Eighth House

Dean Hethcock had this house built next door to his parents after having served in the United States Navy during in World War II. He was married and had four children.

Ninth House

Earl Stephens Reed and his family lived at 339 Dunn Street. He and his wife, "**Teenie**," had two children: a daughter, **Jackie**, and a son, **Steve**. Earl Stephens was one of the sons of Mr. and Mrs. B.F. Reed, Sr.; "Teenie" Duncan was a sister of Gene Duncan, who lived on the east side of Atlanta Street. See *Reed* and *Duncan, Atlanta Street, from Mrs. Mazie's to Pearce Matthews.*

Mrs. Estelle Addison McDaniel

Mrs. **Estelle Addison McDaniel** and her children, **Bob**, **Travis**, and **Latrelle** moved to 339 Dunn Street in 1943. Having married in 1930, Estelle was widowed in 1942, when John, at age 38, was killed in an automobile accident while returning from an agricultural meeting in Macon. See *Addison, west side of Dunn Street.*

Travis tells that both of the Addison and McDaniel families were very strong on education. "My dad, John Robert McDaniel, grew up on a small farm in Laurens County (South Georgia). Due to the hardships of helping his father provide for a family of five children, Daddy was not able to attend school regularly. He was persistent, however, and graduated from high school when he was 21. With a minimal $50.00 initial loan, obtained through his high school agriculture teacher, and working odd jobs, he put himself through the University of Georgia. He graduated with a Bachelor of Science degree in Agriculture in 1930.

"My mother initially attended the Normal School (also in Athens), but in her sophomore year transferred to the University of Georgia, where she met Daddy. They began dating and were married upon his graduation and at the end of her junior year. After Daddy's death, Mama found herself a 32-year-old widow with three children to raise. She immediately began work on credits to finish her Bachelor of Science degree in Home Economics.

"Mama finished her degree in 1943, mostly through correspondence— and with help from her sister, Hazel. (We were living in Smyrna by that time.) All three of her children saw her graduate! After graduation she worked as a Home Demonstration Agent in Cobb County until she remarried in 1946. After that, she taught at Fitzhugh Lee School."

John Robert McDaniel, Jr., known as "Bob,"soon after graduation from Fitzhugh Lee High School, married Virginia Gann, the daughter of Ed and Irene Gann, a well-known Smyrna couple. They had five children, John Robert McDaniel III, known as "Butch," Joanie, Ricky, Melanie, and Robin, 12 grandchildren, and 10 great-grandchildren. "Bob" later received his Bachelor of Business Administration degree from Georgia State University, in Atlanta. His entire career was with Southern Bell Telephone Company, now BellSouth. See *ninth house, north side of Powder Springs Street.*

Travis McDaniel, a graduate of Campbell High School, majored in Wildlife Management at the University of Georgia and worked for the United States Fish and Wildlife Service. He married Joyce Mason, who at the time of their marriage, was a teacher at Campbell High School. Joyce and Travis had three children, Cindy, Laurel, and Travis, Jr., and four grandchildren. In 1991, while serving as a Girl Scout leader, Laurel was killed in a bus accident in California.

Mrs. McDaniel was the former Joyce Mason, daughter of Jackie and L.B. Mason, known as "Buddy." She graduated from Cedartown High School, and Georgia State Teachers College in Statesboro, now Georgia Southern University. Joyce moved with her family from Cedartown to Smyrna in 1953. Joyce and Travis now live in Dawson County.

Jackie and "Buddy" Mason also had four sons: Johnnie, Kippy, Jerry, and Barry. In 1953 "Buddy" began working for Lockheed Aircraft Corporation. After his retirement, he became employed as First Baptist Church's Building Superintendent. Jackie Mason taught at Smyrna Preschool and First Baptist Kindergarten.

Latrelle McDaniel, a 1957 graduate of Campbell High School, married Doug Allen, a graduate of Roosevelt High School in Atlanta. While in high school, Latrelle was a member of the Rainbows, an affiliate of the Eastern Star. Trained as a medical technician, she worked at several area hospitals including the Radiology Department of Cobb General, now Wellstar Cobb Hospital, from where she retired. Doug Allen, who received his degrees from the Atlanta Division of the University of Georgia, now Georgia State University, taught at Dykes High School in Atlanta before going into administration with the Cobb County Public School System. His last position before retiring was as Principal at Lassiter High School in East Cobb County. Latrelle and Doug had two children, Kevin and Tanya, and three grandchildren.

Mr. and Mrs. W.J. Pennington

In 1946, Estelle Addison McDaniel married **W.J. Pennington**, known as "Bill." They lived in this house on Dunn Street until 1956, when they moved to East Lee Road, in the Oakdale community. A manager of the produce department with A&P, "Bill" had an avocation of turning his four-acre enclave into an azalea-covered haven and growing tomatoes and vegetables for friends and neighbors. "Bill" and Estelle had one daughter, **Sandra**, who married Mike DeLong; they had one son, Scott. The Penningtons were members of First Baptist Church.

Tenth House

Pat P. Shaw
Mayor Protem
1951
Smyrna City Councilman
1948-1951

Mr. and **Mrs**. **Pat Shaw** were residents of this house. They had two daughters: **Angelina** and **Margaret**. Mr. Shaw built many houses in Smyrna during the 1950s, especially in the Forest Hills community, including one on Pretty Branch Drive, to which he and his wife moved. Pat Shaw served on the Smyrna City Council, 1948-1951. He was Mayor Protem in 1951.

Angelina Shaw married Mr. Abercrombie. A writer for the *Smyrna Neighbor* for many years, Angelina resided a long time on the east side of Lee Street. Later on, Angelina married Harry Holliday, who served as President of the Bank of Smyrna for many years. Harry's death preceeded that of Angelina, who died in 2002. See *Abercrombie, east side of Lee Street.*

Eleventh House

Margaret Shaw, the daughter of Mr. and Mrs. Pat Shaw, lived in this house, next door to her parents.

Twelfth House

Mr. and **Mrs**. **Wilton Carson** resided in this house, at the bottom of the hill, for a long time. Mr. Carson was known as "Wit." See *Carson, south side of Love Street.*

Thirteenth House

Mr. and **Mrs**. **Jim Manning** lived here. Mr. Manning was known as "Soapy." In the early 1950s, the Mannings' son, Sidney, and son-in-law, "Pete" Williams, built this house for the Mannings, who were residents here the rest of their lives. See *Manning, north side of Gilbert Street.*

Fourteenth House

Stella Mae and **J.C**. **Austin,** who resided here, had three children: **Carol, Johnny**, and **Don**. Carol is married and lives in Texas; Johnny lives in Smyrna, where he attends First Baptist Church; Don died when he was still a young man. J.C. and Stella lived the rest of their lives in this house. See *Austin, south side of Bank Street* and *North Cooper Lake Road.*

Next to the Austin house was a vacant lot owned by Mr. Jones, who lived on Lee Street. He raised a garden on this property for many years

Fifteenth House

Mr. and **Mrs**. **I.D**. **Buice**, **Sr**. had this house built and moved from Buford to it about 1950. Mrs. Buice was the former Ruby Jones, of Flowery Branch. They had three children: **Linda**, **Mary Ann**, and **I.D**., **Jr**., known as "Butch."

I.D. Buice, Sr., was a flagman and conductor for Southern Railroad. Ruby Buice first worked for Lockheed Aircraft Corporation and then for the Internal Revenue Service (IRS), from which she retired.

Linda Buice married Earl Smith, who has operated a television and appliance business in Cobb County for 36 years. They had one daughter, Teri, who married Fred Stanfield, and one grandson, Bryce.

Mary Ann Buice married Eric Kimmerling, and had one son, Brandon. Dr. Eric Kimmerling, who has practiced pulmonary medicine in Dalton for many years, is the son of Dr. Richard Kimmerling, a Cobb County surgeon, who had two other sons, Craig and Kirk, one of whom is a dentist.

I.D. Buice, Jr., is married to Margaret.

Linda Buice Smith and "Dot" Cook shared this neat story of how I.D. and Ruby Buice met. "They were riding through Tallulah Falls Covered Bridge—each of them in a car with with a group of friends. The two cars met in the middle of the bridge, and neither driver would consent to back out. After an extended period of time, sitting there and being stubborn, I.D. and his friends got out of the car and started talking with Ruby and her friends. That is how they met, and ever thereafter, until I.D.'s death, they both were that stubborn." See *Cook, east side of Lee Street.*

Sixteenth House

Mr. and **Mrs. Ferd Brown** moved from Atlanta Street to this house in the very early 1950s. Mrs. Brown was the former Mary Ruth Sorrells. They had two sons: **Ronnie** and **Jerry**. See *Brown, 8th house* and *Sorrells, 15th house on Atlanta Street, from Marlowe's to Creatwood,* and *Magbee, 5th house, east side of Access Highway.*

Ferd Brown was employed by Paradies Wholesale Company in Atlanta's Bellwood community.

Mary Ruth Sorrells Brown worked for The Telephone Exchange on Atlanta Street in downtown Smyrna. She was an operator before the dial system was instituted.

Ronnie Brown, a graduate in the Campbell High School Class of 1957, was a "stand out" in basketball and baseball. He graduated from Rollins College, in Florida; there he had attended on a baseball scholarship. Ronnie married Sally Hinsch, who came to Atlanta via Texas and Louisiana. They had three children, (two sons, Kelly and Casey, and a daughter, Susan), and seven grandchildren. Casey is deceased. Ronnie and Sally are living in North Carolina.

Jerry Brown, a graduate in the Campbell High School Class of 1962, played baseball and basketball while a student there. He married Vickie Hopkins; they had two daughters, Lee-Anne and Alicia, and four grandchildren. Jerry and Vickie are divorced; Jerry is living in Jasper. See *Hopkins, north side of Powder Springs Street.*

I remember much building began taking place in this area about the time I graduated from high school, in 1951, the year Lockheed Aircraft Corporation opened. Dunn Street was extended southward beyond Collier Drive; afterwards, many houses were built on Dunn Street, and newcomers began moving into the area

DUNN STREET
West Side

Dunn Street was the second street to the left off Love Street, and west of Atlanta Street. In the late1940s or very early 1950s, the street was extended beyond Collier Drive. Many of the houses that are currently on Dunn Street from Love Street (now Concord Road) to Legion Drive were there in the days of my youth. Most of the ones from Legion Drive to Collier have been built since 1950, with the exception of the Wilson house and maybe one or two others.

Appreciation is extended to Elizabeth Hethcock Barnes, Wilson McEntyre, and Nancy Wilson Sandifer for sharing their memories of growing up on Dunn Street in the middle of the Twentieth Century to Lynn Martin and Travis McDaniel for information on their families, to Wilson McEntyre, for his memories of the McEntyre Family, and to Palma Ann Guthrie Tempel for sharing her memories about the Guthrie and Reed families; and to Peggy Norton Cochran for information about the Norton Family.

First House

Mrs. Anna Fain Addison, who lived in this house, often rented one of her bedrooms to school teachers. Anna Fain, born in 1876, was raised in the mountains of White and Habersham counties, where she received an advanced education at one of the mountain academies. She first taught school in Westminister, South Carolina, and then in the Red Hill community of Franklin County, Georgia. At Red Hill she met and married Lawrence Addison, a farmer. Since married women were not allowed to teach in 1901, Anna had to give up her teaching career.

NOTE: John Lawrence Addison's mother was a Vandiver; the children of Anna and Lawrence and those of former Georgia Governor Ernest Vandiver were second cousins. Also, Addison Elementary School in East Cobb County is named for Lawrence's brother, W.P. Addison, an educator.

Anna and Lawrence had six children: **Lula Mae**, **Sloan**, **Doyle**, **Estelle**, **Joel**, and **Hazel**. Before her husband's death, Anna had moved into the town of Carnesville in order for her children to obtain a better education. (While their children were still young, Lawrence was killed when his father's gravestone, which he was hauling to the cemetery in a wagon, fell and crushed him.) In Carnesville, with the help of some Democratic friends, Anna was able to secure the position of Postmistress in 1914, during President Woodrow Wilson's administration. In 1917 she borrowed money to buy adjacent to the town square, a large house and turned it into a boarding house. Her sons did odd jobs, and her daughters helped run the boarding house. According to her son, Joel, she lost her Postmistress position in 1923, when she refused to contribute to the Republican campaign—or "buy her job," as she put it! (This was before Civil Service Reform.)

Anna Addison was determined to see that all of her children received an education adequate for making a good living. As each one finished his/her education, he/she was expected to help put the next one through school. Anna and her youngest child, Hazel, moved to Smyrna after Hazel had graduated from college and had begun teaching at Fitzhugh Lee Elementary School. In the generations that have followed, 22 members of Anna's extended family have became teachers or members of a school board, mostly in Cobb County. Anna was active in First Baptist Church until her health failed.

Lula Mae Addison graduated from the Norma School, in Athens, in 1922. She then began teaching in Pacolet Mills, South Carolina. There she met and married W.A. Burgess, a widower. W.A., a mill store manager, also operated a peach orchard. Lula Mae worked at the mill for several years.

Sloan Addison attended Draughon's Business School in Atlanta. Later he worked in sales and owned various business enterprises. He married Lassie Bearden of Woodstock and settled in the Oakdale community, south of Smyrna. He and Lassie, active members of Locust Grove Baptist Church, had two daughters: Peggy Jo and Anna Katherine. Sloan later built a large enclave on East Lee Road.

Peggy Jo Addison married Phillip Walker; they were16 years of age when they married later in the year after they graduated from high school. Peggy graduated in the Class of 1951 from Fitzhugh Lee High School, and Phillip from Smyrna High School, in the Class of 1951. (Phillip and I went through school together.) They had two children: Kathy and "Chuck," three grandchildren, and three great-grandchildren. Peggy and Phillip, for many years, were members of Locust Grove Baptist Church, where she played the piano and Phillip, with a beautiful bass voice, sang as a soloist and as part of the choir. In the early 1980s, the Walkers moved their membership to First Baptist Church. See *Bacon, east side of King Street, Walker, south side of Spring Street* and *Worley, south side of Church Street.*

Anna Katherine graduated from Campbell High School and Auburn University. She and her husband, Vern Davis, live in Atlanta's Buckhead community. They had two children, Vern, Jr., and Peggy Elizabeth, and five grandchildren. Anna, a well-known expert on the growing and care of roses, writes extensively on these subjects.

Doyle Addison, having attended Draughon's Business School in Atlanta, married Margaret Hanky, known as "Gret." Making their home in Decatur, they had one adopted son, Larry, and two grandchildren. Doyle had a long career with Southern Bell Telephone Company, now BellSouth.

Estelle Addison married John R. McDaniel. See *McDaniel, east side of Dunn Street.*

Joel Addison attended Draughon's Business School in Atlanta, as did his brothers, and later married Pauline Cheek, known as "Polly." They had two children, Joel, Jr., and Paul, and four grandchildren.

Hazel Addison graduated from Piedmont College in Demorest. Since Hazel was the last child at home, her mother went with her to Demorest, where she lived in a small rented cottage. After graduation, Hazel taught at McEachern High School in Cobb County before accepting a position at Fitzhugh Lee High School, where she taught music, piano, glee club, and chorus and rhythm band. It was at this time that her mother bought this house on Dunn Street.

A talented musician, Hazel was for many years a pianist in First Baptist Church. There she played the piano when my sister, Hilda Wood, married Grady Chaffin, in 1950. She also taught piano. Janet Brown's husband, Ray, remembers taking lessons from her at Fitzhugh Lee School and going to this house in Smyrna for lessons in the 1940s.

Hazel Addison married Conrad Petit in 1944. They had no children. Hazel moved to Miami in the late 1950s, after her mother died. After marrying her second husband, Howard Kerns, she continued teaching music and chorus in Miami until she retired

Mr. and Mrs. Toombs

Mr. and Mrs. Robert Toombs moved here after the Addisons vacated. Mrs. Toombs, whose given name was Joann, taught at Smyrna School.

Second House

Mr. and Mrs. Otho Norton resided here; they had four daughters: **Mary Lou, Gladys, Emilene,** and **Betty**. Mrs. Otho Norton was the former Ethel Harris, who grew up on Harris Road, west of Smyrna. An excellent seamstress, Mrs. Norton sewed for the public. Mr. Norton worked for Standard Oil Company.

Otho and Ethel Norton in 1929 moved to Dunn Street, where they lived until 1943, when they moved to the Virginia/Highlands area of Atlanta. After retiring, they built a house on Harris Road; there they lived until their deaths.

Otho Norton was the son of Oliver and Linnie Norton, who raised their large family on Church Road, west of Smyrna. See *Norton, Church Road, North Cooper Lake Road,* and *Medlin Street.*

NOTE: Betty Norton Cox, who was born in this house on Dunn Street, currently resides on Harris Road. She provided the aforementioned information.

Third House

Mr. and **Mrs. E.T. Bradley** were residents of this house, (which is still standing) on the northwest corner of Dunn and Hunter streets. Three of their adult children, **Ben**, **Archie**, and **Mary Ann**, lived here also. The Bradleys were faithful members of First Baptist Church, where Mrs. Bradley and Mary Ann were active in the Women's Missionary Union (WMU). From her early childhood, Mary Ann has been faithful to the missions program through the church. The Bradleys had another son, remained in the North Georgia Mountains area where the Bradleys had lived before they moved to Smyrna. Later on, the Bradleys had a brick ranch house built on Dunn Street, back toward Love Street from this house and on the same side of the street where the elder Bradleys and Ben lived the rest of their lives. Mary Ann sold her property on Dunn Street in the 1990s and moved to Presbyterian Village, a retirement community in South Cobb County; there she currently resides.

Fourth House

Howard L. McEntyre, Sr.
Smyrna City Councilman
1948-1951

Mr. and **Mrs. Howard L. McEntyre, Sr.**, lived at the southwest corner of Dunn and Hunter streets. They had three sons: **Howard, Jr.**, **Lewis**, and **Wilson**. Mrs. McEntyre was the former Florence Wilson, who grew up on Maple Avenue in Marietta. Florence Wilson McEntyre was a childhood playmate of Mary Phagan, who was murdered in the pencil factory in Atlanta in the early part of the Twentieth Century.

Mr. McEntyre operated Sunlight Bakery on the Square in Marietta before coming to Smyrna. Here he opened their first bakery in Smyrna, on the west side of Atlanta Street, about mid-way between Bank and West Spring streets. The McEntyre Bakery in Jonquil Plaza Shopping Center in Smyrna is owned and operated today by Steve McEntyre, the third generation McEntyres to run the bakery. See *Howard McEntyre, Jr., below.*

Mrs. Florence McEntyre, in her senior years worked in the baby nursery at First Baptist Church. She was one of the few people that Lillie would allow to keep our children when they were little. Mrs. McEntyre was a genuine lady on whom we knew we could depend. Lillie and I mourned the passing of Mrs. McEntyre.

Members of the McEntyre Family have been very faithful to First Baptist Church through the years.

Howard McEntyre, Jr., who operated McEntyre's Bakery after his dad, married Carolyn Medlin. They had one son, Steve. Carolyn, the daughter of Mr. and Mrs. William Medlin, grew up in Atlanta. Her family moved to Concord Road when she was a teenager. Her dad was a member of the Medlin Family who earlier in the Twentieth Century had farmed land in the area from Concord and King Springs roads to Medlin Street.

Louis McEntyre's wife, Joan, was from McDonough. Louis and Joan had four children: Bradley, Sharon, Scott and Maria. The Louis McEntyres were active members of First Baptist Church, where they both were faithful to workers in the Preschool Department.

Wilson McEntyre married Mary Sanders. They had two children: Jennifer and John. Mary, the daughter of Mr. and Mrs. Warren Sanders, had a twin sister, Martha, and a brother, Charles; the three grew up on Concord Road near the intersection of Concord and Hurt roads. The Sanders Family were faithful members of First Baptist Church. After her marriage, Martha relocated with her family to Louisiana. Charles and his family reside in Marietta, where they are faithful members of First Baptist Church of Marietta. Wilson and Mary live in the Smyrna area; they are both still active members of

First Baptist Church, where Wilson is a Deacon. See *Sanders, south side of Concord Road, The Country Road.*

Jennifer McEntyre married but divorced.

John McEntyre married Stephanie Williams. They had one son, Scott Nixon McEntyre. Stephanie, the daughter of Larry and Gail Williams, and her family were active members of First Baptist Church.

Mary Sanders McEntyre's dad, Warren Sanders, and his brother, Bill Sanders, along with B.C. Castellaw, founded a funeral home in Smyrna: Sanders Funeral Home. It was located on the north side of Concord Road in the vicinity of the present Vickery Ace Hardware Store. When that partnership was dissolved, Bill Sanders and his wife, Juanita, opened a funeral home on the corner of Church and King streets. That funeral home is currently owned and operated by Randy Carmichael, who has been in business there for more than a quarter of a century.

B.C. and Hellan Castellaw and their family formed another partnership upon opening a funeral home on Church Road near South Cobb Drive; they have been in business for 40 years. B.C. and Hellan had a daughter, Gale, and a son, Coleman Castellaw. B.C. Castellaw retired in 1996; his daughter, Gale Castellaw Baker continues the day-to-day operation of

CHOOSING UP SIDES
by Wilson McEntyre

"When I was a kid, boys would go to the park or some other open space and play ball. We had a system called 'Choosing up Sides.' It worked like this: We would take the ball bat and two boys, one from each side. The first boy would grip the bat about midway with his left hand; the second boy would grip with his right hand above the first boy's hand. This procedure would be followed and the last person to grip the bat at the top would get the first choice of players. The other boy would get second choice. Each boy would pick in this order until all the boys had been chosen. Using a taped-up bat and ball, we would play ball!"

Fondly remembering the above procedure, Wilson has memories that involve summers at Brinkley Park before there was Little League or other organized youth groups. In the summer when school was out, boys would show up at Brinkley Park, a neighborhood field, or a vacant lot. Some boy that owned a ball or bat would say, "Let's play ball tomorrow"; then a certain time would be named.

Mr. and **Mrs. A.T. Parks**

Mr. and **Mrs**. **A**.**T**. **Parks** were residents of this house after the McEntyres moved across the street. They had four daughters: **Andrea Jeanette**, **Beth**, **Sherri**, and one son, **Tracy**.

<u>Fifth House</u>

Joe and **Maggie Wrublesky**, who lived here, had three sons: **Joseph**, **Bobby**, and **Billy**.

<u>Sixth House</u>

Hoyt Brinkley and his wife, **Marie**, resided in this house. They had two children: **Ben** and **Howard**. Hoyt, the son of Mr. and Mrs. P.F. Brinkley, grew up on the north side of Love Street; he worked for the railroad. See *north side of Love Street.*

Dallis and **Colene Guthrie**

Later on **Mr**. and **Mrs**. **Dallis Guthrie** moved to this house. Mrs. Guthrie was the former Colene Reed. They had two children: **Rufus** and **Palma Ann**. They moved from this house to Bank

Street before their children started to school. Mrs. Guthrie was a teacher in the Atlanta School System. See *Atlanta Street, from Marlowe's to Creatwood;* the *south side of Bank Street,* and *Atlanta Street, from Mrs. Mazie's to Pearce Matthews.*

Seventh House

Mr. and **Mrs. Jones** and their son, **Charles**, lived in this house, which was directly across the street from Mr. and Mrs. Eskew.

Mr. and Mrs. Wright

The **Wright Family** lived in a house in this area. Though I cannot recall all of the members of this family, I know the Wrights had a daughter, **Jimmie Lou**.

Eighth House

Mr. and **Mrs. George Britton Wigington**, known as "G.B.," resided in this house, on the northwest corner of Dunn and Pine streets, with their son, **George**. Mrs. Wigington's was the former, Freida Wehunt. "G.B.," who worked for the Smyrna Post Office, had a brother, Sherman, who lived on Dixie Avenue. See *Wigington, Dixie Avenue.*

Ninth House

Miss Darrinda Martin lived alone here, on the southwest corner of Dunn Street and Legion Drive. From my earliest memories, her house was not originally on a corner. At one time she owned the land where the American Legion Post #160 was built and Pine Street was cut, put Miss Darinda's house on a corner. (Pine Street was later named Legion Drive.) Miss Darrinda Martin was a very active member of the First Methodist Church; but, according to one of her close friends, "Miss Darrinda Martin was baptized in the Baptist Church upon her request."

I remember that Miss Martin, an avid member of the Cobb County Temperance League, made a big impression on me in the days of my youth. A number of ladies in our community were active in the Temperance League. In fact, one year they enlisted me to serve as President of the Junior Temperance League in Cobb County. I took a lot of kidding about that because I was in school; perhaps you know how my contemporaries were! However, I do not regret serving, for it became part of my growing-up and maturing experiences. Unfortunately that organization ceased to exist. (Surely it wasn't because of my leadership abilities!) I have a feeling it was because of the passing of notables that included Miss Darrinda Martin and Mrs. Mary Nations. They were a staunch group of ladies who knew what they believed. I also think they had something there.

The Temperance League ladies always became active during election year. Usually a candidate would run on a "wet" or "dry" ticket. In Smyrna, a "dry" city in those days, there was always one group that wanted to sell alcohol in the City. That group eventually won. With the problems in our society today, we could benefit from Miss Darrinda's and Mrs. Nation's voicing their principles loudly and clearly—keeping the rest of us in line. I always had a lot of respect for Mrs. Nations and Miss Martin, who, you might say, were "activists" of their day.

Mr. G.W. Nations and his wife, Mary, lived on the south side of King Springs Road just west of South Cobb Drive and outside the City; there they had a farm. Mr. G.W. Nations was one of the first Rural Free Delivery men in the Smyrna area. Mrs. Nations, one of the strong mission-minded ladies of First Baptist Church of that day, lived to be quite an elderly lady.

Mrs. Leila Wilson

Mrs. Leila Wilson and her son, **George**, in 1938, moved into a garage apartment behind Miss Darrinda's house. They were living there when George entered the United States Army he became a Staff Sergeant during World War II while he was based in the Philippines. Mrs. Wilson and George at that time were members of First Baptist Church, known in those days as the Baptist Church. They earlier had had their membership at First Baptist Church of Marietta.

George married Ruby Wilson in 1946, just after he was discharged from military service. See *eleventh house.*

Tenth House

Jean Skelton Davis, the sister of Frances Skelton, resided here. See *Skelton, north side of Sunset Avenue*

Eleventh House

George and **Ruby Wilson** had two children: **Nancy** and **Larry**. George and Ruby met at church, while he was stationed in the United States Army, in Virginia near where Ruby grew up; they married in 1946. In 1947, they built and moved to this house where they raised their family. Ruby and George celebrated their 50th wedding anniversary before he died, in 1996. Ruby is still an active member of First Baptist Church, where she was a long-time teacher in the Junior Department and has been an active participant in the Women Missionary Union, (now known as Women on Missions, or (WOM). Ruby was hired as the first full-time paid secretary of First Baptist Church. She is still living in her home on Dunn Street.

George Wilson worked at Fort McPherson Army Installation, 1951-1970, in the Telecommunications Department. After he retired from Fort Mac, he started a rubber stamp, engraving, and locksmith business. Having serviced several banks, a department at the Social Security Administration, and other businesses, he retired from this occupation after 14 years.

George Wilson was one of my dad's best friends. Like Jesse Cook, George could do almost anything he was asked to do. He was extremely adept at electronics; it might be said that he was before his time. At First Baptist Church, George set up the first sound system, which he operated for many years. Anything that had to do with electronics he could do. He was a natural!

Nancy Wilson married Perry Sandifer of Macon. They had one son, Tim. Perry Sandifer, who is an ordained Methodist Minister in the South Georgia Conference, presently directs an adult day care for people in the early stages of Alzheimer's disease. He works through the State of Georgia in the Griffin and Jackson areas. Nancy works part-time at the public library in Barnesville.

Tim Sandifer, who married Suzie Woelfel from Illinois, finished his Masters degree in Religious Studies from Vanderbilt University in the summer of 2004. Tim and Suzie now reside in Godfrey, Illinois, where he is Youth Minister at a church, and Suzie teaches first grade.

Larry Wilson married Patty Hicks, who had one daughter, Renee, and two grand- daughters, Alexis and Ashleigh. Patty Wilson, a histologist (a nurse who reads tissue), is employed in the laboratory at Saint Joseph's Hospital in Atlanta. Larry, a photographic artist who specializes in black and white design, works with Meteor in Atlanta. Both Larry and Patty are active in First Baptist Church, where Patty sings in the choir.

Twelfth House

Mr. and **Mrs. Sidney Manning** lived in this house, where Mrs. Manning still resides. See *Manning, east side of Gilbert Street.*

Thirteenth House

Mrs. Laura Howard Martin and her two younger children, **Rex** and **Billy** were residents here. Mrs. Martin's three oldest children, **Hazel**, **Howard**, and **Lynn**, were grown at the time, and Laura's husband, Edward Martin, was deceased

Lynn Martin, in the 1950s, bought this house on Dunn Street for his mother and two younger brothers, Rex and Billy. He assumed from Mr. Baldwin a 4½ percent GI loan of $12,000.00.

The Martin Family, in the early 1940s, moved to Richardson Road, located between Smyrna and Fair Oaks. Mr. Martin, after retiring from the Bell Bomber Plant, bought land in Forsyth County and moved his family there. He died less than a year later.

Edward Martin was a World War I Veteran, having served in France as part of the United States Army's American Expeditionary Forces. Having been left with declining health after being gassed, he thereby suffered from lung problems the rest of his life.

Hazel Martin married Cleon Bennett in 1940.

Howard Martin married Jacquie Ball, who was from Philadelphia, Pennsylvania, but was raised in Ohio. They had three children: Ann, Bobby, and Nancy. Jacquie's father, Norman Ball, was a master electrician who helped build the Bell Bomber Plant, in Marietta.

Howard Martin was born in Forsyth County in 1922. A graduate of Cumming High School, Howard served in the United States Navy, during World War, where he was attached to Seabees. While aboard ship, he was seriously injured. Almost losing a leg, he was left with a physical disability. From this injury Howard suffered the rest of his life. For 18 years he was manager of Smyrna American Legion Post #160, and established in 1964 Howard's Delicatessen being located on Pat Mell Road, north of Cobb Center. After his death, his son, Bobby, relocated the Delicatessen to Cobb Center and still later to the south side of Concord Road, west of South Cobb Drive and near the site of the Hollis Hill Dunton home place; it is now known as Howard's Restaurant.

Ann Martin, a graduate of Campbell High School and Massey Business College, married Harold Rowe from Georgetown, South Carolina, in 1967. They had two sons: Brad and Brian.

Brad Rowe, born in 1968, graduated from Campbell High School and attended Young Harris College and the University of Georgia. Brad married Nicole Gilbert, also a Campbell High School graduate. They had one son, Derrick.

Brian Rowe was born in 1970. A graduate of Jacksonville State University, he is unmarried at this time.

Bobby Martin married Jane Melon of Smyrna in 1969; both were graduates of Campbell High School. Bobby attended the University of Georgia and Southern Polytechnic Institute, now Southern Polytechnic State University, in Marietta, and Kennesaw State College, now Kennesaw State University. They had one child, Deborah, born in 1971.

Deborah Martin graduated from Campbell High School and Southern Polytechnic Institute, in Marietta. She married Ken Rabitch of Statesboro; they had two children: Maggie and Spencer. Deborah and Ken now live in Savannah.

Bobby Martin is now to married Sandra O'Neal of Alabama, who from a previous marriage had a daughter, Sherrie, born in 1970.

Sherrie O'Neal, who graduated from Campbell High School, married Andy Preston of Smyrna. They had three children: Audrey, Garret, and Connor.

Nancy Martin, a graduate of Campbell High School and the University of Georgia married Robert Gsegner of Marietta in 1973. They had two children: Adam and Amanda. Nancy is now married to Kenny Jones, whose mother, Becky Jones, owns Becky Jones School of Dance.

Adam Gsegner, born in 1979, graduated from Campbell High School and Mercer University.

Amanda Gsegner, born in 1987, graduated from Campbell High School and is attending Auburn University.

Lynn Martin, attended Smyrna High School but completed his high school studies while in the United States Navy. After attending Gupton Jones College of Mortuary Science and John Marshall Law School, in 1956 he married Arletta Field of Jesup; they had two children, Tana and Brent.

Tana Martin, a graduate of Campbell High School and the University of Georgia, married William Parks and had one daughter, Cason Lynn. After her divorce, Tana married Steve Greer; they live in Canton.

Brent Martin, a graduate of Campbell High School and the University of Georgia, is currently living in Savannah.

Rex Martin, a graduate of Cumming High School, in Forsyth County, owned and operated Oakdale Thriftown Grocery Store, in the Oakdale community, south of Smyrna, for 22 years. He and his wife, Charleen, had two sons: Terry and Scott.

Terry Martin, a graduate of Campbell High School, married Pam Jones of Smyrna. They had two sons: Ryan and Russ.

Scott Martin, a graduate of Campbell High School and Southern Methodist University, married Christy French of Knoxville, Tennessee. They had one son, Alex.

Billy Martin, a 1959 graduate of Campbell High School, attended Southern Polytechnic State University. He and his wife, the former Brenda Turner, a graduate of South Cobb High School, had two children: Kelley and Todd. Billy owned and operated Hallmark Office Supply for 20 years, and now is owner/broker of Vinings Realty.

Todd Martin, a graduate of Campbell High School, lives in Smyrna.

Kelley Martin, a graduate of Campbell High School and Emory University, received a Masters in Business Administration degree from Columbia University, where she is now employed. Kellie married Robert Blanco; they reside in New York City.

CHAPTER THIRTEEN

CONCORD ROAD

North Side

Appreciation is extended to Bob Baldwin, Tom Camp, Bob Fowler, Kathy Hardage Hatcher, Mary Lou Redd Cochran, Benny Lou O'Bryant, and Mike Terry for sharing information about their families and others that lived on Concord Road, where Bobby, Kathy, and Tom grew up. Mary Lou moved to Concord Road when she was in the eighth grade and lived there until shortly before she graduated from high school, in the late 1940s, when her family moved to King Springs Road. Mike Terry is a grandson of Mr. and Mrs. John Baldwin. Bob Fowler, who grew up on King Springs Road, furnished information about Miss Della Dunton, and Benny Lou O'Bryant Tackett, who grew up on Concord Road, The Country Road, shared her knowledge about the Lusk and Swain families.

First House

Mr. and **Mrs. Early L. Cooper** resided on the west side of Concord Road in the first house, a nice brick one that is currently occupied by Love Street Gift Shop and Gardens. I remember that Mrs. Cooper, whose given name was Viola, was with my mother in the Homemaker's Sunday School Class at First Baptist Church.

After the Coopers had moved, this became the home of Mrs. Lena Turner, who had two grandsons living with her: Charles Turner and "Buddy" Cooper. The mother of "Buddy" later married Mr. Harbuck after which time "Buddy" Cooper became known as "Buddy" Harbuck.

Second House

The Shetter Family

The **Shetter Family** lived in a large, white frame house, located on the northwest corner of Medlin Street and Concord Road. They had six children: **Dorothy**, **Edwin**, **Donald**, **Robert**, known as "Bobby," and twins, **Ruth** and **Ruby**. The twins were my age. The Shetter home is now an art and frame shop.

When we were in high school, the Shetter Family moved from Concord Road to a farm located in the Godfrey community of Morgan County. Mr. Shetter, who worked for the railroad, died in the mid 1950s, while he was still a young man. Mrs. Shetter, who lived into her 90s, died in 2002.

The Wheeler Family

Idelle and **Howard Wheeler** are remembered by Mary Lou Redd Cochran as living in this house after the Shetters had moved. She recalls Howards being a World War II Veteran, who had received, during the War, injuries that left him an invalid. See *Wheeler, Atlanta Street, from Mrs. Mazie's to Pearce Matthews.*

The Otis White Family

Mr. and **Mrs. Otis White** were the last family that I knew to reside in the aforementioned house. The Whites had two sons, **Joe** and **Jimmy**. Joe served as choir director at First Baptist Church during the late 1950s and early 1960s. Jimmy married Joann McDowell, who was a member of the Smyrna High School Class of 1951. Mrs. White, whose given name was Jewell, was a very attractive lady, always well dressed and adorned with a hat. I especially remember her and my mother's marching in Atlanta's Easter Parade to show off their hats; a very colorful event, that parade was held close to the Easter season for many years. See *McDowell, Dixie Avenue*

Third House

Mr. and **Mrs. Nemory Chadwick** owned and operated a neighborhood grocery store on the southwest corner of Concord Road and Medlin Street. Mrs. Chadwick was the former Mary Dinsmore. They had a daughter, Loma. I remember the Chadwicks were very nice, accommodating people.

Loma Chadwick married Douglas Redd, who lived on King Springs Road. They had three children: Glenn, Weldon, and Mary Lou. Loma and Douglas resided with the Chadwicks in the living quarters at the rear of their store, from the time Mary Lou was in eighth grade until just before she graduated from high school, in the late 1940s. At that time the Redds moved to Mr. Redd's parents' home, on Kings Springs Road. See *Redd and Chadwick, west side of King Springs Road.*

Mary Lou Redd married Bobby Cochran. They had three children: Steve, Donna, and Charles, known as "Charlie." Bobby, the son of B.B. and Dessie Cochran, grew up on Elizabeth Street. See *Elizabeth Street.*

Steve Cochran married Mary; they had three children: Katie, Megan, and Abby. Steve later married Donna Brown; they had no children.

Donna Cochran married Larry Milford. They had two children: Nolan and Amanda.

"Charlie" Cochran married Laura Dashielle. They had four children: Christin, David, Charlie, and Ben.

By 1955 Roy and Sue Robinson had bought the Chadwicks' store and named it Corner Grocery. From previous marriages, Sue had a son and a daughter, and Roy had a son.

Fourth House

Mr. and **Mrs. Joe Camp** lived here. Mrs. Camp's given name was Jewell. They had three children: a daughter, **Mary Ellen,** born in 1924; and sons, **Mac**, born in 1928, and **Tom,** born in 1932. The Camps were very active in First Baptist Church. Mrs. Camp, a teacher and office worker, also worked at the Bell Bomber Plant during World War II. Mr. Joe Camp, brother of Aletha Hardage, who lived next door, and of Mary B. Carson, who lived on South Atlanta Road, was a disabled World War I veteran.

Mac Camp entered the United States Marine Corps after World War II and moved to California.

Tom Camp, along with Bobby Fowler and John Porterfield, joined the United States Navy in 1950; they served throughout the Korean Conflict. Tom married and had two children. He later married Pam Bush; they live in the Bennett Woods subdivision, not far from Lillie and me. Pam, long-time treasurer of the Bennett Woods Garden Club, and Tom are active in the Smyrna Historical and Geneological Society, the Friends of the Smyrna Library, and First Baptist Church.

Fifth House

George and **Aletha Hardage** and their three children, **Janis**, **Mike**, and **Kathy**, resided in this house, originally numbered 314 Concord Road but changed to 1229, was built by Aletha Hardage's dad, James Newton Camp, known as "J.N." Mr. Camp, ordained a Deacon at First Baptist Church on June 27, 1907, was also a member of the building committee at the time of the construction of the rock church, which was completed in 1924. Mrs. Hardage was a sister of Joe Camp, who lived next door, and Mary B. Carson (Mrs. Heery), who lived on South Atlanta Road, near the Spring Hill Streetcar Stop.

George Hardage was a pharmacist; Aletha Hardage taught at both Smyrna Elementary and High School and Campbell High School. At First Baptist Church Mrs. Aletha Hardage for many years taught the Homemaker's Sunday School Class, of which my mother, Dora Wood, was a member.

Janis Hardage married Gerald Tache; they had one son, Garett. Janis and Gerald live in Annapolis, Maryland.

Mike Hardage married Rosemary Nally of Smyrna. They had two children: Andrew and Katie. Mike and Rosemary live in the Oakdale community, south of Smyrna.

Kathy Hardage married B.J. Hatcher. They had three children: Mike, Erin, and Mary Beth.

Michael Hatcher, known as "Mike," was married and had a daughter, Chloe. Living in Smyrna, he works for SunTrust Bank.

Erin Hatcher, a graduate in the Campbell High School Class of 1985, married Ken Turner, the son of Reverend and Mrs. George Turner and a graduate of Wills High School. They had four sons: Landon, Reed, Cullen, and Caleb. Erin passed away in 2003.

Mary Beth Hatcher, who works for Coca-Cola Company, lives in Palo Alto, Calfironia. She is married to Dana Carpenter of Atlanta, a graduate student of Stanford University in California.

B.J. and Kathy Hatcher, who live in the Forest Hills community in Smyrna, are active in First Baptist Church. They own and operate Hatcher and Son Construction Company, located in the Oakdale community.

Sixth House

Mr. and **Mrs**. **Wayne Giles** were residents of the next house. Mrs. Giles was the former Ruth Jones. Ruth and Wayne had two children: **Herbert**, known as "**Herby**," and **Seymour.** The Giles Family lived in a garage apartment behind the main house. **Mrs**. **Jones**, Mrs. Giles' mother, lived in the main house. Mrs. Jones had five other children who lived in Cobb County: Frank and Paul Jones, and twin sons, Bill and Glenn Jones, and daughter, Kathryn Jones Short.

Mr. Wayne Giles was ordained a Deacon at Smyrna First Baptist Church January 5, 1955. When King Spring Baptist Church was constituted, the Giles Family was among First Baptist Church families who moved their membership to King Spring Baptist.

Mrs. Ruth Giles was a secretary for a railroad union; Mr. Giles, a radio and television repairman, had a shop that was located at the old Georgia Power substation on Atlanta Street, across from the Smyrna Woman's Club. He later moved his business to the Sunnyside Inn building, across the street from Campbell High School.

"Herby" Giles is deceased.

Seymour Giles married Rosalyn Bronson of Marietta. They had two daughters: Robyn and Melanie. In their later years, after their daughters were grown, Seymour and Rosalyn, through the Cobb County Department of Children and Youth, were foster parents. Now retired, they live in The Villages, Florida.

Seventh House

Mayes Hamby
Mayor of Smyrna
1942-1944
Smyrna City Councilman
1940-1942, 1952-1953

Mr. and **Mrs. Mayes Hamby** lived next door to the Giles Family. Mayes and his wife, Lola, had four children: **Charles, Joyce, Joy**, and **Jeri Lynn**. (Joyce and Joy were twins.)

Mrs. Hamby was a long-time member of the Homemaker's Sunday School Class at First Baptist Church and the Eastern Star. Lillie and I were privileged to attend Mrs. Hamby's 95th birthday celebration in May 2004; she died September 13, 2004.

Mr. Hamby, who worked for the railroad for a very long time, served on the City Council and was Mayor of Smyrna in the 1940s and early 1950s. He was a member of the Nelms Masonic Lodge and First Baptist Church, where his family was active in Sunday School and Church organizations and where Mayes was ordained a Deacon in 1957. Both he and his wife, Lola, in the 1950s were very active in the selling of bonds to build the present First Baptist Sanctuary. The Hambys, in the early 1970s, moved their church letters to King Spring Baptist Church, where they were faithful members the rest of their lives.

Charles Hamby was married to Mary Jo Clark of the Oakdale community, south of Smyrna. He died as a young man due to complications from diabetes.

Joyce Hamby married Donald Parks, who grew up on Elizabeth Street. They live on Kathy Lane, in the Forest Hills community. See *Parks, Elizabeth Street.*

Joy Hamby married Ed Hamby of Smyrna.

Jeri Lynn Hamby, a 1960 graduate of Campbell High School, married Richard Burman. They had eight children, six of whom were adopted, including two Chinese daughters. The Burmans live in Carrollton.

NOTE: Charles, Joy, and Joyce Hamby graduated from Smyrna High School.

Eighth House

D.A. and **Mary Hamby** resided in the next house. Mrs. Hamby was the former Mary Vaughn Bell, the daughter of Mr. and Mrs. Homer Bell, who lived on Reed Street. D.A., a plumber, was the son of Mr. and Mrs. Judson Hamby, Sr., who lived on Love Street. See *Hamby, south side of Love Street,* and *Bell, east of Reed Street.*

Ninth House

Mr. and **Mrs. Johnnie J. Terry** and their son, **John Michael**, known as "**Mike**," lived in this house during the days of my youth. Their son, **William Patrick**, known as "Pat," was born after they moved. (Mary, the former Mary Jeanette Baldwin, the daughter of Mr. and Mrs. John Jacob Baldwin, married Johnnie Terry June 18, 1938.) The Terry dwelling was a rock house, which, according to family information, was built by Mary's brother, Robert Baldwin, in 1933. Mary and Johnnie moved from this house to Collier Drive in the Forest Hills community in 1949. There, Mary lived until near the end of her life, when she required assisted living. See *Terry, Forest Hills*

I was closely associated with Mary Terry for many years. When I was Chairman of the Budget and Finance Committee at First Baptist Church, she was the financial secretary. During those years we had much association with each other. She was a lovely Christian lady. I still miss her!

NOTE: Mary Baldwin grew up on the Baldwin Farm, which was on the opposite side of Concord Road from the rock house. With Mary's family members living on both sides of the road, this area of Concord Road could easily have been called "The Baldwin Family Compound." Mary's parents' property, on the south side of Concord, was later sold to American Legion Post # 160.

Mike Terry, a graduate of Campbell High School and Jacksonville State University, in Jacksonville, Alabama, had one son, Christopher, and two grandchildren: John and Annabelle. Mike married Sue Bingham, the daughter of Owen and Betty Bingham. (Sue, born in Maryville, Tennessee, grew up in the Hickory Hills community in Smyrna. Due to her dad's working for Lockheed Aircraft Corporation, the family had previously lived in Tennessee and Oklahoma, before moving to Smyrna.) Sue, a graduate of Campbell High School and The University of Georgia is a master gardener, currently involved with the Root House in Marietta; she is also a member of the Jonquil Garden Club. Mike and Sue are involved with the Forest Hills Neighborhood Association. They live on Pinetree Drive, in the Forest Hills community.

Mike Terry is now serving as Chairman of Smyrna's Planning and Zoning Board, Past President of the Smyrna Golden "K" Kiwanis Club, and Treasurer and Historian of the Taylor-Brawner House Foundation. Some of Mike's favorite projects are M.U.S.T Ministries and mentoring children at the local schools. He has contributed many articles and pictures for use in this book. Mike was honored with the "Mr. Smyrna" Award in January 2006 by the Smyrna Moose Lodge for his outstanding contributions to the community.

John Christopher Terry, along with his wife, Jeanna, and their children live just off King Springs Road.

Pat Terry and his wife, the former Pamela Housley, reside on Dunn Street. Pamela and Pat were married in 1979 at Roswell Street Baptist Church, in Marietta. They have no children. Pamela, the daughter of E.O. and Helen Housley, was born April 7, 1956, in Meridian, Mississippi. When she was three years old, her family moved to Atlanta, where her father worked for Southern Railway; in 1967 her family moved to Smyrna. Pamela owns and operates a successful interior design business: Pamela Terry Designs.

Pat Terry was born February 17, 1952. Having attended Smyrna Elementary School, he was a 1970 graduate of Campbell High School. As a child he became interested in popular music; though never formally trained, he became a professional song writer. In 1973 he formed The "Pat Terry Group," signed as one of the pioneer contemporary Christian bands to the fledgling Myrrh Records label. From 1974 to 1980 The Pat Terry Group traveled to perform at churches and colleges and in concert halls across America; they recorded five nationally recognized albums. Other artists became aware of Pat's song writing abilities during this period: in 1976, pop singer B.J. Thomas recorded Pat's gospel song "Home Where I Belong," which became an early contemporary gospel standard.

In 1980 Pat disbanded The Pat Terry Group. Performing as a soloist, he recorded three albums co-produced by artist/producer Mark Heard, a long-time friend and Macon native.

With song writing still being his first love, Pat Terry retired from touring in 1986 and began spending time in Nashville, Tennessee, where he pursued a writing career. Though never moving from Smyrna, he enjoyed a fruitful working relationship with Nashville's song writing community and found success in the country music field. His songs have been recorded by a diverse list of well-known national and international artists, including Travis Tritt, western stars Roy Rogers and Dale Evans, The Oak Ridge Boys, Tanya Tucker, Kenny Chesney, Sammy Kershaw, and John Anderson. In 2004 Pat wrote "Where Dreams and Jonquils Grow," a song in tribute to his home town, Smyrna, where he debuted it October 22, 2005, at the first benefit held for the restoration of the Taylor-Brawner House.

Smyrna Mayor Max Bacon and City Council members honored Pat by naming December 19, 200 "Pat Terry Day" in Smyrna.

ROCK HOUSE
1933-2002
by Mike Terry

From resting places in open fields, forested ravines, and creeks that traversed the old hom place, 28-year-old Robert Lee Baldwin carefully selected every stone that would be used to constru his rock house. Paying attention to color and shape, he muscled the stones into a wagon and slowl moved them several miles to the building site on Concord Road. How long it must have taken t select, load, transport, and unload the tons of rocks needed! How many backbreaking trips did h make? Of course, there is no real answer, as Rob rarely talked about his remarkable project—though suspect he was proud of what he had accomplished.

Rob learned stone masonry, house framing, and plumbing from his father, John Baldwin. H and his "Papa" and older brother, Voss, had built and sold several houses in Smyrna, each one for small profit; thus Rob had no reservations about building his own home. But he wanted his home to b unique, and unique it was! Having the exterior constructed entirely of native stone, he then place Civil War artillery shells into the mortar on either side of the front door. Next, he selected a heart-pine arts-and-crafts style front door and added appropriate hardware. The entrance, with its rock archway was unusual. It wasn't "grand," just different from any other home in Smyrna. Locals watched as th house took shape. The name "Rock House" was quickly given to it.

As was his nature, Rob had taken his time; thus the house was not completed for severa years. This had allowed Rob to focus on the details of construction as well as to pay cash for all th building supplies. (W. P. Stephens Lumber Company supplied all the building materials, and he pai as he went.) Rob moved into his new home in the late 1930s, but family circumstances would caus him to move out just a few years later.

In 1938 Rob's youngest sister, Mary, was married to her long-time beau, Johnnie Terry Residing in a small apartment in Marietta, they really wanted (and needed) a bigger place. Rob, still single man, agreed to move back in with his Mama and rent the Rock House to Mary and Johnnie "After all," Mary told him, "we'll have a place of our own some day, and you can move back into you house."

It was not until 1950 that the Terrys built their own home, and Rob once again occupied th Rock House. Mama Baldwin moved in with Rob a few years later and lived with him until her death in 1962. Rob was not without female companionship for long. He had dated Carrie Rivers, a widow from Atlanta, for several years, and just one year after Mama Baldwin's death, he and Carrie married Rob was 62-years-old, and this was his first-and-only marriage. Carrie passed away in 1989, after 2 good years with Rob, who continued to live in the Rock House until he was forced to move into retirement home in 1996. He passed away in 1997 at age 95.

The Rock House stood unoccupied until being sold in September 2002. It was demolished to make way for the development of the Laurel Springs Townhome community.

One clear morning, just a week before the demolition was to begin, I parked my truck between the large oaks and stately pecan trees that shaded Rob's back yard. I slowly walked the entire property—pausing to listen, touch, and experience what I knew would soon fall victim to "progress." I studied the stones and remembered the life of the man that lifted them into place. I snapped a few pictures, as insurance against the inevitable failings of memory. I don't regret losing the Rock House, for it was time for it to go. I just hope my son and his son will have a "Rock House" in their lives some day.

Rob Baldwin
1902 – 1997
He built the Rock House.
Photo Courtesy of Mike Terry.

The Rock House on Concord Road
Built by Mr. Rob Baldwin in the 1930s.
Picture courtesy of Mike Terry.

Johnnie Terry and son **Mike**
In front of the Rock House
Circa 1945 – Photo courtesy of Mike Terry

Mike Terry, Summer 1945 with dad, **Johnni**
Rock House on Concord Road
Photo courtesy of Mike Terry

Mary Baldwin Terry and her mother, **Mrs. John (Jennie Legg) Baldwin**
in the Rock House, December 1957
Photo courtesy of Mike Terry

Home of Mr. and Mrs. Voss Baldwin
Corner of Concord Road and Dunton Street, next door to the Rock House
Photo courtesy of Mike Terry.

L-R: **Lois Baldwin** and **Maude Baldwin Paris**, after church in the late 1940s
Courtesy of Mike Terry.

NOTE: The above story was written by Mike Terry, the son of Mary and Johnnie Terry an nephew of Mr. Robert Baldwin, who built the Rock House. Mike was born in the rock house o Concord Road, but was raised on Collier Drive in the Forest Hills community.

Tenth House

Mr. and **Mrs. William Voss Baldwin**, known as "Voss," lived on the corner of Conco Road and Dunton Street, next door to the "Rock Baldwin, House." Mrs. Baldwin was the former Lo Frances Day. They had three children: **John William**, **Robert Max**, known as "Bob," and **Patrici Mae**, known as "Patty."

John William Baldwin married Norma Dobbs; they had four children. Having chosen military career, John retired from The United States Army with the rank of Major. He passed awa recently.

Robert Max Baldwin, known as "Bob," married Martha Burns, known as "Martie." They ha one daughter, Lee Ann. "Martie" died March 20, 2001.

Lee Ann Baldwin married Bob Schooner; they had two sons and a daughter.

Robert Max Baldwin, known as "Bob" retired from Lockheed Aircraft Corporation. He an his second wife, the former Patricia Durham live in the Lost Mountain community, west of Marietta just off Dallas Highway. See *Durham, south side of Powder Springs Street.*

Patricia Mae Baldwin, known as "Patty," married Jim Crandall, a minister from Sout Georgia. They currently live in Brunswick.

"Bob" Baldwin related a story that indicated how resourceful the youth of Smyrna could b in making spending money. "In 1940 my dad, William Voss Baldwin, worked for nearly a week laying brick, to earn the money to buy the double-seated bicycle that John William and I had wanted How we would ride it that bicycle through Belmont Crossing and over to the site of the runways fo the new Bell Bomber Plant (later becoming Dobbins Air Force Base). On Sundays we could mak good pocket change by letting people ride that double bike on those long, level runways."

Eleventh House

Adella Dunton, known as "Della," the sister of Jesse Macaulay Dunton, who lived on th south side of Concord Road, resided here. "Della," who never married, owned much property. Nea her home, she maintained extensive flower gardens with a variety of plants. She grew chrysanthemum in abundance; each autumn people in the area would buy them to wear to the football games. See *Dunton, south side of Concord Road.*

NOTE: The following statement was lifted from the minutes of the regular meeting of the City of Smyrna Mayor and Council, dated February 1, 1951: "City Councilman Howard Hames made a motion and it was seconded by Councilman C.W. Jones to accept a project of Bennett Realty Company, located on property known as Della Dunton Property, Concord Road to Medlin Road to Dunton Street and Evelyn Street, in City Limits, assuring City of Smyrna the building of 92 homes and in turn City to furnish sewerage and water; sewer taps $100.00 each and water meters $50.00 each to be paid by Bennett Realty Corporation. City agrees to run trunk sewerage line around west side or inside City Limits and extend line to new project. Voted unanimous." Mayor J.M. (Hoot) Gibson Councilmen; P.P. Shaw, C.W. Jones, Howard Hames, and H.L. McEntyre. Martha Theodocian was City Clerk." This Vote broke the half-mile circle, which had been the Smyrna City Limits.

Twelfth House

Mr. and **Mrs**. **Henry Swain** and their family lived in this house, which was located in the vicinity of Vickery Ace Hardware. B.C. Castellaw, Bill Sanders, and Warren Sanders opened Sanders Funeral Home in this house in the 1960s. Sanders' Funeral Home was not the first funeral home to open in Smyrna. Vickers Funeral home opened on Sunset Avenue in the Ed Skelton house, was in operation for about two years, in the mid 1950s. By way of local chatter, I heard that, earlier in the century, an embalming room was located behind one of the houses on the west side of Atlanta Street, between Church and Love streets. See *Vickers, Sunset Avenue* and *Swain, north side of Church Street.*

Thirteenth House

Mr. and **Mrs**. **Lusk** resided here. They had two children: **Joyce** and **Roger**. The house faced Lusk Drive, which was a small street off the north side of Concord Road, and now the entrance into Concord Square Shopping Center.

Joyce Lusk married Lamar O'Bryant.

Roger Lusk's grandson, Jeffrey, died while he was still a child. I recall that when the Lusk Family sold the property on Concord Road to a developer for building of houses, Roger stipulated that his grandson be remembered in some way. The Hampton Place subdivision, entered via Jeffrey Place, is named for Roger's grandson. When I travel down Concord Road, which is often, and see that street, I think about Roger, Joey, and the Lusk Family.

McArthur Concrete Company

Sometime in the early 1950s after I graduated from High School, the McArthur Family began operating McArthur Concrete Products Company in this location. The best I remember, it was located behind where the Lusk house had stood. This business operated in this location until the property was acquired for the building of Concord Village Shopping Center where the K-Mart store operated for many years. McArthur Concrete in now located in Acworth. Some of the McArthur family lived in Forest Hills

CONCORD ROAD
South Side

Concord Road in the days of my youth began where Love Street Interiors, Gifts, and Gardens is today; the section of Concord that runs from the gift shop to Atlanta Street was called Love Street.

Appreciation is extended to Mary Lou Redd Cochran and Emma Jean Faucett Barden, who shared their memories of the people residing on Concord Road in the middle of the Twentieth Century. Mary Lou grew up on Concord Road and Jean on Medlin Street. Carolyn Medlin McEntyre, who related memories of her family, the Medlins; Jimmy and Janice Pitts for information about Jimmy's family, Mr. and Mrs. Bill Pitts; Mike Terry and Bob Baldwin, for reminiscences of the Baldwin Family, some of whom lived on Concord Road for most of the Twentieth Century; Edd Gann, whose parents, late in life, moved here from North Cooper Lake Road, and Patsy McAdams Barnett, for data about the Brown Family, for whom Brown Elementary School is named.

First House

Emmett Marcellus Hamby and his second wife, **Carrie Loutilla (Hamby Barrett) Hamby**, lived in the first house on the south side of Concord Road. They had one son, Harry, who married Elizabeth Adair of Marietta, and a daughter, Harriett.

Carrie Hamby was the fifth child of Benajah Judson Hamby and his wife, the former Emma Pope Hudson. Emmett Marcellus Hamby was the first child of Virgil Stewart Hamby, who was the older brother of Benajah Hudson Hamby; thus Carrie Hamby and her husband, Marcellus, were fir cousins.

Carrie Hamby was first married to Mr. Barrett; they had two children: a son, Willie, and daughter, Emma Lou. See *Hamby, south side of Love Street.*

Emmett Marcellus Hamby first married Alice Fuller; they had twelve children: David A known as "D.A.," William, Bertha, Kate, Gertrude, Grace, Emmett Faye, Guy Marcellus, Alton Jacl Prentice, Charles Mayes, and Thomas Leo. See *Hamby, north side of Concord Road, east side* *Roswell Street, north side of Spring Street,* and *south side of Love Street.*

David A. Hamby, known as "D.A.," married Emma Lou Barrett, the daughter of his father second wife, Carrie Loutilla Hamby Barrett. "D.A." and Emma Lou were both second cousins an step-siblings. See *D.A. Hamby, Jr., south side of Love Street.*

Second House

Mr. and **Mrs**. **Warren Cargal**, **Sr**., and their son, **Warren Cargal**, **Jr**., resided in thi second house, which was a nice, brick one. Mr. Cargal was the manager of Plant Atkinson, a Georgi Power generating plant off the Access Highway, later renamed South Cobb Drive. The Cargal Famil attended First Baptist Church.

Warren Cargal, Jr., married Sue Scoggins, the daughter of Mr. and Mrs. Howard Scoggins Warren and Sue had five children: Warren Jr., Connie, Bill, William, and Matthew. In the 1950 Warren and Sue moved to Albany. See *Scoggins, south side of Bank Street.*

NOTE: After the death of Warren Cargal, Sr., his son became known as Warren, Sr., and hi grandson became known as Warren, Jr.

The Bill Pitts Family

Later on **Mr**. and **Mrs**. **Bill Pitts** and their sons, **Billy** and **Jimmy**, lived here. Mrs. Pitts wa the former Frances Jones. The Pitts moved from Clinton, South Carolina, to Smyrna in 1952, whe they rented a room in the "old Quarles House," on Atlanta Street, from Martha Quarles. Mr. and Mrs Pitts operated Sam's Cleaners in downtown Smyrna. See *Quarles, Atlanta Street, from Marlowe's t* *Creatwood.*

Jimmy Pitts, though playing several sports, was an outstanding basketball player at Campbel High School, where, in the early 1960s, he earned All-State honors in basketball. In 1961 he earned a athletic scholarship to the University of Georgia, where he became an All-Southeastern Conferenc player and graduated.

After attending Emory University School of Dentistry, Jimmy established a dental practice i Smyrna, where he has been very successful through the years.

Jimmy Pitts married Janice Carden. They had five sons: Jimmy, Jr., Jonathan, Jeff, Jennings and Joey. Their oldest son, Jimmy, Jr., grew up with my son, Stephen. Jimmy and Janice and thei three oldest sons are graduates of Campbell High School; the youngest sons, Jennings and Joey, ar graduates of The Lovett School in Atlanta.

Janice Carden Pitts, the daughter of Jewel and Carl Carden, who also had a son, Gene. Afte the Cardens moved from Rockmart to Smyrna in 1955, Jewell Carden worked for many years a Administrative Assistant to Harry Holliday, President of the Bank of Smyrna. Carl is deceased.

Jim Pitts shared, "One of my fondest summer memories is of meeting at Brinkley Park and playing baseball all morning. After finishing, we then would go to Robinson's Corner Grocery Store, on the corner of Concord Road and Medlin Street."

NOTE: Corner Grocery Store in other parts of this book is known as Chadwick's Store.

Jimmy Pitts, Jr., married Stephanie Myers, a graduate of Wills High School; they had two children: James and Chloe. Jimmy, Jr., a graduate of Georgia State University, where he was an outstanding tennis player, and Medical College of Georgia School of Dentistry, has his dental practice in Jasper, Tennessee.

Jeff Pitts married Sharon Elkins, a graduate of Campbell High School, They had three children: twins, a son, Grayson, and a daughter, Carly, and another son, Alden. Jeff, a graduate of Kennesaw State University, is employed as the accountant and bookkeeper for Davis Construction Company in Cobb County.

Jonathan Pitts married Lori Mullins, a graduate of Campbell High School. They had two children: Abby and Austin. Jonathan is employed by Georgia Power Company.

Jennings Pitts married Kimberly Glaser, of Atlanta. A graduate of The Lovett School and Furman University, Jennings received his Masters degree from the University of Georgia. Also an outstanding tennis player while in college, Jennings is a Certified Public Accountant with Bennett and Thrasher. Jennings and Kimberly had a son Patrick, and a daughter, Veyton Elizabeth.

Joey Pitts, a graduate of The Lovett School is also a graduate of the University of Georgia and Medical College of Georgia School of Dentistry, where he was an outstanding tennis player. Currently he is in dental practice with his dad, on Concord Road. Joey married Jacy Wade of Douglas.

Third House

Mr. and **Mrs. Winston Medlin** moved from Medlin Street, named for Winston Medlin, to this house. Mrs. Medlin's given name was Effie. They had two children: **Jesse** and **Marie**. Winston was a brother of Carolyn McEntyre's grandfather, who lived at one time near the southwest corner of Concord and King Springs roads. Aubrey McIntosh later built there a brick house, which was razed in 2005 for Ed Hatcher to build The Cottages at King Springs.

Carolyn, her mother and her brother moved from the Morningside area of Atlanta to this house in the mid 1940s. Carolyn's dad, **William Medlin**, who worked for the City of Atlanta, was head of the Signal Department, on Courtland Street. (Mr. Medlin's name is on a plaque on the front of the City of Atlanta Signal Department building.) Because at that time the City of Atlanta required him to maintain residence in Atlanta as long as he was a City employee, Mr. Medlin would stay in Atlanta through the week, then spend the weekends with his family in Smyrna.

In their elder years, Mr. Winston Medlin and his wife, Effie (William's uncle and aunt) needed help in order to remain in their home. Carolyn, her mother, and her brother moved in with them.

In 1947 Carolyn Medlin married Howard McEntyre, who grew up on the west side of Dunn Street; they had one son, Steve. Howard, having worked with his dad in McEntyre's Bakery in Smyrna, later ran the bakery. Today Steve is the owner and operator of the bakery. See *McEntyre, Dunn Street.*

Bill Medlin married Virginia Ruff. Active members of Bethany Methodist Church on Hurt Road they had three children: Kathy, Andrea, and Dave. Virginia passed away in 2003; Bill still lives in the Smyrna area.

Fourth House

Mr. and **Mrs. Travis Alexander Gann**, quite elderly when I was growing up, moved fro their home place on North Cooper Lake Road, to this house, which stood on the northeast corner Concord Road and Hunter Street. Mrs. Gann's given name was Mabel. They had four children: **Trav H.**, **Harold**, **Edgar**, known as "Edd," and a daughter, **Mary**, all of whom were much older than I.

Travis married Opal Bartlett, who, over the years, was a close friend of my wife, Lilli through Sunday School. Opal preceded Lillie as teacher of the JOY Sunday School Class at Fir Baptist Church. Opal and T. H. are buried in the Gann Family Cemetery, on North Cooper Lake Roa See *North Cooper Lake Road*

Fifth House

Mr. and **Mrs. James Edward Hiatt** lived in this house with their five children: **Lois**, **Ga Karen**, **Jimmy**, and **William Paul**, known as "Billy." "Jimmy" Hiatt remembers that the family's fir phone number was 87R.

James Edward Hiatt, also known as "Jimmy," originally from Mississippi worked durin World War II for Federal Reserve Bank in Atlanta, where he was in charge of the War Bond Divisio He died at a young age, due to complications from his heart's having been damaged by rheumat fever when he was a child. James Edward was the son of Mr. and Mrs. William Paul Hiatt, who live south of Smyrna, between Oakdale and the Chattahoochee River. William Paul, an arbiter, worked f Long Stockyards, located in Northwest Atlanta. James Edward shared with his children his memori of having lots of bacon to eat during the Depression years because of his father's employ with th stockyards.

Mrs. James Edward Hiatt, the former Marjorie Ennis, moved from Milledgeville to Atlant where she graduated in the Girls High Class of 1931. She attended Georgia State College for Wome at Milledgeville, she received a Bachelor of Arts Degree and did graduate work at Emory Universit After James Edward's death, she began teaching at Smyrna High School, in 1944, and was a columni for *The Smyrna Herald,* in which she wrote social events. Later in her life, Marjorie married "Happy Collins, whose family were long-time residents of Roswell Street. See *Collins, east side of Roswe Street.*

Lois Hiatt married Jim Durrell of Cherokee County. They had five children: Ben, Da Brandi, David, and Bill. Bill at one time served as Mayor of Woodstock.

Gail Hiatt, married Charles Fouts. They had three children: Angela, known as "Tootsie, Jane, and Patricia, known as "Patty." Gail later married James Roloff. See *Fouts, Atlanta Street, fro Mrs. Mazie's to Pearce Matthews.*

Karen Hiatt married Allen Johnson, who was employed by the Bank of Smyrna; they had n children. Karen and Allen live in Watkinsville.

Jimmy Hiatt married Malinda Fain; they had a daughter, Jamie, and a son, Chris. All of th family graduated from Campbell High School. Malinda, the daughter of Sarah and Ed Fain, had brother, Paul, and a sister whose name I do not recall. Employed by the City of Smyrna for man years, Malinda held the office of City Clerk, from which position she retired. After Jimmy an Malinda divorced, Jimmy, a long-time member of the Moose Lodge, married again and had a so Wayne.

Jamie Hiatt, a graduate of the University of Georgia, married and had a daughter, who live in Dunwoody.

Chris Hiatt, a graduate of Southern Polytechnic State University, formerly known as Southern Tech, married and had two sons: Stephen and James.

"Billy" Hiatt died in 1991.

Sixth House

Mr. and **Mrs. William F. Waldron** resided in this house. Mrs. Waldron was the former Mildred Arrington. Married December 25, 1925, in New Orleans, Louisiana, Mildred and William had ten children: **William**, known as "Bill," **Samuel M.**, known as "Sam," **Helen Elizabeth**, known as "Betty," **Marie, Frank, Frances, Lynda Mae, Henry William**, known as "Buddy," **Albert**, and **Sandra**. Mr. and Mrs. Waldron moved from Macon to Smyrna in 1942, when Mr. Waldron became employed by the Bell Bomber Plant; he was one of the last people to work there after World War II had ended and the plant was closed. Mr. and Mrs. Waldron were active members of First Baptist Church, where William was ordained a Deacon in September 1952.

William F. Waldron, known as "Billy" and/or "Tony," was born August 17, 1900, and died March 14, 1956; Mildred Arrington Waldron was born June 17, 1902, and died October 4, 1984. As of June 2004, the Waldrons had 35 grandchildren, 52 great-grandchildren, and 4 great great-grandchildren.

William Waldron, known as "Bill," married Pat Durham, who grew up on Powder Springs Street. They had two children: Beverly and John. The Waldron and Durham families attended First Baptist Church, where Beverly served as pianist for many years.

Beverly Waldron married Philip Johnson. They had three daughters: Melissa, Lara, and Nicole. The Johnson Family are members of First Baptist Church. See *Durham, south side of Powder Springs Street.*

John Waldron, a very talented young man, served First Baptist Church for many years by performing drama roles and helping to produce musical programs. He married Darlene Whatley of Douglasville, where they now live. They had one son, Bryant Wesley Waldron.

William Waldron, know as "Bill," later married Margaret Newbern, who had four children from a previous marriage, whom she and "Bill" raised.

Samuel M. Waldron, known as "Sam," married Mary Thomas of Macon. They had two children: Margie and "Sam," Jr., who are both married. At First Baptist Church "Sam" was called into the gospel ministry. Later he and Mary, as missionaries commissioned by the International Mission Board (formerly the Foreign Mission Board) of the Southern Baptist Convention, served in the Philippine Islands for 28 years. Now retired, Sam and Mary live in Macon.

Helen Elizabeth Waldron, known as "Betty," married Marcellus Hamby, who also grew up in Smyrna. They had two daughters: Marsha and Frances. See *Hamby, south side of Love Street.*

Marsha Hamby married Max Bacon; they had two children: Ashley and Ty. After Max and Marsha divorced, Marsha married Hayward Savage. A very talented artist, Marsha signed her earlier art "Marsha Bacon" and her later art "Marsha Savage."

Frances Hamby and her husband, Allen Moore, were married July 26, 1971. Both, at 18 years of age, died in an automobile accident December 26, 1971.

Marie Waldron married Albery Elrod, who grew up on Pat Mell Road in Cobb County. They had three children: Jackie, Danny, and Wayne. Marie lives in the Smyrna area.

Frank Waldron married LaDon Long of Dawsonville. They had one daughter, Sonja. Fra and LaDon live in Dawsonville.

Frances Waldron married Jerry Williams of Villa Rica. They had six children. Frances a Jerry are currently living in Carroll County.

Lynda Mae Waldron married Eddie McLeroy of Atlanta; they had three sons. Lynda Mae a Eddie reside in Marietta.

Henry William Waldron, known as "Buddy," married Jeanine Rabaduex from the Belmo Hills area of Smyrna; they had three children: Annette, Craig, and Angela. "Buddy," a graduate Southwestern Seminary, Ft. Worth, Texas, served several years as associate pastor of Vinings Fi Baptist Church. He is currently serving in Christian ministry in Newnan, where he and Jeanine no live.

Albert Waldron married Linda Kraft from Arkansas. They had two children: Cindy a Albert, Jr., known as "Bert." Albert and Linda live in Sparta, Tennessee.

Cindy is a civilian truck driver in Iraq.

Bert served in the United States Navy during Desert Storm.

Sandra Waldron married Larry Dunn of Smyrna; they had two children: Lee and Lisa. Aft Sandra and Larry divorced, Sandra married again and had four children; she lives in Tennessee.

Seventh House

Mr. and **Mrs. Charles Pitner Dorris** were residents of the seventh house. They had tw daughters: **Elizabeth**, known as "Beth," (Fairley) and **Susan Amanda** (Johnson). Mrs. Dorris was t former Catherine Elizabeth Baldwin, a daughter of Mr. and Mrs. John Jacob Baldwin. The Dorr dwelling was another one of the "Baldwin Family Compound" homes accompanying those of Mr Dorris' sister, Mary Terry, and her brothers, Voss and Robert Baldwin. (Their sister, Maude Baldwi Paris, lived just off Concord Road, on King Springs Road.)

Mr. Dorris, as a professional, worked for Georgia Power Company. He also opened hardware store in downtown Smyrna after World War II. My dad, Roy Wood, bought the two lots ea of our house on Bank Street from Mr. Dorris after World War II. To my knowledge, Mrs. Dorri whom I remember as a very nice and attractive lady, did not work outside the home.

Eighth House

Mr. and **Mrs. John Jacob Baldwin**, who married June 14, 1889, lived on the hill and in th curve just past the Dorris house. Mrs. Baldwin was the former Jennie Belle Legg, the daughter of M Thomas Ephrain Legg and his wife, Amanda Legg, two of the four charter members of First Bapti Church

NOTE: The other two charter members were Mr. Benson A. Bell and his wife, Fanny Be First Baptist Church was then known as Smyrna Baptist Church.

Mr. and Mrs. John Jacob Baldwin, who raised their family in this house, had five childre **William Voss**, **Robert Lee**, known as "Rob," **Maude Mae**, **Catherine Elizabeth**, and **Mar Jeanette**. Each of the Baldwin offspring lived out his/her life in or near the family farm house, and a of the Baldwin Family were members of First Baptist Church.

Mr. John Jacob Baldwin succumbed in December 1933; Mrs. Jennie Belle Baldwin died in Novemb 1962. After Mrs. Baldwin's death, the Baldwin Home was used first as a teen cantee

Home of Pitner Dorris and his wife, Catherine Baldwin Dorris
Corner of Concord Road and Legion Drive, Circa 1940s
Photo courtesy of Mike Terry.

Susan Dorris with Nanny**, Ms. Sellers**
At the Dorris Home – 1945
Photo courtesy of Mike Terry.

operated by the City of Smyrna. Its later use was for a kindergarten, operated by Mrs. Jackie Mas and Mrs. Dorene Dunn. (I believe the property by this time belonged to American Legion Post #16 See *C. J. Dunn, north side of Powder Springs Street,* and *Travis McDaniell, east side of Dunn Street.*

"Bobby" Baldwin, the grandson of John Jacob and Jennie Baldwin, related: "The Baldw farm was purchased from Mr. Gautchy, who was licensed to operate the 'Pearl Springs Distille there until the effects of prohibition in the United States made it unprofitable for him to continue operation. The blocks used to build the Gautchey house on Atlanta Street were made on the site t later became the Baldwin Farm."

NOTE: Prohibition was a national action. In 1913 the United States Congress passed Webb-Kenyon Law that stopped the shipping of liquor from a "wet" state to a "dry" state. By July 1919, 31 states were "dry" or had voted a statewide prohibition on a certain date. See *World Bo Encyclopedia,* Volume 15. Chicago: Field Enterprises Educational Corporation, 1974.

THE BALDWIN FARM
by Mike Terry

The family of John Baldwin lived in several houses in the Smyrna area, but the house that family members call "home" was the one located on the corner of Concord and Kings Springs roa Built between 1880 and 1900, it had a large front porch, three bedrooms, a large kitchen, living roo and parlor. The last Baldwin to move out was Grandma Jennie Baldwin, who sold the property American Legion Post #160 in 1962.

The house stood on 15 acres that included a large barn, smoke house, spring house, stora and repair shed, and, of course, an outhouse; a fresh water well was conveniently located next to t back porch. It was one of the few houses in Smyrna that had a circular driveway and its own wa storage tank.

The first occupants of the house were the Gautchy Family. Mr. Gautchy, who had brought h family from Germany, needed an ideal location from which to run his business. He selected this s for his new home and business because of its ample supply of fresh water and its location near the r line. Mr. Gautchy, a liquor distiller, had planned to build and operate, from this site in Smyrna, t first legal liquor distillery in Cobb County.

The liquor business was quite successful, even though many of the local churches objected its presence. With success came wealth, and Mrs. Gautchy pressured Mr. Gautchy to build her a ni home, one more fitting to their newfound wealth. Thus he constructed the landmark residence that st stands on Atlanta Street, across from Jonquil Plaza Shopping Center and next door to CVS Pharmac His next move was one that included relocating his liquor business to Vinings and eventually in Atlanta, where he operated until the Federal Government passed prohibition legislation, whi outlawed the manufacturing of all alcoholic beverages.

The house on the corner of Concord and King Springs roads was purchased by John Jac Baldwin about 1910. His last child, Mary, was born in this house in 1915. The Baldwins, farming t land behind the house, raised corn, wheat, and cotton. They also had a milk cow, a mule, chickens, a rabbits. In addition to being a farmer, John Baldwin was Smyrna's only rural mail carrier for ma years. Once the town became large enough, the postal service decided to build a larger post office a have its own postmaster. John, having applied for the position, was considered to be the obvio choice for the job. However, he died from a heart attack just a few days before his likely appointme He, at 60 years of age, was buried on his birthday, December 24,1933.

Ninth House

The **Medlin Farm** was on the corner of Concord and King Springs roads.

The Baldwin Farm
Corner of Concord and King Springs roads
Circa early Twentieth Century
Photo courtesy of Mike Terry

Seated: **Amanda Legg**, her daughter, **Jennie Legg Baldwin**, standing with Jennie's oldest son, **Voss**, and his son, **John Baldwin**, in the 1930s.
Courtesy of Mike Terry.

Mary Baldwin (Terry)
Smyrna High School Graduation Picture 1933.
Photo courtesy of Mike Terry.

Tenth House

Mr. and **Mrs. Jesse Macaulay Dunton** owned a farm on Concord Road in the middle of t Twentieth Century. Mrs. Dunton was the former Ruth Cooper of Atlanta's Bolton community. Th two children, Jesse and Dovia, named for their grandparents, grew up in this house. See *Coop Pickens Street* and *Fowler, King Springs Road.*

The Dunton property extended from the Medlin property to the Brown property, wh Tillman Memorial Methodist Church now stands. On this property Mr. Dunton owned two ren houses, one of which was located in the area now known as Concord Circle.

The Dunton house was on the site where Georgia Power Company is currently located a was locally known as the "Dunton Place." Jesse Macaulay Dunton, a farmer, grew large patches sweet potatoes, and many youth in the community worked seasonal jobs on this farm.

Jesse Dunton married JoAnn Paris. They had two children: Jesse Macaulay, named for h grandfather, and Tina Marie. Jesse Macaulay is deceased.

Tina Marie Dunton married Ken Smith. They had a daughter, Christy, and tw grandchildren.

Dovia Dunton married Bill Cox of Marietta. They had seven children: six daughters: Ali Cynthia, Jackie, Billie Ann, Patrice, and Katrina, and one son, Donald. Both Dovia and Bill a deceased.

NOTE: When the Dunton property was developed in the late 1940s and/or the early 195 McCauley Street was named for Mr. Jesse Macaulay Dunton. Unfortunately, the street is spell differently from Mr. Dunton's name: Macaulay versus McCauley, respectively.

Mr. Jesse Macaulay Dunton had a sister, Adella Dunton, known as "Della," who nev married. She lived on the north side of Concord Road. See *Dunton, north side of Concord Road.*

Benny Lou O'Bryant Tackett remembers Mr. Coby Norton's driving the school bus up t large hill in front of the Dunton house. "One day when it was raining and the road was very mudd Mr. Norton went to the front door of Mr. and Mrs. Dunton's house and asked Mrs. Ruth Dunton if could drive the school bus around their circular driveway to bypass the hill in front of their house; s gave him permission to do so. Afterwards, on days like that, we always rode on the Dunton driveway. This kept us children from having to get off the bus and walk up the hill."

Eleventh House

The **Brown Family** lived in a beautiful, white, ten-room house that was on the property the present Tillman Memorial Methodist Church, the revival of the old Tillman Church Chap located three miles west of Smyrna on Concord Road The Country Road. The chapel was named honor of James LaFayette Tillman, a noted evangelist/singer of that period. The property where t Chapel was located was deeded to the North Georgia Conference of the Methodist Church about 18 and abandoned in the 1930s. See *Tillman Chapel, north side of Concord Road, The Country Road.*

Mr. and **Mrs. Gregory Billups Brown** had two children: **Ida Lee** and **Alton Park Brown**. Mr. Brown was a potato farmer.

Ida Lee Brown, who never married, was a school teacher. A member of First Methodi Church, Ida Lee lived in the family home until age required smaller accommodations. She then mov to Collier Drive, in the Forest Hills community, where she resided the rest of her life.

Gregory Billups Brown House
south side of Concord Road
(Present site of Tillman Memorial Methodist Church)
Picture courtesy of Tillman Memorial Methodist Church.

Alton Parker Brown, Sr., and his wife, Virginia, known as "Ginny," had two children: Alton Parker, Jr., and Katherine.

Virginia Brown later married William A. McAdams, known as "Mack." See *McAdams, eleventh house, south side of Spring Street.*

Both Brown School and Brown Road were named in honor of the Gregory Billups Brown Family. Miss Ida Lee Brown, the last resident of the house, in her later years handled the disposition of the Brown property: to Tillman Memorial Methodist Church; the Cobb County Board of Education for the building of Brown Elementary School; Cobb County, for the building of Brown Road. It has been called to my attention that Sharon Baptist Church was also built on part of the Brown Farm.

NOTE: The information regarding Tillman Memorial Methodist Church was gleaned from a scrapbook (containing the history of old Tillman Chapel and Tillman Memorial Methodist Church) loaned to me by Tillman Memorial Methodist Church.

It has been mentioned that **"Preacher Howard"** lived in a house (near the southeast corner of Access Highway) facing Concord Road. During the days of my youth, Clybe Dunton's Garage, on the southeast corner of Concord Road, faced Access Highway.

CONCORD ROAD
The Country Road
North Side

When I was a kid growing up in Smyrna, Concord Road, also called the "Covered Bridge Road," was an unpaved country road, sparsely populated and synonymous with Ruffs' Mill. The road ran then, as it does today, from the Access Highway (now South Cobb Drive), through the Concord Covered Bridge, and to Floyd Road, Concord Road ended at Concord Baptist Church. (The Access Highway, which was also referred to as "Bomber Plant Road," was built during World War II to accommodate traffic going to the newly built Bell Bomber Plant in Marietta.) I knew some of the families that lived out toward the bridge. All of the children east of there attended Smyrna Elementary and High schools.

Appreciation is extended to John Dickson, Ann Pickens, Linda Ruff Smith, and Benny Lou Tackett, all of whom grew up on Concord Road west of the Access Highway. (John Dickson and Benny Lou O'Bryant Tackett have lived on Concord Road 61 and 62 years, respectively.) Appreciation also goes to Stephen Ruddell and Alice Gibson Vaughn for sharing their memories of the Patterson Family and to Rosemary Moon for data on the Moon Family.

First House

The **Simmerson Family** lived in this small house, on well-kept property. They had a son, **Charles**. Benny Lou O'Bryant Tackett remembers that after her family moved to North Cooper Lake Road, in December 1942, she and Charles, both in the fourth grade, rode the same bus to school.

T.L. Dickson
Cobb County Commissioner
1967-1974

Mr. and **Mrs. T.L. Dickson** and their sons, **Lamar** and **John**, (one of the prominent families on Concord Road in the days of my youth), purchased this house, which was a small well-kept place at that time. After moving here, they renovated it into a very nice, upscale home in that era. (Mrs. Dickson was the former Ruth Jolly from Rockmart.) Prior to coming to Smyrna in 1943, Mr. and Mrs. Dickson owned and operated a grocery store in Atlanta, not far from the State Capitol. See *Jolly, west side of Old Concord Road.*

T.L. Dickson purchased acreage on both north and south sides of Concord Road west of the Access Highway (now known as South Cobb Drive). He built a shopping center near the southwest corner of the Access Highway at Concord Road. According to Dickson Family information, it was known to be the first shopping center in Cobb County. Definitely the first one in Smyrna, it was in operation many years before the opening of Belmont Hills Shopping Center, in 1954. Mr. Dickson operated a grocery store in Dickson Shopping Center until the 1960s, at which time he leased the building and property south of the shopping center to Atlantic and Pacific Tea Company, whose grocery store (A & P Food Store) was operated there for many years. (This building still stands just north of Smyrna Hill Drive.) A community leader in many ways, T.L Dickson served as a Cobb County Commissioner, 1966-1974.

On the north side of Concord Road, about two blocks from the intersection of the Access Highway, was the Dickson House. Later on, John and Lamar (in my generation), built their homes alongside Lamar, on the east side of his parents, and John, on the west side; there each son raised his own family. I would say there was a "Dickson Family Compound" within those two blocks, now ending at Lamar Circle.

NOTE: The Dickson House, still standing, is currently the site of Roeske Chiropractic Clinic.

Lamar Dickson married Peggy Duncan, the only child of Mr. and Mrs. D. Eugene Duncan, who lived on South Atlanta Road. Peggy and Lamar, both graduates of Smyrna High School, had two children: Cindy and Cliff. With the family's having moved from the "Dickson Family Compound" to McEachern Farms in West Cobb County, their children graduated from McEachern High School, in that area. Both Peggy and Lamar are deceased.

John Dickson married Marlene Hall from Moultrie. They had two daughters: Debbie and Donna. (John and Marlene are members of First Baptist Church.) After the intersection became more commercial, John and Marlene moved their house farther out Concord Road, just west of the Bennett Woods subdivision.

John loves to tell the story about the first time he ever saw Marlene. Visiting with her sister and brother-in-law, Hilda and John Moore, Marlene dropped by John's dad's grocery store to buy a loaf of bread. John, who was working there, said, "That was the most expensive loaf of bread I ever sold."

After his dad's death, John assumed the operation of Dickson Shopping Center. The shopping center (now called Dickson Center), where Marlene and Debbie own and operate a florist, is a vibrant, successful area in the commercial life of Smyrna.

T.L. Dickson, John, and other members of the Dickson Family have been a driving force in the success of the shopping center at South Cobb Drive and Concord Road for more than 60 years. Their contribution to the business life of the city has been a strong and lasting one.

Second House

Mr. and **Mrs. Grover Cleveland Patterson,** in the late 1940s purchased property on the north side of the road, in the area between what we know today as Lamar Circle and Old Concord Road. Eventually several members of Mr. Patterson's family built houses in this area; the last members of this family sold their property for the development of Concord Lakes subdivision. See *Patterson, north side of Medlin Street.*

Third House

The Redd Dairy

Mr. and **Mrs. Claude Redd** lived in this rock house, located in the area where Dr. Jim Pitts has his dental office. The Redds had five children: **Douglas**, **Gene**, **Maxie**, **Herbert**, and **Hoyt**. Mrs Redd was the former Ethel Samples. In the 1930s and 1940s, the Redds owned and operated Redd's Dairy Farm in the area north of Concord, Old Concord, and Hurt roads. Mary Lou Redd Cochran remembers walking from the home and grocery store of her maternal grandparents, Mr. and Mrs Nemory Chadwick, on the north side of Concord Road, (nearer Smyrna), to her paternal grandparents' dairy farm. See *west side of King Springs Road* and *west side of Concord Road.*

NOTE: According to information from Redd Family members, in the 1940s the Redds moved their dairy to Hightower Road in Atlanta.

Mr. and Mrs. Spear Stone

Mr. and **Mrs. Spear Stone** moved to this rock house after the Redds had vacated. Here they, too, operated a dairy farm. Mrs. Stone's given name was Vinnie. They had one son, **Hoyt**, whose wife's name was Annie. Spear was a brother of Henry Grady Stone.

I remember Spear Stone very well, particularly as a regular checker player (along with my dad, Roy Wood, and others) at Paul Clayton's Gulf Service Station, on the east side of Atlanta Street. Paul had a bench with a checkerboard in the center. Two players would sit "straddle legged" across the bench, where, in some cases, they would play for hours.

Fourth House

Mr. and **Mrs. Henry Grady Stone**, of Gainesville, in the late 1940s purchased a farm which extended from about where the Concord Office Park is currently located to the beginning of Hurt Road, almost directly across from North Cooper Lake Road. Along with his brother, Spear, Henry Grady operated a dairy business. Mrs. Stone was the former Mamie Nalley. They had two daughters: **Jewel** and **Kathryn**.

Mr. and Mrs. Henry Grady Stone moved from Concord Road in the early 1950s to a 100-acre farm they bought in the northeastern area of Marietta.

Jewell Stone married Winton C. Coker of Gainesville; they had three children, Ronald C., H. Ryan, and Nancy Renee, and eight grandchildren.

Ronald C. Coker, Sr., married Elaine Eskew; both were Campbell High School graduates, as were their children: Ronald Coker, Jr., known "Ron, Jr.," and Rhonda. Ronald C. Coker joined his uncle, Ed Wait, who established Artistic Pools, Inc.; they have been in business 48 years. See *Eskew, east side of Dunn Street.*

Ronald Coker, Jr., known as "Ron," a graduate of the University of Georgia, married Julie Lollar of Colorado. They had four daughters: Haven, Ceely, Olivia, and Georgia. Ron, Jr., upon graduating from college, joined his dad in his business, Artistic Pools, Inc.

Rhonda Coker graduated from Auburn University, in Montgomery, Alabama. She married John Sillesky; they had two daughters: Eliza and Emmy. Rhonda, a former Cobb County teacher, now teaches in Dawson County.

Ryan Coker married Lily O'Conner of Marietta. Both graduates of Sprayberry High School, they had one son, Roger. Ryan and Lily are divorced.

Nancy Coker married Robbie Lee Joines. They had two children: Christy and Matthew.

Kathryn Stone married Ed Wait. They had a daughter, Sheila, who married Colin Thompson. Sheila and Colin had two sons: Christopher and Stephen.

Fifth House

Mr. and **Mrs. LaFelle Ruff** resided on the north side of the road, in the triangle between Concord and Hurt roads. Their house was in the grove, about where the new Masonic Lodge is located. Mrs. Ruff was the former Lucille Glisson of Hawkinsville. The Ruffs had three children: **Vicki Lucille, Rex LaFelle Ruff, Jr.**, and **Linda Louise Ruff**.

Sixth House

Mr. and **Mrs. Wansie Hambrick** moved from Cooper Lake Road, in the 1950s, to this house, located on several acres of land just west of the LaFelle Ruff Family. Benny Lou O'Bryant Tackett, who grew up on Concord Road, remembers this house being referred to as the "Glover Place." Mrs. Hambrick was the former Dorothy Vining of Thomaston. Wansie and Dorothy had four children: **Wayne, Marion, Jesse**, and **Gary**.

Wansie Hambrick, in the sawmill business, worked for Tatum Lumber Company in Oakdale. Because he helped to organize the Smyrna Little League baseball program in the early 1950s, the Little League field at Brinkley Park, named for him, is now called Hambrick Field. Mr. Hambrick died in 1974.

Wayne Hambrick married Rebecca Shirley, known as "Becky." They had three children: Elaine, Shannon, and Kevin.

After Wayne and "Becky" divorced, Wayne married Andrea Alexander Holloway, who had two children from a previous marriage: Nathaniel Holloway, known as "Nat," and Alex. Wayne and Andrea live in Monroe.

Marion Hambrick and his first wife, Penny, had no children. He and his second wife, Barbara, had two children: Amy and Joy. Marion and Barbara live in West Palm Beach, Florida.

Jesse Hambrick, Sr., married Chenita Clonts; they had three children: Jesse Hambrick, Jr., Heather, and Tondy. Jesse and Chenita divorced; Jesse is living in Bremen.

Gary Hambrick married and had one child. He and his second wife, Merian, who had no children, live in Powder Springs.

Seventh House

The Robert Daniell Family

Sara Daniell Godfrey, a great-granddaughter of Robert Daniell, and his second wife, Margaret Fleming, shared the following information. After the Civil War, Robert Daniell built this house, on the north side of Concord Road, on the site where Oak Knoll Drive intersects with Concord Road. The house was a single-story brick one with a basement. The bricks, handmade from clay, were dug and fired on the property. The walls were about 18 inches thick. Off a hall, which went from the front to the back of the house, were bedrooms: on the left, one for company; on the right, the first for Pa and Ma; the next for the girls; and the back one for the boys. The kitchen was beyond the boys' room, and beyond it was a large porch. The house was demolished in the early 1950s; Rem Bennett, Sr., began developing the Bennett Woods subdivision across the street in the very early 1960s.

NOTE: There is some dispute as to when Robert Daniell came to Cobb County, but the traditional history says it was about 1850. However, the U.S. Census for that year shows his living in Clarke County. Robert's sister, Rachel, married William Barber; they moved to Cobb County in the 1830s. Speculation is that William Barber told Robert and his brothers about the attributes of Cobb County, and thus the two brothers came here to live. Steven Daniell settled in the Mableton area. Two other brothers, Alfred and Moses Daniell, settled in Douglas County.

When Robert Daniell moved to Cobb County, he built his house by Nickajack Creek, near the Covered Bridge. He and Martin L. Ruff developed an industrial complex: the Concord Woolen Mills, a gristmill for flour and meal, and a sawmill all powered by water from the creek. The Concord Woolen Mill was constructed from stones from the banks and bed of Nickajack Creek. On the property today stands the ruins of three buildings, not accessible to the general public.

NOTE: The gristmill is still standing, but the machinery was removed in the 1920s. The covered bridge, built by Robert Daniell, is still standing. This area is much more visible today than in the past because of the adjoining Silver Comet Trail, built along the old railroad bed. This idea, conceived in the early 1990s, is still a work in progress in some areas.

Robert, one of Smyrna's most prominent citizens in the mid 1880s, was born February 2, 1813, and died June 21, 1881. An elder in the Primitive Baptist Church, Robert Daniell often preached at both Maloney Springs and Collins Springs Primitive Baptist churches.

Robert Daniell and his first wife, **Naomi Barnett**, had nine children: **Martha, Olive Ann, William, Catherine, Greenberry, George Lumkin, Robert P.**, **John Sidney**, and **Pickney Young**.

Robert and his second wife, **Margaret C. Fleming Daniell**, had seven children: **David Patman**, **Pliney Franklin**, **Mary Naomi**, **Jesse Layden**, **James Jordan**, **Ida**, and **Amanda Jane**, known as "Jennie."

According to family information, Robert Daniell was mentioned in Sarah Gober Temple's book *The First Hundred Years, A Short History of Cobb County*. More information about Robert Daniell and his family is available in the Smyrna Museum

Mr. and Mrs. Pliney Frank Daniell, Sr.

Mr. Pliney Frank Daniell, Sr., known as Frank, was born August 25, 1867, in the Daniell home (on Concord Road), built by his father, Robert Daniell. Frank Daniell lived in this home most of his adult life, and all of his children were born here. Late in his life, Frank moved to Bank Street, where he died in 1947. He is buried in the Daniell Cemetery, located at the intersection of Cloudland Drive and Havilon Way, in the Bennett Woods subdivision, off Concord Road. The land for this cemetery was given by Robert Daniell, as inscribed near the entrance to the cemetery: "This property, 300 feet square deeded by Robert Daniell revised platt book number 1, page 80 to the white citizens within 1 ½ miles of same cemetery purposes."

Pliney Frank and his wife, **Frances Elmira Carmichael**, known as "Fannie," married on Frank's 22nd birthday, August 25, 1889. Fannie, born January 6, 1868, and Frank had eight children: **Brent, Ewell, Mazza, Ethel, Carl, Pliney Frank, Jr.**, **Alma**, and **Jewell**. See *Daniell, east side of King Springs Road.*

Frances, a member of the Carmichael Family in Oakdale, south of Smyrna, died July 30, 1910, from a reaction to drugs administered for an asthma attack.

P.F. Daniell Home on Concord Road, Circa 1902
The Daniell House was built in 1872 by Robert Daniell.
L-R: **Brent**, **Ethel**, **Fanny**, (she was pregnant with P.F., Jr.)
Frank, Sr., **Carl**, **Mazza**, and **Ewell**

Homer Black and **Ronnie Cochran**
Brinkley Baseball Park
Circa Probably 1980s
Courtesy of Ronnie Cochran
Cochran Floor Coverings

Ewell Daniell
Casualty of War
World War I

Ewell Daniell, the oldest son of Frank and "Fannie," was drafted into the United States Army during World War I. He died in combat. Before his death, he had married an English girl; they had one son, Ewell Daniel, Jr. Ewell's English wife chose to stay in England after the War. Therefore, the American Daniell Family did not know Ewell, Jr., who also married an English girl, named Frances, and had two children: Pam and David. In 1968 the English Daniells came to America for a visit with their American kin. After returning to England, they packed their possessions and came back to the United States to live. Ewell, Jr. is deceased; Frances and their children live in Marietta.

Sara Daniell Godfrey remembers her grandfather's living on Bank Street when she was a student at Smyrna School in the 1950s. She recalls "slipping away" from school early and going to see her grandfather, a "kindly" gentleman, who did not tell her mother she had "slipped away" from school. Sara treasures those times spent with her grandfather. (Sara Daniell Godfrey says her grandfather's house was on the north side of Concord Road, on a knoll, near the entrance to Bennett Woods North subdivision.)

In 1969 on Havilon Way, in the Bennett Woods subdivision, Lillie and I built a house; (to date, we have lived 36 years in the second house on the east side of Havilon Way, which intersects with Concord Road, across the street from where the Daniell house stood and dead ends at the Daniell Cemetery.) The Daniell Cemetery, a pretty place is well maintained by the Daniell descendants. When Clint Buckner, one of my neighbors died, in 2002, his family chose this cemetery for his burial place. Tommy Harper, another long-time Havilon Way resident, is also buried there.

My editor, Joyce Reagin, said that when she and her family moved to Cloudland Drive, in the Bennett Woods subdivision, her daughter, Kathy, six years old at the time, chose a bedroom because the view would be the Daniell Cemetery. She also shared that a few days after they moved into their house, she missed Kathy and her older sister, Elizabeth, but soon found them, picking blackberries at the entrance to Daniell Cemetery.

NOTE: John W. Meeler shared that his father, James Oscar Meeler, purchased the above house and 80 acres of land from P.F. Daniell, March 10, 1922. Mrs. Meeler sold the property to Rufus Pritchet, August 5, 1943.

Mr. and **Mrs. Dewey Wilson**
by Benny Lou O'Bryant Tackett

Mr. and **Mrs. Dewey Wilson** moved to this house after the Daniells vacated. The Wilsons had several children who attended Smyrna School with her: **Martha Sue**, **Charles**, **Bobbie Neal**, **Merle**, and **Lewis**. Merle, the sweetest and most loving child, was a special one, suffering from Down's Syndrome. Martha Sue, being the oldest child in the family, was given the responsibility of taking care of Merle, who, seeming to get such joy from just being around us older children, would laugh and clap his little fat hands. Lewis Wilson was born after the family moved to this house. A beautiful, chubby, blond-haired baby, he was also in Martha Sue's care.

Martha Sue Wilson married Ezell Coxe, who worked for Pfarner's Cabinet Shop, located on Concord Road and behind Dickson's Service Station. When Pfarner's Cabinet Shop closed, Martha and Ezell moved to Forsyth County, where Ezell's family lived. Though crippled (I believe as a result of childhood polio) Ezell was a good-looking fellow and a hard worker. I kept in touch with him and Martha for a long time through mutual friends; I know that Ezell died many years ago, but I do not know where Martha Sue currently lives.

One day when Charles Wilson was in a fifth-grade class, a girl in front of him was sharpening a pencil with a pocket knife. Charles was curiously looking over her shoulder when the knife slipped and went into his eye. It was a horrible accident! I still shudder at the pain he must have endured! He wore a black patch over that eye for a long, long time before getting an artificial eye, to which he never seemed to become accustomed. Often he would take the eye out and lay it on the edge of the desk during class!

Eighth House

The Rock House

The little rock house that stood on the tract of land across from what is known today as Highview Drive was built by **Mr. Rogers**, who, according to Benny Lou O'Bryant Tackett, "gathered the rocks from around the property and other places in the area for building the house himself. It has been said that Mr. Rogers drowned in Cooper's Lake after his boat overturned while he was fishing with G.V. Westbrook.

After Mr. Rogers' death, and at some time in the 1930s, Ralph and Willie Argo bought this property and moved Willie's family, the Blacks from Bartow County, to this house."

Mr. and Mrs. Bart Black

Mr. Bart Black and his second wife, **Bessie**, lived here. Mr. Black and his first wife had four children: a daughter, **Willie**, a son, **Homer**, another daughter, **Clifford**, and another son **Howard.** Mr. Bart Black was a brother of Mrs. Bessie Stone, who lived across the road. See *Stone, south side of Concord Road.*

Willie Black married Ralph Argo. They had one son, Alan. See *Argo, east side of Hughes Street.*

Willie Black Argo and her husband, Ralph, who was a Smyrna policeman at one time, lived on the east side of Hughes Street, where Ralph owned several businesses. The Argos, having plans to build a house on this farm property on Concord Road, would come out often and survey the site of their dream home.

Willie and Ralph, married 18 years without children, had recently learned that they were expecting a baby. One afternoon, upon returning home from visiting Willie's parents and while walking across their future home site, Ralph suffered a heart attack and died. In due time, Willie gave birth to a baby boy, whom she named Alan. Willie returned to work for Sears, Roebuck & Company on Ponce de Leon Avenue in Atlanta, where she was employed until she retired. Though continuing to live on Hughes Street, she kept her property on Concord Road as long as she lived. Never did Willie get to build her dream house; but, in later years, her son, Alan, there built a house where he was a resident for several years.

Homer Black lived in the rock house along with his father and stepmother. I'm sure that every town has its special people, those who add dimension to others' lives by just being there; Smyrna had such a person in Homer Black.

I recall that Homer, having worked for Pete Logan, at Logan Construction Company, had a reputation of being a good employee and being happy wherever he was, even at work. His task was to mix mortar and roll it in a wheelbarrow to the job site. He always wanted to do a good job.

Homer loved most sports, but he especially loved baseball and basketball and seldom, if ever, missed a game. He liked them all, and you could count on Homer's being there. He also loved University of Georgia basketball, and that pleased me. But then, he also liked Georgia Tech basketball. Nancy Argo shared, "When Homer was a child, his dad played semi-pro ball." Homer had his own baseball field in his back yard. If he liked a team, there he would let the players practice.

Homer's speech impediment did not hinder his "rooting" for his favorite team that was playing—which was both sides. I always knew there was someone pulling for me when I played ball. I can hear his yelling now, "Come on, Pete, hit that ball!"

Homer was well known in the neighborhood and throughout Smyrna. He would walk all over town to get to a ball game. Often, however, people would stop to pick him up, especially those on their way to a ball game. I doubt that he missed many games at Brinkley Park, which was his favorite place.

I believe that, if Homer had been born 50 years later, his speech impediment might have been corrected. But I also believe that his quality of life suited him just fine. He was happy.

Homer died a few years ago; for a long time it did not seem right for him not to be at the games or walking around town. Those of us who knew Homer knew the joy of watching a game through our association with him. He made it so much fun! Homer Black, with a terrific memory was a walking encyclopedia when it came to ball games. He never forgot that I played basketball in high school; thus, when Homer would see me, he would always bring up something about a game from the past. I still miss him!

NOTE: The Black/Argo property was eventually sold for the development of Concord Grove subdivision.

A Tribute to Homer Black
by Benny Lou O'Bryant Tackett

Homer Black was a very interesting and well-known resident of our neighborhood. He was about 19 years old when his family moved to Concord Road. I was 10, my brother Lamar was 12, and my brother Reginald was 9. With Homer as our playmate, we spent many hours playing baseball and pitching horseshoes. He was good at both, but baseball was his passion. Homer had a speech impediment that made it difficult for many people to understand what he was saying; but having grown up with him, neither I, nor any of my family, ever had a problem communicating with him. He called me 'Manna Lou' and my brother 'Mar.'

Homer loved all sporting events except 'feetball.' He just never got into 'feetball!' He would attend all the high school basketball games, and he could tell a listener who scored every point. One who also loved Little League baseball, he could always be found at one City of Smyrna baseball park or another during the summer. He had a loud voice, and everybody could hear him all over the park when he cheered for his favorite team.

I have wondered if Homer were only mildly autistic; if so, this might have accounted for his impeccable memory and apptitude with figures. He could remember, for instance, who pitched a certain World Series game 10 to 20 years before, who scored points, and the final score!

Because there were no 'special education' classes for people like Homer, with his handicap, he never went to school. Though never learning to read, he was a genius at math. (He kept everything in his head.) Homer worked for many years as a hod carrier for a brick mason. At the end of each week, he would know exactly how many hours he had worked and how much pay he was due. He had his account at the Bank of Smyrna, and he knew exactly what his balance was at all times. There he would take his check and relate to the teller just how much money he wanted to deposit and how much he wanted in cash; he would tell her his new balance!

He could recall the birth date of every person he knew and would embarrass many of us by yelling out in a crowd: for example, "Manna Lou, you gonna be (whatever my age) on September 23rd." We had a birthday box at Sunday School for many years; on someone's birthday, the person was asked to come up and deposit in the box as many cents as he or she was old. The money was used at Christmas to buy food for the needy or to give a party for the children. Homer never let anyone get away without depositing birthday money. He would start reminding an individual weeks in advance about saving money. On Sunday morning he would yell out, "Okay, (person's name), put your money in the box. Your birthday was last (Wednesday or whatever day)." If one happened to be absent on his or her birthday, Homer would remind that person the next Sunday or the next month. He did not forget, nor did he let anyone else forget, a birthday!

Homer walked everywhere, but he was so well known that he would not get far from home before someone would offer him a ride. He liked to hang around Dickson Shopping Center or Belmont Hills and just talk to people. Folks new to the areas did not always understand Homer; thus there were some complaints about him, and he was asked not to frequent some business places. Little did many know he was a simple, hardworking man who loved people and life and made the best of what God had given him!

Clifford Black, the second daughter, was married and lived in Atco (in Bartow County).

Howard Black was married and lived in White, where he owned property and was a businessman.

Ninth House

The Clay Families

The Clay property abutted the Black property on the east side and extended westward, connecting with the J.Y. Wooten property. The following information about the Clay families was furnished by Benny Lou O'Bryant Tackett.

"The sons of **Mr.** and **Mrs. Henry Clay** were our neighbors on Concord Road. I do not know when Mr. Henry Clay died, but Mrs. Clay had died a year or two before we moved into the neighborhood. The Clays, who owned much acreage along both sides of Concord Road, had four sons: **Roy**, **Robert**, **Walter**, and **John**. Roy left the family farm when he married Sara and moved to a small town in South Georgia. After Sara died, Roy moved back and lived with Robert until his death. Because a sister, Josie, died shortly before we moved to the neighborhood, we never knew her. The Clays were hog farmers; often in the summer months our neighborhood took on a distinctive but not altogether pleasant odor! The Clays were wonderful people who had lived in the neighborhood for years. Only one of the Clay sons had children." See *Hollis Dunton, south side of Concord Road, The Country Road.*

Mr. and Mrs. Walter Clay

"**Walter Clay** was married late in life to a fine woman named **Fannie Brand**, who came to reside with him in the original Clay home, which stood on the site of what is now the entrance to Deerwood sudivision. A beautiful old home with a long, wide front porch and an "L"-shaped porch on the west side, it is another house that I grieve for—not only for its history but also for the beauty and elegance with which it adorned the land. It was bulldozed to make room for yet another subdivision!"

Tenth House

"**Robert Clay's** wife, **Lena**, had a daughter named **Martha**. After Lena died, Robert sold his farm property to a developer who built Deerwood subdivision, on the south side of Concord Road. Robert then built another house on the north side of Concord Road, next door to his brother Walter. (Here Robert lived until his death.) On the west side of his new home, Robert also built a house for his stepdaughter, **Martha**, and her husband, **J.D. Kite**, who were residents there for years. After J.D.'s death, Martha became increasingly despondent and was subsequently diagnosed with Alzheimer's disease; she then went to live with her daughter, Mary Brown, and Mary's husband, Jack, in Douglas County. Martha died at the age of 87."

Eleventh House

"**John B. Clay** and his wife, the former **Lucille Sinard**, built this house, on the northeast corner of the property across the street and about 200 hundred yards from the O'Bryant house. John and Lucille had one daughter, **Jane**.

"Jane Clay married Jimmy Adams; they live in Jasper.

"Still standing, the Clay House is currently the home of Sam Whitfield.

"Lucille Clay's mother, Nettie Austin Sinard, was a sister of Mr. Paul Austin and Mr. Chester Austin, Sr." See *Austin, south side of Sunset Avenue* and *west side of North Cooper Lake Road.*

NOTE: The following paragraphs to the Twelfth and Thirteenth houses contain information provided by Benny Lou O'Bryant Tackett. She also furnished the data on Tillman Methodist Church and the one-room schoolhouse.

Twelfth House

J.Y. Wooten
Mayor of Smyrna
1945

"**Mr.** and **Mrs. J.Y. Wooten** were residents farther down Concord Road. Mr. Wooten, the owner of J.Y. Wooten Real Estate Agency in Smyrna, served as Mayor of Smyrna in 1945. The Wootens had a daughter, **Jane**, a principal at Venetian Hills Elementary School, in Atlanta, according to Joyce Reagin. After living here for many years, Jane sold the property for the building of Bentley Park subdivision." See *north side of Medlin Street.*

Thirteenth House

"The **Denny Family** built this house, where they lived until the latter part of the 1990s. Next door and to the rear of this home was property that belonged to Mr. J.Y. Wooten."

Tillman Methodist Church

"The North Georgia Methodist Conference owned property just north of the Denny home. (I believe the bridge over the East-West Connector may have been built about where this property was located.) I remember that, on the property, there was a small building, called Tillman Chapel. After this building burned, the congregation met in the school building next door."

One-Room Schoolhouse

"A one-room schoolhouse, owned by the Cobb County Board of Education, was located next door to the church. Classes were held in the little building until the school was consolidated with Smyrna School. After the school was relocated, Tillman Methodist Church burned completely; the congregation then began holding their services in the school building. The membership finally merged with First Methodist Church in Smyrna.

"The little school building stood vacant for several years, or until a group of people in the neighborhood (John Clay, Ben O'Bryant, G.V. Westbrook, and others, with the sponsorship of First Baptist Church of Smyrna), began holding Sunday School classes in the little school building. Permission from the Cobb County School Board was secured to use the building for a church. The first classes were taught on May 8, 1947, with 11 people from the neighborhood and 4 or 5 members from First Baptist Church of Smyrna in attendance. The congregation grew; in 1949 a new church, first named Happy Hill, then later changed to Sharon Baptist, was built on South Cobb Drive. It is interesting that the property on South Cobb Drive was also purchased from the Browns, who owned a large tract of land on Concord Road, including what is now Brown Elementary School. Later a group of people who had formerly been members of the old Tillman Methodist Church came together and established a new church on the former site of Miss Ida Brown's beautiful home on Concord Road. The church is now known as Tillman Memorial Methodist Church."

Fourteenth House

Mr. and **Mrs**. **Jeff Moon** lived here. They had three children: twin daughters, **Mary** and **Martha**, and a son, **Jeff**, **Jr**., known as "Junior."

Jeff Moon was the son of David Littleton Moon, known as "Lit," an ordained minister, and his wife, the former Ella Crowe. "Lit" and Ella had four other children: Ed, Jeff, Harry, Mary Ella, and George.

Ed Moon married Sally Willoughby. They had three children: Raymond, Betty, and Joe.

Harry Moon and his wife, Margaret, had one daughter, Rosemary. They lived on Cooper Lake Road, near Cooper Lake.

Mary Ella Moon married Carver Smith. They had two daughters: Sarah and Betty.

George Moon, a minister, and his wife, Odene, lived on Matthews Street. See *George Moon, west side of Matthews Street.*

NOTE: Ella Mae Crowe Moon was a sister of Ed and Jeff Crowe. Ed Crowe was the father of my mother, Dora Crowe Wood.

The Mack Greenway Family

Mr. and **Mrs**. **Mack Greenway** resided here with their children: **Jeannine**, **Maxine**, **Billy**, and a son whose name I do not recall.

The Seaboard Railroad Bridge

The Seaboard Railroad right-of-way was converted to the Silver Comet Trail.

Fifteenth House

The **Thorman Famliy** were residents of this house, which is still located on a large hill on the north side of Concord Road, between the Seaboard Railroad Bridge (now Silver Comet Trail) and the Concord Covered Bridge.

The Concord Covered Bridge

The Concord Covered Bridge, now an historic site, listed on the National Historic Register, was constructed before the Civil War. In the Smyrna Museum there is much history regarding this bridge.

CONCORD ROAD
The Country Road
South Side

Appreciation is extended to the following people for furnishing information about the former Concord Road residents during the middle of the Twentieth Century: John Dickson, Benny Lou

O'Bryant Tackett, Jane Brooks Daniel, Carolyn Dunton Flythe, Mary Sanders McEntyre, Charles Sanders, and Rex Ruff.

First House

Mr. and **Mrs**. **Pfarner** lived in this house, located on Concord Road immediately behind Dickson Service Station. The Pfarners owned and operated Pfarner Cabinet Company, located where BB&T Bank presently stands. According to local lore, the cabinet shop is literally buried beneath the bank.

In the middle of the Twentieth Century, between the Pfarner house and cabinet shop, there was a dirt lane, which led southward to three residences: those of the Otwells, Jennings, and Bowmans.

The Otwell Family

Mr. and **Mrs**. **Johnny Otwell**, in 1949, moved to a garage apartment which was located on this property, behind the Pfarner Cabinet Shop. The Otwells had two daughters: Harriett and Mary Ann.

Harriett Otwell married and divorced. She later married Jim McClendon, a widower with four children: three daughters (Cathy, Marcia, Cindy) and a son (Chris). Harriett and Jim, who had a son, Jimmy, live in Smyrna.

Mary Ann Otwell, who married Don Carroll, is employed at Wellstar Hospital Administrative Office. See *Carroll, west side of Roswell Street*.

Johnny Otwell, a member of a large family, was born and raised in the Bethel community, out Spring Road, where he attended Bethel School. He was employed by Myron Dwoskin in Atlanta, where he did interior decorating and painting; his salary was $5.00 per hour.

Before moving to this house in the mid 1940s, the Otwells rented a small house about one-fourth mile off Concord Road. Then they rented one side of Mrs. Ruth Dunton's house; from there they moved to this garage apartment. After living in one rental house or the other, Mrs. Otwell, when her daughters were teenagers and after her divorce, was thrilled to be able to buy a house on Lee Road in the Oakdale community, with $50.00 per month payments. There she lived for many years, or until she had to move to a nursing home.

Mrs. Otwell, the former Virginia Howington, was born in Powder Springs. When she was 14 years old, Virginia and her mother moved to the old part of Smyrna. Virginia, one of the first operators in the Smyrna Telephone Exchange Building, had four sisters and one brother: Molly, Lucile, Annie Mae, Ruby, and William.

Molly Howington married George Tinsley.

Lucile Howington married Floyd Schaeffer.

Annie Mae Howington, who married Watt Gresham from South Georgia, was at one time Postmistress in Helena and McRae.

Ruby Howington married Lamar Couey.

William Howington married Mildred.

The Jennings Family

Mr. and **Mrs. Joseph Franklin Jennings, Sr.** in the late 1940s moved to this residence located behind the Pfarner Cabinet Shop. Mr. Jennings, known as "Joe," and Mrs. Jennings, whose given name was Bertie, had two children: **Joseph Franklin, Jr.**, also known as "Joe," and **Gwen.** After "Joe" graduated from Campbell High School, in 1956, Gwen and her parents moved to Florida, where Gwen graduated from high school.

The Bowman Family

Mr. and **Mrs. Walter O. Bowman, Jr.**, lived in the second small house located behind the Pfarner Cabinet Shop. They had two children: **Walter O. Bowman III**, known as "Pete," and **Margie.** "Pete" Bowman, who graduated from Campbell High School in the Class of 1955, is currently living in Pennsylvania.

NOTE: The postal addresses of the three residences located behind Pfarner Cabinet Shop were Route 2, Concord Road, Smyrna, Georgia.

NOTE: There was some farm land located between the Pfarner property and that of Hollis Hill Dunton.

Second House

Mr. and **Mrs. Hollis Hill Dunton**, in the middle of the Twentieth Century, owned much land which abutted the T.L. Dickson property and extended westward to North Cooper Lake Road. Their property extended southward from Concord Road and encompassed what is now Smyrna Hill Drive and Sherwood Road and included Sherwood Mobile Home Park and Smyrna Home Park, on the northwest side of Sherwood Road. The Dunton home stood near the southeast corner of the intersection of Sherwood and Concord roads; Smyrna Fire Station #2 now stands about where their home was located.

Hollis Hill Dunton and his wife, the former **Leola Clay**, a descendant of Henry Clay, had five children: **Douglas**, known as "Doug," **Hollis Clybe**, known as "Clybe," **Glenn Aubrey**, known as "Aubrey," **Maurice**, and a daughter, **Mary Ella.** See *Clay Family, south side of Concord Road, The Country Road.*

Mrs. Leola Clay Dunton, a college graduate (rare for a lady of her age in the middle of the Twentieth Century) was a prolific artist. Her specialties were landscapes and famous houses. According to some of her younger family members and friends, "she could turn any object into a beauty." One friend told that she remembers that Leola, painting a gallon milk jug, turned it into a beautiful piece of art. Much of her artistry is still enjoyed in the homes of some of her family members and at least one friend, with whom I spoke. Mrs. Dunton also enjoyed reading. In fact, she named her children according to subjects in her favorite books. For instance, Clybe, a Scottish name, means "cliff dweller." At the time Maurice was born, Leola was reading French novels. Mary Ella's name may have been selected from a combination of two books with France as their settings.

<u>Douglas Dunton</u> married Nettie Conley of Alabama. Previously married, she had some children; but she and Douglas had no children. Douglas built, then owned and operated what is referred to as Sherwood Forest Home Park, located on the east side of Sherwood Road, immediately south of Smyrna Hill Drive.

<u>Clybe Dunton</u> married Nellie Humphries of Baldwin County; an accountant, she was working in an Atlanta department store. They had one daughter, Carolyn.

Carolyn Dunton married Watson Flythe of Chatham County. They had one son, Thomas Watson Flythe, known as "Tom," who is a financial consultant.

The Hollis Jewel Dunton, Sr., Family Reunion
Circa 1912
Courtesy of Earline Dunton Pettet

The Family on the left is Elizabeth, holding Raymond, and Job, with their other children – grouped with them. Two daughters in white, and an older daughter in dark clothing, and three sons, including the blond haired boy standing in front of his dad.

Standing in front of the Hollis Hill Dunton House on the south side of Concord Road, The Country Road.

Serving during World War II in the United States Army Air Corps (known today as the United States Air Force) Clybe received an injury which affected his voice for the rest of his life; in his later years, he was not able to communicate orally. His daughter, Carolyn, born late in his life, never remembers her dad's being able to talk. After the War, Clybe, an artistic painter, was very good as an auto detailer. He owned and operated H.C. Dunton Garage, located on the southeast corner of Concord Road and South Cobb Drive. (This property was part of the land holdings of his dad, Hollis Hill Dunton.)

After his marriage in the early 1950s, Clybe built the third house, still standing, on the south side of Sherwood Road from North Cooper Lake Road. Sherwood Road at that time was not much more than a pig trail.

Glenn Aubrey Dunton married and had one daughter, Glenna. According to information from the Dunton Family, Glenn built and operated Smyrna Home Park, located just before the 90-degree curve on the east side of Sherwood Road; there too, he built a nice brick house, where he and his family lived. This mobile home park was located on property, which earlier was part of the land holdings of his father, Hollis Hill Dunton.

NOTE: In the summer of 2005 this mobile home park property was sold for the development of Sherwood Forest subdivision, to have 87 homes.

Maurice Dunton married Evelyn Moody of Smyrna. They had six children: Donnie, Jack, Fred, Evelyn, Patty, and Mary Ann.

Mary Ella Dunton, who married Oliver Rice, had one son. The Rice Family lived in Atlanta.

NOTE: The Pickens Family resided in the first house on the east side of North Cooper Lake Road, just off the corner of Concord Road. They farmed land which belonged to Hollis Hill Dunton. See *Pickens, east side of North Cooper Lake Road.*

Hollis Hill and **Martha Dunton**

NOTE: According to information from the Dunton Family, **Hollis Jewel Dunton**, a farmer, and his wife, **Martha**, in 1860 came from Edgefield, South Carolina, to Cobb County's Lost Mountain community. From there, they moved to District 1017, in Smyrna, to land that Hollis Jewel Dunton had purchased from the Whitfields in 1892.

The second house on the south side of Concord Road, The Country Road was the setting for a family portrait taken in front of the house in 1912. I have been able to establish that the following listed Smyrna residents of the Twentieth Century were daughter and sons of Hollis Jewell and Martha Dunton.

Della Dunton, according to information from the family, never married. See *Dunton, north side of Concord Road.*

Hollis Hill Dunton. See *Dunton, south side of Concord Road, The Country Road.*

Jesse Macaulay Dunton. See *Dunton, south side of Concord Road.*

Hollis Jewel Dunton, Jr., was known as "Joby." See *Dunton, south side of Church Road, The Country Road* and *Dunton, north side of Church Street.*

Job Carroll Dunton. See *north side of Bank Street.*

Third House

Mr. and **Mrs. Martin Ruff, Sr**., and their family lived about one and one-half miles west
North Cooper Lake Road, across the street from the triangle at Concord and Hurt roads. Their hous
was located a little distance off the road, within a grove of trees. Mrs. Ruff was the former Katherin
Watkins of Memphis, Tennessee. The Ruffs, who owned and operated a small dairy on this acreag
had four children: **Martin, Jr**., **Katherine**, known as "Kitty," **Virginia**, and **Rex Robert**. Martin, J
"Kitty," and Virginia graduated from Smyrna High School; Rex graduated from Campbell Hig
School. Rex remembers that he and Jimmie Lou Wright were mascots for the graduating class of h
sister Virginia.

Martin Ruff, Jr., married Dorothy Willis, who grew up in Smyrna; they had one daughte
Paula. After Martin and Dorothy divorced, Martin re-married and had a daughter, Angela. See *Willi
Fleming Street* and *Highland Avenue.*

Katherine Ruff, known as "Kitty," married Gene Daniel of Thomaston. They had four son
Jerry, Ken, Alan, and Stan.

Virginia Ruff married Bill Medlin. They had three children: David, Kathy, and Andre
David's wife's name is Susan, Kathy married Darrell McGlon, and Andrea married Jim Carme
Virginia, a Registered Nurse at Kennestone Hospital (now Wellstar Kennestone) also worked for D
Charlie Underwood. Later she was the Director of Nursing for Brawner Sanitarium. Virginia is no
deceased. See *Medlin, south side of Concord Road.*

Rex Robert Ruff
Juvenile Court Judge
Cobb County
March 12, 1973-June 30, 1985

Rex Robert Ruff, an attorney in private practice in Marietta, was a graduate of Merce
University as well as a graduate of Walter F. George School of Law at Mercer University. He was th
first full-time Juvenile Court Judge in Cobb County, a position he held for 12 years. (Such judgeship i
through appointment by the Superior Court Judges.)

Rex Ruff married Dolores Hightower, who was from Atlanta's Druid Hills area. An educato
in the Cobb County School System, Dolores was the first female President of the Cobb Count
Association of Educators. The Ruffs had a daughter, Rae. Dolores died from cancer while a youn
woman.

Rex Ruff then married Marcia Smith of Marietta, the daughter of Brooks Smith, forme
owner, publisher, and editor of *The Marietta Daily Journal*. Marcia was previously married to And
Morris; they had three children: Drew, Brooke, and Tyler. Together Rex and Marcia have eigh
grandchildren.

Rex Ruff remembers, "Concord Road was not paved; as a young child, I could walk b
myself to Mr. T.L. Dickson's Sinclair Station, located on the corner of the Access Highway an
Concord Road, to buy a snack and walk back home.

"I remember the daily routine of my dad's and brother's working at the dairy and of m
helping deliver milk on occasions. My dad and brother, Martin, Jr., would milk the cows by hand
They would pour the milk into glass bottles which had been sterilized, put on cardboard tops, an
place the bottles in a 3'x 4' wire container, which they placed into the back of the truck and covere
with a tarp. They drove to downtown Smyrna, crossed the railroad tracks, and went to the ice plant
There they backed up the truck and lifted the tarp for the men at the ice plant to shovel ice over th
bottled milk. I would sit in the front seat of the truck; Dad would drive up to a house which was on th

route and hand me the bottled milk; and then I would hop out and take the bottle(s) to the customer's front door."

Rex Ruff shared the following historical facts about his dad's family: The Ruffs of Concord Road. "In the late 1800s the Ruff Family, who lived in the Ruff House, still standing on Concord Road in the Covered Bridge area, gave land to establish a Methodist Church in Smyrna. My parents, Martin, Sr., and Katherine, were married in the Ruff House, where they lived for a short time with my father's parents. My father's sister, Mildred Inez Ruff, was born in 1904 and died in 1930 while giving birth to her daughter, Joan, who was raised by her grandparents. The last person to be buried in the Ruff Cemetery on Concord Road was Mamie Ruff, in 1964."

Rex also related, "My family lived on Concord Road until I was about six years old, at which time we moved to Bank Street." See *Ruff, north side of Bank Street.*

Benny Lou O'Bryant Tackett, who has lived on the south side of Concord Road since 1944, related: "I remember that the cows and a large barn on the Ruff property were sold to Mr. and Mrs. Warren Sanders. I also remember that their three children, Charlie, Mary, and Martha, rode the bus to Smyrna School with me and my brothers."

The Warren Sanders Family

Mr. and **Mrs. Warren Sanders** moved from Atlanta to this third house, which they purchased from the Martin Ruff Family. The Sanders had three children: a son, **Charles**, and twin daughters, **Mary** and **Martha**—all graduates of Campbell High School. Warren Sanders, who was employed by White Provision Company (later Swift), was one of the original owners of Sanders Funeral Home, which was established in the early 1960s in a house on the north side of Concord Road. Mrs. Sanders, whose given name was Blonnie, was from Commerce; Mr. Sanders was from Toomsboro.

Mary Sanders, a Campbell High School graduate, married Wilson McEntyre, the son of Mr. and Mrs. Howard McEntyre, who owned and operated McEntyre's Bakery. They had two children: Jennifer and John. Mary and Wilson still live in Smyrna. See *McEntyre, west side of Dunn Street.*

Martha Sanders graduated from Campbell High School and Georgia State College, (now Georgia State University). She received her Masters and 30 plus degrees at Louisiana Technology in Rushton, Louisiana; taught kindergarten for 31 years, she is retired. She married James Humphreys of Moultrie, who graduated from Georgia Institute of Technology and Candler School of Theology, at Emory University and served as pastor of several churches in Louisiana. They had two children, Jeffrey and Mindy, and two grandchildren. Martha and James live in Louisiana.

Charles W. Sanders married Jane Ballenger, a graduate of Marietta High School. They had two sons, Charles W. Sanders, Jr., known as "Chuck," and Rodney, and four grandchildren.

Charles first attended Georgia State College and then Carson-Newman College, where he received a degree. He then earned his Masters degree from Mississippi State College and his sixth-year degree from the University of Georgia. Employed by the Cobb County Board of Education, Charles taught at Elizabeth Elementary and Osborne Junior High schools; then he served as principal of Harmony-Leland and Hollydale elementary schools. While principal of Powder Springs Elementary School, he was involved in the building of the new school. Charles was later associated with the Cobb County Board of Education's Central Office, from which he retired. He and Jane live in West Cobb County.

Fourth House

Benny Lou O'Bryant Tackett recounted memories of **Ida** and **Lum Henderson**, who lived in an old farm house on a hill that is now the entrance into Ashley Court. "I do not know who owned this house, but I believe it was part of what was known at one time as the Martin Ruff Dairy Farm. Lum farmed the land; Ida did laundry for several housewives in the area, including my mother.

"Ida Henderson, whose maiden name I do not know, was born on the land that was bought in the 1940s by my father. The ruins of Ida's family home could still be seen when we moved there. My brother Lamar remembers the neighbors' telling about a smallpox epidemic earlier in the century and the house occupants dying of the disease. (I assume they could have been Ida Henderson's family, as she told us she was orphaned at an early age and was raised by her grandparents.) I remember the remains of the old house being in our pasture; Daddy finally removed them. Ida became a close friend of our family and especially of my grandmother, Mary Elizabeth (Molly) Brannon, who lived with us.

"The Hendersons walked everywhere they went, as neither of them drove a car. Ida was a devoted member of First Methodist Church. If you were to set out on Sunday morning around nine o'clock, you would see Ida, walking up Concord Road on her way to Church. Usually someone would come along and give her a ride, but I'm sure there were many times when she walked the entire two and one-half or so miles to church.

"The Hendersons later moved to a garage apartment owned by the Jolly Family, on property at the intersection of Concord and Old Concord roads. Lum worked as a gardener and caretaker for the Jolly Family until he reached retirement age. The Jollys furnished Lum and Ida the nice garage apartment which they made their home for many years." See *Jolly, west side of Old Concord Road.*

Mr. and **Mrs. Holcombe**

Mr. and **Mrs. Holcombe** bought this house after the Hendersons had moved. Mrs. Holcomb's given name was **Stella**. The Holcombes had three children: **Virgil, Gail,** and **Vicki**.

Benny Lou O'Bryant Tackett, who remembers the Holcombes well, shared the following memories of them. "They lived here for many years, and all of the children attended Smyrna schools with my brothers and me. While here, Mr. Holcombe worked for the Clorox Company. When he retired, he and his family moved back to the Sand Mountain and/or the Piedmont, Alabama areas, from which they originally came.

"Concord Road at this juncture made a rather sharp, downhill curve just past the Holcombe place. Many accidents happened there over the years, as cars would come over the hill too fast, with the drivers failing to negotiate the curve. More than one car wound up against a tree on the side of the road or in a yard. It is still referred to by those who have lived in the area a long time as 'The Holcombe Curve.'"

"Before the end of World War II, Concord Road was still a dirt road. In the winter, with the occurrence of rain, sleet, and snow, the Holcombe hill and curve would become treacherous. Mr. Norton, the school bus driver, would have the County bring in gravel on a regular basis to try to keep the road passable and safe. Once or twice he had us get off the bus and walk down the hill while he slowly and skillfully drove the bus down. Then he would stop the bus, and we would climb back on and continue the trip to school. As the property on both sides of Concord Road was developed, the hill was graded down and the road was slightly straightened; this somewhat modified the curve and, therefore, reduced the danger.

Fifth House

Mr. and **Mrs. Frazior Trevor Brooks**, who were originally from Forsyth County, moved to East Cobb County in the 1930s and then to this house on Concord Road. Mr. Brooks was known as "F.T."; Mrs. Brooks was the former Estalee Gilleland. They had six children: **J.T.**, **Rupert**, known as "Butch," **Hulett**, **Edna Jane**, **Harold**, and **Benny**. In 1944 they moved from this house back to East Cobb County.

J. T. Brooks married Ellene Daniel; they had three children: Nancy, Johnny, and Beaver.

Rupert Brooks, known as "Butch," married Evelyn Johnson. They had two children: Tony and Phyllis.

Hulett Brooks married Patsy Todd of the Fair Oaks community; they had four children: daughters, Robin and Julie, and sons, Allen and Terry.

Edna Jane Brooks married Robert Daniel. They had two sons: Jerry and Randy.

Harold Brooks married Polly Austin. They had three children: Penny, a son, Chris, and Amy. See *Austin, west side of North Cooper Lake Road.*

Benny Brooks married Barbara Leatherwood. They had two children: Ashley and Lorie. Benny Brooks is an architect.

The Brooks' house stood on a knoll located about two city blocks west of what is known as the intersection of Concord and Hurt roads; it extended between the entrances of Havilon Way and Woodvalley Drive, each being part of the Bennett Woods subdivision. This farm, with about 30 acres of land, had an apple orchard and a pasture, which extended southward toward the Daniell Cemetery. Here Edna Jane Brooks remembers playing with her friend Corrine Austin (Ware-Cates). See *Ware, south side of Sunset Avenue* and *Austin, west side of North Cooper Lake Road.*

Edna Jane also remembers walking westward on Concord Road to the Clay home. The Clays were long-time Concord Road residents, who raised hogs. Mr. Clay, on a regular basis, traveled to Atlanta, where he collected food scraps from some of Atlanta's nicest restaurants. From these scraps, he created what was commonly called "slop" for feeding his hogs. On occasions, mixed in with the food scraps, he would find nice pieces silverware. See *Clay house, north side of Concord Road, The Country Road.*

NOTE: J.T., Rupert, and Hulett Brooks, in the early 1940s, owned and operated Brooks Taxi on Atlanta Street. Later "Papa" Day and his son, Robert Day, owned and operated Day's Taxi in this location. See *Day's Taxi, Atlanta Street, from Miss Mazie's to Pearce Matthews.*

Mr. and Mrs. S.U. Hendrix

Mr. and **Mrs. S.U. Hendrix** later lived in this house. Benny Lou O'Bryanat Tackett recalls that when they moved here, their only daughter, **Edith**, was a student at North Georgia College, in Dahlonega. Upon finishing college, Edith moved back home and went to work for the State Merit System. According to information from former neighbors, the Hendrix's only **son**, while walking, was struck by an automobile and killed.

"The Hendrix house stood upon a ridge where Autumn Lane now intersects with Concord Road. It was a big, beautiful, white house with a long, wide front porch. The interior had a huge front room with the most beautiful mahogany woodwork. I suppose it was originally built for a formal dining room, for between that room and the kitchen that was situated to the back of it, was a serving pantry. It also had beautiful cabinets with glass doors and many drawers. I have often grieved for that beautiful house and thought, 'What a shame it was torn down for yet another subdivision.'"

Sixth House

Mr. and **Mrs. William M. Pressley** lived in this house, which is still standing on the southeast corner of Concord Road and Highview Drive, an entrance to Bennett Woods subdivision. According to the Pressley's son, James, in the early 1930s the Pressleys moved to Bank Street so that he could ride the streetcar to Marietta High School. It is believed, by some who remember, that Mr.

W.M. Pressley built this house in the first quarter of the Twentieth Century. See *Pressley, south side Bank Street*

The Stephens Family

Bennie Lou O'Bryant Tackett related the following, "**Mr.** and **Mrs. James Stephens**, it believed, bought this house from Mr. William M. Pressley, who moved back to Smyrna, on Ba Street. Mr. Stephens died of tuberculosis (TB), and Mrs. Stephens continued to live here with her eig children: **Grace**, **Jewel**, who worked away from home, **Cora Mae**, **Wilma**, **Dorothy**, who worked f the Bell Bomber Plant and rode back and forth with my parents, **James**, known as 'Junior,' and **Anni** a couple of years older than the younger daughter, **Lynette**, who was my age. (She and I were in t same class in school and were good friends during our elementary and high school years.). Not to long after we moved to Concord Road (1944), Mrs. Stephens sold the place and bought a house o Atlanta Road, just north of Pat Mell Road, because her children, grown and working, needed publ transportation to their jobs. The streetcar ran from Marietta to Atlanta via Atlanta Road: thus they ha an ideal place to live. Mrs. Stephens was a wonderful and sweet woman, in whose home I alway enjoyed visiting. Lynette married Ben Maxwell."

Mrs. Bessie Stone

Raymond Stone
Casualty of War
World War II

Mrs. Bessie Stone, a widow, whose son, **Raymond**, had been killed during World War I bought this house from Mrs. Stephens. Mrs. Stone's youngest son, **Randall**, came home after servin in the United States Military during World War II and moved in with his mother.

"Randall went to work for the State Department of Defense, where he had a long an distinguished career. After marrying the 'girl next door,' Edith Hendrix, he bought a house on the ea side of North Atlanta Road, where he and Edith lived for several years. When Edith's father's healt began to fail, Edith and Randall moved in with Edith's parents, on Concord Road. There they reside until Mr. Hendrix died; then Edith and Randall bought a house on Cooper Lake Road and added 'mother-in-law suite' for Mrs. Hendrix. They sold the farm on Concord Road, and Bennett Wood another subdivision was born! At age 50, Randall unfortunately died after a sudden heart attack. Edit who retired from the State Merit System, still lives in the house on Cooper Lake Road.

"Mrs. Stone died in 1965. Upon her death, the **Gene Kane Family** bought the house. Gene, coach at Campbell High School, and his wife had four children. The Kanes lived here for about a yea or until Gene got an offer to coach high school in or near his home town in Tennessee. After the moved, during the summer, Carl and I bought the property. (Bennett Realty Company bought all of th other parts of Mrs. Stone's property except two and one-half acres that fronted Concord Road.) Mrs Stone also sold us an easement for a road to run along the southern edge of her property and th northern edge of our lot. Because our lot had a rather odd configuration, we felt that our house woul be just too close to the new road to be safe or attractive; thus we bought the property from the Kane and negotiated with Bennett Realty Company to put the new road at a more advantageous angle tha previously planned."

NOTE: Mrs. Bessie Stone was a sister of Mr. Bart Black, who lived across the road in th rock house, and of Willie Argo. See *Ralph* and *Willie Argo, east side of Hughes Street,* and *Bart Black north side of Concord Road, The Country Road.*

<u>Seventh House</u>

Mr. and **Mrs. Joseph Benjamin O'Bryant** and their children, **Benny Lou**, **Lamar Reginald**, and **Major Jerry**, known as "Jerry," lived in this farm-style house, still standing on th

Home of Joseph Benjamin and Ethel O' Bryant
208 Concord Road
Circa 1890s house
Courtesy of Lou O'Bryant Tackett

Ethel and **Joseph Benjamin O'Bryant**
208 Concord Road
Circa 1890s house
Courtesy of Bennie Lou O'Bryant Tackett

south side of Concord Road, just west of a Bennett Woods entrance sign. Mrs. O'Bryant was th former Ethel Beatrice Brannon, a niece of Mr. Ernest Brannon, her father's youngest brother. I recal from my childhood, that the O'Bryants had lived off Powder Springs Street in the vicinity of th Earnest Brannon house. See *Brannon, north side of Powder Springs Street.*

Benny Lou O'Bryant, a member of the Smyrna High School Class of 1951, married Ca L.Tackett. She and Carl, in 1954, built their home on what is now the southwest corner of Concor Road and Highview Drive, next door to her parents' home, where Benny Lou grew up. Carl and Benn Lou had three children: Carl L., Julie Anne, and Mark Ellis.

Carl L. Tackett married Eva Brunson of Andulusia, Alabama. With no children, they liv next door to his parents.

Julie Anne Tackett married Mr. Perkerson. They had two children: Tonya, who attend Kennesaw State University, and Brandon, a senior at Campbell High School.

Mark Ellis Tackett married Michelle Phelps; they had two children: Jake Ellis and Haley The Phelps live in Kennesaw.

Emory Lamar O'Bryant married Joyce Lusk, who grew up on the north side of Concor Road, east of South Cobb Drive, now known as Lusk Drive. Lamar and Joyce had three children Emory Lamar, Jr., known as "Marty," Michael Lewis, and Matthew Jack. Lamar O'Bryant is Pastor o First Southern Baptist Church in Pomeroy, Ohio. See *Lusk, north side of Concord Road.*

Reginald O'Bryant married Martha Nunnally, who had two sons, Randy and David, whom Reginald adopted. Reginald O'Bryant died in 1993.

Major Jerry O'Bryant, known as "Jerry," married Sheila Voyles, who grew up on McCaule Drive. They had one son, Joey. Sheila had a daughter, Lisa, whom "Jerry" adopted. Sheila is deceased

MEMORIES ON CONCORD ROAD

by Benny Lou O'Bryant Tackett

Daddy bought the farm, which adjoined at the rear, the place where we lived on North Cooper Lake Road (then known as Cooper Lake Road). We moved here in the fall of 1944. Previously owned by Dr. Berry, who, I believe, practiced medicine in Atlanta, it had been used as a country home

Fronting Concord Road, the house where I grew up bears the address 208 Concord Road. I consisted of 29 acres of farm and pasture land, a smokehouse, a chicken house, a corncrib, a barn, and a big, white six-room house. Daddy paid $2,900.00 for all this—$100.00 an acre! He worked long long hours (sometimes two jobs) to pay for it. When the mortgage was paid off, he bought a additional 70-acre parcel, which lay behind it, for $1,500.00. Off that parcel he had the timber cut to pay for the tract of land. My mother, still owning the property, resided in the house until October 2004 when her health failed and made it impossible for her to continue living alone.

The property was originally part of the G. Lumpkin Daniell Estate. A two-story brick structure, the Daniell house stood on its original site (now the entrance of Bennett Woods North) until the housing boom of the 1960s and 1970s. As a student in Mrs. Lena Mae Gann Green's study hall a Smyrna High School, I was told by Mrs. Green, that the bricks for the old Daniell house were made on the Daniell Plantation by 'slave labor.' Mrs. Green also related that, because Mr. Daniell was a very active Mason, he had made and donated bricks with which the original Masonic Hall in Smyrna was built.

Mrs. Green told me an interesting Civil War story about the original Masonic Hall building It seems that when the Yankees were making their way to the sea, a small skirmish took place in downtown Smyrna, at which time General Sherman's troops had captured the railroad depot According to Mrs. Green's account, General Sherman took up headquarters in the original Masoni

Hall building. The story goes that, during the battle, the General raised up to look out the window, and his hat was shot off his head; that was the closest he came to being killed during the entire war! Mrs. Green also said that the reason the old Daniell place was not burned by Sherman and his men was that Sherman was a devoted Mason, as was Mr. Daniell. See *Daniell, south side of Concord Road, The Country Road.*

Our house supposedly was built in the late 1890s by Robert Daniell, a son of G. Lumpkin Daniell. The Daniell Cemetery encompasses a one-acre tract to the east of the old Daniell home site. There buried are many of the original Daniell family members, as well as several residents of the Bennett Woods subdivision, where the cemetery is located.

Such are my memories of Concord Road and Smyrna, a wonderful place in which to grow up! As with most places, what made it great was *The People.* There was very little crime reported in the City, and juvenile delinquency was not an issue. A few years ago at a memorial service for Mrs. Corrine Hosch, a beloved teacher at Smyrna High School, a classmate and I were discussing how punishment was meted out in our day. He made the remark that discipline was not a problem for us because we respected our elders so much that we were careful not to do anything that would require our having to be disciplined. It was not so much that we feared the discipline but rather the disappointment we would bring to both our parents and teachers. It seems that the key to many of the problems encountered by young people today is not only the children's but also the adults' need for attitude adjustments.

Eighth House

The Ruff Family Estate

On the south side of Concord Road, before the approach to the railroad overpass, is Ruff Cemetery. On the grounds is a beautiful two-story white, framed house, referred to by local citizens as the Ruff House. I do not believe any of the Ruff Family occupied this house during the years I was growing up.

The following information was shared by Linda Ruff Smith, a descendent of Martin Luker Ruff, who built this house in 1851. Linda grew up in another house on Concord Road in the middle of the Twentieth Century. See *Ruff, fifth house on the north side of Concord Road, The Country Road.*

Martin Luker Ruff and Robert Daniell built and operated the Concord Woolen Mill and the gristmill at Nickajack Creek. According to information I received, they also built the Concord Covered Bridge.

Martin Luker Ruff was the son of William Ruff (1769-1836) and Rebecca Martin Ruff (?-1852). Martin Luker Ruff, (1807-1877) married Judith Mead Lovejoy (1813-1885). They had a son, John Wesley Ruff (1849-1907), who married Mary Ella Earnshaw (birth and death dates unknown).

John Wesley Ruff and Mary Ella Earnshaw Ruff had a son, Rex Earnshaw Ruff, (1877-1939), who married Mary Josephine Farren Ruff, known as "Mamie" (1880-1964). Rex Ruff somehow became the owner of the Ruff House on Concord Road. After his death in 1939, my grandmother, 'Mamie,' had to sell the house. At that time there were 80 acres, which she sold for a total of $3,900.00.

My great-grandfather, John Wesley Ruff, developed for hides and skins a new tanning process that Loyds of London wanted to insure. He met with the cattle industry out West but was afraid to write the formula down for fear of its being stolen. John Wesley became ill and died without ever passing the formula along. I have all the handwritten documents to back it. My dad always said, 'We were almost rich!'

The Martin Ruff House
Circa 1851
Photo courtesy of Mike Terry.

The Ruffs and the Daniells had business enterprises in the Concord Covered Bridge area. The uff House was used as a hospital for the injured during the Civil War, and the woolen mills there 'ere used to make uniforms for Confederate soldiers. The Ruff House, built in 1851, was the site of a 'ivil War Battle; partially burned during Sherman's March through Georgia; the house was later ebuilt."

NOTE: Evidence of shots fired into the stone foundation around the house can still be etected, according to Janice Ivester, a former owner/resident, who now lives in Carrollton, her home own.

The Milroys

by Benny Lou O'Bryant Tackett

Other neighbors to the southeast were the Milroys, who lived in the original Ruff House, part f the Ruff Estate. The Ruff Cemetery is still on the property. (The bulk of the property, sold many ears ago, is now the Patricia Place and Heritage Mill subdivisions.) The Ruff House is currently wned by Philip and Lanier Ivester; Lanier is a great-granddaughter of Mrs. Lena Mae Gann Green, 'hom I quoted earlier. I do not know where Mr. Milroy worked, but Mrs. Milroy would take him to tlanta Road, in Smyrna, every morning to catch the bus and would pick him up at the bus stop in myrna at the end of the day.

Just south of the Milroy House was the Seaboard Railroad line, now the Silver Comet Trail. eyond the railroad line is the property of the Ruff Woolen Mill and the Ruff House, built by one of Iartin Luker Ruff's sons at Nickajack Creek, which almost encircles the home. A covered bridge, uilt over the creek, has always been a beautiful and familiar area landmark; it is now designated as The Covered Bridge Historic Site.' The old gristmill still stands to the left of the entrance to the iller's house. When I was growing up, the property was owned by Dr. and Mrs. Clinton Reed, he was physician whose office was in the Candler Building, at the corner of Peachtree and Houston streets, downtown Atlanta,"

NOTE: According to Janice Ivester, Ian and Jennie Milroy came to Smyrna in 1941. During Vorld War II, Ian worked for the Bell Bomber Plant in the Department of Finance. Jennie, an avid orse rider, was an instigator of the founding of the Atlanta Steeple Club. She would travel to New)rleans to purchase antiques, which she would have shipped back to the Ruff House. One of her crown jewels" was a bedroom suite which had belonged to a former governor of Louisiana. Ian had a ast collection of Civil War artifacts (e.g. swords, cannon balls) he had found on the property. This rea was the site of the Battle of Smyrna, with the Ruff Woolen Mill as Sherman's target. Though herman was successful, the Woolen Mill, rebuilt after the war, continued in operation well into the 'wentieth Century. Ian, who was born in England, was returned there for burial.

The Harold Ivester Family

In the 1970s, Harold and Janice Ivester bought this house, restored it, and lived in it until 988. There they raised their three sons: Andrew, Philip, and Michael. Their middle son, Philip, and is wife, the former Lanier Adams, the great-granddaughter of Dr. and Mrs. Grover Cleveland Green, re now the proud owners and occupants of this house. See *Green, south side of Love Street.*

During the days of my youth, the Covered Bridge area was, as it is today, a beautiful setting. n years gone by, it was used for family picnics, dating, and some scavenger hunting."

EARLY WRECKER SERVICE

There is a story told that, during World War II a group of young guys had heard about the Nation's gathering of scrap metal to use for the War effort. Someone had discarded an old automobile omewhere in the Covered Bridge area, and certain guys knew about it. Getting together, they rolled hat old automobile all the way out of the woods onto Concord Road and then turned the car, side over

side, all the way to Smyrna. In doing so, the guys salvaged the scrap metal from that automobile f
the War effort.

Ninth House

Dr. and **Mrs**. **Clinton Reed**, as told by Benny Lou O'Bryant Tackett, died of natural caus within two months of each other. Upon their deaths, their daughter, **Carolyn**, and her husband, **Smil** **Bush**, moved into the house where they lived until Smiley's sudden death, following a heart attack the early 1960s, when he was only in his mid 40s. Carolyn continued living in the old house for seve years, or until she sold it and built a brick house on Covered Bridge Road; she also built one next do to hers for her daughter, Leah, and Leah's husband"

Tenth House

Benny Lou O'Bryant Tackett reflected upon her knowledge of Mrs. Rheta Dowda and h son. "On the west side of the Covered Bridge there was a house that stood upon a hill overlooking t Covered Bridge. Not visible from the road, the house was occupied by **Mrs**. **Rheta Dowda** and h son, **Francis**. (Francis had been a patient at Milledgeville State Hospital for several years when n family became acquainted with he and his mother.) Mrs. Dowda, with a few resources, supplement her 'Old Age Pension' with money made from selling handmade linens: beautifully embroider pillowcases and napkins and crocheted pieces. Because everyone knew of Mrs. Dowda's financ plight, the neighbors frequently carried groceries to her, a dear lady who was devoted to her son.

Shortly after we moved to Concord Road, Francis was allowed to leave Milledgeville Sta Hospital and come home to live with his mother. (Some said he had tuberculosis or TB and that t State sent him home to die, such as was a common practice in those days.) However, fresh, clea country air and his mother's cooking and loving care cured him of TB. Because Mrs. Dowda a Francis attended our church, Daddy or one of the Clay boys would make sure Mrs. Dowda and Franc had transportation each Sunday.

When my brother Lamar became old enough to drive the car, he took on, as his person mission, the responsibility of making sure Mrs. Dowda and Francis had a way to church every Sunda But one Sunday, when Lamar went to pick them up for church, Francis came out and told him th were not going to church that morning because 'The old lady won't get up.' The next day Lamar w contacted by the Cobb County Police and advised that Mrs. Dowda was found dead in her bed (Monday morning. Lamar was required to attend a formal inquest, as he was apparently the la outsider at Mrs. Dowda's house prior to her death. Since there were no living relatives that anyone h known and because Francis had previously been adjudicated insane and made a ward of the Stat Francis was taken back to Milledgeville State Hospital. There he remained a patient until his death few years later; he is buried alongside his mother in the old Ruff Cemetery, on Concord Road."

KING SPRINGS ROAD

East Side

First House

Mr. and **Mrs**. **Bob Cadle** lived in this house, about one block from Concord Road. Bob w a son of Mrs. Floy Eaton, who lived on the west side of King Springs Road. *See west side of Kir Springs Road.*

Second House

Later on **Reverend** and **Mrs**. **M.C**. **Howard** built this house, past the Cadle house. At o time, he was the pastor of Sharon Baptist Church. See *Access Highway*.

Third House

Mr. and **Mrs. Henry Grier** and their family were residents of this house. They had nine ıildren: **James, Willie, Clara Mae, Jeanette, Henry, Jr., Homer, Herbert, Hubert,** and **Gloria.** Ierbert and Hubert were twins.) This property, at one time belonging to the Eaton Family, was sold Mr. Ralph Stephens; he, in turn, sold it to Henry Grier, a custodian at Smyrna School and First aptist Church. The Grier Family lived here well into the last half of the Twentieth Century.

It is my understanding that some members of the Grier Family were active in Cooper Lake aptist Church. One of Mr. and Mrs. Grier's daughters married a minister who preached there.

Fourth House

Mrs. Ethel Daniell Turner, a sister of P.F. Daniell, bought this house, on the corner of King prings Road and Daniell Drive and across the road from P.F.'s house. Behind the Turner House was e Daniell picnic ground, a large area that extended back to the present location of Dunn Street. After eir marriage, Ethel and Charlie Turner lived in Atlanta for a while; they moved back to King Springs oad in the 1940s. Ethel and Charlie had three children: **Dan, Gladys** (Eidson), and **Lois** (Henry). thel resided in Smyrna until 1998, when she died at 100 years of age. She is buried in the Daniell emetery, located in the Bennett Woods subdivision.

Dan Turner currently on Spring Hill Road, in the Smyrna area.

Fifth House

Mr. Pliney Frank Daniell, Jr., known as P.F., married Hazel Berryhill. In 1936 P.F. bought nd located in the area now known as King Springs Road and Daniell Drive, extending from Lee reet southwesterly to the Quillan Petty property, where he built a house in 1937 and moved into it in)38. P.F., along with his brother-in-law, Joe Godfrey, farmed the land and raised pigs. P.F. also orked for Louisville and Nashville Railroad (L&N). When the Daniells moved here, their address as Route I, Cooper Lake Road. After the road was paved, its name was changed to King Springs oad, and the driveway to the Daniell house was made into a street. After Lee and Dunn streets were tended, in the early 1950s, Daniell Drive intersected with Dunn Street and ended at Lee Street. See *obert Daniell Family, north side of Concord Road, The Country Road.*

P.F. and Hazel had four children: **Sara, Jane, Robert,** known as "Bobby," and **Brenda.**

Sara Daniell married Robert Godfrey, a nephew of Joe Godfrey, who married Doris erryhill, a sister of Hazel Daniel. In 1939 P.F. Daniell, Jr., had deeded five acres and a house to Joe d Doris to have family members near by. (In the 1930s King Springs Road was a very rural area.) e and Doris never had children but helped raise the children of P.F. and Hazel. The Godfrey operty, located at the rear of the Daniell home, is now known as Daniell Drive.

Behind their house, the Daniells had a swimming pool that faced their driveway. Beyond the vimming pool was the home of Joe and Doris Godfrey.

On the Daniell property in the 1950s Sara (Daniell) and Robert Godfrey built a house facing ing Springs Road and now facing Tolleson Park.

Sixth House

Mr. and **Mrs. Quillan P. Petty,** who resided here, had four children: **Annie, J.B., Watson,** d **James.** The father of Mrs. Petty, the former Vinnie B. Vietch of Cobb County, ran a blacksmith op on Church Street in Marietta, opposite from the present location of Schillings Restaurant.

The Pettys moved from the Macland area in West Cobb County to Concord Road in 192 They raised their children in the vicinity of King Springs and Concord roads. In the 1940s the fami farmed about 400 acres, located on both sides of Concord Road, from King Springs Road to what now South Cobb Drive.

In 1934 Quillan Petty bought land and three old houses on King Springs Road. The fami lived in one of the houses; the other two were used for sharecroppers. In 1939, for $370.00 he boug the house and property on the corner of what is now Hayes Drive and King Springs Road.

Annie Petty married Mr. Johnson.

Mr. and Mrs. Quillan Petty had three sons who served in the United States Military during World War II. Their son, James, served during the Korean Conflict. Two of their sons were taken Prisoner of War: Watson, in World War II and James, in Korea.

Watson Petty has shared: "In 1940 I enlisted in the United States Army because I wanted do something other than plow with a mule. I was in the Army when World War II began and serv with a tank company in Europe, where I was taken as a Prisoner of War."

Watson Petty
Prisoner of War
World War II

Watson Petty, married Dorothy Cranshaw, known as "Dot," who grew up on Love Stre Currently living on the King Springs Road property that was part of Watson's family's farm, Wats and "Dot" are members of First United Methodist Church. Watson is a member of the Vetera Memorial Association in Smyrna and American Legion Post #160; "Dot" is a member of the Easte Star. See *Cranshaw, south side of Love Street.*

J.B. Petty., in the United States Army, served during World War II in North Africa a several other theaters.

James Petty
Prisoner of War
Korean Conflict

James Petty served in the United States Navy during World War II. He returned to Smyr Later he served in the United States Army during the Korean Conflict, when he became a Prisoner War. James, upon returning home came from Korea, was honored by the City of Smyrna in a b parade and through the presentation of an automobile. Sara Daniell Godfrey remarked, "The para was the biggest event I had ever seen in Smyrna."

KING SPRINGS ROAD
West Side

Appreciation is extended to Gerald Eaton, Robert Fowler, and Sara Daniell Godfrey f sharing information about their families: the Daniells, Eatons, Cadles, Fowlers, and Godfreys—all whom lived on King Springs Road. Appreciation also is extended to Gerald Eaton for relating h memories of the Sellers Family.

Medlin Farm

The **Medlin** home at one time was located on property near the intersection of King Springs a Concord roads. **Ed Medlin** grew up here. When the Medlins were residents here, the street was call Cooper Lake Road. (According to family information, Ed's family moved from here to Spring Street.

The Log Cabin, property of
Emory and Maude Paris on King Springs Road
Demolished in 2004 to build the cottages of King Springs
Courtesy of Mike Terry.

The Log Cabin, property of
Emory and Maude Paris on King Springs Road
Courtesy of Mike Terry

Home of Mr. and Mrs. Emory Paris
King Springs Road, west side
Photo courtesy of Mike Terry.

The Nehemiah Chadwick House
King Springs Road
Circa early 1920s – Photo courtesy of
Mary Lou Redd Cochran

According to long-time residents of the area, after the road had been paved, the rural postal route was changed to King Springs Road.) See *Medlin, south side of Concord Road and Hann, west side of Roswell Street.*

NOTE: The following fourt houses were razed in 2005; builder Ed Hatcher, President of Hatcher Homes, constructed 11 houses in this area, now called the Cottages at King Springs.

First House

Aubrey and **Hazel McIntosh** purchased property and built this brick ranch house, located about a half block off the southwest corner of Concord Road. They had one son, **David**, who married Sandy Gober, the daughter of Gayle Martin Gober and Phil Gober. Gayle Martin Gober grew up on Bank Street, near Aubrey's parents' home. See *Gober, south side of Bank Street.*

I am not sure when Aubrey and Hazel moved to King Springs Road, but I think it may have been in the early 1950s. Aubrey and Hazel were very faithful members of First Baptist Church. Hazel is deceased.

Second House

Mr. and **Mrs. Emory Paris** resided in the second house. Mrs. Paris, the former Maude Baldwin, was one of the daughters of Mr. and Mrs. John Jacob Baldwin on Concord Road. Emory and Maude married May 3, 1941, and moved to this house soon afterwards; here they lived the rest of their lives. See *east side of Concord Road.*

Mr. Emory Paris had one son, Emory Duane. See *north side of Bank Street.*

Third House

Mr. and **Mrs. Nemory Chadwick** were residents here. The Chadwicks owned and operated a neighborhood grocery store on the southwest corner of Concord Road and Medlin Street. That store in later years became known as Corner Grocery Store. The Chadwicks were Mary Lou Redd Cochran's maternal grandparents. **Mary Lou** and **Bobby Cochran** later lived in this house—until 2005, when they sold it for the building of the Cottages at King Spings. See *west side of Concord Road.*

Fourth House

Mr. and **Mrs. Redd**, the paternal grandparents of Mary Lou Redd Cochran, lived in this house in the 1940s. At one time, the Redds ran a dairy farm a few miles outside Smyrna, on the north side of Concord Road and west of Old Concord Road. See *west side of Concord Road, The Country Road.*

Fifth House

Mr. and **Mrs. Camp**, who had three children, in the 1940s resided in this house, set farther back off the road than the other houses in this area. Later on, Mr. A.Q. McLean, having bought this house from the Camps, converted it into a cabinet shop. See *McLean, Stephens Street.*

Six House

A family named **Allen** built this house in the late 1940s or early 1950s. Later on the **McDonald Family** lived here.

Seventh House

Bill and **Frances Scoggins**, having moved to this house in the early 1950s, were living here when their son, Bill, Jr., was born. See *south side of Bank Street.*

Eighth House

Mr. and **Mrs**. **A.S.** **Beavers** lived in this house. Mr. Beavers, known as "Scott;" and Mrs. Beavers, whose given name was Hattie, had one son.

Ninth House

Bill Cadle
Casualty of War
World War II

Floy Eaton Cadle, and her sister, **Amber Eaton,** were residents about a half mile down the road, on the west side. Their house was located in the vicinity of Rem Bennett's first-built brick housing development in Smyrna and near the present-day intersection of Pinedale Drive and King Springs Road. Floy and Amber were sisters of Mr. R.A. Eaton, who lived on King Springs Road, just south of them.

R.A. Eaton and his sisters were first cousins of P.F. Daniell, Jr. Their mothers, who were sisters, were members of the Carmichael Family on Log Cabin Drive, in the Oakdale community. See *P.F. Daniell, Sr., north side of Concord Road, The Country Road* and *P.F. Daniell, east side of King Springs Road.*

Floy Eaton Cadle had three children: a daughter, who was called "Little" **Floy**, and two sons, **Bill** and **Bob**. Bill was a United States Army Air Corps (now United States Air Force) training pilot during World War II. He was on a training mission when the plane crashed. Both Bill and the trainee were killed.

Floy Cadle attended Young Harris College. Afterwards she taught school and married, but she never returned to Smyrna to live.

Bob Cadle, having attended college away from home, married and had two children: Larry and Diane. He returned to Smyrna with his second wife, Margaret, and lived on King Springs Road. They had one son, Bill. See *first house, east side of King Springs Road.*

Amber Eaton never married. She and Floy lived in the home on King Springs Road until the 1950s. After the property had been sold and the house razed, brick homes were constructed on the property. On Lee Street, Amber and Floy built the house where they lived until their deaths. Floy, Amber, and Bill Cadle are buried in the New Smyrna Cemetery, on Hawthorne Avenue.

Tenth House

Mr. and **Mrs**. **Rufus A. Eaton** were residents of this house, located on the northwest corner of King Springs Road and what is now Oakdale Drive. They had eight children: **Eleanor**, **Charles Ray**, **Larry**, **Edwin**, **Gerald**, **Jackie**, **Kenneth**, and **Saundra**.

Eleanor Eaton married Miles Willis, who lived on Highland Avenue and Fleming Street at different times. Eleanor and Miles, who built a house on Collier Drive in the Forest Hills community, currently live in Kennesaw. See *Evans, north side of Fleming Street*, and *west side of Highland Avenue.*

The R.A. Eaton House, West side of King Springs Road
Circa 1940 Courtesy of Gerald Eaton

Miles and I had a lot of association through the years, both in business and civic life. In the late 1950s and 1960s, we both belonged to the Jaycees; also, we were in the banking business. Miles was employed for a long time at Lockheed Aircraft Corporation, where he retired. Then he worked for Security National Bank, which was later bought by the Trust Company of Georgia. (This bank, located on South Cobb Drive, south of Concord Road, is currently SunTrust Bank.)

Charles Ray Eaton married Joyce Meaux (pronounced "Mo") from Louisiana. Charles Ray is deceased.

Larry Eaton never married.

Edwin Eaton married Betty Jean Watkins of Smyrna.

Gerald Eaton married Barbara Barrett, the daughter of Bill and Dot Barrett, of Marietta. Gerald and Barbara, both graduates of Campbell High School, 1956 and 1960 respectively, had two daughters, Michelle and Jennifer. They live in Smyrna, where Gerald was a postman for the United States Post Office, from which he retired. (When Lillie and I lived on Pinehurst Drive, he delivered our mail; at that time he was a walking postman.)

Jackie Eaton married Paul Owenby of Marietta. Jackie is deceased.

Kenneth Eaton, known as "Kenny," married Joan Keenum from Birmingham, Alabama. Kenny and Joan live in Virginia.

Saundra Eaton married Bill Barrow of Smyrna.

Mrs. Rufus Eaton was the former Myrtis Parnell, the daughter of Mr. and Mrs. John Fletcher Parnell, who lived on the west side of King Street. See *Parnell, west side of King Street*.

Mr. Rufus A. Eaton was the son of Mr. and Mrs. R.A. Eaton. The elder Mr. Eaton, a farmer, owned land from what today is Pinehurst Drive, to McCauley Road down to what is now Starline Drive, and over to King Springs Road.

Rufus A. Eaton was a first cousin of Pliney Frank Daniell, Jr., who lived on the east side of King Springs Road. Each of their mothers was part of the Carmichael Family, (from the Oakdale community), who ran a grocery store on Log Cabin Drive. See *Daniell, west side of Concord Road* and *Daniell, east side of King Springs Road.*

Eleventh House

The Sellers Family property joined, on the north side, with the Eatons. It began at what we know today as Starline Drive, connected on the south side with the Gordon Fowler property, and extended through to the west side of the Access Highway (now known as South Cobb Drive). A day care center, which is located on the west side of South Cobb Drive, (adjacent to Walton Park Apartment Homes), is on part of the former Sellers property.

Rosa Belle and **Ed Sellers, Sr.**, lived here with their family. They had several children, among whom were **Ed, Jr.**, **Tom, Henry**, **Johnny**, **Guy**, **Mollie**, and **Lizzy**.

Ed Sellers, Jr., who worked as a custodian at the Georgia State Capitol, moved to Davenport Town.

Tom Sellers left Smyrna. It is believed that he went to Detroit or Chicago.

Mollie Belle Sellers' husband, Mr. Johnson, was killed in an automobile accident.

The following information was furnished by Gerald Eaton, a member of the Rufus A. Eaton Family: "The Sellers Family is an African-American Family, some of whose ancestors were living on the Eaton Farm when the Civil War ended. At that time Mr. R.A. Eaton deeded 40 acres on King Springs Road to the Sellers Family. The property stayed in the Sellers Family until the 1990s, when a portion of the land was sold for the building of a housing development, Sutherlin Park, on King Springs Road, and the day care center on South Cobb Drive."

"The 40 acres of land were not given to the Sellers by the Eatons. The Sellers, sharecroppers on the land, paid Mr. Eaton for the land over a period of time. From the end of the Civil War to the middle of the Twentieth Century, the Sellers were among the very few "Black" families who owned property in Cobb County. They managed to keep this land in their family through the boll weevil, World War I, the Great Depression of the 1930s, and World War II. Some members of the Sellers Family still own a part of the original 40 acres of land."

Twelfth House

Mr. and **Mrs. Gordon Fowler** resided here, where King Spring Baptist Church is currently located. Mrs. Fowler was the former Cora Cooper, the daughter of Mr. and Mrs. Jesse Cooper. Gordon and Cora had two children: **Robert**, known as "**Bobby**," and **Maurice**. *See Pickens Street.*

"Bobby" Fowler married Doris Bailey, who grew up on Highland Avenue. They had three daughters: Lisa, Leslie, and Lauren. See *Bailey, Highland Avenue.*

After he graduated from high school, "Bobby," along with Tom Camp and John Porterfield, enlisted in the United States Navy at the same time, in 1949.

Maurice Fowler married Hulon Leathers, who grew up on Highland Avenue. They had four children: Renee, Patrice, Lori, and Forest.

Forest has been in Hollywood for 30 years. An art director specializing in special effects, he created all of the special effects for the *Mighty Joe Young* Show and Janet Jackson's videos.

Gordon Fowler, an accomplished electrician, served during World War I in the European Theater, where he was assigned to a United States Navy troop ship. Mr. Fowler was the second Commander of American Legion Post # 160. In the 1940s, Gordon served as Chairman of the Building Committee for the Legion home, where his picture, along with others of those who have served as commanders, now hangs.

Mrs. Cora Cooper Fowler, who worked for American Hat Manufacturers on Trinity Avenue in Atlanta, rode the streetcar to her job.

NORTH COOPER LAKE ROAD
East Side

North Cooper Lake Road in the days of my youth was far out into the country. The road ran from Concord Road, as it does today, across the railroad (now the Silver Comet Trail), through to where Cooper Lake Road now intersects with the East West-Connector. A country road, it was very isolated in some areas. I seldom went out that way. Bennie Lou O'Bryant Tackett shared that, when her family moved to this road in 1942, it was referred to as Cooper Lake Road.

Appreciation is extended to Vera Austin Blackburn and Corrine Austin Ware Cates for imparting their knowledge of the North Cooper Lake Road residents from the 1930s to the early 1950s; to E.S. Gann, known as "Edd," for information about his family, the Ganns on North Cooper Lake Road; to Odelia Norton Rogers and Peggy Norton Cochran for information about the Norton Family; to Ann Pickens Causey for data about the Pickens Family; and to Cecil Pickens and G.V. Westbrook for their memories of the area.

First House

Mr. and **Mrs. James Gilbert Pickens** lived on the east side of North Cooper Lake Road, jus off the corner of Concord Road. Mrs. Pickens was the former Leila Gaddis Webb. They had two son and five daughters: **Marian Inez, John Daniel, James Cecil, Ruby Mae, Bobbie Louise, Charlott Ann**, and **Myrtle Marie**, all born and raised in Smyrna. For 40 or more years, after the Pickens ha moved, Sparkey's Package Store was located on this site, where there is now a barber shop. Th Pickens' house and farm were located on property which belonged to Hollis Hill Dunton, whose lan holdings in the area extended from the Pfarner property westward to North Cooper Lake Road an encompassed all that we know today as Sherwood Road. Mr. Pickens, a sharecropper, farmed in thi area. See *Dunton, south Side of Concord Road, The Country Road; south side of Concord Road; nort side of Church Street;* and *south side of Church Road, The Country Road.*

NOTE: Sharecropping was a common form of farming: a tenant farmer's giving a share (o shares) of his crop to the landowner in exchange for the use of his land.

James Gilbert Pickens was born in 1894 and died in 1973. Mrs. Leila Gaddis Webb Picken was born 1n 1903 and died in 1975.

Marian Inez Pickens married Edwin Kennedy. They had one daughter, Cynthia.

John Daniel Pickens married Frances Medlin. They had three children: Donald, Ricky, an Nancy.

John Daniel Pickens later married Claudine Blankenship. They had three sons, John Christopher, Gilbert, and two daughters, Jennifer, and Jody.

James Cecil Pickens married Merlene Livingston. They had one son, James David.

Ruby Pickens married J.C. Cogburn. They had three sons: John, Ronald, and David.

Bobbie Louise Pickens married Vernon Moody from South Carolina. They had two children Paula and Victor.

Charlotte Ann Pickens married James J. Evans. They had three children: Stephen, Jimmy and Scott.

Charlotte Ann Pickens later married Ronald Causey; they had a daughter, Rhonda.

Myrtle Marie Pickens married Ronal Stephens. They had no children.

Mr. Pickens contracted with Mr. T.L. Dickson to build a house on property now known a Smyrna Hill Road and Radcliffe Drive. The Pickens Family moved from their house on North Coope Lake Road, to the newly built house.

For nearly 50 years, Cecil Pickens has owned and operated Concord Body Shop on the sit where his dad, Mr. James Gilbert Pickens, had the family house built at Smyrna Hill and Radcliff drives.

NOTE: James Gilbert Pickens had three brothers and three sisters who grew up in Smyrna.

MEMORIES

by Cecil Pickens

Cecil Pickens shared that, during the years his family lived in this house, occasionally, he an his brothers, along with other neighborhood boys, would "take" eggs from Mrs. Ola Dunton's he house. Although there were times Mrs. Dunton would come out of her house, screaming "Cecil Pickens, you younguns get out of my chicken house," we would take the eggs home, boil them and have a feast. We always got the freshest eggs from that hen house; sometimes they were still warm.

"When I was a child, Mrs. Dunton, a prolific artist, loved to smoke cigarettes, her favorite being Lucky Strikes. Many times, when I would be walking by her house, I would hear her call to me 'Cecil, while you're at the store, get me a pack of Lucky Strikes, and don't open them.' I guess she thought I might smoke some of them!"

"Mr. Hollis Hill Dunton always had a watermelon patch. It never occurred to me to ask him if I could have a watermelon. Some of us kids would just go into the patch and help ourselves. Another one of our neighbors, Mr. Gann, who lived farther out North Cooper Lake Road, didn't see it that way; he called it "stealing." One time some of us boys were in his watermelon patch, helping ourselves when T.H. and Harold Gann saw us and began chasing us toward the creek. We were better at forging that creek than they were. With watermelons in hand, the last we saw of T.H. and Harold was their trying to get out of that creek. After that creek episode, we did not go back to Mr. Gann's watermelon patch!"

NOTE: In 1955 Mrs. Hollis Hill Dunton, Leola, known as "Ola," sold all that tract of land, beginning at the southeast corner of Concord and North Cooper Lake roads and extending to the northeast corner of Sherwood and North Cooper Lake roads, to Lewis E. Hardy. For the land, Mrs. Dunton received $65.00 a month for the next ten years.

Second House

The Lewis Hardy Family

Mr. Lewis Hardy and his wife, the former **Ethel Fuller**, moved to Hill Street in 1951 for Mr. Hardy, a Veteran of the United States Army, to work for Lockheed Aircraft Corporation. From there they moved to McLinden Avenue and then to Concord Road into the home with Mrs. Hollis Hill Dunton. After purchasing property that faced North Cooper Lake Road from Mrs. Dunton in 1955, the Hardys moved to a house they built, facing North Cooper Lake Road near the northeast corner of Sherwood Road. The Hardys had three daughters: **Sandra**, who was stillborn, **Brenda**, and **Janice**. The Lewis Hardy Family were members of Sharon Baptist Church.

After leaving Lockheed Aircraft Corporation, Lewis trained as an Emergency Medical Technician. Afterwards working for Grady Hospital, in Atlanta, he drove an ambulance on emergency calls; his # was 727. From there, he retired.

Brenda Hardy, a graduate of Wills High School, married Harold William McGee of Smyrna. They had three children: Barbie, Angie, and Hal. Brenda was a nurse for 25 years. Later, she married Jimmy Southers and moved to Powder Springs, where she continues to live.

Janice Hardy, a graduate of Campbell High School, married Gary Brown, the son of Herbert and Nellie Brown, who lived on Dixie Avenue. Janice and Gary had twin sons: Jacob and Justin.

Janice Hardy Brown, now married to J.D. Calhoun, lives in Hiram.

The Gann Family Cemetery

The Gann Family Cemetery is on the east side of North Cooper Lake Road, a short distance off Concord Road. (In the Smyrna area are many descendents of the Ganns, an old family of Smyrna.) This cemetery dates back to the Revolutionary War, and many of the people who are buried within fought in the Civil War.

Alexander Gann, in the Georgia Calvary during the Civil War, was the father of Travis Alexander Gann, who lived on North Cooper Lake Road. Alexander is buried in the Gann Cemetery.

Third House

Mr. and **Mrs. Travis Alexander Gann** lived with their family on the east side of North Cooper Lake Road, in the area not far from the Gann Cemetery. Mrs. Gann was the former Martha Mable Johnson from Polk County. They had three sons and one daughter: **Travis Hiram**, known as "T.H.," **Harold**, **Edgar Sewell**, known as "Edd," and **Mary Estelle**, all of whom were educated in Smyrna School.

Travis Hiram Gann, known as "T.H.," married Opal Bartlett, the daughter of a circuit preacher with the Methodist Church. They had no children. During World War II, Travis served with the United States Army on several islands in the Pacific, where he fought in many battles; he was awarded several medals for his service to his country during that War. Born November 7, 1921, "T.H." died June 5, 2004. (Well known to my family, "T.H." was the only person Lillie ever knew to have the same birthday as hers.)

Harold Gann married Edith Duke of Griffin. They had two daughters: Jenny and Susan. Serving in the Tank Corps of the United States Army during World War II, Harold fought in the Battle of the Bulge in Belgium.

Jenny Gann, who married Greg Whitiker, lives in West Cobb County. She worked for Coca-Cola Company.

Susan Gann married Mr. Dadich; they had one son, Bryan. Susan is employed by IBM in South Carolina.

Edgar Sewell Gann, known as "Edd," married Louise Lovvorn, who graduated from Smyrna High School in the Class of 1949. "Edd" and Louise retired from Southern Bell Telephone Company, now BellSouth, in their late 40s, and then established a wholesale jewelry business, which they operated for the next 20 years. Now they are truly retired!

"Edd" Gann shared this heart-warming story with me: "When I was ready to graduate from Smyrna High School, Mrs. Corrine Hosch stated that, with my strong work ethic, I should enroll in college right away. I didn't see how I could do that because of my parents' age and economic condition. But I decided to try it anyway. I remember working hard to try to come up with the college tuition when, without any notice, T.H. and Opal paid my tuition. They kept much to themselves; but when there was a need in the family, Opal and T.H. were always there."

"Edd" served in the United States Marine Corps during the Korean Conflict. A Shriner for over 40 years, he is currently serving as Director of Public Relations for the North Georgia Shriners.

Mary Estelle Gann married Ira L. Spier. The Spiers had one daughter, Diane, who married Troy Parks of Smyrna. Diane and Troy had a son, Robbie.

Fourth House

Mr. and **Mrs. Coby Norton**

Mr. Coby B. Norton and his wife, **Dovie**, had six children: **Vera, Parker, Otis, Velma, Volia**, and **Sarah**. Mr. and Mrs. Norton owned a large farm that encompassed land down North Cooper Lake Road, south of what is now Highview Drive, to Honeysuckle Drive and then eastward, covering the Reed Road area. Peggy Norton Cochran remembers that her Uncle Coby Norton drove a school bus.

<u>Mr. and Mrs. Parker Norton</u> and their family lived on North Cooper Lake Road. Mrs. Norton was the former Pauline Harbuck from Atlanta. They had two daughters: Patricia, known as "Pat," and Paula. Mr. Parker Norton worked for A&P, (I remember him as always dressing professionally). Their house, which is still there, is located on the northeast corner of North Cooper Lake and Reed roads. I am not sure when this house was built; but, according to family information, it is located on land that was part of the Coby Norton Farm. Pauline and Parker Norton moved from Concord Road, where the Clay Family had lived, to this house.

Patricia Norton married Jack Levings.

Paula Norton married Charles Lesley, known as "Butch," who grew up on Spring Street. The son of Mary and Claude Lesley, "Butch" had a sister, Barbara, who married James Burson. Paula and "Butch" Lesley had three sons: Chad, Alec, and Brett. See *Lesley, north side of Spring Street.*

Both Patricia and Paula still live in the Smyrna area.

<u>Volia Norton</u> and Vera Austin (Blackburn) were close friends. Vera remembers that Volia's brother drove the school bus and one of the older Norton daughters played the piano. She also recalls a time when, as a teenager, Mrs. E.C. Bird at First Baptist Church invited her and Volia Norton to sing at a missionary meeting. "When we started singing 'Let the Lower Lights Be Burning,' every light in the church went out. We were in the basement of the rock building, where the Sunday School rooms of that day were located, and it was really dark!"

NOTE: The City "Dump" was located on the east side of North Cooper Lake Road, about a mile past the Nortons, across from the Westbrook home, and near the location of Nowlin Drive. The garbage dump has been abandoned for many years, and the City of Smyrna is contemplating developing that property into a park.

NORTH COOPER LAKE ROAD
West Side

<u>First House</u>

Appreciation is extended to Very Austin Blackburn, Corrine Austin Ware Cates, Benny Lou O'Bryant Tackett, G.V. and Wynelle Westbrook for sharing information about their families, who lived on North Cooper Lake Road in the Middle of the Twentieth Century.

Mr. and **Mrs**. **Paul Austin** lived in this house. Mrs. Austin was the former Eva Adair. They had six children: **J.C.**, **Vera**, **Robert Joseph**, known as "Bob," **Alvin Chester**, **Corrine**, and **Virginia Pauline**, known as "Polly." Mr. and Mrs. Austin lived on Stilesboro Road in Kennesaw when their first three children were born. In 1923 they moved to Smyrna, where their three youngest children were born. This family, whom I knew very well, moved from Sunset Avenue, which was the street directly behind my house on Bank Street, to North Cooper Lake Road. According to one Austin Family member, "We grew up all over Smyrna—that is, until we moved to North Cooper Lake Road, where we established deep roots." The Austin Family attended First Baptist Church. See *Austin, south side of Sunset Avenue.*

The Austin Family home was on the west side of North Cooper Lake Road, about a half mile from Concord Road. The house, still there, is the second one past the southwest corner of North Cooper Lake Road and Pineview Drive. According to a family member, "The house has been changed so much that it doesn't look as it did when we lived there."

NOTE: When Austin Drive was cut in the 1960s, Mr. and Mrs. Paul Austin built a house and moved there.

Mr. and **Mrs. Paul Austin**
(Former Eva Adair)
50th Wedding Anniversary, March 13, 1966
Photo courtesy of Vera Austin Blackburn.

Mr. and **Mrs. Paul Austin**
(Eva Adair)
50th Wedding Anniversary, March 3, 1966.
Austin Drive
Six Children and Spouses
L-R: **Harold** and **Polly Brooks**, **Corine** and **Spurgeon Ware**,
"Jim" and **Vera Blackburn**, **Alvin** and **Jackie Austin**,
"Bob" and **Lucille Austin**, and **J.C.** and **Stella Austin**.
Courtesy of Vera Austin Blackburn.

J.C. Austin., a graduate of Smyrna High School, married Stella Mae Chandler, whose family lived on Austell Road in Southwest Cobb County. With three children, J.C. and Stella were members of First Baptist Church, which J.C. joined in the revival service that was conducted in April and May of 1932. See *south side of Bank Street* and *east side of Dunn Street.*

Vera Austin married Jim Blackburn and lived for years in Florida. They had no children. After both Jim and his mother died, Vera returned to Smyrna (1990) to be near her family. Having graduated from Smyrna High School in 1934, at the age of 15, Vera said: "I remember my dad's having to pay $3.00 per month tuition for me to go to school. Our country was in the midst of the Great Depression, and Cobb County did not have the money to fund the school system without help from the students. When I finished school, I started to work for Holeproof Hosiery Company in Marietta."

Vera shared a memory of attending First Baptist Church when she was about 10 years old. "The Church toilet, which was referred to as the 'outhouse,' was behind the Church building. Sometimes I would take my little brother, Alvin, who was 4 years old, with me to Sunday School. He would sometimes act up and thus embarrass me. One day I told Mother, 'If he acts up today, I am going to take him to the 'outhouse' and spank him.' He acted up, and I did what I said I was going to do. (This was before the Church had restrooms.)"

Vera joined First Baptist Church during the revival service held in April and May of 1932. After living in Florida for many years afterwards, she returned to Smyrna and First Baptist Church, where she is still active.

From the days of her youth, Vera remembers the so-called restrooms in Smyrna School: "In reality they were 'inside outhouses.' In the basement of the school building, which was the two-story building on Church Street, the 'outhouses' were several cubicles in a row. Some kind of tank was used; it had to be emptied regularly. (It was probably a small septic tank.) When we had to go to the restroom, we would say, 'I need to go to the basement.' I remember that one year, when I had a young male teacher, that I was always embarrassed to tell him that I needed to go to the basement. Therefore, I just did not go."

Robert Joseph Austin, known as "Bob," a graduate of Smyrna High School, married Lucille Hanson, who grew up on Love Street. They established their home on the south side of Bank Street, where thy raised their children. "Bob" was baptized at First Baptist Church June 28, 1936. See *Austin, south side of Bank Street*, and *Hanson, south side of Love Street.*

Alvin Chester Austin, a graduate of Smyrna High School, was known on the baseball team as "Burr." He married Jackie Bennett and moved to South Georgia; they had no children.

Corrine Austin, a graduate of Smyrna High School, married Spurgeon Ware, who grew up on Sunset Avenue. The Wares, who lived on North Cooper Lake Road (on the opposite side of Corrine's family home place) had no children. Spurgeon is deceased.

Now re-married, Corrine and her husband, Walter Cates, still live across the street from her family home place; their house is on the northeast corner of Austin Drive and North Cooper Lake Road. Austin Drive is a semi-circle street with its name derived from the Paul Austin Family.

Virginia Pauline Austin, known as "Polly," a graduate of Smyrna High School, married Harold Brooks, who also grew up in Smyrna. They live in West Cobb County, where they are members of Macland Baptist Church, on Macland Road. See *Brooks, south side of Concord Road, The Country Road.*

Second House

Mr. and **Mrs. Joseph Benjamin O'Bryant** resided in the second house on the west side of what was then called Cooper Lake Road. This house was located about halfway between where Highview Drive and Colonial Drive currently intersect with North Cooper Lake Road.

Appreciation is extended to Benny Lou O'Bryant Tackett for her reminiscing the family's living on North Cooper Lake Road in the middle of the Twentieth Century. At that time residents referred to the road as Cooper Lake Road. "We moved to Cooper Lake Road in 1942 when I was in the second grade. I loved living on Cooper Lake Road because I had such wonderful playmates there! The first house on Cooper Lake Road was occupied by Paul and Eva Austin, who had three daughters and three sons. Polly Austin and I, the same age, became great friends. We had some wonderful times playing with my brothers, Lamar and Reginald, and Polly's sister, Corrine. While all three Austin boys were away during World War II, I remember Mrs. Austin's visiting our home and eagerly telling my Mother about the letters she had received and what her sons had to say. Sometimes the letters were censored by the military, and thus she would try to guess what was in the blackened- out spaces.

"Across the street from our house lived Parker Norton and his wife, Pauline. A year older than I, Patsy, their daughter and I played together almost every day. Next door to the Nortons lived Parker's parents. Parker's father, Mr. Colby Norton drove the school bus for Smyrna School; my brothers and I rode his bus, first grade through high school. As soon as he backed the school bus out of the 'bus barn' in the mornings, he would blow the horn long and hard; that was our cue to get to the bus stop. (He left promptly at 7:00 A.M. every day.)

"The property about a half mile south of our house was owned by the Ferman Westbrook Family, originally from Forsyth County, where Mother and Daddy had known them for many years before we moved to Smyrna. Our family spent a good bit of time with them. They were just like family to us. I remember that Mr. Westbrook, a farmer, who raised the biggest and best watermelons that I've ever tasted! G.V., the Westbrooks' son still lives on the family farm, on North Cooper Lake Road. The Westbrooks' daughter, Wynelle, and I, close friends while growing up, still keep in touch." See *Ben O'Bryant, north side of Powders Springs Street* and *south side of Concord Road, The Country Road.*

Third House

Mr. and **Mrs. J. Ferman Westbrook** lived out North Cooper Lake Road, in a deep curve on the west side of the road. Mrs. Westbrook was the former Mae Durham of Cherokee County. They had four children: **G.V.**, **Margaret**, **Thelma**, and **Wynelle**. On the property were a large, white farm house and several farm-related buildings. (The house still looks very much as I remember it from the days of my youth. I recall vividly the apple trees on this property!)

Appreciation is extended to G.V. Westbrook and his sister, Wynelle, for sharing with me information about their family, who moved to North Cooper Lake Road in the early 1930s. They remember the street at that time was called Cooper Lake Road.

In 1934 the Westbrooks had moved from the two-story frame house on Powder Springs Street, where the Henry Gann Family later lived, to 4240 North Cooper Lake Road. At that time, their youngest child, Wynelle, was two years old. Family members recall that, when the Westbrook Family moved here, they had no electric lights or inside bathrooms. (Wynelle remembers the house as being very dark at night during her childhood.)

G.V. Westbrook married Edna Ruth Holcomb of Cold Mountain, near Forsyth; they had no children. G.V., in the United States Army during World War II, served in the European Theater Operations. The troops sailed to Europe on *The Queen Elizabeth* and landed in Scotland; from there they worked their way through England, France, and Germany during a period of 18 months. G.V., though never being in combat, saw it from a distance and was very close on many occasions.

Margaret Westbrook married Mr. Newberry. They had three children: Mary Ellen, Michael, and Bobby. The Newberrys lived near Augusta.

Thelma Westbrook married Herschel Godsey. They had four children: Frances, Kenneth, Warren, and Jerry. In 1954 the Godseys moved to North Cooper Lake Road, just north of the Westbrook home place and on part of the Westbrook estate. Thelma is deceased.

Wynelle Westbrook, a member of the Smyrna High School Class of 1950, married and had three daughters: Kathy, Jeanie, and Edith, known as "Edie."

Fourth House

Adolph Turley
Causalty of War
World War II

Mr. and **Mrs. Turley** resided about a block or two away, on a road that turned to the right in front of the Westbrook House. (It was located very near the site of West Smyrna Swim and Tennis Club.) The Turleys had a son, "Tubby," who was a few years older than I.

NOTE: Wynelle Westbrook remembers that the Blair Cemetery was located down the road and toward the Turley House. She believes that the Blair Family built the Turley house, lived there for a while, and then moved back to Marietta.

The railroad was about a mile farther down North Cooper Lake Road from the Westbrook House. The area was very isolated, and the roads were unpaved.

NOTE: According to the Cobb County Parks & Recreation Department, Seaboard Railroad managed the Silver Comet passenger train line. But prior to the development of the Silver Comet Trail, the rail line had been acquired by CSX Railroad.

G.B. Westbrook, who, at the age of 85, still lives in the family home on North Cooper Lake Road, has provided the following invaluable information. "After crossing the railroad on North Cooper Lake Road and traveling about two or more miles to the end of North Cooper Lake Road, one would approach Cooper Lake, located in the area where North Cooper Lake and Cooper Lake roads of that day intersected. To locate the approximate site of Cooper Lake, go south and travel up the hill from the East/West Connector to the first new bridge. Underneath that bridge and northward from the bridge that spans the Southern Railroad is a low area that was, in the days of my youth, the site of Cooper Lake. When I was a young man, the lake became stagnant, and area citizens began getting sick. (Both my dad and I became sick twice.) The Corps of Engineers came in and dynamited the lake. I believe they burst that dam about 1937 or 1938."

OLD CONCORD ROAD
The Country Road
East Side

I do not recall any houses on the east side of Old Concord Road in the days of my youth. Though there may have been some, this was an area that I did not frequent. According to family information, T.L. Dickson and Herman Jolly purchased land on the east side of Concord Road in the late 1940s and built a fishing lake, which is still here. Later on many families built houses on this side of Old Concord Road; some that I knew were **Louie** and **Montez Davis**, **Pete** and **Ethel Logan**, **Joe** and **Nancy Logan**, and **T.G.** and **Ruth Rogers**.

I do remember the house on the northeast corner of Old Concord and Church roads. It was the Nickajack community meeting place before **Richard Cobb** lived there. See *Virgil Cobb Family, west side of Old Concord Road*

First House

Nell and **Leland Williams**, who previously lived on Hill and Church streets, built this brick house across the street from Nell's parents' home on Old Concord Road. The former Nell Cobb, she and Leland had one daughter, **Virginia Lenell**. Leland died in early part of the Twenty-first Century. Nell is still living in this house

Leland worked at Atlantic Steel Company in Atlanta. When I was a young boy, I remember that Nell and Leland would attend the ball games played by the Smyrna Amateur Team, managed by my dad, Roy Wood. See *Virgil Cobb, west side of Old Concord Road* and *Hill Street, Cobb north side of Church Street.*

Virginia Lenell Williams married Leroy Martin. In the late 1950s or early 1960s, Virginia and Leroy built a white brick house, still standing, next door to Virginia's parents, Nell and Leland Williams. The Martins had three children: Jana, Andy, and Stephen.

Second House

Carl Cobb and his wife, **Nina Foster Cobb**, at one time resided diagonally across from Marion Cobb. They had four children: **Jerry**, **George Ronnie**, **Thomas**, and **Diane**. The Carl Cobb Family later moved to the Fair Oaks community.

NOTE: Their house was on the northeast corner of Old Concord Road and Powder Springs Street. Central Church of Christ is currently located on this site.

Jerry Cobb married Patricia Mauldin.

Ronnie Cobb married Nancy Wehunt.

OLD CONCORD ROAD
The Country Road
West Side

Old Concord Road in the days of my youth was an unpaved country road. (Lucile Cobb, who grew up on Old Concord Road, remembers its being paved in 1955.) Running from Concord Road, on the south end, it crossed the Access Highway, (now South Cobb Drive), and connected with Atlanta Road in the vicinity of the present Naval Air Station.

I want to thank Beverly Cobb Amacker, Lucile Cobb Crowe, John Dickson, and Nell Cobb Williams for furnishing information about their families on Old Concord Road. Beverly Cobb Amacker, the granddaughter of Mr. and Mrs Virgil Cobb, is currently living in Marietta. Lucile, who grew up on Old Concord Road, still lives a short distance from Church Road. John Dickson, a nephew of Mr. and Mrs. Jolly, and the owner and operator of Dickson Shopping Center, lives on the south side of Concord Road, between South Cobb Drive and the Concord Covered Bridge. Nell Williams grew up on Old Concord Road, where she still lives. Nell and Lucile, sisters, are the daughters of Mr. and Mrs. Virgil Cobb.

First House

Mr. and **Mrs. McCollum**, who had at least two sons, resided here when the Pecks moved next door, in 1937. Martha Peck Theodocian remembers that at least one of the sons was in the tobacco business.

Mr. and Mrs. Herman Jolly

Herman and **Mary Jolly**, who had no children, lived in the first house on the northwest corner and facing Old Concord Road. Mr. Jolly, a brother of Mrs. T.L. (Ruth Jolly) Dickson, and Mrs. Jolly moved from West Paces Ferry Road in Atlanta to Smyrna. He had the house built with red brick but painted them white before he moved in. Having lived on West Paces Ferry Road in the Buckhead section of Atlanta, where he was accustomed to seeing many homes with painted brick, he liked the style.

Mr. Jolly was a Southern Spring mattress dealer who traveled to furniture stores throughout his territory and stocked them with mattresses. Mr. and Mrs. Jolly were of the Baptist faith.

After the Jollys moved to Old Concord Road, Mr. Jolly bought all of the property across the road and in front of his house. This tract of land, which covered most of the property between Concord and Church roads, included a four-acre lake behind the large church that is on part of the property today. At a later date his brother-in-law, T.L. Dickson, bought an interest in some of the aforementioned property, including the lake.

Herman and his sister, Ruth Jolly Dickson, grew up in Rockmart.

The Marshall Family

Later on, **Dr. Don Marshall** and his wife, **Janice**, bought the Jolly house, on the northwest corner of Concord and Old Concord roads; there they raised their children: **Kirk**, **Richard**, **Robert**, **Scott**, and **Barbara**, (Richard and Robert are twins).

Dr. Marshall, a dentist, now retired, operated a dental office on the northwest corner of King and Stephens streets, in downtown Smyrna for 40 or more years of the Twentieth Century. Scott and Barbara, also dentists, are currently practicing in their dad's office.

The Marshalls are long-standing members of the First United Methodist Church. Janice, an accomplished musician, was a part of the music ministry for many years, playing both the organ and piano in First United Methodist Church and Cumberland United Methodist Church. She also taught piano and organ lessons to several generations of Smyrna students.

Dr. Marshall was a long-time member of the Smyrna Lions Club. See *Atlanta Street, from Mapps to the R & M Café.*

Second House

Mr. and **Mrs. T.J. Peck**, having come from Atlanta's West End community in 1937, moved to this house on 27 acres, which they named "Peck's Acres." Mr. Peck paid $2,700.00 for the house and the land. There was no electricity, and the outhouse was on the outer edge of the back yard. The well on the back porch furnished their water. The Pecks had one daughter, **Martha**, who married **Sam Theodocian**.

Mr. Peck grew up in Gainesville, where his family was very active in Peck's Chapel Baptist Church. I remember Mr. Peck as a short, very nice man who was a streetcar conductor, and I recall often riding on the streetcar that he operated. I also remember his coming to Smyrna School, where many of the school children referred to him as "Granddaddy." (According to information from his family, the reason for Mr. Peck's frequent visits to the school was to pick up from the school cafeteria leftovers to feed his animals.)

Mrs. Peck, the former Cora Palmour of Gainesville, was a short, quiet and very reserved lady (at least that is the way I remember her). One of her uncles was Dr. Artilius Palmour, who practiced medicine in Gainesville, where another uncle owned and operated a hardware store.

The Theodocians

Sam and **Martha Theodocion** had four children: **Charlotte, Dan, Bud,** and **Ben**. I first remember their living with Mr. and Mrs. Peck in the aforementioned house on Old Concord Road. Bud and I, the same age, attended Smyrna Elementary School together; however, he attended Marietta High School, where he played football for Coach James ("Red") Pressley, and I attended Smyrna High School.

Martha Theodocion was a businesswoman. I remember that she was a member of the Smyrna Business and Professional Women's Association and served as Smyrna City Clerk in the late 1940s and early 1950s. She later worked at Belmont Hills Shopping Center (opened in 1954) and afterwards for the Federal Reserve Bank in Atlanta, from which she retired.

Martha shared that, during World War II, she, along with some other ladies in Smyrna, operated a nursery school to meet the demands of mothers going to work at Bell Bomber Plant. See *north side of Stephens Street.*

Sam Theodocion was a second generation Greek, for his parents migrated to this country early in the Twentieth Century. He had three brothers: Louis, Paul (a pharmacist in Atlanta's West End community), and Theo, who shortened his name from Theodocian to Theos. (I knew Mr. Theo Theos' son, Fred Theos, who was one of my customers when I worked at Fulton National Bank.) Mr. Theodocian also had three sisters: Frosa, known as "Rosa," Sophia, and Helen. Some of Sam's siblings were first generation Greek immigrants.

For many years Sam Theodocion operated the Cobb House Restaurant, on the northwest corner of Jones Shaw Road (now Windy Hill Road) and South Cobb Drive. Sam also ran a package store at South Cobb Drive and Benson Poole Road. He and/or his sons, Benny and Dan, operated this store for more than a quarter of a century. In his neighborhood, Sam was famous for his beautiful gardens and delicious fruits and vegetables.

Charlotte Theodocion attended Smyrna School, where she was a member of the Class of 1949. She graduated from Wesleyan College in Macon with a degree in social work, and received her Masters degree from Tulane University, in New Orleans, Louisiana. Charlotte, employed with United Way, supervised social workers in three counties: Cobb, Gwinnett and Douglas. She passed away in 2002.

Dan Theodocian graduated from Marietta High School, where he played football for Coach "Red" Pressley. He attended Georgia Institute of Technology on a football scholarship. After a two-year interlude with "Uncle Sam," in the United States Army, he returned to Georgia Institute of Technology and there earned his degree.

Dan Theodocian, married but separated, lives in Smyrna.

James Pete Theodocion, known as "Bud," married Ruth Kelley from Tennessee. They had two children: Kelley and Pete, and two grandchildren, Pete is an attorney; Kelley is a school teacher.

Bud Theodocian earned his degree for teaching at the University of Florida in Gainesville, Florida where he attended on a football scholarship. Having been a teacher and football coach at Dykes High School in Atlanta, he moved to Clayton County, where he coached a number of years at Morrow High School, which won a football State Championship under his leadership. After retiring from the Clayton County School System, Bud was a coach at Woodward Academy, from which he retired. Bud Theodocian died July 29, 2005.

Ruth Theodocian, "Bud's" wife, has been associated with Mary Kay Cosmetics for 30 years; she is now a national sales director, the highest position that can be attained with the company. Ruth lives in McDonough.

Ben Theodocian married Frances Hightower of Iptania, Mississippi; they had two sons, Jimmy and Nicholas, known as "Nick." Ben graduated from Marietta High School and attended Auburn University on a football scholarship. Transferring to Southwestern University in Louisania, he earned his degree. Frances, who taught at Osborne Junior High School, and Ben live in Marietta.

Both the Pecks and the Theodocians were members of First United Methodist Church, where Martha still attends.

NOTE: The Peck/Theodocian home was located next door to the Jollys. In more recent years a new street, Charlotte Circle, (which was named for Charlotte Theodocian) was built on the north side of the Theodocian home; on it many new homes were constructed. Two other streets in the development, which were built on property formerly owned by the Pecks and Theodocians, were James Street and Dan Place, named for "Bud" and Dan Theodocian.

Third House

The **Hester Family**, in the days of my youth, lived for a while in a house across the creek, on the northwest corner of Old Concord and Church roads. This house, which was occupied by several different families through the years, was razed; a new brick house was built on the same site.

Fourth House

Mr. and **Mrs. Edgar Peyton Logan**, **Sr**., were residents of this house, built by Mr. Logan for his family. Mrs. Logan's given name was Ethel; Mr. Logan was known as "Pete." The Logans had three sons: **Joe**, **Orrin Brown**, known as Brown, and **Edgar Peyton**, **Jr.**, known as "**Eddie**." (Joe and Brown were twins.)

Joe Logan married Nancy Cooper of Smyrna. They had two sons: Joseph Mark and Scott Daniel. Joe and Nancy first lived on the south side of Church Road. Later on, they built the house where they still live, on the east side of Old Concord Road just east of his parents' home. See *Cooper, north side of Bank Street.*

Joseph Mark Logan married Donna Roland from Greensboro. They had two children: Katie Leigh and Joseph Roland. Donna is deceased. Mark and his children live in Marietta.

Scott Daniel Logan married Colleen Marie McGetterick from Chattanooga, Tennessee. They had two children: Brandon Scott and Hanna Marie. The Logans live in West Cobb County.

Orrin Brown Logan, known as Brown, married Myra Milam of Smyrna. They had three children: Barry Michael, Cheryl Diane, and Sandra Arlene. Brown and Myra built a house on the south side of Church Road, between South Cobb Drive and Old Concord Road, where they lived next door to Joe and Nancy. Brown and Myra divorced in 1976.

Barry Michael Logan married Susan Dillard, the daughter of Bill and Elinor Dillard, who lived in the Bennett Woods subdivision for many years. Barry and Susan had three children: Jenna, Michael, and Abby. Barry, a building contractor in West Cobb County, and his family live in Marietta.

Cheryl Diane Logan married Tony Camp of Smyrna, They had two children: Kristen and Alex. After their divorce, Diane married Dennis Underwood of Austell, where Diane, Dennis, and their five children live.

Sandra Arlene Logan, known as "Sandy," married Wesley Kay of Smyrna: they had two sons: Joe and Max. Wesley died while on the job with Smyrna Cable in 1987. "Sandy" and her sons live in Aiken. South Carolina.

Orrin Brown Logan, in 1977, married again to Catherine Day of Covington; they had or daughter, Lorrin Day. Brown Logan died in December 2002 from complications due to pulmonar fibrosis.

Lorrin Day Logan married Jerry Scott. They had three children: Ryan, Kaitlyn, and Loga The Scotts live in Temple.

Brown and Joe Logan, together, worked with their dad, Pete, in building and developmen The last subdivision Joe and Brown developed together was Covered Bridge Crossing, off South Hu Road.

Peyton Edgar Logan, known as "Eddie," and his wife, Janice of Florida, had a daughte Krissy. After Eddie and Janice divorced, Eddie married Frances; they lived in North Carolina whe Eddie, a chicken farmer, died in 1990.

This house, where the Logans first resided, is located just past Nickajack Creek on the we side of Concord Road. Builders, "Pete" and sons constructed many homes in the Smyrna area over th years. Lastly, "Pete" built another house on the east side of Old Concord Road about one-half mil from the intersection of Concord and Old Concord roads, in front of the lake that T.L. Dickson an Mr. Jolly built. This house, where he and his wife, Ethel, later lived, is still standing, just south of an next door to Highpoint Christian Tabernacle.

The Logan Family were members of First Baptist Church. Mrs. Ethel Logan, originally fror Indiana, was Director of the Cradle Roll Department. When my son, Stephen, was born, in 1968, Mr Logan visited and enrolled him. (Her signature is on his certificate.) At the time of her death, in 199 at the age of 85, Mrs. Logan was living in her own home in Jupiter, Florida.

Edgar Peyton Logan, known as "Pete," and his first wife, Ethel, divorced. He then marrie Mildred Walker, who still resides in the Smyrna area, in their home, which "Pete" built off Gray Roac "Pete" died in 1990 from complications due to cancer.

"Pete" Logan grew up on Log Cabin Drive, across the street from the Log Cabin Sunda School, south of Smyrna. His parents were Orrin Brown and Ruth Logan, who had four sons: Brown Edgar Peyton, known as "Pete," William, known as "Billy," and Robert. Robert Logan currently live on Cumberland Drive in the Smyrna area. See *Logan, Brown Circle*.

Fifth House

Mr. and **Mrs. William Virgil Cobb** lived on 400 acres of farm land in a white, two-stor farm house with a large porch; set on a hill, on the west side of the road, it was above Nickajac Creek, just north of Church Road. The Cobbs had six children: **Cecil**, **Lucile**, **Howard**, **Ralph** **Richard**, and **Nell**. (Richard and Ralph were twins.) Mrs. Virgil Cobb was the former Rubie Hill, th daughter of Mr. and Mrs. Reuben Hill of Vinings and a cousin of Mr. Judge Hill, who lived on Ban Street. See *north side of Bank Street.*

Mr. Cobb purchased this house from Mr. Parker M. Rice, who, having inherited the lan from his father, Z.A. Rice (a Colonel in the Confederate Army). Parker M. Rice had this house built i 1891 for his bride.

NOTE: The Oaks of Concord, a townhome community, was built on the Cobb Farm durin the last quarter of the Twentieth Century.

Virgil Cobb, who was born and raised in Union County, came to Cobb County on a assignment for the Internal Revenue Service. As an agent for the Federal Government, he was sent t various locations to gauge whiskey. He met Rubie Hill, his future wife, when he was assigned to Ros Distillery, founded by Rufus Rose and located on the present-day Stillhouse Road in Vinings. Rufu named his brand of whiskey "Four Roses" after the four generations of men in his family who had been involved in the distilling of whiskey. (Seagrams later owned and marketed "Four Roses.)"

In Vinings, Virgil and Rubie resided in a house on what is now Paces Mill Road; it was across the street from the present Vinings Methodist Church, near Rubie's parents. All of their children except Nell were born in Vinings; Nell was born after they moved to Smyrna.

Later, in Vinings, Virgil Cobb owned and operated a general store, which had a post office. With the Cobbs' planning to relocate to Murphy, North Carolina, Virgil sold the store to his father-in-law, Reuben Fleming Hill.

NOTE: The Vinings Inn now occupies the building that had once been Virgil Cobb's store.

Virgil and Rubie moved from Vinings to Murphy, N.C., where they lived for a short period of time. Coming back to Smyrna, the Cobbs moved to a house on Roswell Street, south of what was known as the Shipp House. They relocated from Roswell Street to a house on the northwest corner of Church Street and Memorial Place, where Virgil had bought much land; in fact, at one time he owned most of the land at Memorial Place and down Church Street, including the house where his son, Ralph Cobb, later lived. In 1918 the Cobbs moved once again to Old Concord Road, where they were residents the rest of their lives.

Cecil Cobb, a writer, married Otis Wesley. (She and Otis lived in Maryland before moving to the Buckhead section of Atlanta.) They had two children: Cecile, who married Bobby Dobson, and Hawthorne, who married Betty Nied.

Lucile Cobb married J.B. Crowe, the son of Mr. and Mrs. Samuel Jefferson Crowe, who lived on Church Street. Lucile and J.B. had no children. Lucile worked at Bell Bomber Plant during World War II and later at Dobbins Air Force Base; J.B. worked at the Atlantic Steel Plant in Atlanta. Lucile and J.B. lived with her parents, on Old Concord Road. See *Church Street* and *Old Roswell Street.*

During World War II, J.B. Crowe was in a car pool. When it was his turn to drive, Lucile was left without a car; because no family owned two cars back then, she would ride her horse, a Tennessee Walker, named Prince, to Smyrna. Leaving Prince at a mill in Smyrna, she rode a streetcar to work. J.B.'s brother, Elmer, who worked the night shift at Atlantic Steel Plant, would ride the streetcar to Smyrna and then ride Prince home. Lucile would come home with J.B. in the evening.

The Cobb Family were active members of First Methodist Church, where many Cobb family members are still regular attendees. Lucile still lives in the Smyrna area, off Church Road, not far from where she grew up. She celebrated her 100th birthday in 2006.

Howard Cobb married Curtis Pace, who for many years worked at Miller's Department Store in Marietta. Howard and Curtis, who had two sons, Douglas and Eddie, moved to West Cobb County.

Douglas married Joan Mayes and then Margaret Manos.

Eddie married Delores Lee.

Richard Cobb married Estelle Housley Millsap. They had a daughter, Carol, who married George Jordan. Richard worked at Simmons Mattress Company in Atlanta.

Ralph Cobb married Edna Ledbetter. They had three daughters: Beverly, Ann, and Nancy. Ralph, who had worked for N.C. & St. L Railroad, which later merged with L & N Railroad, died after a courageous battle with cancer. See *north side of Street, south side of Fleming,* and *Grady Street.*

Nell Cobb married Leland Williams. Nell worked at Davison's Department Store in Atlanta. Leland was employed by Atlantic Steel Company in Atlanta. They had one daughter, **Virginia Lenel** and three grandchildren. Nell and Leland Williams were active members of First Methodist Church. See *Hill Street; north side of Church Street;* and *Williams, east side of Old Concord Road.*

NOTE: Beverly Cobb Armacker stated: "Some of the information in this section came from my aunts, Lucile Cobb Crowe and Nell Cobb Williams, daughters of Virgil Cobb. The information about Rose Distillery came from the article entitled, 'Walking through Historic Vinings,' in the *Vinings Gazette,* December, 1997, page 7. The information about the original Parker Rice house came from the article 'Alert Developers Treasure Home's History,' by Randy Jay, on page 4F of the October 20, 1983, edition of '*Cobb Extra,*' a special publication included weekly in *The Atlanta Journal and Constitution.*"

Sixth House

Mr. and **Mrs. Hayes Cobb** resided here. Mrs. Cobb, whose given name was Emma, and Hayes had four sons and one daughter: **Vivan**, **Marion**, **Ruth**, **Carl**, and **Earl**. Their white farm house, which was located just north of the Virgil Cobb home, was razed; a nice brick ranch, house built on the same site, is still standing.

Vivan Cobb married Fannie Mae Wills, an artist. He and Fannie Mae had three children: Marjorie, known as "Margie," Bobbie and Mark. Vivan Cobb operated a grocery store in Atlanta; he and Fannie Mae lived on Lee Street in Smyrna. See *Cobb, west side of Lee Street* and *Wills, east side of Lee Street.*

Margie Cobb married Donald Levesque.

Bobbie Cobb married Harry Nix.

Mark Cobb married Mary Jane Peacock.

Earl Cobb married Hazel Ray; they had two children: Ray and Joe. Earl owned and operated Earl Cobb Shell Service Station in Smyrna during the days of my youth. See *Lee Street.*

Ray Cobb married Rena Ann Sheppard.

Joe Cobb married Judith Mary Jones.

Seventh House

Marion Cobb and his wife, the former **Beatrice Dobbins**, had five children: **Doris**, **Johnny**, **Norma Jean**, **Larry**, and **Randy**. Marion and Beatrice resided in this house, just north of Marion's parents' house. On Old Concord Road, this nice, white frame dwelling stood on Old Concord Road west of where Powder Springs Road turns 90 degrees northward. The Marion Cobb house was razed in 2005 for the building of a small subdivision, Hickory Springs Estates.

Doris Cobb married Gerald Choate.

Johnny Cobb married Jackie Jones.

Norma Jean Cobb married William Key.

Larry Cobb married Pat Hayworth.

Eighth House

Robert and **Louise Pope** lived on the northwest corner of Old Concord and Smyrna Powder Springs roads. (Their house stood where Hickory Lakes apartment homes are now located.) The Popes had three children: **Robert**, **Ellen**, and **Martha**. I believe Mr. Pope worked for Sears, Roebuck, and Company, in Atlanta, where the family later moved.

Ninth House

The **Hester Family** at one time were residents in this house which was located just south of today's intersection of Old Concord and Windy Hill roads. This house also stood on land that is now occupied by Hickory Lake apartment homes.

Tenth House

The **Merritt Family** resided for a long time in a house on Old Concord Road before it reached South Cobb Drive. This house stood on the hill on the northwest corner of the intersection of Old Concord and Windy Hill roads. The Merritts had two daughters, one of whom was Irma Jean, who attended Smyrna School with Beverly Cobb at Smyrna.

CHAPTER FOURTEEN

MEDLIN STREET

North Side

Appreciation is extended to Alice Gibson Vaughn, Sandra Ruddell Garvin, and Stephen and Gayle Ruddell for their memories of the Gibson and Patterson families, who lived on Medlin Street in the middle of the Twentieth Century.

First House

Fred and **Irene McRae** lived in this house within the curve, just before the Davenport House. Mrs. McRae was the former Irene Holleman. They had two children: **Steve** and **Susan**. See *south side of Love Street.*

Second House

Mr. and **Mrs**. **V.A. Davenport**, known as "Pete" and Elaine, were the residents of the house west of the big curve. They had two children: **Annette** and **Ben**. Mrs. Davenport, whom I remember as being a very pretty woman, was a good friend of my mother.

Mr. Davenport, a barber, worked on the ninth floor of the First National Bank Building in downtown Atlanta, where "Pete" cut and styled the hair of many downtown bankers, lawyers, and executives. An appointment was required to get service at the barber shop where he was employed.

The Davenports were members of Smyrna Presbyterian Church, where "Pete" sang in the choir.

Annette Davenport married Ronald Clark. They currently live in Florida.

Ben Davenport married Bobbie Hoffman from Little Rock, Arkansas. They had one daughter, Elizabeth.

Third House

Mr. and **Mrs**. **Winston Medlin** lived in this house. They had two children: a son, **Jesse**, and a daughter, **Marie**. Mrs. Medlin, whose given name was Effie, and Mr. Medlin in their elder years moved from this house to the east side of Concord Road, where Carolyn Medlin (McEntyre) and her family resided with them. Medlin Street is named for Winston Medlin. See *east side of Concord Road.*

NOTE: Winston Medlin was a brother of Carolyn Medlin McEntyre's grandfather, who owned a farm in this vicinity earlier in the Twentieth Century.

Mr. and Mrs. Grover Cleveland Patterson

Mr. and **Mrs**. **Grover Cleveland Patterson**, affectionately known as "Miss Pat" and "Pat," moved to this house after the Medlins had vacated. Mrs. Patterson's given name was Alice. The Patterson Family lived here for several years in the 1940s before moving to a house on the east side of Concord Road, where the Nichols office buildings are currently located. Afterwards, in the late 1940s, Mr. and Mrs. Patterson bought a house and some property on Concord Road, The Country Road; they moved to this location, about one-half mile west of the Access Road (known today as South Cobb Drive). The property they purchased extended from what is known today as Lamar Circle to the Dunton property, which was later purchased by Mrs. Patterson's daughter and her family. See *north side, Concord Road, The Country Road.*

Mr. and Mrs. Grover Cleveland Patterson had children from their first marriages. M Patterson was an engineer for Southern Railroad (known today as Norfolk Southern), from which h retired.

Mr. Grover Patterson's First Family

Mr. Patterson, from his first marriage, had four daughters: Geneva, Leola, Clara, and Ruby.

<u>Geneva Patterson</u> married Aubie Hendrix; they had two daughters: Carolyn and Audrey. Th Hendrix Family lived in Howell Station in Atlanta.

Carolyn Hendrix married Charles Fetterolf; they had two children: Carol and David.

Audrey Hendrix married Tommy Roberson ; they had two daughters: Karen and Connie.

<u>Clara Patterson</u> married J.C. Gilley, known as "Jan." They built a house on the corner o Concord Road and Lamar Circle, on property purchased from Mr. Patterson. The Gilleys had thre children: Segrid, Janice, and David.

Segrid Gilley married Larry Ray; they had one son, Scotty.

Janice Gilley married Robert McElreath; they had two sons: Jay and Marty.

David Gilley married Nancy Kemp; they had three children: Tammy, Kathy, and David. Se *Kemp on Main Street.*

<u>Ruby Patterson</u> married Herbert Ruddell. Living on the west side of Access Highway (nov South Cobb Drive), about a block from Cooper Lake Road, they had two children: Sandra an Stephen. The Ruddell Family were active members of Locust Grove Baptist Church in Oakdale. Bot Herbert and Ruby Ruddell are deceased.

Sandra Ruddell married George Earnhart, known as "Buddy"; they had two children: Lis and Becky. After "Buddy's" death, Sandra married George O. Garvin, known as "Bud."

Lisa Earnhart married Michael Gallagher. They had two children: Jenny and Jessica.

Becky Earnhart married Toney Johnson of the Oakdale community.

Stephen Ruddell married Gayle Colquitt. They had three children: Russell, known as "Russ," Jeffrey, known as "Jeff," and Leslie. Gayle was the daughter of Mr. and Mrs. Hubert Colquitt. Se *north side of Bank Street.*

Jeffrey Ruddell married Mandy Phillips of Vinings. They had two sons, Chandler an Chapman.

Leslie Ruddell married Brandon Moore.

Mr. and Mrs. Herbert Ruddell and family moved to Smyrna in 1950. Herbert worked fo Sears, Roebuck and Company, from which he retired after 45 years of service. Herbert's parents, Ome and James Alfred Ruddell, came from Howell Station in Northwest Atlanta to Smyrna and lived o property directly behind Herbert's family. Their driveway is now the entrance to Ivy Glen townhomes which are on James Alfred Ruddell's old home place. James Alfred built the first service station on th corner of Access Highway (now South Cobb Drive) and Cooper Lake Road; later he built a house nex door to the station.

Leola Patterson married Roy A. Flowers. They had three children: Marvin, Louise (who never married), and Grace. Mr. and Mrs. Flowers were residents on Atlanta Road in the Oakdale community and operated a drug/grocery store in a block building at the corner of Atlanta and Camp Highland roads. Having later resided in California, they returned to Smyrna in 1956 to live in West Smyrna Heights, a community built by Rem Bennett on the west side of South Cobb Drive, south of Dickson Shopping Center.

Marvin Flowers married Joan Bray of Atlanta; they had seven children: Paul, Donna, Patrick, Carl, Linda, John, and Troy.

Grace Flowers married Kenneth D. Coombs; they had two children; Gregory and Kandy.

Mrs. Alice Cook Patterson's First Family

Mrs. Alice Cook Patterson, from a previous marriage, had two children: Claude and Tommie Cook.

Claude Cook married Alice McClure and had one son, Ben.

Tommie Cook married Otis Bourn. They had three daughters: Virginia, Janette, and Claudia.

Otis and Tommie Bourn in 1949 bought from H.H. Dunton six acres next door to the Pattersons on the north side of Concord Road. They built a house, facing Concord Road, and moved there in 1950. As their three daughters married, each built a home on one of the other three lots. The entire family sold their homes in 2004 for the development of Concord Lakes subdivision. See *west side of Concord Road.*

Virginia Bourn married Franklin Coggins; they had two children: Franklin and Peggy. After Franklin died, Virginia married Ray Jones.

Janette Bourn married Andrew W. "Corky" Hudgins. They had two children: Mike and Vickie.

Claudia Bourn married Jay Shumpert. They had two children: Jerri and Angelia, known as "Angel."

Fourth House

Though I am not sure who lived in this house, I know that it existed.

Fifth House

J. M. "Hoot" Gibson
Mayor of Smyrna
1949-1952
1958-1959

J.M. Gibson, known as "Hoot," and his wife, **Lucy**, had four daughters: **Margaret**, **Colleen**, **Shirley Ann**, and **Alice**. They moved to the fifth house after the Pattersons had vacated.

Margaret Gibson married W.B. Barrett. They had one son, John Donald. Margaret died in 2005.

Colleen Gibson married Francis Cooke, known as "France." They had two children: Michael Arthur and Cynthia Frances.

Home of the "Hoot" Gibson Family
270 Medlin Street
Circa late 1940s
Courtesy of Alice Gibson Vaughn.

Mayor and **Mrs. "Hoot" Gibson**
City Hall on Bank Street
Completed July 1958
Dedicated September 1958
Courtesy of Alice Gibson Vaughn.

Shirley Ann Gibson married Don Walker of Smyrna. Shirley later married Benson Plunkett; hey had one daughter, Laura Denise, known as "Dee." Shirley Ann's third marriage was to Michael Ioltzclaw.

Alice Gibson married Steven Douglas Vaughn from Atlanta. They had two children: Steven Chadwick, known as "Chad," and Aliceson Courtney, known as Courtney. Steven Douglas lived on ite at the Atlanta Water Works, where his dad, Lindsey G. Vaughn, was employed for 40 years.

I really liked Mrs. Lucy Gibson, always a very nice lady. "Hoot" worked for the Southern Railroad Company, where he was a conductor. "Hoot" was a brother of Lois Barden, the mother of Don and Harry Barden. See *Pickens Street.*

"Hoot" served as Mayor of Smyrna, 1949-1952 and 1958-1959. He was serving as Mayor during the 1940s and 1950s "big building boom," which escalated when Lockheed opened at the ormer Bell Bomber Plant in 1951. The Gibson family, were long-time members at Smyrna Presbyterian Church.

A colorful guy, "Hoot" Gibson was very political in nature and always enjoyed a good 'hassle" while he served the City of Smyrna. Under his leadership, many of the streets were paved; water and sewer lines installed; City Limits tripled; and the City Hall on Bank Street was built and dedicated in September 1958. (The City Hall served the citizens of Smyrna well for the next 35 years.) It was an exciting time to be in political office in Smyrna!

"A lot of people have loved Smyrna through the years," but according to "Hoot's" daughter, Alice, "no one loved Smyrna more than my dad!"

Sixth House

Mr. and **Mrs. Hardy Bailey** in the earlier part of the Twentieth Century lived in a log house ocated somewhere on the north side of Medlin Street. Hardy was an older brother of Jesse Bailey, who, coming from Flowery Branch, moved to Pickens Street, on property owned by Hardy in late 1940 or early 1941. See *Bailey, west side of Pickens Street* and *west side of Roswell Street.*

According to information from Doris Bailey Fowler, her Uncle Hardy owned much land in his vicinity, extending from Pickens Street, where he owned several rental properties, and down the north side of Medlin Street to his cabin home. Doris remembers that, as a child, she went to the log house on many occasions. She also fondly remembers the picnics held there, and the many singings, where shaped notes were used. According to Doris' memories, this log house stood near the creek on Medlin Street. (This creek may be the one that runs from Flagler Circle and under Church Road, east of the present Smyrna Senior Aquatic Center. If so, this is probably the area where B.F. Reed, Jr., built many houses in 1950s and 1960s.)

MEDLIN STREET
South Side

Medlin Street in the days of my youth was a short east-west street, running from Concord Road to Dunton Street. Later on, it was extended westward for several blocks.

Appreciation is extended to Emma Jean Faucett Barden, Mary Lou Redd Cochran, Barbara Bryant Emmett, Alice Gibson Vaughn, and Peggy Norton Cochran for sharing their memories of the esidents on Medlin Street in the middle of the Twentieth Century.

Mr. and **Mrs. Nemory Chadwick** owned and operated a store on the corner of Concord Road and Medlin Street. He and Mrs. Chadwick resided in quarters in the rear of the store. Mr. and Mrs. Chadwick had four daughters and one son: **Loma** (see *Redd, first house*), **Irene** (see *Bryant, first* *house*), **Inez** married Charles Foster, they had two children, Mickey and Reggie, **Grace** (see *Langsto fourth house*) and **Broughton** (see *Chadwick, third house*).

First House

Loma Chadwick married **Douglas Redd**; they had three children: **Glenn**, **Weldon**, ar **Mary Lou**. Mr. Nemory Chadwick built this house on his property to the rear of his store, where h daughter Loma and her family lived. Loma and Douglas moved from this house to King Springs Roa

Glenn Redd married Betty Lou Fortner. They had five children: Rita, Terry, David, Vicke and Pam. See *Fortner, north side of Powder Springs Street.*

Weldon Redd married Bobbie Gaines from Moultrie. They had two children: Andy an Tony.

Glenn and Weldon Redd both served in the United States Military, during World War II.

Mary Lou Redd married Bobby Cochran. See *Chadwick* and *Redd, King Springs Road* an *Cochran, Elizabeth Street.*

Mr. and **Mrs. Paul Bryant**

Irene Chadwick married **Paul Bryant**. They had two children: **Joan** and **Sandra**. Paul an Irene moved to this house after the Redds vacated. *See Bryant, Pickens Street.*

Mr. and **Mrs. Louis Bryant**

Mr. and **Mrs. Louis Bryant** had five children: **Clifton**, **Clyde**, **Paul**, **L.M.**, and **Barbar** who was the only one living at home when they moved here. Mrs. Bryant, the former Lula Williams Dawson County, and Mr. Bryant, originally from Cherokee County, from where they moved Pickens Street, with their son, Paul, and his family. From Pickens Street they moved to this house 1950. See *Paul Bryant, west side of Pickens Street.*

Mr. Bryant, who worked for McNeel Marble Company and Georgia Marble Compan helped to build the "Singing Tower" (now known as the Bok Tower) in Lake Wales, Florida.

Clifton Bryant died when he was 12 years old.

Clyde Bryant married Lois Groover of Marietta. They live in North Carolina.

Paul Bryant lived on Pickens Street with his family. See *Bryant, west side of Pickens Street.*

L.M. Bryant and his wife, Delene, lived in Austell. According to information from the Brya family, L.M., who played country music, was inducted into the Atlanta Country Music Hall of Fame.

Barbara Bryant, a graduate of the Smyrna High School Class of 1951, married Georg Herman Emmett. They had two sons: Derrick and Darrell. Barbara was a gospel singer and member c the Harmonettes Trio, which was inducted into the Atlanta Country Music Hall of Fame. See *Emmet east side of Anderson Circle.*

Second House

Mr. and **Mrs. Henry Norton** resided in this house. Mrs. Norton was the former Mildre Lamb of Marietta. They had four children: **Lucille**, known as "Lucy," **Marshall**, **Peggy**, and **Lynd** All of the Norton children are graduates of Campbell High School. The Norton Family were membe of Spring Street Baptist Church. Mildred Norton was a sister of Edna Lamb Chadwick. See Norto

rth side of Church Road, The County Road, east side of North Cooper Lake Road, west side of Dunn reet, and Chadwick, third house on Medlin Street.

"Lucy" Norton, who never married, passed away in 2001.

Marshall Norton married and had a daughter, Christina, who graduated from Campbell High chool. Marshall passed away in 1978.

Peggy Norton married Ronald Cochran, who grew up in the Oakdale community, south of nyrna. Peggy and Ronald, both graduates of Campbell High School, had two children, Darren and indy, who graduated from Sprayberry High School in Marietta.

Darren Cochran and his wife, Kim, live in Acworth. They had two children: a daughter, bby, and a son, Austin.

Cindy Cochran married Jerry Lucas; they had two sons: John and Chandler. The Lucas amily lives in Acworth.

Peggy Norton Cochran shared, "Our children know about Smyrna only through having nversations with us and being around their cousins. When they played and cheered against Campbell igh School, it was so hard for Ron and me to root for Sprayberry; we felt like traitors. It was a joke ith our family that we were 'turncoats.'"

John Steely
Smyrna City Councilman
1980-1981
1988-1991

Lynda Norton married John Steely. They had two sons, Greg and Gary, who graduated from ampbell High School, as did both their parents. When my son, Stephen, married, Greg was a oomsman.

Third House

The **Chatham Family** lived here after the Bryants. They had two sons: **Lamar** and **Joe.**

Mr. and **Mrs. J.Y. Wooten**

Mr. and **Mrs. J.Y. Wooten** were residents of this house. They had a daughter, **Jane**. See *'ooten, north side of Concord Road, the Country Road.*

Mr. and **Mrs. Broughton Chadwick**

Broughton Chadwick married Edna Lamb; they had two sons: **Donald** and **Clay**. roughton began employment with Atlanta Paper Company when he was 16 years old and worked ere until he retired. Atlanta Paper Company later became Sonoco. See *Norton, second house on 'edlin Street.*

Fourth House

Hoyt and **Grace Langston** resided in this house. Grace was the daughter of Mr. and Mrs. emory Chadwick, who owned and operated the Chadwick's Store. Mr. Langston was a policeman for e City of Smyrna. Grace and Hoyt, who had no children, were active members of Spring Street aptist Church. See *Chadwick's Store, corner, Concord Road and Medlin Street.*

Emma Jean Faucett's four year old birthday party
In front of the Faucett House on Medlin Street
March 1938
Boys: L-R: **Lamar** and **Joe Chatham**
Girls: L-R: **Betty McManus** in print dress, **Emma Jean Faucett** (Barden) in plaid skirt, **Doris McLarty**, taller girl in back, **Betty Jo Ellis**, dark haired girl with bangs, **Jeanette Hanson** (Taylor), with hands to the mouth.

Fifth House

Mrs. Agnes Baldwin Faucett and her daughter, **Emma Jean**, lived in the next house. Mrs. aucett's husband, Emmett, was deceased.

Emma Jean Faucett married Don Barden, who also grew up in Smyrna. They had three sons: 'harles Edwin, known as "Chuck," Stephen Donald, known as "Steve," and Sanford William, known Sandy." Jean worked as the secretary to the principal of Griffin Middle School; Don worked for The tlanta Newspapers. Jean Faucett, a graduate in the Smyrna High School Class of 1951, and I were lassmates throughout our school years. See *Barden, west side of Pickens Street.*

"Steve" Barden, a graduate of Georgia State University, married Amanda Glosson; both of iem graduated from Campbell High School. They had two children: Sean Michael, known as "Sean" nd Christopher Thomas, known as "Chris."

"Chuck" Barden graduated from Kennesaw State University.

"Sandy" Barden is a graduate of Kennesaw State University.

Emma Jean Faucett Barden shared the following memories about her mother, Agnes aldwin Faucett Barden Feely. "My mother, Agnes Baldwin, was born in Douglas County, December 1, 1904. Her parents were Mr. and Mrs. Larkin Baldwin; she had one sister, Opal Anderson, and one rother, Olin Baldwin. Mother's dad, Larkin Baldwin, was a cousin of Robert Baldwin, whom I did ot know because he died when I was little, but we always called his wife 'Aunt Cousin Jenny,' why, I on't know. See *Baldwin, west side of Concord Road.*

"Mother was strong spiritually, and her faith never wavered. She taught me to love and trust ie Lord by daily living her faith and through her attending church regularly. My brother Sanford mmett Faucett, Jr., died in 1935, when he was five years old. My dad, Sanford Emmett Faucett, Sr., ied in 1940, when I was six years old. Mother, going back to school, took a business course so that he could get a job in the business world. During this time she continued to be Director of the Junior epartment in Sunday School at First Baptist Church, a position she held for approximately 40 years. he then became a director of an adult department; still later, she taught the Homemaker's Sunday chool Class, 1972-1984. Mother was active in Sunday School until a year before she died, at age 91.

"Since her death, I have had many people tell me, 'She was instrumental in leading me to 'hrist when I was in the Junior Department.'

"Mother was also a school teacher in her young adult years. I have received reports from ome of her students that she taught them at Smyrna School in the late 1920s.

"Widowed for many years, Mother was married the second time to Mr. J. L. Feely, who was lso a member of First Baptist Church."

NOTE: I knew Mrs. Faucett (Feely) very well, for I, as a part of the Junior Department of irst Baptist Church, was one whose life she impacted.

PICKENS STREET
East Side

First House

Miss Lena Crowe and **Mrs. King** lived in the first of the two houses on the north side of ickens Street. They were living there when they died.

Second House

Cecil Christopher and **Earnestine Cantrell**, known as "Tina," lived in this house. M Cantrell was the former Earnestine Bryant. Cecil Cantrell came to Smyrna from Pickens County, 1930. They had two children: **Barbara** and **Don.** The Cantrell Family were faithful members of Fi Baptist Church.

Barbara Cantrell, a graduate of Campbell High School, married Fowler Martin of Walk Street, who also graduated from Campbell High School. They had three children: a daughter, Dale, a two sons, Danny and Doug. Barbara later married Mack Davis; they had one son, Jeffrey. See *Mart Walker Street.*

Dale Martin married Greg Webster. They had two children: Mandi and Chris. Dale and Gr are divorced.

Doug Martin lives and works in Atlanta, where he is a Bank of America Vice-President.

Danny Martin was killed in a car accident when he was a little boy.

Jeffrey Davis is the head mechanic at Forest Park Bowling Alley. He lives in Marietta.

Barbara Cantrell Davis worked for the Bank of Smyrna on Atlanta Street, 1956-197 afterwards, she transferred to Cobb Exchange Bank in Marietta, which became First Bank and Tr and then National Bank of Georgia. After leaving National Bank of Georgia, she became employed Cobb Federal Savings and Loan Association. Barbara retired from First Union Bank in 2000, after years in the banking business. While working at First Union, she began as a part-time cashier for Wi Dixie Grocery Store, later known as SaveRite Grocery, where she worked from 1990 until the sto closed in 2005.

I recall seeing Barbara and her parents at church and fondly remember how faithful she w to take them to church during their senior years; after her mother passed away, she continued to ta her dad. She was a devoted daughter.

Don Cantrell married Lillie Jean Tillery from the Oakdale community. They had o daughter, Kim. Don and Lillie Jean graduated from Campbell High School. Later, Don married Jo Vansant, also a graduate of Campbell High School. They currently reside in Smyrna.

PICKENS STREET
West Side

Pickens Street, a very short street runs from Medlin Street, which runs off Concord Roa through to Nichols Street.

Appreciation is extended to Emma Jean Faucett Barden, Harry Barden, Millie Clayt Broyles, Sue Sargent Cantrell, Barbara Cantrell Davis, Ruby Cooper, Jesse Macaulay Dunton, Nan Cooper Logan and Bobby Fowler, for sharing memories of their families on Pickens Street.

First House

Harmon and **Azzilee Ellis** and their four children, **Ovalene**, **Peggy Jean**, **Betty Jo**, a **Charles,** lived in the first house on Pickens Street. They later moved to a house on King Springs Ro and next door to the Chadwick/Redd house. See *King Springs Road* and *east side of Roswell Street.*

The Paul Clayton Family

After the Ellis Family had moved, **Paul** and **Ida Mae Clayton**, and their two daughters, **Iildred**, known as "Millie," and **Pauline**, moved into this house on Pickens Street. Paul's mother ved with them.

"Millie" Clayton Broyles shared the following memory from her childhood. "For a short me, when I was a small child and my family lived on Foster Street in Smyrna, there was the murder f a woman and her young son. On the day of their funeral, which was conducted in Spring Street aptist Church, I was playing in my yard; I remember how afraid I was when I saw a group of Ku lux Klansmen entering the Church." See *north side of Bank Street.*

The Jess Sargent Family

Mr. and **Mrs. Jess Sargent** and their four daughters, **Margaret Lucile**, **Annabelle**, **Minnie ou**, known as "Sue," and **Frances**, resided here after the Claytons had moved. Mrs. Sargent was the ormer Ella Rosalee Huggins. The Sargents and Huggins came to Cobb County from the Ellijay, Blue idge, and Ballground areas. Mr. Jess Sargent worked for Tate Marble Company, in Tate, and later for IcNeal Marble Company, in Marietta.

Margaret Lucile Sargent married L.E. Green. They had three children: "Sonny," Annette, and ancy.

Annabelle Sargent, known as "Ann," married Charlie Thomas Martin. They had three hildren: Larry, Joann, and Patsy.

Minnie Lou Sargent, known as "Sue," married Olin Cantrell, who grew up on the southwest orner of Reed and Love streets. They had one son, Kenneth Edward. See *Cantrell, Reed Street.*

Kenneth Edward Cantrell married and had two children: Carli and Missey.

Frances Sargent married Wesley Liebergesell and had two children: Michael and Anita.

Second House

Mr. and **Mrs. Charlie Stephens** lived in the second house on Pickens Street. Her maiden ame was Corene Akins. They had four children: **Charles, Jr.**, **Juanita**, **Edward**, known as "Donnie," nd **Gloria**.

The Goss Family

After the Stephens had vacated, **Mr.** and **Mrs. Goss** and their daughter, **Henrietta**, resided in his house. They moved from here to Highland Avenue. See *Highland Avenue.*

Mr. and Jewell Barden

Mr. and **Mrs. Jewell Barden**, the former Lois Gibson moved to this house in 1947. They ad two sons: **Donald** and **Harry**.

Donald Barden, known as "Don," married Emma Jean Faucett, who grew up on Medlin treet. They had three sons: Charles, known as "Chuck," Steve, and Sandy. Donald and Jean are nembers of First Baptist Church.

Harry Barden married Norma Coleman, the daughter of Lewis, known as "Luke," and hristine Melton Coleman, from the Center Hill community in Northwest Atlanta. Norma graduated from West Fulton High School. They had two sons: Glen and Donny. Harry and Norma were membe of First Baptist Church before becoming members of Mt. Harmony Baptist Church in Mableton.

NOTE: Lewis Coleman was a member of the large Coleman Family in Oakdale communit south of Smyrna.

Mr. and Mrs. Barden were from Atlanta but moved to Virginia during World War II. Whe they returned to Georgia in the late 1940s, they moved to this second house. Lois Barden was a siste of " Hoot" Gibson, who served two terms as Mayor of Smyrna. See *Medlin Street.*

<u>Third House</u>

Paul and **Irene Bryant** moved to this house in 1941 with their daughters: **Joan** and **Sandr** (Later on, Paul and Irene obtained legal custody of their foster son, **Charles Sanders**.) Both Paul an Irene worked for National Biscuit Company, where Irene retired. Paul was stricken wit mysethenia/gravis which caused him to go on disability. They were members of Spring Street Bapti Church. After Paul's death, Irene continued living here for many years.

<u>Joan Bryant</u> married Clarence Hobgood; they had two daughters: Paula and Melody. Joa later married Ernest Eubanks; they had a daughter, Ginger. Joan has six grandchildren and two grea grandchildren. Joan, who lives in Cobb County, retired with 32 years of service, from J.C. Penney.

Paula Hobgood married Jimmy Burson; they had one son, Shayne, and a grandson, Tyle Paula later married Edward Ritter; they had one son, Paul.

Melody Hobgood, who never married, lives in Florida.

Ginger Eubanks married Lee Nelson; they had a daughter, Jenna, and one grandchild. Le Nelson had three children, Heather, Ashley, and Jessica, from a previous marriage.

<u>Sandra Bryant</u> married Lewis Hall and had a daughter, Renee.

Renee Hall married Erwin Traylor; they had a son, Matthew. Renee later married Jame Smith, and had a daughter, Jamie, who married Derek Dougherty, and had a son, Dylan.

Renee worked as a LPN at Smyrna Hospital for many years. She died in 1996 from cancer.

<u>Fourth House</u>

The **Manus Family** who lived here had several children. One was close in age to Emma Jea Faucett (Barden). See *Medlin Street.*

The Shipp Family

The **Shipp Family** lived here after the Manus Family had vacated. The Shipps had tw daughters: **Betty** and **Sarah**.

<u>Fifth House</u>

Mr. and **Mrs. Jesse Bailey** moved to this house from Gainesville in late 1940 or early 194 Her given name was Lois. They had two children: **Doris** and **Roger**. This property and other parce on Pickens Street, along with many acres down Medlin Street was owned at that time by Hardy Bailey Jesse's older brother. It was from this house that Doris Bailey, in the middle of the first grade, starte to school in Smyrna. See *Bailey, north side of Medlin Street and west side of Roswell Street.*

Mr. and Mrs. Jesse Cooper

Mr. and **Mrs. Jesse Cooper** resided in this house. She was the former Dovia Gordon. They had seven children: **Lois**, **Cora**, **Ruth**, **Maggie**, **Gideon**, **Carl,** and **Dudley**. Mr. Jesse Cooper, a farmer, tilled the land on the north side of Concord Road where Rem Bennett later built the small white frame houses. This area today includes Dell and McLinden avenues and Medlin Street. The houses on Dell Street and McLinden Avenue are located on land where Mr. Cooper's potato patch was located.

Lois Cooper married Jeff Moon and had two daughters, Mary and Martha, and one son, Jeff Moon, Jr., known as "Junior." Later Lois married Fred Daniel of the Oakdale community, south of Smyrna. They had one daughter, Terry Lee. Lois is now deceased.

"Junior" Moon, with limited reading and writing skills had a desire to join the military during World War II. Bobby Fowler remembers that "Junior" asked Bobby's dad, Gordon Fowler, if he would go with him to the recruiting office. Gordon signed him in. "Junior" joining the United States Navy, served the duration of the War, where the ship he was on was destroyed by a Japanese suicide bomb, "Junior" was injured but survived.

Cora Cooper married Gordon Fowler. They had two children: Maurice and Robert, known as "Bobby." Cora and Gordon lived on King Springs Road, on the site where King Spring Baptist Church is currently located. In 1947 their house was struck by lightning and burned. Afterwards, they built another house on the King Springs. Gordon Fowler had a heart attack in downtown Smyrna at Sanders Drug Store and died. See *Fowler, west side of King Springs Road* and *Bailey, west side of Roswell Street,* and *north side of Medlin Street.*

Maurice Fowler married Hulon Leathers. See *Highland Avenue*

"Bobby" Fowler married Doris Bailey. See *west side of Roswell Street.*

Ruth Cooper married Jesse Macaulay Dunton, who lived in the large white house on the southeast side of Concord Road where the Georgia Power Company is currently located. They had two children, a son, Jesse Macaulay, and a daughter, Dovia, each named for a grandparent. Macaulay Street off Concord Road, is named for Mr. Dunton. Because the developer spelled the name differently, the street is now known as McCauley. See *Dunton, east side of Concord Road.*

Maggie Cooper married Mr. McMichen. They had two daughters, Jeane and Louise. Later on, **Maggie Cooper McMichen** and her daughter, **Louise**, and her husband, **James Harris**, lived here for several years after the Coopers were gone.

Mr. and Mrs. James Harris had ten children: two daughters and eight sons including one set of twins. The oldest son was named David, the name of one of the daughters was Jean. James Harris was from Texas. After Maggie McMichen died, the Harris family moved to Texas.

Gideon Cooper married Cora Mae Hayes from Atlanta. They had one son, Ronnie. Gideon farmed on Concord Road, west of the Access Road, which is now South Cobb Drive. Gideon Cooper was a Mason.

Dudley Cooper married Nell Tatum of Atlanta's Bolton community. They had three daughters: Sylvia, Nancy, and Sue. See *Cooper, north side of Bank Street* and *Logan, east side of Old Concord Road.*

Carl Cooper married Ruby Fuller of Atlanta's Bolton community. They had four children: two sons, Cary and Randy, and two daughters, Carlene and Susan. Carl drove a truck for a living until 1951, with the opening of Lockheed he worked there until he retired. Ruby Fuller Cooper's stepfather was a preacher, known as "Brother" Wilson.

Cary Cooper married Kay Johnson. They had three children, Michael, Kimberly, an Christopher, and five grandchildren.

Michael Cooper, a Baptist minister in Utah, and his wife, Sherry, had a son, Michael Austin.

Kimberly Cooper married Todd Chambers; they had two sons, Nick and Ben.

Christopher Cooper and his wife, Melonie, had two children: Katelyn and Austin.

Randy Cooper married Betty Kendrick. They had two children, a son, Jeffrey, and daughter, Jessie.

Carlene Cooper married Bud Meers. They had one child, Melissa, and two grandchildren After Bud's death, Carlene married Harold Cheek.

Susan Cooper first married Jim Strayhorn, an attorney. They had two sons: Clay and Adam After Jim's death Susan married Stanley Cochran.

The Cooper House was located at the end of Pickens Street, near the curve into Nichol Street.

NICHOLS STREET

Nichols Street was cut at the end of Pickens Street in the 1940s. As a child, I do no remember this street as being here.

First House

Mr. and **Mrs. Cooper**, an older couple, moved to this street when it was new. They were th parents of Jesse Cooper, who lived on the south side of Pickens Street. See *Cooper, south side o Pickens Street* and *north side of Bank Street.*

Mr. and Mrs. Carl Davis

Mr. and **Mrs. Carl Davis**, both of Cedartown, moved to this house in 1949, after the Coopers vacated. Mrs. Davis, the former, Mary Jackson, and Carl had five children: **Carolyn**, **Larry** **Marilyn**, **Darlene**, and **Linda**. See *Clintes Davis, Walker Street.*

Carl, a preacher at Spring Street Baptist Church, later helped organize Temple Baptis Church (on South Cobb Drive), where he served as pastor. Before coming to Smyrna, Carl worked a Goodyear Mill in Cedartown for 27 years and afterwards for Tumpane, an independent contractor fo Lockheed Aircraft Corporation. He also did painting, and later worked at Kelly Chrysler-Plymouth Carl is deceased.

Mary Davis was employed for 17 years at Davisons, in Atlanta, and at Richs' Cobb Cente respectively. She now resides at Smyrna Towers.

Carolyn Davis married Richard Newton. They had two children, Debra and Timothy, five grandchildren, and five great-grandchildren.

Larry Davis married Bobbie Lewis and had two children, Dawn and Ross, and two grandchildren.

Marilyn Davis married Curtis Boren and had one son Kevin. Curtis, from a previous marriage, had three children: Becky, J.C., and Tyler. Marilyn and Curtis had three grandchildren.

Darlene Davis married Almarine Martin. They had a daughter, Cynthia, who died at the age f 20, and a son, Randall, and four grandchildren. Almarine, along with his mother, Shirley Martin, nd his sisters, Barbara Ann and Delores Martin, moved from Dawnsonville to Smyrna in the late 940s, by which time, Shirley's husband had died. Shirley later married Johnny Johnson. See *Martin, wenty-first house, east side of Roswell Street.*

Linda Davis married Tony McEntyre. They had four children, two daughters, Michelle and Kelley, and two sons, Dennis and Steven, and 11 grandchildren.

Second House

Mr. and **Mrs. George T. Hill** moved from Atlanta to this house in the early 1950s. George vas originally from Covington; Mrs. Hill, the former Martha Quigley, was a native of Atlanta. George vorked for Lockheed Aircraft Corporation for 30 years. He and Martha had six children: **Joyce**, **eonard**, **Robert**, known as "Bobby," **Roger**, **Daniel**, known as "Danny," and **Gordon**, known as "Gordy."

Joyce Hill, a graduate of Campbell High School, married Tommy Harper. See *Harper, south ide of Church Street.*

Leonard Hill married and divorced.

"Bobby" Hill, a graduate of Campbell High School, married Ann Weldon; they had one son, Dean.

Roger Hill married Elaine Dudley; they had two daughters: Crystal and Tiffany.

"Danny" Hill, a graduate of Wills High School, married Susan White; they had two daughters: Haley Daniel and Tatum.

"Gordy" Hill, a graduate of Campbell High School, married Pam Goodson; they had two hildren: Nancy and Mark.

HUNTER STREET

In the late 1940s and early 1950s Hunter Street was, as it is today, a short street running from Dunn Street to Concord Road.

Harry and **Lucy Evans** lived in the only house I can remember as being on Hunter Street. Harry was the son of Mr. Evans who lived on Fleming Street. His dad's widow, Mrs. Grace Evans, ater moved to the south side of Bank Street. Lucy was the daughter of Dr. and Mrs. Claude W. Mitchell. (Mrs. Mitchell's given name was Louise.) See *Mitchell, Atlanta Street, from Marlowe's to reatwood; Evans, Fleming Street,* and *Highland Avenue.*

Brinkley Park is bounded on the north side by Hunter Street and on the south side by Pine Street. After American Legion Post #160 was built, Pine Street was renamed Legion Drive.

In the 1970s, Jim Nichols built a business park in this area,

PINE STREET/LEGION DRIVE

Pine Street was a short street that ran from the east side of Concord Road through to Dunn Street. After **American Legion Post #160** building was erected, the street was renamed Legion Drive. Brinkley Park was on the north side of Pine Street. On the Park property stood the **Boy Scout Hut**, ocated behind the house which stood on the northwest corner of Dunn and Pine streets. As a boy, I

Mary Wills Girl Scout Hut
Legion Drive
Circa 1950s
Courtesy of Mike Terry.

The American Legion
Pine Street / Legion Drive
Circa late 1940s
Courtesy of Smyrna Museum

Boy Scout Hut
Brinkley Park
Circa 1950s
Courtesy of Mike Terry.

Smyrna's First Kindergarten

This picture taken in 1942 shows eleven six-year-old students who made up the first kindergarten in Smyrna. Mrs. Agnes Faucett (later Mrs. Lester J. Feeley) of 233 Medlin Street was the teacher. The class met in the Boy Scout Hut in Brinkley Park, shown in the background. **L-R: Front Row**: Victors Griggers, Henrietta Goss, Nancy Candler, and Jeane Pavolvsky. **L-R: Second Row**: Jesse Dunton, Gail Hiatt, Jean Magness, Betty Clayton, Julia Gibbs, Shirley Foster, Lila Lewis, Mrs. Faucett is standing on the right. This picture, which belonged to Mrs. Jay Foster, appeared in the *Marietta Daily Journal*, August 1962.

The newspaper article is courtesy of Mike Terry.

remember, I went to Scout meetings in this building, which was here before the American Legion building was constructed in 1947. See *Brinkley, west side of Dunn Street.*

NOTE: In the early 1970s, the original ball field at Brinkley Park was named Hambrick Field in honor of Wayne Hambrick, who dedicated himself for more than 20 years to Little League Baseball, which began at this park in the mid 1950s. See *Hambrick, north side of Concord Road, The Country Road.*

Prior to World War II, Veterans who were members of American Legion Post #160 conducted their meetings in various locations. With no Legion building and Smyrna area veterans returning from World War II, there was substantial community interest in raising money to build an American Legion home; therefore, fund raisings (e.g. barbecues and selling of raffle tickets, etc.) were held. The Legion's building was completed in 1947.

The **Mary Wills Girl Scout Hut** is located on Pine/Legion Drive, behind Mr. and Mrs. Pitner Dorris' home, which stood on the southeast corner of Concord Road and Pine Street. This hut, built in the late 1940s, primarily used for Girl Scout activities; occasionally was used by other groups. See *Dorris, south side of Concord Road.*

The Girl Scout Hut was an old building used during World War II. Surplused by the United States Government, it was relocated here by American Legion Post #160 and named in honor of Mary Wills because of her involvement in the American Legion Auxiliary.

NOTE: At the time of this writing, the Girl Scout Hut is standing.

CHAPTER FIFTEEN

GILBERT STREET

East Side

Appreciation is extended to the following people for sharing their memories of the people who lived on Gilbert Street in the days of our youth. Betty Burruss Brown for sharing her memories of Reverend Lawler and his family; to Carolyn Patrick Amburn, and Gwendolyn Patrick Rainwater, who grew up on Gilbert Street in the middle of the Twentieth Century, for information on their family and to Joycelyn Wallace Fain, for memories of her grandparents, the Green Berry Wallace Family. Appreciation also to Janice McDaniel, who furnished information on the Blackstone Family, into which her mother married; to Maxcine Gibson, who purchased the Gilbert House in 1961, which she razed in the late 1960s, and she built a house where she lived until 2005. At that time, Maxcine sold her property, which along with the Blackstone property and others, is being developed.

First House

Mr. and **Mrs. Hugh McCollum** lived here with their two daughters: **Patricia Ann** and **Andrea Lee**. According to neighbor information, the first house on Gilbert Street was built much later than the Gilbert House. Mrs. McCollum was the former **Clara Bell Anderson**. Clara Bell and her family moved to Florida, where she died August 6, 1991. See *Andersons of Roswell Street* and *Andersons, west side of Roswell Street.*

Patricia Ann McCollum married Robert W. Elling. They had three children.

Andrea Lee McCollum married John Linster.

Second House

The second house on the east side of Gilbert Street from Roswell Street was built by Mr. M.S. Gilbert in 1900, and known as the "Gilbert House." This was a large wood frame house without insulation. It had a sixty-foot long porch across thje front and extended twenty feet on each side of the house. The entry hall had a bedroom on the right. The "parlor" was on the left, with ten-foot pocket doors. Maxcine Gibson said her children called it the "funeral parlor." The next room on the right was the living room with a door opening to the side porch. The next room on the left was a bedroom with a door out to the side porch. I am told this room was available to the itinerant preacher who would just let himself in and spend the night. Behind the living room was the dining room and another bedroom across the hall. A kitchen was on the right side of the house with a porch behind it. The well that furnished their water was on the back porch. Across from the kitchen was another bedroom. When Maxcine purchased the house, a bathroom had been added at the end of the front hall, and another bathroom behind the back bedroom with a small kitchen. Two large mantles were in the parlor and dining room, and two small "ladies" mantles, one in the living room, and one in the preacher's bedroom. The ceilings were eleven feet high. The original Gilbert house burned; the one described above was built in 1900, in the same location. I am told this house had an enormous attic. The Gilbert family lived in this house in the first part of the Twentieth Century. According to long time Smyrna residents, at least one and possibly two of the Gilbert daughters lived on King Street, next door to Mrs. Agnes Flynn. One long time resident remembers when the Gilbert sisters, Miss Alma, Miss Leila and Miss Lula lived here.

The Gilbert Family were members of First Baptist Church. According to *A Beacon for Christ*, A Centennial History of First Baptist Church, the church minutes in 1888 show that Mr. M.S. Gilbert contributed $5.00 toward the preacher's annual salary of $135.00. Mr. M. S. Gilbert also served as a Smyrna City Councilman.

M. S. Gilbert
Smyrna City Councilman
1903

In the early days Gilbert Street ended just past Mr. Gilbert's property and the street was just the driveway. The house was very close to the street and their "yard" was on the other side. There were four stone steps at the front of the lot going down to the street.

According to information from residents on Gilbert Street, the Gilbert house in the 1940s and 1950s was divided into apartments and used as a rejntal house. Many people lived there through the years.

Maxcine Gibson bought the house in 1961 from a realtor. She tore the house down in 1977 and built the house in which she is currently living. Maxcine retained the mantles. She shared that once when she was a Girl Scout troop leader, she had thirty-six girls spend the night. "We cooked out and they slept in sleeping bags on the porch."

Maxcine is an active member of the First Baptist Church, where she is an officer in the LLL Club. Maxcine has two daughters, one son, three grandchjildren and four great-grandchildren. Her daughter, **Sherrill Williams**, lives with her.

NOTE: Maxcine Gibson's house, along with the Blackstone House, and several others were demolished in 2005, to build a new subdivision.

Third House

Mr. and **Mrs**. **Homer Blackstone** and their son, **Thomas Clyde**, lived in this house. Clyde and his wife, Evelyn, had two daughters: **Shirley** and **Jean**. Shirley is deceased.

Homer Blackstone worked for the railroad from which he retired. He later worked as a night security guard at Cobb Center Mall on South Cobb Drive.

Thomas Clyde Blackstone worked for Lockheed Martin. Later on, he married Pearl Cornman whose daughter, Janice Cornman McDaniel, was the last ownjer and occupant of this house.

The Blackstone residence was a nice red brick house, with a screened front porch and a side carport, which was very rare in the days of my youth. It had four fireplaces with mantles and two bathrooms that were installed when the house was built. For this reason, we believe this house had to be built after 1920. The first inside bathroom to be installed in a house in Smyrna was the Edwards house on Roswell Street in 1917. I delivered the elder Blackstone's paper in the 1940s they were always nice to me. See *Edwards, east side of Roswell Street.*

Mrs. Pearl Cornman Blackstone was a volunteer at the Smyrna/Adventist Hospital. She was also an employee with the Cobb County Board of Education lunchroom program.

Fourth House

Mr. and **Mrs**. **Bishop** and their son, **Don**, lived in this house. Don married Marie Turner. See *M.N. Turner Family, Dixie Avenue.*

Fifth House

About mid-way between Roswell Street and Marston Street was the home of **Reverend** and **Mrs. Clyde Lawler** and their children: **Jack, Marvine**, and **Carolyn**. He was the pastor at Smyrna Second Baptist Church on Atlanta Street. He performed the wedding ceremony of Betty Burruss and

The Blackstone House
East Side of Gilbert Street
Reportedly built in the 1930s
Demolished in 2005 to build a subdivision.
Picture taken by Lillie Wood

Home of Mr. and Mrs. Lamar H. Patrick
272 Gilbert Street, East Side
Courtesy of Carolyn Patrick Amburn.

Richard Brown in 1955, in the Second Baptist Church. See *Whelchel, north side of Walker Street*, and *Lacy, north side of Spring Street.*

Sixth House

Mr. and **Mrs. Green Berry Wallace**, known as "G.B.," lived in this house, which was a large white two-story wood frame house. They had seven children: **Bessie**, **Lucille**, **Ruby**, **Edna**, **Green Berry**, **Jr.**, known as "G.B.," **Sarah**, and **Fred**. The Wallace children were in my parents' generation. Mr. Wallace was known as "Uncle Green" in his family and also to the children in the neighborhood. He was a brother to Mrs. Della Tinsley who lived across the street. See *west side of Gilbert Street.*

Bessie Wallace married C. T. Conn, they had one son, Earl.

Lucille Wallace married Waymon Sorrells. They had five children: Emma Jean, Edith, Harold, JoAnn, and Beverly. The Sorrells moved to Jacksonville, Florida.

Ruby Wallace married Howard Akins. They had two sons, Billy and Lamar. See *south side of Bank Street.*

Edna Wallace married Herbert Wallace. They had four children: William, Joycelyn, Martha, and Neal. (Edna and Herbert were not related.) See *Foster Street.*

Green Berry Wallace, Jr., known as "G.B.," married Garderlee Land. They had four children: Barbara Ann, Wayne, Brenda and Venita. After Garderlee died, "G.B., Jr.," married again and moved to northwest Atlanta. They had no children.

Sarah Wallace married Robert Tolbert. They had two daughters, Patricia and Judy and two sons who died at birth.

Fred Wallace died at the age of fifteen due to complications from a ruptured appendix.

The Gunnels

Mr. and **Mrs. William Eugene Gunnels** had two daughters: **Judy** and **Betty**. Mrs. Gunnels given name is Mildred. They first moved to Smyrna in the early 1940s, during World War II, for Mr. Gunnels to work at the Bell Bomber Plant. After the War ended, they moved back to Griffin, where they lived for several years.

The Gunnels returned from Griffin to Smyrna in 1951, for Mr. Gunnels to work for Lockheed Aircraft Corporation, which opened that year. They renovated this house on Gilbert Street, which they bought and lived in for many years, before moving to the southwest of Concord Road and Concord Circle. The Gunnels were active members of First Baptist Church.

NOTE: The above house on Gilbert Street was designed for multiple family living.

Mr. and **Mrs. T.L. Dunn**

T.L. and **Margaret Dunn** lived in an apartment in the above house when they were newly married. She was the former Margaret Tanner. They moved from here to the Belmont House on Dixie Avenue. Later on they bought a house on Gilbert Street. See *west side of Gilbert Street.*

Mr. and **Mrs. McWaters**

Mr. and **Mrs. B.H. McWaters** and their son, **Alvin**, lived in this house. I delivered their paper during the World War II years and knew Alvin well.

The "Soapy Jim" Manning Family

I believe the sixth house is the same one that the "Soapy Jim" Manning family lived in when they first came to Smyrna in 1948.

Jim and **Sybil Manning** along with two of their four children: **Mary Faith** and **Sandra**, moved to Smyrna in 1948. The Mannings had two older children, Rrona, who was married before the Mannings moved to Smyrna, and Sidney, who was in the United States Army at that time. Jim and Sybil later had fifteen grandchildren and twenty-two great-grandchildren.

Jim Manning worked for John Smith Chevrolet as a car salesman. Almost immediately after moving to Smyrna, he became interested in politics and after a short while became active in several political campaigns, including the campaign of his friend, Cobb County Commissioner, Herbert McCollum. He was also involved in the campaign of Joe Lee Thompson when he first entered the political arena in the early 1960s.

Jim's favorite "hangout" was Atkins Pharmacy on Atlanta Street. It was here that he and several of his friends would meet daily to drink coffee and discuss local events, the topics of the day, and to see his good friend Bill Atkins who owned and operated the pharmacy. Another one of Jim's favorite people was newspaperman Bill Kinney and he read Bill's articles regularly. If Bill Kinney printed it, Jim Manning read it. On Saturday morning you could usually find Jim drinking coffee at the home of Mayor George Kreeger "discussing," what else but politics.

When Bill Atkins moved his drug store to Spring Road, then to Concord Road, it is reported that he kept the counter stool and coffee cup that Jim Manning used for many years.

Jim Manning had some interesting jobs during his long and colorful career. He once ran against Tom Linder for Commissioner of Agriculture and gained more popular votes than his opponent, but lost the race due to the county unit rule. At one time he was the youngest licensed rate expert with the Georgia Public Service Commission under Governor Eugene Talmadge. He went on to become Vice-President of the Trailways Bus System in Chicago and later founded the Jim Manning Chemical Company. He sold mattress covers, shoes, cleaning, and other supplies to businesses, cities, schools, and prison systems throughout the State of Georgia. It was when he was in the chemical business that he picked up the nickname "Soapy Jim." He met and had many friends throughout Georgia, which are too numerous to mention.

After Jim retired, his wife, Sybil, went to work as a bailiff for the Cobb County Court System. For many years she served as bailiff for the late Judge Luther Hames.

Jim and Sybil Manning moved from Gilbert Street to Belmont Avenue. Later, they moved from Belmont Avenue to Bank Street, between the Dallis Guthrie and the Austin Atkins families. When their son, Sidney, retired from Lockheed Martin in 1970, Sidney and his brother-in-law, Pete Williams, built a new home for Jim and Sybil near Sidney's house on Dunn Street. They lived there until Jim's death November 12, 1972 at the age of 67. His wife Sybil lived there until her health required her to be moved to a nursing facility in 1997. She died February 11, 1999.

Sidney Manning was born March 24, 1926. He died September 8, 1994. Sidney Manning never lived on Gilbert Street. He was serving in the United States Army when they moved here. He married after his family moved to Belmont Avenue.

Rrona Manning married before her family moved to Smyrna. She was born July 28, 1928 and died December 1, 2002.

Mary Faith Manning was born July 24, 1938. She married Pete Williams. They live in Smyrna. Mary Faith and all of her children graduated from Campbell High School.

Sandra Manning was born November 18, 1943. She married Don Caswell, who also grew up in Smyrna. He was the son of "Chick" and Edith Caswell. Sandra, Don and their children graduated from Campbell High School. His mother, Edith Caswell, worked at the Bank of Smyrna from where she retired. His dad, "Chick" Caswell, owned and operated an auto parts business on Pat Mell Road for many years.

Jim and Sybil Manning and their family were members of First Methodist Church, which was located at that time on Atlanta Street at Church Street. Reverend Roland Walker was the pastor. Before they moved to Smyrna they were members of the Baptist Tabernacle in Atlanta.

"Soapy Jim" Manning's parents lived directly across the street. They rented quarters in the Tinsley home at # 2601 Gilbert Street.

Seventh House

Mr. and **Mrs. Lamar H. Patrick**, known as "Pat," lived in this house. She was the former Gertrude Tinsley, the daughter of Olin and Della Tinsley who lived on the west side of Gilbert Street. They had three children: **Gwendolyn**, **Carolyn** and **William Edward**. The Patricks were active members at the First Baptist Church. Their street address was #148.

Gwendolyn Patrick married Frank Rainwater. They had one daughter, Cheryl.

Carolyn Patrick married Jerry Amburn. They had one son, Kent.

Edward Patrick married Nancy Thomason. They had twin sons: Tyler and Todd.

Gertrude Tinsley Patrick was a homemaker. Mr. Lamar H. "Pat" Patrick worked for Yancey Brothers Company. During World War II, he worked at the Bell Bomber Plant and rode his bicycle to work.

Eighth House

This house was owned by Frank Jones, to sold it to Mr. and Mrs. R.J. McCurry. They had moved into the house next door (where the Horsleys later lived) in 1955. Mr. McCurry remodeled this house then moved into it.

Ninth House

Mr. and **Mrs. Horsley** lived here with their son, **Dan**, who was close to my age. R.J. McCurry purchased jhis house and moved here in 1955.

R. J. McCurry
Smyrna City Councilman 1960-1965
Cobb County Board of Education 1969-1972
Smyrna Planning and Zoning Board Sixteen Years

R.J. and **Virginia McCurry** moved to this house on the northeast corner of Marston and Gilbert Street in the 1960s. R. J. shared with me that this area is known as Gilbert Heights Subdivision. He and Virginia lived in this house at 2601 Gilbert Street until May of 2004.

Virginia McCurry was the former Virginia Lackey from Gainesville, Georgia. They had one daughter, **Vicky Lynne**. R. J. grew up in the Hickory Flat Community just east of Canton, Georgia. He served on the Smyrna City Council from 1960-1965. He served four years on the Cobb County Board of Education and sixteen years on the Smyrna Planning and Zoning Board. He worked for The Berkeley Pump Company and Virginia worked with the Agri-Chem Division of Swift and Company.

He is a charter member of the Smyrna Optimist Club, which was chartered in 1962. They are faithful members of the King Spring Baptist Church.

Vicky Lynne suffered from cerebral palsy. For forty years she was loved and cared for by her adoring parents. She was one of God's "Special Angels" on earth. During her lifetime, R.J. and Virginia treated her as if God had sent her as "*His someone special*" for them to care for. Vicky Lynne was born on Valentine's Day in 1952. She passed away in October 1992. R. J. and Virginia have honored Vicky Lynne by helping some of her cousins to realize their dream of a higher education.

GILBERT STREET
West Side

Gilbert Street runs north and south parallel with Atlanta Street. It is a short street about three or four blocks long, from Roswell Street just past where G.B. Williams' Park is today to Hawthorne Avenue. Some long time residents remember Hawthorne Avenue being referred to as Hawthorne Street in the 1940s.

Appreciation is extended to Mary Faith Manning Williams for sharing information on her family who lived on Gilbert Street in the late 1940s. Appreciation is also extended to Carolyn Patrick Amburn, Gwendolyn Patrick Rainwater, Warren Day, and Janie Dunn, who all grew up on Gilbert Street. Janie still lives on Gilbert Street in the house where she grew up.

First House

Mr. and **Mrs**. **Manus** lived here. They had a daughter, **Nancy**, and a **son**.

Second House

Mr. and **Mrs**. **Don Atkinson** lived here. He was the Fire Chief for the City of Smyrna. They had two children: **Maureen** and **Gary**. Janie Dunn remembers seeing the red fire truck parked at this house on occasion.

Third House

At one time, **Mr**. and **Mrs**. **Robert Day** lived here. Mrs. Day's given name was Myrtice, they had two children: **Warren** and **Betty**. Mr. Day worked at the Warren Company making bomb shells during World War II. Later on, he owned and operated Day's Taxi Service in Smyrna and Day's Grading Service. The Day family later lived on Lee Street in the Hickory Hills area.

Warren Day graduated from Campbell High School in the class of 1960 and served in the United States Navy. He was married and had four sons, a daughter, and two stepchildren. Warren is presently living in Grantville.

Betty Day married William F. Smith, known as "Skeeter," a graduate of Marietta High School. They had four children: Bill, Sandy, Susie, and Danny. They live in the western United States. "Skeeter" was a brother to Wylene Cochran. See *Day, north side of Sunset Avenue*, and *Cochran, south side of Powder Springs Street.*

Fourth House

Mr. and **Mrs**. **Thomas Lee Dunn**, known as "T.L.," lived here. They had three children: **Janie Lee**, **Debbie Lynn** and **Marvin Daniel**, known as "Danny." Mrs. Dunn was the former Margaret Tanner of Smyrna. T.L. Dunn was in the United States Army during World War II. He served in the European Theater, was wounded and lost his leg in combat. He served as Commander of the Smyrna American Post #160. Janie Dunn recalls when she was a little girl she marveled how her dad could march in the parades with the American Legion. Even with his one leg, he could keep time with the others who were marching. She also said that having one leg did not keep him from swimming. He loved to swim and he was good at it.

T.L. Dunn began working for Lockheed Martin Corporation when they opened in 1951. He retired from there. Margaret Dunn worked for the Cobb County Board of Elections and Registration. Janie Dunn works for Sears at Cumberland Mall.

The house the Dunns lived in had a basement and a livable attic area. When Margaret and T.L.'s children were small, Margaret's parents, Mr. and Mrs. Morris Tanner, lived in the house with them. Margaret's grandparents, Mr. and Mrs. Jonathan Poss, lived in the basement apartment. Mrs. Poss' given name was Gennie. Margaret's two brothers, Johnny Tanner and Morris Tanner, Jr., known as "Buck," lived in the attic quarters.

Fifth House

Mr. and **Mrs**. **Frank McCutchen** lived in this house. They had three daughters, **Peggy**, **Betty**, and **Sarah**, and a son, **Billy Joe**. Billy Joe was killed in an automobile accident in Oakdale when he was a young man.

Mrs. McCutchen was the former Ruth Mathis, the daughter of Mr. and Mrs. John Mathis of the Mt. Olivet area off Paul Samuel Road in West Cobb County. In addition to Ruth, Mr. and Mrs. Mathis had five other children: daughters Eloise, who married Glenn Martin of the Oakdale Community, Ruby, who never married, and three sons, Everett, Earl, and Carl. Mr. John Mathis later lived in the Oakdale community south of Smyrna.

Frank McCutchen and Earl Mathis were baseball players.

NOTE: Frank McCutchen had a relative, an old umpire, "Red" McCutchen, who was hated by Atlanta Cracker fans.

Sixth House

Mr. and **Mrs**. **Olin F**. **Tinsley** had five children: **Isaac**, known as "Ike," **Calvin**, **Walter**, **Gertrude** and **Ed**. Mrs. Tinsley was the former Della Wallace, a sister to Green Berry Wallace. "Granny" and "Grandpa" Tinsley, as they were known, built this large yellow wood frame house. He was a farmer and also had a cow and sold milk to the neighbors. Ed Tinsley and his wife, Louise, moved here from Fleming Street after both his parents died. Louise still lives in this house. See *Wallace east side of Gilbert Street,* and *Ed Tinsley, north side of Fleming Street.*

Isaac Tinsley, known as "Ike," had one daughter, Roslyn, who married Edgar Benton.

Calvin Tinsley had two children: Douglas and Beatrice.

Walter Tinsley had no children.

Gertrude Tinsley married Lamar Patrick, known as "Pat." They had three children. See *east side of Gilbert Street.*

Ed Tinsley married Louise Brown. They had one daughter, Winifred, who married Richard Gazaway. Mr. and Mrs. Ed Tinsley ran an upholstery business on Atlanta Road south of Smyrna. Their business was located next door to Mr. and Mrs. Fuller Daniel's home, across from where Campbell Middle School is currently located. At one time, Louise and Ed Tinsley lived on Fleming Street.

Home of Mr. and Mrs. Olin F. Tinsley
143 Gilbert Street, West Side
Courtesy of Carolyn Patrick Amburn.

Mr. and Mrs. Manning

Mr. and **Mrs. Manning** lived at 2601 Gilbert Street. They lived in a section of the home of Mr. and Mrs. Olin F. Tinsley. Mr. and Mrs. Manning were the parents of "Soapy Jim" Manning who lived directly across the street. See *east side of Gilbert Street.*

Note: Mr. and Mrs. Olin Tinsley rented an apartment in their home to many families through the years.

The next five houses were built around 1953 to help meet the housing need created by the opening of Lockheed Aircraft Corporation in 1951. The following people lived in these houses in those early years: Doris Day, the Roarks, James and Hazel Brown, and their two sons: Roger and Sammy, and Mr. and Mrs. Earl Sheppard. After Peggy and Earl Sheppard came to Smyrna she began teaching in the new Campbell High School. Earl was an air traffic controller at the Atlanta Airport, (which is now Hartsfield-Jackson.) See *Watson, south side of Spring Street.*

A. C. and Josephine Shepherd also lived in one of the above mentioned five houses. Josephine was a registered nurse and served in the United States Armed Forces during World War II, and A.C. was the Executive Director of the Smyrna Chamber of Commerce. While he was in that position, he drew a map of Smyrna of that time. See *a copy of the map in the Smyrna Museum.*

Lila and Dick Baker also lived here at one time with their young family. She was the daughter of Mr. and Mrs. Sam Lewis. See *Highland Avenue.*

HIGHLAND AVENUE

East Side

First House

Mr. and **Mrs. Bob Brewer** lived on the east side of Highland Avenue. They had one daughter, **Mary Ann**. The Brewers lived almost directly across the street from the Sam Lewis Family. Mary Ann married Paul Caldwell. I remember Mary Ann because she worked at the Smyrna Telephone Exchange. I always knew when she answered the telephone. She was a very expressive person on the phone and I was always glad when she answered. This was when we had the party line system and an operator answered and transferred the call. I remember that she and Paul lived with the Brewers for a long time after they married. The Brewers had some other children, but they were much older than I.

Mr. Brewer had a small grocery store behind his house.

To my knowledge, this family was not related to my grandmother, Callie Brewer Crowe.

Second House

Mr. and **Mrs. Leathers** lived on the east side of Highland Avenue. They had a son, **Hulon**. Hulon married Maurice Fowler, who grew up on King Springs Road. See *west side of King Springs Road.*

Third House

Mr. and **Mrs. Davenport** lived in the next house. They had several sons and one daughter. I recall that **Leonard Davenport**, was one of their sons.

Fourth House

Mr. and **Mrs. Jim White** had one son, **Milton**, who married Virginia Norton. The daughter of Charlie and Nell Norton, Virginia grew up on Church Road. Milton was in the Class of 1951 at Smyrna High School. He worked for the Georgia State Highway Department from where he retired.

Jim White was a bricklayer. That was his occupation and he was very good at it. I remember that he had a reputation of being among the best. He and Jesse Bailey worked together. I believe they did some developing and building together. I remember that Jim White did some building in Bennett Woods after it was developed in the 1960s. He built at least one house on Havilon Way, the street where Lillie and I live.

I understand that Milton has owned this property on Highland Avenue through the years since his parents passed away. Their house on Highland Avenue was torn down in the middle of May 2004 and three houses were built there.

HIGHLAND AVENUE
West Side

Appreciation is extended to Rita Lewis Nowlin and Robert Lewis for sharing information about the Sam Lewis and Marcus Lewis families on Highland Avenue; to Sally White Foster for sharing information on the Jay Foster family; and Paula Robinson Lewis for information on her grandchildren; to Margie Miles Jones for information on the Jones family.

From Spring Street at the railroad, Highland Avenue is the second street to the left off Roswell Street. In the days of my youth it was an unpaved street. When the streets were paved the homeowners had to pay half the cost. This street was paved in the late 1940s or early 1950s.

First House

Mr. and **Mrs. Jimmy Jones** lived in the first house on the west side of Highland Avenue. They had four children: **Buddy, Marion, Laura Ann**, and **Betty**. Buddy was a little older than I. He played football at Marietta High School. He also played baseball for my dad on the Smyrna amateur team. Buddy was a good ball player.

Buddy Jones is married and has a son, Evan.

Marion Jones graduated from Marietta High School. He married Margie Miles, a Campbell High School graduate. She is a member of a large family from the Oakdale Community. They had five children: Bill, Glenn, Matt, Mark and Susan.

Laura Ann Jones married Kelly Motter who grew up on Spring Road at what is now Cumberland Parkway near Bethel Baptist Church. See *south side of Spring Road.*

Betty Jones married Garland Cook. They have four sons: Benny, David, Douglas and Stephen.

Mr. Jones was a big baseball fan. I remember that he attended all of the ball games. He worked in Atlanta, but I'm not sure where. The Jones family were members of the First Baptist Church.

Second House

Mr. and **Mrs. Jay Foster** lived in next house. Her give name was Edna. I remember her well. She was a very friendly lady and always nice. They had four children: **Shirley**, **Don**, **Richard**, known as "Dickie," and **Mary Ellen**.

Shirley Foster married Eddie Strickland. They had two children: Keith and Connie. Connie married Mr. Duncan.

Don Foster married Polly Sinclair from Marietta. They had three sons: Matt, Brad and Whit.

Richard Foster, known as "Dickie," married Sally White of Smyrna. They had two sons: Robbie and Andy.

Mary Ellen Foster married Mike Leonard. They had one daughter, Paige.

Shirley, Dickie and Mary Ellen live in Smyrna. Polly, Don's widow, lives in Augusta, Georgia.

The Fosters were active members at Smyrna First Baptist Church. Mr. Foster died in 2003. He attended church until a short time before he died. He was a good and faithful Christian man.

When I was a kid, Mr. Foster worked for D.C. Osborn as a mechanic. Another person that worked with him at D.C. Osborn's station was Cecil Pickens. Mr. Foster later made a career working for the Georgia Power Company at Plant Atkinson off South Atlanta Road.

Mrs. Edna Foster was in the Homemaker's Sunday School Class with my mother.

In the later years of Mr. Foster's life, Lillie taught in the senior ladies' Sunday School class for a number of years. She knew Mr. Jay Foster and his second wife, Lenore, well. Lenore was a very nice, intelligent lady. She was faithful to attend church through the years with Mr. Foster and also after his death.

Third House

The Willis/Evans Family: **Mrs. Grace Willis** lived in south Georgia. She had two children, **Miles** and **Dorothy Willis**. Her first husband died while she was pregnant with Dorothy, and after Dorothy was born, Mrs. Willis moved to Tilton, near Dalton where she met **Mr. John W. Evans** whose first wife had died. He had three young sons,. **Harold**, **Kenneth**, and **Harry** After Mrs. Willis and Mr. Evans married, they moved to Highland Avenue. Later on, they moved from Highland Avenue to Fleming Street. After Mr. Evans' death, Mrs. Grace Evans and her family moved to Bank Street, to the house that was formerly the home of the Howard Scoggins family. See *Willis/Evans, north side of Fleming Street.*

Fourth House

Mr. G. P. Blount and his wife, **Mary Lester Matthews,** lived in this house, in the days of my youth. Mr. and Mrs. Blount, both previously married, were in their senior years when they married. However, from my earliest memories they were married to each other. See *Pritchard, Twenty-third House, east side of Roswell Street.*

I remember that Mr. Blount would dress every day in a shirt, tie, and dress pants. He was one of the men that would sit on the ledge at Walker Akins Grocery store and talk politics with Mr. B.F. Reed, Sr., my grandfather, Ed Crowe, and his brother, Uncle Jeff Crowe. Mr. Blount was a distinguished, kindhearted gentleman. He always made me feel very special. All of the men that sat on that ledge were that way. I knew that they liked me and were keeping an eye on me.

I never knew what Mr. Blount did because he was retired as long as I could remember. He died while I was still a young boy. Mrs. Blount worked at the Arrow Shirt Factory, which was known as Cluett & Peabody. The Cluett & Peabody plant was located on Murphy Avenue in East Point. She would ride the streetcar to Five Points in Atlanta and transfer to the College Park Line. A lot of people who lived in Smyrna, and worked in Atlanta or Marietta, rode the streetcar in those days. The Blounts attended church at Smyrna First Baptist.

Mrs. Mary Lester Blount's first marriage was to a Mr. John Matthews. They had a daughter, **Margaret**, and a son whose name I never knew. In the early 1940s, Margaret and my Uncle **Tom Tucker**, married. They lived on Highland Avenue with Mr. and Mrs. Blount. They lived there for a long time. Mr. Matthews had some other children, whom I never knew.

Tom and Margaret Tucker had one son, Guy. The Tuckers moved to Cherokee Trail in the 1950s after the development started on Cherokee Street, which is now Windy Hill Road. There they lived for a long time before moving to Pineview Drive off North Cooper Lake Road. Tom Tucker played on the Smyrna Amateur Baseball Team with my Dad. See *R.H. Tucker, west side of Roswell Street.*

Guy Tucker married Patricia Clark. She also grew up in Smyrna. They had two daughters, Ann and Mary. Guy is the only person that I know that is still in the paper route business. He has made a profession of it. I respect him, for I know about that paper route work. He and his dad, Tom Tucker, did that together for a long time. Tom died suddenly on New Years Day, 1991.

Guy and his family lived on the south side of Smyrna-Powder Springs Road west of South Cobb Drive. After his parents' deaths, Guy and his family moved to Tom and Margaret's home on Pineview Drive, where they raised their daughters. Guy and Pat attend church at Smyrna First Baptist.

Fifth House

Mr. and **Mrs. Kerr** lived in the next house.

Sixth House

Mr. and **Mrs. Marcus Dudley Lewis** lived in this house. She was the former Minnie Burns. They had five children: **Glen, Ruth, Sam, "Tink,"** and **Sarah**.

Mr. Marcus D. Lewis was a dairy farmer. At one time he had a dairy in the vicinity of where the Russell Elementary School is presently located. He and his son, Sam Lewis, farmed the land beyond Sam and Edna's house on Highland Avenue.

Glen Lewis married Alma Pass. They had two children: Ralph and Emma Jean.

Ruth Lewis never married.

Sam Lewis married Edna ParnellThey had twelve children. See *eighth house.*

"Tink" Lewis married Clayton Pass. They had two children: Rex and Marie. Clayton Pass was a brother to Alma Pass who married Glen Lewis.

Sarah Lewis married Chesley Parnell. They had two children, Max and Madge. Sarah and Chesley Parnell lived here in this house on Highland Avenue for a long time. Later on they moved north of Smyrna in the Dixie Avenue area. Mr. "Chess" Parnell operated a laundry pickup service in Smyrna. It was for one of the laundry services out of Atlanta. He would pick up laundry the first of the week and deliver it back later in the week. I don't think his pickup service was limited to Smyrna.

Madge Parnell married Arvis Moore. Arvis was a pilot in World War II. He flew in the Pacific in the Army Air Corp.

Max Parnell
Prisoner of War
World War II

Max Parnell married Virginia Duckett from Vinings. He graduated from Georgia Tech. Max was a pilot with the United States Army Air Corp. This was before the Air Force was established as a separate branch of service after World War II. Max flew with the Flying Tigers during World War II in Asia, China, and Burma. He was shot down in the China Sea and captured by the Japanese and held as a prisoner of war. Max was a prisoner when the atomic bomb was dropped. He was rescued and admitted to a hospital ship. While he was a patient he could see the USS Missouri where the papers were signed that ended the war. During the war, Max flew P40s, and later on he also flew P51s. After the war, Max worked for the National Cement Company as a sales person. At one time he was a partner with Jack Dobbins in a sporting goods store in Marietta. Max and Virginia Parnell were members of the Smyrna First Methodist Church.

Max is one of Smyrna's celebrated citizens who served in World War II. His name is engraved on the War Memorial in Smyrna.

Seventh House

A family named **Stephens** built this house and lived here for a few years. Afterwards many other families lived here over the years.

Eighth House

Mr. and **Mrs. Sam Lewis** lived here. Mrs. Lewis was the former Edna Parnell. They had a large family and probably have more descendents in the Smyrna and Cobb County area than anyone else that I know. They had twelve children: **John D.**, **Claire**, **Robert**, **Nanette**, **Lila**, **Ann**, **Jerry**, **Wayne**, **David**, **Rita**, **Sammy**, and **Jenny**. Sam and Edna Lewis were members of the First Baptist Church and reared their family in the faith. Mrs. Edna Lewis was a homemaker.

Mrs. Lewis was the daughter of Mr. and Mrs. John Fletcher Parnell who lived on the southwest corner of Church and King Streets. See *west side of King Street.*

Mr. Lewis worked for the railroad. He was the son of Mr. Marcus Dudley Lewis and Minnie Burns Lewis, who also lived on Highland Avenue. See *sixth house.*

John D. Lewis married Mary Ruth Evans. They had four children: Gary Lewis, Judy Lewis Stafford, Connie Lewis Glass and Tim Lewis.

Claire Lewis married Archie Helton. They had three children: Randall, Karen, Fain, and Stan. Claire and Stan are deceased.

Robert Lewis married Sue Ingle. They had two daughters: Marsha and Mary Jane. Sue grew up on Bank Street next door to my family. Robert Lewis is now married to Barbara Carroll. They live off Church Road and are very active at Norton Park Baptist Church. I remember at one time, Robert was the soda jerk at Landers Drug Store on Atlanta Street.

Marsha Lewis married Snyder Turner who also grew up in Smyrna. They have two sons: Spencer and Brent. Tyler is the Administrator of the Calvary Children's Home in West Cobb County. Calvary was founded by Snyder's dad, the Reverend Ben Turner, who was the pastor of Calvary Baptist Church on Belmont Avenue in Smyrna. The home was located near Calvary Church for more than twenty-five years. It was relocated to West Cobb County in the 1990s. According to family information, before Reverend Ben Turner became pastor at Calvary he was the pastor at Spring Street Baptist Church.

Mary Jane Lewis married a Dulaney.

Nanette Lewis married Dr. Van Houton. They had one daughter, Angela Houton (Williams).

Lila Lewis married Dick Baker. They had one daughter: Lisa Baker, and three sons: Ted, Greg, and Chris. Lisa married Shane Cannon. See *Burruss, Atlanta Street, from Miles Stop to the Motters.*

Ann Lewis married Frank Denson. They had two children: Bruce and Mike.

Jerry Lewis and Pat had two children: Marc and Cindy (Leaf). Marc was a missionary to Thailand and is currently serving as youth minister at Orange Hill Baptist Church in Austell.

Wayne Lewis married Paula Robinson. They had a son and a daughter: Bryan Lewis and Gina Lewis

Gina Lewis married Bobby Booth and they had eleven children.

Bryan Lewis married Jill Taylor, the daughter of Judy and Tom Taylor of Smyrna. Bryan and Jill live in Orlando, Florida.

David Lewis and Mandy Lewis had two children: Matthew and Laura. David later married Diane, who had a daughter, Lauren.

Rita Lewis married Lloyd Nowlin, and they have two sons: Jeff Nowlin and Nathan Nowlin. Rita and Lloyd are members of the Smyrna First Baptist Church. They have been faithful through the years in the Sunday School, working with five year olds. They raised their sons at First Baptist. Lloyd also grew up in Smyrna and graduated from Campbell High School.

Sammy Lewis and his wife, Patsy, had one daughter, Samantha Lewis (Wamble).

Jenny Lewis, is married to Wayne Moody, they had no children. Jenny and Wayne are members of the Smyrna First Baptist Church. She served on the pulpit committee when Reverend Bud Abbott was called to pastor the church.

All of the Lewis children are still living except Claire. She died while she was still a young woman, from cancer.

Mrs. Edna Parnell Lewis died May 21, 2004. She was ninety-seven years old. Her funeral service was held May 23, 2004, at the Smyrna First Baptist Church. Like her grandmother, Gina Lewis Booth has a large family. She and her husband Bobby Booth have eleven children. They are a beautiful, talented family. The entire Booth family sang at Mrs. Edna Lewis's funeral. The second daughter, Anna, played the piano before the service and the violin as the family was being seated. The two older sons, their dad, and Jerry's son, Marc, sang *Beulah Land,* at the end of the service. Another grandson-in-law, Shane Cannon, also sang in the service. It was a beautiful, worshipful occasion.

At the present time, 2006, Jenny Lewis and her husband, Wayne Moody, live in the house on the north side of Mrs. Lewis' house. So, after seventy or more years, there is still a Lewis family member living on Highland Avenue.

NOTE: The older Lewis children from John through Nanette, graduated from Smyrna High School, the younger ones from Lila through Jenny, graduated from Campbell High School.

OLD ROSWELL ROAD

East Side

Appreciation is extended to Sam Crowe and Lamar Davenport, for the information they furnished on their families on the west side of Old Roswell Road.

First House

William Thomas Crowe, known as "Sugar," and his wife, **Loueva,** lived in the first house on the east side of the street from Roswell Street. They had two sons: **Lanier** and **Wayne**. See *second house on Old Roswell Road, and south side of Church Street.*

"Sugar" Crowe worked for the Atlantic Steel Plant on 14th Street in Atlanta. I remember he rotated shifts there. I don't know why I remember that. He later worked for the Georgia Power Company, from which he retired.

Lanier Crowe married Frances Chastain of Fair Oaks. They had two children: Jeff and Jill. Lanier and Frances live in Marietta.

Wayne Crowe married Carolyn Hardin and they had two children: Lori and Ashley. Wayne and Carolyn live in Powder Springs.

Second House

Mr. and **Mrs. Samuel Jefferson Crowe**, known as "Jeff," lived here early in the 1940s. Mrs. Crowe was the former Effie Lenora McWaters. They had eight children who were in my parent's generation: **Gertrude**, **Dave**, **J.B.**, **Eva**, **Samuel Joseph**, known as "S.J.," **Elmer**, **Wilmon**, and **William Thomas**, known as "Sugar." See *south side of Church Street, and first house on east side of Old Roswell Road.*

Gertrude Crowe married Herbert Barfield. They had two sons: Herbert Lee and Rex.

Dave Crowe married Clyde Elgin. They had no children.

J.B. Crowe married Lucile Cobb. See *west Side of Old Concord Road.*

Eva Crowe married Bill Poss. They had four children: Ed, William, known as "Buck", Hazel, and Edna Mae.

Hazel Poss married Charles Coleman who lived on Camp Highland Road, in the Oakdale area south of Smyrna.

Edna Mae Poss married Glenn Cantrell who lived on Gilmore Road, in the Oakdale area south of Smyrna.

NOTE: Bill Poss had several brothers, who lived in and around Smyrna: Jess, Lee, Claude, Joe, Ike, and a sister, Sarah. See *Fouts Brothers, Atlanta Street from Mrs. Mazie's to Creatwood.*

Elmer Crowe married Emma Lou Scoggins. They had five children: Eugene, Betty, Eula Mae, Larry and Tommy.

Samuel Joseph Crowe, known as "S J.," married Ethel Cochran. They had one son, Samuel Joseph Crowe, Jr., known as "Sam."

Samuel Joseph Crowe, Jr., known as "Sam," married June Durrett of Marietta. They had three children: John, Michele, and David. David is deceased. Sam and June had five grandchildren, and one great grandson.

Wilmon Crowe married Mary Morgan. They had two children: Jerry and Ronald. Wilmon and Mary lived on Grady Street where she still lives.

William Thomas Crowe, known as "Sugar." See *First house.*

Third House

Mr. and **Mrs. Will Davenport** lived here. Mrs. Davenport was the former Iona Arrowood. She had two brothers, Eb and Ed, who lived on Matthews Street. The Davenports had eleven children: **James**, **Carl**, **Clifford**, **Haydon**, **Leonard**, **Lamar**, **Willie Mae**, **Faye**, **Pauline**, **Catherine**, and **Janell**.

James Davenport married Annie Mae Quarles.

Carl Davenport's wife's name was Ruby.

Clifford Davenport married Nan Bridwell.

Haydon Davenport married Marie Pittman. Later on, Hayden married a second time to Grace.

Leonard Davenport married Jean Black.

Lamar Davenport never married.

Willie Mae Davenport married Monroe Dunn. See *Dixie Avenue.*

Faye Davenport married A.W. Loudermilk.

Pauline Davenport married Lonnie Coker.

Catherine Davenport married Herman Echols.

Janell Davenport married Leroy Skinner.

Mr. Will Davenport was a brother to John Davenport who was the father of Melvin Y. Davenport, known as "Sonny". Mr. Will and Mr. John's other siblings were Jean Davenport Poss, (who married John Poss) and, Lizzie Davenport (Zimmerman).

Fourth House

This house was built later but I believe it was there in the late 1940s. A family named **Kensey/Kinsey** lived here. They had two sons and a daughter.

Fifth House

Mr. and **Mrs. Carl Mohan** lived here. This was another large family, some of the children are as follows: **J.C.**, **Robert**, **Jack**, **Mary**, and **Jackie**. Jack and Jackie were twins. There may be other children in this family whose names we do not recall.

OLD ROSWELL ROAD

West Side

There may have been more houses on this street than I remember. I have listed these houses according to information I received from neighbors who grew up in that area, and from my own memories. I delivered papers on this street in the mid 1940s.

Appreciation is extended Ruby Langley Hunter, for the information she shared about the Alton Langley Family.

First House

Mr. and **Mrs. Joe Anderson** lived here. She was the former Mae Conn. They had eight children: **Gene**, **Lois**, **Sammy**, **Lillian**, **Mack**, **Dan**, **Neal**, and **Kenny**. Lois Anderson was in the Class of 1951 at Smyrna High School. See *Conn on Foster Street.*

Second House

Mrs. Henry Jenkins lived in the second house. She had two children: **Nora Mae** and **Henry**.

Later on, **Mr.** and **Mrs.** Mulkey lived in this house. They had two children: **J.C.** and **Ethel.**

Third House

Mr. and **Mrs. Alton Langley** lived in this house on the southwest corner of Old Roswell and Hawthorne streets. They had six children: **Mary Ellen**, **Sue**, **Ruby**, **Alton**, **Jr.**, **Christine**, and **Clara Nell.**

Uncle Alton, as we called him, was my Grandmother Tucker's brother. I remember going to see them a lot. Uncle Alton managed the ice plant. I can see him in my mind's eye, walking back and forth from his home to the ice plant on Roswell Street.

Aunt Ethel was the former Ethel Fraser. She was the daughter of Mr. and Mrs. William Earnest Fraser. They lived on the south side of Powder Springs Street. See *thirteenth house* on *south side of Powder Springs Street.*

Mary Ellen Langley married A.M. George, Jr., from Birmingham, Alabama. They had no children. A.M., Jr., retired from the Federal Aviation Administration as supervisor of the Birmingham Tower at the Birmingham Airport.

Sue Langley married Fred Knox. See *Knox North Matthews Street.*

Ruby Langley married Jack Hunter of Marietta and they had one son, Jack Jr. Ruby graduated from Marietta High School in 1944. She retired from the First National Bank of Cobb County in Marietta after twenty-seven years service. After her retirement, Ruby worked as a real estate sales associate.

Jack Hunter graduated from Marietta High School in 1934. While Jack was a student at Marietta High School, he played football with James "Red" Pressley of Smyrna. Jack was captain of the football team and "Red" later became the football coach at Marietta. Jack served in the United States Navy, with only two years shore duty, and retired with twenty years service in 1954. He was stationed at Pearl Harbor on December 7, 1941, when Pearl Harbor was bombed. Jack worked for Lockheed Aircraft for twenty-three years and retired in 1977. He died August 3, 1990.

Alton Langley married Emialee Anderson of the Oakdale Community south of Smyrna. They had three children: Tim, Tom, and Donna.

Tim Langley is a Doctor of Chiropractic. He was married and had two children: Christopher and Megan.

Tom Langley married Georgia Childers of Marietta. They had two sons: Matt and Michael. He owns Tom Langley Auto Accident Reconstruction Company.

Donna married James Fennell of Acworth. They had one daughter, Alice. Donna works at Kennesaw State University and James works for the J.O. Stephenson Exterminating Company of Kennesaw.

Christine Langley married Walter Smith, Jr., known as "Snuffy," from the Oakdale Community south of Smyrna. They had four children: Toni, Barbara Ann, David and Stevie. "Snuffy" was pitcher for a farm team of the St. Louis Cardinals.

Toni Smith married and had two children: Kimberly and Christopher. Toni is manager of McCoy's Adult Day Care Center, in Mt. Dora, FL, which is owned by her daughter and son-in-law.

Barbara Ann Smith married Paul Turlington. They have four children: Laura Ann, Brook, Trei, and Sammy. Paul is a master chef. He and Barbara Ann make their home in Tavares, Florida.

David Smith died in 1992 from injuries sustained in a diving accident.

Stevie Smith and his wife, Mary Lee, had two children, Johnny Mack and Angie. Stevie and Mary Lee live in Longwood, Florida.

Later Christine married Johnny Farmer from Jacksonville, Florida. Johnny retired from APAC of Florida. They are living in Sanford, Florida.

Clara Nell Langley married Gene Brooks from Smyrna. They had three children: Terry Jean, Gene, Jr., and Mark. He attended school in Smyrna. His family lived on Highland Avenue, off Roswell Street in Smyrna. Clara Nell was in the class of 1951 at Smyrna High School.

Clara Nell later married Jack Beavers from Fair Oaks. Both Clara Nell and Jack retired from Lockheed Aircraft Corp. Clara Nell passed away in 2005, Jack lives in Marietta.

Terry Jean married Bill White of Marietta, Georgia and they had one daughter, Tracie.

Terry Jean married again to Rodney Hanes from Cocoa Beach, Florida. Terry Jean is employed at Chattahoochee Technical College in Marietta, and Rodney works for the City of Marietta.

Gene Brooks, Jr., married Donna Cox of Atlanta. They had two children: Gene III, and Joanne. Gene is Chairman and CEO of Project Time and Cost, which is a cost estimating consultant firm in Vinings.

Mark Brooks married Cyndi Baca from Banning, California and they had one daughter, Summer. Mark was in the U.S. Navy stationed in San Diego, California, when he met and married his wife. Mark is a Division Manager for Science Application International Corporation, a research and development technology corporation in San Diego. They still live in San Diego.

EARLY CHILDHOOD EDUCATION

By Ruby Langley Hunter

"There were five girls and one boy in the Alton Langley family. I was the third girl. My sister Sue and I were extremely close. We played together and did hardly anything independent from the other. She is sixteen months older than I.

"When my sister Mary, who was the oldest, started to school, it did not bother me very much because I still had Sue. But the year that Sue started to school I cried every day for two weeks. Finally, one day my mother said, 'Why don't you go to school with her?' I did!

"The Smyrna school had two first grades. They were in an addition to the big building on the Reed Street side of the school. That morning I got up and got ready for school. At that time, we were living in a little house on what was later called Cherokee Road. I am not sure that it had a name when we lived there. It was 'kind of a country road.' It is now Windy Hill Road. We were about two or three blocks from Atlanta Road in the vicinity of the rear of where Belmont Hills Shopping Center is today.

"The bus picked us up at Atlanta Street. I boarded the bus and nobody questioned me. When we arrived at school, they put me in the opposite first grade from the one that Sue was in. But that was okay. I was so happy to be in school and was doing the same work as my sister. I was making good grades and loved being there.

"My birthday was in September. I turned five years old after I started the first grade. I stayed in school until November. One day the teacher discovered that I was only five years old. She reported to the principal that I was too young to be in school. She insisted that I be taken out of school and sent home to my Mother that day.

"The principal was Mr. Homer Bell. I will never forget that he told me he was taking me home. We walked down Atlanta Street to the road to my house, which later became known as Cherokee Road. I was scared to death and cried all the way home.

"I remember Mr. Bell as being a tall, handsome man. I seem to remember that he was very nice to me during that walk home. But I was terrified and also very upset that I could not go to school anymore.

"Atlanta Street was the main U.S. Highway from Miami to Canada. It was very busy. I was frightened enough with Mr. Bell holding my hand and walking me home. The cars were whizzing by very fast, and a noisy train passed by also. I remember Fuller's Hill seemed so steep. When we reached my house, I ran straight up the steps to the porch as fast as I could. Mother had red peppers hanging on the back porch to dry. Somehow, when I ran out on that porch, I got pepper juice in my eyes. My face was swollen for days. I remember that I could not see. The whole experience was very traumatic for me. I did go back to school when I was old enough and graduated from Marietta High School in 1944."

MARSTON STREET

North Side

Going north on Gilbert Street, Marston is the last street to the left before you get to Hawthorne Avenue. There were no houses on the south side of Marston Street in the days of my youth.

Appreciation is extended to Diane McCollum Whelchel for sharing her memories of her family on Marston Street, where she grew up, in the middle of the Twentieth Century.

NOTE: In the days of my youth, there were three houses on the north side of Marston Street.

First House

Hugh L. Marston
Smyrna City Councilman
1928-1929

Mr. and **Mrs. Hugh Marston** lived in the first house on the north side of Marston Street from Gilbert Street. They had no children. Mrs. Marston was the former Lula Dunn, the daughter of Mr. and Mrs. J.D. Dunn who were active members of First Baptist Church in the early part of the

Twentieth Century. Their picture is in *A Beacon for Christ*, A Centennial History of First Baptist Church.

Mr. Marston was a deacon at the First Baptist Church and Mrs. Marston was active in Sunday School and the Women's Mission Programs. The mission program was known as the W.M.U. I knew Mr. and Mrs. Marston well when I was growing up. They were "pillars" at First Baptist Church. In fact, when I was a kid, I thought he was appointed by God to run the church forever.

Mr. Marston worked in Atlanta. I'm not sure that I ever knew where, but I recall that he always drove a nice car. It was a Packard or something like that. I remember delivering Mr. and Mrs. Marston's paper and they were always very nice to me.

<u>Second House</u>

John Worth McCollum
Smyrna City Councilman
1925,1932-1933

Mr. and **Mrs. John Worth McCollum** lived next door to the Marstons. Mrs McCollum was the former Callie Lacy. They had seven children: **Reed**, **Vietta**, **Howard**, **Ed**, **Cecil**, **Martha**, and **Herbert**. All of Mr. and Mrs. J.W. McCollum's children were in my parents' generation. I remember Mrs. Callie McCollum and all of her children, except Vietta well. I was still a child when the elder Mr. McCollum died, I barely remember him. Mr. McCollum was ordained a deacon at First Baptist April 13, 1919.

According to family information they moved to Smyrna about 1916. Mr. McCollum ran a blacksmith shop in the heart of Smyrna on West Spring Street.

Reed McCollum
Smyrna City Councilman
1934-1937

<u>Reed McCollum</u> married Mary Austin from Acworth, Georgia. They had no children. Reed was the oldest of the McCollum children and outlived all but one of his brothers and sisters.

Reed and Mary McCollum were faithful members at First Baptist Church where he served on the Board of Trustees in 1947. Reed was the church treasurer from 1946-1950, and was ordained a deacon on September 1, 1952. See *McCollum, south side of Bank Street.*

<u>Vietta McCollum</u> married Tommy Walker. They had two children: Virginia and Tommy.

<u>Cecil McCollum</u> never married. He lived in the family home on Marston Street until his death. Cecil was very attentive to his mother in her aging years.

<u>Martha McCollum</u> was a very attractive lady. She never married. Martha was an active member at the First Baptist Church. I remember that she had a car and she would bring her mother to church. They were both active in the Women's Missionary Union and Sunday School. She lived in the family home on Marston Street until her death. Along with Cecil, Martha was very attentive to her mother in her aging years.

Martha McCollum was an intelligent lady, who worked for Standard Oil Company from the time she was seventeen years old until she retired. I recall that she rode the streetcar to and from her job until the streetcar line shut down; then she rode the bus.

Herbert McCollum
Cobb County Commissioner
1957-1965

Herbert McCollum married Jessie Dockery from Dahlonega, Georgia. They lived in Marietta. Herbert served as Commissioner of Cobb County from 1957 to 1965. He was the last Commissioner to serve before the county set up the multiple county commission, as it is known at the present time.

Third House

Howard McCollum
Smyrna City Councilman
1947-1949
Mayor Protem 1949

Mr. and **Mrs. Howard Putnam McCollum** lived next door to his parents with their three children: **William H. McCollum**, known as "Bill," **Shirley**, and **Diane**. Mrs. McCollum was the former Cordelia Casey from Cave Springs, Georgia. Her dad was a Baptist preacher. Howard McCollum, born in 1910, was about six years old when the family moved to Smyrna. Howard and Cordelia raised their family in this house.

"Bill" McCollum married Valerie Leffew from the Oakdale community. They had two children: Angie and Kennon. Bill married again and lives in Buchanan.

Shirley McCollum married Weyman Hinton. They had three daughters: Tamara, Kayla and Lysha. Shirley is widowed. Shirley lives in Cobb County.

Diane McCollum married Martin R. Whelchel, known as "Rudy", from Atlanta. They had three children: Jodi, Martin R., Jr., known as "Marty," and Mitchell. They all live in Cobb County. Diane is a registered nurse. She is retired from Wellstar Cobb Hospital in Austell, where she was a nursing supervisor.

Diane McCollum Whelchel shared some of her memories of growing up in Smyrna. "I remember as early as six years old, my sister and I walking to Smyrna without supervision. We would go by City Hall and see our dad, Howard McCollum, who was the superintendent of the Smyrna Water Department. Dad would give us a nickel, and we would go to Collins Drug Store and buy an ice cream cone.

"Other times we would walk to Jonquil Theater and go to the movies. We would use a Capitola flour token for admission and dad would give us ten cents and we could have popcorn and a coke with that." Diane asked the question, "Can you imagine two little girls walking up Atlanta Street today from across the railroad and spending the entire afternoon in town unsupervised? That was life in Smyrna in the 1940s. It was the normal thing and it happened all the time. We had lots of friends doing the same thing."

Janet Brooks Brown remembers that Cordelia McCollum was active in the Eastern Star and the Smyrna Rainbow Assembly, which was organized in the 1950s.

The Howard McCollum Family were active members of the First Baptist Church.

CHAPTER SIXTEEN

MATTHEWS STREET

East Side

Matthews Street runs from Spring Street northward to Six Points, at Roswell Street. The street is basically the same today as it was in the days of my youth except that, through the years, some other houses have been built.

I want to thank Sonny Davenport for his information about the residents of Matthews Street. (He and his wife, Mae, good customers on my paper route, moved from Matthews Street to Highview Drive in one of the new subdivisions that Rem Bennett, Sr., developed off North Cooper Lake Road in the 1960s.) Appreciation is also extended to Fred Anderson, who grew up on Matthews Street.

First House

Mr. and **Mrs. Stephen D. Byrd** lived in the first house on the east side of Matthews Street. Mr. Byrd was known as "Steve"; Mrs. Byrd was the former Bertha Simpson, a member of the Simpson Family who owned much acreage out Spring Road. "Steve" Byrd was a brother of Mr. Dick Byrd. See *north* and *south sides of Spring Road* and *south side of Spring Street.*

Mrs. Bertha Byrd was first married to Mr. John Davenport, who died in 1918. They were the parents of Agnes Davenport Quarles and Melvin Y. Davenport, known as "Sonny," who also lived on Matthews Street. Mrs. Byrd had four grandchildren. See *Davenport* and *Quarles, Matthews Street.*

I remember that Mrs. Bertha Byrd was an active member of Bethel Baptist Church on Spring Road. On my paper route, she was always very kind to me. I remember her as a lady being of average stature and having gray hair. Mrs. Byrd was the grandmother of June Quarles, a member of the Smyrna High School Class of 1951. When June was a child, she spent much time at Mrs. Byrd's house, a white frame one that was located far off the road, at a distance that mattered to a paper boy.

Mr. "Steve" Byrd was employed with the NC&St.L Railroad, from which he retired after 42 years. He was a member of both Bethel Baptist Church and Nelms Lodge # 323. See *south side of Spring Street.*

Second House

Mrs. Curtis Ione Anderson, along with her four children (**Mary Evelyn**, **Lillian Herlene**, **James Neil**, known as "Jake," and **Gary Fred**) resided here. Mrs. Anderson, the former Curtis Ione Hill from the Sardis community, was widowed at age 29, when her husband, James Anderson, a member of the William David Anderson Family on Roswell Street, died; the Anderson children were nine, seven, five, and three, respectively, at the time. Prior to her marriage and after her sister Odene left to teach at New Salem and New Hope Schools, Curtis taught at Bold Springs School.

Curtis Anderson worked at the restaurant owned by her brother-in-law, James W. Bentley, and located on Washington Street in Marietta, across the street from the Cobb County Court House. (Curtis and my mother were friends; in their later years they talked often to each other.) The Anderson house, very nice, was set a little closer to the street than that of Mrs. Byrd. This was important to me as the Andersons' paper boy. See *Will Anderson, east side of Roswell Street* and *Andersons of Roswell Street.*

Fred shared, "Church attendance was very important to my family. Mother's family was Methodist; but she adopted Spring Street Baptist Church, partly because her brother-in-law, George Moon, was the pastor but primarily because it was the closest church within walking distance of our home. In later years, we children attended First Baptist and/or First Methodist churches.

"We as a family were very good friends with our neighbors, especially the Byrds, Spradleys, Davenports, and Quarles. In fact, Ruby Spradley always referred to herself as 'Fred's Other Mother,' a title of which I have always been exceedingly proud."

Mary Evelyn Anderson married Chester Garland Tapp from Chamblee; they had one son: Chester Garland, Jr., known as "Gary," who became a medical missionary administrator. Evelyn and Chester now live in Jasper.

Gary Tapp married Judy Emory on June 5, 1971. A graduate of the University of Georgia School of Pharmacy, he attended New Orleans Baptist Theological Seminary and later received a Masters degree in Business Administration from Kennesaw State University. Judy Tapp received an Associate's degree in Religious Education from New Orleans Baptist Theological Seminary and an Associate of Science degree in Nursing, with RN status. She and Gary had two children: Bethany Gail and Andrew Emory.

Bethany Gail Tapp is employed as a children's minister directly contracted to an international church in Dubai, United Arab Emirates.

Andrew Emory Tapp graduated from Wake Forest University. He is pursuing post graduate studies while he works as a veterinary assistant in Winston-Salem, North Carolina, where he and his wife, Anna Cox from Maryland, live.

Judy and Gary Tapp were appointed as missionaries of the Foreign Mission Board (now International Mission Board) of the Southern Baptist Convention November 6, 1979. They have served in Palestine, Jordan, Tanzania, Kenya, Sudan, Ethiopia, Djiboupia, Somalia, Yemen, and the Arabian Peninsula, where they are currently assigned.

Lillian Herlene Anderson married Ralph Austin Morris from Atlanta. Ralph worked for Lockheed Aircraft Corporation and later for Cobb County Government. They had one daughter, who was stillborn.

Herlene was named for both her grandmothers—Lillian, for her American kin, and Herlene, for a German relative. Because her maternal great-grandparents immigrated from Bavaria, Germany, they gave some of their children born in America, American names as well as German names; such became a family tradition.

After graduating from Smyrna High School, Herlene graduated from a business college in Atlanta and worked for an engineering design and sales company, also in Atlanta, with which she became a partner. Mrs. Ruby Spradley later was employed with her at that firm.

Subsequently, Herlene and Ralph owned and operated Morris' Gift Shop in Marietta and a retail grocery store in Kennesaw. After selling those businesses, Herlene, tired of retirement, took a job in the Cobb County Sheriff's Department and became one of the first female Deputy Sheriffs in Cobb County.

According to her brother, Fred, "Herlene attributed much of her ultimate career successes to the business acumen acquired while working with Ruby Spradley. They were always the very best of friends." Herlene died May 12, 2001.

James Neil Anderson, known as "Jake," married Rebecca Smith; they had one daughter, Catherine Marie, known as "Cathy."

"Cathy" Anderson married Paul Epting; they had four sons: Jonathan Paul, Michael James, David Russell, and Tyler Garrett. Paul, who owns and operates Epting Enterprises, a software consulting firm, and "Cathy," a registered nurse, live in Cordova, Tennessee. "Cathy" and Paul are graduates of Gardner-Webb University in Boling Springs, North Carolina.

Fred Anderson shared, "My older brother, 'Jake,' and I were paper boys; together we elivered *The Atlanta Constitution* in the morning and the *Atlanta Journal* in the afternoon. We started e first *Marietta Journal* route in Smyrna. Prior to that time, the *Marietta Daily Journal* customers ceived their papers the next day through the mail; they were glad to get their paper the same day of ublication.

"As a child 'Jake' was diagnosed with rheumatic fever, which dashed his dream of joining e military and becoming an officer. When he was 12 years old, he joined Boy Scouts of America and edicated much of his life to that organization as a member of Troop #156 when Sherwood, known as Cotton' Pierce was the Scout Master. 'Jake' became the first Eagle Scout in the history of Smyrna; arold Bowen was the second one. The awards ceremony was held in the old Cobb County Court ouse, in Marietta. and was attended by all BSA Troops in Cobb County.

" 'Jake' and James Davis, founders of the Explorer Scout Troop in Smyrna, were the leaders ho planned and supervised the activities of the Explorers, which included trips to the Boy Scouts of merica regional and national jamborees and many boat/camping excursions in the Southeast, specially canoe trips into the rivers of Florida and journeys into the Great Smokey, and Yosemite. hey also made trips to Canada. The Explorers visited both public and private caves, primarily in the outheast. Jasper Griffin and Andy Anderson, no relation to 'Jake' participated in some of the trip-king." See *Davis, north side of Church Street.*

" 'Jake' and James chartered the Kennesaw Mountain Archery Club, which was active in the 950s and 1960s. 'Jake' worked for Railroad Publications Services, Inc., formerly Southern Freight ariff Bureau (a railroad agency) in Atlanta until his death (from a heart attack), February 15, 1992."

Gary Fred Anderson married Joyce Dameron of Kennesaw. They had two daughters: eborah Ellen, known as "Debbie," and Freda Michelle, known as "Mickie."

After high school, Fred worked for Southern Freight Association (a railroad agency) in tlanta and attended night classes at Georgia State University. He also attended Woodrow Wilson ollege of Law, where he received a Bachelor of Law degree. He continued his career in ansportation management with Continental Can Company and United States Gypsum Company efore becoming Transportation Manager for BellSouth Telecommunications, from which he retired in 998.

Joyce Anderson, having retired from Lockheed Martin Aircraft Corporation, is now Assistant the President and Chief Executive Officer of Lockheed Georgia Employees Federal Credit Union.

"Debbie" Anderson graduated from Kennesaw State University with a Bachelor of Business dministration degree. Having also been certified to teach, she owns and operates Debbie's Day Camp nd Learning Center. "Debbie" married David Casteel of Kennesaw, who graduated from DeKalb ollege with paramedic certification and is employed by the Georgia Department of Transportation; ey had one son, Denver Frederick.

"Mickie" Anderson graduated from Kennesaw State University with a Bachelor of Business dministration degree. She earned a Master of Religious Arts degree and a PhD degree in Christian sychology from Logos Graduate School, in Jacksonville, Florida. "Mickie" married Christopher enton Metcalf, known as "Chris," who grew up in the Hollydale community, west of Marietta. A raduate of New Orleans Baptist Theological Seminary, he is now Senior Pastor of Lihue Baptist hurch in Kauai, Hawaii; he is pursuing a Master of Divinity degree. "Chris," the founder, and Mickie" are Co-Directors in the Agape Outreach Ministries. "Mickie" and "Chris" had four children: hristopher Andrew, known as "Drew," Laurel Ashten, Carah Michelle, and Coren Nicholas, known s "Corey."

Because Fred Anderson and I were in the Smyrna High School Class of 1951, I have see him through the years at class functions: e.g. our 50th Class Reunion on May 19, 2001, at Howard' Restaurant, in Smyrna.

Curtis Ione Hill's paternal grandfather, Curtis Jefferson Hill, was born August 8, 1837, i Cobb County. In Marietta he enlisted into Confederate States of America Company F, Ga. Reg March 19, 1861. He was wounded and hospitalized in Savannah July 20, 1861. He died in Mariett April 8, 1892, and is buried in Sardis Baptist Church Cemetery in Marietta. A marker ther commemorates his service to the Confederate States of America.

Curtis Ione's father, Israel Edward Hill, was born February 1, 1880, in Cobb County, an died March 15, 1944, in Atlanta. He married Alice Herlene Lutz in Cobb County September 27, 1903.

Curtis Ione Hill's maternal grandfather was Lawrence Frederick Lutz, known as "Lorenze, born March 3, 1843, in Bayern (Bavaria), Germany. Leaving Bavaria via the Port of Bremen, he an his family arrived in New Orleans, aboard the bark *Oldenburg,* December 12, 1853. They settled i Jasper, Indiana.

Lawrence returned to New Orleans, where he worked before joining the Confederate Army' E, 1st Louisiana Infantry. Having been shot through the ankle at Chickamauga, he drew a pensio Lawrence later was Postmaster of Seaborn, at Powers Ferry and Mt. Paran roads in North Fultc County. He married Elizabeth Morris; they had six children, including Alice Herlene Lutz, mother c Curtis Ione Hill. Lawrence Frederick Lutz, having died October 30, 1909, in Milledgeville, is buried Sardis Baptist Church Cemetery in Marietta; a marker commemorates his service to the Confedera States of America.

Curtis Ione Hill's parents, Alice Herlene Lutz and Edward Hill, married September 27, 190 in Cobb County: they had seven children: Lawrence Hill, Mary Odene, Lena Elizabeth, Curtis Ion Alice Ruby, Edward Dorsey, and Minnie Lou. Alice Herlene Lutz, was born November 17, 1873, i Fulton County, and died March 9, 1958, in Cobb County.

Third House

Mr. and **Mrs**. **James Spradley** resided in this house. Mrs. Spradley was the former Rub Moseley from Camden, South Carolina. The Spradleys had three children: **Jimmy**, **Peggy**, and **And** all of whom were younger than I.

James and Ruby Spradley came to Smyrna from Camden, South Carolina, in 1943 for Jame to work at Bell Aircraft Corporation. He became employed by Lockheed Aircraft Corporation ju after its opening in 1951; from there he retired.

Mrs. Ruby Spradley, having first been employed by Bell Aircraft Corporation, bega working for First Methodist Church in the 1950s; there, until 1976, she worked as secretary to thes pastors: Roland Walker, Frank Echols, James W. Scarborough, Fred Shelnut, and Larry Caywoo respectively. " I really enjoyed my years at First Methodist Church and working with some wonderf people," Ruby related.

Jimmy Spradley married Lois Tillison from Atlanta. They had four children: Scott Thoma James Gregory, Laurey Ann, and Kerrie Beth. Jimmy worked for CSX Railroad, where he wa Director of Industrial Development. Through his position with the railroad, he was instrumental i helping the Nissan Plant to relocate to Smyrna, Tennessee. Jimmy, Lois, and their family were ver involved in their church, Antioch Methodist in Nashville, Tennessee. At age 54, Jimmy passed away i 1993 due to complications from a brain tumor.

Peggy Spradley married Alec Smith, who was in my class in school. They had tw daughters: Carol and Dorothy. Alec, spending his career in the United States Marine Corps, attaine

L-R: **James** and **Ruby Spradley**, with **Peggy** and **Jimmy**
At their home on Matthews Street
Circa 1946 or 1947
Courtesy of "Dot" Bacon.

L-R: **James** and **Ruby Spradley** and **Andy**
At their newly renovated home on Matthews Street
Circa 1957
Courtesy of "Dot" Bacon.

the rank of Colonel. Now retired, he and Peggy are living in Richland, North Carolina. I see them occasionally when they are here to visit their families.

Andy Spradley and his wife, Karon Marie Harber from California, had no children. They are currently living in Ashville, North Carolina, where Andy works for Biltmore Estates. There he and Karon also run the Corner Oak Manor Bed and Breakfast Inn, located about a half mile from the entrance to Biltmore Estates.

Mr. and Mrs. Spradley, very nice people, were also good paper customers. Mrs. Spradley was a homemaker. The Spradley Family were long-time, active members of First Methodist Church.

Mrs. Spradley and Dorothy "Dot" Bacon, who lives on Bank Street, are sisters. (I have enjoyed a great relationship with both Mrs. Spradley and "Dot" throughout my adult life.) Some years after Mr. Spradley died, Mrs. Spradley married Austin Atkins, the United States Postmaster in Smyrna and the father of former Georgia State Representative Bill Atkins. The Atkins were also long-time members of First Methodist Church. See *Atkins, south side of Bank Street.*

Fourth House

Mr. and **Mrs. Melvin Young Davenport** lived in this house, which was very much like the other houses on the street, a white frame one, close to the street, and well maintained.

Mr. Davenport was known as "Sonny"; Mrs. Davenport was the former Artie Mae Ransom, known as "Mae." "Sonny" and "Mae" had three children: **William M.**, known as "Johnny," **Patsy**, and **Susan**. See *Byrd, first house.*

William M. Davenport, known as "Johnny," married Martha Carolyn Ashe from Canton. They had two sons: David Raye and Stephen Michael. "Johnny," who retired from Louisville and Nashville Railroad (L&N, now CSX), and Martha live in Canton.

David Raye married Gail Ann Whitney; they had one daughter, Savannah Raye. David, employed by CSX Railroad, makes the fourth generation of men in his family to work there.

Patsy Davenport married Clarence Cole from Atlanta; they live in Kennesaw.

Susan Davenport married Thomas Mathis from Chattanooga, Tennessee. They had two sons: Matthew and Marcus. Susan, a school teacher, is deceased.

I remember Johnny, Patsy, and Susan when they were young and going to the ball games.

"Sonny" worked first for Atlantic Steel Company and later on for L&N Railroad (now CSX).

"Sonny," a good friend of my dad, played baseball on the amateur team that Dad managed from 1938 to about 1942. By that time World War II was in full force, and some of the men either had been drafted or had volunteered for active duty. Those that stayed behind worked longer hours and/or were involved in defense work. It was hard to have a team under those circumstances, particularly with Smyrna's being a small town in those days and losing several of the key players; in fact, it was impossible to continue to exist.

After the War ended, in 1945, and the men started returning home, by 1946, the team reassembled. Before long the team was reorganized, with my dad as the manager. They played into the early 1950s.

Because "Sonny" had a car and my dad did not, when the games were away, Sonny would always drive; my family would ride with him often. Sonny's 1937 Ford must have been driven a million miles!

All of my life I was privileged to know "Sonny" and "Mae" Davenport, who were really good friends to my parents. In fact, in the last 30 plus years of their lives, they resided on Highview Drive, off North Cooper Lake Road, near Lillie and me. I always counted "Sonny" and "Mae," fine people, among my good friends.

In earlier years, the Davenports were faithful members of Bethel Baptist Church on Spring Street; later, and for many years, they were faithful members of Fellowship Baptist Church off Atlanta Road, south of the Oakdale and Log Cabin communities. "Sonny," a 50-year member of Nelms Lodge #323 and a Past Master, passed away July 22, 2004. Artie Mae Davenport, a member of the Smyrna Chapter of the Order of the Eastern Star, from which she received a 50-year pin, passed away June 4, 2004.

As was mentioned earlier, "Sonny" Davenport played on the Smyrna Amateur Baseball Team, managed by my dad, Roy Wood. This was a great amateur baseball team, and "Sonny" was a great hitter. The team and the fans depended on his coming through in a tight place. (Of course, no one can do that all of the time.) On August 19, 1946, after a big game, Ralph Cobb wrote the following poem, depicting "Sonny" Davenport at bat. This poem, fashioned after the baseball myth of "Casey at the Bat," is used by permission of the Davenport Family. See *Ralph Cobb, north side of Church Street.*

SONNY AT THE BAT
by Ralph Cobb

It looked extremely rocky for the Smyrna nine that day; the score stood two to four, with but an inning left to play. So when Cooney died at second and Burrows did the same, a pallor wreathed the features of the patrons of the game.

A staggering few got up to go, leaving there the rest, with that hope which springs eternal within the human breast. For they thought, "If only Sonny could get a whack at that," they'd put up even money now with Sonny at the bat. But Flynn preceded Sonny, and likewise so did Blake; and the former was a puddin,' and the latter was a fake. So, on that stricken multitude a death-like silence sat, for there seemed but little chance of Sonny's getting to the bat.

But Flynn let drive a "single" to the wonderment of all, and that much-despised Blakely "tore the cover off the ball." And when the dust had lifted and they saw what had occurred, there was Blakey safe at second and Flynn a-huggin' third.

Then from the gladdened multitude went up a joyous yell; it rumbled in the mountaintops, it rattled in the dell. It struck upon the hillside and rebounded on the flat; for Sonny, **Mighty Sonny**, was advancing to the bat.

There was ease in Sonny's manner as he stepped into his place; there was pride in Sonny's bearing and a smile on Sonny's face. And when responding to the cheers, he lightly doffed his hat; no stranger in the crowd could doubt 'twas Sonny at the bat.

Ten thousand eyes were on him as he rubbed his hands with dirt; five thousand tongues applauded when he wiped them on his shirt. Then when the writhing pitcher ground the ball into his hip, defiance glanced in Sonny's eye; a sneer curled Sonny's lip.

And now the leather-covered sphere came hurtling through the air, and Sonny stood a-watching it in haughty grandeur there. Close by the sturdy batsman the ball unheeded sped; "That ain't my style," said Sonny. "Strike one," the umpire said.

From the benches black with people, there went up a muffled roar, like the beating of the storm waves on the stern and distant shore. " Kill him, kill the umpire!" shouted some one in the stand, and it's likely they'd have killed him had not Sonny raised his hand.

With a smile of Christian charity great Sonny's visage shone. He stilled the rising tumult; he bade the game go on. He signaled to the pitcher, and once more the spheriod flew; but Sonny still ignored it, and the umpire said, "Strike Two."

"FRAUD" cried the maddened thousands, and the echo answered "Fraud"; but one scornful look from Sonny, and the audience was in awe. They saw his face grow stern and cold, they saw his muscles strain, and they knew that Sonny wouldn't let the ball go by again.

The sneer is gone from Sonny's lip, his teeth are clenched in hate; he pounds with cruel vengeance his bat upon the plate. And now the pitcher holds the ball, and now he lets her go; and now the air is shattered by the force of Sonny's blow.

Oh, somewhere in this favored land the sun is shining bright; the band is playing somewhere and somewhere hearts are light. And somewhere men are laughing; and somewhere children shout, but there is no joy in Smyrna—Mighty Sonny Has Struck Out!

NOTE: As my dad always said, "You lose some, you win some—and some get rained out!"

"Sonny" Davenport died July 22, 2004.

Fifth House

Lee and **Agnes Davenport Quarles** resided in this house with their daughter, **Mary June**. Agnes Quarles was Sonny Davenport's sister and Mrs. Steve Byrd's daughter. The Quarles also attended Bethel Baptist Church. Lee worked for Atlantic Steel Company, beginning in 1931 and continuing for 47 years. Agnes, who worked for Lockheed Aircraft Corporation, from which she retired, always attended the ball games.

Mary June Quarles, a member of the Smyrna High School Class of 1951, married W.E. (Bill) Fortner from Marietta. They had two children: Barry and Melissa. Both June and Bill are deceased.

Sixth House

Mr. and **Mrs. Carl Carson** were residents of this house. In the generation of my parents, the Carsons had no children. Early on Mr. Carson worked for Cannon Casket Company. Later becoming a barber, he worked in Smyrna Barber Shop, on the east side of Atlanta Street. At some time in my life Mr. Carson cut my hair.

Mrs. Carson had a mentally challenged sister, **Mollie**, who lived with Mr. and Mrs. Carson. Mollie had scarlet fever when she was eight years old—it stopped Mollie's mental growth. The Carsons, good people, kept up their home and paid their paper bill. I liked Mrs. Carson very much; a nice lady, she gave me cookies when I collected for the paper.

Seventh House

Mr. and **Mrs. Frank Dunton** lived in this house. Mrs. Dunton was the former Bertha Holcombe. The Duntons had five children: **Ernest**, **Billy**, **Charles**, **Virginia**, and **Carolyn**. Mr. Dunton retired from the United States Post Office. I delivered the Duntons' paper in 1944; they always paid their paper bill. See *Holcombe, Alexander Street.*

Billy Dunton has worked for NAPA Auto Parts Company on South Cobb Drive for many years.

Eighth House

Earl and **Mary Moon** and their daughter, **Edna Earl**, were residents next door to the Duntons. Mary, the former Mary Reed, and my mother were friends, both through the church and school.

All the years that I can remember, Mary worked for Georgia Power Company, from which she retired. I remember that she rode the streetcar and/or the bus to Atlanta. Earl Moon, a painter, owned a painting contracting business in Smyrna for many years.

Mary and Earl resided in this house on Matthews Street until Earl died. Continuing to live here into her upper years, Mary later married Andrew Lewis; they moved to North Cooper Lake Road, where they were residents for a long time. The Moons were active members of First Baptist Church; after their marriage, Mary and Andrew Lewis were also active there.

Edna Earl Moon, a member of the Smyrna High School Class of 1948, went all the way through school with my sister, Hilda. Edna Earl married H.O. Scoggins, known as "Buddy," who grew up on Bank Street. "Buddy" and Edna, after they married, lived here with the Moons for a time. They later moved to Jane Lyle Road, south of Smyrna, where they raised Dani Beth, their daughter.

Hugh O. "Buddy" Scoggins, the son of Mr. and Mrs. Howard Scoggins, worked at Lockheed Aircraft Corporation and owned and operated Scoggins Real Estate Company, in Smyrna, for many years. "Buddy" and Edna were active members of First Baptist Church while residing in Smyrna. "Buddy" was the public address announcer at Campbell High School football games in the 1950s and 1960s—and maybe even into the 1970s. The Scoggins moved in the late 1980s or early 1990s to Clarkesville. See *Scoggins, south side of Bank Street.*

Dani Beth married Brad Whitecotton. They had two children: Jeff and Mary Elizabeth. The Whitcottons live near Dani's parents, in Clarkesville.

Ninth House

Fred Brown
United States Army
Casualty
World War II

Mr. and **Mrs. Brown** lived here. Their son, **Fred**, was killed in action during World War II. According to information from the neighbors, Mr. and Mrs. Brown were also the parents of Dovie Brown Whelchel, Clara Brown Lawler, Edna Brown Lacy, and J.T. Brown. See *Lacy, north side of Spring Street,* see *Whelchel, north side of Walker Street,* see *Lawler, east side of Gilbert Street,* see *Lacy, north side of Spring Street*

Tenth House

Mr. and **Mrs. Earl Arrowood** and **Mr.** and **Mrs. Eb Arrrowood**, brothers and their wives, together with their families, resided in this house, which was the last one on the eat side of Matthews Street. (A third brother, **Marvin**, may have lived here also.) Painted white, the house was large and could well accommodate both families. Eb and Earl worked at King Plow Company, on Marietta Street in Atlanta.

Mr. and Mrs. Earl Arrowood had a son, **Jerry**, who was younger than I. The Arrowood family attended First Baptist Church. I remember Mrs. Gladys Arrowood well; a Sunday School teacher for a long time at First Baptist, she was a very nice lady. Because she always handled the paper business, I never had to worry about getting paid. (In fact, all of the Arrowoods were nice, quiet, and kind-natured citizens. Though I do not know where they all are now, I do know the oldest Arrowood family members were residents of Smyrna into their upper years.) See *Bourne, Access Highway.*

NOTE: The area where Roswell Street, Hawthorne Avenue, Matthews Street, North Matthews Street, and Davenport Street intersect is called Six Points. In the days of my youth, Hawthorne crossed Roswell Street and connected with Davenport Street, about two blocks east of Six Points.

MATTHEWS STREET

West Side

First House

Mr. and **Mrs. Walker Franklin Conn**, senior citizens, lived in the first house on the west side of Matthews Street. Mrs. Conn was the former Kate Smith. They had six children, all adults when I was delivering papers on Matthews Street: **Hazel**, **Dot**, **Jeanette**, known as "Chick," **Betty**, known as "Jack," **Mae**, and **Ernest Ed**, known as "Ted." Another daughter, **Catherine**, had died as a small child. See *Gibson and Richards, north side of Walker Street.*

Hazel Conn married "Huey" Gibson.

Dot Conn married Hunter Richards.

Jeanette Conn, known as "Chick," married Ray Richards, brother to Hunter Richards

Betty Conn, known as "Jack," married Mr. Petty.

Mae Conn married Joe Anderson. See *Anderson, Old Roswell Road.*

Ted Conn married Lillia Wood. See *Foster Street.*

The Conns had previously lived on Spring Street. Because the Conns did not subscribe to the paper, therefore, I did not have much contact with them.

Mr. Conn's grandson, Willis Conn, remembers that his grandfather, a farmer, would take to Marietta a wagon loaded with cotton to sell. Mr. Conn also worked at Smyrna Taxi for many years.

Second House

George Moon, a first cousin of my mother, Dora Wood, and his wife, the former **Odene Hill**, resided in this house, which was located about a block north of Whitfield Street. They had four children: **Thomas**, known as "Tom," **Gerald**, **Dean**, and **Larry**. George, Odene, Tom, Gerald and Larry are deceased.

The Moon house was located about a block past Whitfield Street. All of the land between the Conn house and Whitfield Street was vacant.

George Moon, a minister, preached at several Baptist churches in Cobb County: Haney Grove Baptist Church on Franklin Road in Marietta, Bethel Baptist Church on Spring Road, and Spring Street Baptist Church, where he was the pastor for many years. (George was also a carpenter.)

According to information from members of her family, Odene, in her younger years, taught at Bold Springs, New Salem, and New Hope schools. During my childhood I always knew her to be a homemaker; one of her daughters-in-law remembers that she was a substitute school teacher. The Moons were among my good paper customers.

My mother and Odene were good friends until Mother died. In fact, Odene was the last person known to talk with Mother: they talked on the Saturday night before Mother died the next morning. Mother had taken her medications due at 8:00 a.m. and gone back to sleep—or so it was thought because her 8:00 a.m. medicine had been taken; she died around 10:00 a.m., February 9, 1992.

Third House

Mr. and **Mrs. C.F. Light**, very good paper customers, lived next door to the Moons. In the Fair Oaks community the Lights operated a trailer park which, I believe, they owned. They furnished the trailer homes for those employed at Bell Bomber Plant because there was such a big demand for housing in those days, as people had moved from many areas of the country to work at the plant.

NORTH MATTHEWS STREET
East Side

North Matthews Street, a short street, ran from Roswell Street, at Six Points, northward to the Government property, a large tract of land purchased by the United States Government in the early 1940s for defense purposes during World War II. (The area now encompasses Lockheed Aircraft Corporation, Dobbins Air Reserve Base, Naval Air Station Atlanta, Fox Creek Golf Course, Legacy Golf Course, and the area of Windy Hill Road south of the two golf courses.)

Appreciation is extended to Ruby Langley Hunter and Jackie Knox Cash for sharing information about the Fred Knox Family, who lived on North Matthews Street, where only a few people lived during the days of my youth.

First House

Mr. W.G. Graham, known as "Buckles," and his wife, the former **Betty Hann**, resided here. They had four children: **Ann**, **Carol**, **Bill**, and **Bonnie**. Betty Hann Graham was the daughter of Mr. and Mrs. Claude Hann, who lived on the corner of Roswell and North Matthews streets. "Buckles" worked for Scott Electric Company in Atlanta.

NOTE: There was much open land between the Graham and Knox houses.

Second House

Mr. and **Mrs. Fred Knox** were residents here. Mrs. Knox was the former Sue Langley, the daughter of Mr. and Mrs. Alton Langley, Sr. They had six children, **Larry**, **Dickie**, **Jackie**, **Freddie**, **Johnny**, and **Jimmy**, twelve grandchildren, and nine great-grandchildren. See *Langley, Old Roswell Road* and *Fraser, South Side of Powder Springs Street*.

Sue and Fred built this house, on the east side of North Matthews Street after World War II ended. It was about three blocks from Six Points at Roswell Street (near the edge of the United States Government property). They lived in this house on North Matthews Street into the 1990s.

Larry Knox married Wanda Goodgine from Smyrna. They had two daughters, Michelle and Bridget.

Dickie Knox married Kerry Grokett, a neighbor of Wanda Goodgine. They had three children: Kellie, Lisa, and Michael. Dickie and Kerry are divorced.

In 1996 Dickie married Judith O'Daniel, who had two sons from a previous marriage; they live in Hiram. After 33 ½ years with AT&T Dickie retired as manager of their large customer service center in Jacksonville, Florida.

Jackie Knox, the only daughter, married Gary Cash of Smyrna. They had two sons: Jason and Jeremy. Jackie was a paralegal for the attorneys at Allstate Insurance Company in Atlanta. She is now retired.

Freddie Knox married Carolyn Lee of Smyrna. They had two daughters, Shea and Maggi, and one son, Mick.

Johnny Knox married Frances Threat of Smyrna. They had two sons: Christopher and Paul.

Jimmy Knox, the youngest child of Sue and Fred, lives in Marietta.

Fred grew up in the Fair Oaks area, where his parents, Mr. and Mrs. William Knox, lived in a nice brick house on the north side of Barber Road. Mr. William Knox was a supervisor with Georgia Power Company, from which he retired. My mother was well acquainted with the Knox Family, for she also grew up in Fair Oaks.

Fred served in the United States Navy during World War II. I remember that Sue was pregnant with their first child when Fred was in the Navy, and I remember going to her house with her brother, Alton Langley, Jr., to see her. Because Sue needed some things from the store, Alton, Jr., and I went shopping for her. Their son, Larry Knox, was born a short time later—maybe within a day after we went by her house. The Knox house was on Garrison Road, off Access Highway, in Marietta, near where Chattahoochee Technical College is today. Alton and I would walk from there to the Langley house in Smyrna and back. (It was not unusual to walk that far in those days.)

Alton Langley and I had lots of fun! We would walk from Smyrna to one of the theaters (Strand, Cobb, or Legion) in Marietta. I always felt very welcome at the home of Uncle Alton and Aunt Ethel. I don't think I ever went by their house that Aunt Ethel, very hospitable, did not offer me food or beverage.

At first, Fred owned and operated Knox Electric Company in Marietta for many years. In 1974 Fred's son, Larry, joined the company. After Fred and Sue retired, Larry bought the company. At the present time Wanda, Freddie, Johnny, Jimmy, and Johnny Knox's son, Chris, all work for Knox Electrical Contractors: thus three generations of the Knox Family are employees there.

Fred, Past Commander, is a loyal member of American Legion Post # 160. Sue, having been very active in the American Legion Auxiliary, has served as President and District President of the Ladies' Auxiliary.

NOTE: Carrington Park subdivision, which faces Windy Hill Road and is across from the Fox Creek Golf Course, now occupies the property where the Knox Family home stood.

NORTH MATTHEWS STREET

West Side

Appreciation is extended to Cecile Akins Martin for sharing information about the Walker and Cecil Akins families and the Posey and Moon families who lived on North Matthews Street in the middle of the Twentieth Century.

First House

Mr. and **Mrs. Moon** were residents of this house at one time. To my knowledge, they were not related to the Moon families on Matthews Street and Concord Road, The Country Road.

Second House

Bessie and **Louie Posey** resided here with their three sons: **Melvin**, **Ronnie**, and **Terry**. Mr. Posey operated an automotive business, but I do not recall its location. One of the neighbors remembers that Mr. Posey drove a fuel truck.

Third House

Mr. and **Mrs. Cecil Akins** lived in the house next door to Cecil's parents. Mrs. Akins was the former Margie Simpson. They had three daughters: **Cecile**, **Geneva**, and **Elaine**. I liked Mr. and Mrs. Cecil Akins very much, for they were good paper customers and always nice to me.

Margie Akins worked for Bobby Landers at Smyrna Drug Store. Cecil Akins, who had served in the United States Navy during World War II, worked for L&N Railroad, from which he retired.

Margie Simpson Akins was a member of the Simpson Family, big "land barons" on Spring Road in the last part of the Nineteenth Century and into the 1930s. According to information from family members, the Simpsons gave acreage to their children and donated some property for the building of Bethel Baptist Church. (Most of the Simpson Family, who came from Alabama, are buried in the Bethel Church Cemetery. Mrs. Simpson, who was formerly a Mitchell, also came from Alabama.)

Cecile Akins, a Campbell High School graduate, married Hugh Doyle Martin, a graduate of Osborne High School. They had three children: Andy, Patty, and Sheri.

Andy Martin married Angela Long from the Oakdale community, south of Smyrna. They had two children: Alyssa and Austin. Andy, a graduate of the Georgia Institute of Technology, was commissioned a 2nd Lieutenant into the United States Marine Corps. A veteran of the Desert Storm War, he served in the War on Terror in Iraq and is now a Lieutenant Colonel in the United States Marine Corps Reserves.

Patty Martin married Ricky Beckham; they had one child, Patrick. After her divorce, Patty married Dave Cox.

Sheri Martin married Billy Pendley; they had two sons: Mitchell and Justin.

Geneva Akins, a graduate of Campbell High School, married Larry Bean, also a graduate of Campbell High School. They had two daughters: Debbie and Beth. Geneva later married Hans Milo from Holland.

Debbie Bean, currently not married, lives in Marietta.

Beth Bean married Steve Lavin; they had two sons: Alex and Chris. Beth Bean is deceased.

Elaine Akins married Douglas Townes; they had no children. At one time Elaine and Douglas owned and operated Townes Tiffany Antique Shop in the same building where Mr. Walker Akins Grocery Store was located in the middle of the Twentieth Century. After many years of job-related traveling to both Italy and Egypt, where Elaine was employed by the American Embassy, Elaine and Douglas are now residing in Atlanta.

After Margie died, Cecil married Mollie Presley of Hiawassee. Following Cecil's selling of the property on Matthews Street, he moved to Hiawassee, where he died years later.

Walker Akins Home
North Matthews Street
Circa 1940s
Courtesy of Cecile Akins Martin.

Cecil and **Margie Akins**
North Matthews Street
U.S. Navy, World War II
Courtesy of Cecile Akins Martin.

Walker and **Lila Akins**
April 21, 1940
North Matthews Street
Courtesy of Cecile Akins Martin

Fourth House

Mr. and **Mrs**. **Walker Akins**, who had a son, **Cecil**, were residents of the last house on the west side of North Matthews Street before the Government fence. Mrs. Akins, the former Lilla Emory, was an artist who early on was self-taught but who, in her later years, took lessons from several different artists. Mrs. Akins, for many years, was also the pianist at Spring Street Baptist Church, where Mr. Akins, the choir director there, was a vocalist in a trio that included Mr. and Mrs. Lowe; Mrs. Akins was the trio's accompanist. Mr. and Mrs. Akins operated Walker Akins Grocery Store, on the corner of Bank and Atlanta streets. (It seemed to me that Mrs. Akins was always working in the store.) Walker was a brother of Howard Akins, who lived on Bank Street, across the street from my house. See *Akins, North Avenue*.

In the late 1930s and early 1940s, Walker Akins, working as a building contractor, was responsible for the construction of several houses west of Smyrna School. In addition to being a building contractor, he owned and operated a Texaco Service Station. Walker later retired from the Cobb County Water Department.

During World War II, when I delivered Mr. and Mrs. Akins' paper, I saw a star hanging in their window; it represented their son, Cecil, serving in the United States Navy. After the War, Cecil worked for the Atlanta Casket Company for a brief time. Later, having worked for L&N Railroad for more than 40 years, he retired.

NOTE: The entrance into Carrington Park subdivision, which faces Windy Hill Road and is across from the Fox Creek Golf Course, now occupies the site where the Akins house stood. The Posey property was also used for the building of this subdivision.

CHAPTER SEVENTEEN

WHITFIELD STREET

North Side

Whitfield and Walker streets run angularly from Roswell Street to Matthews Street. The first streets to the right off Roswell Street from the railroad, they are separated by a stone marker. Walker Street veers to the right and Whitfield Street veers to the left. There was a large vacant area of land, or open field, before the first house, where new houses were later built.

First House

Mr. and **Mrs. Paul Caldwell** lived in the first house on the north side of Whitfield Street from Roswell Street, directly across the street from the Carter Family. Mrs. Caldwell's given name was Mary Ann. They had one son, **Pete**. See *Old Roswell Road.*

The Bearden Family

Mr. Raymond Boyd Bearden, known as "Pete," and his wife moved here after the Caldwells had vacated. Mrs. Bearden, was the former Wynelle Burdine, the widow of Hoyt Crawford who died in a car accident at the age of twenty-five, had a daughter, **Beverly Crawford**. Pete and Wynelle who raised Beverly, had one son, **Ray Bearden**. The Beardens and the Crawfords were born and raised in Dawsonville. Raymond Bearden was a brother of Maude Parks who lived on the opposite of Whitfield Street. In the late 1950s, the Bearden Family moved to Terrell Mill Road.

Beverly Crawford graduated from Campbell High School in 1954. She married Byron Reeves. After her divorce from Byron, Beverly married Walter Dockery of North Carolina. They had four children: Brian, Sharon, Susan, and Andrea. Beverly graduated from American University in Washington, D.C., with a degree in nursing. Now divorced from Walter, she is retired and living in Kennesaw.

Beverly remembers the Fred Carter Family had fig trees in their yard, and a horse, which they kept behind their house, across the street. She also remembers the next door neighbors, the Mannings, had goats, which they contained with an electrified fence. (Beverly remembers the way the goats smelled.) Once, while her mother was giving her a home perm, they heard yelling, looked out the door, and saw Knox Manning caught in the electric fence. They had to run next door to get Lois, his wife, to turn off the electricity. Knox was slightly injured.

Beverly remembers the fun times on the street, playing Tarzan and Jane, with neighborhood children, among who were Carlton Harris and Larry Babb.

Ray Bearden's wife, Pat, was from the North Georgia area. They had two daughters: Jessica and Kimberly. Ray and Pat divorced. Ray married again, he and his wife, Dixie, live in Mississippi.

Larry Babb remembers that at one time Beverly Crawford was a nurse at Kennestone Hospital.

Second House

Mr. Roach resided in this house before the Mannings moved here.

Mr. and Mrs. Knox Manning

Mr. Knox Manning his wife, **Lois**, lived here with their two children: **Freida** and **Joyce**. The Manning Family previously were residents of the fifth house on the south side of Whitfield Street.

Third House

Mr. and **Mrs**. **Hugh Christian** lived in this house. Mrs. Christian's given name was Catherine. They had three children: **Dido**, **Daphne**, and **Thor**. All of their children were named for a Greek god or goddess. Dido, in the same class in school with me, was a very bright girl, the top student in the Smyrna High School Class of 1951, and a graduate of the Georgia Institute of Techology.

Mr. Christian was a professor, but I do not recall where he taught. I remember the Christians as being courteous people and very intellectual. Always nice to me, when I delivered their paper, they were punctual with their paper bill.

One particular thing I remember about the Christian Family was that their house was very different from the norm, almost as if it were designed to be underground; at least it had that appearance. For some reason I just remember that.

NOTE: In this area there was an alley that ran from Whitfield Street to the east side of Roswell Street; later it was named Crumbley Drive.

Fourth House

Mr. and **Mrs**. **Carl Crumbley** and their family lived here. According to Billy Flowers, their house stood to the rear of the Christian house. Their driveway later became a street that came out at "Pinky" Morris' house on Roswell Street. Mrs. Crumbley, formerly Velma Proctor, and Carl had four children: **Jesse**, **Rachel**, **Elsie**, and **Evelyn**. The Crumbley Family were Baptists.

Jesse Crumbley married Betty Hilton; they had two children: Steve and Jackie. Jesse is now deceased.

Rachel Crumbley married Marvin Barber. They had four children: Mike, Jeff, Linda, and Susan. Rachel is divorced and lives in Calhoun.

Elsie Crumbley married Andy Anderson. They had twin sons: Felton and Lelton. Andy is deceased. Elsie lives in Smyrna.

Evelyn Crumbley married Joe Blalock. They had two children: Billy and Bobby. Joe is deceased. Evelyn lives in Austell.

The Crumbley Family moved to Smyrna in 1942 from Carrollton, for Mr. Crumbley to work for the Bell Bomber Plant. He later worked for Lockheed Aircraft Corporation, from which he retired.

Mrs. Crumbley worked for Slater Systems, which operated the cafeteria at Lockheed Aircraft Corporation. Both Mr. and Mrs. Crumbley are deceased.

Rachel Crumbley Barber remembers that when she and her family first moved to this house, there was no electricity. "We used kerosene lamps for our lighting. Dad attempted unsuccessfully—to get some of the neighbors to give rights of way so that we could have electricity in our house. Finally someone at Smyrna City Hall told Dad 'you have a right of way that can be opened; open up that road and you can get electricity.' The road was opened, and finally we got our electricity. The road, which was named Crumbley Drive, was later paved."

Whitfield Park

NOTE: In the 1960s, when my dad, Roy Wood, was on the Smyrna City Council, there was a bond referendum that allowed the city to buy a large tract of open land between the second and third houses for a City park. Named Whitfield Park, it is a community playground geared toward younger children.

The City of Smyrna was very fortunate to have far-sighted city fathers that bought land for parks as properties became available. According to information from the Barnes Family, this property was purchased from Mr. Homer Barnes, who lived on Roswell Street.

WHITFIELD STREET
South Side

Whitfield and Walker streets run east and west from Roswell Street to Matthews Street, and are divided by a stone marker, which is located in front of Dr. and Mrs. Collins' house. Walker Street veers to the right, and Whitfield Street veers to the left.

Appreciation is extended to Larry and Mike Babb, Rachel Crumbley Barber, Janet Brooks Brown, Beverly Crawford Dockery, Nadine Carter Ellenburg, Bill Flowers, Steve Harris and Joann McDowell for sharing their memories of the residents of Whitfield Street .

First House

Mr. and **Mrs. Charles Flowers**, who lived here, had one son, **Billy**, now known as "Bill." Mrs. Flowers, whose given name was Virginia, known as "Jennie," was the daughter of the first Mr. and Mrs. Henry David Motter. The Flowers, on my paper route, were very good customers. Later on, Billy built a house on Walker Street, which backed up to his mother's house. See *First family of Henry David Motter, north side of Spring Road.*

"Bill" Flowers, a Smyrna High School graduate, married Norma Jean Cagle from Talking Rock. They had two children: Mike and Angela.

Billy later married Sue Sanders Dunn who had two children from a previous marriage: Ken and Kara Dunn. Bill is retired from Lockheed and has ten grandchildren.

Second House

Mr. and **Mrs. G.T. Hamby** were residents of this house. They had one daughter, **Vannie**. Mrs. Hamby was the former Sadie Peeples Chambers. Mrs. Hamby's son from a previous marriage, **Weldon Chambers**, also lived here. I remember Mrs. Hamby working at the dry cleaners in Smyrna. See *Hamby, south side of Love Street.*

The McDowell Family

Mr. and **Mrs. Joe McDowell** lived here. They had three children: **Howard**, **Joann**, and **Shelba**. Mrs. McDowell was the former Sadie Robinson, who grew up on the north side of Spring Street. See *McDowell, Dixie Avenue* and *Robinson, north side of Spring Street.*

Nadine Carter Ellenburg remembers that the McDowells would sit in their yard, play music, and sing.

Third House

Mr. and **Mrs. Peeples** lived next door to the McDowells. Mrs. Peeples given name was Bess. They had one daughter, **Sadie**. She married Mr. Chambers and they had a son, Weldon. See *Hamby, second house.*

Mike Babb, a neighbor, remembers that Mr. Peeples was a retired locomotive engineer from the days of steam engines. See *Mike's Memories under Babb.*

Ray Bearden on Whitfield Street
In front of the Carter's boat
Circa 1950
Courtesy of Mike Babb.

L-R: **Mike Babb** and **Ray Bearden**
Mid – 1950s on Whitfield Street
Courtesy of Mike Babb.

L-R: **Ray Bearden**, **Mike Babb**, and **Gary Carter**
On Whitfield Street
Notice the Roy Rogers Cowboy Boots
Early 1950s
Courtesy of Mike Babb.

Gary Carter seated, and **Mike Babb** standing,
Holding "Rex," the banty rooster.
Carter camper in the background
Circa early 1950s
Courtesy of Mike Babb.

L-R: **Gary Carter** and **Mike Babb**
On Whitfield Street
During snowstorm of 1958.
Courtesy of Mike Babb.

Fourth House

Mr. and **Mrs. James Carlton Babb** lived between the Peeples and Carters. They had three children: **James Larry**, **Ara Jane**, and **Walter Michael**, known as "Mike." Mrs. Babb, the former Dorothy Mae Hyde, and her husband (both from Dalton) moved here in 1942, immediately after World War II began. Mr. Babb, who worked for Nashville, Chattanooga and Saint Louis Railroad (NC&St.L), had been transferred here from Dalton, because of changes made in the company due to the War. The Babbs, good paper customers who always paid their paper bill on time, were members of Second Baptist Church.

Mrs. Dorothy Babb had a sister, Kate Hyde Moore who, with her husband, Charlie, resided in a house next door to Second Baptist Church, on Atlanta Street. They had two daughters: Linda and Charlotte. Charlie Moore worked for the railroad. His family at one time lived on Spring Street, across from the Groce House. Mrs. Babb also had a brother, James Hyde, who worked for the railroad.

James Larry Babb, known as "Larry," was born in Dalton in 1939. He attended Campbell High School through the tenth grade and then transferred to Mt. Berry School for Boys from which he graduated. He married Marian Quinn of Dalton. They had two children: Andy and Amy, both of whom are schoolteachers. Larry, who spent eight years in the United States Air Force, is retired from Shaw Industries and lives in Dalton.

Larry remembers being baptized in a small concrete pool located at the rear of Second Baptist Church.

Ara Jane Babb, known as "Jane," born in 1944, was named for her maternal grandmother, Ara. "Jane" graduated from Campbell High School and married David Wayne Whitaker of Crossville, Tennessee. They had two children, David, Jr., and Diane, and three grandchildren. Jane recently retired from the Cobb County Board of Education, administrative offices. Jane and David are divorced. She is currently living in Marietta.

Walter Michael Babb, known as "Mike," was born in 1949 while his family resided on Whitfield Street, where he lived until 1971. Because of the tremendous growth in the area, "Mike" attended three different elementary schools Smyrna, Belmont Hills, and Hawthorne, and three different high schools Pebblebrook, for the ninth grade, Campbell, and then Wills High School, where he graduated. "Mike," a 1971 graduate of Georgia State University, married Karen Thomason of Dalton. They had three children: two daughters, Kim and Kelly, and a son, Corey, and two grandchildren. They live in Rocky Face. "Mike" who is employed for Mohawk Industries, just finished eight years on the Whitfield County Board of Commissioners.

Memories by Mike Babb

"I remember our neighbor, Knox Manning, worked the night shift at Lockheed Aircraft Corporation and grew the 'best' garden every summer. He had a well under his house that pumped water to his garden.

"Every time it snowed, Knox got his old four wheel drive jeep and took it over to the Four Lane and made money pulling people's cars out of ditches.

"I remember Mr. Peeples, who was an elderly man. He would nail wooden ladders together to trim his trees, maybe 50 feet off the ground so his yard would get lots of sunlight. Today those trees look very strange, there are bare of limbs very high up.

"There was a field across the street from our house that was the playground for the community children. I remember some of the boys building an underground fort. They dug holes big enough for them to get into to hide and put boards over it to help conceal it. When the owner of the property came to bush cut the field it almost tore up his tractor when it fell in the hole."

Memories by Larry Babb

"I remember when the peddler came in his pick-up truck with vegetables to see to our neighbors. All the ladies on the street met him to buy his fresh vegetables.

"I remember the day I started first grade at Smyrna School. Later in the day, Mother was called because they could not find me there. I along with a neighbor, Daphne Christian, had decided at 10:30 that we had enough of school, we went home.

"I remember that a girl in our neighborhood had polio. She had to go away for awhile. When she returned she was wearing braces and crutches. Thanks to Dr. Salk, our classmates do not have to face this anymore.

"There were two large trees in our front yard when we lived there. One of them fell a long time ago, but a second one fell on the bedroom of the house recently. Some minor damage was done, cracked rafters, etc. I remember helping my dad build the addition to that house, which included that bedroom. It was real wood!"

Larry stated, "My grandfather, Thad Babb, taught school in Whitfield County for 40 years without missing a day!"

Fifth House

Mr. and **Mrs. Fred Carter** lived in this house. Mrs. Carter's given name was **Ara**. They had two children: **Nadine** and **Gary**. I remember their children were very small when I delivered their paper. In those days, Fred was the manager of the Sunnyside Inn; because he worked so much and Mrs. Carter was always busy with the children, I hardly ever saw him at home! The Carters were good paying paper customers.

Ara Carter was a daughter of Mrs. Maude Parks, who owned Sunnyside Inn. She along with her two two sons, A.T. and Fred, managed the business, which was located on South Atlanta Road.

Nadine Carter married Stan Bourne; both graduated from Campbell High School. They had one daughter, Sandy, who married Phillip Hughes. After Nadine and Stan divorced, Nadine married Jim Ellenburg of Atlanta; Nadine and Jim live at Lake Allatoona. See *Bourne, Access Highway*.

Gary Carter married Gail Overton; both graduated from Campbell High School. They had two daughters: Jennifer and Cheryl. Gary and Gail now reside in Clearwater, Florida.

Steve Harris recalls that the Carters purchased the first television on Whitfield Street. All the other residents were in awe.

Sixth House

The **Carlton Harris Family**, and Mrs. Harris' parents, **Mr.** and **Mrs. John Petty**, lived in this house. This was before Carlton Harris built the house next door for his family. See *Harris, seventh house and Petty, south side of Spring Street.*

NOTE: According to information from other residents of the area, Mr. Harris owned much property on this street.

Mrs. Clara Hulsey

Later **Mrs. Clara Hulsey** and her sons, **Horace** and **Mickey**, lived in this house after the Harris' moved to their new one. **Mr.** and **Mrs. West**, Clara's parents, also lived here in accommodations which Clara had prepared for them.

Horace Hulsey, who graduated from Berry High School in Rome, married Peggy Burruss. They had one daughter, Jennifer. See *Burruss, Atlanta Road at Miles Stop.*

Seventh House

Mr. and **Mrs. Carlton Harris** later lived next door to the Hulseys. Mrs. Harris was the former Dorothy Petty. They had four children: **Carlton, Jr.**, **Margaret**, **Steve**, and **Carole Ann**. Mrs. Harris was a lovely lady whom I remember well. The Harris Family were members of First Baptist Church, where Dorothy was a member of the Homemaker's Sunday School Class. See *sixth house* and *Petty, south side of Spring Street.*

Carlton Harris, Jr., married Ann Diggs; they had one son, Michael, and one granddaughter, Christina. Carlton is now deceased.

Margaret Harris married A.T. Parks. Along with his sister, Ara, and her husband, Fred Carter, A.T. operated the Sunnyside Inn on Atlanta Street, south of Smyrna. See *Carter, fifth house.*

Mr. and Mrs. Harris, on my paper route, were some of my favorite people. Mrs. Harris was always nice to me when I would go by to collect.

After Lillie and I married, Lillie and Mrs. Harris became friends. Mrs. Harris died suddenly in the late 1960s.

Steve Harris shared that his family and the Christian Family "had the only brick houses on Whitfield Street. Whenever a storm would come up, Mrs. Flowers and Mr. and Mrs. Anderson would come to our house and stay until it was over." Steve married and had children.

Steve also shared, "Smyrna was a wonderful place to grow up." I share those sentiments also.

Carole Ann Harris is deceased.

Eighth House

Mr. and **Mrs. Willis Weaver Anderson** were residents of this house. They had a son, Bill. Mrs. Anderson, the former Annie Bell Dawson, along with her husband, Willis, were natives of the Hopewell community. Moving here from Atlanta, they bought this property, on which to build this house, from Arthur Willis.

"Bill" Anderson married Joyce Gleeson from Roswell. They had two sons: John Larry and Alan Gleeson. Bill was already married and working for Zachry's men's clothing store in Atlanta when his parents built their house. I remember buying suits from Bill for many years when I was in the banking business, downtown. Bill Anderson is deceased. Joyce still lives in Smyrna.

John Larry Anderson and his wife had two children and two grandchildren.

Alan Gleeson Anderson and his wife had two children.

Mrs. Annie Bell Anderson's mother, Julie, was a sister of Arthur Cochran. Willis Anderson was a brother of "Toad" Anderson Cochran. See *tenth house on Whitfield Street,* and *Cochran, twelfth house on east side of Roswell Street.*

I remember Mrs. Annie Bell Anderson as being a beautiful lady.

NOTE: To my knowledge Willis Weaver Anderson was not related to the large Anderson Family on Roswell Street.

Ninth House

Arthur and **"Toad" Anderson** lived here. She was the former "Toad" Cochran. See *eighth house on Whitfield Street* and *Cochran, east side of Roswell Street.*

"Dusty" and **Martha Rhodes**

"Dusty" Rhodes
Smyrna City Councilman
1960-1962

James Beauregard Rhodes, known as "Dusty," from a farm in the Alpharetta/Roswell area, and his wife, the former Martha Gray Carithers, of Ft. Valley, moved to this house in the early 1950s. The Rhodes had four children: **Marna Carol**, **Jim**, **Gay**, and **Etta Wylie**, all of whom graduated from Campbell High School. All earned college degrees, and Etta and Marna Carol earned Masters degrees. The Rhodes were members of First Methodist Church, where Martha is still active.

Marna Carol Rhodes, a graduate of Campbell High School, met and married John F. Melcher at North Georgia College, where they both received a degree. They had three sons, and an adopted daughter: John, Jim, Jason, and Valerie. A registered nurse still working, and divorced, Marna Carol lives in St. Simons.

Etta Wylie Rhodes, a graduate of Campbell High School, met and married Joe G. Raines of Moultrie, at North Georgia College, where they both graduated. Etta is a school counselor. She and Joe had two children, a son, Joey, and a daughter, Roben, and four grandchildren. The Raines live in Jacksonville, Florida.

Jim Rhodes, a graduate of Campbell High School, married Elizabeth Lord of Marietta. They met while both were attending North Georgia College, from where she graduated. Jim transferred to the University of Georgia, from where he graduated. They had two children, Daniel and Anna Kate, and two grandchildren. They are now retired and living in Marietta.

David Decker, Sr.
Casualty
Vietnam

Gay Rhodes, a graduate of Campbell High School, married David Decker, known as "Dave." Gay met "Dave," who was from Pennsylvania, at North Georgia College, where she graduated. He graduated from Georgia Institute of Technology. They had two sons: Christopher and David.

David, Sr., a Captain in the United States Army, 82nd Airborne, was killed in action, in Vietnam. He was hit by sniper fire trying to rescue his radioman, and was awarded the Silver Star.

Gay had two grandchildren, and is expecting the third one. She is retired from The Coca-Cola Company, where she was secretary to the President of Coca-Cola U.S.A. When the formula was changed, she received many calls from customers, complaining about the change. Gay, a resident of Hawaii, is currently in Smyrna with her mother.

Martha Rhodes was a secretary in the engineering division of Lockheed Aircraft Corporation; was named Citizen of the Year by the Smyrna Civitan Club in 1964.

"Dusty" Rhodes was Director of the Seventh Congressional District of Georgia. This was a paid position. He worked with Congressman John Davis and others of that era. Later on, "Dusty" headed up the Miscellaneous Tax Department for the State of Georgia. He served on the Smyrna City Council, 1960-1962.

Tenth House

Mr. and **Mrs**. **George Crowe** lived in this house. Mrs. Crowe was the former Martha Lo Williams. They had three children: **Mary Jean**, **George**, **Jr**., and **Peggy**. Martha Lou was a sister o G.B. Williams who owned and operated G.B.'s Place. See *south side of Powder Springs Street.*

Eleventh House

Mr. and **Mrs**. **A.M**. **Poston**, moved here in 1952. Mrs. Poston's given name is **Clifford**, an Mr. Poston was known as "Red." The Postons later moved to Northview Place, in the Forest Hill community, where Clifford has lived for fifty years. They had three children: two sons, **Milburn** an **Bill**, and a daughter, **Marion**. See *Poston Realty, Atlanta Street, from Mapps to R. & M. Café.*

Mr. and **Mrs. Marvin Reese**

Mr. and **Mrs**. **Marvin Reese** resided here after the Postons vacated. Mrs. Reese was th former Elise Parks, a sister of Ara Carter and A.T. Parks. Marvin and Elise had four children: **Denise** **Roger**, **Benny**, and **Wayne**. Marvin Reese was a brother of Montez Reese Matthews who late married Joe Barnes, a member of the large Barnes family on Roswell Street. Montez Reese Barne lives in Atlanta's Bolton community. Marvin and Elise are both deceased. See *east side of Roswel Street.*

Twelfth House

Mr. and **Mrs**. **Will Wright** lived in this house. They had two sons: **Thomas** and a **son** wh died at birth.

Thomas Wright married Nema Ransom. They had two daughters: Thelma and Elsie. Nem Ransom was the daughter of Mr. and Mrs. Bill Ransom. See *Ransom south side of Spring Street.*

Mr. Will Wright was the Chief of Police in the early 1940s.

The Wright Family had a dairy at the end of Whitfield Street, near Matthews Street. The also farmed and raised hogs. Billy Flowers remembers his family buying milk and butter from th Wrights. He also remembers that, after the Wrights killed hogs in the fall of each year, his parent would also buy sausage from them.

WALKER STREET
North Side

Walker Street and Whitfield Streets veered to the right off Roswell Street. These were th first streets off Roswell Street to the right after you crossed the railroad. Walker Street veered to th right and Whitfield Street to the left. The streets are divided by a stone marker, which stood in front o Dr. and Mrs. Collins' house. The Marker is still there.

NOTE: Harold Smith, Smyrna Historian, interviewed Mr. Hugh Marston, who served on th Smyrna City Council in the 1920s and 1930s. He told Harold that, while he was serving in office, th city council voted to name the streets in this area after homeowners who lived here. (At that time non of the streets were named or paved.)

Appreciation is extended to Martha Barnett Akins for sharing her memories of the Akins an Lee Black families, and to Janet Brooks Brown for furnishing information about her neighbors o Walker Street, where she grew up in the 1940s and 1950s. Appreciation is also extended to Lind Whelchel Bennett, Johnny Black, Jerry Black, Gladys Black, Durron Davis, Jerry Davis, Bill Flowers Betty McNelley Harris, Patricia Tolbert Jones, Brenda Gibson Johnston, Brenda Pass Massey, an

Ernest "Buddy" Painter for contributing memories of their families, who lived on Walker Street, in the Middle of the Twentieth Century.

First House

Aubrey and **Clara Parson** lived here with their six children. Clara Parson was a sister-in-law of James Lovern. The Parsons later moved to Cheney Woods Farm, the area where Cheney Woods subdivision was later developed. See *Lovern, south side of Powder Springs Street.*

Mr. and **Mrs. Robert David McNelley**

Mr. and **Mrs. Robert David McNelley** moved from the Fair Oaks area in 1942 to this house. They had two children: Betty and Robert. See *McNelley, east side of Lee Street.*

Mr. and **Mrs. William G. McNelley**

Mr. and **Mrs. William G. McNelley** lived in a small house, which was located to the rear of the main house. Mrs. McNelley, the former Augusta Olemacher, the daughter of immigrants from Germany, was raised in Sandusky, Ohio. In addition to Robert David, William and Augusta had two other sons: Wesley and Henry. William G. McNelley was originally from Dahlonega, where he was the editor of a newspaper. Prior to the years of the Great Depression they lived in Atlanta where he was very prosperous. From there they moved to a farm in Dallas, which was worked by their three sons and their families. By the time the family moved to Smyrna, the elder Mr. McNelley was an invalid. After his death, Mrs. McNelley lived among her three sons.

Mr. and **Mrs. Grady Pass**

Mr. and **Mrs. Grady Pass** moved here after the McNelleys vacated. Mrs. Pass was the former Edna Terry of Forsyth County. They had two children: **Brenda** and **Jerry**. Brenda Pass Massey currently lives in this house. Grady Pass was a diesel mechanic for Greyhound Bus Lines.

Brenda Ann Pass married Robert Massey, whose dad worked at Creatwood Dairies. After her divorce Brenda married Billy Dunton. They had two children: **Becky** and a son, **Marty**. Brenda Pass Massey married again to Jack Martin and had a daughter, **Katie.** In 1979, Brenda and Robert Massey remarried and had twin sons: **Michael** and **Mitchell**. Brenda Massey had 14 grandchildren and one great-grandchild. Brenda, who is currently living in this house, worked for 25 years in the LPN Mother/Baby unit at Kennestone Hospital.

Robert Massey, from a previous marriage, had two children: Roberta and Bobby. He also had four brothers who lived in the Smyrna area: Homer, Edward, Terrell, and Johnny.

Jerry Pass who worked for Greyhound Bus Lines, is currently living in the second house. Jerry married Sheila Cash; they had a daughter, Diane, who has a son, also named Jerry.

Jerry Pass later married Loretta Tucker who had two sons from a previous marriage: Robbie and Anthony. Robbie had two sons, and Anthony had three daughters.

NOTE: At one time, Edna's sister and brother-in-law, Ada Terry and William Thomason, lived in this first house, built in 1932, which they owned, before moving to Deering Road in Atlanta. Edna's brother, E.J. Terry, and his wife, Ruth, at one time lived in a garage apartment attached to this house.

Second House

Mr. and **Mrs. Wes Pass** resided here with their son, **Harold**. Mrs. Pass, the former Clyde Turner, was the daughter of Sam and Ella (Osburn) Turner. Wes and Clyde were also the parents o Grady Pass, who lived next door.

NOTE: According to information from members of the Pass Family, their family record show this house was built in 1910. Members of this family occupied this house for over half of th Twentieth Century and Jerry Pass, and his wife, Loretta, are currently living here.

Third House

Mr. and **Mrs**. **Lee Black** lived in this house. Mrs. Black was the former Ida Akins, th daughter of Mr. and Mrs. Virgil Homer Akins. Lee and Ida had a daughter **Betty Lee**, who marrie Wendall Bradfield. See *North Avenue, North Matthews Street, South Side of Bank Street,* and *Sout Side of Spring Street.*

Lee Black was a brother of Harry Black who, along with his brother-in-law, Sam Webb, wa a partner in the Black and Webb Grocery Store on Atlanta Street in Smyrna. Harry lived on Hill Stree at South Atlanta Road in the Oakdale community, south of Smyrna. He had a daughter, Evelyn, a ver close friend of Martha Barnett Akins during Evelyn's lifetime. Martha Barnett Akins and her parents Milton and Lucille Brooks Barnett, lived in one of the houses Harry Black had built in Oakdale for hi family. They were very close neighbors with the Blacks in the middle of the Twentieth Century Evelyn passed away in 2003.

Roy Black, another brother of Lee, and his family lived out Terrell Mill Road in the vicinit of Interstate-75's crossing Terrell Mill Road, where he owned large acreage. Roy was the father o Clarence Black, known as "Shorty," who worked for J.D. Daniel for many years in J.D.'s grocer store, located in Jonquil Plaza Shopping Center. "Shorty" Black married Grace Wall of Riverdale; the had one son, Jerry, a talented musician, whose specialty was the organ, he played for many are churches. Jerry married Charlise Mallory of Atlanta. See *"Shorty" Black,* under *City Jail, Atlant Street, Mrs. Mazie's to Peace Matthews.*

Hubert Black, another son of Roy Black, married Mary Brooks who was a member of th large Brooks family on the east side of Roswell Street. *See Brooks, east side of Roswell Street.*

NOTE: This Black Family was not related to Reuben or Casson Black then living on Sprin Street, or the Black Family in the Seventh House on the north side of Walker Street.

Fourth House

Mr. and **Mrs. John Martin** lived in this house. They had five children: **Raymond**, **Fowler** **Maxie**, **Willie**, and **Margie**. Mrs. Martin was the former Bessie Akins, the daughter of Mr. and Mrs Virgil Homer Akins. The Martin house was actually located behind Mrs. Ida Black's house. (The thir house.) See *North Avenue, south side of Bank Street, North Matthews Street,* and *south side of Sprin Road.*

Mr. Martin worked for the railroad. Though I do not remember what his job was, I remembe he rode the trains.

Fowler Martin married Barbara Cantrell, the daughter of Cecil and Earnestine Cantrell. believe the Martin family attended First Baptist Church. *See Pickens Street.*

Margie Martin married Weyland Adams, known as "Buddy." See *twelfth house* and *nort side of Spring Road, the Country Road.*

Fifth House

Mr. and **Mrs. Robert Tolbert** lived here. Mrs. Tolbert was the former Sarah Wallace. They had two daughters: **Patricia**, known as "Pat," and **Judy**. Mrs. Tolbert was the daughter of Mr. and Mrs. Green Berry Wallace. See *east side of Gilbert Street, south side of Bank Street*, and *Foster Street.*

The Tolbert Family were members of Spring Street Baptist Church, where Mr. Tolbert was a deacon. Here Patricia Tolbert was baptized. Later the Tolberts transferred their membership to First Baptist Church, where they worshiped the rest of their lives.

Mr. Tolbert was the professional type: he wore a suit and tie to work each day, I remember. He retired from Boyle Mid-Way. The Tolberts, in the 1960s, moved to Ashwood Drive.

Patricia Tolbert, known as "Pat," a graduate of Campbell High School, married John Lee Jones of Blakely. They had two daughters: Debra and Tonya. Patricia is now deceased.

Debra Jones married John Cooper; they had two children, a son and a daughter.

Tonya Jones married Jeffrey Nail; they had two sons.

Judy Tolbert married William Bailey; they had two daughters: Audra and Leslie.

Sixth House

Newman and **Jewell Wallace** were residents of this house. They had two children: **Norman** and **Beverly**. Mrs. Wallace was the former Jewell Wood, also, known as "Cricket." Mrs. Wallace's parents also resided in this house at one time. Mrs. Wallace's half-brother, (they had different dads) Leonard "Critter" Crider, was a long-time loyal employee and manager of G.B.'s Place. His chili recipe is still famous. I worked with him at G.B.'s Place when I was in my middle teenage years. See *north side of Bank Street.*

Norman Wallace, who was married, died in 1982.

Beverly Wallace, a graduate of Campbell High School, married Weldon Chambers. They had three children: Neal, Carla, and Matthew. Beverly and Weldon divorced. Having married again, Beverly lives in Fairmont. See *Hamby, south side of Whitfield Street* and *Hamby, south side of Love Street* and *Crider, north side of Bank Street.*

Seventh House

Mrs. Dolly Black, the widow of Reuben Black, lived here with her sons: **Earl** and **Troy**. Mrs. Black, the former Dolly Akins, was the daughter of Mr. and Mrs. Virgil Homer Akins. See *Akins, north Matthews Street* and *south side of Bank Street.*

Reuben Black was the son Mr. and Mrs. Casson Black, who had seven children: Elsie Mae, Ada, Reuben, Tom, Claude, Daniel, and Carrie Lou. See *Bowles, north side of Spring Street.*

Elsie Mae Black married Mr. Spinks.

Ada Black married Mr. Theodore Dwight Frisbee. See *Stephens, north side of Walker Street.*

Reuben Black married Dolly Akins.

Tom Black married Sarah Elizabeth Frisbee, a sister of Ada's husband. See *Tom Black, west side of Roswell Street.*

Claude Black later on lived on Pinehurst Drive, off King Springs Road, in Smyrna Heights, one of the subdivisions built by Rem Bennett in the early 1950s. Mr. and Mrs. Black had one son, Charles.

Daniel Black and his wife, Myrna, from Atlanta's Bolton community, had three children, two sons, Alfred, known as "Mutt," and Garel; and a daughter, Earline.

Alfred Black married Gladys McPherson and had two children: Barbara and Jimmy. Gladys was a sister of Imagean McPherson Poss. See *Poss, Davis Road.*

Carrie Lou Black first married Mr. Neary. Later she married Mr. Newton.

Eighth House

Mr. and **Mrs. Huey D. Gibson** and their family resided in this house, which stood past the creek at the bottom of the hill. Mr. Gibson, was known as "Hoot" at Lockheed Aircraft Corporation, from which he retired. Mrs. Gibson was the former Hazel Conn, a member of the large Conn Family on Matthews Street. The Gibsons had a small grocery store in part of their house at one time; Mr. Gibson also had a "rolling store." Huey and Hazel Gibson had six children: **Huey**, known as "Sonny Boy," who died when he was two and one-half years old, **Donald**, **Mary Kate**, **June**, **Beatrice**, known as "**Blondie**," and **Brenda**. See *Conn, west side of Matthews Street.*

Donald Gibson married Delia Cato, they had four children: Yvonne, Ricky, Rena, pronounced Renee, Sandy, and four grandchildren. Delia is deceased. Donald and his second wife, Linda, live in Henry County.

Mary Kate Gibson first married Miguel Billes of Puerto Rico; they had one son, Tony. Mary Kate later married S.D. Weeks, known as "Don;" they had three children: Debra, Donnie, and Mary Delores, known as "Sissy." Mary Kate had nine grandchildren and four great-grandchildren. Mary Kate's third marriage was to Franklin Reece, known as "Junior;" they had one son, Franklin, known as "Frankie." Mary Kate and Donnie are deceased.

June Gibson married James A. Reece; they had three children: James Bryan, Sherry Lyn, and Travis Wade. James is deceased. Sherry Lynn died in infancy, James and Travis Wade are also deceased.

Beatrice Gibson as a child was known as "Blondie." Now known as "Bea," she married Curtis Green; they had three children: Kim, Michael, and Lori, and seven grandchildren.

Brenda Gibson married David E. Johnston; they had one child, David Russell Johnston, and three grandchildren. David E. Johnston is deceased.

Ninth House

Mr. and **Mrs. Hunter Richards** lived here. Mrs. Richards, the former Dot Conn, was a sister to Hazel Gibson, who resided next door. Dot and Hunter had three children: **Patsy**, **Joey** and **Keith**. See *Conn, west side of Matthews Street.*

Tenth House

Mr. and **Mrs. Loren Joseph Austin, Sr.**, and their family were residents here. Mrs. Austin was the former Pauline Hill, and Mr. Austin, known as "Bearcat," was a brother of Mary McCollum, who lived across the street from my family, on Bank Street. I remember "Bearcat" had a truck that I was very impressed with.

"Bearcat" and Pauline had four children: **Helen**, **Hazel**, **Betty**, and **Loren Joseph Austin, Jr.**, known as "L. J."

Helen Austin married Wilson Keyes. They had three children: two sons and a daughter.

Hazel Austin married Herman McRae; they had one daughter, Cheryl. Herman, a printer, worked with Clarence Brooks in the Trust Company of Georgia building in Atlanta. Hazel and Herman McRae live in Blairsville, Georgia.

NOTE: My friend, Hoyt Dorris, worked with Clarence in the Trust Company of Georgia building in Atlanta. Hoyt, a graduate of the Smyrna High School Class of 1951, died just before Christmas in 2003.

Betty Austin first married Paul Hunter. Her second marriage was to Pat Bryant. She currently lives in Florida. She had no children.

L. J. Austin, Jr., known as "Little Bearcat," married Dorothy Holden. They had two sons, Wayne and Robert, who live in Florida. "Little Bearcat" and Dorothy, who had moved to Florida, are both deceased.

NOTE: In the 1940s, Smyrna's City Limits ended at the top of the hill on Walker Street, which was not paved until 1950. Pavement ended at Wright Street.

Eleventh House

Mr. and **Mrs. James L. Whelchel** built a house next door to "Bearcat" Austin. Mrs. Whelchel was formerly Ruth Brown of South Carolina. They had a daughter, Linda. Mr. Whelchel retired from Southern Bell Telephone Company, now known as BellSouth, after 30 plus years. Mrs. Whelchel worked for the Cobb County School lunchroom program.

Linda Whelchel married Murphy Bennett, from West End in Atlanta and then Oakdale, They had two daughters: Tonya and Denise. Linda and Murphy live in Dallas.

Tonya Bennett married Michael Burruss, the son of Mr. and Mrs. "Buddy" Burruss, who was a member of one of Smyrna's large families. See *Atlanta Road, from Miles Stop to the Motters.*

Denise Bennett married Aaron Hunnicutt.

Twelfth House

Mr. and **Mrs. Walter Whelchel** lived in this house which was located behind the James L. Whelchel house. Mrs. Whelchel was formerly Dovie Brown, a sister of Clara Brown Lawler, Edna Brown Lacy, J.T. Brown, Milton Brown, and Fred Brown. See *Lawler, east side of Gilbert Street, Lacy, north side of Spring Street.*

After Mrs. Ruth Whelchel's death, Mr. Whelchel married Runell Fowler of Dahlonega. Mr. Whelchel is now deceased; Mrs. Runell Whelchel moved back to Dahlonega.

Milton Brown, Ruth Brown Whelchel's brother, still lives in this house.

Thirteenth House

Mr. and **Mrs. Weyland Adams** built this house. Mr. Adams was also known as "Buddy." Mrs. Adams was the former Margie Martin. They had three children: **Samuel**, known as "Sam," **Weylene**, and **Mark**. See, *Martin, north side of Walker Street, Adams, east side of Anderson Circle,* and *Adams, north side of Spring Road, the Country Road.*

Samuel Adams was married and had four children: Marti, Amy, Samuel, and Sarah. He lives in Marietta.

Weylene Adams married Ken Branscombe; they had two daughters: Jackie and Jenson. Ken and Weylene lives in Norcross.

Mark Adams is deceased.

NOTE: At the City Council meeting, December 5, 1947 the following property owners on Walker Street and Walker Court agreed to pay seventy-two cents per running foot of their property fronting on the street to be paved, (payment 20% upon completion and balance in four annual payments). The property owners were: F.C. Dabney, Jr., M.L. Collins, R.D. Tolbert, C.B. Campbell, James V. Sanders, W.D. Pass, Dolly Black, A.B. Carter, James R. Ferrell, Ida A. Black, Mrs. C.W. Flowers, R.E.Goins, H.D. Gibson, H.W. Richards, J.L. Huddleston, and W.S. Adams.

WALKER STREET

South Side

Walker Street runs east off Roswell Street to Matthews Street. Rather winding or crooked, short and very narrow, it is less than a half-mile long. In the days of my youth, the homes, all very modest, were white frame houses. It was a stable community, for the people who lived in those houses remained there for a long time. This was true for many residential areas of Smyrna in the days of my childhood and youth. I think this may be why I remember so many of the people. Until I was a big child, I thought that people always lived where they lived!

Appreciation is extended to Janet Brooks Brown for the information she provided about the residents of Walker Street, where she grew up the late 1940s and early 1950s. Her input has been invaluable in remembering the many residents who lived in this area in the middle of the Twentieth Century.

A special thanks is extended to the memory of Georgia Gillham Brooks. Through her love of Smyrna, she felt the need to preserve history where she found it. In her post child rearing years, walking around her beloved Smyrna was her therapy. Another of Georgia's hobbies was checking the discarded items at the *Smyrna Herald* office. Her diligence of saving memorabilia such as pictures, newspaper articles, obituaries and other related items, gave us much information which otherwise might have been lost.

Janet Brooks Brown remembers, "when all Cobb County students, in the 1951-1952 school year, were issued 'dog tags' with chains similar to those issued to military personnel. These metal tags had the student's name, address, date of birth, and religious preference. Mine had a 'P' for Protestant stamped into it. The tag had a hole in one end and an indention in the opposite end. My husband Glenn Ray Brown, remembers the students his age swapping tags with the boyfriends or girlfriends—a lot of good the tags would do them in case of an emergency! Bomb drills were also common for school kids in addition to tornado drills.

"About the same time Civil Defense Fallout shelters were designated in particular buildings. The old Locust Grove Baptist Church building on South Atlanta Road, built of Stone Mountain granite, still has the sign posted."

Another one of Janet's memories is, "I remember while living in the Belmont house (about four years old) walking with Mother and a two year old brother along Dixie Avenue beside the railroad and picking up coal that bounced off coal cars on the train. (Mother made it like an Easter egg hunt.) I assume the coal was used to help heat the house.

"I also remember walking to Smyrna to the Post Office to pick up our mail. (This was before it was delivered to the house up in the 1950s.) I would walk up to the postal clerk and ask for my daddy's mail. About six years of age, I would reach up to retrieve the mail and the clerk would say with a friendly voice, 'How are you today?' or 'you look very pretty today.' They would always call me by name, and that would make me feel so important. Our mail was addressed to Clarence Brooks, Smyrna, Georgia. Later on in the 1950s, after the mail was delivered to our house, we had a box attached to the house beside the front door and the mailman would walk up and place the mail in the box. We had no air conditioning and the windows were always open in the summer. As a teenage girl I always knew about when the mailman would come. I would get up and get dressed, make sure my hair was brushed and apply lipstick. There was a chance the mailman might be a 'cute guy'—maybe Gerald Eaton or Charles Pritchett. I would always be at the door to get the mail. I do not believe they ever noticed me!"

First House

The **Raymond Parks** Family lived here.

Second House

James Camp
Casualty of War
World War II

"B" and **Ethel Camp** were residents of this house. They had four children: **Dorothy Lee**, **Otis**, **Robert**, who was stillborn, and **James**, who served in the United States Military during World War II. Ethel's mother, **Maude Turner Kill**, who lived with them, was a sister of Clyde Pass, who lived across the street. Mrs. Kill was known in the neighborhood as "Aunt Maude." See *Pass, north side of Walker Street.*

Third House

PFC Gary William Painter
Casualty of War
Vietnam

Mr. and **Mrs. Hoke Painter** lived here. Mrs. Painter was the former Eva Goins. They had one daughter: **Ivajean**, and two sons, **Ernest**, known as "Buddy," and **Gary**. PFC Gary Painter was killed in Vietnam February 28, 1968.

The Painter Family were members of Second Baptist Church on Atlanta Street; Mr. Painter worked for Lockheed Aircraft Corporation in Marietta.

Ivajean Painter married James Beaver; they had no children. Ivajean's second marriage was to James Reily; they had two children, Michael and Pam, and one grandchild.

Ernest Painter, known as "Buddy," a graduate in the Campbell High School Class of 1959, married Hilda Reagan. They had a daughter, Anderia. Ernest later married Linda Silver; they had a son, Brian. Ernest is the proud grandfather of five grandchildren.

Gary Painter was a graduate in the Campbell High School Class of 1966. Before enlisting in the United States Marine Corps, in May 1967, Gary was first employed with A & P Store and then by Mayes, Sudderth and Etheredge, Inc., an engineering company in Marietta. A native of Smyrna and a member of Spring Street Baptist Church, Gary married Julie Smith nine days before he departed for duty in Vietnam, where he was killed February 28, 1968. According to the newspaper article concerning his death, his wife received his Purple Heart, the National Defense Service D Medal, the Vietnam Service Medal, and the Vietnam Campaign Medal.

NOTE: I have been told the **Lawler family** lived in this house before the Painters.

Fourth House

Everett and **Ruth Richards** were residents here with their children: **Janice** and "**Buddy**."

Fifth House

Janice Tilley and her family lived in this house. In Smyrna, Janice attended school with Janet Brown and "Buddy" Painter.

NOTE: Walker Court was cut from Walker Street to Spring Street in the late 1940s. Much later a stop sign was erected. See *note, end of north side of Walker Street.*

Sixth House

Bobby Butler, and his mother, **Mrs. Butler**, lived around the curve from the Tilley House. Mrs. Butler was killed in the Atherton Drug Store (Marietta on the Square) explosion on Halloween 1963.

The Davis Family

Mr. and **Mrs. Clintes Davis**, of Cedartown, moved to the sixth house after the Butlers vacated. Mrs. Davis was the former Marteal Brock. Mr. Davis, a "lay" minister, preached at Spring Street and Second Baptist churches, among others. Marteal and Clintes had four sons: **Jerry**, **Duron**, **Kayward**, and **Stacy**. Clintes Davis retired from Lockheed Aircraft Corporation. See *Davis, Nichols Street.*

Clintes Davis had a sister, Herstine Davis Slafton of Cedartown. His brother, Carl, was also a "lay" minister, at times pastoring and preaching at churches in the Smyrna area. Marteal Brock Davis had two sisters, Lucille Brock Dean and Mozelle Brock Reynolds, of Cedartown.

Jerry Davis who served in the United States Air Force in the 1950s, married Micheline Manzuri of Mar-la-tour, France. They had four daughters: Sylvia, Amanda, Karen, Marlene; and a son, Regis; nine grandchildren; and three great-grandchildren.

Duron Davis married Lynn Darnell, both of whom were graduates of Campbell High School. They had four sons, Kyley, Brock, Ryan, Justin, and a daughter, Evie, and three grandchildren.

Kayward Davis, a graduate of Campbell High School, married Glenda Fulton, a graduate of Osborne High School. They had five daughters, Kim, Kristi, Kathy, Karla, and Kelly, and nine grandchildren. Kayward and Glenda live in Lynchburg, Virginia.

Stacy Davis married Belinda Bert, both of whom were graduates of Wills High School. They had three children, a son, Casey, and two daughters, Courtney and April, and one grandchild. Stacy and Belinda are divorced, he is living in White.

Seventh House

Clarence and **Georgia Brooks** lived here. Mrs.Brooks was the former Georgia Gillham. They had five children: **Janet**, **Jimmie**, known as "Jim," **Joan**, **Judy**, and **Joel**. Georgia Brooks was the daughter of Mr. and Mrs. William Pierce Gillham, who lived on Broad Street, off Dixie Avenue, north of Smyrna. See *Gillham* on *Broad Street,* and *Fleming*, on *Fleming Street.*

Home of Clarence and Georgia Brooks
Walker Street
1950s

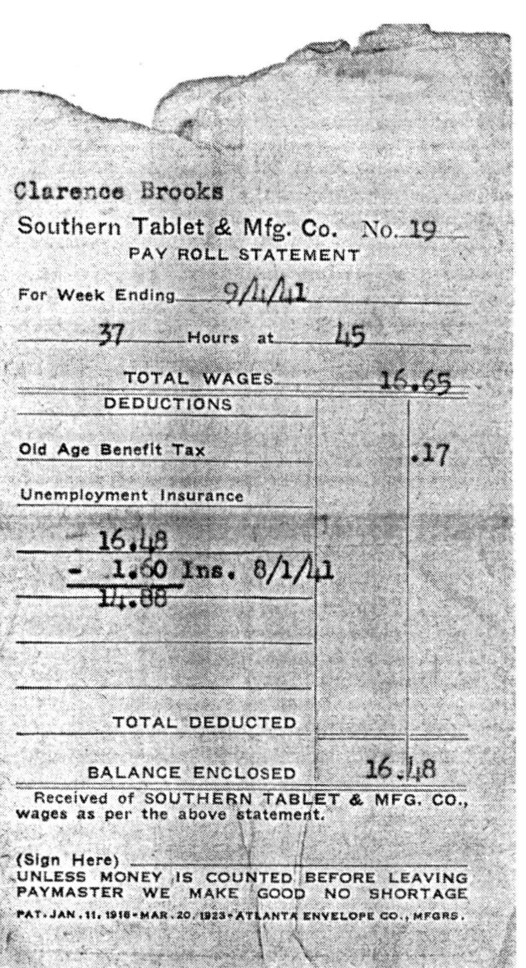

Clarence Brooks

Southern Tablet & Mfg. Co. No. 19

PAY ROLL STATEMENT

For Week Ending 9/4/41

37 Hours at 45

TOTAL WAGES 16.65

DEDUCTIONS

Old Age Benefit Tax	.17
Unemployment Insurance	
16.48 - 1.60 Ins. 8/1/41 14.88	
TOTAL DEDUCTED	
BALANCE ENCLOSED	16.48

Received of SOUTHERN TABLET & MFG. CO., wages as per the above statement.

(Sign Here) ______

UNLESS MONEY IS COUNTED BEFORE LEAVING PAYMASTER WE MAKE GOOD NO SHORTAGE

PAT. JAN. 11, 1916 - MAR. 20, 1923 - ATLANTA ENVELOPE CO., MFGRS.

Clarence Brooks was in the printing business. He worked in the basement of the old Trus Company of Georgia building on the corner of Edgewood Avenue and Ivy Street in Atlanta. Se *Brooks, east side of Roswell Street.*

Clarence Brooks and Roy Wood played baseball together in their young adult life, and late on the Smyrna Amateur Baseball Team that Roy managed. Later on Clarence was one of th organizers of the Smyrna Girls Softball Association, in which he was active for more than on generation. A softball field was named for Clarence at Jonquil Park. The plaque honoring Clarenc was removed when the Girls Softball Association disbanded in 1985, and the park became a socce field. Clarence and Roy were both very involved and interested in the activities for the youth i Smyrna. On the grounds of Jonquil Park, a marker still stands on Spring Road, dedicated to th memory of Roy Wood.

After all of her children were in school, Georgia Gillham Brooks began work for the Cob County School lunchrooms. After working in several schools, she retired from Argyle Elementar Among those with whom she worked were Louise Bell, Jennie Whitener, Gertrude Loudermilk, an Edna Ledbetter Cobb.

Janet Brooks married Glenn Ray Brown, known as "Ray," of the Oakdale community, sout of Smyrna. Janet graduated in the Campbell High School Class of 1959; Ray graduated from Campbe High School in the class of 1955, and played on Campbell's first football team. (The Panthers firs game was in September of 1952.) Ray continued his education at Georgia State College, nov University, in Atlanta, where he received a Bachelor of Business Administration degree in 1967—afte eight years of night school and Janet was awarded a PHT (Putting Husband Through) Diploma.

Janet and Ray had two children, Todd and Tracy. The Browns, first active members of th Locust Grove Baptist Church in Oakdale, are now active at Mt. Harmony Baptist Church, in Mableton

Todd Brown graduated in the Campbell High School Class of 1982 and received a Bachelo of Business Administration degree from the University of Georgia. He married Rebecca Bounds o Smyrna, also a Campbell High School graduate, who attended Kennesaw State College. Rebecc earned a Bachelor of Fine Arts degree and a Masters in Art Education, from Georgia State University They had two children: a son, Carson, and a daughter, Ansleigh. Todd works for John Weilan Homes; Rebecca Brown is an upper school art teacher at Whitefield Academy in Cobb County.

Tracy Brown graduated in the Campbell High School Class of 1984. Tracy continued he education at the University of Georgia, in Athens, where she received a Bachelor of Arts degree i Journalism. She worked for the Arthritis Foundation, where she was an editor of *Arthritis Today*. Sh married Michael Ballew of Smyrna; they had two children: Savannah and David. Michael is a graduat of Campbell High School and the University of Georgia, where he received a Bachelor of Busines Administration degree. He is a partner with Tanner, Ballew, and Maloof Insurance Agency, in Atlanta.

Ray Brown's parents, Mattie Lee and Glenn Brown, along with Mattie Lee's sister and he husband, Elizabeth and Virlyn Herren, operated B & H Recreation Center (skating and bowling), o South Cobb Drive, in the Oakdale community, during the 1950s. The Browns and Herrens were ver active members of Locust Grove Baptist Church, also in the Oakdale community.

NOTE: Felton Brown, Ray's grandfather, who lived on Camp Highland Road, was th Justice of the Peace in Oakdale in the 1940s and 1950s. Earlier, Felton's brother, Tom, who lived o Gilmore Road, held this office.

Memories

by Janet Brooks Brown

Janet Brooks Brown remembers that, in the late 1940s, her family bought milk from thei next door neighbor, Mrs. Ada Stephens. She also recalls that she and her family affectionately calle

Mrs. Stephens, "Aunt Ada;" they also called Dolly Black, who lived across the street, "Aunt Dolly." This was a fairly common Southern tradition, which showed respect for "special" people.

"Aunt Dolly," who had a small clothesline on her back porch, sometimes used the Brooks' outside clothesline for larger items. The neighbors' lives were intertwined through day to day activities; it was also a common practice to share vegetables from the garden, or other commodities, when available.

Jimmie Brooks, now known as "Jim," married Jane Reed, of Moncton, New Brunswick, Canada. He and Jane met and married while "Jim" was stationed in Bermuda, where Jane was working as a newspaper reporter. He was in the United States Air Force, where he served as a loadmaster during the Vietnam War, and retired after 20 years. Still later, "Jim" retired from the United States Post Office. He and Jane had a daughter, Tara, a son, Drew, and two granddaughters. Along with their family, "Jim" and Jane now live in Dover, Delaware.

Joan Brooks, a 1965 graduate of Campbell High School, married Elton Lawrence of Florida. They had one son, Paul. Joan worked for BellSouth for thirty-five years. She and Elton divorced.

Paul Lawrence graduated from Campbell High School in 1991 and afterwards from the Art Institute of Atlanta. He married Robin Spritzer, a graduate of Lassiter High School.

Judy Brooks married Johnny Bryson. Judy, a 1967 graduate of Wills High School, and Johnny had two daughters: Kelly and Kerry. Johnny is deceased.

Kelly Bryson, a 1986 graduate of Wills High School, married Lee Patrick; they had one daughter, Brooke. Kelly and Lee are divorced.

Kerry Bryson graduated from Smyrna High School in 1990. (This was the year when Campbell High School and Wills High School were combined and named Smyrna High School. After one year, the school was renamed Campbell High School.) Kerry married George Fowlkes; they had a son, Josh, and a daughter, Jennifer.

Joel Brooks married and had one daughter, Jenna. His wife is deceased.

Eighth House

Mr. and **Mrs. John T. Stephens** resided in this house. Mr. Stephens was a Smyrna Policeman in the 1940s. At one time, Mrs. Ada Stephens, was employed by Brumby Manufacturing Company, in Marietta. Mr. and Mrs. Stephens were members of Spring Street Baptist Church.

Mrs. Stephens, the former Ada Black, and her previous husband, Theodore Dwight Frisbee, had three children: a son, **Woodrow Dwight**, and two daughters, **Olive Elizabeth**, known as "Ollie," and **Margaret Mae**, known as "Margie." See *Bowles, north side of Spring Street,* and *Blacks, west side of Roswell Street* and *north side of Walker Street.*

Woodrow Frisbee married Jewel Whitworth. They had one son, Hoyt. Woodrow later married Blanche Mason; they had four children: Barbara, Dwight, Patricia, and Steve. Steve is deceased.

Olive Frisbee, known as "Ollie," married John K. Huff; they had four children: Melvin, Louise, Don, and Eugene, known as "Gene." Both "Ollie" and John Huff were employed by Coats and Clark Thread Mill in Clarkdale. Later "Ollie" worked for Colonial Baking Company, in East Point and John later drove a truck for Dr. Pepper Bottling Company. John K. Huff is deceased.

Melvin Huff married Brenda Barnes; they had three children: Kenneth, Kevin, and Kristina, and two grandchildren.

Louise Huff married Milton Bartlett; they had three children, Elizabeth, Johnny, and Jimmy, and seven grandchildren. Milton is deceased.

Don Huff married Kathie Petty Fowler, who was previously married to Mr. Fowler and had a daughter, Nina. Don and Kathie had one grandchild, Rebecca.

"Gene" Huff married Judy Bell. They had three children, Michael, Lori, and Debbie, and three grandchildren.

"Margie" Frisbee married Claude Poss. After Claude's death, she married Jerry Fouts. She and Jerry had two daughters: Sara, who married Mr. Wilder, and Carolyn. See *Fouts, Atlanta Street, from Mrs. Mazie's to Pearce Matthews.*

Mr. and Mrs. Carl Phillips

After the death of her mother, Ada Frisbee Stephens, and her stepfather, John T. Stephens, "Ollie" Frisbee Huff inherited this house. "Ollie" later Olive Frisbee married Carl Phillips who then moved to this house. After Carl's death, she lived until it was sold in 1996. "Ollie" is now deceased.

WRIGHT STREET

Wright Street is a short, narrow one that runs between Walker and Spring streets. There are only two houses located on it, and they are on the east side.

First House

Mr. and **Mrs. James Huddleston** lived at the top of the hill, on the corner facing Wright Street. Mrs. Huddleston was the former Louise Blan. They had two sons: **James Gerald**, known as "Buddy," and **Ray Lewis**. Reverend Huddleston was the pastor of several churches in the area, including Harvest Baptist Church on North Cooper Lake Road, near the railroad (which is now the Silver Comet Trail). Later on his son, Ray Huddleston was also pastor there. In addition to his church work, Reverend Huddleston worked for Simmons Mattress Company in Atlanta, and later for Cleveland Electric Company. Mrs. Huddleston's first employment was with an insurance company, and later she was a hairdresser. See *Blan, south side of Spring Street.*

The Huddlestons moved from here to a house they built on the south side of Walker Street, across the creek from Mrs. Ada Stephens.

In their later years, Reverend and Mrs. James Huddleston lived in the triangle at North Cooper Lake Road and Nowlin Drive, where they resided for many years.

NOTE: The Harvest Baptist Church, built many years past the middle of the Twentieth Century, was recently razed for the building of new homes.

James Gerald Huddleston, known as "Buddy," graduated from Campbell High School in 1961. He married Carlene Trucks of Marietta. They had three children, Mary Elizabeth, Kyle, and Amanda, and four grandchildren. Mary Elizabeth died when she was nine months old of a streptococcus infection. "Buddy," who owns and operates Huddleston Heating and Air Conditioning, and Carlene live in Buchanan. "Buddy" shared that he remembers the carnival held on Walker Street, between Wright and Matthews streets, in the late 1940s.

Ray Lewis Huddleston married Sarah Cox of Austell, a South Cobb High School graduate. They had two sons, Ray, Jr., and Joseph, and three grandchildren.

Ray, Sr. was among the Smyrna students who were transferred several times due to the changing of the school attendance lines. He attended Smyrna Elementary School through fifth grade, Hawthorne for the sixth grade, and then Osborne Junior High School, before graduating from Campbell High School in 1966. Ray attended Gwinnett/Hall Bible College. He is now an ordained Baptist Minister, serving as President of Harvest Baptist Church Ministries, Incorporated, a non-profit organization devoted to assisting retired pastors. Ray, Sr. owns and operates a business, Huddleston Construction and Grading Company. Ray and Sarah live in Dallas.

NOTE: James Huddleston was the son of Mr. and Mrs. Durwood Huddleston. His mother, the former Essie Quarles was a sister of Lee Quarles who lived on the east side of Matthews Street. Durwood and Essie Huddleston, including James, had seven children: D.W., Effie Lee, Thomas, Callie Mae, James, Inez, and George. Mr. Durwood Huddleston worked for Georgia Power Company. See *Quarles, east side of Matthews Street.*

Janet Brown remembers that, when the carnival came to town in the late 1940s, it was located in an open field on the right side of Walker Street, between Wright and Matthews streets, all of which were outside the City limits at that time. "Buddy" Huddleston remembers when the carnival came to town, his brother, Ray, fifteen months old, was sick with typhoid fever. Mrs. Huddleston recalls that Lorena Pace Pruitt, Mayor of Smyrna, owned this property where the carnival was located.

Mr. and Mrs. Hoyt Ellison

Mr. and **Mrs. Hoyt Ellison** and their daughter, **Elaine**, moved to this house on Wright Street after the Huddlestons vacated. Mrs. Ellison was the former Geneva Coker, a sister of Blanche Ables, whose husband, J.B. Ables, served as Mayor of Smyrna. Hoyt and Geneva still live in the Smyrna area. See *Ables, east side of Lee Street.*

Second House

Mr. Glenn Denson, whose wife was deceased, and who was a brother of Mrs. Mattie Blan, and his children moved to this house. It was built by his brother-in-law, W.A. Blan, who lived on the north side of Spring Street. The Densons had four children: William, Ada, Andrew, and Brady See *Blan, south side of Spring Street.*

The Elbert Parker Family

The **Elbert Parker Family** was residents of this house at one time.

Mr. and Mrs. Magness

Mr. and **Mrs. Magness** and their two daughters, **JoAnn** and **Roberta**, were the third family to reside here.

Roberta Magness married Ray Pruitt. Much later in the century, the Pruitts lived in the Eaton home place, on the corner of Oakdale Drive and King Springs Road.

NORTH AVENUE

North Avenue was a short street that lay between the seventh and eighth houses on Whitfield Street, which only had one house located there.

Mr. and Mrs. Virgil Homer Akins

This house was built for **Mr.** and **Mrs. Virgil Homer Akins** in their senior years, by two of their sons, Walker and Howard. Mrs. Akins, the former Mary Dunn, and Mr. Akins had ten children: Walker, Homer, Howard, Dolly, Ida, Bessie, Angie, Eula, Charley, and Virgil, all of whom were grown and married before Mr. and Mrs. Akins moved to this house. The Akins siblings were in my parents' generation.

Walker Akins married Leila Emory. See *North Matthews Street.*

Howard Akins married Ruby Wallace. See *south side of Bank Street and Gilbert Street.*

Dolly Akins married Reuben Black See *north side of Walker Street.*

Ida Akins married Lee Black. See *north side of Walker Street.*

Bessie Akins married John Martin. See *north side of Walker Street.*

Angie Akins married Bill Ransom. See *Ransom, south side of Spring Street.*

Eula Akins married Judge Emory.

Virgil Akins died from pneumonia at the age of eighteen.

NOTE: Mary Dunn Akins was a sister of George Dunn, who was the patriarch of the large Dunn Family who lived on Dixie Avenue. One of her nephews, Charles Dunn, has lived across the street from Lillie and me for more than thirty years. He married Sara Burruss, who grew up on Atlanta Road. See *Dixie Avenue* and *Atlanta Road, at Miles Stop.*

The Motter Family

Later on **David** and **Louise Motter** and their daughter, **Peggy**, were residents in this house. See *east side of Anderson Circle.*

MORRIS CIRCLE
East Side

There were two houses on this side of Morris Circle.

Appreciation is extended to Billy Flowers and Ray Ferrell for their memories of their families on Morris Circle.

First House

Eugene and **Sybil Green** were residents of this house, with their two children: **Patricia** and **Johnny**. Johnny still lives here.

MORRIS CIRCLE
West Side

Morris Circle, a short street off Walker Street, is the first street to the right traveling north on Roswell Street. There were six houses on the right side of the circle. I have been able to identify only two families who lived here in the middle of the Twentieth Century.

First House

Roy and **Irma Ferrell** were residents of the first house, which was on the southwest corner of Walker Street and Morris Circle. Roy was from the Lost Mountain area of West Cobb County; Mrs. Ferrell, the former Irma Crowley, was from Savannah.

Roy bought Buna Walker's garage, that was located on the west side of Atlanta Street in the triangle with what is now Memorial Drive. Roy later worked for Lockheed Aircraft Corporation.

Roy Ferrell was the second son of Mary and Grady Ferrell, of Powder Springs, who had other children living in the Smyrna area: Fred, Ruth, and Ray. Fred Ferrell married Hattie Olliver. Ruth Ferrell married Simms Boudreau. Ray Ferrell married Betty Pool. Fred and Ray bought Earl Cobb's service station on Atlanta Street. See *Ferrell's Garage, Atlanta Street, from Mapps to R & M Café.*

Mr. and **Mrs. Neely**

Mr. and **Mrs. Neely** moved to this house after the Ferrells had vacated. Mrs. Neely was Dr. Robert Mainor's nurse in his medical office on West Spring Street. See *West Spring Street.*

Second House

The **Taylor Family** lived here. Mrs. Taylor was also a nurse in Dr. Robert Mainor's office.

CHAPTER EIGHTEEN

DIXIE AVENUE

Dixie Avenue runs north and south and parallel with the railroad, from Hawthorne Avenue to just north of where Pat Mell Road intersects with Atlanta Road and Dixie Avenue. When the Arthur Bacon Bridge was built at the intersection of Atlanta and Windy Hill roads, therefore, some houses in this area were lost in the process. Therefore, I was not able to establish for certain the exact location of each house because of the drastic change in the neighborhood over time. Of course, all the houses on Dixie Avenue were on the east side of the street.

Appreciation is extended to Betty Burruss Brown and Doris Haygood Boring for their assistance in remembrance of the people who lived in this area in the days of their youth and to Edmond Mingo and James Wigington for sharing information about their families. Appreciation is also extended to Joann McDowell for sharing information about her family, the McDowells, who moved to Dixie Avenue in the late 1940s. Many members of families who lived in this area still reside in Smyrna and its environs.

The Mingo Family

Mr. Edmond Leo Mingo, Sr., from upstate New York, and his wife, the former **Lula Barnett** from Charleston, West Virginia, with their two sons, **Edmond, Jr.**, and **Louis**, moved to 2425 Dixie Avenue in 1947. Mrs. Mingo, from a previous marriage, had a daughter who never lived here.

Mr. Mingo, Sr., originally from Quebec, Canada, was a farmer in Ticonderoga, New York. He entered the bakery business in West Virginia, where he met his wife. Edmond and Lula moved to Smyrna to assist Lula's sister, Mae Rust, who owned Rust Cheese Company on Atlanta Road, south of Smyrna.

Edmond M. Mingo, Jr., a graduate of Campbell High School, married Martha Jean White from Nashville, Georgia. They had two sons, Stan and Craig, and three grandchildren.

Louis M. Mingo, who attended Campbell High School, and his wife, Mary, had three children, Lisa, Robbie, and Mark, and five grandchildren. Louis died in 2005.

The Sherman Wigington Family

Sherman Wigington and his wife, the former **Myrtle Fulton**, both of Jasper, moved into this old house at 106 Dixie Avenue; it received extensive restoration during their residency, from 1944 to the mid 1980s. Sherman and Myrtle had three children: **Mildred**, **James**, and **Shirley**.

NOTE: Sherman Wigington had a brother, George Britton Wigington, known as "G.B., who lived on Dunn Street. See *Wigington, west side of Dunn Street.*

The Wigington Family had lived on Smyrna's Bank Street in the 1920s. After moving back to Jasper, where they resided for more than 10 years, they returned to the Smyrna area, to live (1941 to 1944) near Gilmore Streetcar Stop, on Atlanta Road, south of Smyrna. (At that time Atlanta Road was United States Highway 41.)

Mr. Wigington, a barber in Oakdale and an ordained minister, and his family worshiped at Spring Street Baptist Church.

Mildred Wigington, a graduate of Fitzhugh Lee High School, married Otis Thomason of Jasper. They had two daughters: Madge and Nancy. Madge never married. Nancy married Edward Patrick; they had two sons: Todd and Tyler.

James Leslie Wigington married Hazel Starnes. They had one son, Stephen. A graduate of Pebblebrook High School, Stephen married Ginger Dinsmore; they had a daughter, Brittany. James, who is retired from Stone Container Company, lives in Smyrna.

After Hazel's death, James Wigington married Hazel's first cousin, Dolores Starnes. Dolores had four children from her previous marriage to Mr. Jackson: Terrence Jackson, Nancy Jackson (Reardon), Penny Jackson (Cox), and Betsy Jackson (Hester). Together, James and Dolores had seven grandchildren.

Shirley Wigington married Edward Massey. Both Campbell High School graduates, they had three daughters: Alice, Rhonda, and Carol. Alice married Doyle Powell and had two children; Rhonda married Don Segassie; and Carol married Robert Jenkins. After Edward's death, Shirley married John I. Duncan, known as "J.I."

The Belmont House

The Belmont House, standing on the southeast corner of Dixie Avenue and Davis Road in the days of my youth, was a very large white two-story house, which was rented to the people who lived there. It had long ceased to be the central attraction of what, at one time, was a very prosperous and well-known estate. When I was a kid, it was still very imposing, across the railroad near the Belmont Streetcar Stop, on Dixie Avenue, north of Smyrna. All of the property surrounding the house at one time was connected to Belmont Farm.

My mother's maternal aunt, Minnie Brewer Dunn, and her husband, Uncle George Dunn, resided in the Belmont House at one time with their son, "T.L.," and daughter, June. They had previously lived on North Cooper Lake Road near the railroad, now known as the Silver Comet Trail. Later on, after "T.L." came home from the United States Army, following World War II, he bought a house on Atlanta Street, across the railroad, for himself. He moved Aunt Minnie and Uncle George from the Belmont House to a Gilbert Street dwelling, which was right behind his house. "T.L." really looked after his parents.

Aunt Minnie was my Grandmother Brewer's sister; they were daughters of Newton Andrew Brewer and Martha Jane Petty Brewer of Marietta. (This family is mentioned in Sarah Temple Gober's book, "*The First Hundred Years, a Short History of Cobb County in Georgia*," written in 1933.) Aunt Minnie, small in stature and very hospitable, smiled a lot. I would say she was very "home spun"—the grandmotherly type.

The Belmont House

by Diane Dunn Savage

My memories of the Belmont House are about a lot of music and my grandparents. At one time my family, along with 'Granny' and 'Gramp' Dunn, lived there. (My grandfather Dunn was born in Marietta but lived most of his life in Smyrna, as did my grandmother.) Aunt June, her husband and daughter, and 'Granny's' brother, whom we called 'Uncle Buck,' resided in a small house behind the large one, where, in 1946, I was born.

Before we moved to the Belmont House, I was told that the little house, which had a basement, was actually where crops were stored from the Belmont Farm's earlier years.

All of the brothers of my dad, George Monroe Dunn, including himself and his father 'Gramps,' played several instruments. When they would get together, they would almost always play and everyone else would listen. Even in later years at family reunions, they would play—therefore, I grew up around a lot of music.

Minnie (Brewer) and **George Preston Dunn**
Married January 27, 1907.
They had been married 55 years in 1962,
when this picture was taken.

Also in the little house, Dad's brother, Hugh, and his family lived in the downstairs apartment. Aunt Lois, Daddy's sister, and her family either resided there or in the Belmont House. (I cannot remember which.)

Some of my family lived in this area from the 1930s until my parents died. This was my home, and I knew all of the people who lived in and around the Belmont House, a stately place. I hated to see it razed!

The George Dunn Family

The **George Dunn Family** was one of Smyrna's large families. Their children were as follows: **Henry Andrew**, **Hugh Edwin**, known as "Buster," **George Monroe**, **Mabel Elizabeth**, **Harold Stephens**, **Lois Martha-Margarite**, **Albert Hoyt**, **William Crafton**, **Thomas Lee,** known as "T.L," **Charles Lucious**, **Joyce Mae**, and **Sarah June**. The George Dunn Family was a "good time" family, with much talent distributed among them. I think all of the men played a musical instrument of some kind, as did June. George was a fiddler, but he played several other instruments; he also had a good singing voice. Actually the group was made up of George, his sons, and one daughter, June. Playing for years in the area, they performed at the American Legion and other places. The Dunns were a close-knit family, to whose home I remember going with my mother when I was a child.

Henry Andrew Dunn married Ada Fortner. They had four children: Henry Lee, Hugh Donald, Charlotte Ann, and Alan Ray.

George Monroe Dunn married Willie Mae Davenport. They had five children: Joyce Mae, James Larry, Jacqueline Diane, James Thomas, and Jimmy Anthony, who served in the Vietnam War.

George Monroe Dunn was a member of the Dunn Brothers Band that was formed in 1940. They later changed their name to Pioneer Ramblers, played over WFOM Radio in Marietta, and made several recordings. They also appeared on Freddy Miller's "*Stars of Tomorrow*," a local talent show, on Channel 5 in Atlanta. Monroe played several instruments, including bass fiddle, drums, and banjo. When "Boots" Woodall and his band were playing at the Atlanta Sports Arena, the Pioneer Ramblers were playing there also and witnessed the Woodall Band's "backing up" a tiny girl singer, who became the famous Brenda Lee.

Harold Stephens Dunn married Myrtle Florence Turner. They had three children: Horace Wayne, Linda Faye, and Christopher Scott Dunn.

Lois Martha-Margarite Dunn married Henry Latimore Dunn (no relation). They had seven children: Carolyn Louise, Martha Jean, Thomas Eugene, David Earl, Jerry Alvin, Kenneth LeRoy, and Janet Elaine.

Albert Hoyt Dunn married Wilene Gilliam. They had three children: Troy Lee, Bobby Joe, and Stevie. The Albert Dunn Family lived in Oklahoma City, Oklahoma.

Albert Hoyt was a Medic, driving an ambulance during World War II, while in the United States Military. He tells of flying 200 miles, from France to England, to visit his brother, "T.L.," who was wounded in action.

Thomas Lee Dunn, known as "T.L.," married Margaret Tanner, a member of the Smyrna High School Class of 1949. They had three children: Janie Lee, Deborah Lynn, and Marvin Daniel. See *west side of Gilbert Street.*

"T.L.," having fought in World War II, was awarded a Purple Heart. Part of an interview that a reporter had with "T.L.," who lost a leg due to injuries he received in battle, appeared in *The Marietta Journal* on the 40th Anniversary of the D-Day invasion. "American troops landed on the western beaches, code named Utah and Omaha. Those landings at Omaha suffered terrible casualties–

western beaches, code named Utah and Omaha. Those landings at Omaha suffered terrible casualties–almost the entire first wave of Allied Troops was destroyed. I landed in one of the later waves at Omaha Beach. A month after D-Day, I fought in the battle of Lt. Lo, at which the Allies broke through the German defenses despite furious suicide attacks by fanatical *Nazi SS Stormtroopers*. I lost my leg in this fight." Dunn was asked if he would do it all over again and he said he would if freedom were again at stake. "I'm no hero," Dunn said, "I think the heroes were the dead ones."

Charles Lucious Dunn married Sarah Burruss; they had two children: Judy Amlinda and Charles Lucious Dunn, Jr., known as "Chuck." Sarah's large family lived near the Miles Crossing Streetcar Stop. Charles and Sarah have lived across the street from Lillie and me on Havilon Way for 30 years; we are very close to them. When our children were growing up in the 1970s, their two grandsons, Shane and Shawn Cannon, would come from school to Sarah's and Charles' house. They would always check in with Lillie because she was at home when the children arrived from school; thus Lillie became very close to those boys. Shane and Shawn, who also have good voices, used to sing in church and at events. See *Burruss, Atlanta Road, from Miles Stop to the Motters.*

Sara June Dunn married Robert Ford Dunn. They had three children: Robert Stanley, Richard Alan, and Michael Timothy.

Robert Stanley Dunn, a graduate of Campbell High School, married Vickie Hillhouse from Woodstock. They had two children: Robert Kyle and Staci Lynn.

Richard Alan, known as "Ricky," a Campbell High School graduate, married Lynette Darlene Tinsley of Marietta. They had two daughters: Melissa and Jennifer.

After "Ricky" and Darlene divorced, "Ricky" married Shannon Howell Sibilia. From a previous marriage, Shannon had two daughters: Alyssa and Emily Sibilia.

June Dunn and her sister, Lois Dunn, married men whose last names were also Dunn. Though the men were related to each other, they were not kin to the George Dunn Family.

Sara June Dunn, known as "June," worked in retail for 25 years: W.T. Grant Company, F.W. Woolworth, Kesslers at Cobb Center; later she was employed in the Cobb County School Lunchroom Program, from which she retired. Robert Ford Dunn, who had worked in vending service, with Servmation Company, retired from YKK Zipper company.

Many other families over the years were residents in the Belmont House. Janet Brooks Brown tells me that she, living in the Belmont House with her family when she was a child, remembers that the rear of the house was high off the ground. Also, she relates, "As children, we were able to go up under the house to play."

As can be seen, much change has come onto Dixie Avenue and the area around the Belmont House. But for me, as a little boy, the Belmont House, always a landmark in my memory, still exists.

A Short Story

by Betty Burruss Brown

Before the McDowells moved to this house, on the northeast corner of Dixie Avenue and Davis Road, across the street from the Belmont House, Dr. Yancey, a dentist who had a dental chair in his house, and his wife lived here. I do not know how many patients he had. In our early days, people did not go to the dentist often as they do today.

Dr. Yancey, a very nice man, seemed to love children. Every afternoon he would walk with his dog; sometimes some of us would walk with them. I remember Dr. Yancey's showing us his dental chair. We were so interested and excited to be invited into his house to see it!

The Joe McDowell Family

Mr. and **Mrs**. **Joe McDowell** moved to Dixie Avenue in the late 1940s. Their house was located on the northeast corner of Dixie Avenue and Davis Street, north of the Belmont House. They had three children: **Howard, Joann, and Shelba**.

Memories of Dixie Avenue

by Joann McDowell

I remember our being neighbors with the **Austin Atkins Family** on Dixie Avenue before they moved to Bank Street. The **Sisson Family** also lived on Dixie Avenue before moving to Hughes Street. See *Atkins, south side of Bank Street* and *Sisson, west side of Hughes Street.*

The memories of my early years in the town of Smyrna are warm and pleasant. Although I could not have described my feelings then, I remember sensing a pervasive spirit of mutual respect, gentleness, and helpfulness among people. A special memory from my childhood during World War II is of neighbors' visiting and sharing letters from loved ones in strange-sounding places.

Of three children, I was the middle child born during the Depression years of the mid 1930s to Joe and Sarah "Sadie" Robinson McDowell. I was named Alice Joann: the name "Alice" in honor of my maternal grandmother, who died about a year before I was born. My brother, Howard Lewis McDowell, was almost seven years older than I, and my sister, Shelba McDowell, is four years younger. All of us, with the exception of my father, were born less than a mile from the traffic light at Spring and Atlanta streets.

My mother's families, the Robinsons and the Cannons, were in Smyrna before the Civil War. Mother, the sixth of seven children, was born in 1908 to Georgia Alice Cannon Robinson and William Oliver Robinson at the family home on Spring Street, which is now the site of the new Ivy Springs townhomes. My grandfather, a carpenter and a roofer, built the home on Spring Street more than a century ago. My mother's oldest sister, Annie Mae Robinson, married Oliver Lawrence Pinson; they built a home on the same property. Their children, Ruby Pinson Camp and O.L. Pinson, Jr., grew up next door to my mother and seemed more like her siblings than niece and nephew.

Several of my maternal grandmother's relatives, the Cannons, are buried in Smyrna Memorial Cemetery. Some of the women and children left the area during the Civil War as the Union Army approached Smyrna. They stayed with relatives elsewhere but returned to rebuild after the War. Among these was my great-grandmother, Sara Jane Brown Cannon, whose father and older brother lost their lives in the Civil War.

My father, the youngest of ten children, was born in 1908 to John Henry and Mary Jane Privette McDowell near Cedartown (in Polk County). John Henry was a farmer, and there were enough children and other relatives to farm the land and provide enough food to survive during the Depression. My grandparents named my father "Joe Brown" after the Georgia Governor (with that name), who was elected the year my father was born.

The McDowells, always known as Scotch-Irish, were in Georgia before the Civil War. Certain characteristics of the Scotch-Irish heritage were evident in spoken words and phrases in this family but were especially present in the music that was always a part of family gatherings. (One of my first cousins became the "Original Blue Grass Boy," hired by Bill Monroe in the late 1930s.) Both of my great-grandfathers on that side of the family fought for the Confederacy.

Around the year 1925, when my father was about age 17, he moved away from the farm in Polk County to find work and a different lifestyle near Atlanta. Several family members had preceded him; he moved into the home of an older sister and her husband on Spring Street in Smyrna. There was easy access to Atlanta by way of streetcar, but there was even easier access to become acquainted with the Robinsons, who lived just across the street. Young Joe McDowell, had found work at Atlantic

Steel Company, began to call on the young woman across the street, Sadie Robinson. They were married in December 1926. Joe continued to work for Atlantic Steel until his retirement, nearly 40 years later. My mother, Sadie, was a homemaker who took her calling very seriously.

During my childhood we lived in several rental houses in Smyrna, including dwellings on Whitfield, Foster, and Elizabeth streets. Those were the Depression years, and I believe many people, including my parents, were fearful of buying on credit. During the rather lean years, I have come to believe, humor and music saved us from undue sadness. My father's sense of humor, along with that of my brother, Howard, and cousin, O.L., kept us amused and distracted; also there was always music in the house. In 1948 we moved to the Dixie Avenue house which my father had purchased. My parents continued to live there until the construction of the Windy Hill connector forced them to sell their property and move. In 1982 they built a log house in West Smyrna and enjoyed this residence for several years.

Always affiliated with Baptist churches, we never missed a service except for serious illness or some extreme emergency. We were all involved in music at church. Both of my parents, who taught Sunday School, were serious students of the Bible, and I treasure what I learned from their discussions of the Scriptures. We were members of two small Baptist churches during my early years, or until we joined First Baptist Church in the mid 1940s. When my brother, Howard, became Pastor of Vinings First Baptist in the 1950s, we moved our membership to be with him.

Some of my fondest memories are the Smyrna Elementary and High school music teachers who took a special interest in us. Miss Bennett taught me piano and voice lessons in elementary school, and Mrs. Maxine Blair was my music teacher in high school. I reconnected with Mrs. Blair some years later, after she had moved back to Creston, Iowa. We stayed in touch until her daughter notified me of her death several years later. Another special teacher who directed our high school Glee Club was Rev. G. Aiken Taylor, then also Pastor of Smyrna Presbyterian Church. (Since the choir at his church was quite small, on special occasions he would invite me to sing alto with his choir. After Sunday School at First Baptist, I would hurry over to the Presbyterian Church choir room to find a robe and fall into place.) Indeed, these are very special memories.

Only in my adult years have I recognized a special gift I received from my brother, Howard, during my childhood. Having learned to play the guitar as a teenager, he studied diligently to be able to accompany himself as he sang. The lyrics to hundreds of songs, from grand opera to country music, are stored in my memory from hearing him sing in the next room as I went to sleep each night.

The sense of community during my early years in Smyrna was a valued gift that I learned from the interaction with the merchants as I accompanied my parents down Atlanta Street. There was Mr. Johnson's Shoe Shop, Rogers Grocery Store, Landers Drug Store, Collins Pharmacy, Mr. Tribble's Feed Store (across from the Depot) and, of course, G.B.'s Place.

What I, along with my siblings, learned during these years surely provided a foundation that became an asset as we grew into adulthood. I worked for Southern Bell Telephone Company (now BellSouth) for 34 years. My brother taught school for a few years before becoming Pastor of Vinings First Baptist Church, where he served 34 years. My sister, Shelba McDowell, became a registered nurse and recently retired from the State of Georgia

Having now been divorced for a number of years, I was free to pursue an education and enjoy being part of the academic community. I earned my undergraduate degree from Oglethorpe University while being employed with Southern Bell Telephone Company. After retirement, I went to graduate school to prepare for a career as a professional counselor. After completing my studies at Georgia State University, I worked part time for six years for the Dekalb Community Service Board.

My daughter, Beth, and my three grandchildren live in Reno, Nevada, a very beautiful area, which I have visited several times. My brother, Howard McDowell is survived by his widow, Beverly Walden McDowell, who grew up on Spring Hill Road, a son, daughter, and three grandchildren.

In writing this historical account I have been aware that I am omitting many difficulties and heart-wrenching events that occurred during my adult life. At the same time, I have realized that without the strength of the lessons learned in childhood, I might not have survived so well to this stage in my life. I can truly say, "'Tis Grace hath brought me safe thus far." I will be forever grateful for my kind and gentle parents, to my God, and for what I learned about stability, values, and community from the citizens of my home town, Smyrna, Georgia."

NOTE: Joann McDowell was a member of the Smyrna High School Class of 1951, the last class to graduate from Smyrna High School.

Mr. and Mrs. M.H. Gwin

Mr. and **Mrs. M.H. Gwin** and their two daughters, **Gina** and **Ellen**, were residents here. Mr. Gwin was a mail clerk for the railroad, traveling back and forth on the train while sorting mail. The Gwins were members of First Baptist Church, where Mr. Gwin was a deacon.

The Jeff Garner Family

Mr. and **Mrs. Jeff Garner** resided on Dixie Avenue next door to the Gwins. (The house is still standing.) They had three children: **Morris**, **Talmadge**, and **Eleanor**. The Garners were members of First Baptist Church. During World War II Mr. Garner converted chicken houses and a big barn on his property into apartments for many who came to the area to work temporarily at the Bell Bomber Plant. A builder, Mr. Garner also constructed the Carney House on Dixie Avenue.

Eleanor Garner married Hansel Parks, who grew up on Elizabeth Street. They had two daughters: Debbie and Sherrie. See *Elizabeth Street.*

Talmadge Garner passed away when he was 12 years old because of complications from juvenile diabetes.

The Stephens Family

The **Stephens Family** lived in this house, still standing. They had two children: **Dorothy** and **James**.

The Eldridge Family

The **Eldridge Family** were residents of this two-story white house, still standing. They had one daughter, **Ethel**, who married "Dub" Westbrook. Betty Burruss Brown shared with me that she cleaned house for Mrs. Eldridge. (It was common in those days for high school students to work after school hours for families in the community.) She remembers that Mrs. Eldridge was especially particular about keeping the baseboards in her house clean.

Mr. and Mrs. Earl Hatfield

Earl and **Eunice Hatfield** lived on the northeast corner of Dixie Avenue and Davis Road, with their house facing Dixie Avenue. Earl worked for Georgia Power Company; Eunice was employed as a registered nurse at Marietta Hospital.

The Robert Ingram Family

Frances and **Robert Ingram** moved to this house after the Hatfields had vacated. They had three children: **Rosemary**, **Bobby**, who died in childhood, and **David**. Several years later, the Ingrams moved to White Oak Drive, off Smyrna-Powder Springs Road (Cobb County). The Ingrams were active members of First Baptist Church, where Robert was ordained a Deacon November 23, 1963. See *Diemer/Ingram, Main Street*

The Coltrane Family

Mr. and Mrs. Coltrane and their daughter and son lived here.

Mr. and Mrs. Hubert Davis

Mr. Hubert Davis and his wife, the former **Edna Freeman**, were residents next door to the Coltranes. They had two sons, **Gary** and **Bobby**. Mr. Davis retired from Cleveland Electric Company, in Atlanta.

Gary Davis, a graduate in the Campbell High School Class of 1956, married Willene Hunt of Atlanta. They had three daughters: Cynthia, Melissa, and Patty.

Cynthia Davis married Glen Rahn. They had two sons: Steven and Eric.

Melissa Davis married Tim Huey. They had a son, Bo.

Patty Davis married Richard White. They had a daughter, Madison, and a son, Mitchell. After Patty and Richard divorced, Patty Davis married Phillip Durrett, who had children from a previous marriage.

Gary Davis, as a youngster, was a paper boy. Afterwards he worked at the Smyrna Drive-in and then for Western Auto in Smyrna. He retired from Cleveland Electric Company, in Atlanta. He and his wife, Willene, live in Powder Springs.

Bobby Davis, a graduate of Campbell High School, married Linda Hubbard, a graduate of Osborne High School. They had three children: two daughters, Kathy and Stacy, and a son, Brad.

Mr. and Mrs. Ramsey

Mr. and **Mrs. Ramsey** resided next door to the Davis Family.

Mr. and Mrs. Howard Carney

Mr. Howard Carney, originally from Jasper, and his wife, the former **Cleo Reese** of Talking Rock, lived here. They had five children: **Marie, Don, Glennis, Genevieve**, known as "Ginny," and **Carolanne.** Mr. Carney worked for the State of Georgia Department of Transportation.

Marie Carney married George Berenze. They had three children: George Martin III, known as "Trey," Rhea, and one whose name I do not know.

Don Carney and his wife, the former Jane McBerry, both graduates in the Campbell High School Class of 1955, had three sons: Michael, James Steven (now deceased), and Scott, who died as an infant.

Glennis Carney married John Hartman. They had no children.

Ginny Carney married Don Bell. They had two children: Frank and Katrina. Ginny later married Ed Simmons.

Carolanne Carney married Roger Hank Finger. They had four children: Shirley, Howard, Rebecca, and Chavon.

The Doris Haygood Family

Mr. and **Mrs**. **Doris Haygood** resided here. Mrs. Haygood's given name was **Lilla**. They had two daughters: **Doris** and **Ellen**. Doris Haygood was named for her father, who was a salesman.

Ellen Haygood married James Emmett Marler. They had two sons: Don and Ron. James, an executive with Standard Brands Company until he retired, was a member of the Marler Family in Marietta; one of his brothers owned and operated Marler Oil Company in Marietta.

Don Marler is a graduate of Darien High School, in Darien, Connecticut. He married Judy Holder of Marietta. They had five children: Kerry, Doug, Jenni, Becky, and Jake, and nine grandchildren.

Kerry Marler married and had two children: Christian and Lily. Now divorced, he lives in Huntsville, Alabama.

Doug Marler married Shannon Doyle. They had two children: Chase and Channing. Don and Shannon live in Sarasota, Florida.

Jenni Marler married Tony Lattanzi. They had two children: Reid and Olivia. Jenny and Tony live in Lula, where Jenni is a teacher.

Becky Marler married David Welch, a Major in the United States Army. They had two children: Miranda and Maggie. Becky and David live in Ft. Leavenworth, Kansas.

Jake Marler married Nicole Robertson. They had one son, Owen. The Marlers live in Woodstock.

Ron Marler married Sharon Costine of Lakeland, Florida. They had three sons: John, David, and Seth. John works for a law firm in New York City; David is married and lives in Atlanta; and Seth, not married, played pro football with Jacksonville Jaguars.

Ron and Sharon Marler live in Gwinnett County. Ron is employed with Schwan Bakery Company in Atlanta.

Doris Haygood married Luke Boring. They had two daughters: Lea and Lynn. Luke was employed by Georgia Power Company. Doris and Luke are members of First Baptist Church, where their daughters had also been members.

Lea Boring married Brian Panosian. Lea works with Georgia Power; Brian is associated with medical sales. They had four children; Luke, Jack, Colleen and Cara. (Jack and Colleen are twins). The Panosians live in Smyrna.

Lynn Boring married Ken Martin. They had three children, Mandy, Amy, Jeffrey, and four grandchildren. Lynn and Ken live in Chattanooga, Tennessee.

Mandy Martin married Danny Hindman. They had three children: Brittany, Callie, and Tyler.

Amy Martin had one child, Devin.

Jeffrey Martin is currently in college.

The J.T. Whitfield Family

Mr. and **Mrs**. **J.T**. **Whitfield** lived here in the middle of the Twentieth Century. Mrs. Whitfield, the former Azzalee McDonald, grew up in Roswell. While a young person, her parents,

Mr.and Mrs. C.L. McDonald, moved to Atlanta Road, at Gilmore Streetcar Stop, in the Oakdale community; Mrs. Whitfield had a sister, Frances, and two brothers, Earl and Van. Mr. Whitfield grew up in Cobb County, in the vicinity where I-285 and Interstate 75 currently intersect south of Smyrna. Mr. Whitfield was employed with Railway Express. See *Nunnally, north side of Church Street.*

The Marcus Nelson Turner, Sr. Family

Marcus Nelson Turner, **Sr**., known as "M.N.," and his wife, the former **Ollie Pruitt**, resided on the southeast corner of Dixie Avenue and Main Street. They had 12 children: **Ruby**, **Mildred**, **Regina**, **Wilma**, **Marcus Nelson**, **Jr**., known as "Mark," **Marie**, **Carolyn**, **Janice**, **Randy**, **Lynn**, **Freddie**, and another son who was stillborn.

The Turners, who previously lived in Matt, a small community bordering the Dawson/Forsyth County line, decided, after farming for one year, that there had to be a better way of making a living. In 1924 they moved to Dixie Avenue, in Smyrna. "M.N." soon established himself in the egg business, which he operated out of his garage apartment behind his house. The Turners lived in this house until 1955, then moved to one of the rental houses that Marcus, Sr., had built in 1941 on Belmont Circle and Turner Drive.

NOTE: In 1948 "M.N." Turner moved his egg business to Atlanta Road, into a former Georgia Power Substation building, in the Fair Oaks community. It was here that his son, Marcus, took over the business in 1958 and sold it in 1968.

Ruby Turner, a graduate of Smyrna High School, never married.

Mildred Turner, a graduate of Smyrna High School, married Sherman Westbrooks, who lived on Davis Road. They had four children: Linda, Bonnie, Sherman, Jr., known as "Chuck," and David.

Regina Turner, a graduate in the Smyrna High School Class of 1950, married Grady Howard of South Georgia. They had one son, Stan.

Wilma Turner, a graduate in the Campbell High School Class of 1954, married Clint Boling of Forsyth County. They had five children: Janet, Judy, Jimmy, Steve, and Mary Ann.

Marcus Nelson Turner, Jr., known as "Mark," was a graduate in the Campbell High School Class of 1957. Marcus married Elnora Silvils, a graduate of Austell High School. They had three children: a daughter, Leslie, a son, Marcus, and another daughter, Robin.

Marcus and Marie were twins.

Marie Turner, a 1957 graduate of Campbell High School, married Don Bishop, also a Campbell High School graduate, who grew up on Gilbert Street. They had four children: Donna, Fran, Wanda, and Alan.

Carolyn Turner, a graduate in the Campbell High School Class of 1962, married Reggie Glaze of Hall County. They had three children: Jennie, Grant, and Griff.

Janice Turner, known as "Jan," a graduate of Campbell High School, received her Master's degree as Specialist in Administration from West Georgia College (now West Georgia State University in Carrollton). She married Ted Holley, a 1961 graduate of Atlanta's Fulton High School. Having attended Louisiana Baptist University, Ted received his Master's of Religious Education degree from New Orleans Baptist Theological Seminary and his Doctorate of Divinity degree from Holy Trinity Seminary. Janice and Ted had three sons: Jeff, Chris, and Ben. Jan Turner Holley is employed by Cobb County Board of Education, and her husband, Dr. Ted Holley, is Pastor of Vinings First Baptist Church.

Randy Turner, the youngest of the Turner children, born in 1949, died of leukemia 1955.

Lynn Turner, another son, died at 18 months of age.

Unnamed son, stillborn.

Freddie Turner, at one month of age, died as the result of a childhood disease.

Mr. and Mrs. Thomas Jefferson Turner

Mr. and **Mrs. Thomas Jefferson Turner**, the parents of **Marcus Nelson Turner, Sr.**, lived in a house located at the end of Main Street. Mrs. Turner was the former Sarah Elizabeth Ravan. Thomas Jefferson Turner was known as "Tommy." He operated an egg business in their garage located to the rear of their house.

In addition to Marcus Nelson, "Tommy" and his wife had 10 other children, among whom were daughters Lottie, Laura Minerva, and Essie and sons Hoyt, Jewell, and George. According to a grandson, Ken Turner, when Thomas Jefferson died at 93 years of age, there were 44 grandchildren and 100 great-grandchildren. Following are a few of those descendants.

Lottie Turner married Carl Fouts. They had eight children: C.J., Jerry, Charles, Richard, known as "Bud," Alvin, Barbara, Shelba, and LaVerne. See *Fouts Brothers, Atlanta Street, from Mrs. Mazie's to Pearce Matthews.*

Laura Minerva Turner married Spencer Savage. They had four children: Sarah, James, Joyce, and Haywood.

Sarah Savage married Don Westbrook. They had four children: Sharliss, Donald, Stephen, and Spencer.

James Savage married Janie Cochran. They had two children: Kim and Kelly. James later married Diane Dunn.

Joyce Savage married Aaron Camp. They had two children: Jody and Joyia.

Haywood Savage married Diane May. They had one daughter, Heather. Haywood later married Marsha Hamby Bacon. See *Hamby, south side of Concord Road.*

Essie Turner married Leonard Childers. They had two sons: Wayne and Clain.

Hoyt Turner married Lillie Mae Milford. They had three children: Doyle, Cloyce, and Wanaza. The Hoyt Turner Family lived on Main Street.

Jewell Turner married Lucille Burruss. They had four children: Ken, David, Nancy, and Renee. The Jewell Turner Family lived on Main Street.

Ken Turner, a 1961 graduate of Campbell High School, married Lana Curry from Louisiana. They had three children: Kim, Karl, and Brooke. Ken served in the United States Army during the Vietnam War, when he was wounded and lost a leg. For many years Ken was employed by Carmichael Funeral Home in Smyrna, where he retired.

David Turner, also a graduate of Campbell High School, married Sue Chastain from McCaysville. They had two sons: Randy and Shannon.

Nancy Turner, a graduate of Wills High School, married Jerry Marstall from Topeka, Kansas. They had no children.

Renee Turner, a graduate of Wills High School, married Tony Dutton from Austell, the son of Reverend Cecil Dutton, Pastor of Second Baptist Church. They had two children: Hannah and Jarred.

George Turner. See *south side of Broad Street.*

HAWTHORNE AVENUE

North Side

Hawthorne Avenue runs from Atlanta Road at Dixie Avenue east to Six Points. In the days of my youth, the area was sparsely populated, with just much farm land and The New Smyrna Cemetery. In the mid-to-late 1950s some development occurred on Hawthorne Avenue. Today the profile of the street is beginning to change, with new- style homes being built in the neighborhoods on the east side of the railroad.

No one seems to know how Hawthorne got its name. It may have been named by the Indians, who at one time inhabited this land, or maybe there were numerous Hawthorne trees there. Perhaps someone who reads this has information!

Beyond the railroad crossing at Atlanta Street, the **Samuel J. Adams Family** owned much acreage on the north side of the street. I knew the Adams' son, "**Buddy**," who married Hilda Motter. See *Spring Road, the Country Road.*

Mr. and Mrs. Jack Pearson

Jack Pearson and his wife, the former **Helen Marr**, in 1941 built a two-story garage apartment, which was located almost directly across the street from the intersection of Gilbert Street and Hawthorne Avenue. This was the first house to be built on Hawthorne Street between the railroad and the New Smyrna Cemetery. Jack and Helen had two children: **Carl William**, known as "C.W.," and **Nancy**. The Jack Pearson Family were members of First Methodist Church.

"C.W." Pearson, a 1954 graduate of Campbell High School, married Martha Isley, who graduated in the Campbell High School Class of 1955. Martha, who grew up in the Oakdale Community, had a brother, Eddie, and a sister, Mary. Martha's family owned and operated the Isley Sand Company in Oakdale. "C.W." and Martha had five children: four sons Carl, Jr., Christopher, Cregg, Danny, a daughter, Lynn, and nine grandchildren. "C.W.," who works for the United States Post Office, and Martha live in Maysville.

Nancy Pearson, a 1956 graduate of Campbell High School, married Verlyn Black, who grew up on Terrell Mill Road, east of Smyrna. He had a sister, Jean, who graduated in the Smyrna High School Class of 1951. Nancy and Verlyn had three children: Anthony, Cheri, and Cynthia, and four grandchildren.

Nancy recollects that her parents built a garage apartment on the back of their lot with the intention of building a brick house on the front part of their property at a later time; instead they added onto the garage apartment. Nancy also remembers, at that time, Hawthorne Avenue was a dirt road and not in the City Limits of Smyrna. She has called Hawthorne Avenue a "muddy mess" when it rained.

Recalling her family's first moving to Hawthorne Avenue, Nancy stated, "We had water at the road but had to carry water from there to the garage apartment. Finally water lines were run to the house, and we got an inside bathroom."

Mr. and Mrs. Carl Pearson

Carl Pearson, who was from Marble Hill, and his wife, the former **Joeita Cochran** of Waleska, in 1947 built a house next door to Carl's brother, Jack. Carl and Joeita had one daughter, **Carolyn Jo**. The Pearsons lived in this house for nine years before moving to Wills Street.

Carl was an employee of a construction company before he began working for Lockheed Aircraft Corporation when it opened in 1951. Joeita, who taught in Marble Hill, also taught for 18 years at Smyrna Elementary School and afterwards, for 14 years at Belmont Hills Elementary School, from which she retired. The Pearson Family, active members of Second Baptist Church, were also active in Nelms Masonic Lodge and the Smyrna Order of the Eastern Star; they were also involved with the Rainbow organization.

Carolyn Jo Pearson married Martin Lockhart. They had two children: Wendy and Diane.

Mr. and Mrs. Wilkie

One of the families that I recall living on Hawthorne Avenue was the **Wilkie Family**, who had a large farm beyond the New Smyrna Cemetery—about where Hawthorne School is located. (The school was built in the mid-to-late-1950s.) I knew **Grady Wilkie**, a son in this family.

Mr. and Mrs. Sam Reed

Mr. and **Mrs. Sam Reed** resided past the Wilkie Farm. Mrs. Reed was the former Ollie Mohon. Sam and Ollie had six daughters, **Annie Mae**, **Mattie Lou**, **Sara**, **Joyce**, **Betty**, and **Ethel**, and four sons, **Baby Boy**, **Thomas**, **A.G.**, and **W.R.** In downtown Smyrna, Sam ran the Sinclair Service Station, which later became Fouts Brothers Sinclair Station. Later on, he ran a grocery store at Little Six Points. The Reed Family were members of Haney Grove Baptist Church. See *Fouts, Atlanta Street, from Mrs. Mazie's to Pearce Matthews.*

Annie Mae Reed died at age 16 due to heart problems.

Mattie Lou Reed married Lemon Dewey Priest, who lived on Elizabeth Street. They had two children: Ronnie and Brenda.

Sara Reed married Lamar Maloney. They had two children: Tony and Kim.

Kim Maloney married John Stegall.

Joyce Reed married Deward Cash of Banks County. They had four sons: Jerome, David, Sam, and John, and 10 grandchildren.

Joyce was a telephone operator in Smyrna, until she was transferred to Atlanta when the dial system was instituted. She later worked for Allstate Insurance Company, from which she retired. Deward Cash retired from the National Linen Company.

Jerome Cash married Pam Parks. They had two children: Chris and Sarah.

David Cash married Kay Patterson. They had three children: Michelle, Heather, and Ryan.

Sam Cash married Lisa Reibel; they had three children: Katherine, Gresham, and Rebecca.

John Cash married Kelley Hair, who had a daughter, Kaula Dye, from a previous marriage. John and Kelley together had one daughter, Kaycee Reed Cash.

Betty Reed married Jack Howard. They had one son, Reed. He and his wife, Patty, had three sons.

Ethel Reed married and had one son, Eric Regan.

Eric Regan, a star football player at Campbell High School, married Tina Pounds. They had three sons: Tanner, Josh, and Ryan.

Baby Boy Reed died as an infant.

Thomas Reed, known as "T.C.," married Oveline Slay from the Oakdale community, south of Smyrna. They had two sons: Robert and Earl. See *Hoepner, Brown Circle.*

A.G. Reed, known as "Pat," married Mary Sweatt from the Oakdale community, south of Smyrna. They had one son, Steve.

W.R. Reed, known as "Bill," and his wife, Gloria, had three children: Jimmy, Ralph, and Jan. After Gloria's death, "Bill" married Judy.

The Woody Family

The **Woody Family** lived near Mr. and Mrs. Reed. Though good customers to whom I delivered their papers, I did not know them well.

WATERMELONS

In 1943 Mr. Grady Wilkie and his sisters, who owned several acres in this area, lived on Hawthorne Avenue; their property adjoined the New Smyrna Cemetery. The Wilkie house was about where Hawthorne Elementary School is today.

There was a "Black" man named Rich Berry, whom the Wilkies permitted to grow a garden on part of their land. Rich, planting here for several years, was a good farmer and he could grow the prettiest, sweetest watermelons you ever would eat.

It so happened that there were, on that side of the railroad some " big" kids who had some time on their hands. One Saturday night they made a truck available for themselves. They went to that watermelon patch and picked every melon in it. That truck was loaded!

Everything went well until they got back to the house where the truck belonged. About that time, a dad came out of that house. It was late! He stated, "You kids been up to Rich Berry's watermelon patch?"

"Yes sir," somebody said!

"Well, you are going back and put every one of those watermelons into a pile at the entrance of that patch. I don't want Rich Berry having any trouble loading them onto his wagon."

On Monday morning, bright and early, came Rich Berry into Smyrna, selling those watermelons that he didn't have to pick.

HAWTHORNE AVENUE
South Side

A church building standing on the southeast corner of Hawthorne Avenue and Old Roswell Road has been there all of my life; its corner stone reads that it was erected in 1921. I do not have a history of the denomination of people who built this church. What I do know is that in 1938, when the "race riot" occurred in Smyrna, the "Colored" people, as was said then, were worshiping there.

A group of Assembly of God parishioners was meeting in the home of "Buckles" and Betty Graham, who lived in the area. The group decided there was a need for an Assembly of God church in Smyrna. At that time, the Assembly of God Tabernacle in Atlanta, whose pastor was Reverend Jimmy Mayo, collected $500.00 toward the purchase of this church building, the renovation of its sanctuary, and pastor's quarters on the second floor. See *Graham, east side of North Matthews Street.*

According to information from Mrs. Myrtice Spinks, the widow of Reverend Lewis Spinks, the Assembly of God Church bought this property in 1954 and started conducting services there. In addition to the sanctuary, the building included living quarters which at that time consisted of two bedrooms, a kitchen, and a small bath. The church added a living room and two new bedrooms.

Reverend Lewis Spinks was the first pastor, 1954-1959. The second pastor was Brother Hardy; the third one was Brother Harris Fennell. The Assembly of God maintained a church here until about 1966, when they sold this church building and bought the Presbyterian Church building on Memorial Drive; they used it until their new building was constructed on King Springs Road. At that time the property on Memorial Drive was sold to First Baptist Church of Smyrna.

In the early part of the Twenty-first Century, First Baptist Church allowed a Hispanic congregation to worship in this church building.

DAVIS ROAD

Outer Circle

Davis Road was a semi-circle street, extending from Dixie Avenue, at the Belmont House, and re-entering Dixie Avenue about one-fourth mile northward, near Miles Streetcar Stop.

Appreciation is extended to Betty Burruss Brown and Juanita Gantt Pratt for sharing their memories of living on Davis Road in the days of their youth. (Betty's family moved from Cumming in the middle of the 1930s to Broad Street, then to Davis Road, and later to Atlanta Street at Miles Streetcar Stop.) Appreciation is also extended to Chad Williams for his furnishing information about the Thompson Family, who were his great-grandparents. See *Burruss, Atlanta Street, from Miles Streetcar Stop to the Motters* and *Williams, north side of Powder Springs Street.*

A large tract of land behind the Belmont House and on the east side of Davis Road, extending down into the semi-circle, was purchased by the United States Government during World War II.

Mr. and Mrs. Floyd Little

Mr. and **Mrs. Floyd Little**, originally from Pickens County, moved in 1946 from the Oakdale community, south of Smyrna, to this house, located on the north side of Davis Road (past the Government property) with their four children: **Bernice**, **Jack**, **Catherine**, and **Wayne**. Mrs. Little was the former Julia Townsend. Floyd drove a streetcar and later a trolley.

Bernice Little married Charles Stanford.

Jack Little first married Betty Gentry and then Reba Waldrep.

Catherine Little married Jack Reed.

Wayne Little married Barbara Fouts; they had three children, Dennis, Michael, and Cheryl, and seven grandchildren. See *Fouts, Atlanta Street, from Mrs. Mazie's to Pearce Matthews.*

Dennis Little married Sheila Stover; they had two children: Justin and Elizabeth.

Michael Little married Mary Harris. They had three children: Christopher, Brandon, and Lauren. Michael's second wife's name is Karen.

Cheryl Little married Jeff Baldwin. They had two children: Adam and Lindsey.

Mr. and Mrs. John Jacob Richards

Mr. and **Mrs. John Jacob Richards** lived here. They were the parents of Allene Durham, who lived next door. See *Richards, north side of Powder Springs Street.*

Mr. and **Mrs. M.T. Phillips**, who moved to this house in the 1940s after the Richards had moved to Powder Springs Street, had two sons. Mrs. Phillips, whose given name was **Erma**, began teaching in First Baptist Church Kindergarten in the 1950s, when it was a new school, and retired in the 1970s. --See *Richards, north side of Powder Springs Street.*

Mr. and Mrs. Homer Durham

Mr. and **Mrs. Homer Durham** resided here. Mrs. Durham was the former Allene Richards, whose parents lived next door. Allene and Homer had two children: Patricia and Richard. See *Durham, south side of Powder Springs Street.*

Mr. and Mrs. Chesley Burruss

The **"Chess" Burruss Family** moved from Broad Street to this house and then from this house to Atlanta Street near Miles Streetcar Stop. See *Burruss, Atlanta Street, from Miles Stop to the Motters.*

Mr. and Mrs. Earl Hatfield

Earl and **Eunice Hatfield** lived in the last house before the re-entering of Dixie Avenue. They had moved from the corner of Davis Road and Dixie Avenue to this house, which they had built on property behind their Dixie Avenue home.

DAVIS ROAD
Inner Circle

Mr. and Mrs. Paul Gantt

Mr. and **Mrs. Paul Gantt**, originally from Ballground (Cherokee County), moved to this house in 1942 or 1943, after purchasing it from Mr. Garner, who at that time lived on Dixie Avenue. Their residence was located behind the McDowell house, which stood on the northeast corner of Davis Road but faced Dixie Avenue. Mrs. Gantt was the former **Thelma Rusk**, first cousin of Dean Rusk, former Secretary of State. The Gantts had five children: **Billy**, **Juanita**, **Mary Ruth**, **Ricky**, and **Wayne**.

Mr. Gantt at one time worked in the oil fields in Saudi Arabia. Mrs. Gantt worked first at W.T. Grant Company and then for the Cobb County School System in the lunchroom at Campbell High School. In the 1960s Mr. and Mrs. Paul Gantt, who had been members of Second Baptist Church, moved to East Marietta.

Billy Gantt, who worked at Day's Taxi during high school, joined the United States Navy in 1954. He married Carol Strom, a graduate in the Campbell High School Class of 1955; they had two children: Michael and Cindy. Billy later married Gay Walker; they had one son, Michael. Now divorced, Billy has retired from the Jones County Sheriff's Department and lives in Jones County.

Wayne and **Juanita Gantt**
Quonset Huts in the Background.
Circa Early 1950s
Courtesy of Juanita Gantt Pratt.

Juanita Gantt, known as "Nita," was a graduate in the Campbell High School Class of 1956. She married Robert Pratt, a graduate in the Osborne High School Class of 1957. They had four children: Anna, Robert M., Jr., Eric, and Pamela, known as "Pam."

Anna Pratt, a graduate in the Osborne High School Class of 1979, attended Berry College and Kennesaw College (now Kennesaw State University), where she earned her nursing degree. She married Darron Findley from Macon; they had three children: a daughter, Morgan, and two sons, Mason and Marshall. The Findleys live in Acworth.

Robert Pratt, Jr., known as "Bob," was a graduate in the Osborne High School Class of 1982. Having served six years in the United States Navy Submarine Service, on nuclear subs, he received a degree from Michigan State University. Robert married Tina Sands of North Dakota; they had three children: Joseph, Aaron, and Rebekah. Robert, Jr., service manager for a HVAC Company, lives in Cherokee County.

Eric Pratt, a graduate in the Osborne High School Class of 1984, obtained an undergraduate degree from Vanderbilt University and both a Master's degree and a Doctoral degree from New Orleans Baptist Theological Seminary. He is currently Vice- President and Professor at Mississippi College. Eric married Penny Hubbard of Dillon, South Carolina; they had three children: Grace, Paul, and Charles, known as "Chip."

Pamela Pratt, known as "Pam," a 1987 graduate of Osborne High School, earned an undergraduate degree from Berry College and a Master's degree from West Georgia College (now West Georgia State University). She is the Media Specialist at Pitner Elementary School in Cobb County. "Pam" married Ritchie Morris; they had two children: a son, Logan, and a daughter, Kathryn.

Mary Ruth Gantt married C. J. Sanford; both were graduates in the Campbell High School Class of 1960. They had two daughters: Katherine Grace and Paula Louise.

Katherine Grace Sanford was a graduate in the Campbell High School Class of 1979. She married Robert Dickerson; they had two sons: Ben Walters and Ross. The Dickersons live in Austell.

Paula Louise was a graduate in the Wills High School Class of 1982. She married Curtis Breazeale from Cheyene, Wyoming; they had two daughters: Marinda and Claudia. Paula and Curtis live in Dallas.

Ricky Gantt died at age 11 from leukemia.

Wayne Gantt, a graduate of Wheeler High School, is not married. He lives in Griffin, where he has his own floral business.

NOTE: Between the McDowell House, which was on the corner of Dixie Avenue and Davis Road, and the Gantt house, there was a driveway to a section of Belmont Farm. During World War II, two quonset huts (oval, metal, pre-built buildings) were parked on the driveway between these two houses. Mr. Kirkpatrick lived in one and stored his possessions in the other. Former neighbors do not remember Mr. Kirkpatrick's occupation, but he rode the bus to work every day.

Mr. and Mrs. Pannell

Mr. and **Mrs. Pannell** lived in the house next door to the Gantts.

Mr. and Mrs. Pirkle

Mr. and **Mrs. Pirkle**, who moved from Cumming to this house in the 1930s, were related to the Chess Burruss and Corn families, Mrs. Pirkle's given name was Vesta.

Mr. and Mrs. Albert Patron

Mr. and **Mrs. Albert Patron** and their two children, **Phyllis** and **Albert, Jr.**, were residents next door to the Pirkles. Mrs. Patron, whose given name was Toledo, worked first in the lunchroom of Smyrna School and then in the cafeteria at Campbell High School. Albert Patron, from New Orleans, worked for Atlantic Steel Company and then for Lockheed Aircraft Corporation, from which he retired. Albert and Toledo were members of Hill Street Baptist Church in Marietta.

Phyllis Patron, a 1956 graduate of Campbell High School, married Dilmas Morris, a 1955 graduate of Osborne High School. They had three children: two daughters, Sonya and Kelley, a son, Preston, and five grandchildren. Phyllis was a member of Second Baptist Church.

Albert Patron, Jr., graduated in the Campbell High School Class of 1958. He married Nell Medlock and had two children: Susan and Sandra. After Nell's death Albert married Mary, who had three children from a previous marriage: Tony, Michelle, and Bobby, whom Albert helped to raise as his own. Albert Patron, Jr., was a member of Second Baptist Church.

Mr. and Mrs. Claude Poss

Mr. and **Mrs. Claude Poss** lived on Hillside Drive, a street that Mr. Garner had cut between the homes of the Patron and Lee Poss families. This street was located near the middle of the circle between Davis Road's entrances to Dixie Avenue, on both the south and north ends. Mrs. Poss, the former Margie Frisbee, after Claude's death married Jerry Fouts. See *Stephens, south side of Walker Street* and *seventeenth House, north side of Spring Street.*

Mr. and Mrs. Robert Lee Poss

Mr. and **Mrs. Robert Lee Poss** and their daughters, **Nell** and **Sandra**, resided on Davis Road, just past Hillside Drive. Mr. Poss, known as "Lee," was employed at Gavin's Cabinet Shop in Cobb County, later by the Smyrna Police Department, and even later by the Cobb County Police Department. Mrs. Poss, the former Imajean McPherson, worked first for Loveable Bra Company in Atlanta and later for Scroll Fabrics. (Imajean was a sister of Gladys Black.) See *Black, west side of Roswell Street.*

Nell Poss first married Jimmy Lacy and later Everett McTyre. See *Lacy, north side of Spring Street* and *Mr. and Mrs. Grover McTyre, in this section of Davis Road.*

Sandra Poss married Garland Oliver; they had two sons: Robert Floyd and Lee Eugene. Sandra later married James Charles Evans, Jr., of Atlanta, and Cleveland, Tennessee. See *Oliver, next house.*

Mr. and Mrs. Lloyd Oliver

Lloyd and **Bessie Oliver**, both from Alabama, lived in this house with their two sons, **Garland** and **Glenn**, and their daughter, **Brenda**. Lloyd and Bessie were both employed at a cotton mill in Atlanta; he worked nights, and she worked days.

Garland Oliver married Sandra Poss. See *Robert Lee Poss Family, previous house.*

Glenn Oliver married Barbara Poss and had one son, Glenn, Jr. (Barbara had several children from a previous marriage). See *Ike Poss Family, next house.*

Brenda Oliver married Ralph Lee of Villa Rica. They had three children: a daughter, Vickie, and two sons, Ricky and Mickey.

Mr. and Mrs. Ike Poss

Mr. and **Mrs. Ike Poss** were residents here. Mrs. Poss was the former Coy Richards. They had five children: **Frances**, **Doyle**, **Barbara Ann**, **Charles**, and **Jerry**. Ike worked for Atlantic Steel Company. See *seventeenth house, north side of Spring Street.*

Mr. and Mrs. Carl Davenport

The **Carl Davenport Family** lived on a small street, Happy Hollow, cut off Davis Road. Mrs. Davenport was the former **Ruby Stephens**. They had four children: **Patricia**, **Scarlett**, **Michael**, and **Gwendolyn**. Carl worked for Atlantic Steel Company. See *Davenport Family, east side of Old Roswell Road.*

Mr. and Mrs. Grover McTyre

Lois and **Grover McTyre** and their two children, **James Everett** and **Jean**, were residents here.

James Everett McTyre married Nell Poss. See *Lee Poss Family.*

Jean McTyre married Lamar Wilson; they had three children: Jimmy, Dennis, and Donna.

Mr. and Mrs. Ellis

Mr. and **Mrs. Ellis** and their daughters, **Geraldine** and **Imogene,** resided here.

Mr. and Mrs. Ephraim Thompson

Mr. and **Mrs. Ephraim Thompson** lived in this house, which was past the arch in the circle and across the street from the Thompson Farm. Most of their farm land was merged with other properties north of Davis Road when the United States Government bought property where the Bell Bomber Plant, Dobbins Air Force Base, and the Naval Air Station were built. (Those installations were vibrant to the growth of both Smyrna and Cobb County.) Chad Williams shared that, after Grandmother Emma Thompson sold her property, she moved to Matthews Street, in the Six Points area. One of her children was **Mary Thompson Curtis**, the mother of Vonceil Curtis, who married G.B. Williams. See *Williams, south side of Powder Springs Street.*

Mr. and Mrs. Marvin Thompson

Mary and **Marvin Thompson** and their daughter, **Dorothy**, lived close to Dixie Avenue. Marvin was the son of Mr. and Mrs. Ephraim Thompson, who were residents next door.

BROAD STREET
North Side

Broad Street is a short street that runs east and west off Dixie Avenue. Several families resided on this street. Appreciation is extended to Betty Burruss Brown and Doris Haygood Boring for sharing their memories of living in this area during their childhood and youth. Those named hereafter were residents on Broad Street during the middle of the Twentieth Century but not necessarily in the order which they are listed.

Mr. and Mrs. Tommy Towns

Mr. and **Mrs. Newbert T. Towns** and their children, **Carol** and **David Towns**, along with Mrs. Towns' two sons, **Jimmy** and **Ronnie**, from her previous marriage to Harold M. Dickerson, lived in this house, which was located on the northeast corner of Dixie Avenue and Broad Street. Mr. Towns was known as "Tommy" and Mrs. Towns was known Eva.

Carol Towns married Bobby Fortner; they live in Marietta.

David Towns married and had a son, Benjamin. David lives in Marietta.

Jimmy Dickerson first married Francille Attaway; they had two sons Spencer and Scott. Spencer was killed when riding a motorcycle while he was in the United States Navy. Jimmy and his current wife, the former Ginger Ripka, had two sons: Craig and Ryan.

Ronnie Dickerson married Cathy Cash; they had two daughters: Cassandra, known as "Cass," and Rhonda. Ronnie and Cathy are divorced. See *Cash/White Family, next house*.

Cassandra Dickerson married David Brown; they had two daughters: Lauren and Lindsay.

Rhonda Dickerson who had a son, Aaron Lovin, lives in Paulding County.

The Cash/White Families

Mr. and **Mrs. Alfred Cash** moved to this house in 1948. Alfred and his wife, the former Frances Gilman of Atlanta, had three daughters: **Cathy**, **Marie**, and **Chris**. Alfred worked for Gulf Oil Company; Frances was employed at Lockheed Aircraft Corporation, where she retired with 37 years of service. After they divorced, Frances married Willis White.

Cathy Cash, a graduate of Campbell High School, married Ronnie Dickerson. Cathy and Ronnie worked for International Business Machines, known as IBM. See *Ronnie Dickerson, previous house*.

Marie Cash, a graduate of Southwest High School in Atlanta, married and had two sons: Todd Harper, Scott Harper, and a daughter, Stacy Harper.

Stacy Harper married David King of Marietta. They had two sons, Evan and Lawson, and a daughter, Sydney. Stacy and David live in Gainesville.

Chris Cash, a graduate of Wills High School, now lives in Dallas, Texas.

The Jones Family

Mr. and **Mrs. James Bradford Jones**, who moved to this newly built house on Broad Street in 1947, had three daughters: **Linda**, **Sybil**, and **Sheryl**. Mrs. Jones, the former Marilyn Miller, was employed first with Marietta attorneys Guy Roberts and Jordan Gardner, and later at Dobbins Air Force Base, where she retired. James Jones, who was from Barnesville, served in the United States Army during World War II, then drove an 18-wheeler truck for Refrigerated Transport Company, and later was employed at Dobbins Air Force Base, from which he retired. Mrs. Marilyn Jones, who was active in the Eastern Star and Rainbow organization, now lives in Marietta with her daughter Linda.

Linda Jones, a 1965 graduate of Campbell High School, married Don Jackson, a graduate of Sprayberry High School in Marietta. They had two daughters: Jennifer and Lauri.

Sybil Jones married David Buckner. They had one son, James.

Sheryl Jones married Tom McClure. They had two children: Melissa and Wesley.

The Blanton Family

Howard G. Blanton, known as "Preacher," and his wife, **Velma**, lived in this house with their children: **Faye** and **Larry**.

The Meeks Family

John and **Mildred Meeks** and their sons, **Paul** and **John, Jr**., were residents here.

The Towns Family

Theodus and **Pearl Towns** resided here with their children, some of whom were **Doddie**, **Sonny**, **Winnie**, **Bobby**, and **Ronnie**.

The Chess Burruss Family

The **Chess Burruss Family** moved to Broad Street in the mid 1930s from Cumming. From here they relocated to Davis Road and then to Atlanta Road near Miles Streetcar Stop. See *Atlanta Road at Miles Stop*.

The William Pierce Gillham Family

Mr. and **Mrs**. **William Pierce Gillham** moved from Fleming Street to this residence and from here to Favor Road. See *Fleming Street.*

BROAD STREET
South Side

Mr. and Mrs. George Turner

George and **Rozelle Turner** and their children, **Hulett**, **Harold**, **Johnny**, and **Sarah Ellen,** lived in this house which fronted Broad Street. There was a small side street that ran between this house and Dixie Avenue. See *Turner, Dixie Avenue.*

MORRIS STREET
East Side

Morris Street, only about two blocks long, ran north and south between Broad Street and Davis Road. Appreciation is extended to Betty Burruss Brown and Doris Haygood Boring for sharing their memories of the people who lived on Morris Street during their childhood and youth.

First House

Mr. and **Mrs**. **Seal**, who lived on Morris Street, owned and operated a "rolling store." In addition, on this street they maintained a warehouse for stocking the "rolling store." Later, the Seals operated a small grocery store from their home.

NOTE: In the early part of the Twentieth Century, "rolling stores" were common across rural areas. (Even in Cobb County in the middle of the Twentieth Century there were many isolated areas.) Because the majority of people did not have automobiles, (new commodities in those days), many people depended on the use of a horse and buggy, horseback, or horse and wagon—depending on their economic status. Therefore, it was a convenience for the housewife to have the "rolling store." Kids liked it, too! In my lifetime, we did not see much of this service in Smyrna because we had grocery stores.

Second House

Mr. and **Mrs**. **Strickland** and their son, **Eddie**, resided here.

Third House

Mr. and **Mrs**. **Frank Pendley** and their daughter, **Kay**, lived for 42 years on Morris Street. Mrs. Pendley, the former Clara Kay, and Kay were very active in First Baptist Church, where Kay was a leader in Young Women's Mission Auxiliary, called *YWA*. (A very effective program in the days of my youth, this was a mission-minded educational program, designed to develop among teenage girls strong leadership and service.) Clara and Kay had a very close mother/daughter relationship.

Clara and Frank Pendley owned and operated The Tasty Grill, a café in Marietta, about a block south of the Square, on the northwest corner of Atlanta and Anderson streets. They kept the restaurant open six days a week but always closed on Sundays.

Kay Pendley, a graduate in the Campbell High School Class of 1958, attended Bessie Tift College, in Forsyth, and Massey Business College, in Atlanta. She worked for Reverend Marion Beaver at Lithia Springs Baptist Church and afterwards for the Georgia Baptist Home Mission Board and the Georgia Baptist Women's Missionary Union (a division of the Georgia Baptist Convention).

Kay married Reverend Hugh Grimmer of Tarboro, North Carolina, a graduate of Wake Forest College (now Campbell University) in Buies Creek, North Carolina and Southeastern Baptist Theological Seminary, in Wake Forest, North Carolina. An ordained Baptist minister, Hugh served several pastorates in North Carolina and Georgia. He retired from Sears, Roebuck and Company.

Hugh and Kay adopted two sons: Jonathan Ray, known as "Ray," and Benjamin Scott, known as "Scott." "Ray and his wife, Heather, had a son, Jacob. "Scott" lives in California.

NOTE: The Strickland and Pendley homes were formerly one large warehouse; it was divided and sold as two homes.

MORRIS STREET
West Side

First House

The **Self Family** were residents across the street from the Stricklands.

Second House

Mr. **Edward Fridell** and his wife, the former **Evelyn Barnett**, and their daughter, **Elizabeth**, lived across the street from the Pendley Family. The Fridell house backed up to that of the Hubert Davis Family on Dixie Avenue.

Third House

The **Coltrane Family** were residents of this house.

PARK STREET

Park Street, a short street, which ran eastward from Dixie Avenue, making an "L" shape northward, ended at Main Street. The following people lived on Park Street in the middle of the Twentieth Century but maybe not in the order in which they are listed.

Mr. and Mrs. Harry A.M. Tuttle

Harry Tuttle from Syracuse, New York, his wife, the former **Thelma Miller** from Woodland, and their son, **Richard**, known as "Dick," resided in this house. Located on the corner of Dixie Avenue; their residence faced Park Street.

Thelma was working for the Standard Milling Company in Griffin, where she diagnosed illnesses in chickens and prescribed medicine for them. Harry, employed by the same company, but in New York, came down to the Griffin facility, where he met Thelma; they fell in love and married. The Tuttles were members of First Methodist Church in Marietta.

Richard Tuttle, known as "Dick," a graduate in the Campbell High School Class of 1959, met his wife, Gloria King of Indianapolis, Indiana, similarly—through their mutual employer—and married shortly after they met. They had two daughters: Angela and Amy.

Angela Tuttle is not married.

Amy Tuttle married Chris Fowler; they had a son and a daughter.

NOTE: Richard Tuttle has said that his dad owned much property on Park Street.

Mr. and Mrs. King

Mr. and **Mrs. King** resided across the street, on the corner of Park Street and Dixie Avenue, with their house facing Park Street. Mr. King retired from Lockheed Aircraft Corporation; in the 1950s he became a crossing guard at Campbell High School.

The Weldon Family

The **Weldon Family** had a daughter, **Ann**.

The Everett Family

The **Everett Family** had a daughter, **Sherrie**, a graduate of Campbell High School.

The Cheek Family

The **Cheek Family** had a son, **Johnny**, who attended Campbell High School.

Mr. and Mrs. Garnett Nunnally

Garnett and **Alice Nunnally** lived here with their sons: **Tommy** and **Pat**.

The Sellers Family

The **Sellers Family** had five pretty daughters— one of whom was named **Carolyn**.

Mr. and Mrs. Earl Ledford

Earl and **Gladys Ledford**, their children, **Terry** and **Rita** lived here. Earl was a mechanic.

Terry Ledford, a 1959 graduate of Campbell High School, married Joyce Grantham of Atlanta. They had four children: two daughters, Chris and Crickett, two sons Troy and Rusty, and seven grandchildren.

Rita Ledford married and had one daughter, Elita.

MAIN STREET

Main Street was the last road off Dixie Avenue in this neighborhood. This street, now closed, is no longer recognizable.

The Ingram/Diemer Family

Mary Wilma Wills of Paulding County married Mr. Ingram, who, from a previous marriage, had a son, **Robert**. Mary Wills Ingram later married Fred John Diemer, Sr., of Toledo, Ohio, while he was a sergeant in the United States Army. (He was discharged at Camp Jesup.) They had four children: **Fred John, Jr.**, **Mary Barbara**, **Eloise**, and **Jack**.

Fred, Sr., was a machinist/tool die maker for Southern Railroad, and Mary Wilma Diemer was a homemaker.

Robert Ingram, known as "Bob," and his wife, Frances, had three children: Rosemary, Bobby, and David. Bobby passed away in his teenage years. When I first knew Robert and Frances, long-time members of First Baptist Church, they lived on Dixie Avenue; later they moved off Smyrna-Powder Springs Road when White Oaks Farm subdivision was developed. According to her daughter, Rosemary, Frances earlier worked at Rich's downtown store and afterwards as a legal secretary at the Security Exchange Commission, in Atlanta. "Bob" retired as a printer for *The Atlanta Journal.*

Fred John Diemer, Jr., and his wife, Edna, who was from Illinois, met while he was in the United States Army, stationed in Indiana. They had three children: Johnny, Mike, and Carolyn.

Mary Diemer married James Miller, who graduated in the Smyrna High School Class of 1941 and served in the United States Navy during World War II. They had one son, Ira Wayne Miller, a retired commander of the Cobb County Police Department. Wayne's wife, Mary Miller, was a special education teacher at Belmont Hills School for many years.

Eloise Diemer married Earl Allen of Tifton. They had one daughter, Ann, who is a registered nurse.

Jack Diemer, a graduate in the Smyrna High School Class of 1949, married Becky Day of Smyrna, a cheerleader and a graduate in the Campbell High School Class of 1956. They had two sons: Alvin and Calvin. Becky and Jack are members of First Baptist Church of Acworth. Jack, a 50-year Mason, is a member of Nelms Lodge in Smyrna. After high school, Jack drove a cab for Day's Taxi and later was a clerk at J.D. Daniel's Grocery Store, on the east side of Atlanta Street. After serving in the United States Army, Jack was employed at Lockheed Aircraft Corporation. On September 28, 1959, at Day's Chevrolet in Acworth, Jack, at the age of 28, became the youngest Chevrolet Dealer in the Southeast. See *Day, north side of Sunset Avenue.*

Alvin Levi Diemer graduated from North Cobb High School, where he ran track and played football. Having attended Middle Tennessee College, he later transferred to Kennesaw College (now Kennesaw State University). Alvin married Sue Staton of Acworth, who also graduated from North Cobb High School. Alvin and Sue had two daughters: Jennifer and Stephanie.

Calvin Diemer and his wife, the former Meleah Barfield, are both graduates of North Cobb High School. Calvin attended Middle Georgia College, in Cochran, on a baseball scholarship; he later transferred to Kennesaw College (now Kennesaw State University). Calvin and Meleah had two sons: Daniel and Andrew.

Both Alvin and Calvin Diemer have been associated through the years with Day's Chevrolet dealership, which their grandfather, Levi Day, established.

MEMORIES
by Jack Diemer

I remember walking every Sunday from my home on Main Street to Brinkley Park to play baseball and then walking home alone after dark. When I graduated from Smyrna High School, I remember my favorite teams were the New York Yankees and Boston Red Sox.

As a member of Spring Street Baptist Church, I remember a great preacher, Emmett Marlowe, who was the pastor there, where great revivals were held with many people being saved during those times. I also remember how upset the members were when "Preacher" Marlowe resigned to go to the seminary. They did not think he needed to go to school, for they thought he was a great preacher without schooling.

The Kemp Family

Mr. and **Mrs. Emmett William Kemp** lived here. Mrs. Kemp was the former Omie Smallwood from Gainesville. Mr. Kemp, from Cherokee County and Atlanta, was one of 11 children who lived in the Atlanta area. (One of his sisters, Inez Kemp Brown had three sons: Terry, Billy Joe, and Junior; the Browns lived in Smyrna. The Brown brothers later on were in the plumbing business in Smyrna.)

Emmett and Omie Kemp had six children: **Hugh**, **James**, **Nancy**, **Ronnie**, and twin sons, **Boyd**, and **Lloyd**. The Kemps moved to this house in the mid 1940s. During World War II, Mr. Kemp worked at the Naval Yard in Charleston, South Carolina. Then, Mrs. Kemp and their two oldest children lived there with him; their third child was born while they lived in Charleston. After moving to Smyrna, the Kemps were members of Second Baptist Church.

Hugh Kemp, a graduate in the Campbell High School Class of 1954, married Valarie Smith. They had three children: Denise, Sonny, and Ty.

James Kemp, a graduate in the Campbell High School Class of 1959, and his wife Brenda, had three children: two daughters, Jamie and Tracy, and a son, Marty. James and his second wife, Gloria, live in Deland, Florida.

Nancy Kemp, a graduate in the Campbell High School Class of 1961, married David Gilley. They had three children: Tammy, Kathy, and David, Jr. See *Patterson, north side of Medlin Street.*

Ronnie Kemp and his wife, Shelby, had two children: Michelle and Shawn.

Boyd and Lloyd Kemp are not married.

CHAPTER NINETEEN

ACCESS HIGHWAY

(South Cobb Drive)
East Side

Southward from what is now Windy Hill Road, three Fortner families lived on the east side of Access Highway, north of Powder Springs Street.

First House

Mr. Truman Fortner and his wife, the former **Virginia Johnson**, were residents here. They had a son, **Robert**, known as "Bobby." See *Johnson, north side of Stephens Street.*

Robert Fortner married Susan Abbott.

Second House

William Tatum Fortner, known as "W.T.," and his wife, the former **Carrie Stover** from Canton, resided here. They had four children: **Craig**, **Chris**, **Donna**, and **Tracy**. "W.T." was employed at the Federal Penitentiary on McDonough Boulevard in Atlanta. The Fortners later moved to Forest Park.

Third House

Robert Fortner, known as "Hoofie," and his wife, **Ann**, and son, **Robert**, **Jr**., known as "Bobby," resided here. "Hoofie" worked at Tumpane Company in Marietta.

"Bobby," a member of the Smyrna High School Class of 1951, and I (also in that class) were good friends during our school days. When he married Betsy Fulford, in Washington, D.C., in 1955, I was his best man; at that time Betsy's dad was a retired United States Naval officer, working for the United States Government in Washington, D.C. Robert and Betsy had two daughters. After their divorce, "Bobby" remarried and had another daughter. See *Fortner, north side of Powder Springs Street* and *Fortner, east and west sides of Access Highway.*

NOTE: Mr. George Fortner, later built a house on the northeast corner of Access Road and Powder Springs Street. From here he sold rabbits and rabbit houses. See *Fortner, north side of Powder Springs Street.*

In the days of my youth, no other houses or buildings, that I can recall, stood on Access Road from Powder Springs Street until one reached the intersection of Concord Road and Access Road.

Clybe Dunton Garage

Clybe Dunton owned and operated **Dunton's Garage and Body Shop**, located in a concrete block building on the southeast corner of Access Highway and Concord Road. Along with his mechanical work, Clybe practiced his skills as an auto detailer at this location. The property where this business stood was part of the large land holdings of Clybe's father, H.H. Dunton, and his grandfather, H.J. Dunton. See *Dunton, south side of Concord Road, the Country Road.*

NOTE: Some of the older people in Smyrna remember Preacher Howard's living at this corner that faced Concord Road when this area was farm land.

Fourth House

Mr. and Mrs. Lacy

Mr. and **Mrs. Lacy** lived somewhere between the Clybe Dunton Garage and Sharon Baptist Church. Mrs. Lacy was a nurse.

The Petty Farm

According to Watson Petty, his father owned much property, beginning at a point past Clybe Dunton's Garage and extending southward toward Sharon Baptist Church. His father farmed this land. See *Petty, east side of King Springs Road.*

Happy Hill Baptist Church

Happy Hill Baptist Church was built in 1949 about a mile south of the intersection of Concord Road and Access Highway. The church later was renamed Sharon Baptist Church.

NOTE: First Baptist Church of Smyrna borrowed money to help defray the cost of the building of this church.

Fifth House

The Magbee Place

Laban Samuel and **Margaret Elizabeth Magbee** owned 40 acres of land located between the property where Sharon Baptist Church now stands and Preacher Moore's property. Magbee Drive, named for this family, runs perpendicularly to Access Road (now South Cobb Drive). The Magbees had four children: Maude, Guy, Laura, and Sid. According to information from a member of the Magbee Family, the following family members grew up on this property.

Maude Magbee married Grayson Ferdinand Brown; they had one son, Ferdinand Trownstein, who was named in honor of a friend. Later on, Maude and Grayson lived on property where Atlanta Terrace was later developed. See *Ferd Brown, east side of Dunn Street.*

Guy Magbee and his son, Fletcher, owned and operated Magbee Lumber Company on Piedmont Road in Atlanta. Laura Magbee, the third child, married Amsel Puckett. They had five children.

Sid Magbee married the former Marie Bradbury. They had two children: Beverly and Samuel.

Beverly Magbee married Reid Gillis. They had two daughters: Missy Marie Gillis (McEliece) and Holly Reid Gillis (Pointer). Reid served on the Wellstar Cobb Hospital Board for many years. After teaching in Atlanta, Beverly taught at Sope Creek Elementary School (in Cobb County), 1975-1987.

Samuel Magbee, a Presbyterian Minister, for many years pastored St. Charles Avenue Presbyterian Church in New Orleans.

Laban Samuel Magbee was a brother of Milton Augustus Magbee, the grandfather of my editor, Joyce Reagin. Milton's wife's name was Leila Augusta (Kutzchan) Magbee.

NOTE: According to long-time Smyrna resident Watson Petty, who grew up on King Springs Road, he and his brother worked for Mr. Laban Samuel Magbee when they were young men. Watson stated, "Mr. Magbee owned 40 acres here, which he bought for the timber. An Atlanta businessman, he also owned a large dry cleaning business on Peters Street. My brother and I would cut as much as one truckload of firewood every morning and haul it to Mr. Magbee's dry cleaning business. Also on this land Mr. John Baldwin owned a steam-powered sawmill."

The Sellers Property

The Sellers Family owned much property, from what is now McCauley Road southward to the rear of King Spring Baptist Church. According to information from the Eaton Family, the Sellers Family purchased this property from Mr. R.A. Eaton after the Civil War had ended. See *Sellers, west side of King Springs Road.*

ACCESS HIGHWAY
(South Cobb Drive)
West Side

Access Highway was built during World War II to handle the flow of traffic from south of Smyrna to the Bell Bomber Plant. The road today is known as South Cobb Drive.

The farms and businesses that are listed in this section were all located between Cherokee and Jones Shaw roads (both roads now named Windy Hill), on the north side of Smyrna, and King Springs Road, on the south side.

<u>First House</u>

The Dorris Farm

Mr. and **Mrs. William Dalton Dorris** lived here with their three sons: **Hoyt**, **Bobby**, and **Don**. Mrs. Dorris, the former Nettie Louise Chaffin, was a sister of Hubert Chaffin, the father of my brother-in-law, Grady Chaffin. The Chaffins, who resided on Shaffer Road, in the Fair Oaks community, had two other children: a son, J.E., and a daughter, Bobbie Ruth.

<u>Hoyt R. Dorris</u>, a graduate of Smyrna High School Class of 1951, served in the United States Army. During high school, Hoyt and I were very good friends. He married the former, Mirilyn Cromer Davis, who from a previous marriage had one son, Eddie Davis. Together, Hoyt and Mirilyn had one son, Jerry. They raised their family in Jonesboro, where Mirilyn still lives. Hoyt died in 2003.

<u>Bobby L. Dorris</u>, a graduate of Campbell High School Class of 1956, served in the United States Army. He married Barbara Wienke, whose family came from California to Marietta for her dad to work at Lockheed Aircraft Corporation. Bobby and Barbara had two sons: Bryan, and William C., known as "Bill." Bobby lives in Marietta.

<u>Donald D. Dorris</u>, known as "Don," served in the United States Army. He married Carlotta Werbell Smith of Powder Springs, who from a previous marriage had a daughter, Ashley Smith. "Don" lives in Powder Springs.

The Dorris' family farm was located near the northwest corner of Access Highway and Jones Shaw Road (now known as South Cobb Drive and Windy Hill Road respectively). Wendy's Restaurant and Walgreen Drug Store are located on the former Dorris property. Bobby Dorris remembers when Windy Hill, then Cherokee Road, was a gravel road and dead-ended at the creek where Old South Barbecue now stands. The reason the Dorris' bought this land was the road divided the previous owner's property when Access Highway was cut for the Bell Bomber Plant access, so he sold this property to Mr. Dorris. In 1957, Mrs. Dorris moved with her sons to property at Sandtown and Jones Shaw Road, (now Windy Hill Road).

The Dorris family, were members of Second Baptist Church. Mr. Dorris, a union painter, drowned at Lake Alatoona, in 1950. Mrs. Dorris worked in the lunchroom at Belmont Hills School after it opened in the 1950s.

Second House

The Bourne Farm

The **Bourne** family farm was located from what was then known as Little Concord Road, now Old Concord Road, to the creek at the bottom of the hill on Cherokee Road, now Windy Hill Road, near Old South Barbecue's present location. The farm extended southward, toward where Belmont Hills Elementary School now stands, and then westward, to Little Concord Road. The Bournes had 20 acres, primarily a truck farm; there the Bourne Family raised vegetables and two to three acres of cotton to sell for cash. Also on the property were pigs, cows, and a mule. Bob Bourne, one of the sons, explained that a 20-acre farm was a one-mule farm and a 40-acre farm was a two-mule one.

Walter Clement Bourne and his wife, the former **Frances Lucille Thornton** of the Grove Park community in Atlanta, lived on this farm with their four children: **Bob**, **Peggy**, **Norma Jean**, and **Stan**.

Bob Bourne graduated from Smyrna High School in 1946 and married Virginia Holmes of Atlanta. They had three children: Robert David, Phillip Dean, and Barbara Denise, and 11 grandchildren. According to Bob, he attended both First Methodist and First Baptist churches with his friends, including the McMullins and the McMillans. After Virginia's death, Bob married Arrettia Winters (Carvelle) (Majeska); they live in Smyrna.

Bob shared the neat little story about his mother's not having decided on a name for him, even while the doctor was still there at his delivery. Therefore, his birth was recorded, but no birth certificate was issued. After he was grown and needed a birth certificate, he had to have the record of his birth legally corrected.

Peggy Bourne married Earl Smith. They had four children: Richard, Earline, Judy, and Steve.

Peggy and Earl Smith owned and operated Earl Smith Flooring on South Cobb Drive, located on part of the Bourne property. After Earl's death, Peggy married James Vaughn. They reside in Florida part time. She still owns Earl Smith Flooring. Her son, Richard, handles the day-to-day operations.

Norma Jean Bourne married Elbert Davidson. They had four children: Byron, Tammy, Danny, and Gary.

Stan Bourne married Nadine Carter and had a daughter, Sandy. See *Carter, Whitfield Street.*

According to information from Bob Bourne, his grandfather, Seaborn Richard Bourne, was at one time Overseer of Belmont Farm. His boss was Colonel Wyatt (not sure if Wyatt was first or last name), the owner/operator of Belmont Farm. Bob also related that when his dad, Walter Clement Bourne, was a small child about five or six years old, living on the Belmont Farm, remembers walking from there to Smyrna to pick up the family's mail. He also recalls that his paternal grandmother, Virginia Catherine Arrowood Bourne, lived with her brother and his wife, Jack and Millie Arrowood, on Matthews Street. See *Arrowood, east side of Matthews Street.*

Mr. and Mrs. Seaborn Richard Bourne had another son, Bertie, who during the 1930s resided in the home place, on the corner of Powder Springs Street and Old Concord Road, where the Central Church of Christ now stands. He and his family moved from this residence to the vicinity of Gilmore Streetcar Stop, in the Oakdale community, south of Smyrna.

Bertie Bourne married Ruth Wellborn. They had two daughters: Martha and Carolyn.

Martha Bourne married John Cagle. They had two daughters: Cathy and Christa.

Cathy Cagle and her husband, Rick Jackson, are graduates of Osborne High School. They had one daughter, Amanda, known as "Mandy."

Christa Cagle, also a graduate of Osborne High School, married Doug Friar, a graduate of McEachern High School. They had two children: Dalton and Anna.

Carolyn Bourne married Ted Brown from the Oakdale community, south of Smyrna. They had three daughters: Debi, Melonie, and Marelda.

Debi Brown married Ted Barker.

Melonie Brown married Luke Adams and had a son: Conner.

Marelda Brown married Chad Garrison. They had two daughters: Amber and Alyssa.

Third House

The Fortner Family

James E. Fortner, known as "Bud," and his wife, the former **Estelle Dobbins** of Marietta, lived here. They had one son, James Wallace, known as "J.W." Their house was located near the northwest corner of Access Highway and Powder Springs Street. (Still standing, it was most recently used as an antique shop.) Before building this house, in the early 1950s, "Bud" and Estelle were residents on Grady Street. The Fortners were members of First Baptist Church.

"Bud" worked during World War II for the Atlanta Metalic Casket Company, in Atlanta, which made hand grenades for the War effort. Later on, after Lockheed Aircraft Corporation opened, Estelle Fortner began working there.

"J.W." Fortner, a graduate in the Campbell High School Class of 1959, married Linda Brown. They had three children: Christopher James, Robin Gay, James Eugene, and seven grandchildren. "J.W." remembers in the 1950s, guys racing cars on Access Highway every Friday night. He especially remembers at that time, the 1940s coupes were "hot."

Fortner "Filling" Station

"Bud" opened a store on Access Highway in the mid 1940s: it was used first as a grocery store and then as a service station (commonly called at that time a "filling" station). The building, still standing, is currently occupied by Smyrna Tire. According to information from a family member, "Bud" and Estelle constructed this building—even from the making of the concrete blocks.

History of the Fortner Family in Smyrna

Levi Franklin Fortner and his wife, the former **Louise Jane Howard**, moved from Black Jack Mountain in Cobb County. Their oldest child, **George**, born in 1890, was four years old. Their house, facing Powder Springs Road, stood near the northwest corner of Powder Springs Road and what we now know as South Cobb Drive.

Levi and Louise settled in Smyrna, in an area known as "Two Mile Branch," which at that time was an area of land extending from Powder Springs Road to Cherokee Road and bordering the Belmont Farm property. Here George Clifton Fortner grew into adulthood.

After Levi and Louise passed away, George was the only one of their children interested in the family farm; therefore, it was set for auction. Because George wanted the farm so very much, he bid 25¢ more each time a bid was made. Out-bidding everyone else, he bought the entire farm for $2,000.00.

As George was bringing a wagon of cotton from the field to bale, he saw Ollie Susan Hamby and one of her sisters playing in the yard of their home. Since George had been doing some work for Ollie's father, he and Ollie were somewhat acquainted. Having fallen in love, they were married November 30, 1912. See *Hamby, Love Street.*

George and **Ollie Fortner** first lived in a small three-room house that stood in the present location of Belmont Elementary School. There their first son, **Robert**, was born July 24, 1912. Their other children were **Evelyn**, born July 12, 1917; **Jamie V.**, born December 4, 1919; **James E.**, known as "Bud," born February 28, 1915; **Truman Lee**, born August 31, 1921; **Henry Thomas**, born January 27, 1923; **Claude**, born November 6, 1925; **Betty Lou**, born January 13, 1929; and **William Tatum**, known as "W.T.," born June 1, 1930. Jamie and Claude were stillborn. See *Fortner, north side of Powder Springs Street.*

On this farm George Fortner plowed with mules and he grew tomatoes, okra, peppers, apples, grapes, watermelons, corn, cotton, and sweet potatoes. (He made a bed on the back of a T-Model car to take his produce to the Farmers Market.) George's routine involved much manual labor: milking the cows, gathering eggs from the chickens, and "slopping" and killing hogs.

Later George built a big white house and a large barn that stood on the corner of Powder Springs Street and South Cobb Drive. The house faced Powder Springs Street. See *Fortner, north side of Powder Springs Street.*

During World War II Truman Fortner entered the United States Marine Corps. By this time, Access Highway, now known as South Cobb Drive, had been cut through the farm as a route to the Bell Bomber Plant. In the early 1950s, George sold to his son, "Bud," and his wife, Estelle, the property on the northwest corner of Powder Springs Street and Access Highway. There, making concrete blocks themselves they built a small store.

After Betty Lou had married and "W.T.," having entered the United States Military, had left to serve in the Korean Conflict, Henry, who suffered from asthma, was the only one left at home. At this time, George decided to downsize his farm. When he began selling parts of the land for subdivisions, he and Ollie moved into a small four-room house on the northeast corner of Powder Springs Street and South Cobb Drive.

Because George still had farming "in his blood," he started raising rabbits, which with rabbit pens, he sold from his house. If you were in Smyrna during that time, you will remember his rabbit pens near both his house and the roadway. Ollie Fortner passed away in August 1971. George stayed busy with his rabbits for the next 10 years, or until he passed away, in 1981, at 92 years of age.

The homes that were in that area are no longer there—but rather the Potter Building, et al. But stop for a moment; see if you can picture that "old dirt farmer," plowing behind those mules all over those hills, (now subdivisions). He raised crops where Old South Barbecue stands beside Windy Hill Road. He had to take water on a sled in barrels to water the crops all the way from the creek that runs under what was then Cherokee Street, now Windy Hill Road, past the Piccadilly Restaurant. Betty Lou Fortner remembers: "Once we had the barrels filled with water the mules pulled it on the sled to the fields; then we had to physically tote the water to the plants. It was hard work!"

NOTE: Sometime in his early life George Fortner was employed by Glover Machine Works in Marietta.

L-R: **Ollie, W.T.**, and **Carrier Fortner**
In front of their house on Powder Springs Street
Note the seam in Carrie's hose
Courtesy of Betty Lou Fortner Circa 1940s

Ann Fortner (Mrs. Robert)
Circa late 1940s
Courtesy of Betty Lou Fortner

Betty Lou and **Evelyn Fortner**
Courtesy Betty Lou Fortner
Circa 1940s

George Fortner driving
Alton, Henry, and **Ruth Fortner**
pushing Old red van to start it.
Courtesy of Betty Lou Fortner
Circa 1951

A FAMILY MEMORY
by Betty Lou Fortner

I remember the large family meals we shared in our home as I was growing up. We always had plenty of eggs, milk, vegetables, and meat. One memory especially stands out in my mind. My brothers, George, Henry, W.T., and Truman, would go out into the fields and pasture and bring back 10 to 14 wild rabbits. My mother, Ollie, would skin and cut them; then, after thoroughly washing them, batter, fry, and serve them along with biscuits and gravy. My dad and brothers needed large meals like this to sustain them while they worked the fields and cared for the livestock.

Fourth House

Mrs. Hunt, a teacher at Smyrna Elementary School, and her son, **Charlie**, and daughter, **Selena**, lived in this house, which stood near the northwest corner of Access Highway, now South Cobb, and Concord Road. The Crossings Shopping Center now occupies this land, which was in Mrs. Hunt's family estate.

Dickson Shopping Center

Dickson Shopping Center, owned and operated by **T.L. Dickson**, began in the 1940s as a service station and small grocery store, located on the southwest corner of Access Highway and Concord Road, the Country Road. A Sinclair Oil affiliate the station in the 1950s was operated by **Lee Dickson**, T.L.'s brother. Lee resided with his wife, **Sadie**, and their three sons, **Jerry**, **Irvin**, and **Milton**, on Lamar Circle, a new street cut off Concord Road, west of South Cobb Drive. Jerry Dickson, now deceased, graduated from North Fulton High School with 12 years perfect attendance. Irvin and Milton are graduates of Campbell High School in Smyrna. Living to be a very aged person, Sadie was extremely healthy, probably due to her being a "stickler" about preventive medicine. See *T.L.Dickson, north side of Concord, The Country Road.*

Fifth House

Twiggs Merritt, a farmer and carpenter originally from Cherokee County, and his wife, **Estelle**, moved from Fulton County, in 1944, to an old farmhouse located on the south side of Concord Road, behind Dunton's Garage. From Concord Road they moved to this house, which they built. The Merritts had eight children: **Harriett**, **Clifford**, **J.T.**, **Floy**, **Twiggs, Jr.**, known as "Junior," **Velma**, **Juanita**, and **Donald**. All of their children, except Donald, had reached adulthood before the Merritts inhabited this house. Twiggs and Estelle moved from this house to Oakdale Road, south of Smyrna, where Twiggs died. Estelle died later in a nursing home.

Harriett Merritt married Sanford Richardson. They had four children: Harold, Barbara Sue, Gaynelle, and James.

Clifford Merritt married Estelle Smith; they had no children.

J.T. Merritt married Ailene Morgan. They had six children: Joyce, Gwen, Irma, Gerald, Marion, and Beverly.

Floy Merritt married Clayton Norton. They had four children: Doyle, Myra, Marilyn, and Dennis.

Mr. and **Mrs. Twiggs Merritt, Jr.**, and their family resided in the house located next door to but farther off the road than that of his parents. This was what one might call a family enclave. Twiggs, Jr., known as "Junior," and his wife, the former Edna Folds, had two daughters: **Sylvia** and **Judy**. Edna Merritt, in 1953, died from complications of tuberculosis.

Don Medlin, Manager, standing in front of T.L. Dickson Groceries and Meats
Second Building, Feed Store, Third building, Mrs. Tipton's Gift Shop;
fifth building not shown in front was S.A. White Gas Station
Courtesy of John Dickson

Dickson Shopping Center – 1952

"Junior" Merritt is a well-known preacher in the Cobb County area. He pastored several churches, with his longest pastorate being at Bethlehem Baptist Church on Powder Springs Road in Marietta.

Reverend "Junior" Merritt later married **Hazel McLarty**. They had six children: **Brenda**, **Sandra**, **Carlene**, **Timothy**, **Tonya**, and **Brandon**.

Velma Merritt. See *sixth house.*

Juanita Merritt married Fostine Barrett. They had one son, Victor.

Donald Merritt and his wife, Naomi, who was from Missouri, had one daughter, Donna. Donald, who served in the United States Army, 1956-1958, and Naomi live in Missouri.

Sixth House

Velma and **Lloyd Monroe** were residents of this house, which was located north of a dirt road, now known as Lake Drive. They had four children: **Theresa**, **Deborah**, **Phyllis**, and **Mark**. Mrs. Monroe was the former Velma Merritt.

Mr. and **Mrs. Wiley Cole**

Mr. and **Mrs. Wiley Cole** lived in this sixth house, on the northwest corner of Lake Drive and Access Highway, after Lloyd and Velma Monroe vacated. Mrs. Cole was the former Cleo Ruddell, the daughter of Mathis and Mary Ruddell of Jasper. In 1947, the Coles and Cleo's mother, Mary Fuller Ruddell, along with their daughter, **Patricia**, known as "Pat," moved to this house. Another daughter, **Deborah**, known as "Debbie," was born while they lived here. Patricia and Deborah graduated from Campbell High School. See *Brooks, east side of Roswell Street.*

Wiley Cole served in the United Stares Army during World War II. Afterwards he worked as an electrician. Cleo Cole worked at Bell Bomber Plant and later at Lockheed Aircraft Corporation. The Cole Family were members of Sharon Baptist Church.

Patricia Cole, known as "Pat," married Tommy Godwin of Powder Springs. They had a son, Wesley Cole Godwin, who died at the age of three months. After their divorce, "Pat" moved to California, where she married Dr. Bruce Sand, who had three sons from a previous marriage. "Pat" and Bruce adopted a daughter, Jennifer, who married and had three sons. After 35 years in California, "Pat" moved back to Georgia; she lives in Dallas.

Deborah Cole, known as "Debbie," married Lamar Buckner of the Oakdale community, south of Smyrna. They had twin sons: Jason and Shane. "Debbie" and Lamar are divorced.

Jason Buckner graduated from South Cobb High School and Mercer University School of Pharmacy, where he received a Doctorate degree. A practicing pharmacist, he lives in Grayson.

Shane Buckner graduated from Douglas County High School and Kennesaw State University. Continuing his education with plans for teaching, Shane lives in Douglasville.

Deborah Cole Buckner is now married to William Johnson, known as "Bill," who from a previous marriage had a son, Casey, a graduate of South Cobb High School and West Georgia State University. "Bill," an employee of the Cobb County Board of Education Transportation Department and a member of the Georgia Army National Guard, has been serving in Iraq.

Seventh House

The **West Family** resided in this house, on the site where a service station is now located.

Eighth House

Mrs. Sadie Sewell lived here with her children: **Lillian, Marie, Wayne**, and **Kathryn**.

Ninth House

WHITE OAKS
by Mike Terry

One of Mary Baldwin Terry's second cousins was an eccentric little man named Roy Gann. Mama said that Roy's family was "part" Cherokee Indian. That may explain his unusual appearance. Roy was born in 1885, just 20 years after the Civil War. Like many people of that era, he was captivated by anything related to that war; over the years Roy amassed a huge collection of Civil War relics, which he displayed proudly and talked about often.

Roy and his wife, Sally, lived on a farm that was located on 20 to 30 acres in the general area of the current home of Wade Ford dealership. Roy owned all of the land down to the northwest corner of South Cobb Drive and King Springs Road. He vowed never to sell any of his land to a "Yankee." Calling his farm "White Oaks," as the picture shows, he erected on his farm, a grand entrance, complete with a painted sign that read "WHITE OAKS Welcomes 'U.'" Roy and Sally harvested logs from their property and hand built a log cabin, where they lived for many years.

As Roy prospered, he was able to build a more proper farmhouse, and he eventually moved all of his Civil War relics to his cabin, which he called his "museum." Word of his collection spread, and newspaper writers from both Atlanta and Marietta, became frequent visitors. A 1961 interview was printed in *The Smyrna Herald.* That interview was probably his last, as he died in 1968 at the age of 83.

I remember trips to visit Roy and Sally and the fun I had poking around in the old cabin. When Roy died, his collection was divided among his family members, including Emory Paris and Rob Baldwin. Sally sold the land to developers—probably Yankees. See *Terry, north side of Concord Road.*

White Oaks
Circa Middle of the Twentieth Century
Courtesy of Mike Terry

CHAPTER TWENTY

FOREST HILLS

This area, about one half-mile south of Smyrna was forest land when I was growing up. During my last two years of high school the area began to change. Over the next five or more years it developed into one of the Smyrna area's most upscale neighborhoods

The actual development of what is now known as Forest Hills subdivision began in 1949, but really escalated in 1951 and 1952 after the start of the Korean Conflict, in 1950. With the Federal Government needing more airplanes, Lockheed Aircraft opened in Marietta and brought an influx of new residents to Smyrna, creating a need for more housing.

The first builder to seize the moment was Pat Shaw, a Smyrna developer. After acquiring land from the Collier Family, he quickly graded and established Collier and Pretty Branch drives, and the part of Lee and Dunn streets south of Collier Drive. (The side streets—Memory Lane, Northview Place, Pinetree Drive, Debra Drive, Forest Drive, and parts of Lee and Dunn streets—would come later and be developed by other builders.) Mr. Shaw chose some of the street names from the many local families in the area and from other well-known landmarks. Collier Drive is obviously named for the Collier Family; Dunn Street which was extended at this time, was named earlier in the century for a family that lived on Love Street (now a part of Concord Road). Ever since Civil War days, Pretty Branch has been the name of the small creek which runs through the area—thus Pretty Branch Drive. See *Dunn Street, Dunn, on Love Street,* and *Collier on Atlanta Street from Marlowe's to Creatwood.*

Appreciation is extended to Michael Terry, known as "Mike," who grew up on Collier Drive in the Forest Hills community. The son of Mr. and Mrs. Johnnie Terry, "Mike" married Sue Bingham, who grew up in Hickory Hills, adjacent to Forest Hills. (They currently live on Pinetree Drive in the Forest Hills community. "Mike" and Sue are both active in the Forest Hills Neighborhood Association, as well as in other organizations in Smyrna.) Appreciation is also extended to Frances Kilpatrick, whose family was among the first ones to live on Collier Drive. See *Terry, west side of Concord Road.*

MEMORIES

by Michael Terry

"Mama, look what I found! It's an arrowhead! I wonder where it came from?"

"Ask your Uncle Rob," Mama said. "He'll know."

"It was 1953, and I had been playing with a friend on the abandoned logging road that ran behind our house on Collier Drive. I looked down, and there it was, a shiny, flint arrowhead, lying on the road that would soon become Pinetree Drive.

"On Sunday, as we were visiting my Uncle Rob, I showed him the arrowhead. He just smiled and said, 'Let me show you something.' From high on a shelf in his bedroom closet Uncle Rob retrieved two large glass jars, each one filled with arrowheads.

"The dominant Indian tribe in North Georgia was the Cherokee," he began in nostalgic tone. "But the Indians that lived in Smyrna were the Creeks. When I was a boy, I used to plow behind a mule, and every time I did, I uncovered arrowheads."

"Rob went on to tell me that the Creek village was located in the area that is now the southeast corner of Concord and King Springs roads. A convenience store is there now. Many years later, Rob's parents (my grandparents) would own a farm on that same property, and Rob and his brother would plow the land and plant the crops that sustained the family. Though my grandmother sold this parcel to American Legion Post #160 in the early 1960s, it is clear from Rob's stories that, many, many years before, Indians had lived in the forest that in 1949 would become Forest Hills subdivision.

"My memories of Forest Hills residents are from my childhood, for I lived here from 1950-1969 (age 5 to 24). Therefore, I knew many of the people very well."

Forest Hills is a community that covers an area encompassed by Collier Drive, Lee and Dunn streets. While these are old streets, the extensions south of Collier Drive were built in the early 1950s.

NOTE: In school many of us studied about our government's decision, in the early 1800s, to relocate the Indian population to the western part of the United States. This forced relocation came to be known as "*The Trail of Tears.*" Michael Terry related that his great-great grandfather had shared in that sad event. Many other current Smyrna residents had ancestors living in the area at that time.

Frances Kilpatrick remembers that the following families were the first to move to Collier Drive: **Johnny** and **Mary Terry**, **Mr.** and **Mrs. Aiken**, **James** and **Evelyn Pressley**, **J.E.** and **Frances Kilpatrick**, **Nick** and **Virginia Mosgovoy**, and **Lois** and **John Matthews**.

A TRIBUTE TO A GOOD FRIEND
by Pete Wood

Though the Mosgovoys moved to Collier Drive in the early 1950s, I first met **Nicholas Mosgovoy**, known as "Nick," in 1956, when I joined the 425th Transportation Group, United States Army Reserve. This was shortly after I was released from active duty. "Nick," a World War II veteran, who had served in the European Theater, at one time was a Russian Interpreter for General Mark Clark. Prior to World War II, "Nick" and his family immigrated from Harbin, Manchuria to New York City; they later moved to Atlanta. When "Nick" and I first became acquainted, he was working as an engineer for the State of Georgia Highway Department and his wife, **Virginia**, was a nurse at Brawner Psychiatric Institute; they had two sons: **Nicholas, Jr.**, and "**Mike**."

"Nick" spoke Russian fluently. During the time I served with him in the United States Army Reserve, he served as an instructor at the United States Army Language School, at Fort Bragg, North Carolina. He would spend two-to-three weeks on teaching tours, usually in the summer, in addition to his duties with the 425th Transportation Group.

In addition to serving in the United States Army and the United States Army Reserve, where he attained the rank of Major, "Nick" was a good citizen in many other areas. He was a member of American Legion Post #160, the Reserve Officer's Association of the United States, First United Methodist Church, Golden K Kiwanis Club, and Campbell High School organizations (while his sons were students there).

Although not born in this country, "Nick" was one of the most devoted United States of America citizens that I have ever known. He was also a fun-loving guy! "Nick" and Virginia both passed away in the 1990s. I miss him!

In conclusion, this book was a collaborative effort by many people. My wife Lillie, Janet Brooks Brown, Joyce Reagin, and Millie Broyles are responsible for a lion's share of the work that made this book possible. I will always be grateful to them and the hundreds of residents and former residents of Smyrna who contributed to this book.

Mike and **Pat Terry**
369 Collier Drive
Summer of 1952
Courtesy of Mike Terry

Johnnie and Mary Terry's home on Collier Drive in Forrest Hills
Circa 1940s Courtesy of Mike Terry

James and **Evelyn** (Edwards) **Presssley** standing on Pinetree Drive in the late 1940s, on property they were considering for a home site. They decided against the property because they would have to pay the installation cost for utilities. Later, in the 1940s, they built on Collier Drive, in Forrest Hills, where they still live. See *Pressley, sixth house, south side of Bank Street, and Edwards, north side of Love Street.*
Courtesy of James and Evelyn Pressley

Hubert and **Frances Colquitt** in the late 1950s.
In their new home on Northview Place, in Forrest Hills.
Courtesy of Gayle Colquitt Ruddell

BIBLIOGRAPHY

But Thou Art Rich, A History of Smyrna First United Methodist Church

A Beacon for Christ A Centennial History of The First Baptist Church of Smyrna, Georgia; by Harold L. Smith

The Atlanta Journal, Cobb Extra, article entitled "Alert Developers Treasure Home's History," October 20, 1983

Presbyterian Church, 75th Anniversary 1914-1989

The Talisman, 1951 Smyrna High School Annual

The People of Smyrna, Centennial Observance, City of Smyrna, 1872-1972 by Bill Miles

The First Hundred Years, A Short History of Cobb County, in Georgia, by Sarah Blackwell Gober Temple

Past…*Present...and Future*, by Mrs. Mazie Whitfield Nelson, early Twentieth Century

Lives and Times, a bi-monthly newsletter published by the Smyrna Historical and Genealogical Society, Editor, Harold Smith

The Original Charter of the The United Daughters of the Confederacy, Phillip's Legion Chapter

A Brief History of Nelms Lodge # 323, loaned by Sam Whitfield.

Gone With The Wind, by Margaret Mitchell

The Smyrna Herald, Editor and Publisher, Bill Miles

Uncle Remus Tales, by Joel Chandler Harris

The Vinings Gazette, article entitled "Walking Through Historic Vinings," December, 1997

ERATTA PAGE

Page 26	Top picture caption should be Pauline Clayton Wood, not Woods
Page 27	Bottom picture should be Diane Bivins, not Betty Clayton
Page 28	Third paragraph Paul Clayton's death was 1987, not 1993
Page 75	Bottom picture should be Hardage, not Yardage
Page 81	Bottom picture should be Colquitt Family, not Culquitt
Page 124	Seventh house, fourth paragraph should be S. B. Love, not S. A.
Page 133	Photo credit should be Claire Curtis, not Clare
Page 178	Last paragraph should read: Some of the children from both of Mr. Motter's families attended classes at old Bethel School. The unpainted school building, not very large, was on the southwest corner of what is now Spring Road and Cumberland Parkway. Raymond Motter, born in 1925, remembers going to school there when he was very small, prior to attending Smyrna School. Raymond thinks Bethel School closed in the late 1920s or very early 1930s, perhaps because of the Great Depression.
Page 195	Mrs. Green's First Family, second paragraph should be John Thurmond, not Thurman
Page 195	Under Susie Castleberry should be the Brysons had ten grandchildren not the Castleberrys
Page 208	Mr. and Mrs. Wallace Knighton, third paragraph should be Dolly Parton, not Partan
Page 223	Should be The Atlanta Journal not the Atlanta Journal
Page 252	The Paul Hensley Family paragraphs one, five, seven, eight and nine should be Sara, not Sarah
Page 320	Third line in caption should be Georgia Gillham, not George
Page 375	Bottom picture, second line should be Grady Chaffin, not Grady Griffin
Page 385	Last line should be Nancy Stricklin, not Strickland
Page 394	First house, seventh paragraph should be Janice Athlene Watkins, not Mitchell
Page 416	Mr. and Mrs. T. P. Holleman, first line, should be Melvin Holleman not Holloman
Page 470	Eleventh house, first paragraph should be James Macaulay Dunton not Jesse.
Page 480	Tenth house, paragraphs one, three, seven and eight should be James Macaulay Dunton not Jesse. Paragraph four the son Jesse is correct, but his son is James not Jesse. James is deceased.
Page 497	Hollis Hill and Martha Dunton fifth paragraph should be James Macaulay Dunton, not Jesse.
Page 522	Caption on bottom picture sixth line should be Corrine, not Corine
Page 547	Mr. and Mrs. James Cooper fifth paragraph should be James Macaulay Dunton not Jesse
Page 588	Bottom right hand picture name is Lilla not Lila
Page 600	Eleventh house should be Marian Poston, not Marion
Page 614	Third line - Walter Akins married Lilla Emory not Lelia
Page 636	Mr. and Mrs. Robert Lee Poss first paragraph should be Imagean McPherson, not Imajean

C

G

H

K

M

Q

R